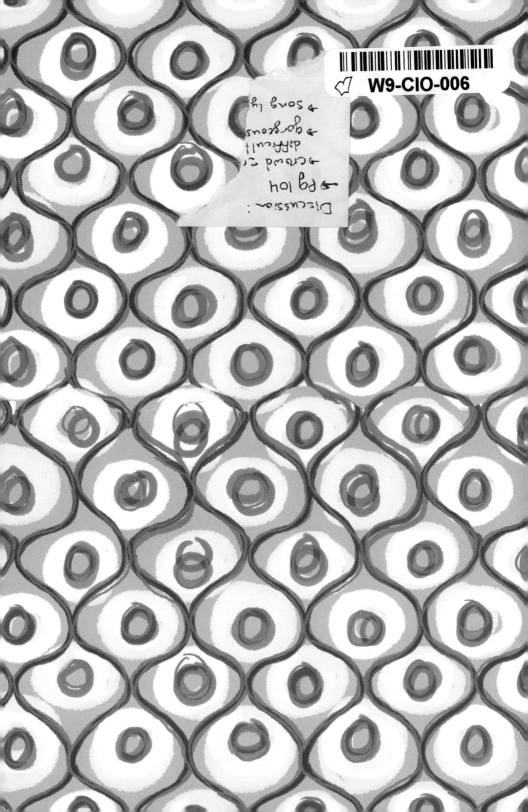

Discussion:
→ pg 104
crowd is
difficult
→ gorgeous
→ song ly

MARGUERITE ABOUET   CLÉMENT OUBRERIE

AYA
LIFE IN YOP CITY

DRAWN & QUARTERLY

Thank you Antoine Delesvaux, Agathe Faucompré, Nina and Patricia N'Gbandjui, Olivier Vitrat, Ernest Odje, Nicolas Merki, Patrick Chapatte, Reynold Leclercq, Mendozza, Christian Ronget, Guillaume Boilève, 1 Jour 2 Mai and Beybson for their beautiful color photos, without forgetting the participation of the Grezaud family.

And, lastly, our gratitude to Hyppolite B. for the music!

Originally published in English by Drawn & Quarterly in three hardcover editions in 2007, 2008, and 2009. Originally published in French by Gallimard Jeunesse as part of the Joann Sfar edited Bayou collection.

drawnandquarterly.com

First paperback edition: July 2012
Second printing: September 2015
Third printing: September 2017
Printed in China
10 9 8 7 6 5 4 3

Library and Archives Canada Cataloguing in Publication
Abouet, Marguerite, 1971–
    Aya: *Life in Yop City* / Marguerite Abouet; Clément Oubrerie, artist.
    1. Teenage girls—Côte d'Ivoire—Comic books, strips, etc.
2. Côte d'Ivoire—Comic books, strips, etc. I. Oubrerie, Clément
II. Title. PN6790.I93A2613 2012   741.5'96668   C2011-907516-4

This work, published as part of grant programs for publication (Acquisition of Rights and Translation), received support from the French Ministry of Foreign and European Affairs and from the Institut français. Cet ouvrage, publié dans le cadre du Programme d'Aide à la Publication (Cession de droits et traduction), a bénéficié du soutien du Ministère des Affaires étrangères et européennes et de l'Institut français.

Liberté • Égalité • Fraternité
RÉPUBLIQUE FRANÇAISE

Drawn & Quarterly acknowledges the support of the Government of Canada and the Canada Council for the Arts for our publishing program.

Published in the USA by Drawn & Quarterly, a client publisher of Farrar, Straus and Giroux; Orders: 888.330.8477
Published in Canada by Drawn & Quarterly, a client publisher of Raincoast Books; Orders: 800.663.5714
Published in the United Kingdom by Drawn & Quarterly, a client publisher of Publishers Group UK; Orders: info@pguk.co.uk

AFRICA
IVORY COAST

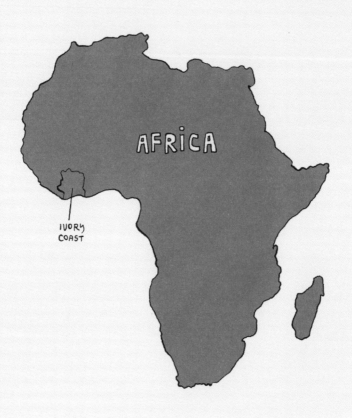

Preface

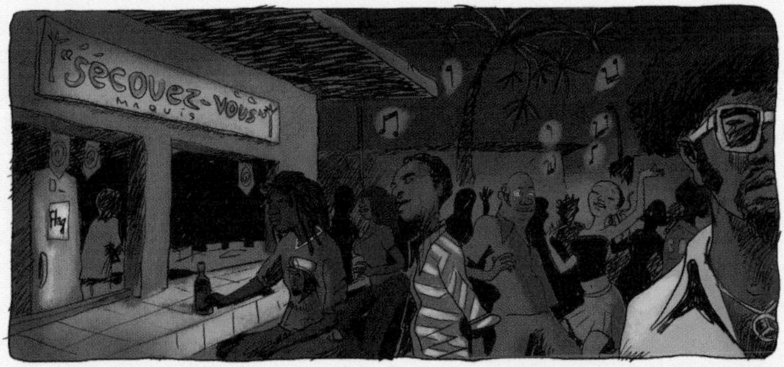

"Sécouvez-vous"
MAQUIS

The amorous hijinks narrated in *Aya* seem so familiar, so nearly suburban in their post-adolescent focus on dance floor flirtations, awkward first dates, and finding just the right dress for a friend's wedding, that to many western readers it may be difficult to believe they take place in Africa. As young Ivorian Myriam Montrat wrote about her homeland in the 1988 essay, "From the Heart of an African," "The vision of Africa in the American mind is shaped by films, music, art, entertainment and the news media...[but] only the news media have the mission to inform. With regard to Africa, the media fail in this mission." Inarguably, the western world is becoming increasingly aware of the myriad cultures on this massively diverse continent, but swollen-bellied children, machete-wielding *janjaweeds*, and too many men and women dying of AIDS continue to compromise the majority of visual images that dominate the Western media.

In the 1970s, however, one exceptional African nation belied the news channels' unremittingly tragic narratives and unsettling images: the Ivory Coast. A French colony for nearly eighty years, the nation was granted independence in 1960, and under the thirty-year leadership of its charismatic president, Félix Houphouët-Boigny, *Côte d'Ivoire* flourished. Instead of concentrating on industrial growth or the more immediate promise of petroleum, as its West African neighbors did, the new government hedged its bets on its sixteen million hectares of virgin forest, and Houphouët-Boigny encouraged industrious migrants to clear it by liberally declaring, "the land belongs to the one who cultivates it." This political masterstroke, as historian Catherine Boon has called it, resulted in a rapidly expanding economy based upon small-scale production of coffee, cocoa, timber, and other agricultural staples such as bananas. In the two decades following independence, the Ivory Coast's economic growth was unsurpassed in the sub-Saharan region, and statistically undeniable: the GNP rose by more than seven percent annually. During the time in which Aya's story takes place, the index of production was the highest in Africa, and what was commonly referred to as the "Ivorian miracle" resulted in unprecedented wealth.

The glamorous capital of Abidjan, often referred to as the "Paris of West Africa," was proof of this success, and not only because of a bridge named after Charles de Gaulle. Chic restaurants, elegant hotels, and world-class golf courses were only a few of this coastal city's many amenities. More than forty thousand French nationals provided economic stability, as "*la présence française*" tended to encourage foreign investment, and perhaps more influentially, granted the city incomparable cultural cachet. Abidjanaise French was the preferred language, *patisseries* and fried plantains peacefully coexisted, and *les filles Afric*aines were more than familiar with the latest couture of Catherine Deneuve. Life seemed promising enough to be pedestrian; Bintou's hip-bumping moves in the open-air *maquis* and Adjoua's make-out sessions at the "1000 Star Hotel" were commonplace teenage pleasures that took place in such working class suburbs as Yopougon. The University of Abidjan flourished, with thousands of students graduating each year, and successfully finding jobs in government or other viable private sectors. Aya's dream of becoming a doctor, while dismissed by her conservative father, was very much a possibility. It was truly, as some wistfully refer to it, *la belle époque*.

Looking back on it, however, many economists wonder if this miracle was only a mirage, and the term "growth without development" is now more commonly accepted to describe this phenomenal period. Houphouët-Boigny's savvy *laissez-faire* policies tended to absorb rather than mobilize any opposition to his rule, and while this one party domination may have left the farmers free to cultivate land as they wished, it also left them politically disenfranchised. Not surprisingly, the real beneficiaries of the Ivorian miracle in the 70s were not the industrious peasants whose crops were responsible for the country's gains, but an urban-based elite, characters not unlike the boss of Aya's father, a man who freely and frequently drops the names of both Houphouët-Boigny and French president Giscard D'Estaing. More problematically, because much of the gain was due more to a rise in the number of smallholders rather than an increase in farm size or individual production, once export prices for key crops declined, the country suffered a serious recession. As the economy began to stagnate in the 80s, social unrest ensued. Student and worker strikes were commonplace; French companies began to pull out, and as dwindling resources began to affect all segments of society, blame and anger began to be directed towards remaining French nationals and non-Ivorian Africans. These conflicts escalated after Houphouët-Boigny's death, when his successor Henri Konan Bédié, resorted to divisive ethnic politics and xenophobia.

The last decade within the Ivory Coast has been dominated by a virulently Franco-phobic generation weaned not on the burgeoning potential of a newly independent nation, but on bloody coups and seemingly endless civil war. Sadly, the easy banter afforded by Aya and her girlfriends now seems a nostalgic anomaly, as the once glittering city of Abidjan falls further into decline. But Marguerite Abouet's gently comic narrative, her sexily piquant recipes, her advice on how to roll one's *pagne* (and one's *tassaba*!), coupled with Clément Oubrerie's vividly colored drawings, remind us of art's power to make another time and place come alive. Brilliantly, *dêh*!

Alisia Grace Chase, PhD
2007

FOR MARGAUX AND EMMANUEL
☆ ☆

The characters

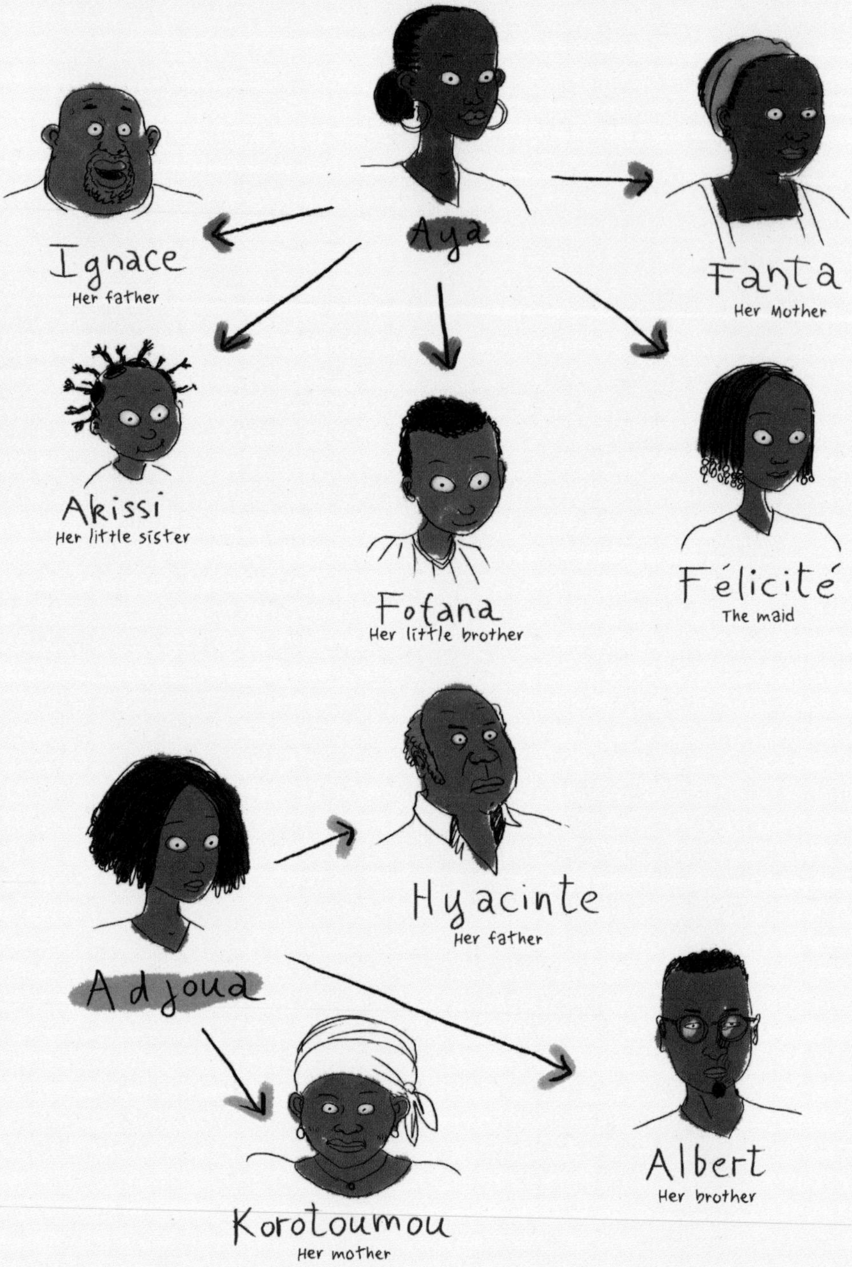

Aya
Ignace
Her father
Fanta
Her Mother
Akissi
Her little sister
Fofana
Her little brother
Félicité
The maid
Adjoua
Hyacinte
Her father
Korotoumou
Her mother
Albert
Her brother

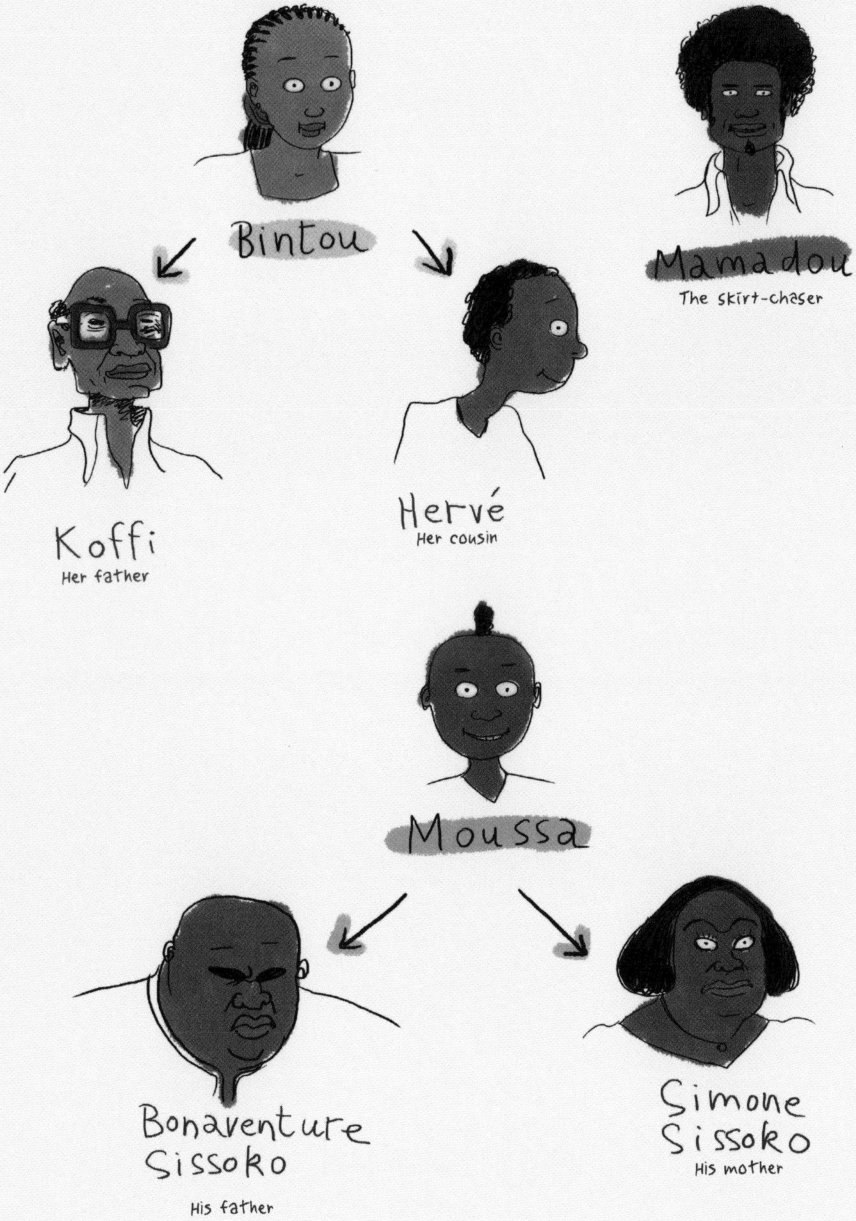

Bintou
Mamadou
The skirt-chaser
Koffi
Her father
Hervé
Her cousin
Moussa
Bonaventure Sissoko
His father
Simone Sissoko
His mother

1978 was the year that Ivory Coast, my beautiful country, got to see its first television ad campaign. It was for Solibra, a local beer popular in all of West Africa. Dago, a comedian who was big at the time, took a swig, and suddenly he had the power to blow by buses on his bicycle.

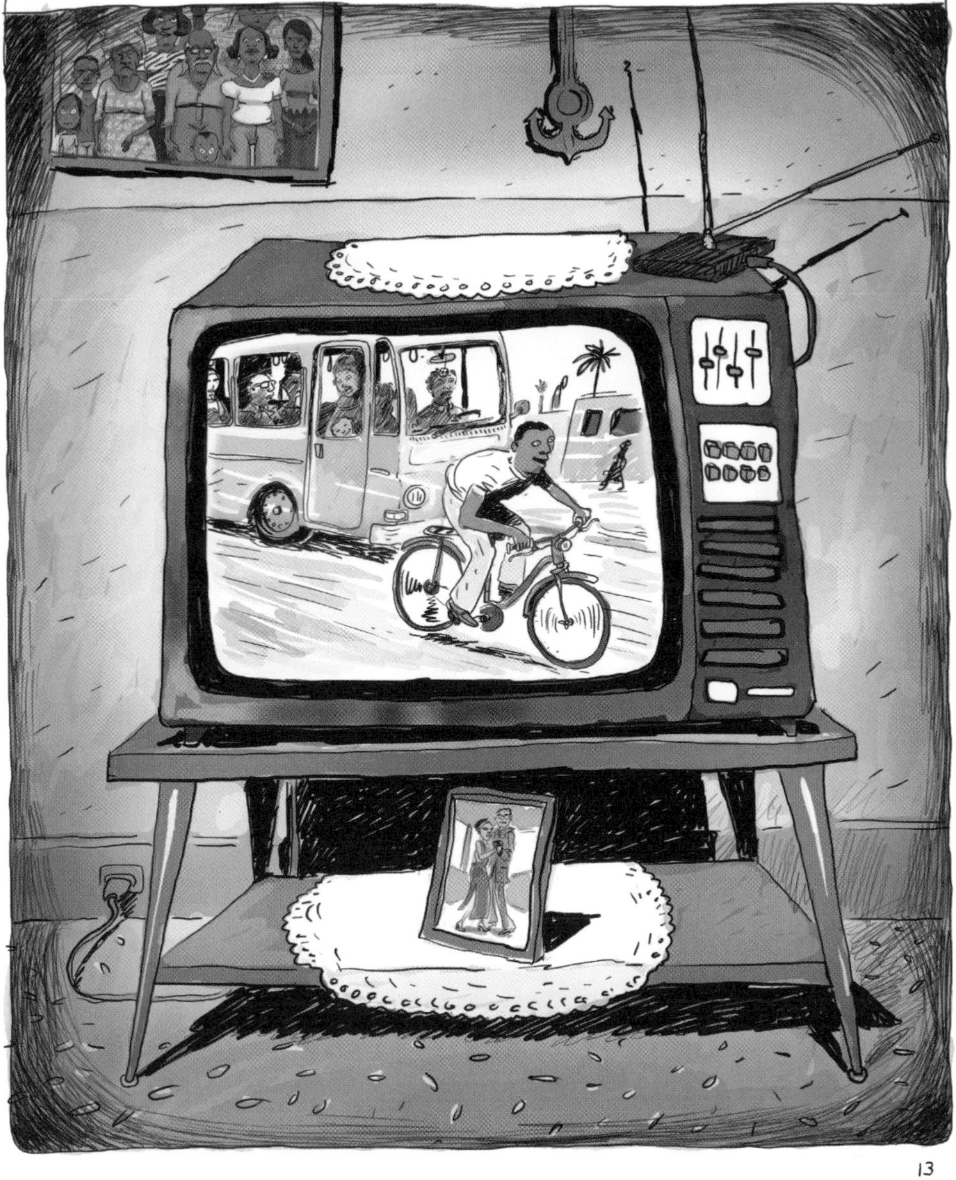

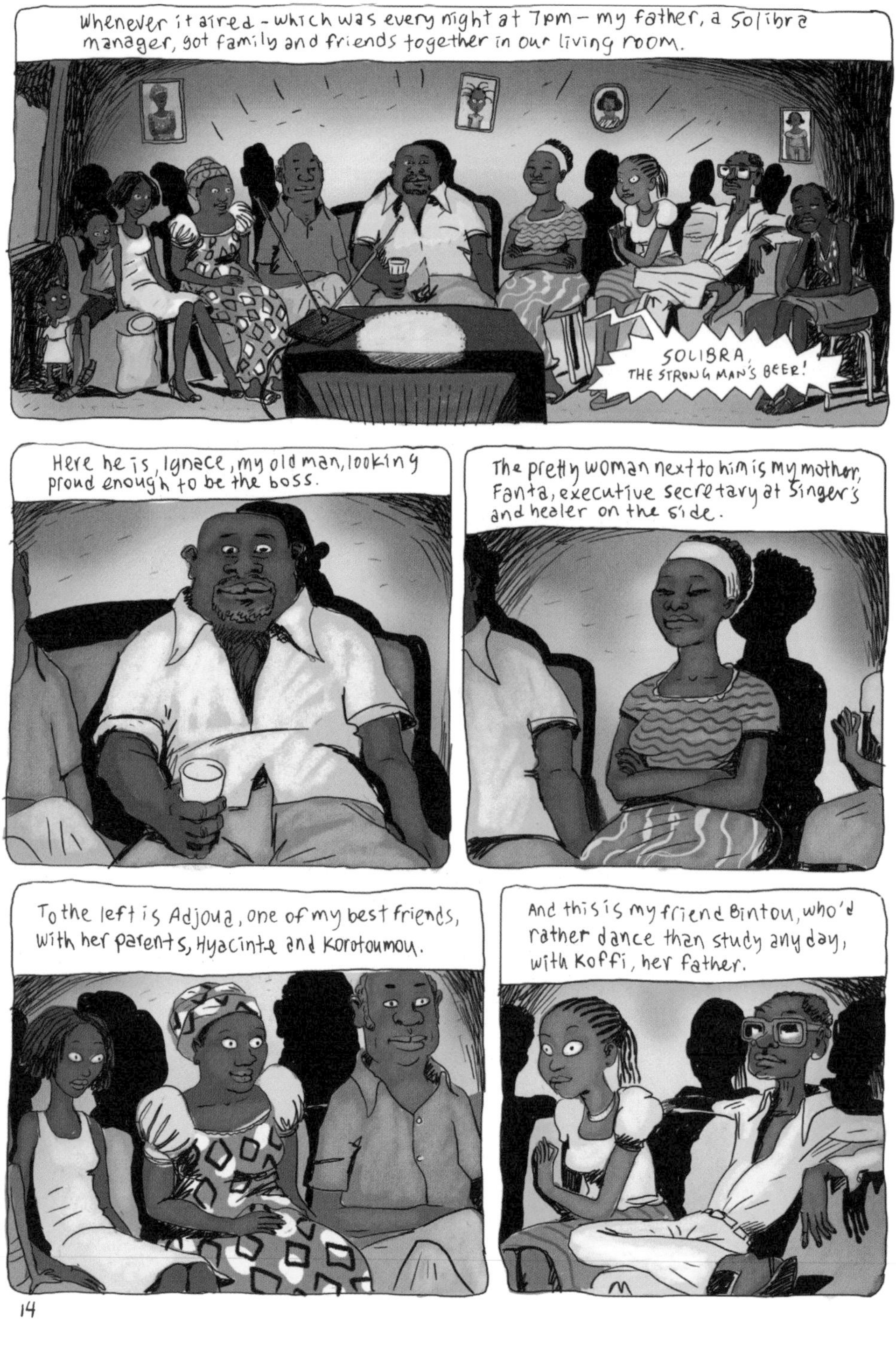
Whenever it aired - which was every night at 7pm - my father, a Solibra manager, got family and friends together in our living room.
SOLIBRA, THE STRONG MAN'S BEER!
Here he is, Ignace, my old man, looking proud enough to be the boss.
The pretty woman next to him is my mother, Fanta, executive secretary at Singer's and healer on the side.
To the left is Adjoua, one of my best friends, with her parents, Hyacinte and Korotoumou.
And this is my friend Bintou, who'd rather dance than study any day, with Koffi, her father.

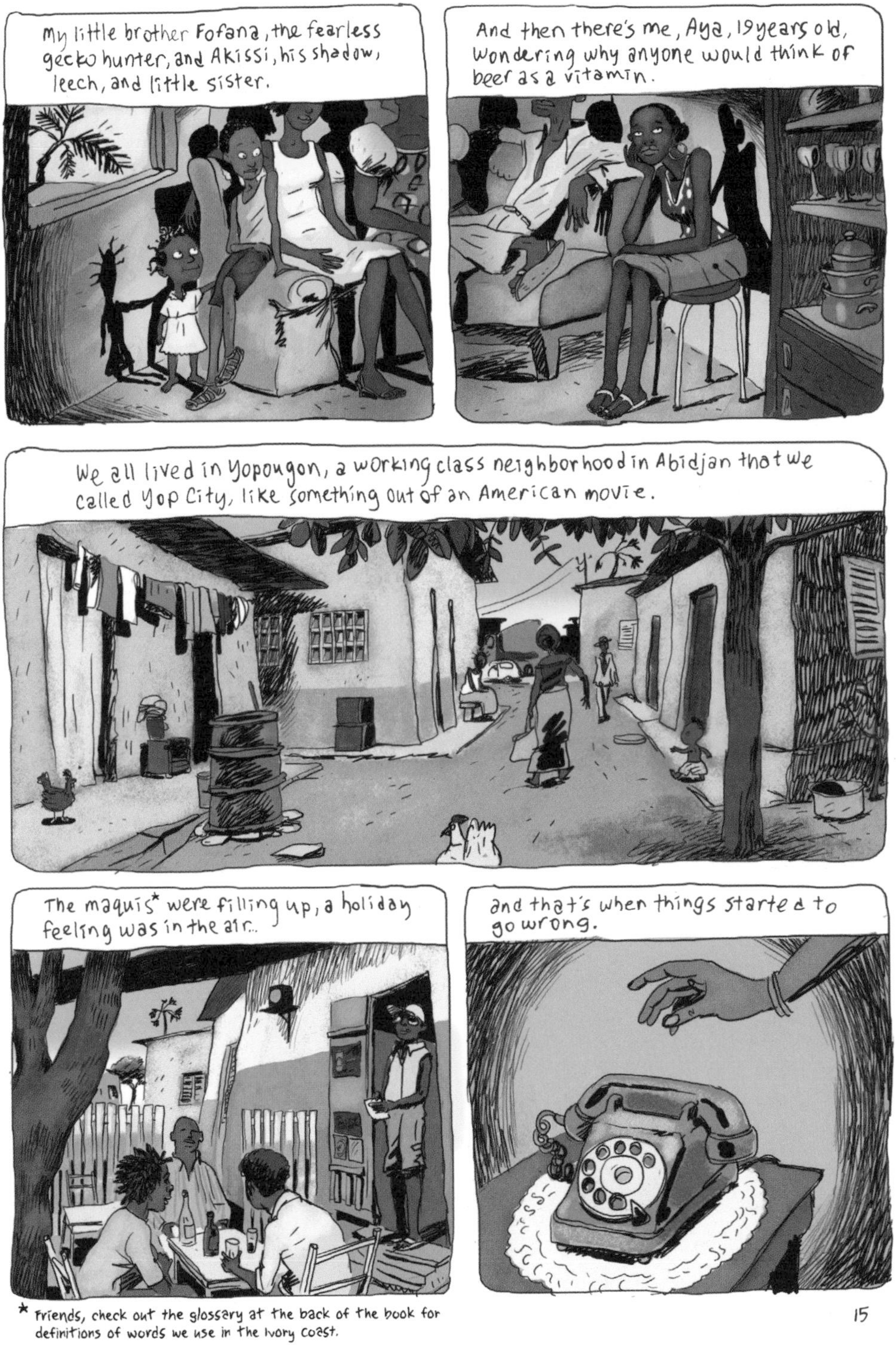
My little brother Fofana, the fearless gecko hunter, and Akissi, his shadow, leech, and little sister.
And then there's me, Aya, 19 years old, wondering why anyone would think of beer as a vitamin.
We all lived in Yopougon, a working class neighborhood in Abidjan that we called Yop City, like something out of an American movie.
The maquis* were filling up, a holiday feeling was in the air...
and that's when things started to go wrong.

* Friends, check out the glossary at the back of the book for definitions of words we use in the Ivory Coast.

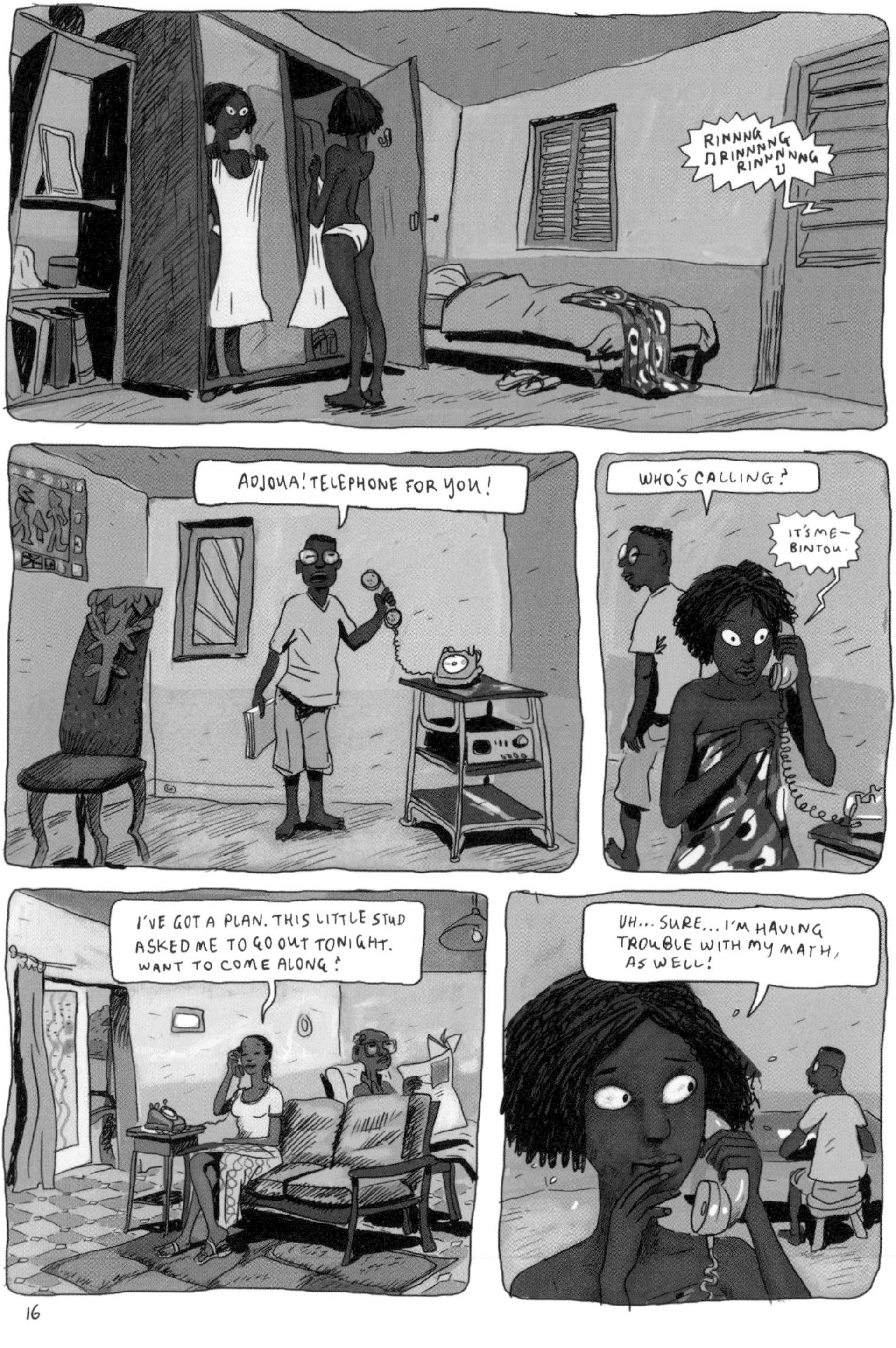
RINNNG RINNNNNG RINNNNNG
ADJOUA! TELEPHONE FOR YOU!
WHO'S CALLING?
IT'S ME- BINTOU.
I'VE GOT A PLAN. THIS LITTLE STUD ASKED ME TO GO OUT TONIGHT. WANT TO COME ALONG?
UH... SURE... I'M HAVING TROUBLE WITH MY MATH, AS WELL!

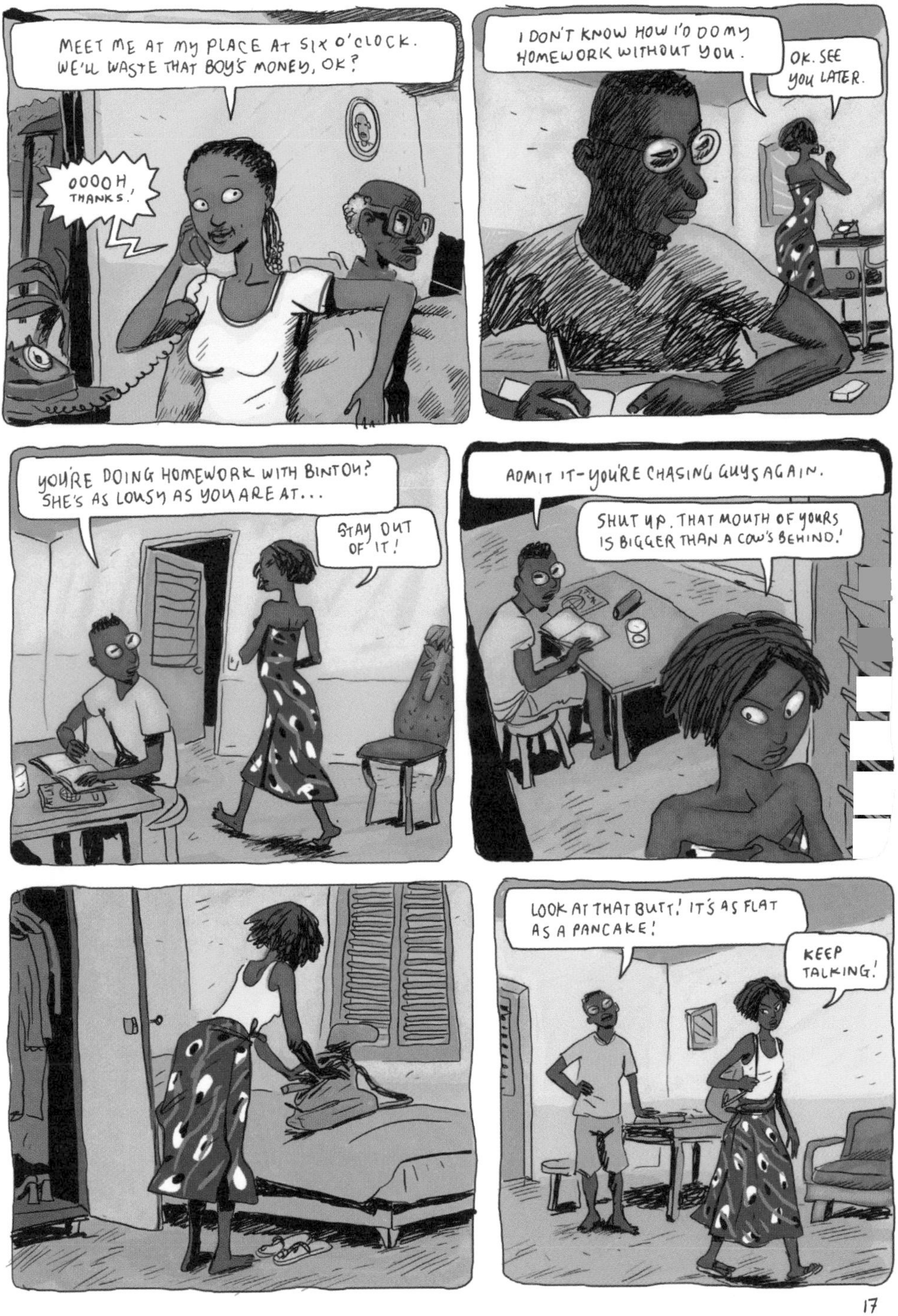

MEET ME AT MY PLACE AT SIX O'CLOCK. WE'LL WASTE THAT BOY'S MONEY, OK?
OOOOH, THANKS!
I DON'T KNOW HOW I'D DO MY HOMEWORK WITHOUT YOU.
OK. SEE YOU LATER.
YOU'RE DOING HOMEWORK WITH BINTOU? SHE'S AS LOUSY AS YOU ARE AT...
STAY OUT OF IT!
ADMIT IT—YOU'RE CHASING GUYS AGAIN.
SHUT UP. THAT MOUTH OF YOURS IS BIGGER THAN A COW'S BEHIND!
LOOK AT THAT BUTT! IT'S AS FLAT AS A PANCAKE!
KEEP TALKING!

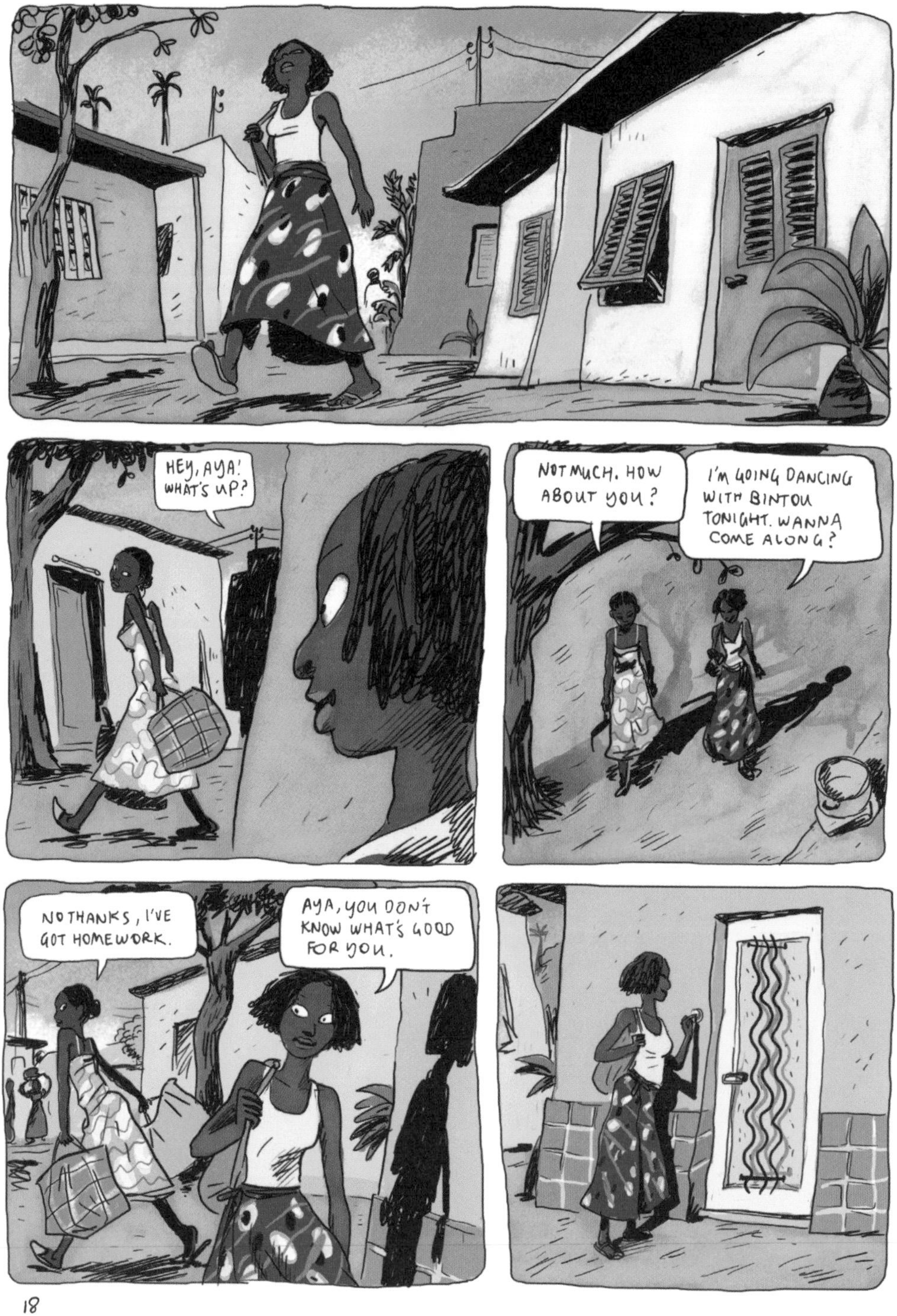
HEY, AYA! WHAT'S UP?
NOT MUCH. HOW ABOUT YOU?
I'M GOING DANCING WITH BINTOU TONIGHT. WANNA COME ALONG?
NO THANKS, I'VE GOT HOMEWORK.
AYA, YOU DON'T KNOW WHAT'S GOOD FOR YOU.

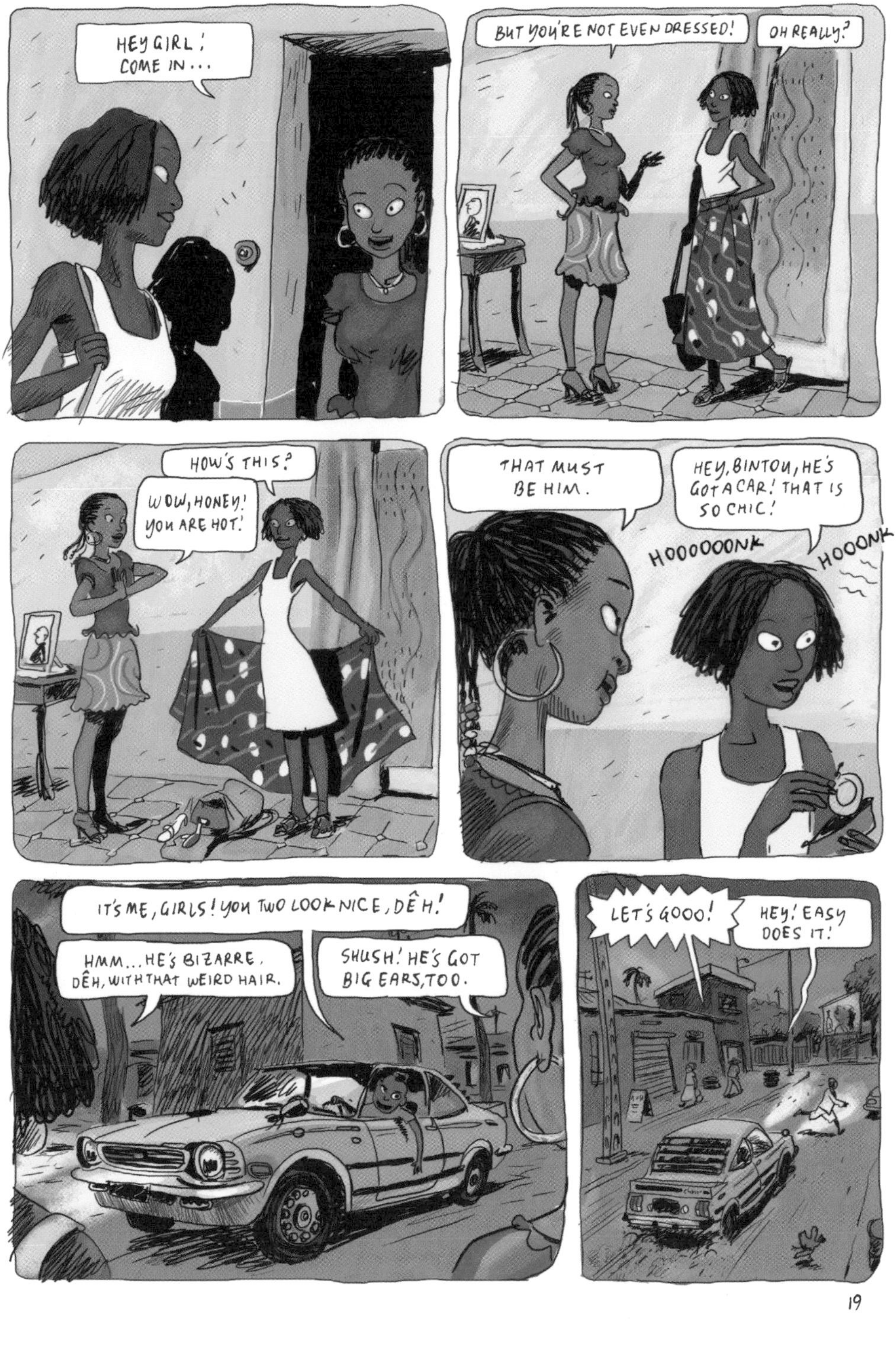
HEY GIRL! COME IN...
BUT YOU'RE NOT EVEN DRESSED!
OH REALLY?
HOW'S THIS?
WOW, HONEY! YOU ARE HOT!
THAT MUST BE HIM.
HOOOOOONK
HEY, BINTOU, HE'S GOT A CAR! THAT IS SO CHIC!
HOOONK
IT'S ME, GIRLS! YOU TWO LOOK NICE, DÊH!
HMM... HE'S BIZARRE, DÊH, WITH THAT WEIRD HAIR.
SHUSH! HE'S GOT BIG EARS, TOO.
LET'S GOOO!
HEY! EASY DOES IT!

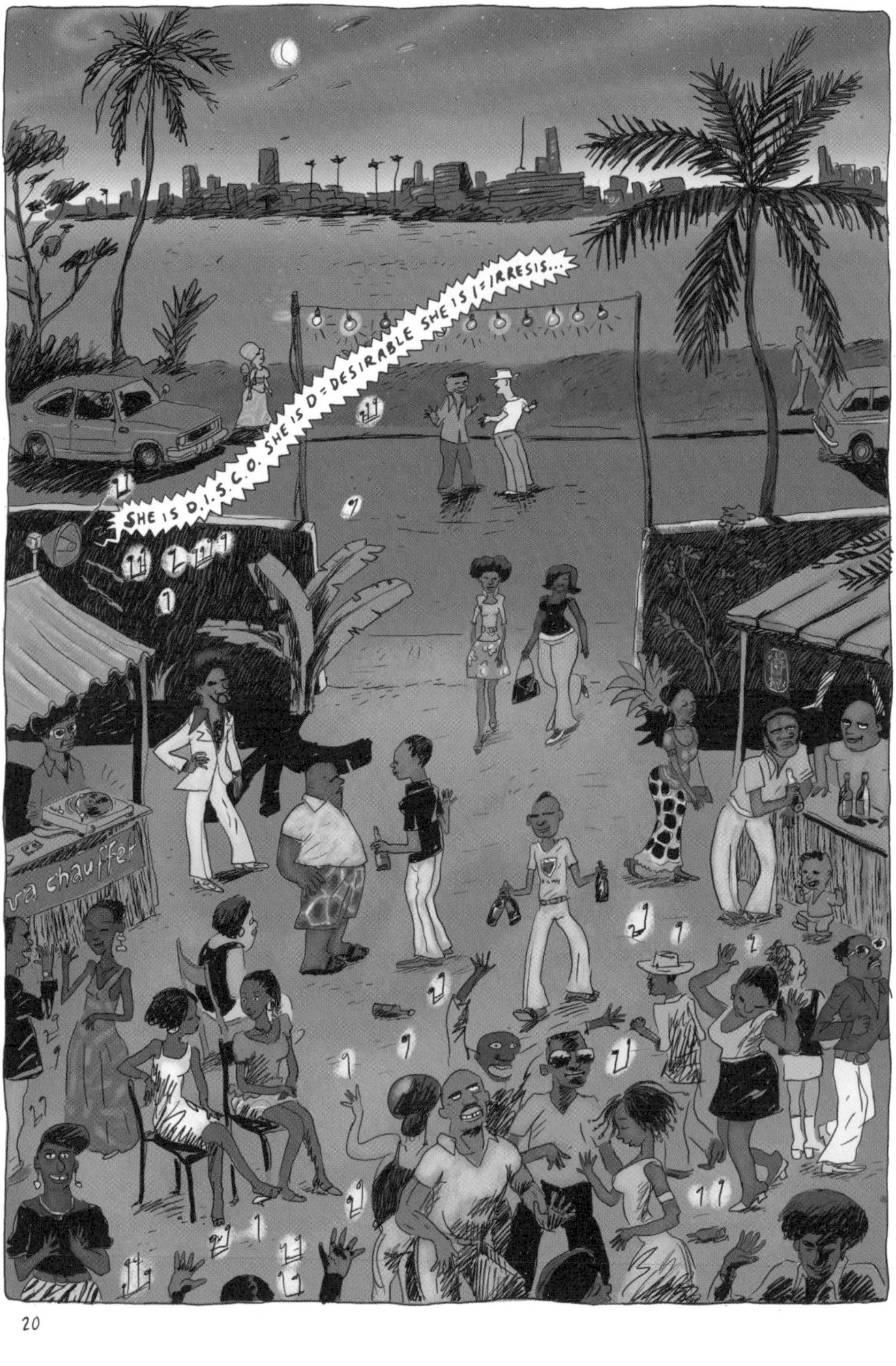
SHE IS D.I.S.C.O. SHE IS D=DESIRABLE SHE IS I=IRRESIS...
va chauffer

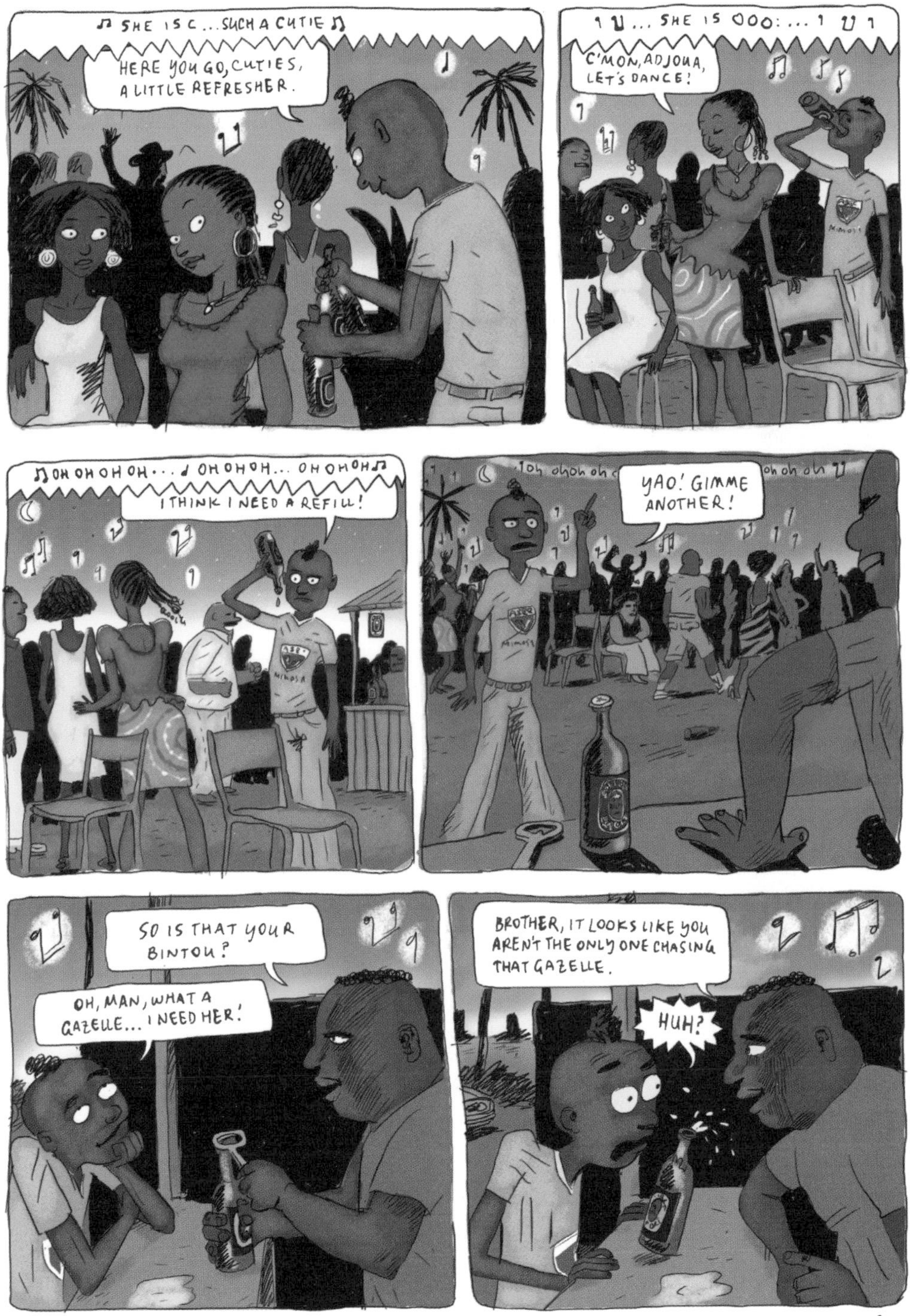
♫ SHE IS C... SUCH A CUTIE ♫
HERE YOU GO, CUTIES, A LITTLE REFRESHER.
... SHE IS OOO: ...
C'MON, ADJOUA, LET'S DANCE!
♫ OH OH OH OH... OH OH OH... OH OH OH ♫
I THINK I NEED A REFILL!
oh ohoh oh
YAO! GIMME ANOTHER!
oh oh oh
SO IS THAT YOUR BINTOU?
OH, MAN, WHAT A GAZELLE... I NEED HER!
BROTHER, IT LOOKS LIKE YOU AREN'T THE ONLY ONE CHASING THAT GAZELLE.
HUH?

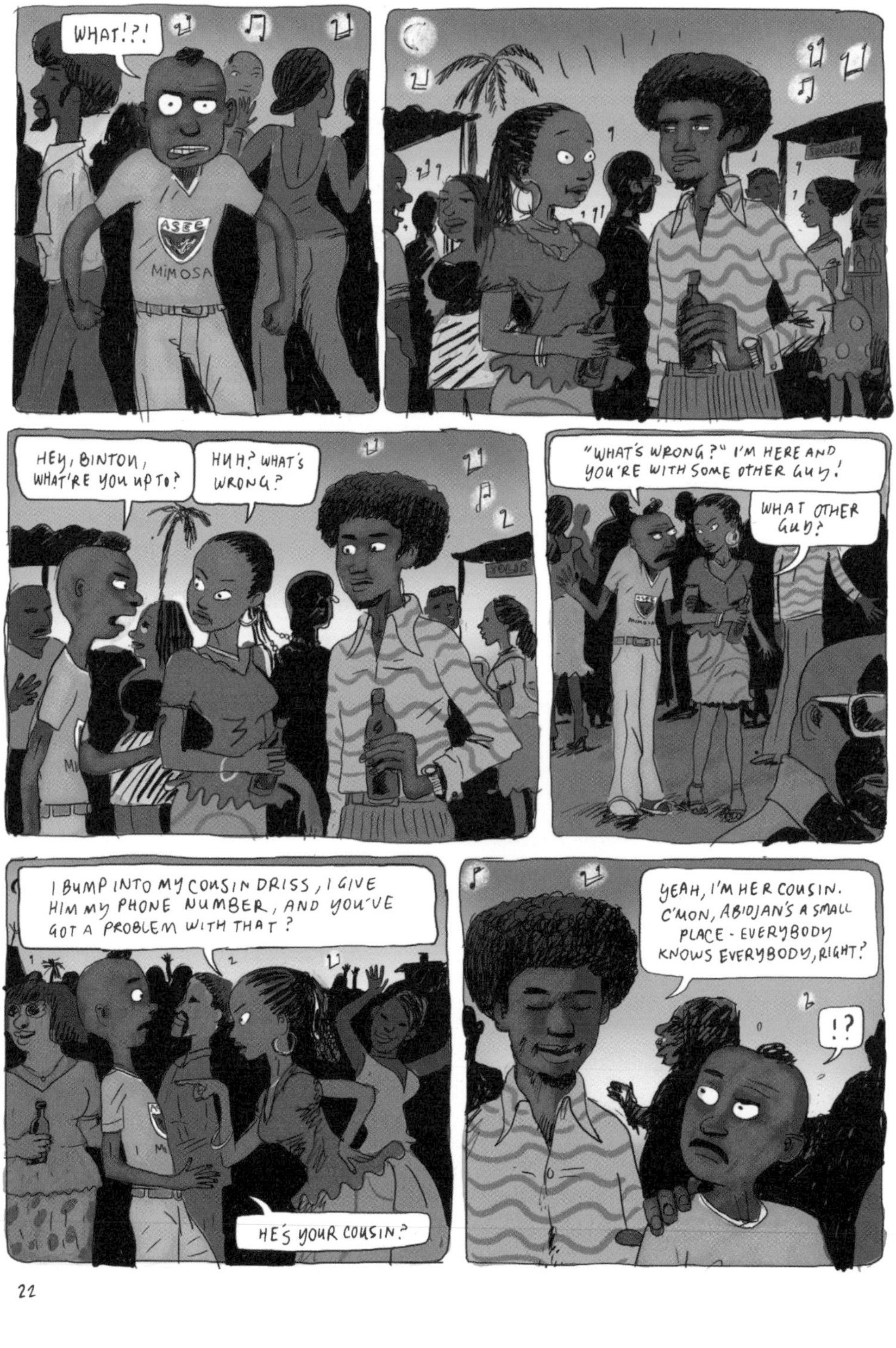
WHAT!?!
HEY, BINTOU, WHAT'RE YOU UP TO?
HUH? WHAT'S WRONG?
"WHAT'S WRONG?" I'M HERE AND YOU'RE WITH SOME OTHER GUY!
WHAT OTHER GUY?
I BUMP INTO MY COUSIN DRISS, I GIVE HIM MY PHONE NUMBER, AND YOU'VE GOT A PROBLEM WITH THAT?
HE'S YOUR COUSIN?
YEAH, I'M HER COUSIN. C'MON, ABIDJAN'S A SMALL PLACE - EVERYBODY KNOWS EVERYBODY, RIGHT?
!?

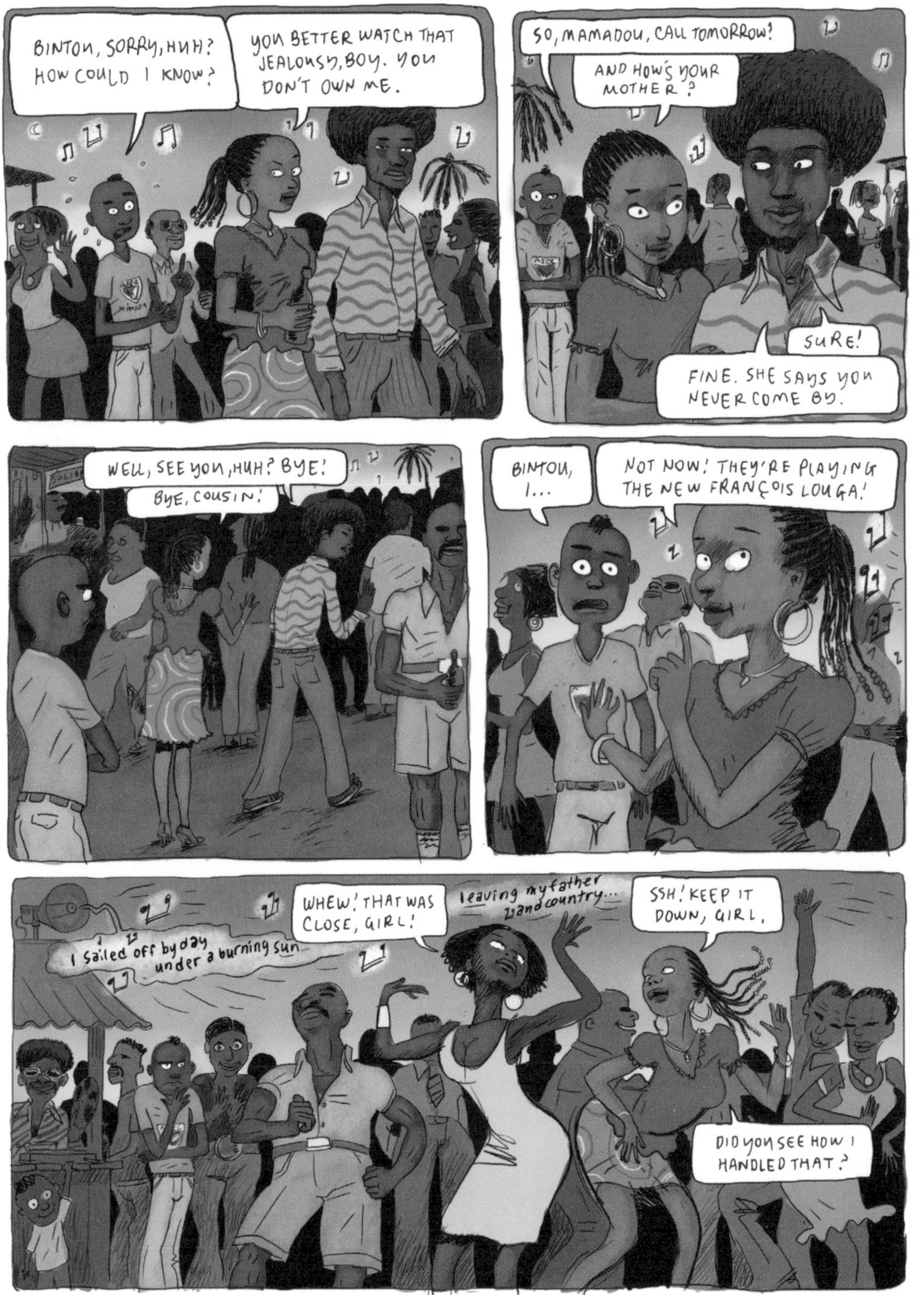
BINTOU, SORRY, HUH? HOW COULD I KNOW?
YOU BETTER WATCH THAT JEALOUSY, BOY. YOU DON'T OWN ME.
SO, MAMADOU, CALL TOMORROW?
AND HOW'S YOUR MOTHER?
SURE!
FINE. SHE SAYS YOU NEVER COME BY.
WELL, SEE YOU, HUH? BYE!
BYE, COUSIN!
BINTOU, I...
NOT NOW! THEY'RE PLAYING THE NEW FRANÇOIS LOUGA!
I sailed off by day under a burning sun
WHEW! THAT WAS CLOSE, GIRL!
leaving my father and country...
SSH! KEEP IT DOWN, GIRL,
DID YOU SEE HOW I HANDLED THAT?

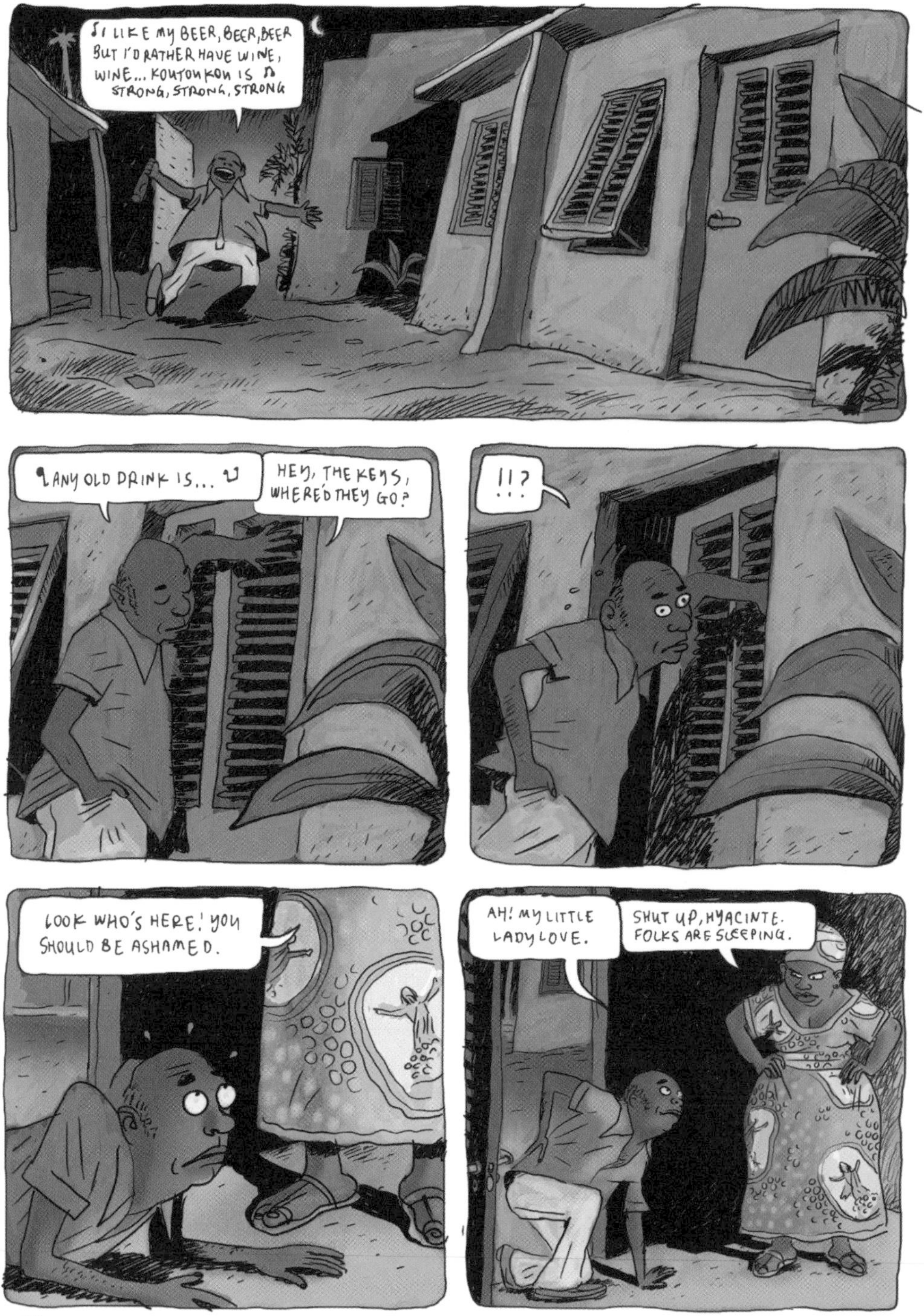
♪ I LIKE MY BEER, BEER, BEER BUT I'D RATHER HAVE WINE, WINE... KOUTOUKOU IS ♫ STRONG, STRONG, STRONG
♪ ANY OLD DRINK IS... ♫
HEY, THE KEYS, WHERE'D THEY GO?
!!? ...
LOOK WHO'S HERE! YOU SHOULD BE ASHAMED.
AH! MY LITTLE LADY LOVE.
SHUT UP, HYACINTE. FOLKS ARE SLEEPING.

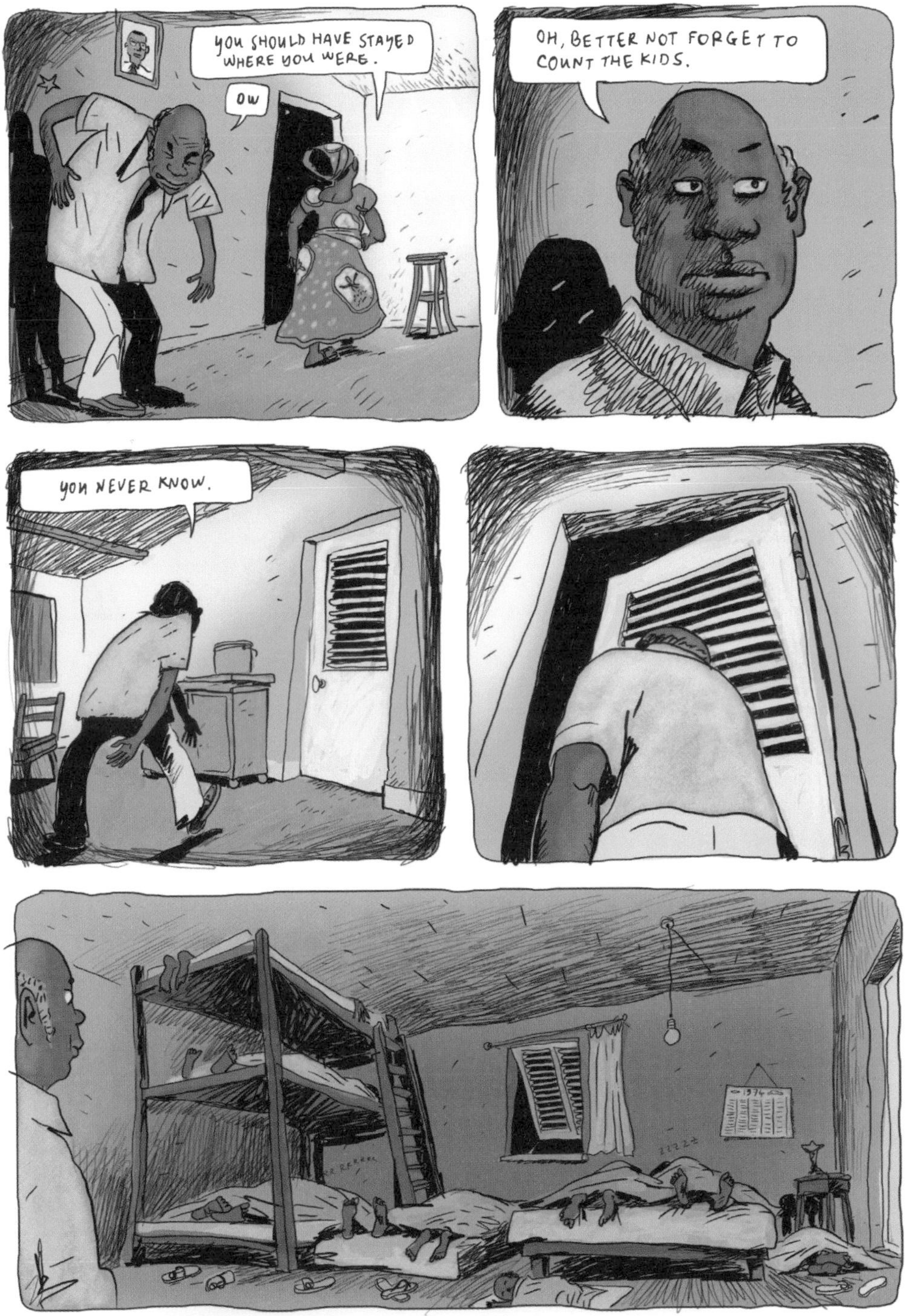
YOU SHOULD HAVE STAYED WHERE YOU WERE.
OW
OH, BETTER NOT FORGET TO COUNT THE KIDS.
YOU NEVER KNOW.

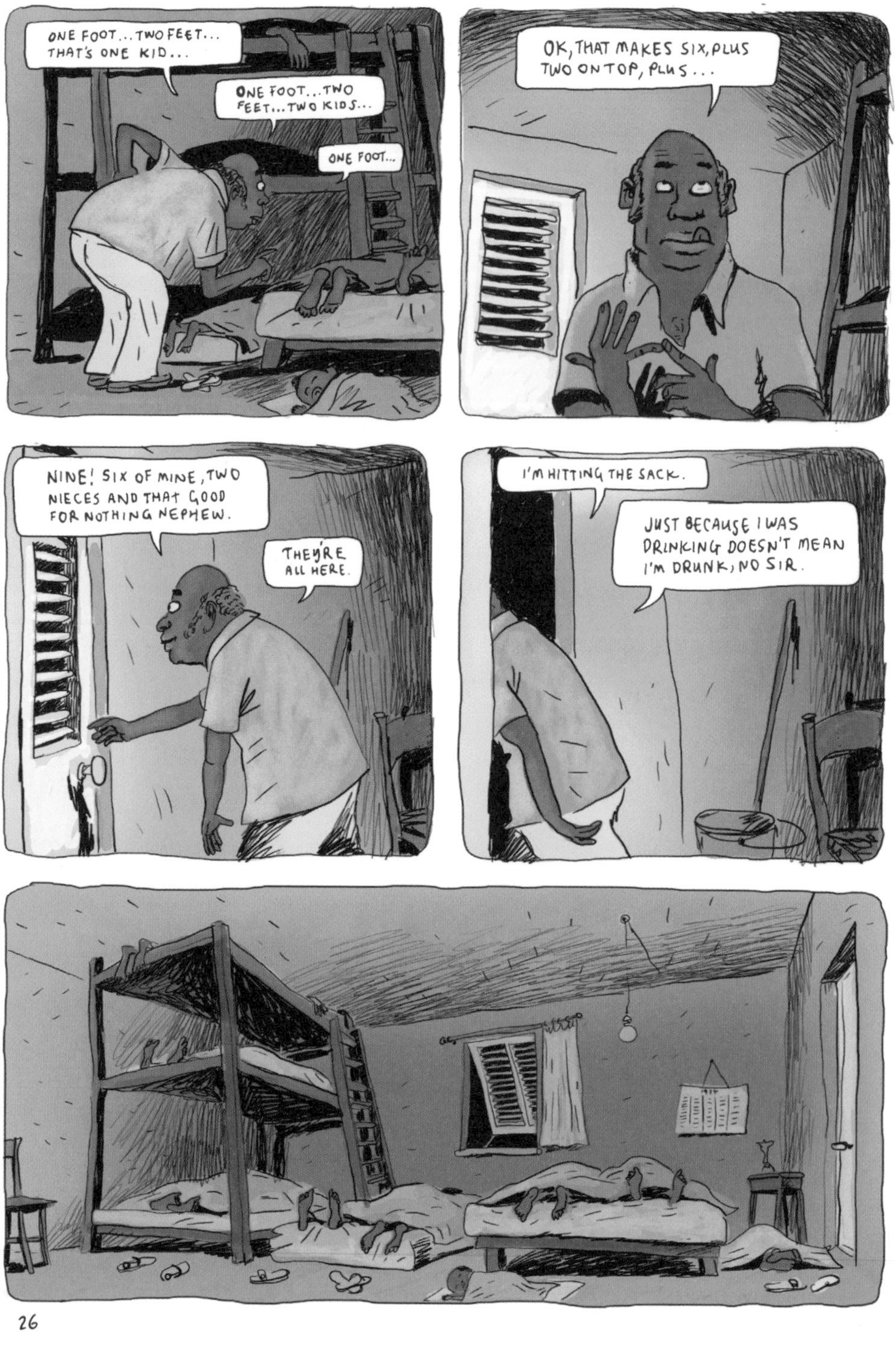
ONE FOOT... TWO FEET... THAT'S ONE KID...
ONE FOOT... TWO FEET... TWO KIDS...
ONE FOOT...
OK, THAT MAKES SIX, PLUS TWO ON TOP, PLUS...
NINE! SIX OF MINE, TWO NIECES AND THAT GOOD FOR NOTHING NEPHEW.
THEY'RE ALL HERE.
I'M HITTING THE SACK.
JUST BECAUSE I WAS DRINKING DOESN'T MEAN I'M DRUNK, NO SIR.

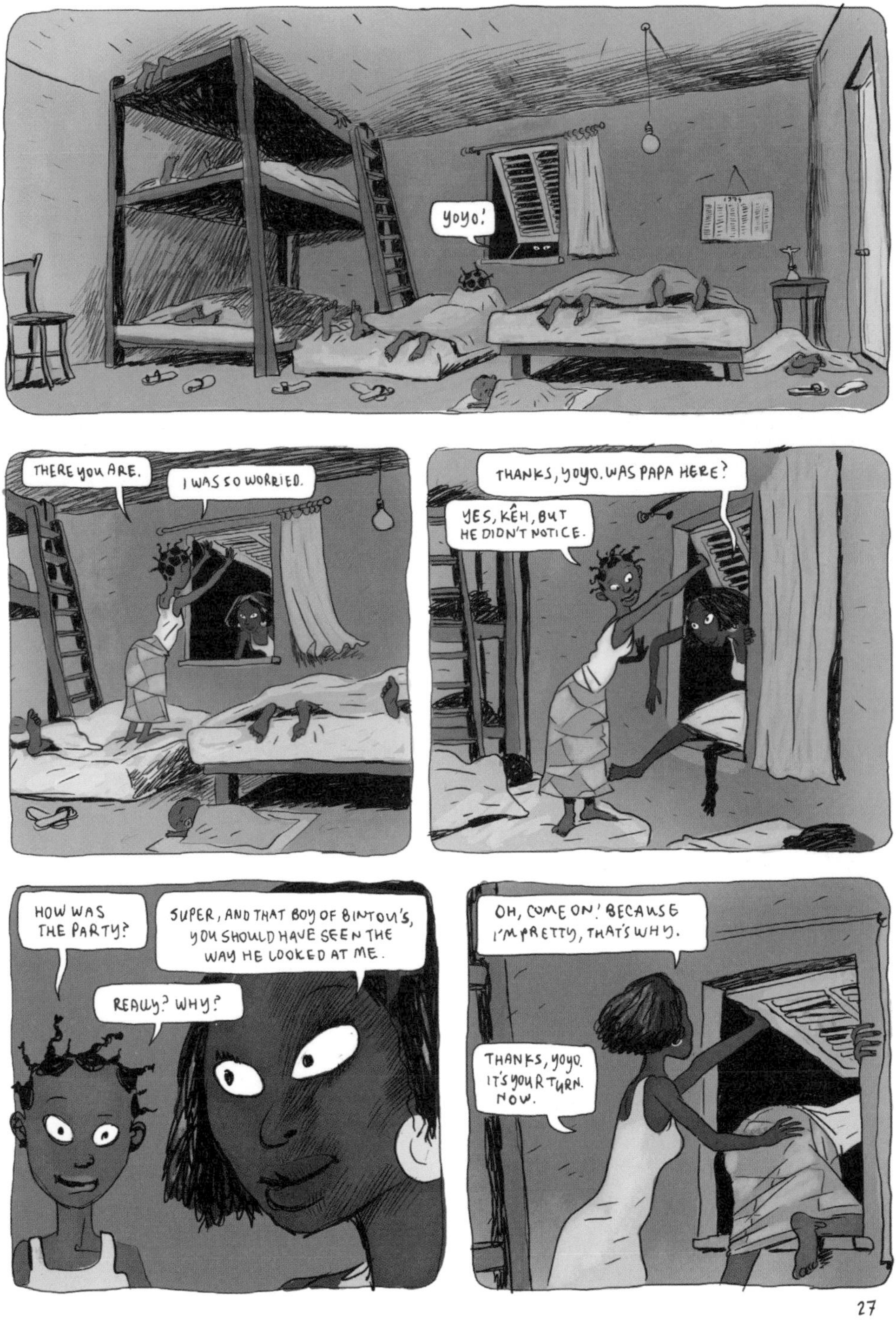
YOYO!
THERE YOU ARE.
I WAS SO WORRIED.
THANKS, YOYO. WAS PAPA HERE?
YES, KÊH, BUT HE DIDN'T NOTICE.
HOW WAS THE PARTY?
SUPER, AND THAT BOY OF BINTOU'S, YOU SHOULD HAVE SEEN THE WAY HE LOOKED AT ME.
REALLY? WHY?
OH, COME ON! BECAUSE I'M PRETTY, THAT'S WHY.
THANKS, YOYO. IT'S YOUR TURN NOW.

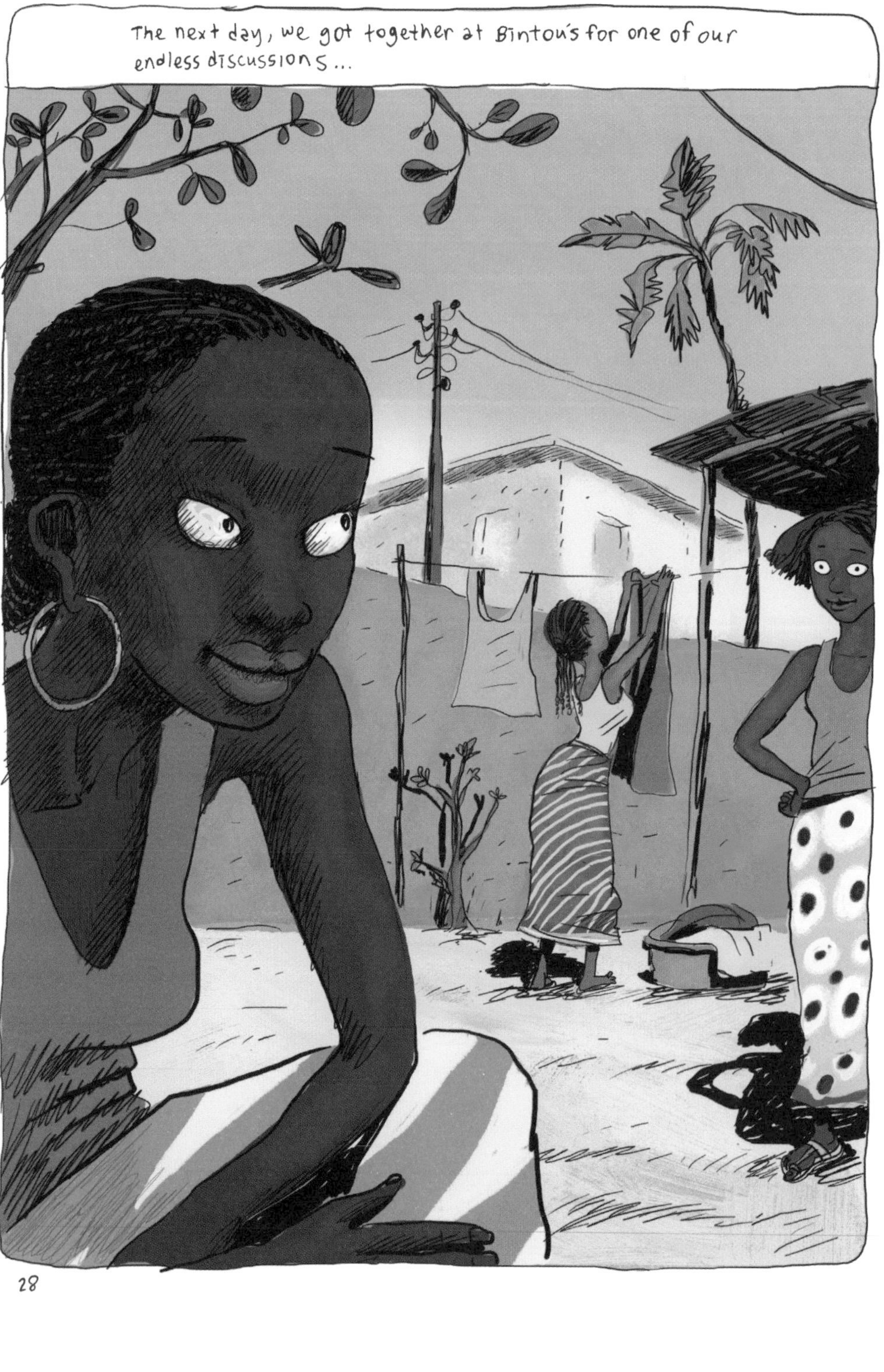
The next day, we got together at Bintou's for one of our endless discussions...

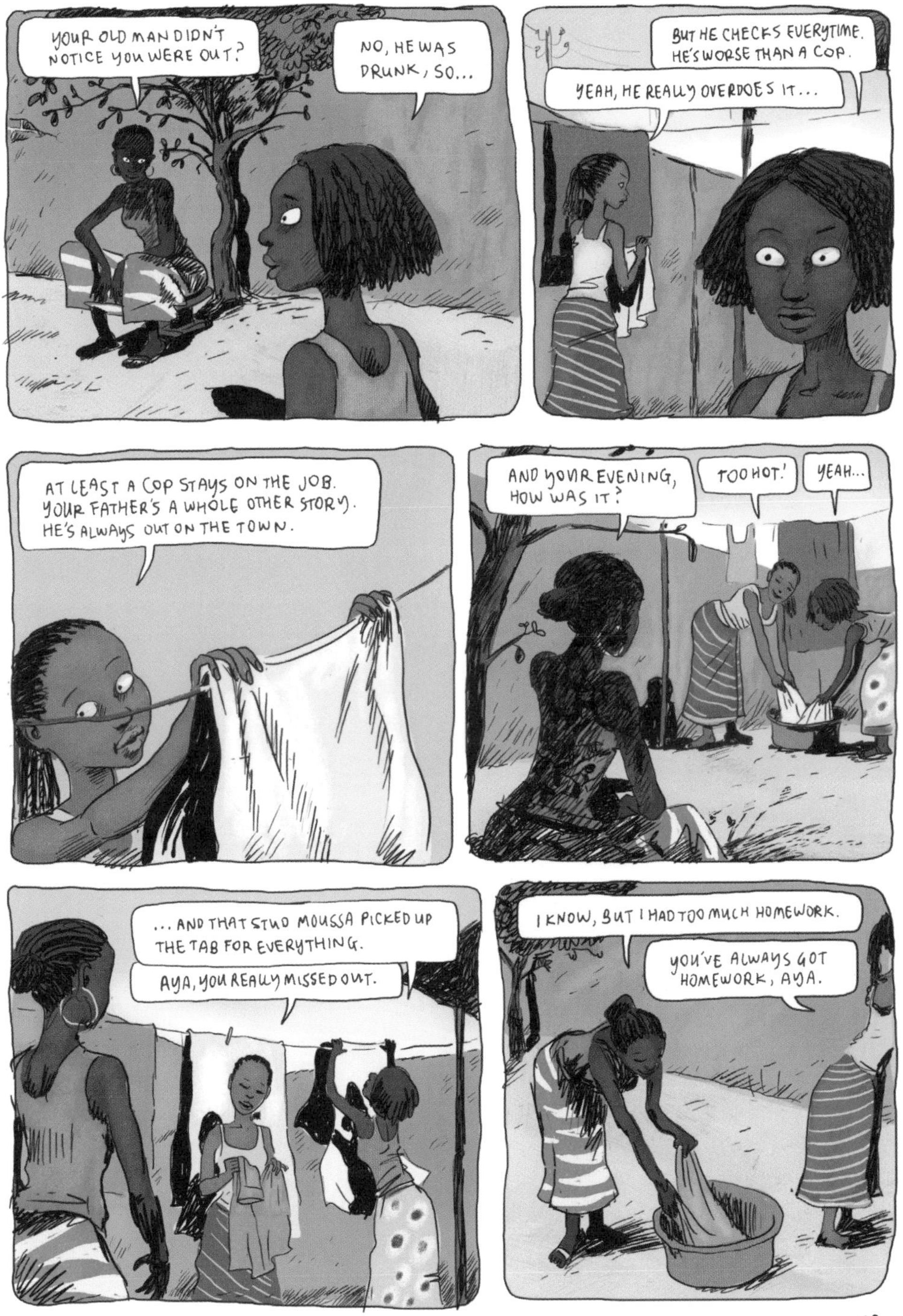

YOUR OLD MAN DIDN'T NOTICE YOU WERE OUT?
NO, HE WAS DRUNK, SO...
BUT HE CHECKS EVERYTIME. HE'S WORSE THAN A COP.
YEAH, HE REALLY OVERDOES IT...
AT LEAST A COP STAYS ON THE JOB. YOUR FATHER'S A WHOLE OTHER STORY. HE'S ALWAYS OUT ON THE TOWN.
AND YOUR EVENING, HOW WAS IT?
TOO HOT!
YEAH...
...AND THAT STUD MOUSSA PICKED UP THE TAB FOR EVERYTHING.
AYA, YOU REALLY MISSED OUT.
I KNOW, BUT I HAD TOO MUCH HOMEWORK.
YOU'VE ALWAYS GOT HOMEWORK, AYA.

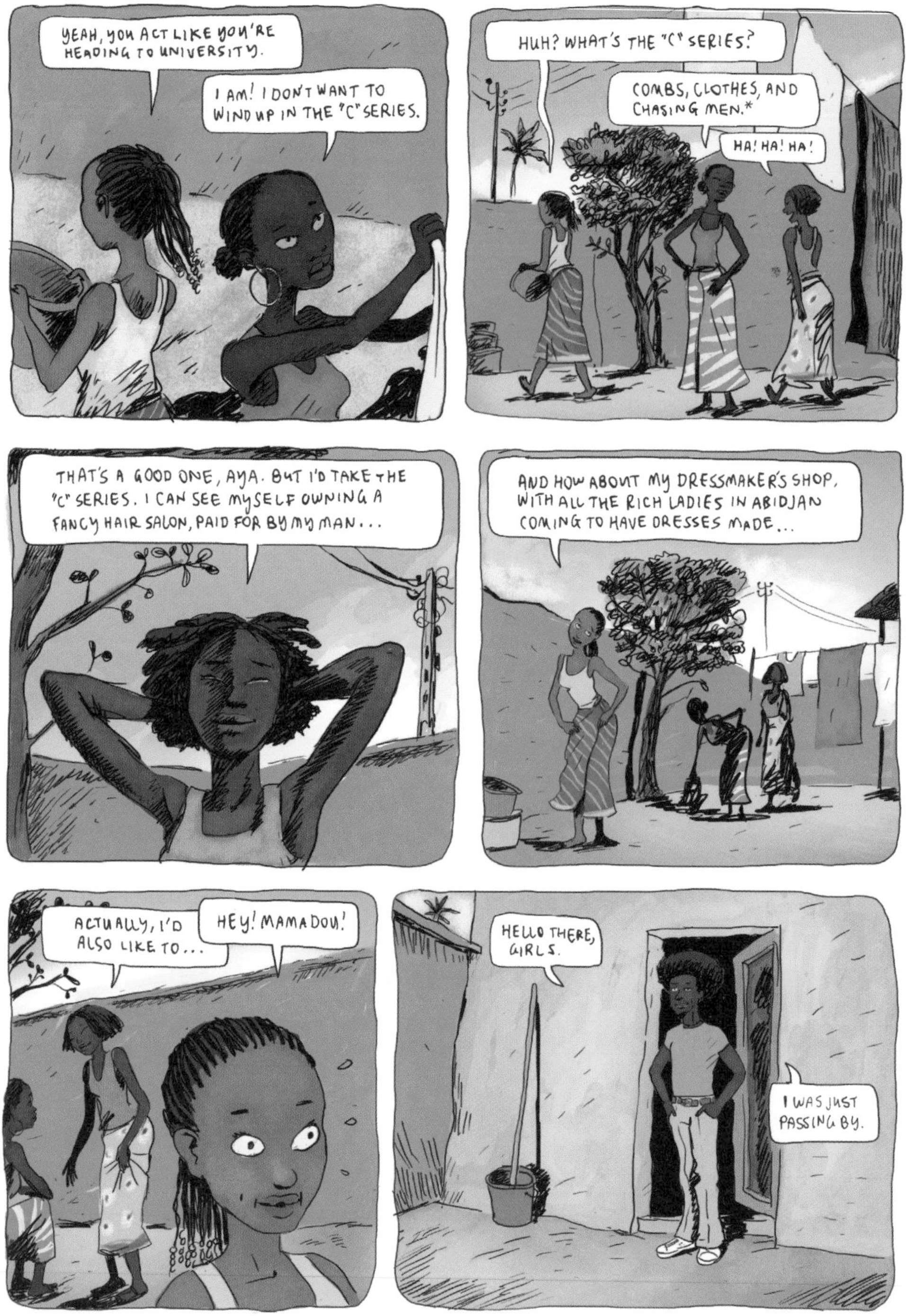
YEAH, YOU ACT LIKE YOU'RE HEADING TO UNIVERSITY.
I AM! I DON'T WANT TO WIND UP IN THE "C" SERIES.
HUH? WHAT'S THE "C" SERIES?
COMBS, CLOTHES, AND CHASING MEN.*
HA! HA! HA!
THAT'S A GOOD ONE, AYA. BUT I'D TAKE THE "C" SERIES. I CAN SEE MYSELF OWNING A FANCY HAIR SALON, PAID FOR BY MY MAN...
AND HOW ABOUT MY DRESSMAKER'S SHOP, WITH ALL THE RICH LADIES IN ABIDJAN COMING TO HAVE DRESSES MADE...
ACTUALLY, I'D ALSO LIKE TO...
HEY! MAMADOU!
HELLO THERE, GIRLS.
I WAS JUST PASSING BY.

*IN SENIOR HIGH SCHOOL, STUDENTS ARE PLACED IN ACADEMIC STREAMS, OR "SERIES," BASED ON SUBJECT MATTER. THE "C" SERIES IS ACTUALLY A SCIENCE STREAM THAT INCLUDES MATH, PHYSICS, AND BIOLOGY.

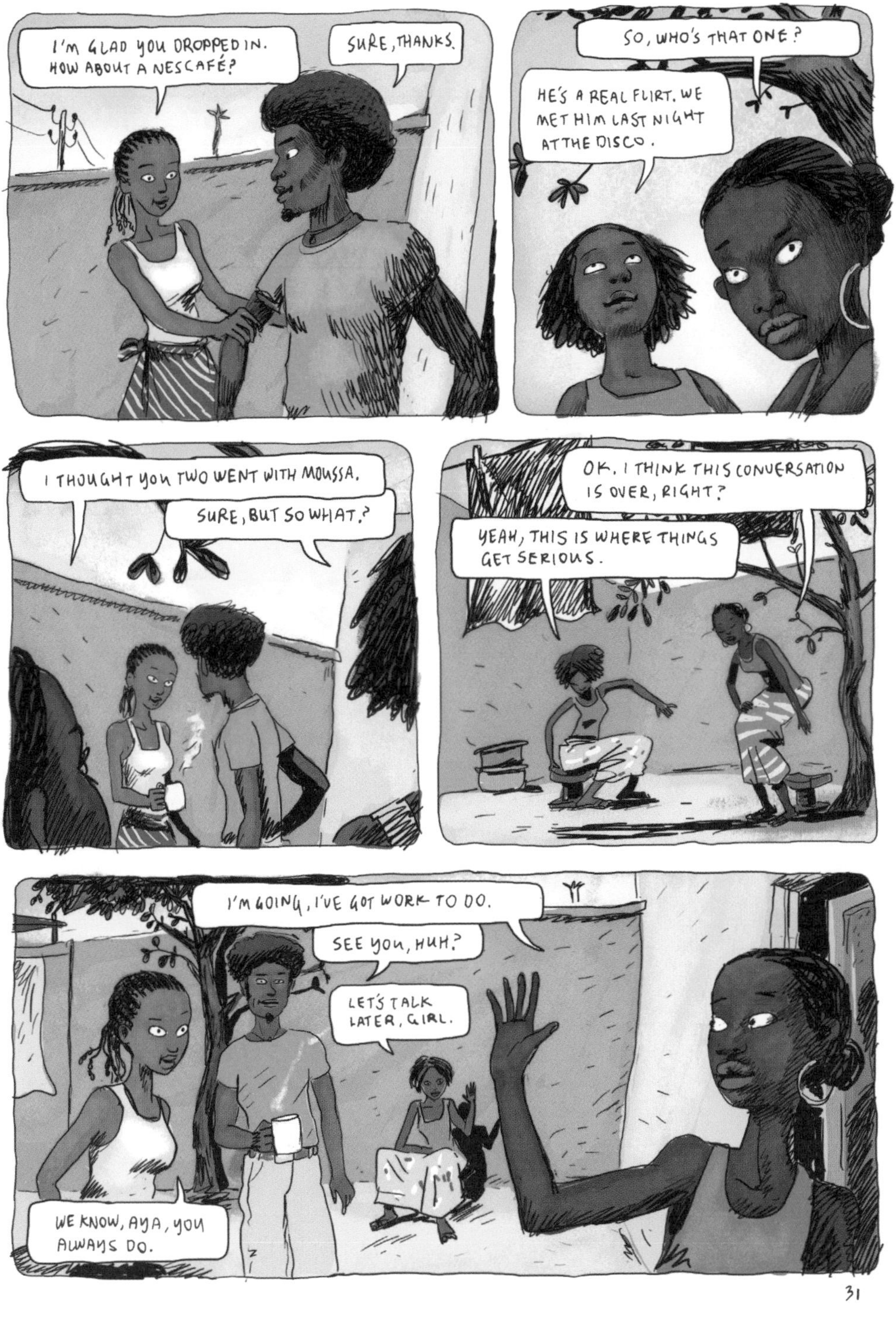
I'M GLAD YOU DROPPED IN. HOW ABOUT A NESCAFÉ?
SURE, THANKS.
SO, WHO'S THAT ONE?
HE'S A REAL FLIRT. WE MET HIM LAST NIGHT AT THE DISCO.
I THOUGHT YOU TWO WENT WITH MOUSSA.
SURE, BUT SO WHAT?
OK. I THINK THIS CONVERSATION IS OVER, RIGHT?
YEAH, THIS IS WHERE THINGS GET SERIOUS.
I'M GOING, I'VE GOT WORK TO DO.
SEE YOU, HUH?
LET'S TALK LATER, GIRL.
WE KNOW, AYA, YOU ALWAYS DO.

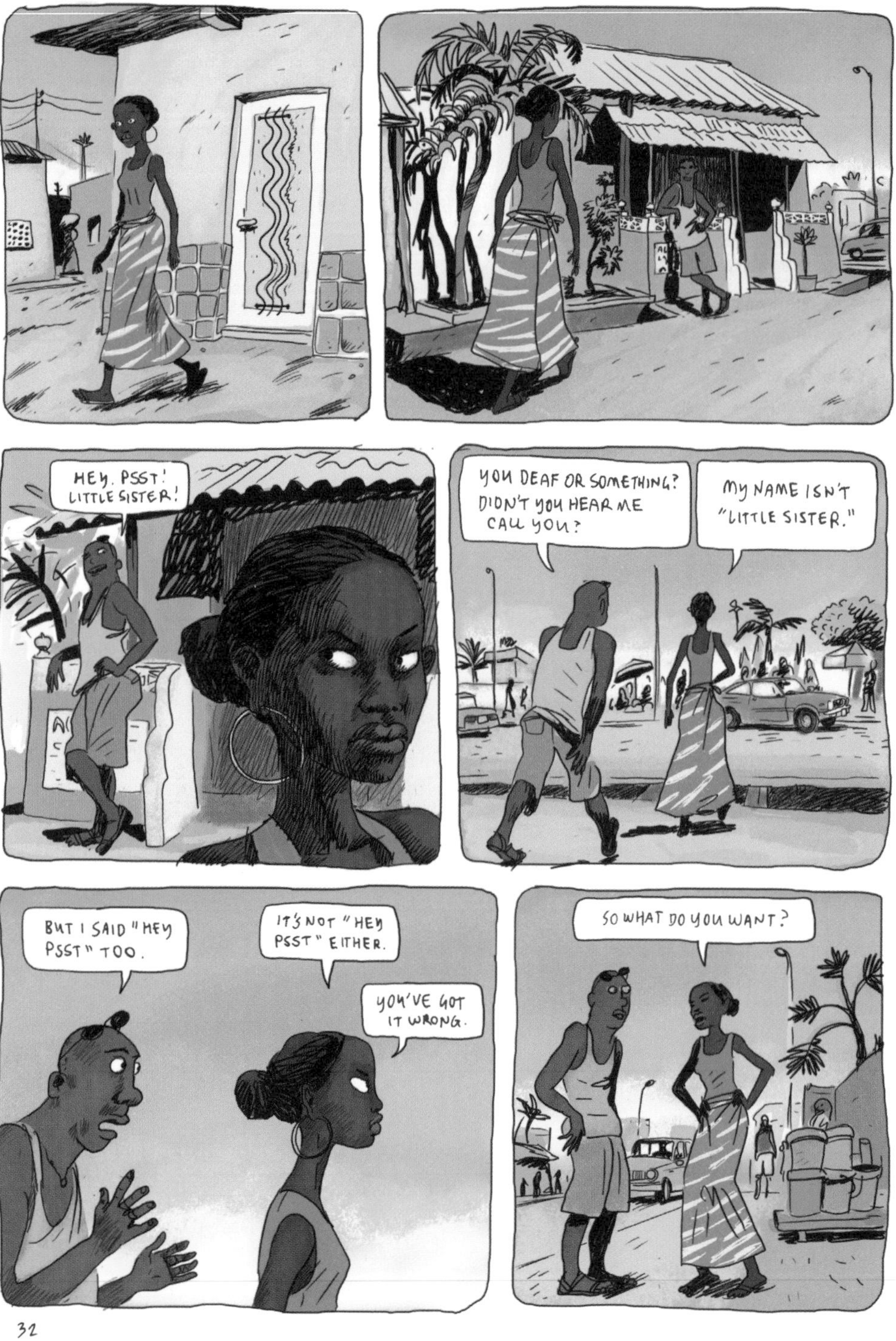
HEY. PSST! LITTLE SISTER!
YOU DEAF OR SOMETHING? DIDN'T YOU HEAR ME CALL YOU?
MY NAME ISN'T "LITTLE SISTER."
BUT I SAID "HEY PSST" TOO.
IT'S NOT "HEY PSST" EITHER.
YOU'VE GOT IT WRONG.
SO WHAT DO YOU WANT?

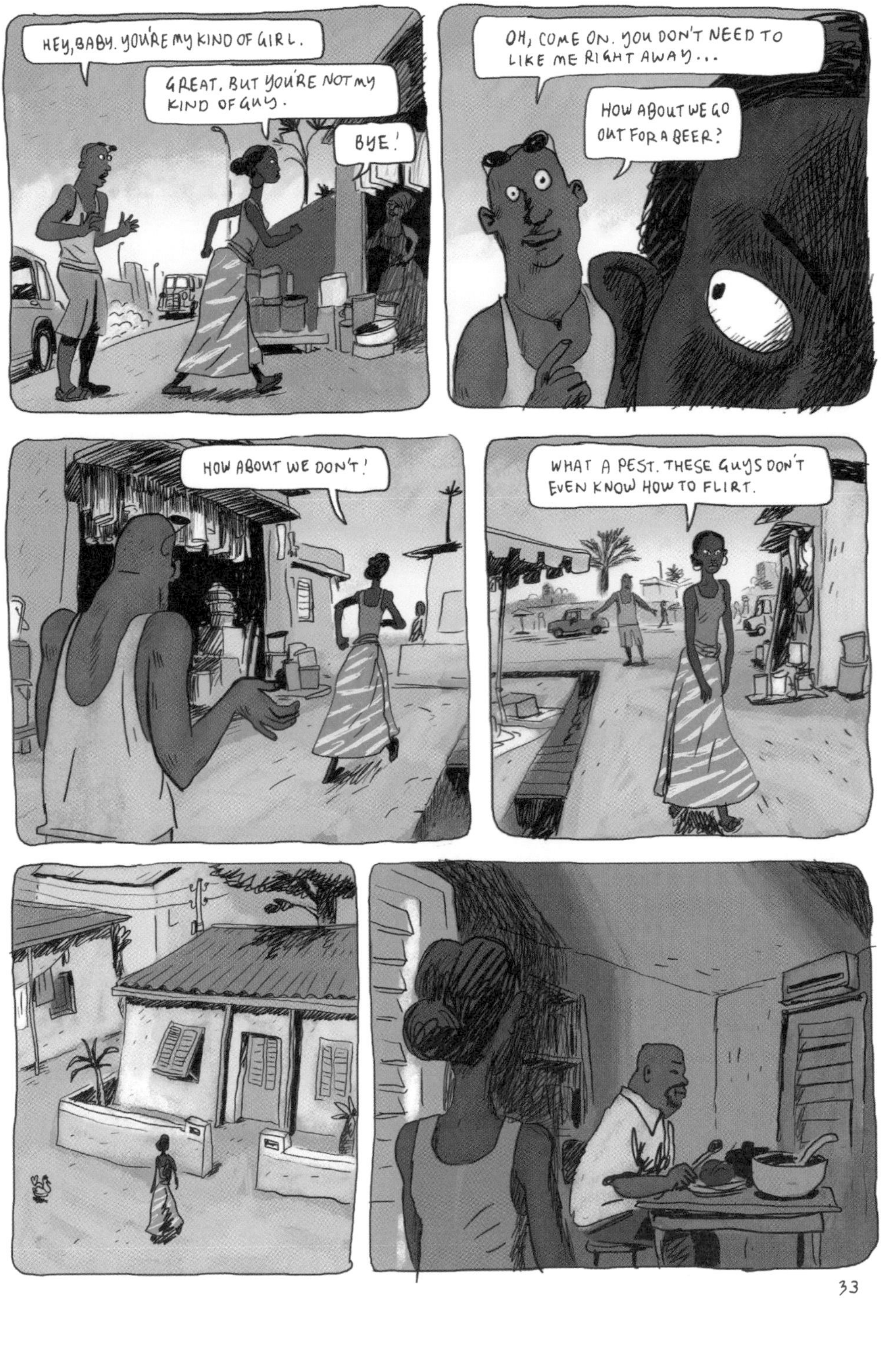
HEY, BABY. YOU'RE MY KIND OF GIRL.
GREAT. BUT YOU'RE NOT MY KIND OF GUY.
BYE!
OH, COME ON. YOU DON'T NEED TO LIKE ME RIGHT AWAY...
HOW ABOUT WE GO OUT FOR A BEER?
HOW ABOUT WE DON'T!
WHAT A PEST. THESE GUYS DON'T EVEN KNOW HOW TO FLIRT.

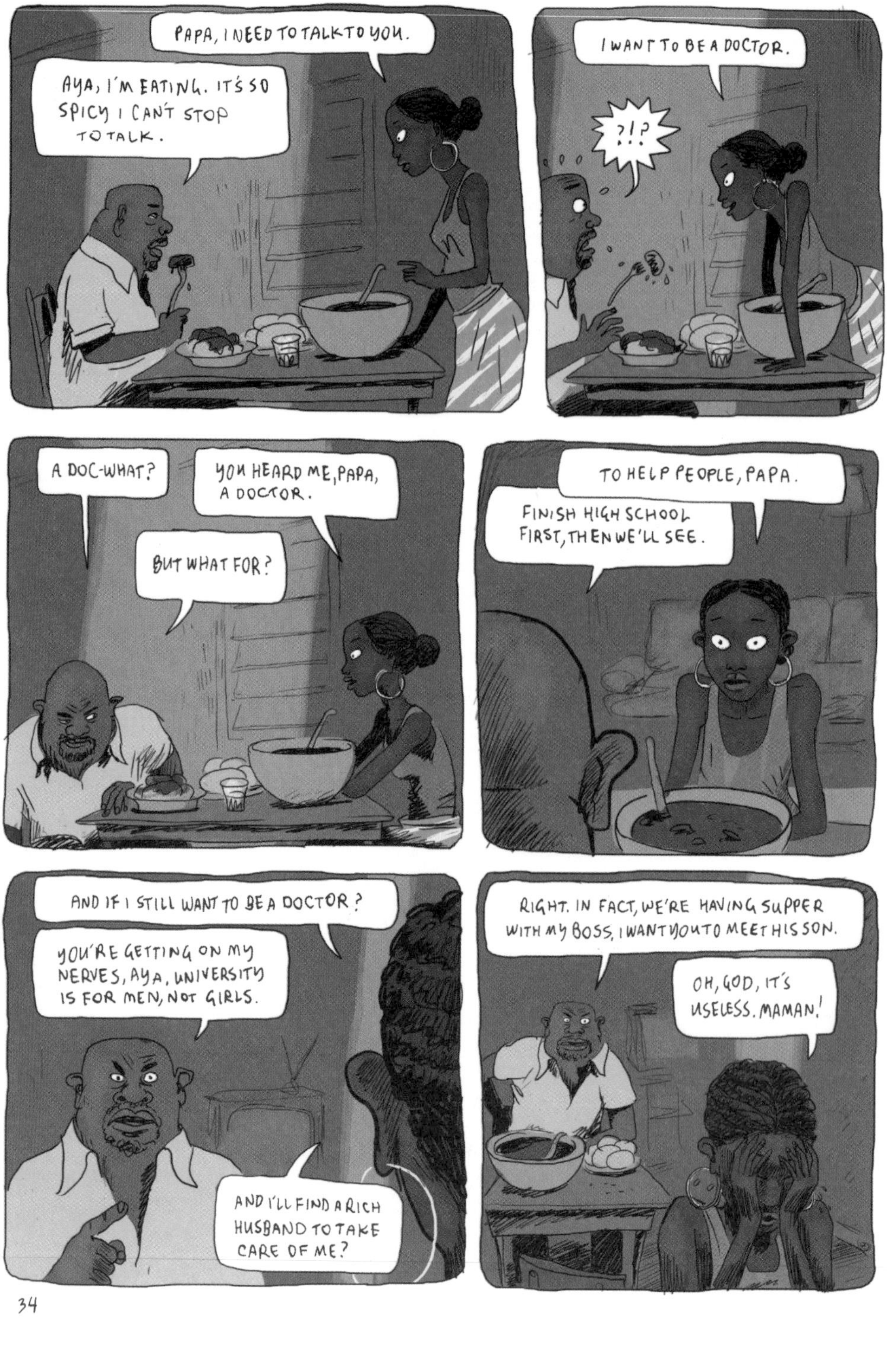
PAPA, I NEED TO TALK TO YOU.
AYA, I'M EATING. IT'S SO SPICY I CAN'T STOP TO TALK.
I WANT TO BE A DOCTOR.
?!?...
A DOC-WHAT?
YOU HEARD ME, PAPA, A DOCTOR.
BUT WHAT FOR?
TO HELP PEOPLE, PAPA.
FINISH HIGH SCHOOL FIRST, THEN WE'LL SEE.
AND IF I STILL WANT TO BE A DOCTOR?
YOU'RE GETTING ON MY NERVES, AYA. UNIVERSITY IS FOR MEN, NOT GIRLS.
AND I'LL FIND A RICH HUSBAND TO TAKE CARE OF ME?
RIGHT. IN FACT, WE'RE HAVING SUPPER WITH MY BOSS. I WANT YOU TO MEET HIS SON.
OH, GOD, IT'S USELESS. MAMAN!

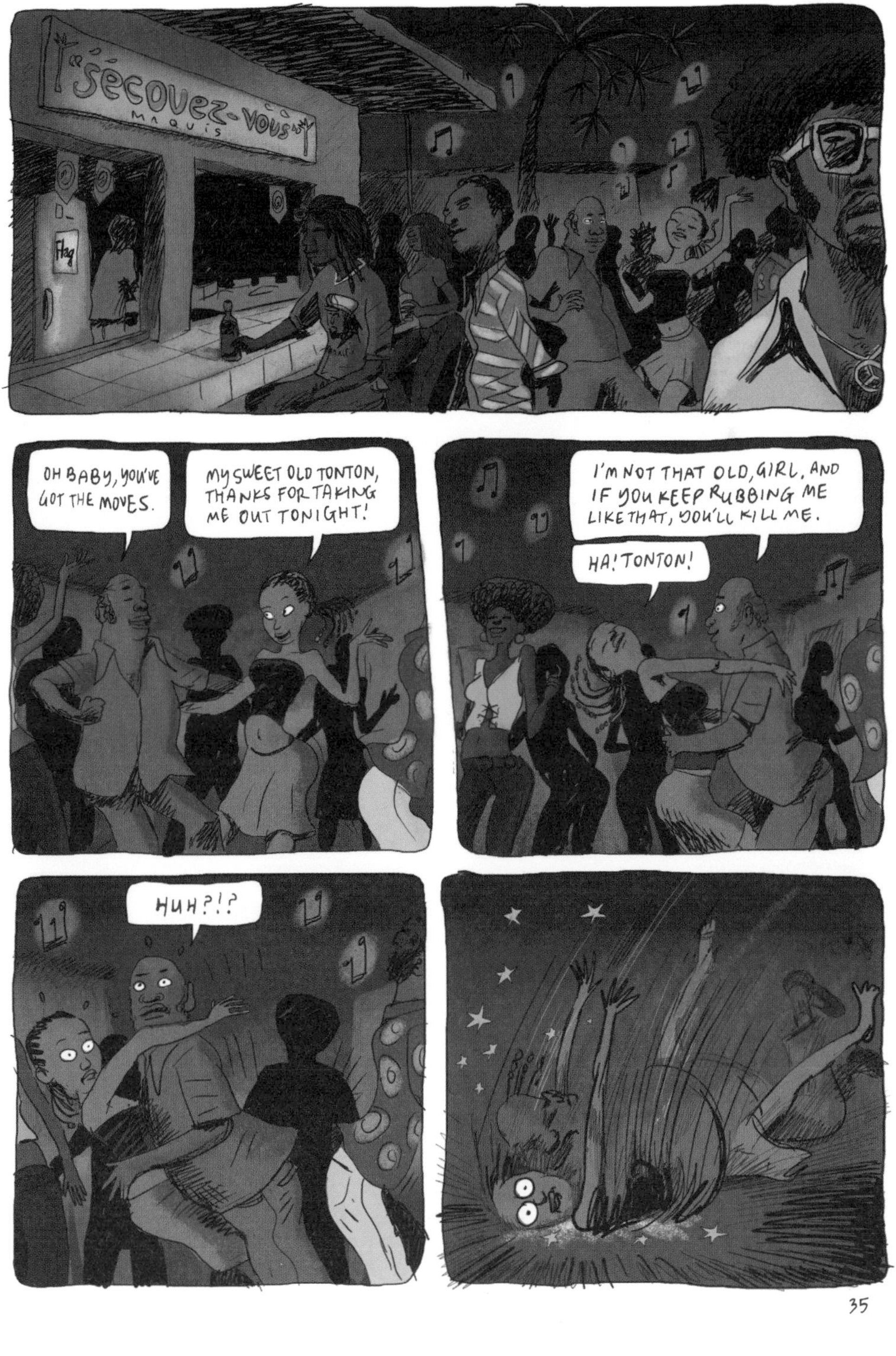
SECOUEZ-VOUS
MAQUIS
Flag
OH BABY, YOU'VE GOT THE MOVES.
MY SWEET OLD TONTON, THANKS FOR TAKING ME OUT TONIGHT!
I'M NOT THAT OLD, GIRL. AND IF YOU KEEP RUBBING ME LIKE THAT, YOU'LL KILL ME.
HA! TONTON!
HUH?!?

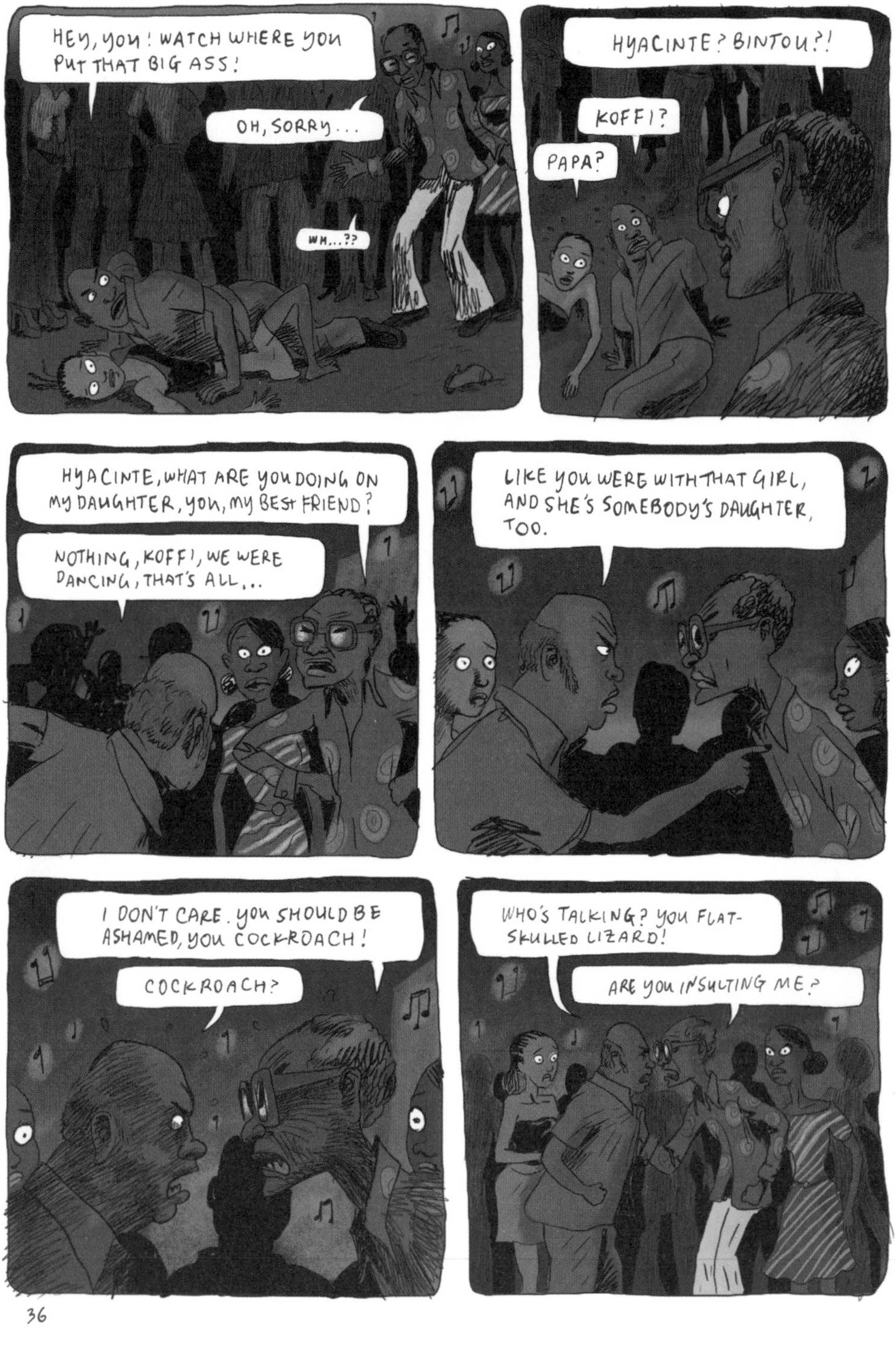
HEY, YOU! WATCH WHERE YOU PUT THAT BIG ASS!
OH, SORRY...
WH...??
HYACINTE? BINTOU?!
KOFFI?
PAPA?
HYACINTE, WHAT ARE YOU DOING ON MY DAUGHTER, YOU, MY BEST FRIEND?
NOTHING, KOFFI, WE WERE DANCING, THAT'S ALL...
LIKE YOU WERE WITH THAT GIRL, AND SHE'S SOMEBODY'S DAUGHTER, TOO.
I DON'T CARE. YOU SHOULD BE ASHAMED, YOU COCKROACH!
COCKROACH?
WHO'S TALKING? YOU FLAT-SKULLED LIZARD!
ARE YOU INSULTING ME?

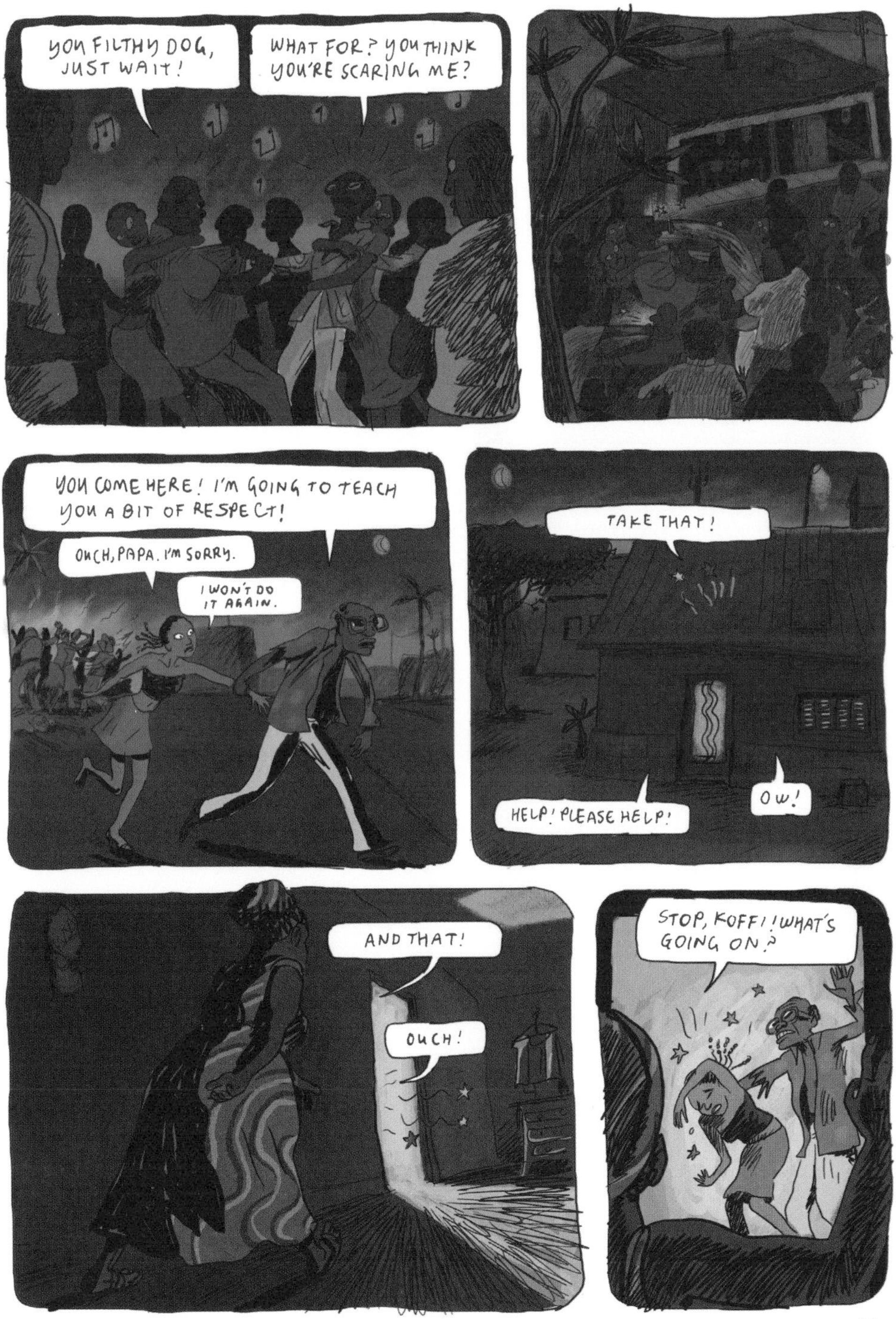
YOU FILTHY DOG, JUST WAIT!
WHAT FOR? YOU THINK YOU'RE SCARING ME?
YOU COME HERE! I'M GOING TO TEACH YOU A BIT OF RESPECT!
OUCH, PAPA. I'M SORRY.
I WON'T DO IT AGAIN.
TAKE THAT!
HELP! PLEASE HELP!
OW!
AND THAT!
OUCH!
STOP, KOFFI! WHAT'S GOING ON?

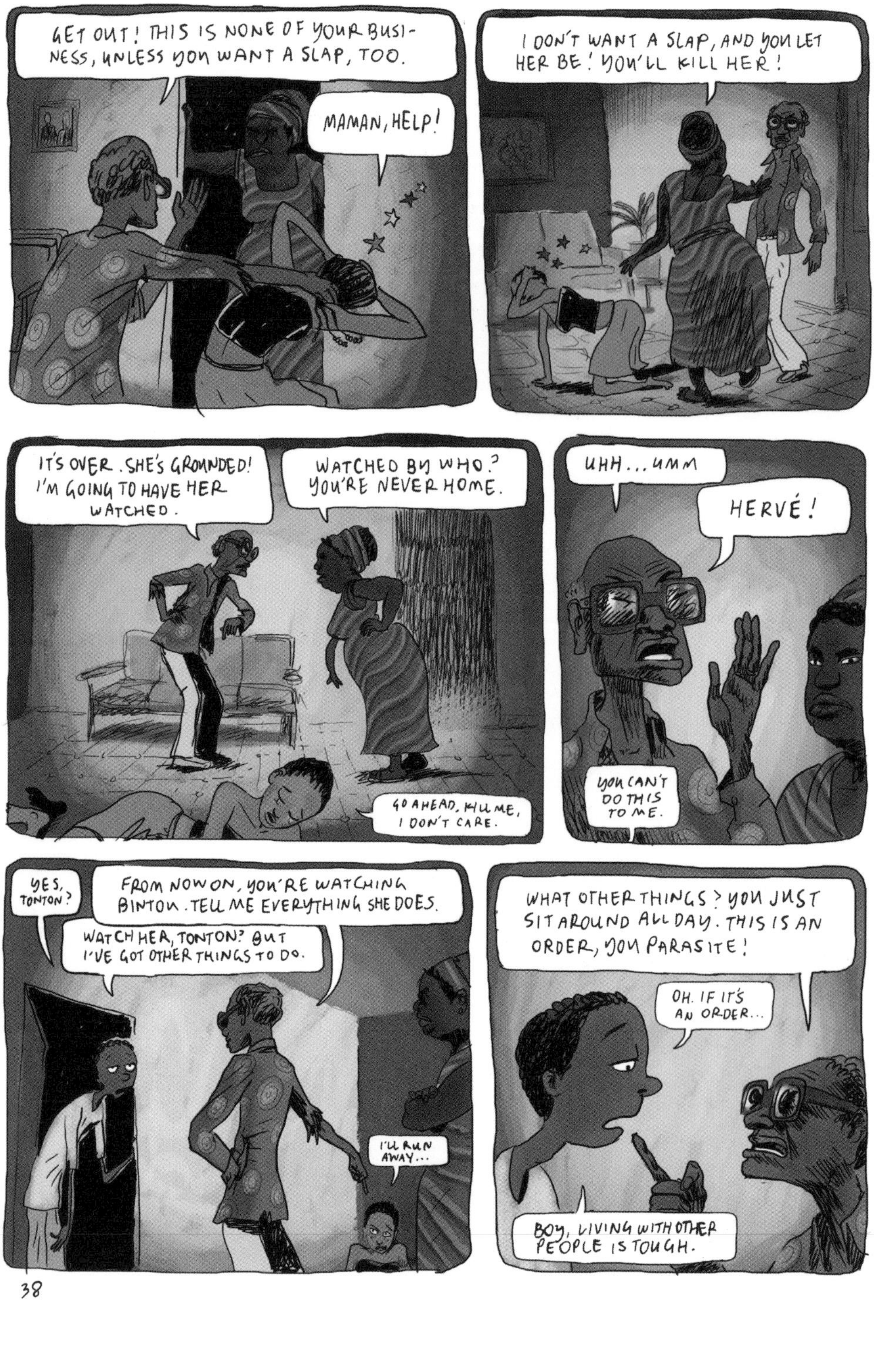
GET OUT! THIS IS NONE OF YOUR BUSINESS, UNLESS YOU WANT A SLAP, TOO.
MAMAN, HELP!
I DON'T WANT A SLAP, AND YOU LET HER BE! YOU'LL KILL HER!
IT'S OVER. SHE'S GROUNDED! I'M GOING TO HAVE HER WATCHED.
WATCHED BY WHO? YOU'RE NEVER HOME.
GO AHEAD, KILL ME, I DON'T CARE.
UHH... UMM
HERVÉ!
YOU CAN'T DO THIS TO ME.
YES, TONTON?
FROM NOW ON, YOU'RE WATCHING BINTOU. TELL ME EVERYTHING SHE DOES.
WATCH HER, TONTON? BUT I'VE GOT OTHER THINGS TO DO.
I'LL RUN AWAY...
WHAT OTHER THINGS? YOU JUST SIT AROUND ALL DAY. THIS IS AN ORDER, YOU PARASITE!
OH. IF IT'S AN ORDER...
BOY, LIVING WITH OTHER PEOPLE IS TOUGH.

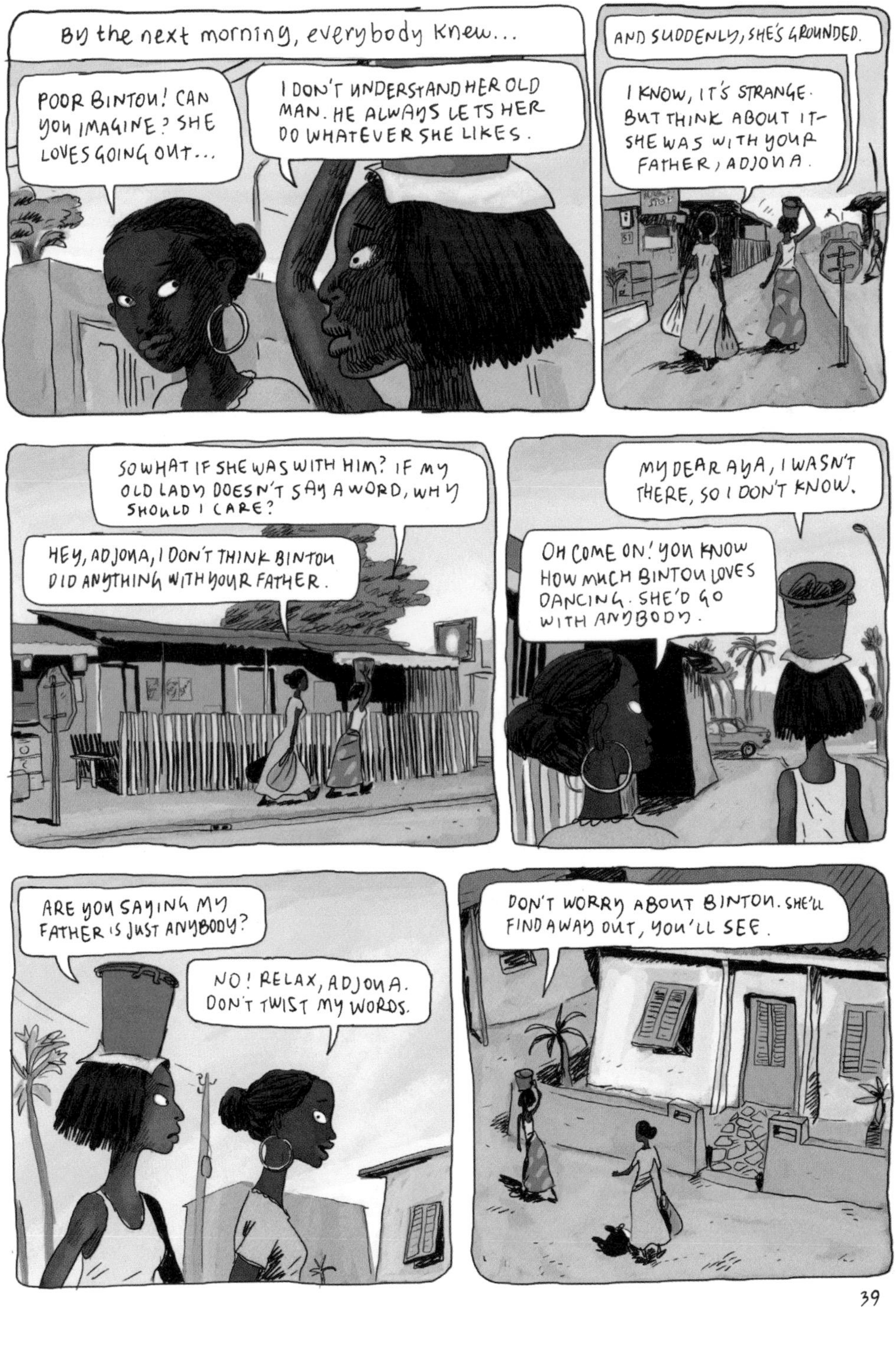
By the next morning, everybody knew...
POOR BINTOU! CAN YOU IMAGINE? SHE LOVES GOING OUT...
I DON'T UNDERSTAND HER OLD MAN. HE ALWAYS LETS HER DO WHATEVER SHE LIKES.
AND SUDDENLY, SHE'S GROUNDED.
I KNOW, IT'S STRANGE. BUT THINK ABOUT IT- SHE WAS WITH YOUR FATHER, ADJOUA.
SO WHAT IF SHE WAS WITH HIM? IF MY OLD LADY DOESN'T SAY A WORD, WHY SHOULD I CARE?
HEY, ADJOUA, I DON'T THINK BINTOU DID ANYTHING WITH YOUR FATHER.
MY DEAR AYA, I WASN'T THERE, SO I DON'T KNOW.
OH COME ON! YOU KNOW HOW MUCH BINTOU LOVES DANCING. SHE'D GO WITH ANYBODY.
ARE YOU SAYING MY FATHER IS JUST ANYBODY?
NO! RELAX, ADJOUA. DON'T TWIST MY WORDS.
DON'T WORRY ABOUT BINTOU. SHE'LL FIND A WAY OUT, YOU'LL SEE.

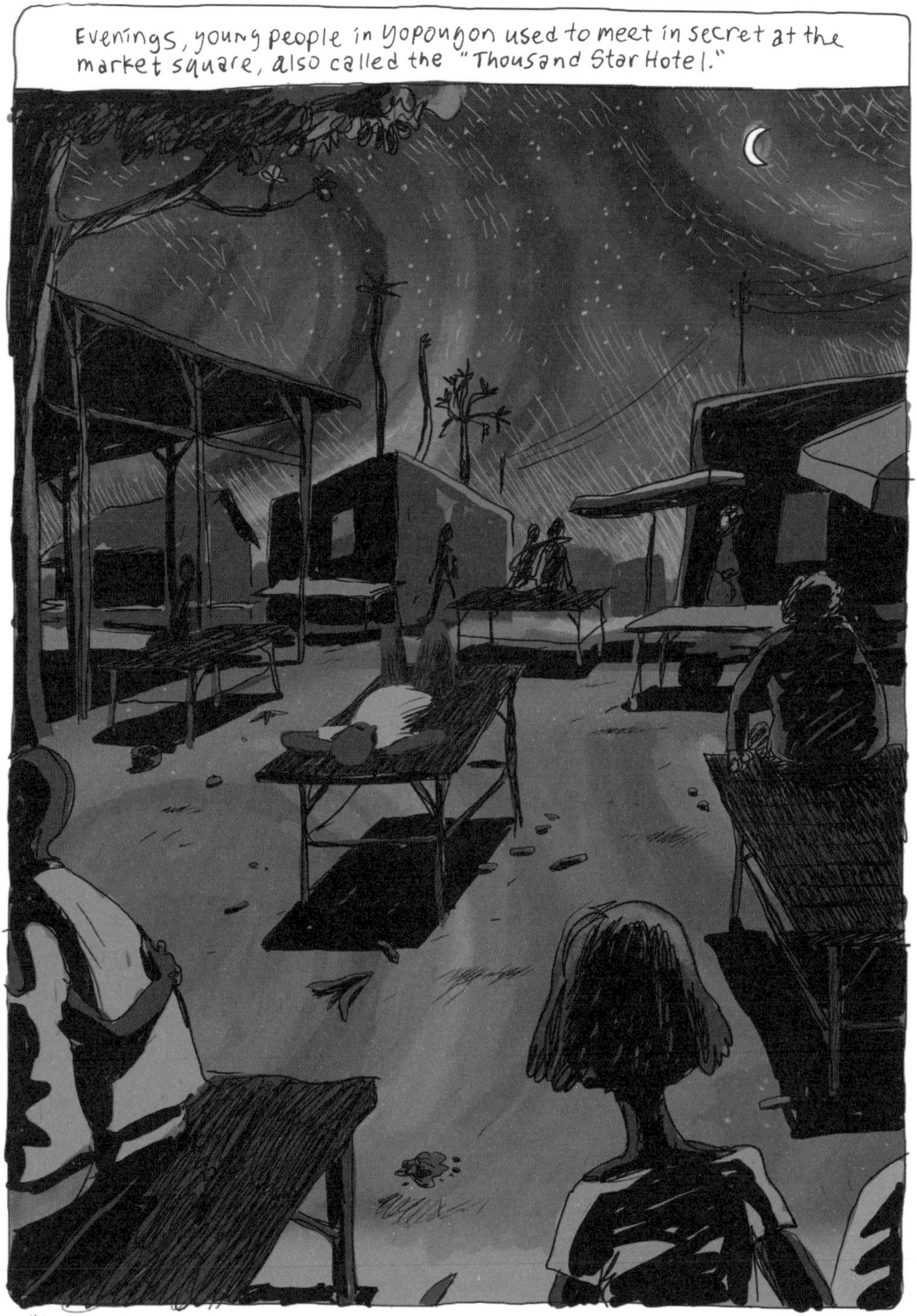
Evenings, young people in Yopougon used to meet in secret at the market square, also called the "Thousand Star Hotel."

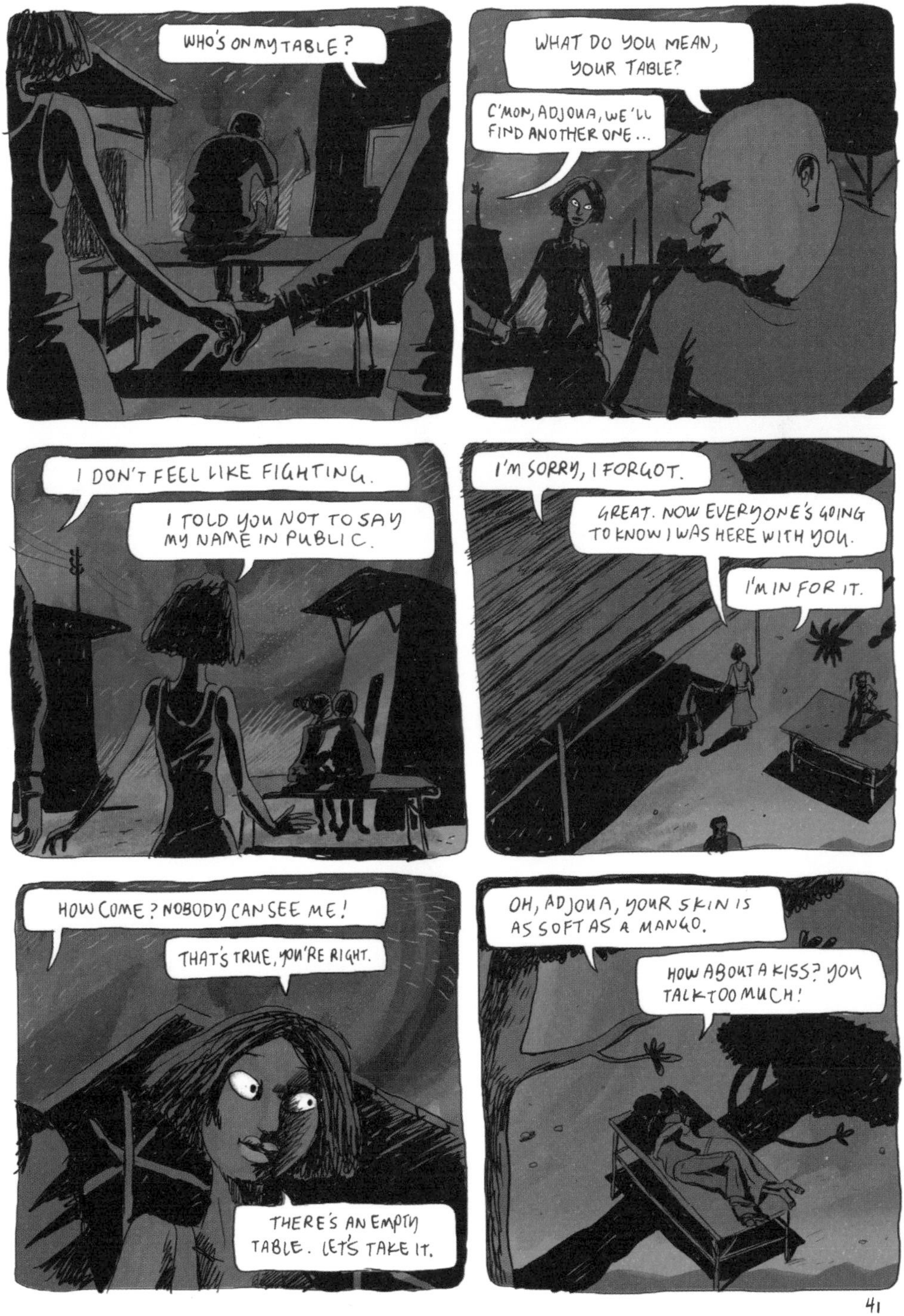
WHO'S ON MY TABLE?
WHAT DO YOU MEAN, YOUR TABLE?
C'MON, ADJOUA, WE'LL FIND ANOTHER ONE...
I DON'T FEEL LIKE FIGHTING.
I TOLD YOU NOT TO SAY MY NAME IN PUBLIC.
I'M SORRY, I FORGOT.
GREAT. NOW EVERYONE'S GOING TO KNOW I WAS HERE WITH YOU.
I'M IN FOR IT.
HOW COME? NOBODY CAN SEE ME!
THAT'S TRUE, YOU'RE RIGHT.
THERE'S AN EMPTY TABLE. LET'S TAKE IT.
OH, ADJOUA, YOUR SKIN IS AS SOFT AS A MANGO.
HOW ABOUT A KISS? YOU TALK TOO MUCH!

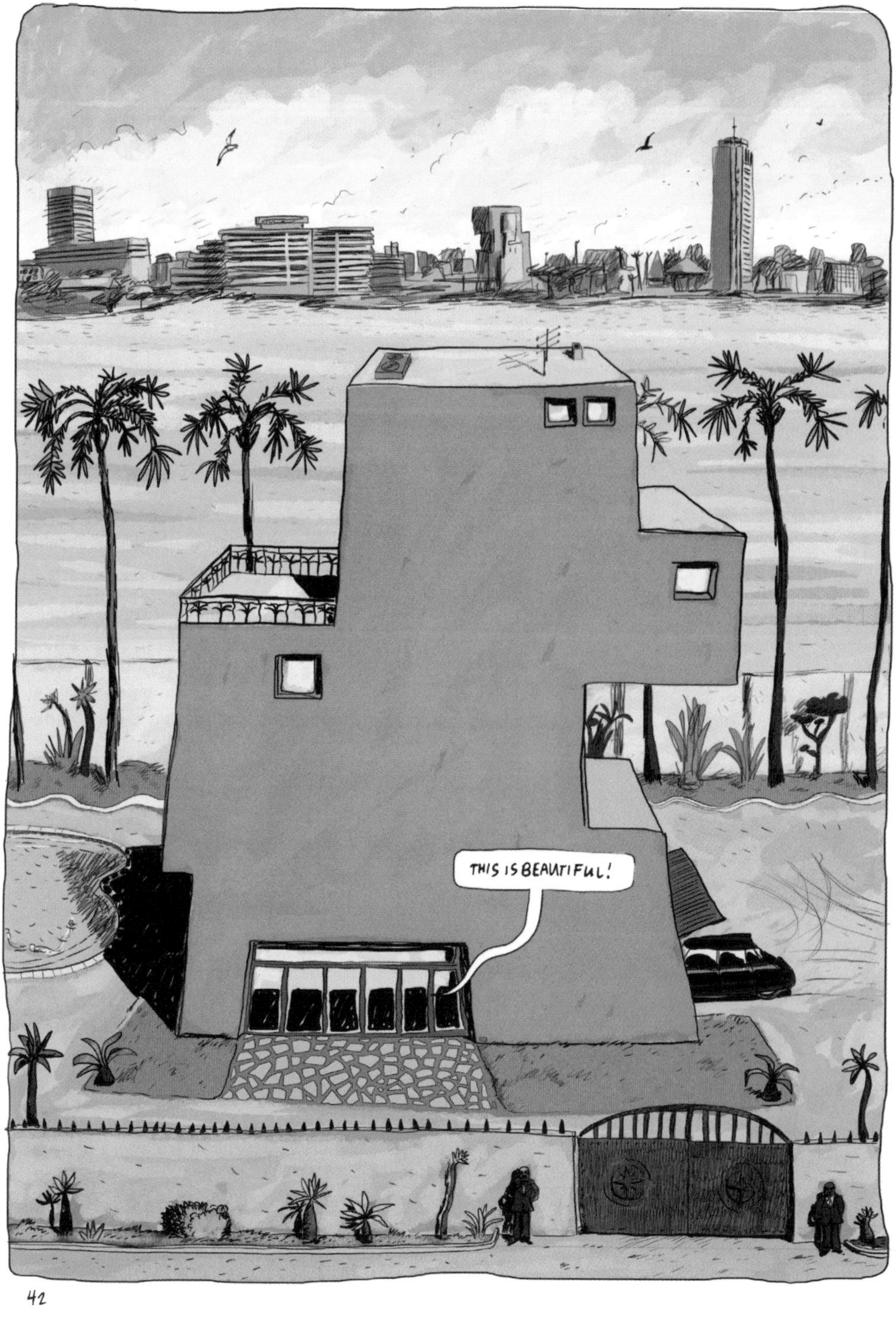
THIS IS BEAUTIFUL!

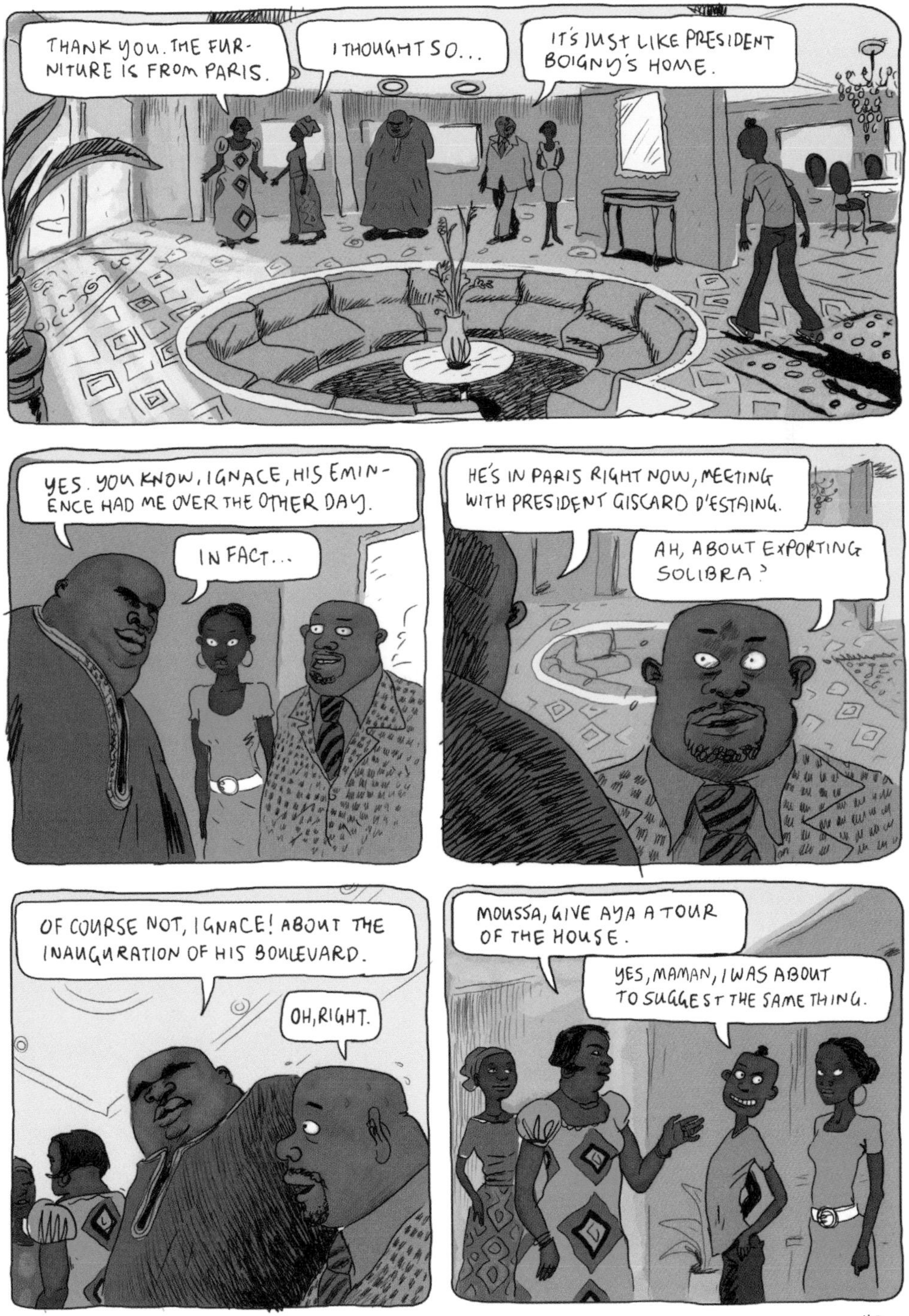
THANK YOU. THE FURNITURE IS FROM PARIS.
I THOUGHT SO...
IT'S JUST LIKE PRESIDENT BOIGNY'S HOME.
YES. YOU KNOW, IGNACE, HIS EMINENCE HAD ME OVER THE OTHER DAY.
IN FACT...
HE'S IN PARIS RIGHT NOW, MEETING WITH PRESIDENT GISCARD D'ESTAING.
AH, ABOUT EXPORTING SOLIBRA?
OF COURSE NOT, IGNACE! ABOUT THE INAUGURATION OF HIS BOULEVARD.
OH, RIGHT.
MOUSSA, GIVE AYA A TOUR OF THE HOUSE.
YES, MAMAN, I WAS ABOUT TO SUGGEST THE SAME THING.

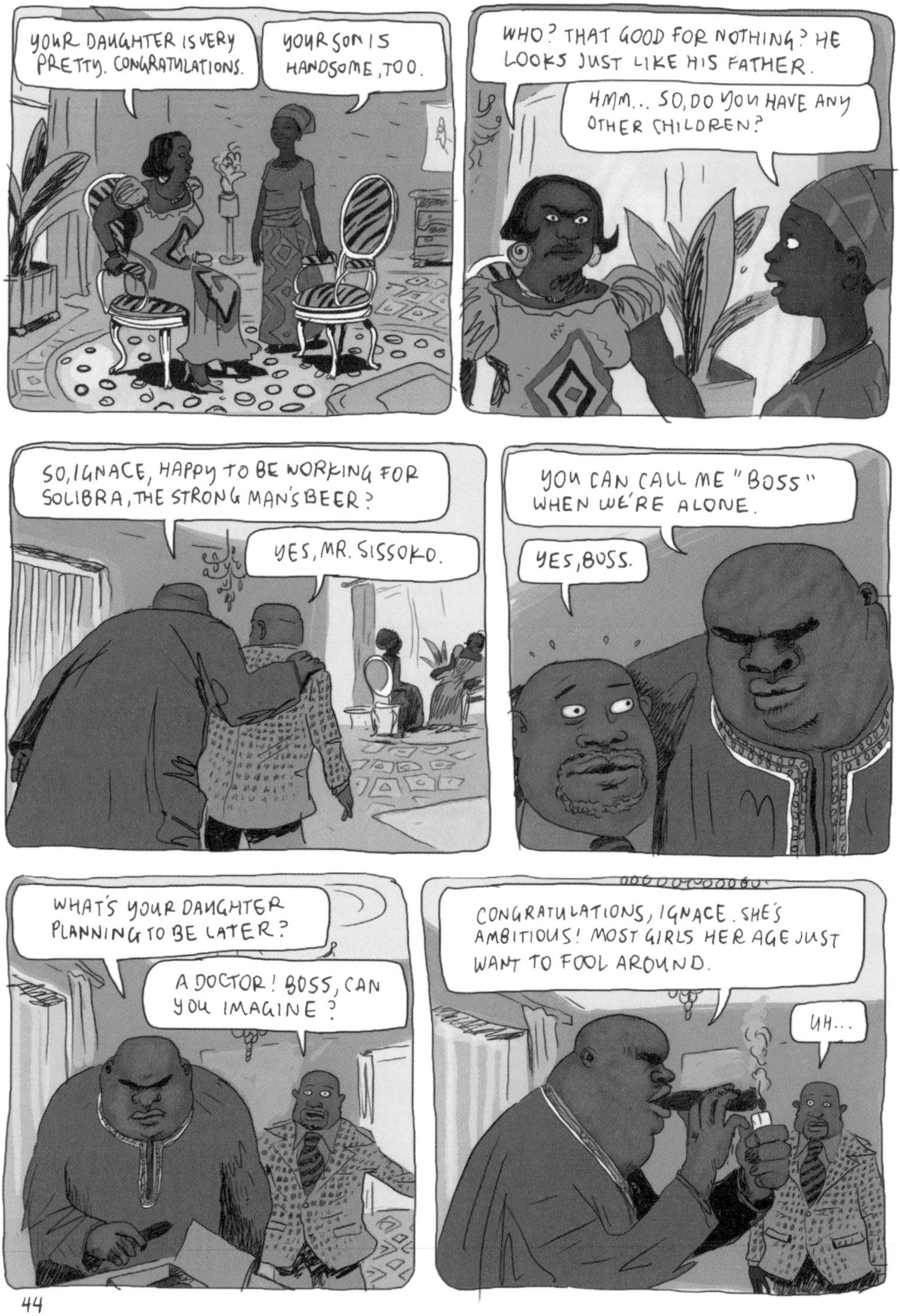
YOUR DAUGHTER IS VERY PRETTY. CONGRATULATIONS.
YOUR SON IS HANDSOME, TOO.
WHO? THAT GOOD FOR NOTHING? HE LOOKS JUST LIKE HIS FATHER.
HMM... SO, DO YOU HAVE ANY OTHER CHILDREN?
SO, IGNACE, HAPPY TO BE WORKING FOR SOLIBRA, THE STRONG MAN'S BEER?
YES, MR. SISSOKO.
YOU CAN CALL ME "BOSS" WHEN WE'RE ALONE.
YES, BOSS.
WHAT'S YOUR DAUGHTER PLANNING TO BE LATER?
A DOCTOR! BOSS, CAN YOU IMAGINE?
CONGRATULATIONS, IGNACE. SHE'S AMBITIOUS! MOST GIRLS HER AGE JUST WANT TO FOOL AROUND.
UH...

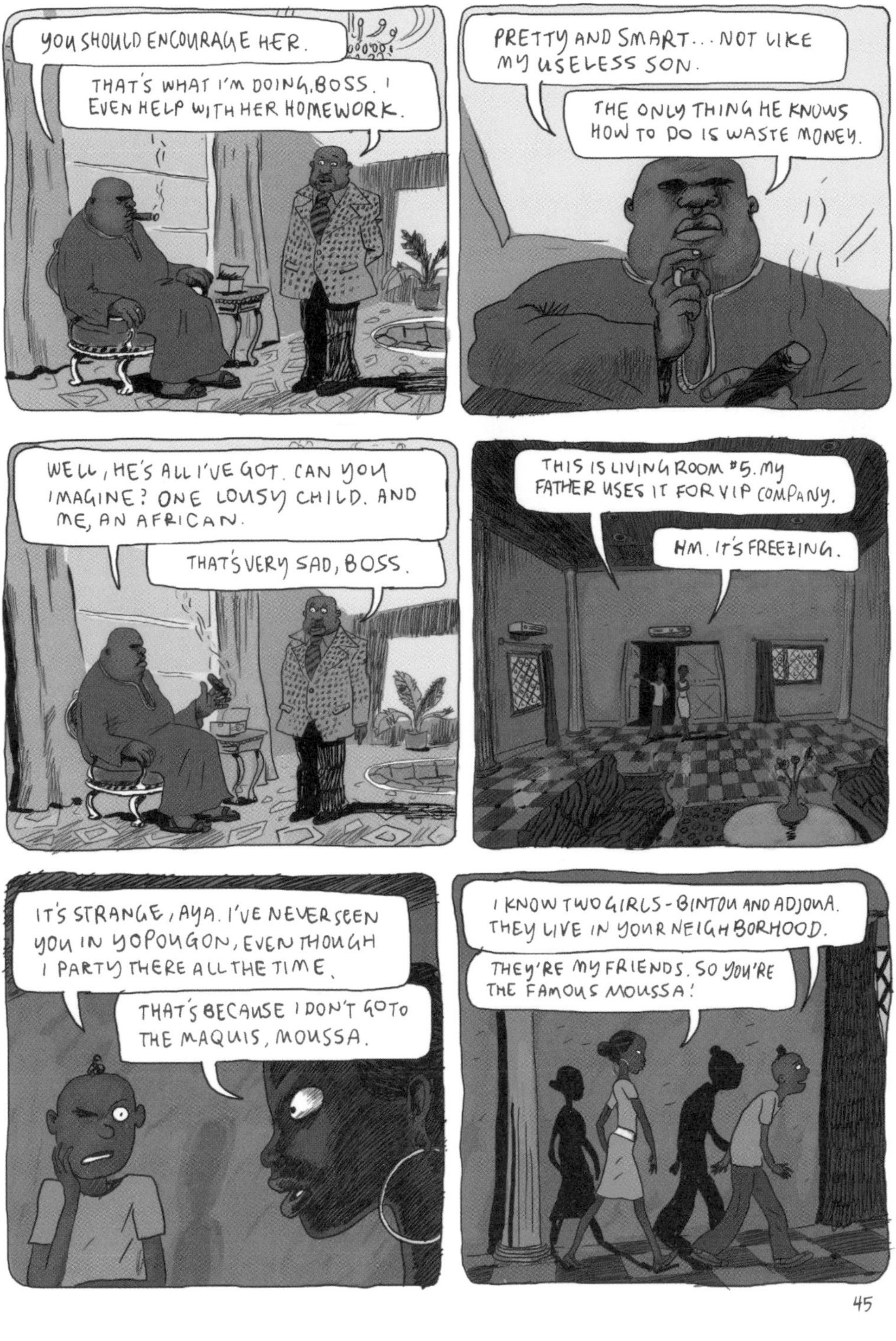
YOU SHOULD ENCOURAGE HER.
THAT'S WHAT I'M DOING, BOSS. I EVEN HELP WITH HER HOMEWORK.
PRETTY AND SMART... NOT LIKE MY USELESS SON.
THE ONLY THING HE KNOWS HOW TO DO IS WASTE MONEY.
WELL, HE'S ALL I'VE GOT. CAN YOU IMAGINE? ONE LOUSY CHILD. AND ME, AN AFRICAN.
THAT'S VERY SAD, BOSS.
THIS IS LIVING ROOM #5. MY FATHER USES IT FOR VIP COMPANY.
HM. IT'S FREEZING.
IT'S STRANGE, AYA. I'VE NEVER SEEN YOU IN YOPOUGON, EVEN THOUGH I PARTY THERE ALL THE TIME.
THAT'S BECAUSE I DON'T GO TO THE MAQUIS, MOUSSA.
I KNOW TWO GIRLS - BINTOU AND ADJOUA. THEY LIVE IN YOUR NEIGHBORHOOD.
THEY'RE MY FRIENDS. SO YOU'RE THE FAMOUS MOUSSA!

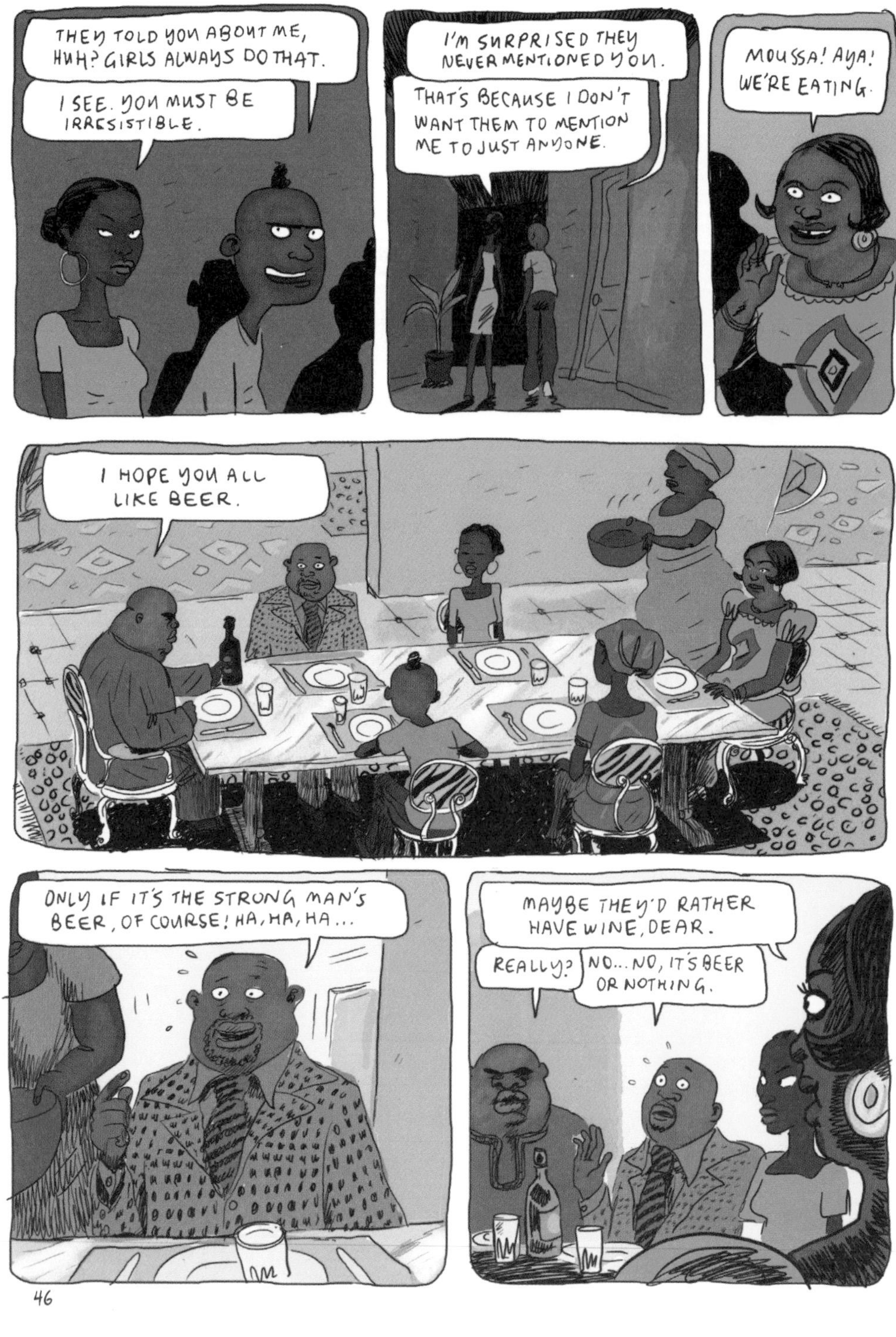
THEY TOLD YOU ABOUT ME, HUH? GIRLS ALWAYS DO THAT.
I SEE. YOU MUST BE IRRESISTIBLE.
I'M SURPRISED THEY NEVER MENTIONED YOU.
THAT'S BECAUSE I DON'T WANT THEM TO MENTION ME TO JUST ANYONE.
MOUSSA! AYA! WE'RE EATING.
I HOPE YOU ALL LIKE BEER.
ONLY IF IT'S THE STRONG MAN'S BEER, OF COURSE! HA, HA, HA...
MAYBE THEY'D RATHER HAVE WINE, DEAR.
REALLY?
NO... NO, IT'S BEER OR NOTHING.

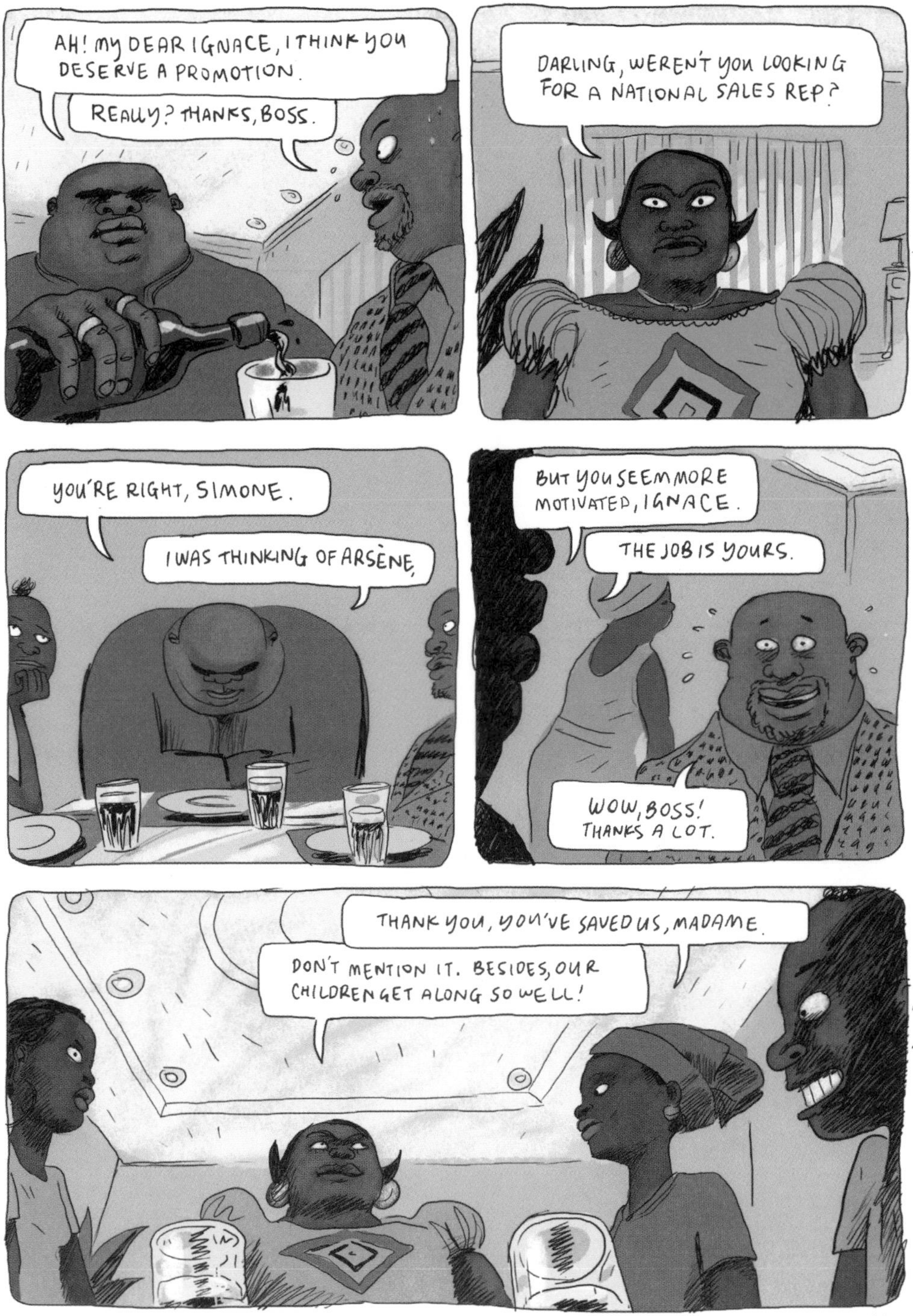
AH! MY DEAR IGNACE, I THINK YOU DESERVE A PROMOTION.
REALLY? THANKS, BOSS.
DARLING, WEREN'T YOU LOOKING FOR A NATIONAL SALES REP?
YOU'RE RIGHT, SIMONE.
I WAS THINKING OF ARSÈNE,
BUT YOU SEEM MORE MOTIVATED, IGNACE.
THE JOB IS YOURS.
WOW, BOSS! THANKS A LOT.
THANK YOU, YOU'VE SAVED US, MADAME.
DON'T MENTION IT. BESIDES, OUR CHILDREN GET ALONG SO WELL!

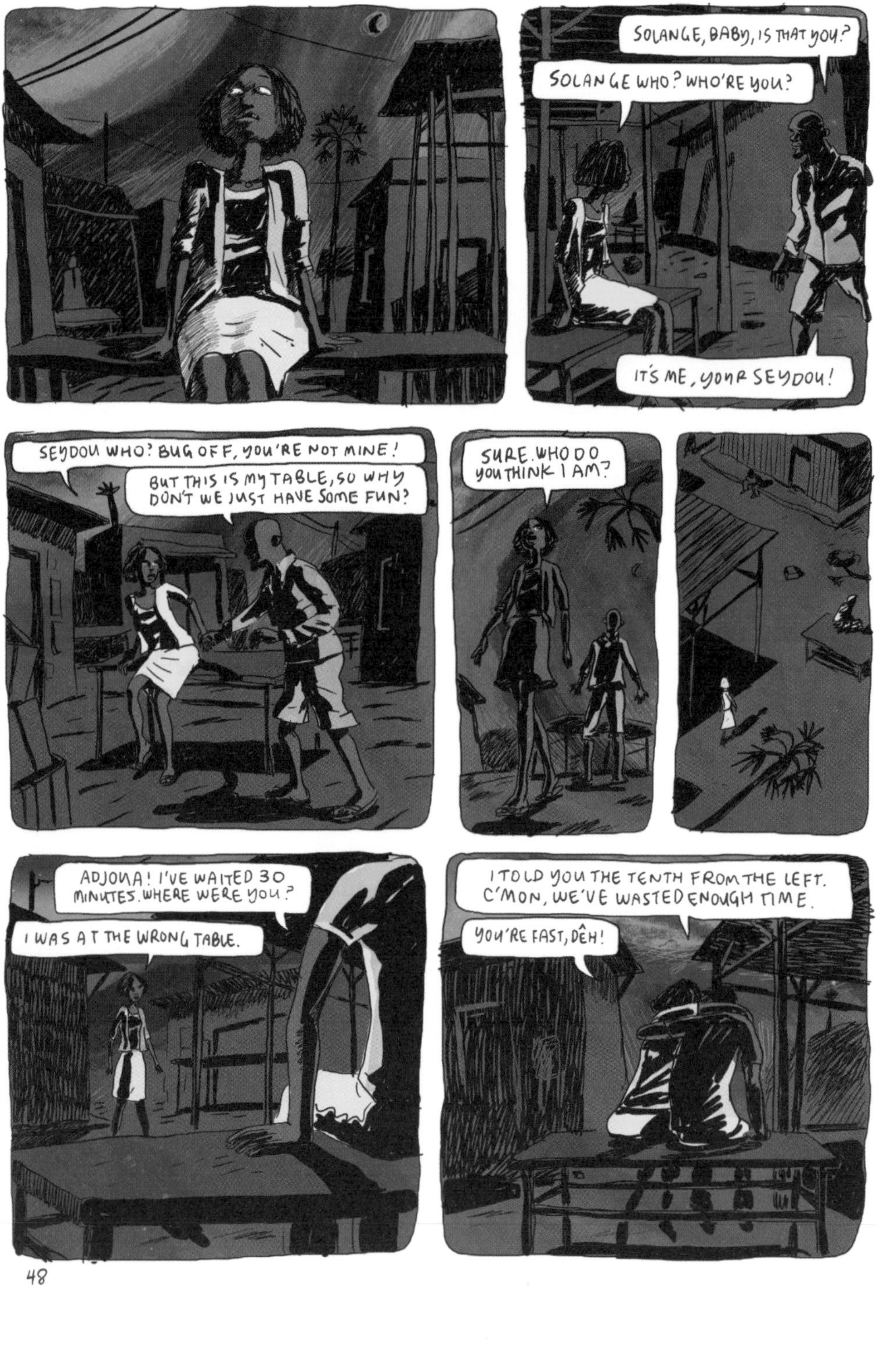
SOLANGE, BABY, IS THAT YOU?
SOLANGE WHO? WHO'RE YOU?
IT'S ME, YOUR SEYDOU!
SEYDOU WHO? BUG OFF, YOU'RE NOT MINE!
BUT THIS IS MY TABLE, SO WHY DON'T WE JUST HAVE SOME FUN?
SURE. WHO DO YOU THINK I AM?
ADJOUA! I'VE WAITED 30 MINUTES. WHERE WERE YOU?
I WAS AT THE WRONG TABLE.
I TOLD YOU THE TENTH FROM THE LEFT. C'MON, WE'VE WASTED ENOUGH TIME.
YOU'RE FAST, DÊH!

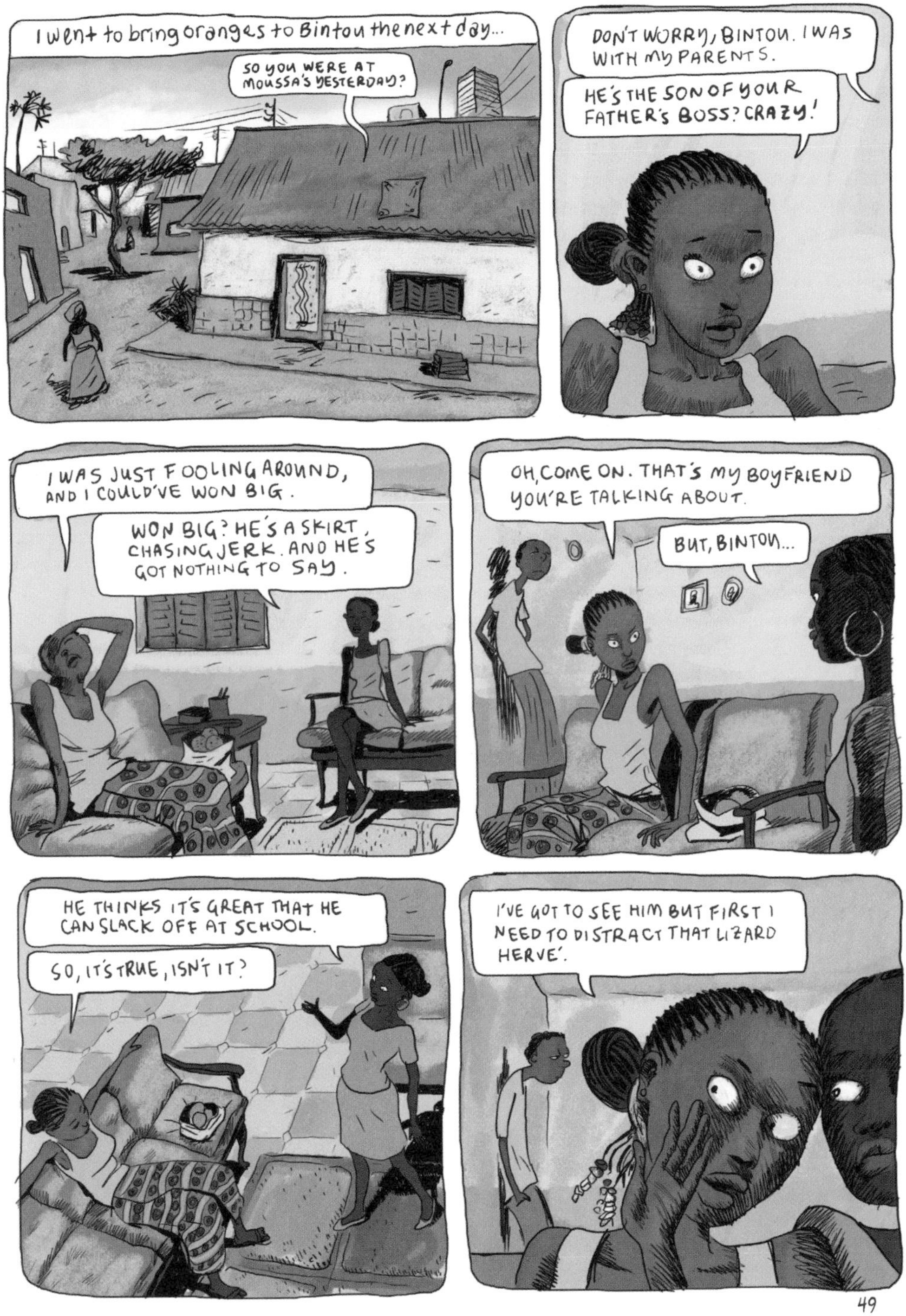
I went to bring oranges to Bintou the next day...
SO YOU WERE AT MOUSSA'S YESTERDAY?
DON'T WORRY, BINTOU. I WAS WITH MY PARENTS.
HE'S THE SON OF YOUR FATHER'S BOSS? CRAZY!
I WAS JUST FOOLING AROUND, AND I COULD'VE WON BIG.
WON BIG? HE'S A SKIRT CHASING JERK. AND HE'S GOT NOTHING TO SAY.
OH, COME ON. THAT'S MY BOYFRIEND YOU'RE TALKING ABOUT.
BUT, BINTOU...
HE THINKS IT'S GREAT THAT HE CAN SLACK OFF AT SCHOOL.
SO, IT'S TRUE, ISN'T IT?
I'VE GOT TO SEE HIM BUT FIRST I NEED TO DISTRACT THAT LIZARD HERVE'.

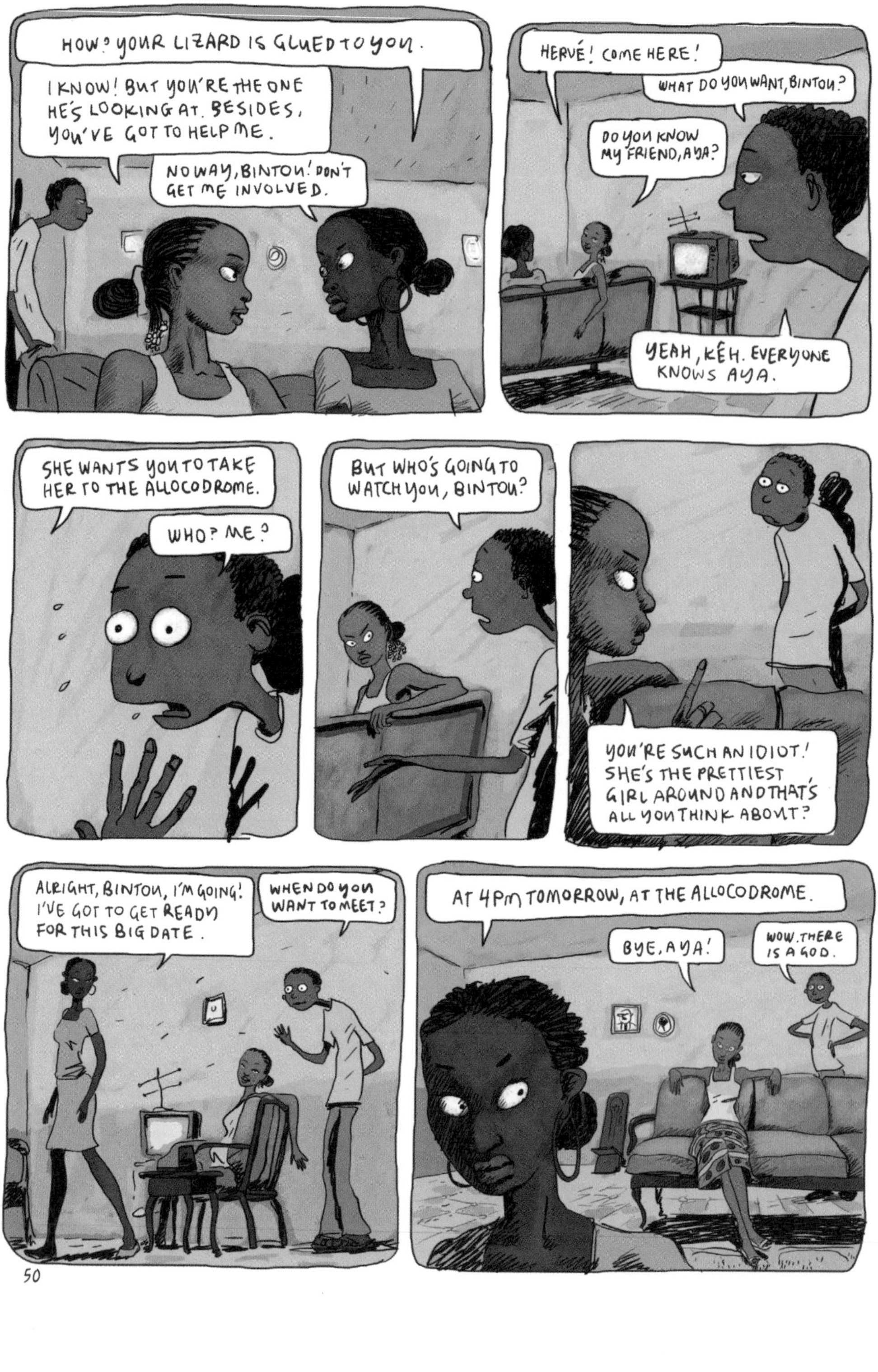
HOW? YOUR LIZARD IS GLUED TO YOU.
I KNOW! BUT YOU'RE THE ONE HE'S LOOKING AT. BESIDES, YOU'VE GOT TO HELP ME.
NO WAY, BINTOU! DON'T GET ME INVOLVED.
HERVÉ! COME HERE!
WHAT DO YOU WANT, BINTOU?
DO YOU KNOW MY FRIEND, AYA?
YEAH, KÊH. EVERYONE KNOWS AYA.
SHE WANTS YOU TO TAKE HER TO THE ALLOCODROME.
WHO? ME?
BUT WHO'S GOING TO WATCH YOU, BINTOU?
YOU'RE SUCH AN IDIOT! SHE'S THE PRETTIEST GIRL AROUND AND THAT'S ALL YOU THINK ABOUT?
ALRIGHT, BINTOU, I'M GOING! I'VE GOT TO GET READY FOR THIS BIG DATE.
WHEN DO YOU WANT TO MEET?
AT 4PM TOMORROW, AT THE ALLOCODROME.
BYE, AYA!
WOW. THERE IS A GOD.

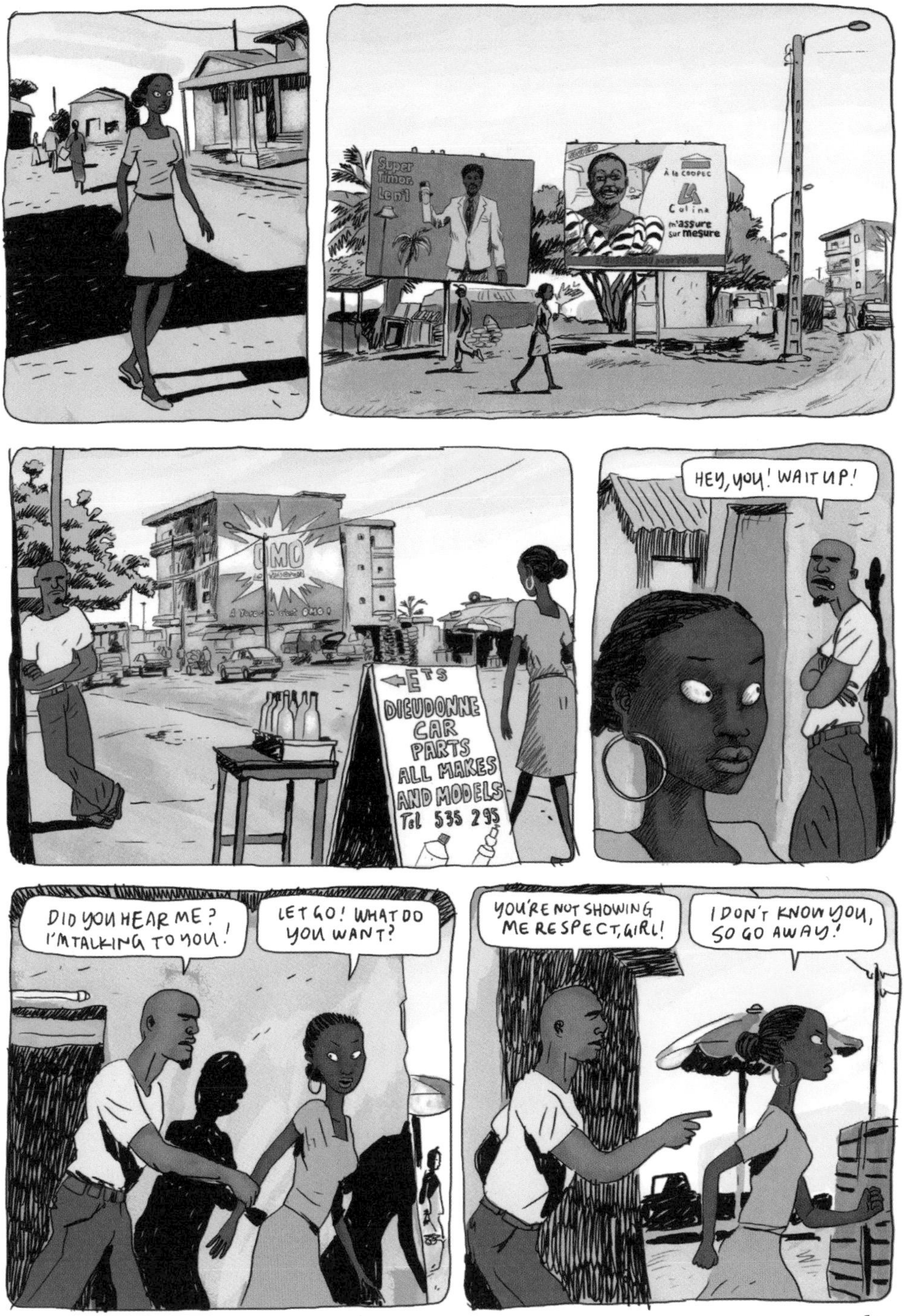
Super Timor. Le n°1
À la COOPEC
Colina
m'assure sur mesure
OMO
ETS
DIEUDONNE
CAR
PARTS
ALL MAKES
AND MODELS
Tel 535 295
HEY, YOU! WAIT UP!
DID YOU HEAR ME? I'M TALKING TO YOU!
LET GO! WHAT DO YOU WANT?
YOU'RE NOT SHOWING ME RESPECT, GIRL!
I DON'T KNOW YOU, SO GO AWAY!

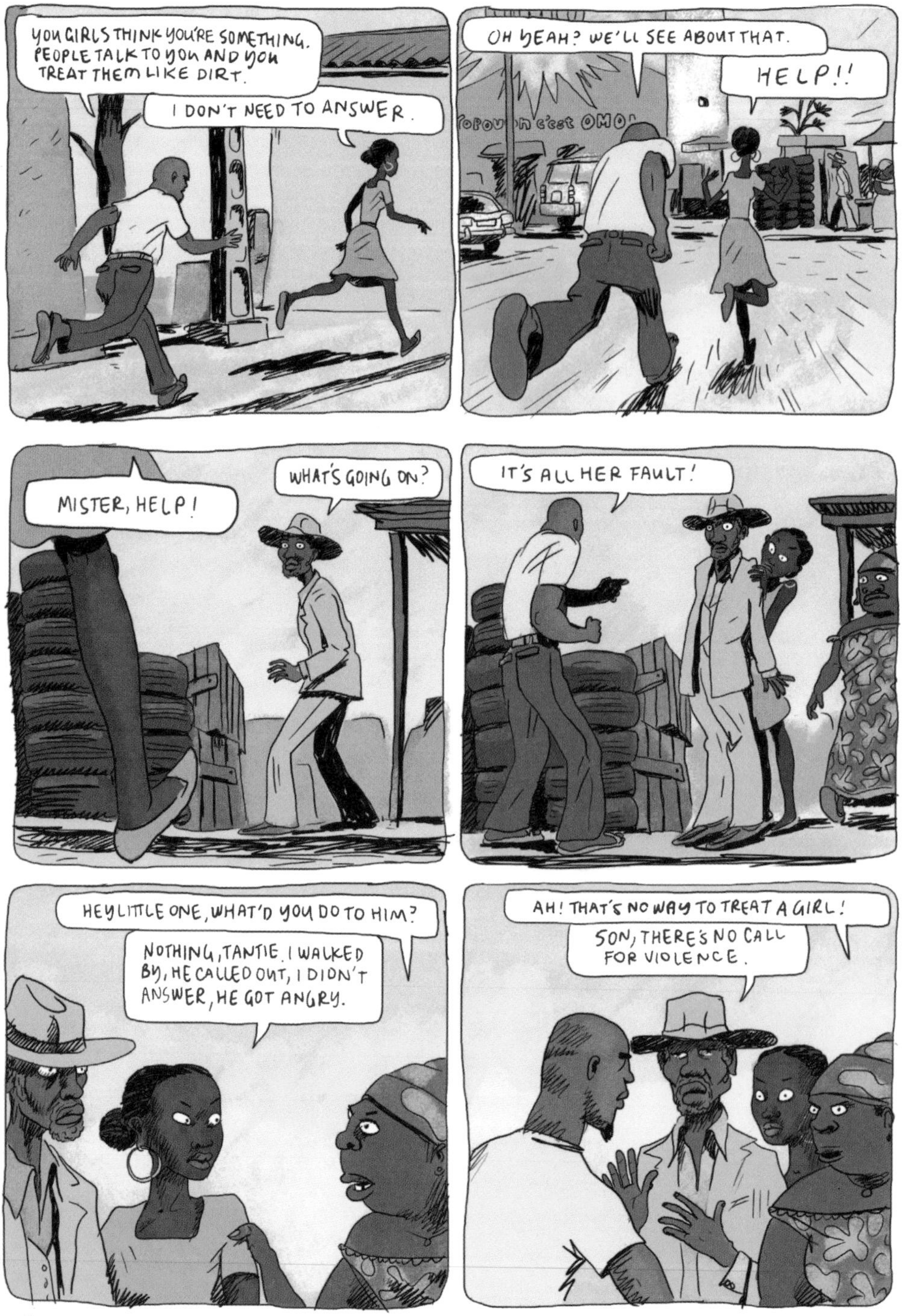
YOU GIRLS THINK YOU'RE SOMETHING. PEOPLE TALK TO YOU AND YOU TREAT THEM LIKE DIRT.
I DON'T NEED TO ANSWER.
OH YEAH? WE'LL SEE ABOUT THAT.
HELP!!
MISTER, HELP!
WHAT'S GOING ON?
IT'S ALL HER FAULT!
HEY LITTLE ONE, WHAT'D YOU DO TO HIM?
NOTHING, TANTIE. I WALKED BY, HE CALLED OUT, I DIDN'T ANSWER, HE GOT ANGRY.
AH! THAT'S NO WAY TO TREAT A GIRL!
SON, THERE'S NO CALL FOR VIOLENCE.

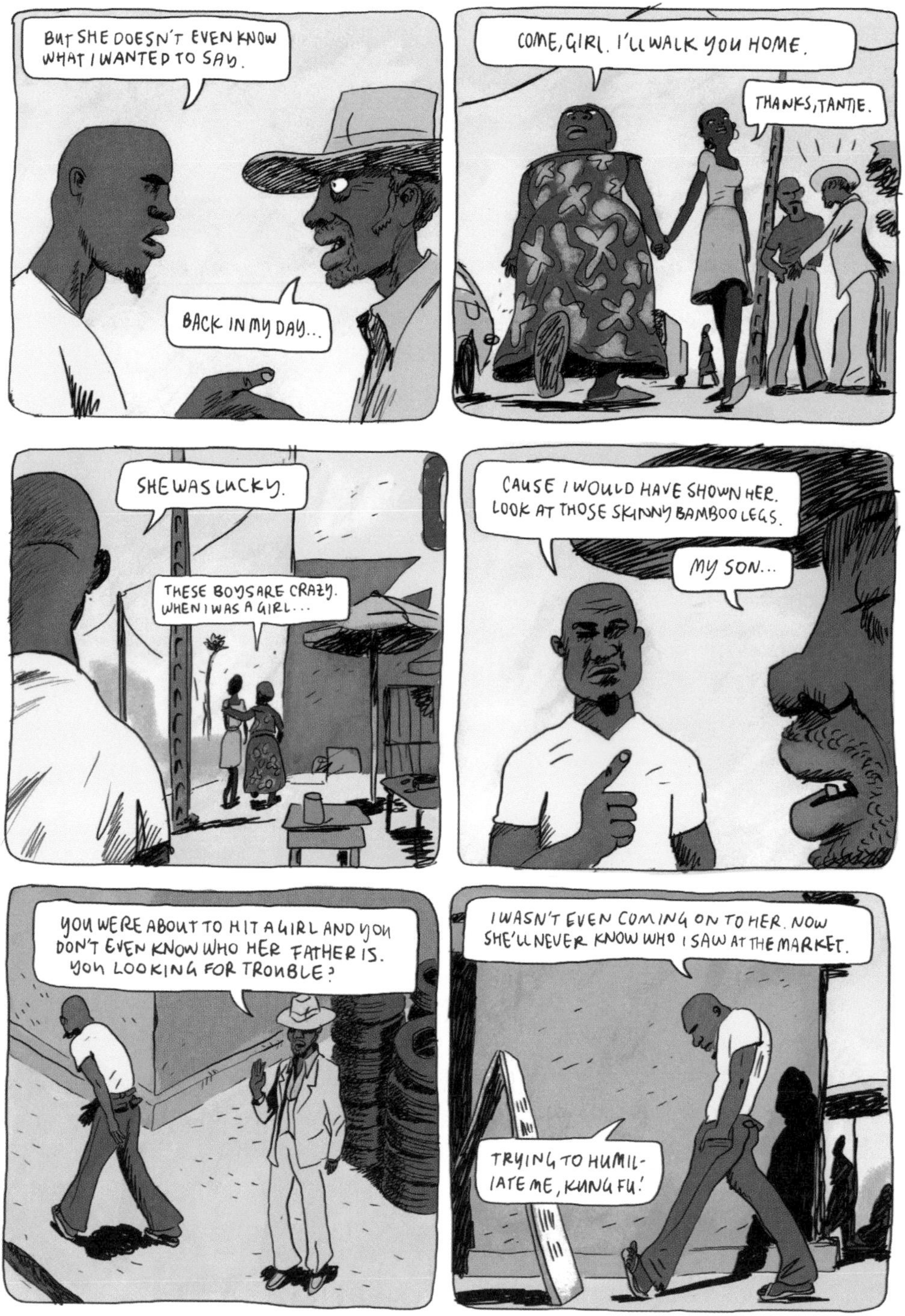
BUT SHE DOESN'T EVEN KNOW WHAT I WANTED TO SAY.
BACK IN MY DAY...
COME, GIRL. I'LL WALK YOU HOME.
THANKS, TANTIE.
SHE WAS LUCKY.
THESE BOYS ARE CRAZY. WHEN I WAS A GIRL...
CAUSE I WOULD HAVE SHOWN HER. LOOK AT THOSE SKINNY BAMBOO LEGS.
MY SON...
YOU WERE ABOUT TO HIT A GIRL AND YOU DON'T EVEN KNOW WHO HER FATHER IS. YOU LOOKING FOR TROUBLE?
I WASN'T EVEN COMING ON TO HER. NOW SHE'LL NEVER KNOW WHO I SAW AT THE MARKET.
TRYING TO HUMILIATE ME, KUNG FU!

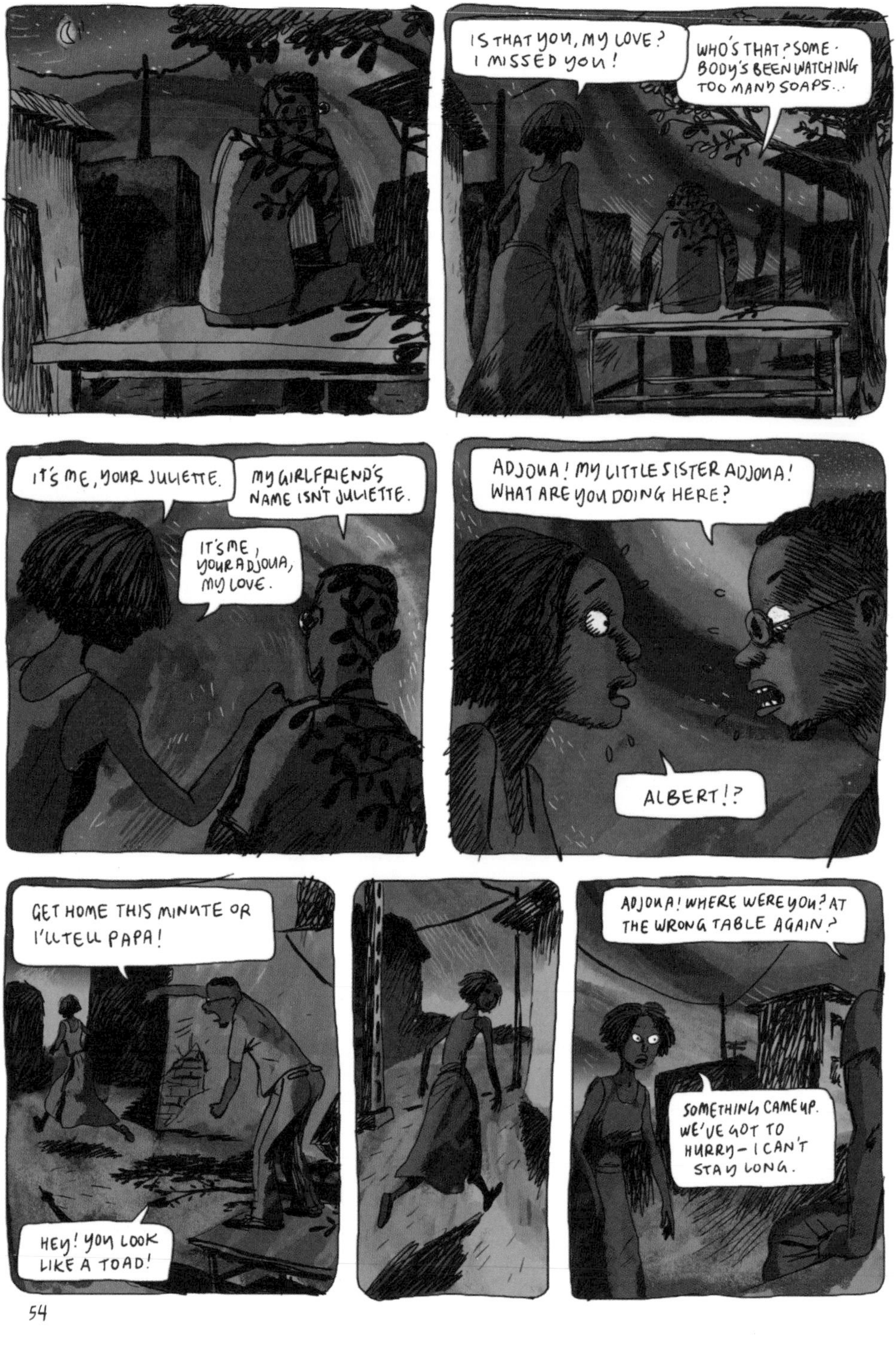
IS THAT YOU, MY LOVE? I MISSED YOU!
WHO'S THAT? SOME-BODY'S BEEN WATCHING TOO MANY SOAPS...
IT'S ME, YOUR JULIETTE.
MY GIRLFRIEND'S NAME ISN'T JULIETTE.
IT'S ME, YOUR ADJOUA, MY LOVE.
ADJOUA! MY LITTLE SISTER ADJOUA! WHAT ARE YOU DOING HERE?
ALBERT!?
GET HOME THIS MINUTE OR I'LL TELL PAPA!
HEY! YOU LOOK LIKE A TOAD!
ADJOUA! WHERE WERE YOU? AT THE WRONG TABLE AGAIN?
SOMETHING CAME UP. WE'VE GOT TO HURRY— I CAN'T STAY LONG.

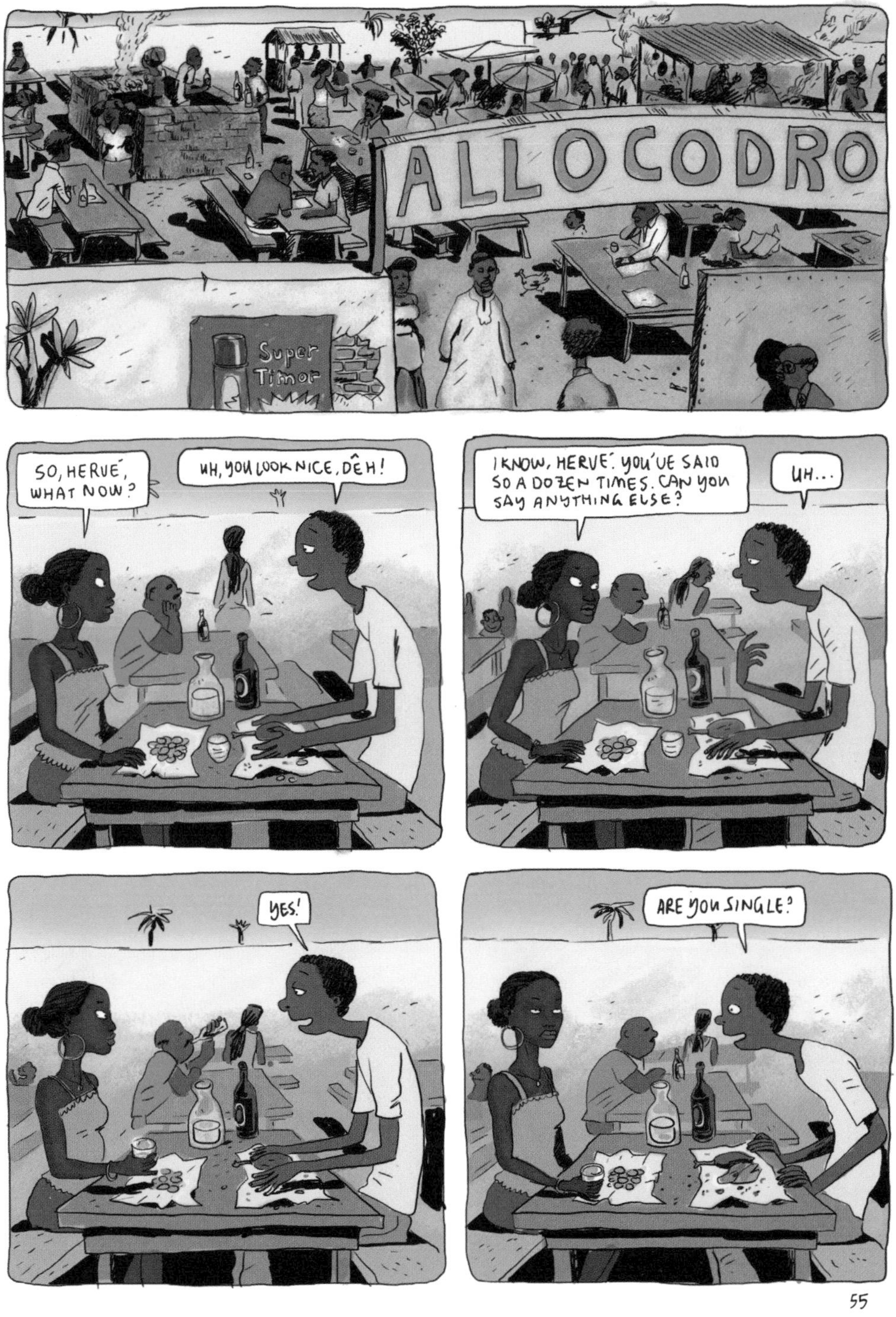
ALLOCODRO
Super Timor
SO, HERVÉ, WHAT NOW?
UH, YOU LOOK NICE, DÊH!
I KNOW, HERVÉ. YOU'VE SAID SO A DOZEN TIMES. CAN YOU SAY ANYTHING ELSE?
UH...
YES!
ARE YOU SINGLE?

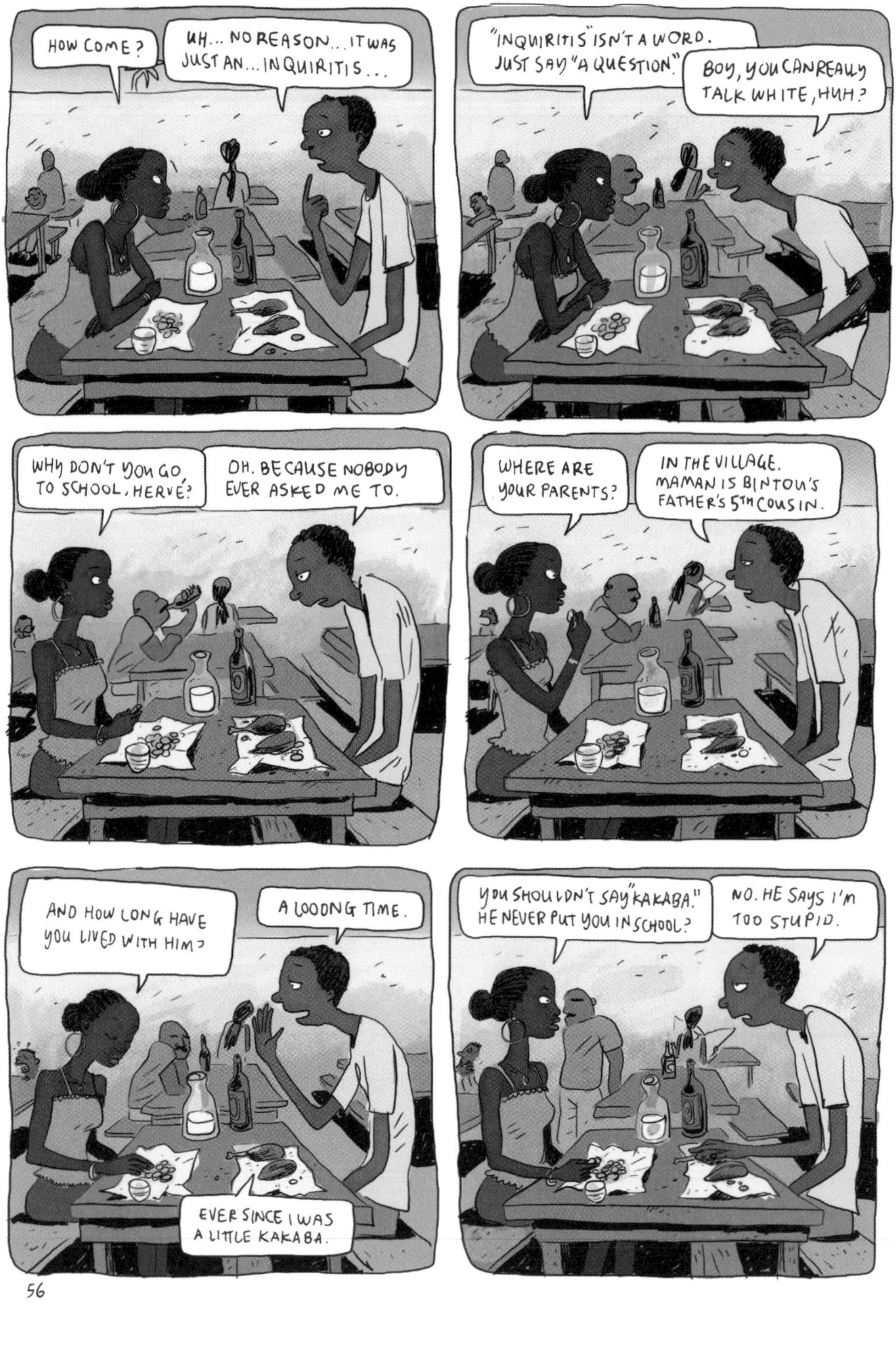
HOW COME?
UH... NO REASON... IT WAS JUST AN... INQUIRITIS...
"INQUIRITIS" ISN'T A WORD. JUST SAY "A QUESTION."
BOY, YOU CAN REALLY TALK WHITE, HUH?
WHY DON'T YOU GO TO SCHOOL, HERVÉ?
OH. BECAUSE NOBODY EVER ASKED ME TO.
WHERE ARE YOUR PARENTS?
IN THE VILLAGE. MAMAN IS BINTOU'S FATHER'S 5TH COUSIN.
AND HOW LONG HAVE YOU LIVED WITH HIM?
A LOOONG TIME.
EVER SINCE I WAS A LITTLE KAKABA.
YOU SHOULDN'T SAY "KAKABA." HE NEVER PUT YOU IN SCHOOL?
NO. HE SAYS I'M TOO STUPID.

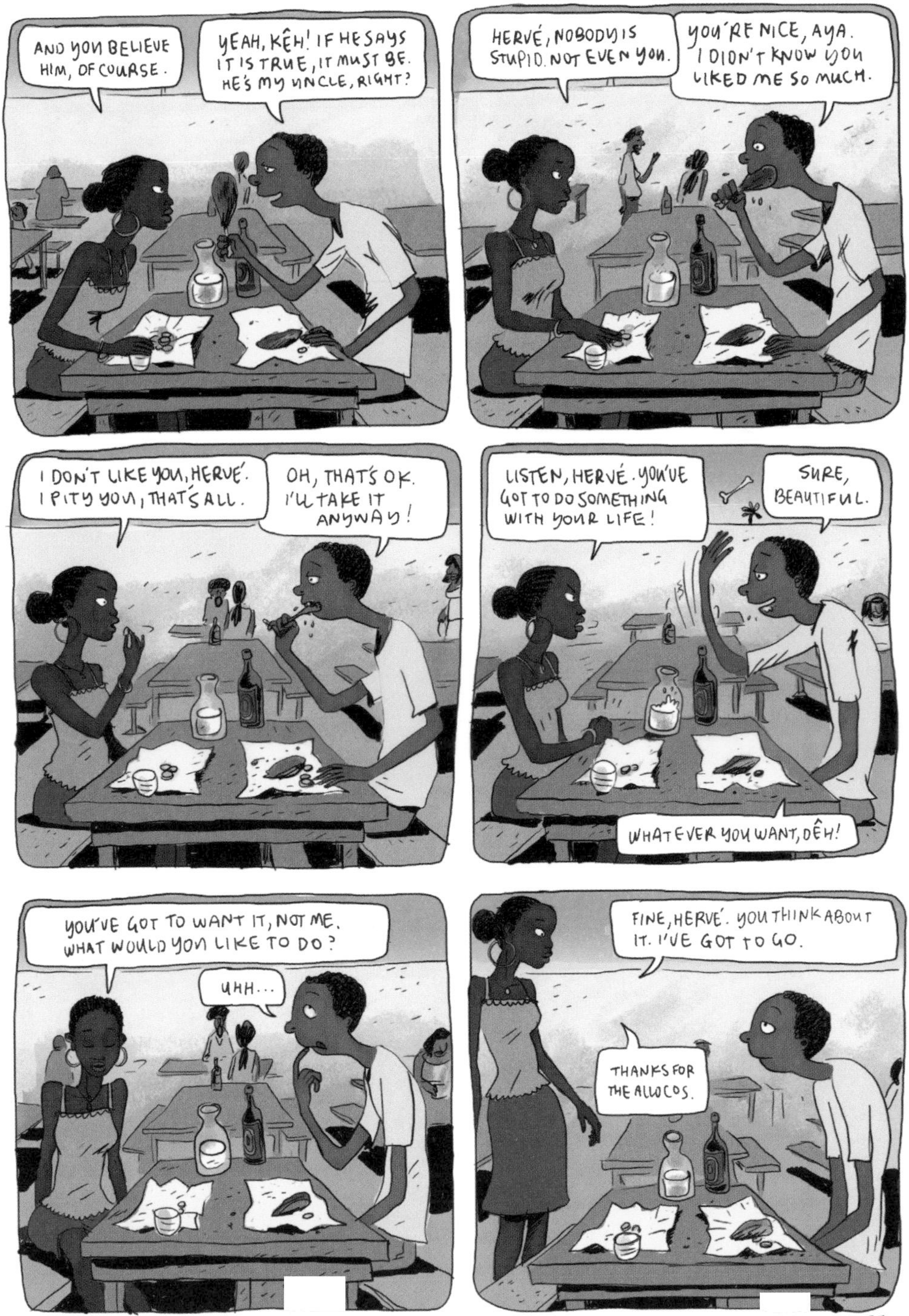
AND YOU BELIEVE HIM, OF COURSE.
YEAH, KÊH! IF HE SAYS IT IS TRUE, IT MUST BE. HE'S MY UNCLE, RIGHT?
HERVÉ, NOBODY IS STUPID. NOT EVEN YOU.
YOU'RE NICE, AYA. I DIDN'T KNOW YOU LIKED ME SO MUCH.
I DON'T LIKE YOU, HERVÉ. I PITY YOU, THAT'S ALL.
OH, THAT'S OK. I'LL TAKE IT ANYWAY!
LISTEN, HERVÉ. YOU'VE GOT TO DO SOMETHING WITH YOUR LIFE!
SURE, BEAUTIFUL.
WHATEVER YOU WANT, DÊH!
YOU'VE GOT TO WANT IT, NOT ME. WHAT WOULD YOU LIKE TO DO?
UHH...
FINE, HERVÉ. YOU THINK ABOUT IT. I'VE GOT TO GO.
THANKS FOR THE ALLOCOS.

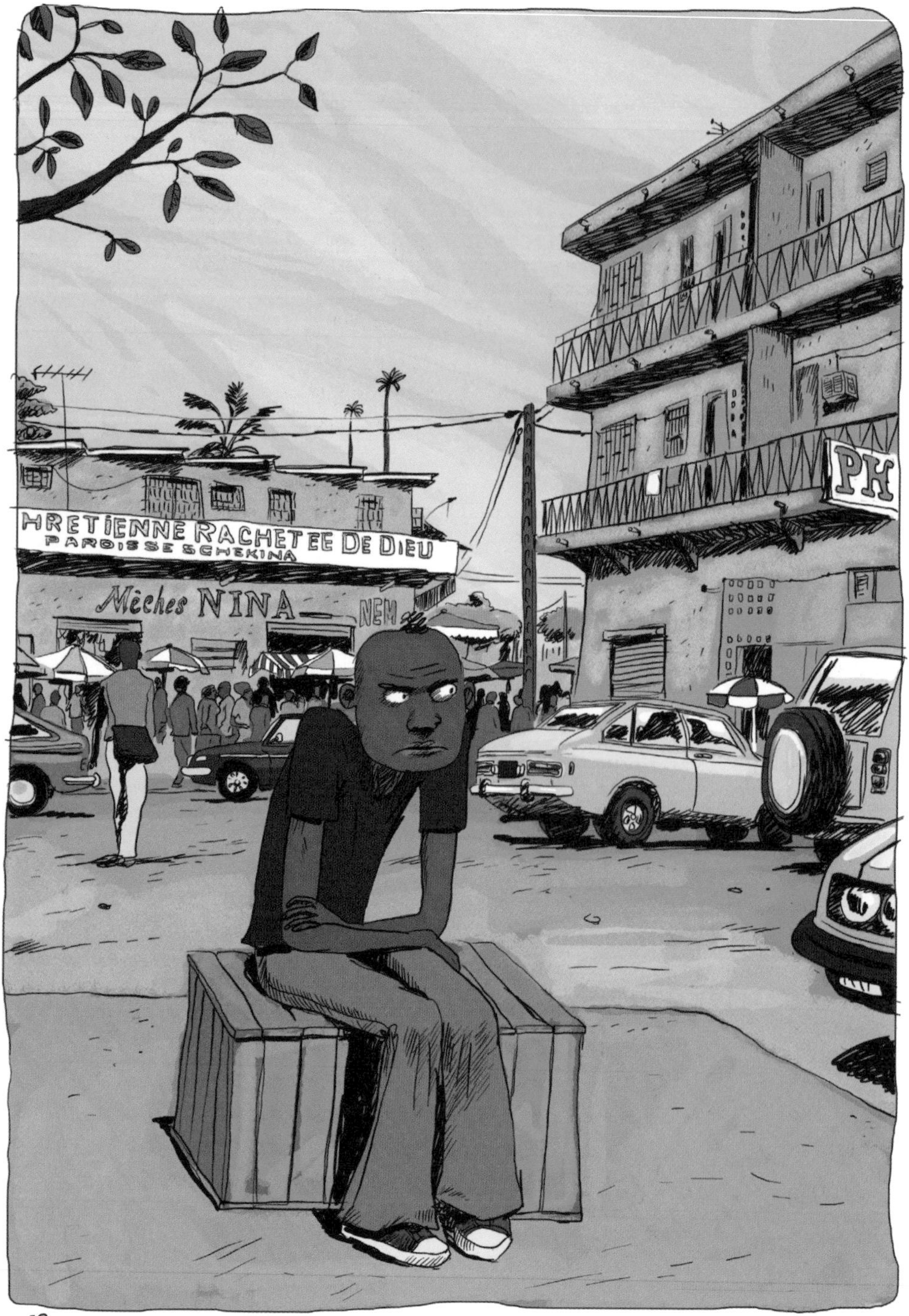
HRETIENNE RACHETEE DE DIEU
PAROISSE SCHEKINA
Mèches NINA
NEM
PK

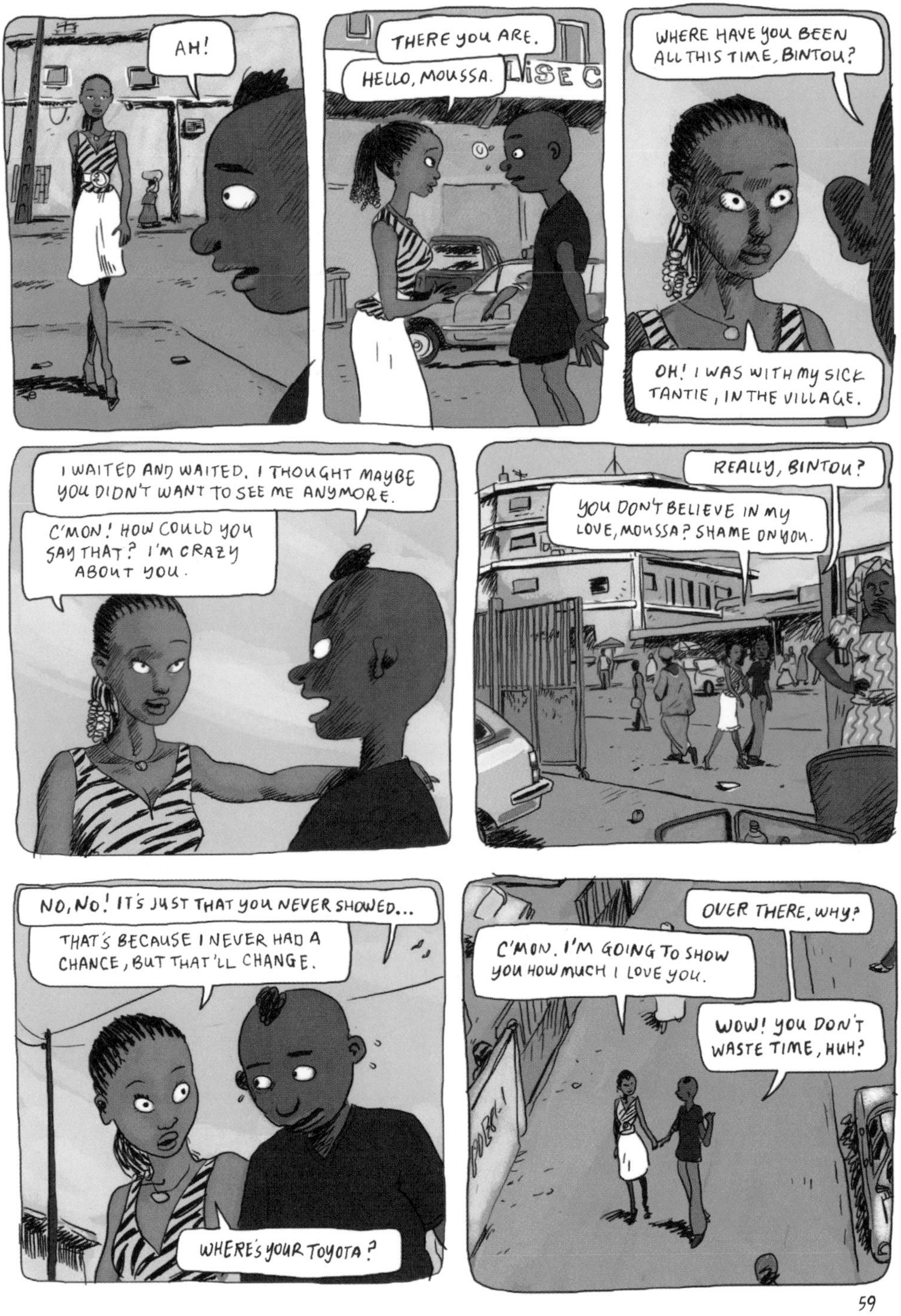
AH!
THERE YOU ARE.
HELLO, MOUSSA.
LISE C
WHERE HAVE YOU BEEN ALL THIS TIME, BINTOU?
OH! I WAS WITH MY SICK TANTIE, IN THE VILLAGE.
I WAITED AND WAITED. I THOUGHT MAYBE YOU DIDN'T WANT TO SEE ME ANYMORE.
C'MON! HOW COULD YOU SAY THAT? I'M CRAZY ABOUT YOU.
REALLY, BINTOU?
YOU DON'T BELIEVE IN MY LOVE, MOUSSA? SHAME ON YOU.
NO, NO! IT'S JUST THAT YOU NEVER SHOWED...
THAT'S BECAUSE I NEVER HAD A CHANCE, BUT THAT'LL CHANGE.
WHERE'S YOUR TOYOTA?
OVER THERE, WHY?
C'MON. I'M GOING TO SHOW YOU HOW MUCH I LOVE YOU.
WOW! YOU DON'T WASTE TIME, HUH?

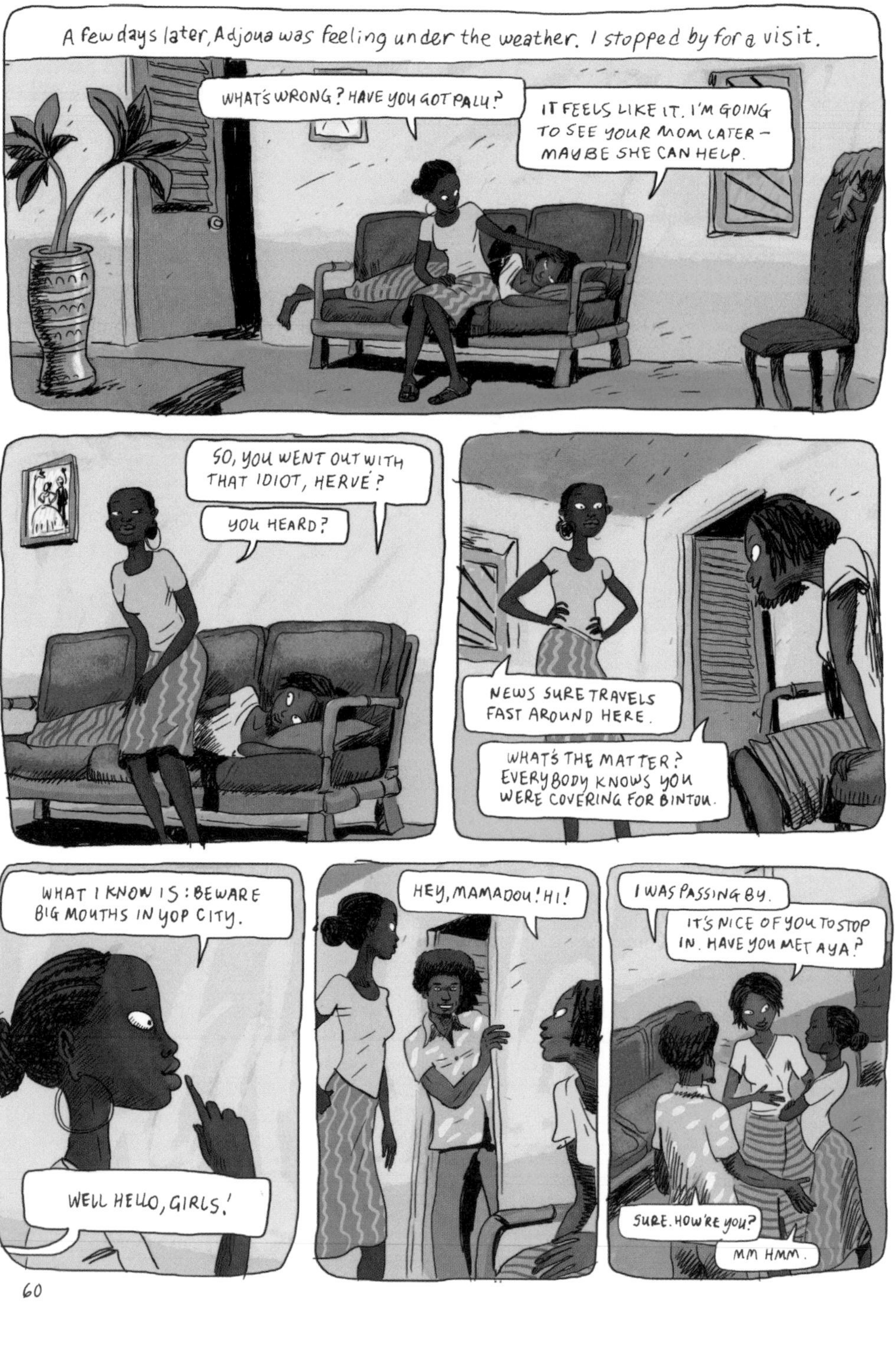
A few days later, Adjoua was feeling under the weather. I stopped by for a visit.
WHAT'S WRONG? HAVE YOU GOT PALU?
IT FEELS LIKE IT. I'M GOING TO SEE YOUR MOM LATER — MAYBE SHE CAN HELP.
SO, YOU WENT OUT WITH THAT IDIOT, HERVÉ?
YOU HEARD?
NEWS SURE TRAVELS FAST AROUND HERE.
WHAT'S THE MATTER? EVERYBODY KNOWS YOU WERE COVERING FOR BINTOU.
WHAT I KNOW IS: BEWARE BIG MOUTHS IN YOP CITY.
WELL HELLO, GIRLS!
HEY, MAMADOU! HI!
I WAS PASSING BY.
IT'S NICE OF YOU TO STOP IN. HAVE YOU MET AYA?
SURE. HOW'RE YOU?
MM HMM.

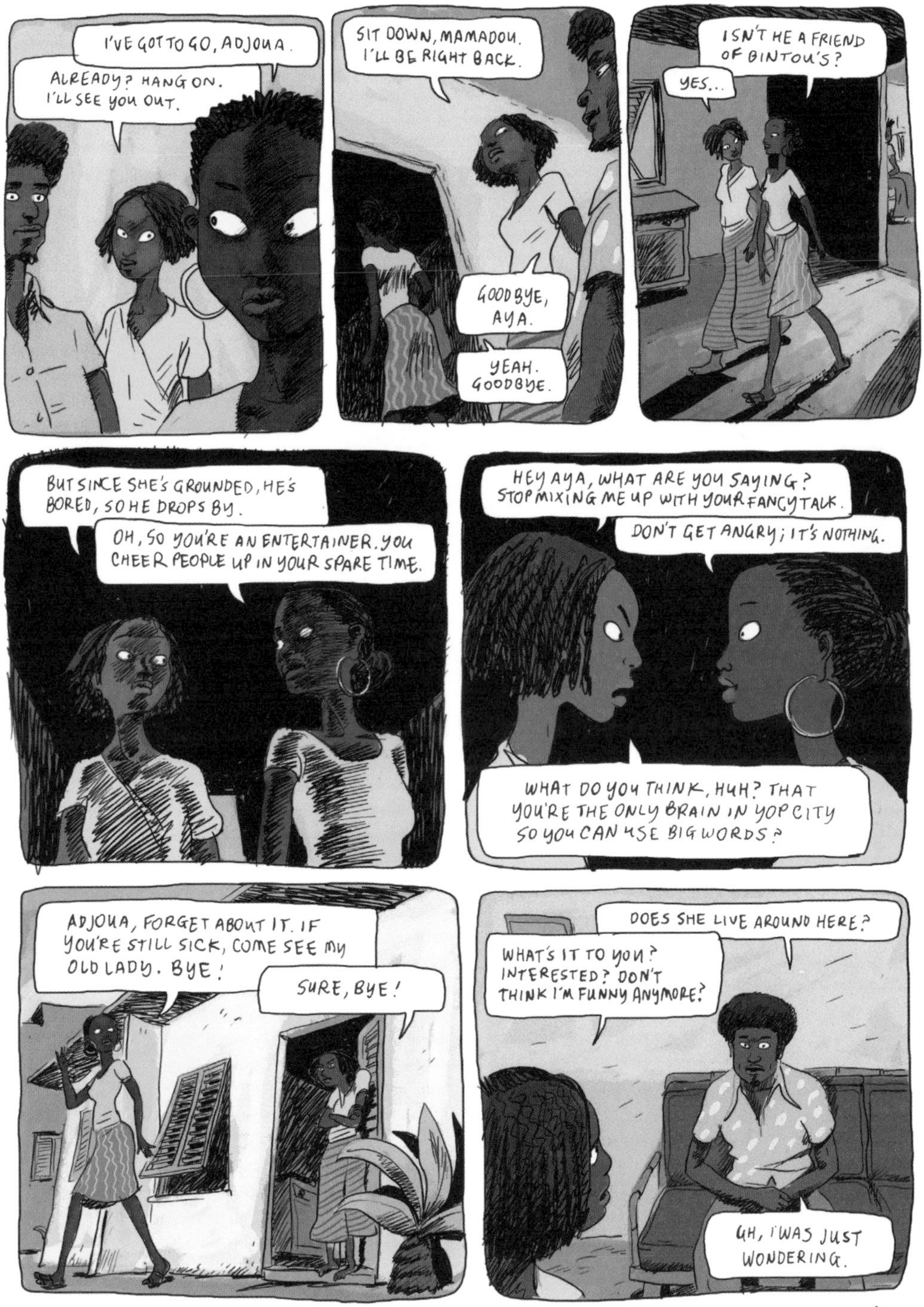
I'VE GOT TO GO, ADJOUA.
ALREADY? HANG ON. I'LL SEE YOU OUT.
SIT DOWN, MAMADOU. I'LL BE RIGHT BACK.
GOODBYE, AYA.
YEAH. GOODBYE.
ISN'T HE A FRIEND OF BINTOU'S?
YES...
BUT SINCE SHE'S GROUNDED, HE'S BORED, SO HE DROPS BY.
OH, SO YOU'RE AN ENTERTAINER. YOU CHEER PEOPLE UP IN YOUR SPARE TIME.
HEY AYA, WHAT ARE YOU SAYING? STOP MIXING ME UP WITH YOUR FANCY TALK.
DON'T GET ANGRY; IT'S NOTHING.
WHAT DO YOU THINK, HUH? THAT YOU'RE THE ONLY BRAIN IN YOP CITY SO YOU CAN USE BIG WORDS?
ADJOUA, FORGET ABOUT IT. IF YOU'RE STILL SICK, COME SEE MY OLD LADY. BYE!
SURE, BYE!
DOES SHE LIVE AROUND HERE?
WHAT'S IT TO YOU? INTERESTED? DON'T THINK I'M FUNNY ANYMORE?
UH, I WAS JUST WONDERING.

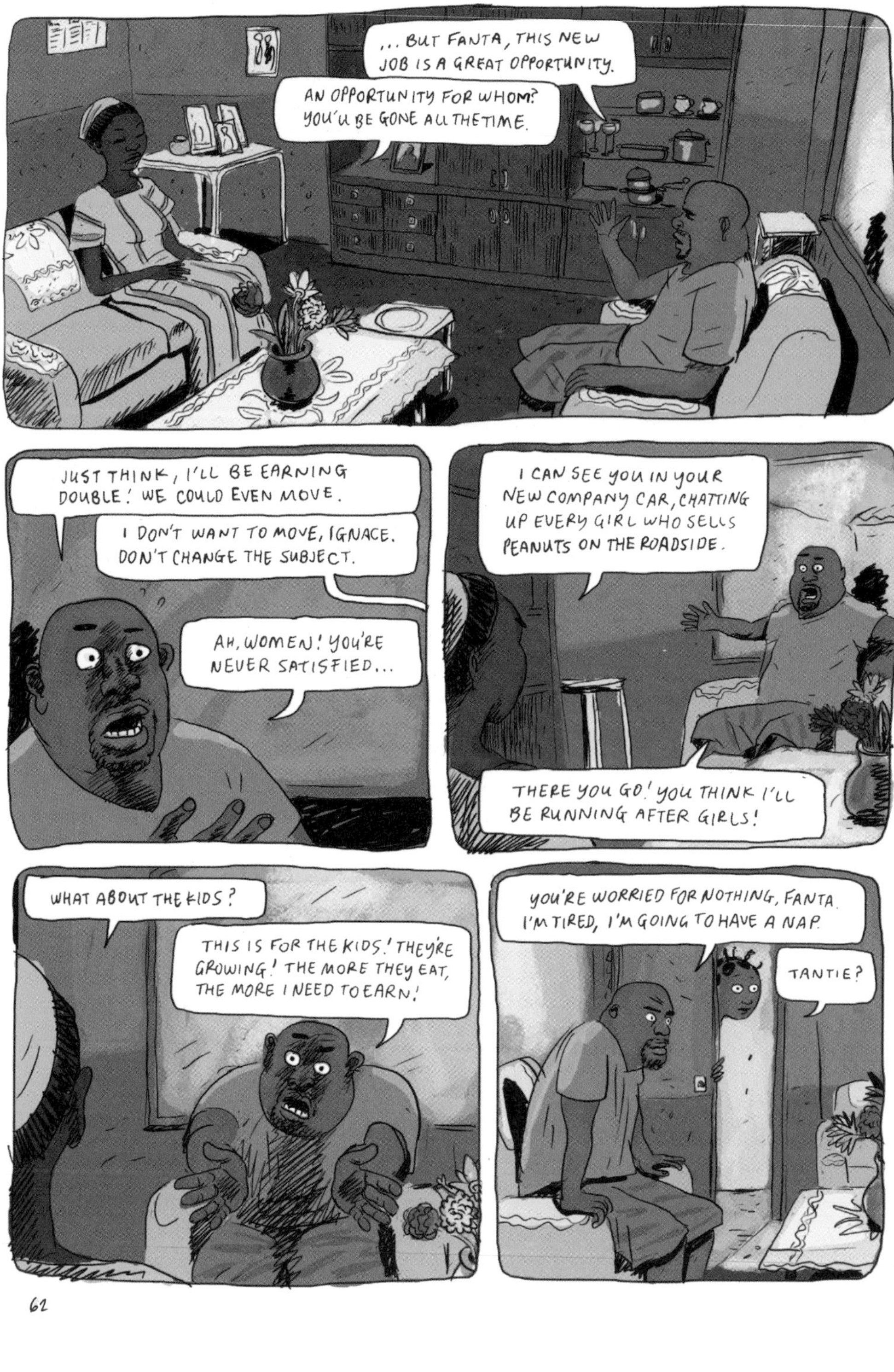
... BUT FANTA, THIS NEW JOB IS A GREAT OPPORTUNITY.
AN OPPORTUNITY FOR WHOM? YOU'LL BE GONE ALL THE TIME.
JUST THINK, I'LL BE EARNING DOUBLE! WE COULD EVEN MOVE.
I DON'T WANT TO MOVE, IGNACE. DON'T CHANGE THE SUBJECT.
AH, WOMEN! YOU'RE NEVER SATISFIED...
I CAN SEE YOU IN YOUR NEW COMPANY CAR, CHATTING UP EVERY GIRL WHO SELLS PEANUTS ON THE ROADSIDE.
THERE YOU GO! YOU THINK I'LL BE RUNNING AFTER GIRLS!
WHAT ABOUT THE KIDS?
THIS IS FOR THE KIDS! THEY'RE GROWING! THE MORE THEY EAT, THE MORE I NEED TO EARN!
YOU'RE WORRIED FOR NOTHING, FANTA. I'M TIRED, I'M GOING TO HAVE A NAP.
TANTIE?

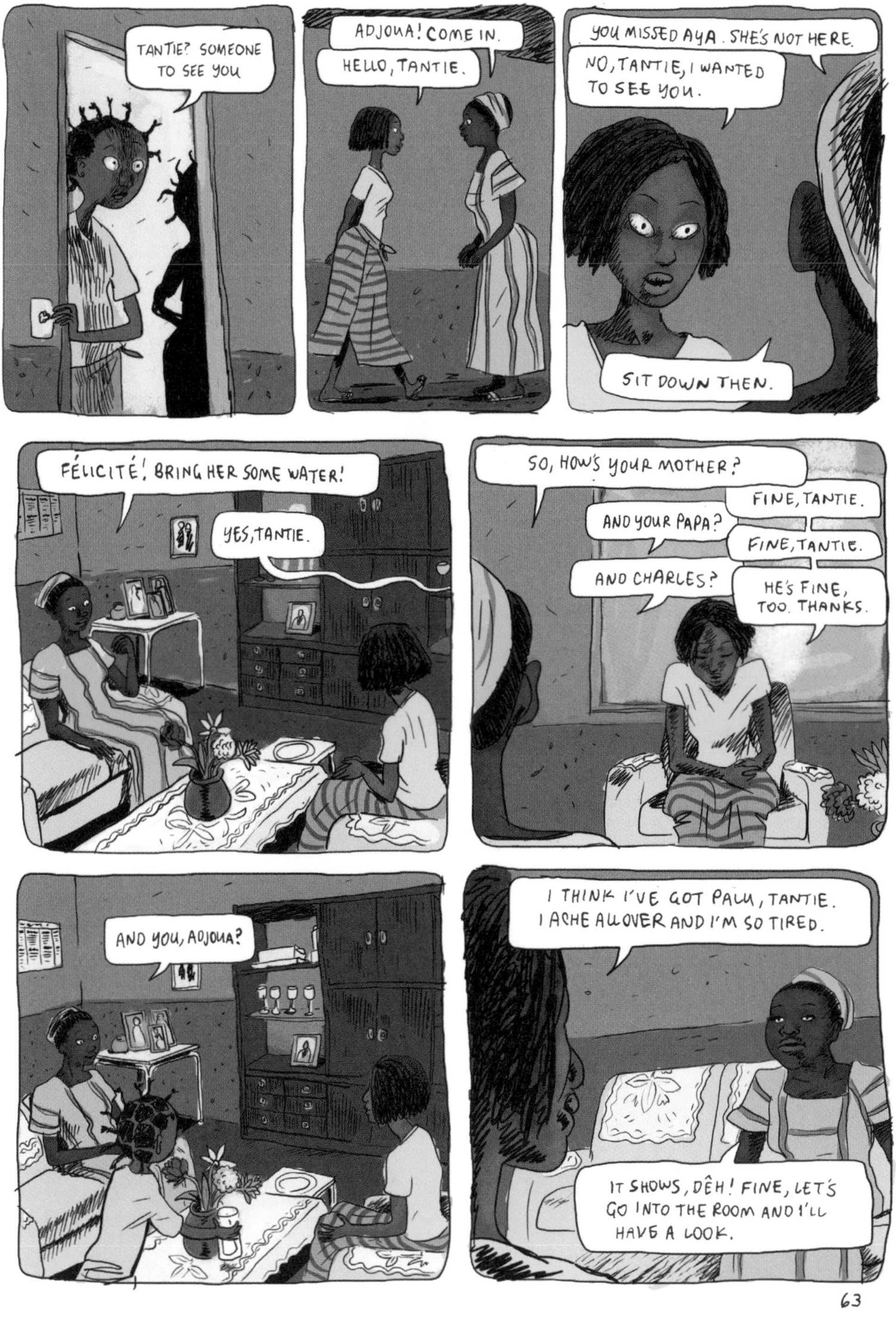
TANTIE? SOMEONE TO SEE YOU
ADJOUA! COME IN.
HELLO, TANTIE.
YOU MISSED AYA. SHE'S NOT HERE.
NO, TANTIE, I WANTED TO SEE YOU.
SIT DOWN THEN.
FÉLICITÉ! BRING HER SOME WATER!
YES, TANTIE.
SO, HOW'S YOUR MOTHER?
FINE, TANTIE.
AND YOUR PAPA?
FINE, TANTIE.
AND CHARLES?
HE'S FINE, TOO. THANKS.
AND YOU, ADJOUA?
I THINK I'VE GOT PALU, TANTIE. I ACHE ALL OVER AND I'M SO TIRED.
IT SHOWS, DÊH! FINE, LET'S GO INTO THE ROOM AND I'LL HAVE A LOOK.

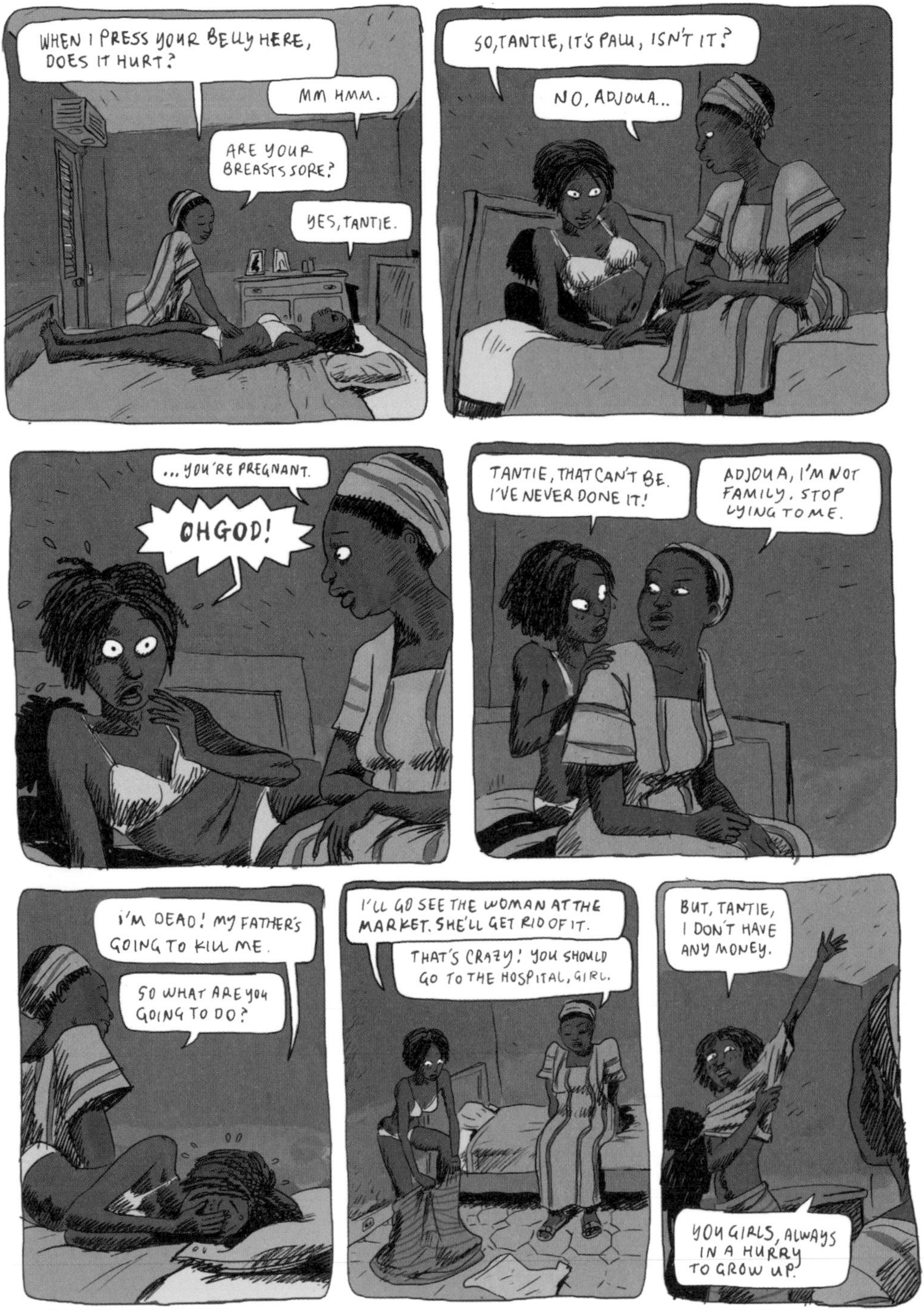
WHEN I PRESS YOUR BELLY HERE, DOES IT HURT?
MM HMM.
ARE YOUR BREASTS SORE?
YES, TANTIE.
SO, TANTIE, IT'S PALU, ISN'T IT?
NO, ADJOUA...
...YOU'RE PREGNANT.
OHGOD!
TANTIE, THAT CAN'T BE. I'VE NEVER DONE IT!
ADJOUA, I'M NOT FAMILY. STOP LYING TO ME.
I'M DEAD! MY FATHER'S GOING TO KILL ME.
SO WHAT ARE YOU GOING TO DO?
I'LL GO SEE THE WOMAN AT THE MARKET. SHE'LL GET RID OF IT.
THAT'S CRAZY! YOU SHOULD GO TO THE HOSPITAL, GIRL.
BUT, TANTIE, I DON'T HAVE ANY MONEY.
YOU GIRLS, ALWAYS IN A HURRY TO GROW UP.

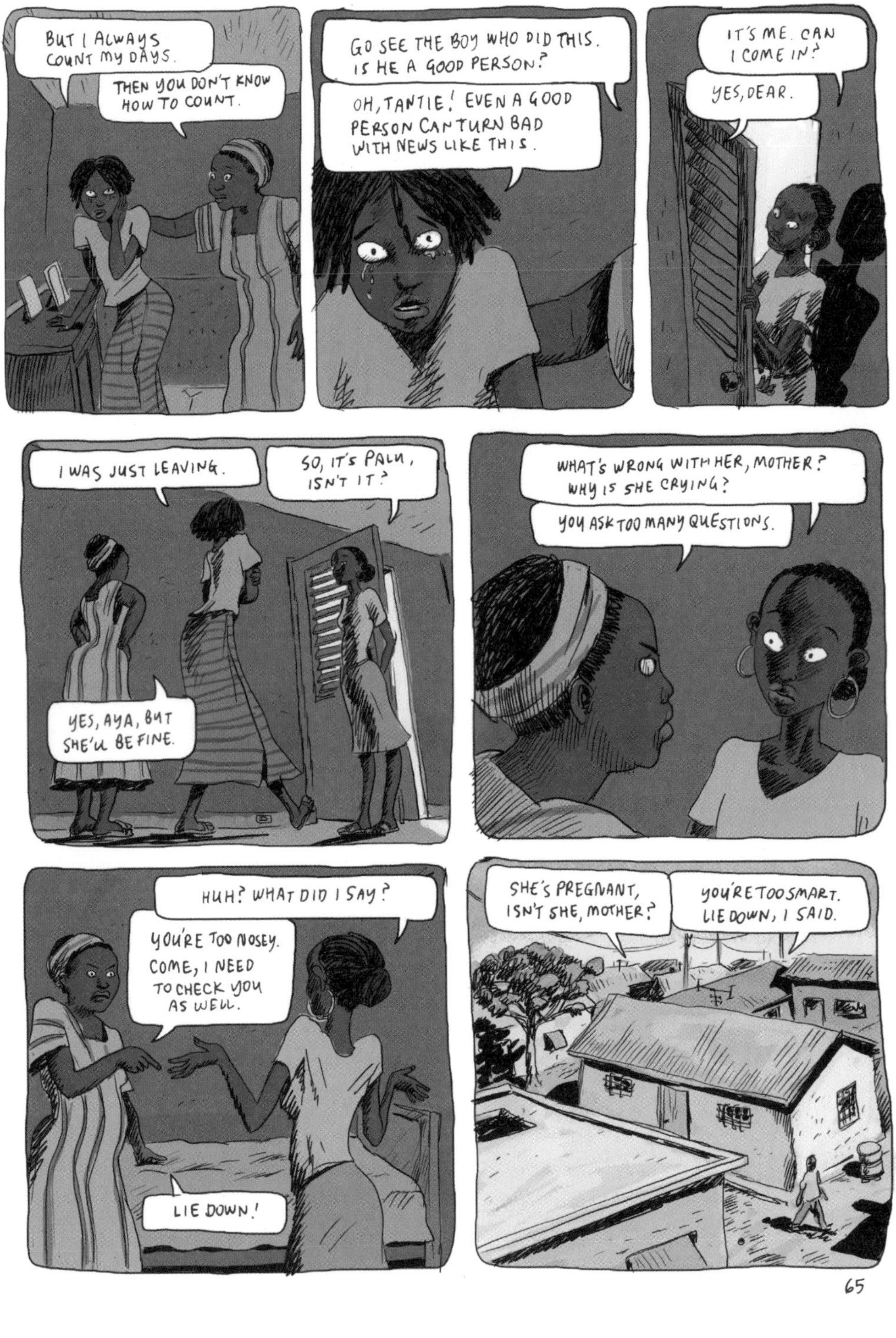

BUT I ALWAYS COUNT MY DAYS.
THEN YOU DON'T KNOW HOW TO COUNT.
GO SEE THE BOY WHO DID THIS. IS HE A GOOD PERSON?
OH, TANTIE! EVEN A GOOD PERSON CAN TURN BAD WITH NEWS LIKE THIS.
IT'S ME. CAN I COME IN?
YES, DEAR.
I WAS JUST LEAVING.
SO, IT'S PALU, ISN'T IT?
YES, AYA, BUT SHE'LL BE FINE.
WHAT'S WRONG WITH HER, MOTHER? WHY IS SHE CRYING?
YOU ASK TOO MANY QUESTIONS.
HUH? WHAT DID I SAY?
YOU'RE TOO NOSEY. COME, I NEED TO CHECK YOU AS WELL.
LIE DOWN!
SHE'S PREGNANT, ISN'T SHE, MOTHER?
YOU'RE TOO SMART. LIE DOWN, I SAID.

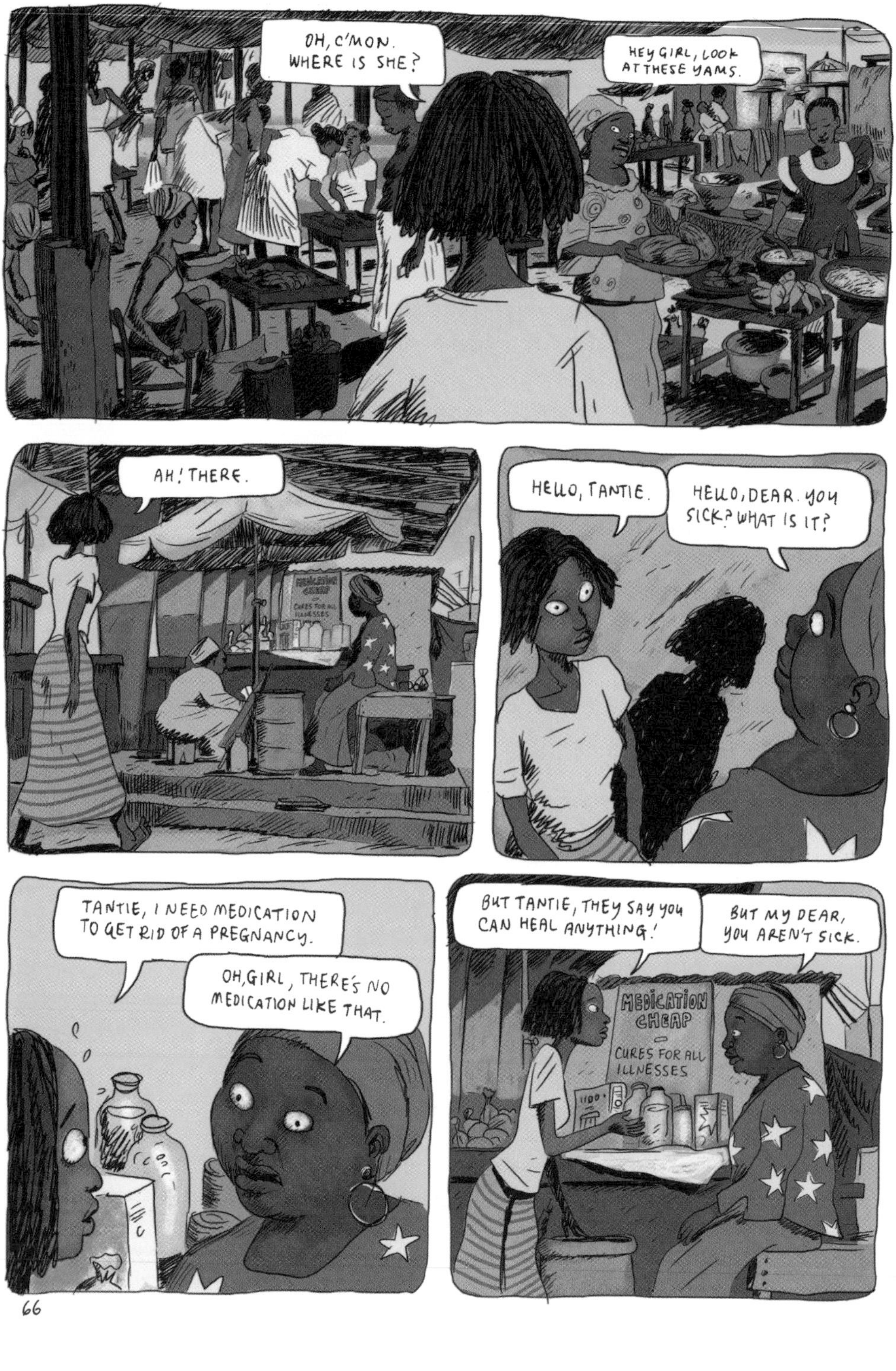
OH, C'MON. WHERE IS SHE?
HEY GIRL, LOOK AT THESE YAMS.
AH! THERE.
MEDICATION CHEAP
CURES FOR ALL ILLNESSES
HELLO, TANTIE.
HELLO, DEAR. YOU SICK? WHAT IS IT?
TANTIE, I NEED MEDICATION TO GET RID OF A PREGNANCY.
OH, GIRL, THERE'S NO MEDICATION LIKE THAT.
BUT TANTIE, THEY SAY YOU CAN HEAL ANYTHING!
BUT MY DEAR, YOU AREN'T SICK.
MEDICATION CHEAP
CURES FOR ALL ILLNESSES

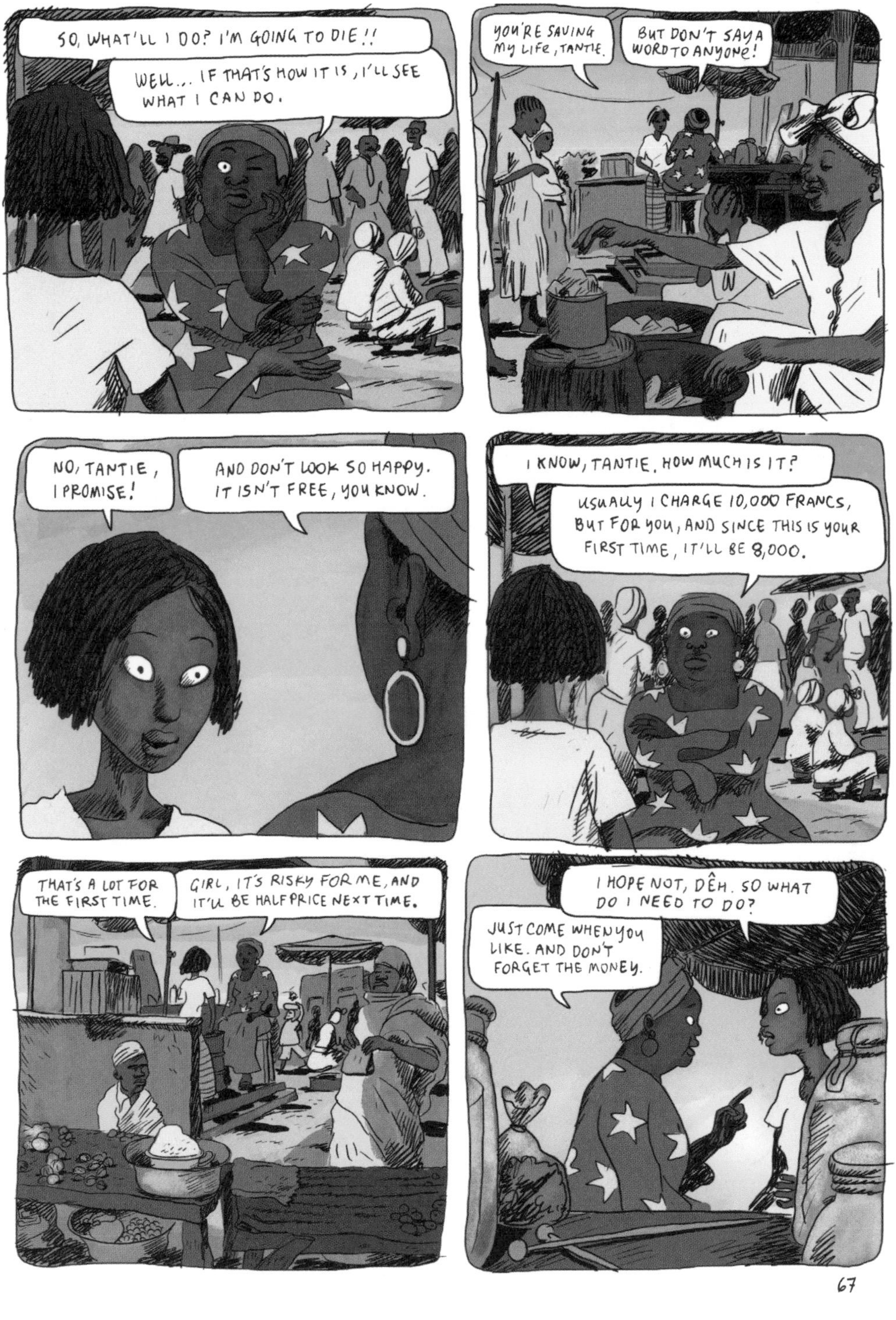

SO, WHAT'LL I DO? I'M GOING TO DIE!!
WELL... IF THAT'S HOW IT IS, I'LL SEE WHAT I CAN DO.
YOU'RE SAVING MY LIFE, TANTIE.
BUT DON'T SAY A WORD TO ANYONE!
NO, TANTIE, I PROMISE!
AND DON'T LOOK SO HAPPY. IT ISN'T FREE, YOU KNOW.
I KNOW, TANTIE. HOW MUCH IS IT?
USUALLY I CHARGE 10,000 FRANCS, BUT FOR YOU, AND SINCE THIS IS YOUR FIRST TIME, IT'LL BE 8,000.
THAT'S A LOT FOR THE FIRST TIME.
GIRL, IT'S RISKY FOR ME, AND IT'LL BE HALF PRICE NEXT TIME.
I HOPE NOT, DÊH. SO WHAT DO I NEED TO DO?
JUST COME WHEN YOU LIKE. AND DON'T FORGET THE MONEY.

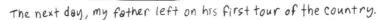

The next day, my father left on his first tour of the country.

WELL, FANTA, LOOKS LIKE I'M OFF. IS EVERYTHING IN MY BAG?

YES, IGNACE, IT'S ALL THERE.

AYA, KEEP AN EYE ON THE KIDS, OK?

MM HM.

AND I DON'T WANT YOU FOOLING AROUND.

YOU TOO, AND DON'T FORGET TO CALL HOME!

HOW COULD I FORGET TO CALL MY DEAR WIFE?

SURE, AND DON'T DRIVE TOO FAST.

DON'T KILL YOURSELF!

AND BRING BACK LOTS OF GIFTS.

OK, AYA, GO TIDY UP THE ROOM.

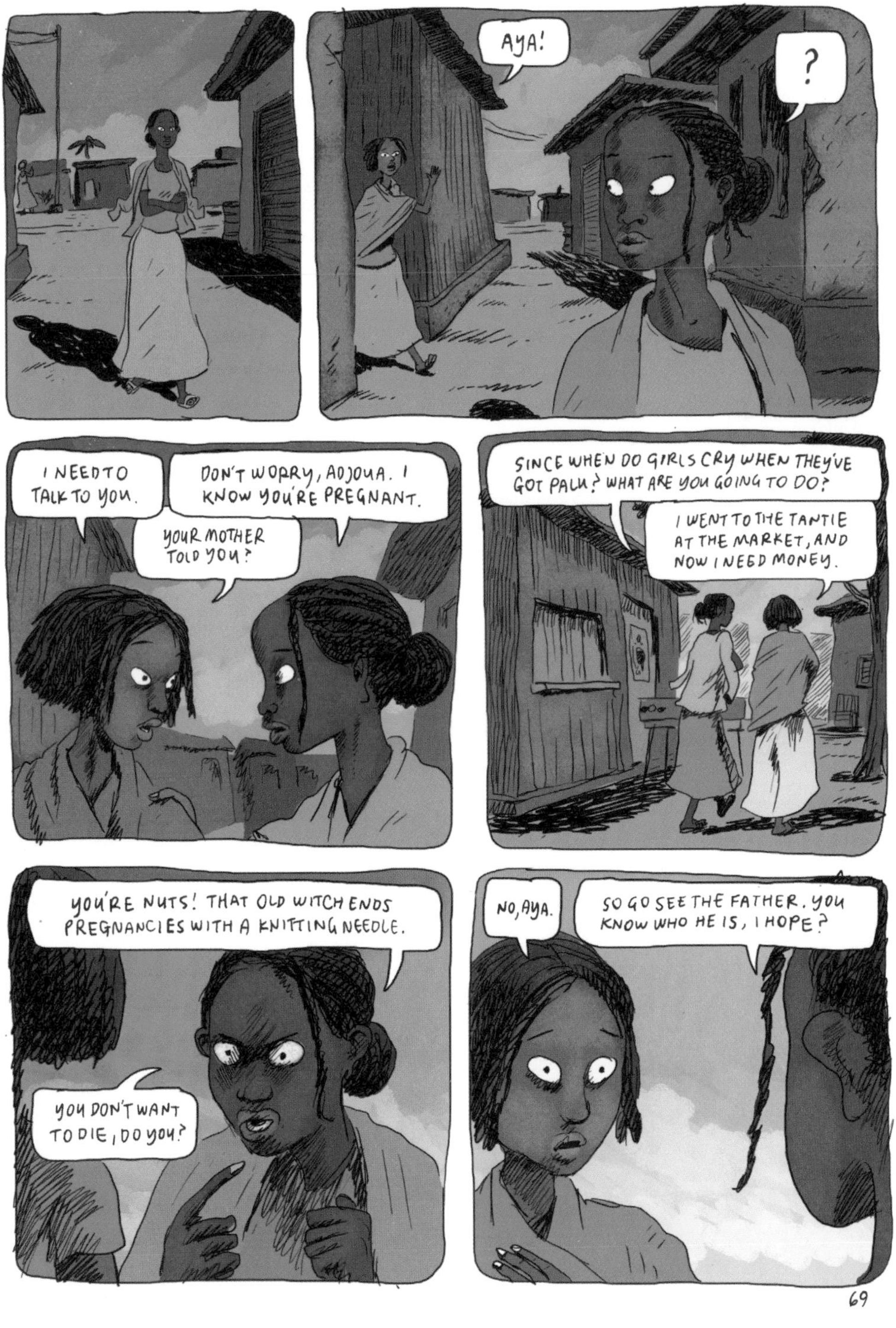
AYA!
?
I NEED TO TALK TO YOU.
YOUR MOTHER TOLD YOU?
DON'T WORRY, ADJOUA. I KNOW YOU'RE PREGNANT.
SINCE WHEN DO GIRLS CRY WHEN THEY'VE GOT PALU? WHAT ARE YOU GOING TO DO?
I WENT TO THE TANTIE AT THE MARKET, AND NOW I NEED MONEY.
YOU'RE NUTS! THAT OLD WITCH ENDS PREGNANCIES WITH A KNITTING NEEDLE.
YOU DON'T WANT TO DIE, DO YOU?
SO GO SEE THE FATHER. YOU KNOW WHO HE IS, I HOPE?
NO, AYA.

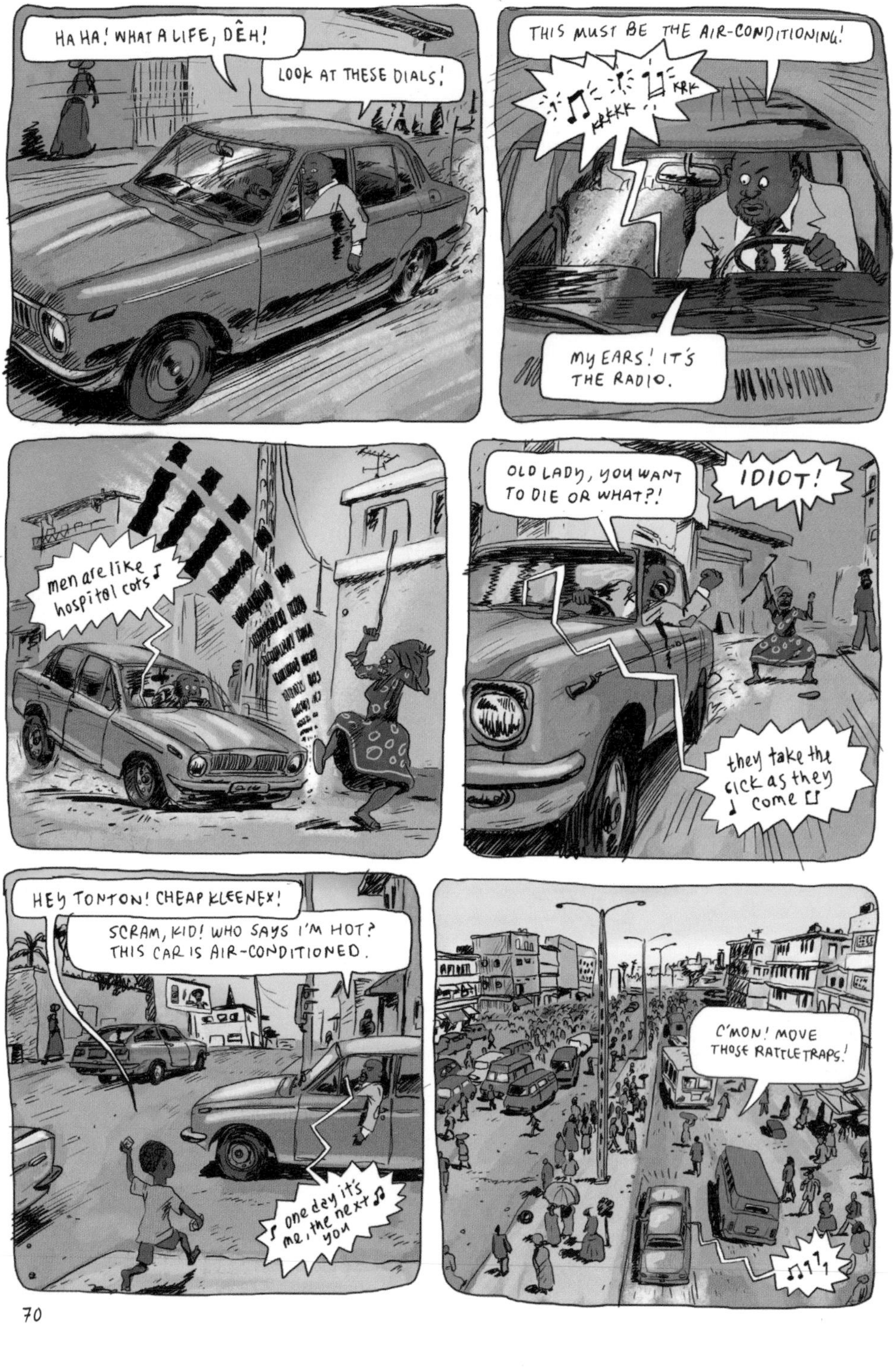
HA HA! WHAT A LIFE, DÊH!
LOOK AT THESE DIALS!
THIS MUST BE THE AIR-CONDITIONING!
KRKKK
KRK
MY EARS! IT'S THE RADIO.
men are like hospital cots
OLD LADY, YOU WANT TO DIE OR WHAT?!
IDIOT!
they take the sick as they come
HEY TONTON! CHEAP KLEENEX!
SCRAM, KID! WHO SAYS I'M HOT? THIS CAR IS AIR-CONDITIONED.
one day it's me, the next you
C'MON! MOVE THOSE RATTLETRAPS!

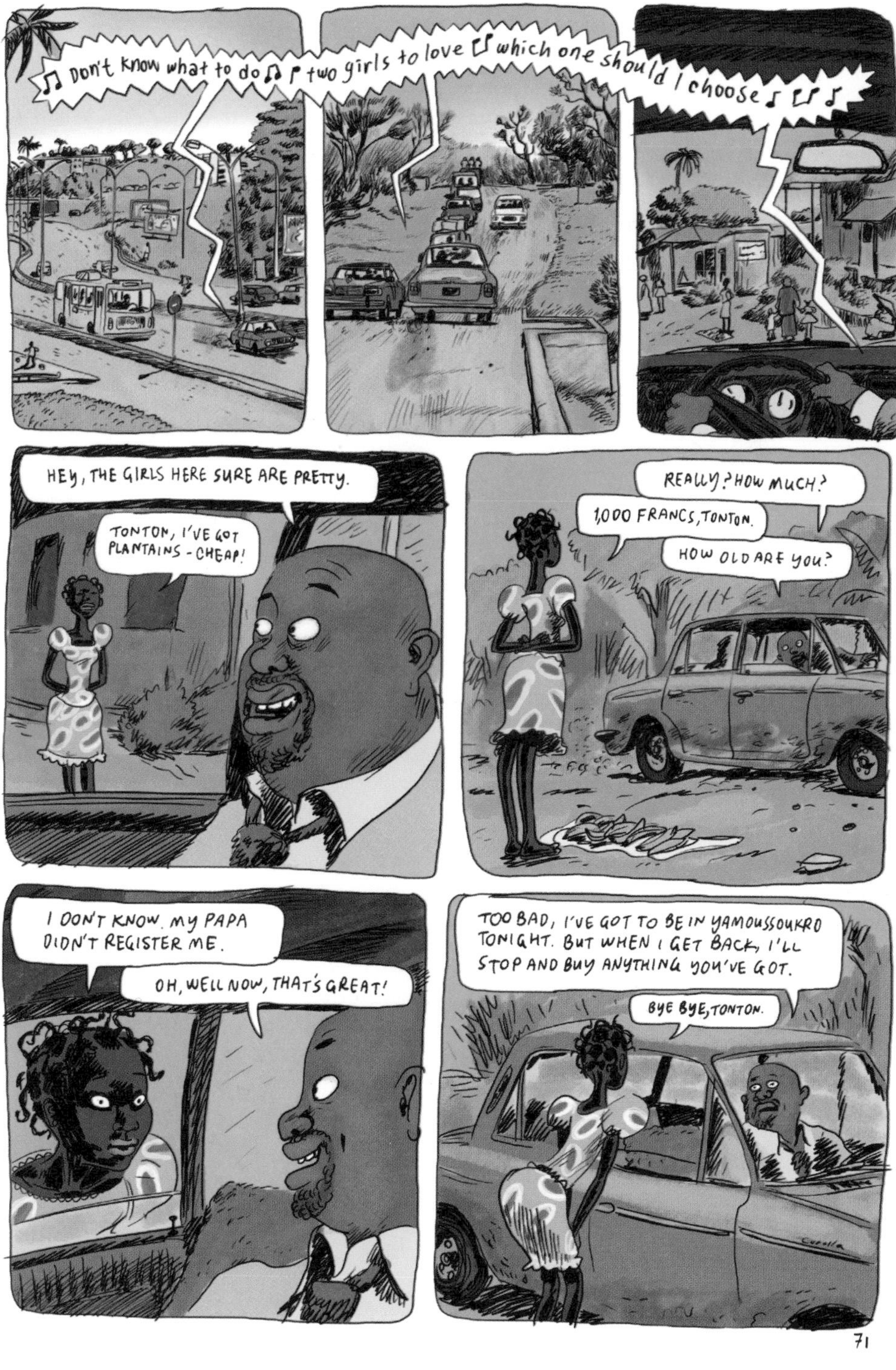
♫ Don't know what to do ♫ ♪ two girls to love ♫ which one should I choose ♪ ♫ ♪
HEY, THE GIRLS HERE SURE ARE PRETTY.
TONTON, I'VE GOT PLANTAINS - CHEAP!
REALLY? HOW MUCH?
1,000 FRANCS, TONTON.
HOW OLD ARE YOU?
I DON'T KNOW. MY PAPA DIDN'T REGISTER ME.
OH, WELL NOW, THAT'S GREAT!
TOO BAD, I'VE GOT TO BE IN YAMOUSSOUKRO TONIGHT. BUT WHEN I GET BACK, I'LL STOP AND BUY ANYTHING YOU'VE GOT.
BYE BYE, TONTON.

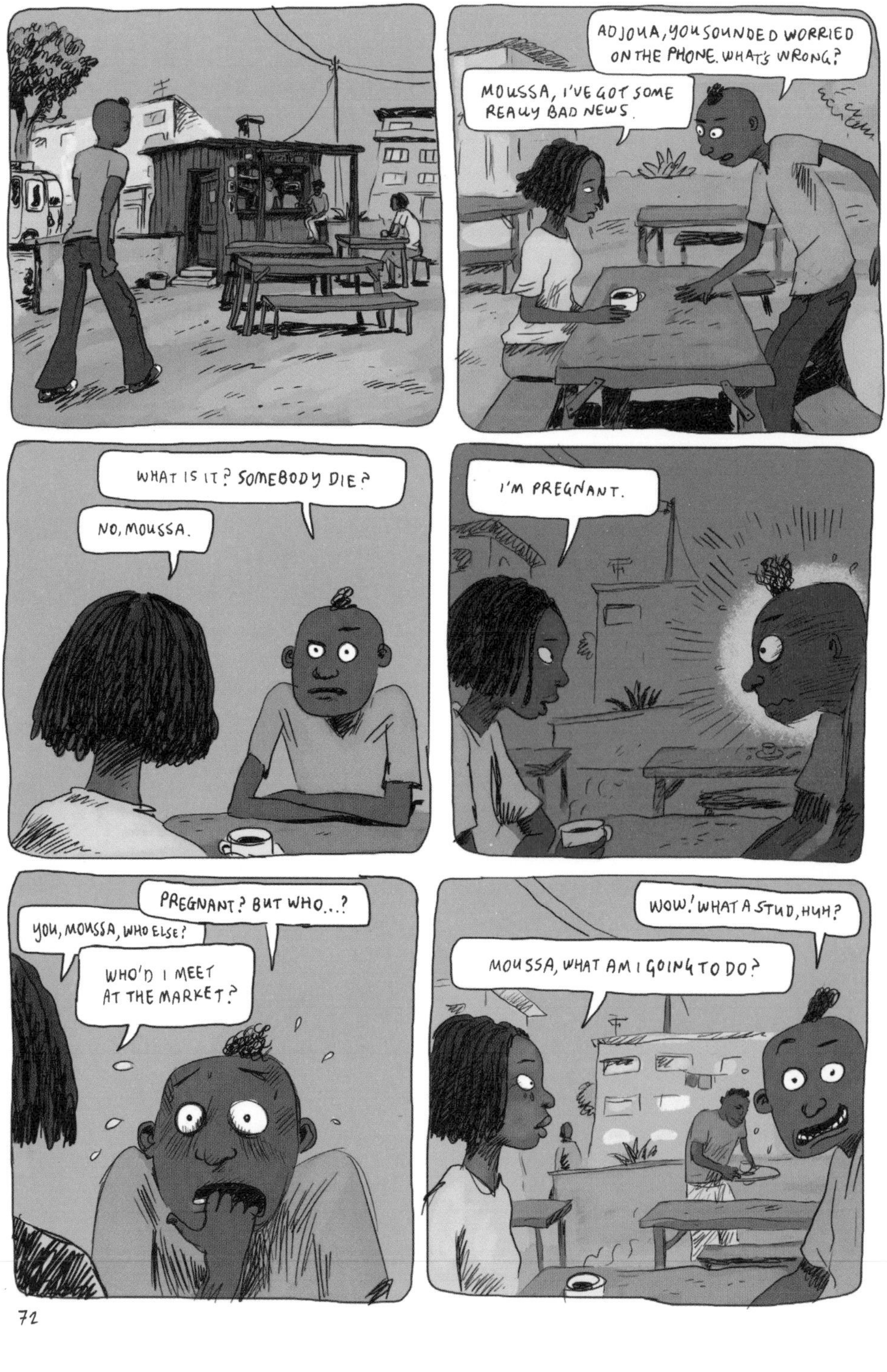

ADJOUA, YOU SOUNDED WORRIED ON THE PHONE. WHAT'S WRONG?
MOUSSA, I'VE GOT SOME REALLY BAD NEWS.
WHAT IS IT? SOMEBODY DIE?
NO, MOUSSA.
I'M PREGNANT.
PREGNANT? BUT WHO...?
YOU, MOUSSA, WHO ELSE?
WHO'D I MEET AT THE MARKET?
WOW! WHAT A STUD, HUH?
MOUSSA, WHAT AM I GOING TO DO?

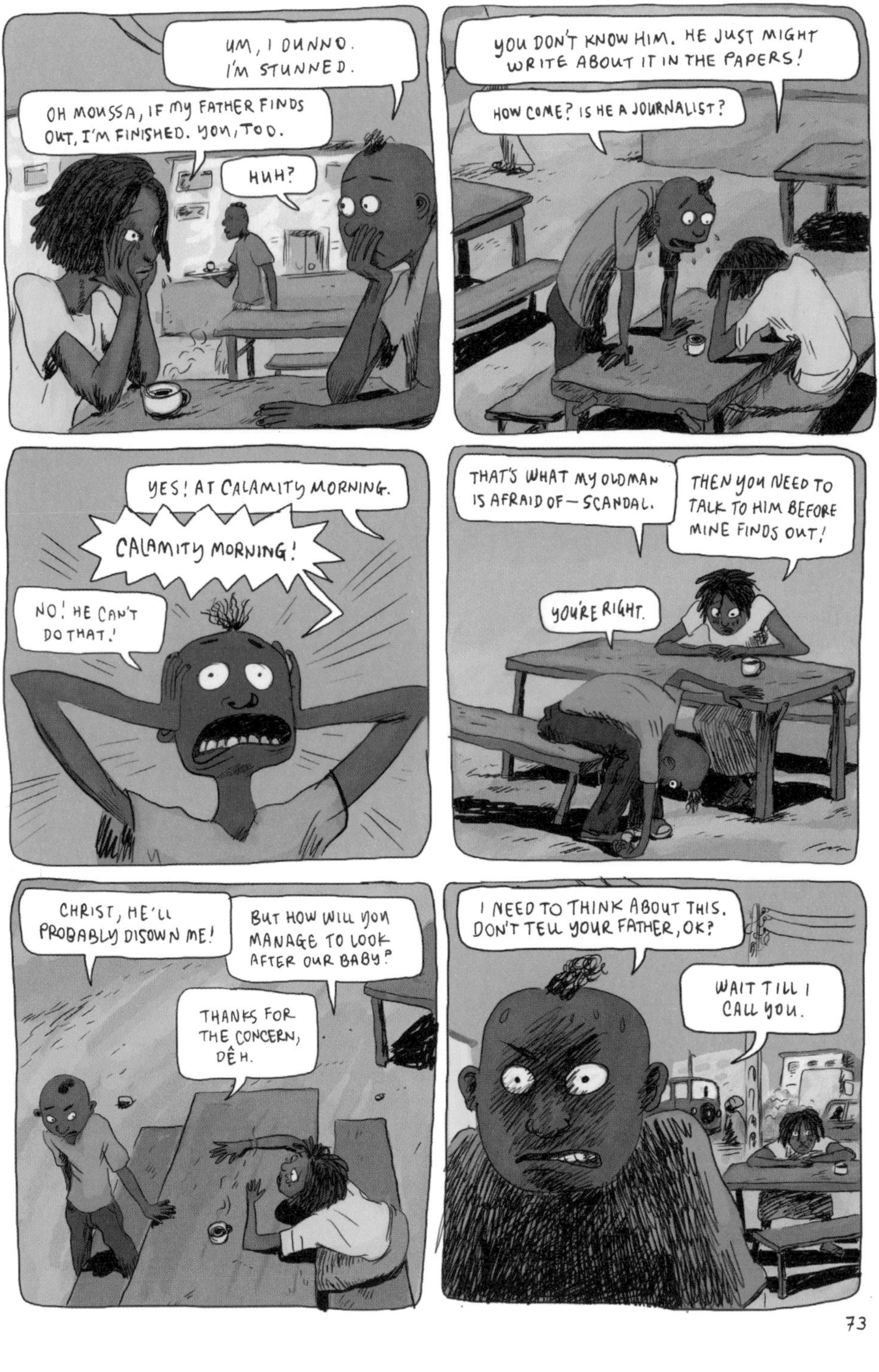
UM, I DUNNO. I'M STUNNED.
OH MOUSSA, IF MY FATHER FINDS OUT, I'M FINISHED. YOU, TOO.
HUH?
YOU DON'T KNOW HIM. HE JUST MIGHT WRITE ABOUT IT IN THE PAPERS!
HOW COME? IS HE A JOURNALIST?
YES! AT CALAMITY MORNING.
CALAMITY MORNING!
NO! HE CAN'T DO THAT!
THAT'S WHAT MY OLDMAN IS AFRAID OF—SCANDAL.
THEN YOU NEED TO TALK TO HIM BEFORE MINE FINDS OUT!
YOU'RE RIGHT.
CHRIST, HE'LL PROBABLY DISOWN ME!
BUT HOW WILL YOU MANAGE TO LOOK AFTER OUR BABY?
THANKS FOR THE CONCERN, DÊH.
I NEED TO THINK ABOUT THIS. DON'T TELL YOUR FATHER, OK?
WAIT TILL I CALL YOU.

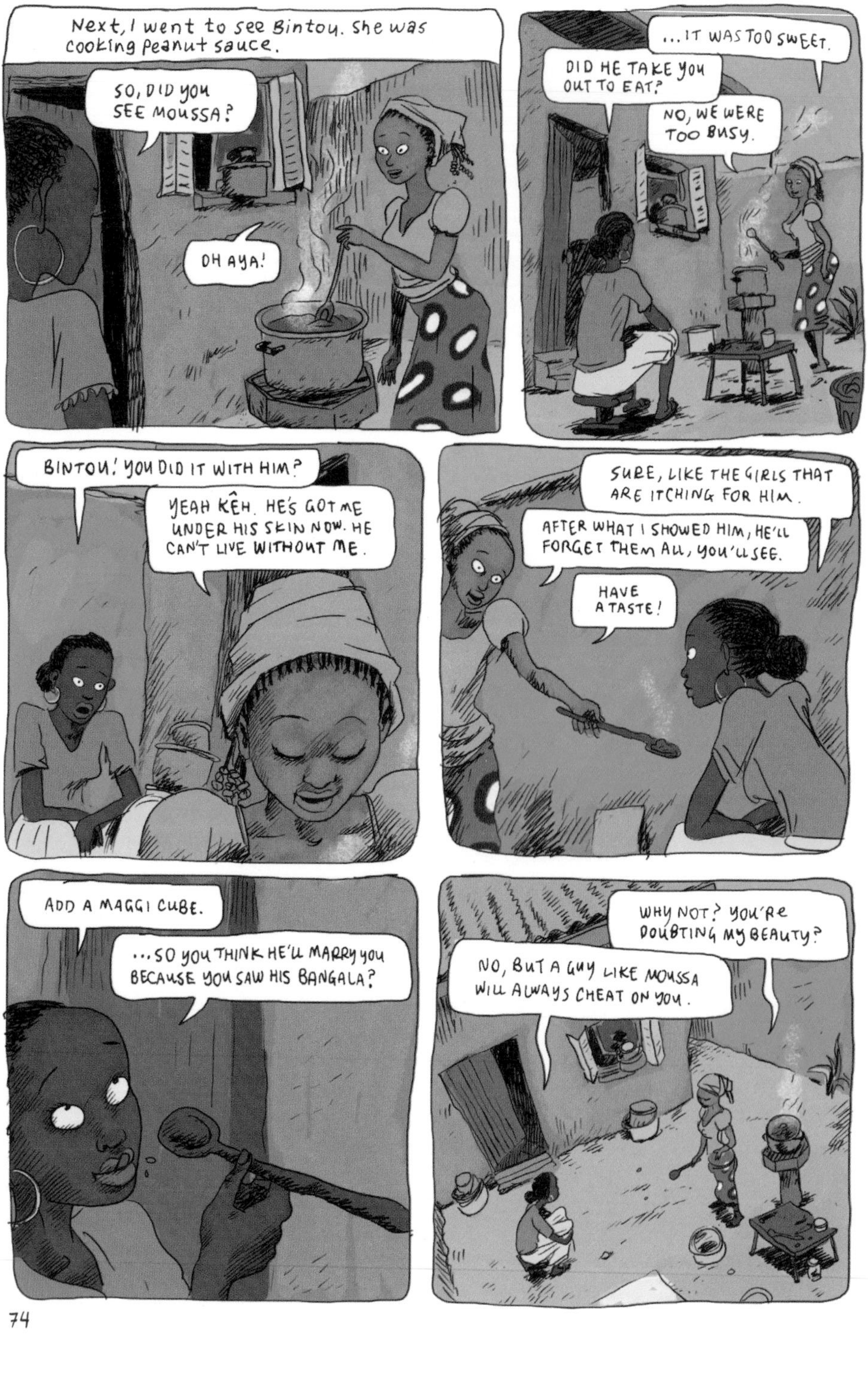

Next, I went to see Bintou. She was cooking peanut sauce.
SO, DID YOU SEE MOUSSA?
OH AYA!
DID HE TAKE YOU OUT TO EAT?
...IT WAS TOO SWEET.
NO, WE WERE TOO BUSY.
BINTOU! YOU DID IT WITH HIM?
YEAH KÊH. HE'S GOT ME UNDER HIS SKIN NOW. HE CAN'T LIVE WITHOUT ME.
SURE, LIKE THE GIRLS THAT ARE ITCHING FOR HIM.
AFTER WHAT I SHOWED HIM, HE'LL FORGET THEM ALL, YOU'LL SEE.
HAVE A TASTE!
ADD A MAGGI CUBE.
...SO YOU THINK HE'LL MARRY YOU BECAUSE YOU SAW HIS BANGALA?
WHY NOT? YOU'RE DOUBTING MY BEAUTY?
NO, BUT A GUY LIKE MOUSSA WILL ALWAYS CHEAT ON YOU.

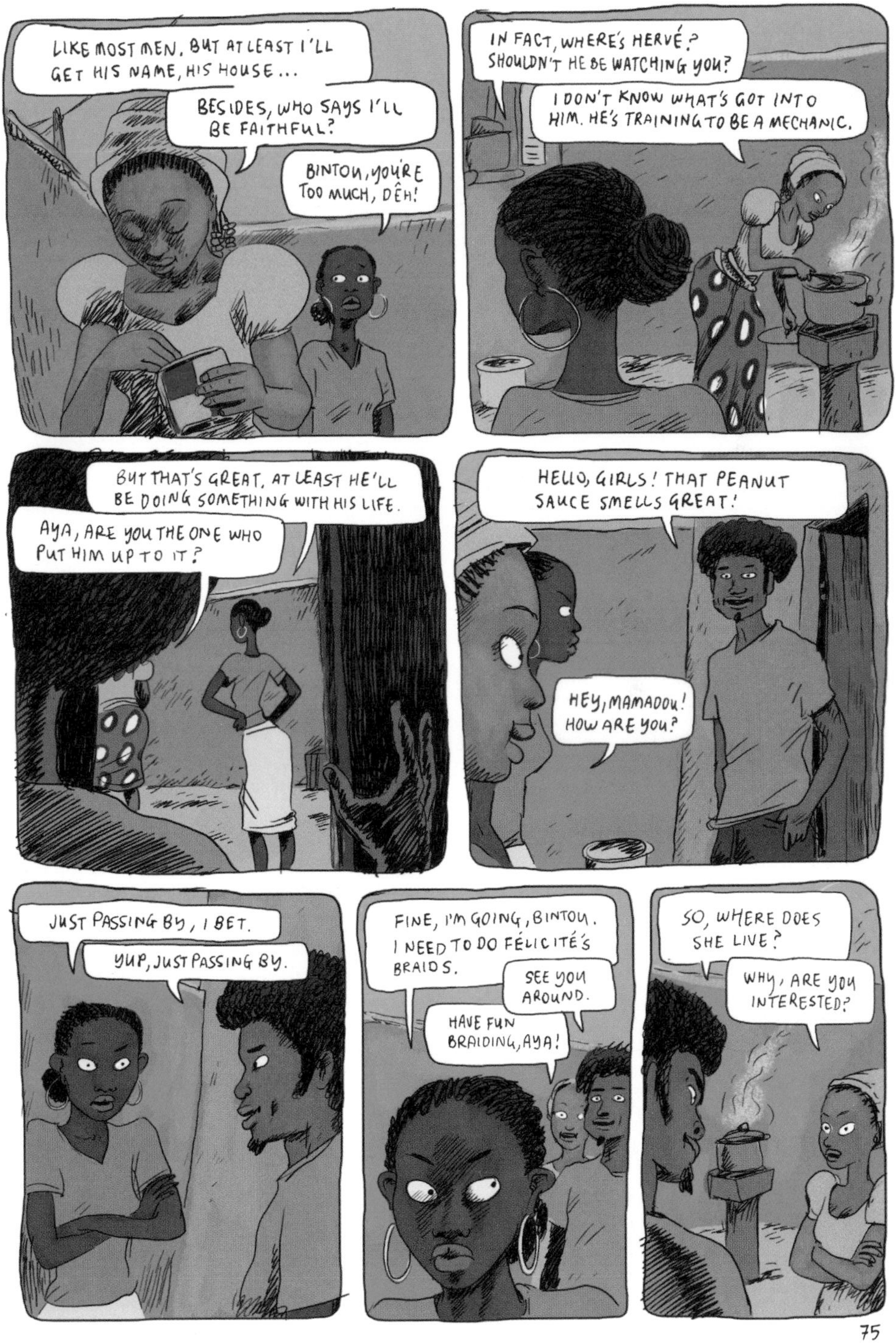
LIKE MOST MEN. BUT AT LEAST I'LL GET HIS NAME, HIS HOUSE...
BESIDES, WHO SAYS I'LL BE FAITHFUL?
BINTOU, YOU'RE TOO MUCH, DÊH!
IN FACT, WHERE'S HERVÉ? SHOULDN'T HE BE WATCHING YOU?
I DON'T KNOW WHAT'S GOT INTO HIM. HE'S TRAINING TO BE A MECHANIC.
BUT THAT'S GREAT. AT LEAST HE'LL BE DOING SOMETHING WITH HIS LIFE.
AYA, ARE YOU THE ONE WHO PUT HIM UP TO IT?
HELLO, GIRLS! THAT PEANUT SAUCE SMELLS GREAT!
HEY, MAMADOU! HOW ARE YOU?
JUST PASSING BY, I BET.
YUP, JUST PASSING BY.
FINE, I'M GOING, BINTOU. I NEED TO DO FÉLICITÉ'S BRAIDS.
SEE YOU AROUND.
HAVE FUN BRAIDING, AYA!
SO, WHERE DOES SHE LIVE?
WHY, ARE YOU INTERESTED?

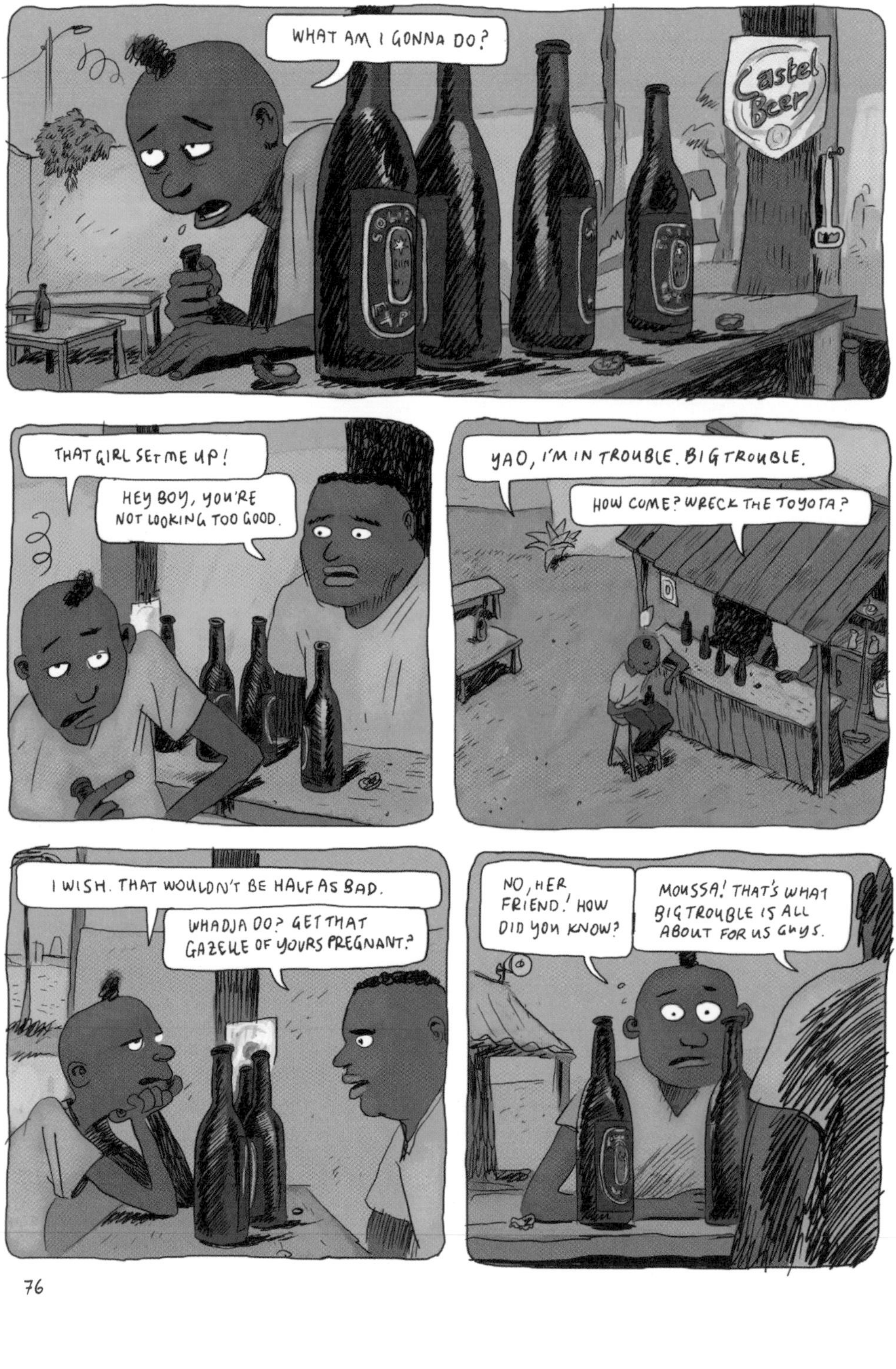
WHAT AM I GONNA DO?
Castel Beer
THAT GIRL SET ME UP!
HEY BOY, YOU'RE NOT LOOKING TOO GOOD.
YAO, I'M IN TROUBLE. BIG TROUBLE.
HOW COME? WRECK THE TOYOTA?
I WISH. THAT WOULDN'T BE HALF AS BAD.
WHADJA DO? GET THAT GAZELLE OF YOURS PREGNANT?
NO, HER FRIEND! HOW DID YOU KNOW?
MOUSSA! THAT'S WHAT BIG TROUBLE IS ALL ABOUT FOR US GUYS.

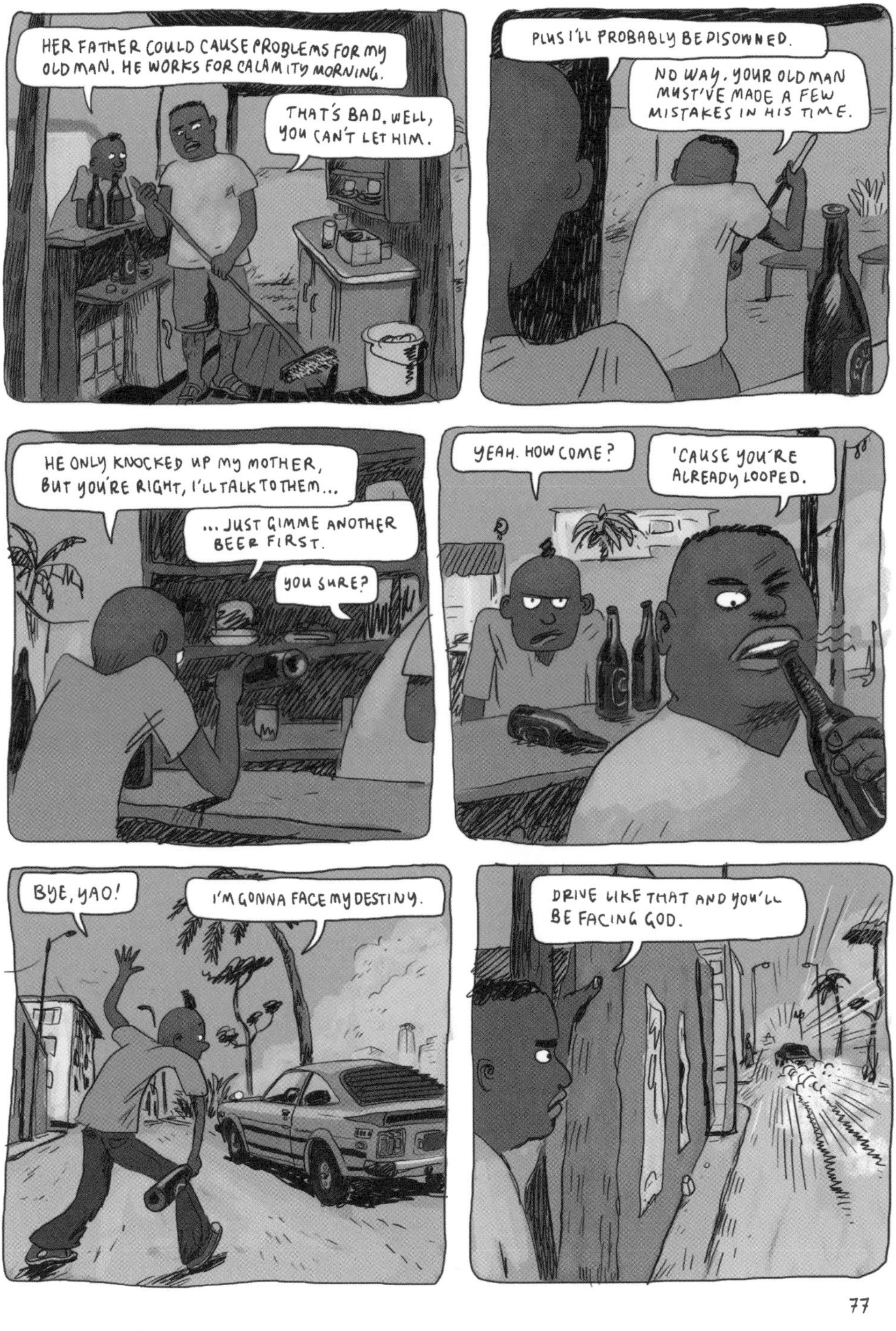
HER FATHER COULD CAUSE PROBLEMS FOR MY OLD MAN. HE WORKS FOR CALAMITY MORNING.
THAT'S BAD. WELL, YOU CAN'T LET HIM.
PLUS I'LL PROBABLY BE DISOWNED.
NO WAY. YOUR OLD MAN MUST'VE MADE A FEW MISTAKES IN HIS TIME.
HE ONLY KNOCKED UP MY MOTHER, BUT YOU'RE RIGHT, I'LL TALK TO THEM...
...JUST GIMME ANOTHER BEER FIRST.
YOU SURE?
YEAH. HOW COME?
'CAUSE YOU'RE ALREADY LOOPED.
BYE, YAO!
I'M GONNA FACE MY DESTINY.
DRIVE LIKE THAT AND YOU'LL BE FACING GOD.

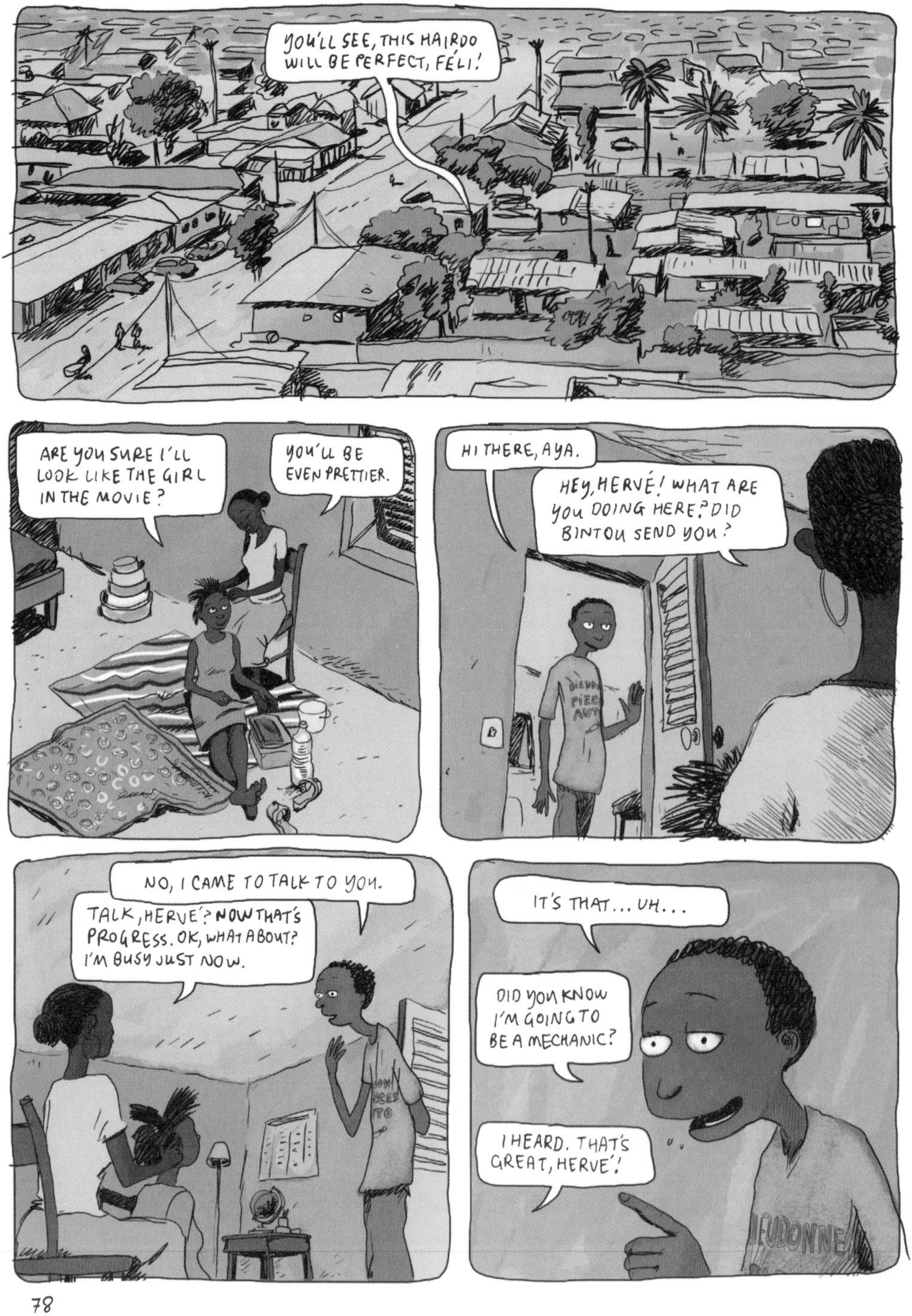
YOU'LL SEE, THIS HAIRDO WILL BE PERFECT, FÉLI!
ARE YOU SURE I'LL LOOK LIKE THE GIRL IN THE MOVIE?
YOU'LL BE EVEN PRETTIER.
HI THERE, AYA.
HEY, HERVÉ! WHAT ARE YOU DOING HERE? DID BINTOU SEND YOU?
NO, I CAME TO TALK TO YOU.
TALK, HERVÉ? NOW THAT'S PROGRESS. OK, WHAT ABOUT? I'M BUSY JUST NOW.
IT'S THAT... UH...
DID YOU KNOW I'M GOING TO BE A MECHANIC?
I HEARD. THAT'S GREAT, HERVÉ!

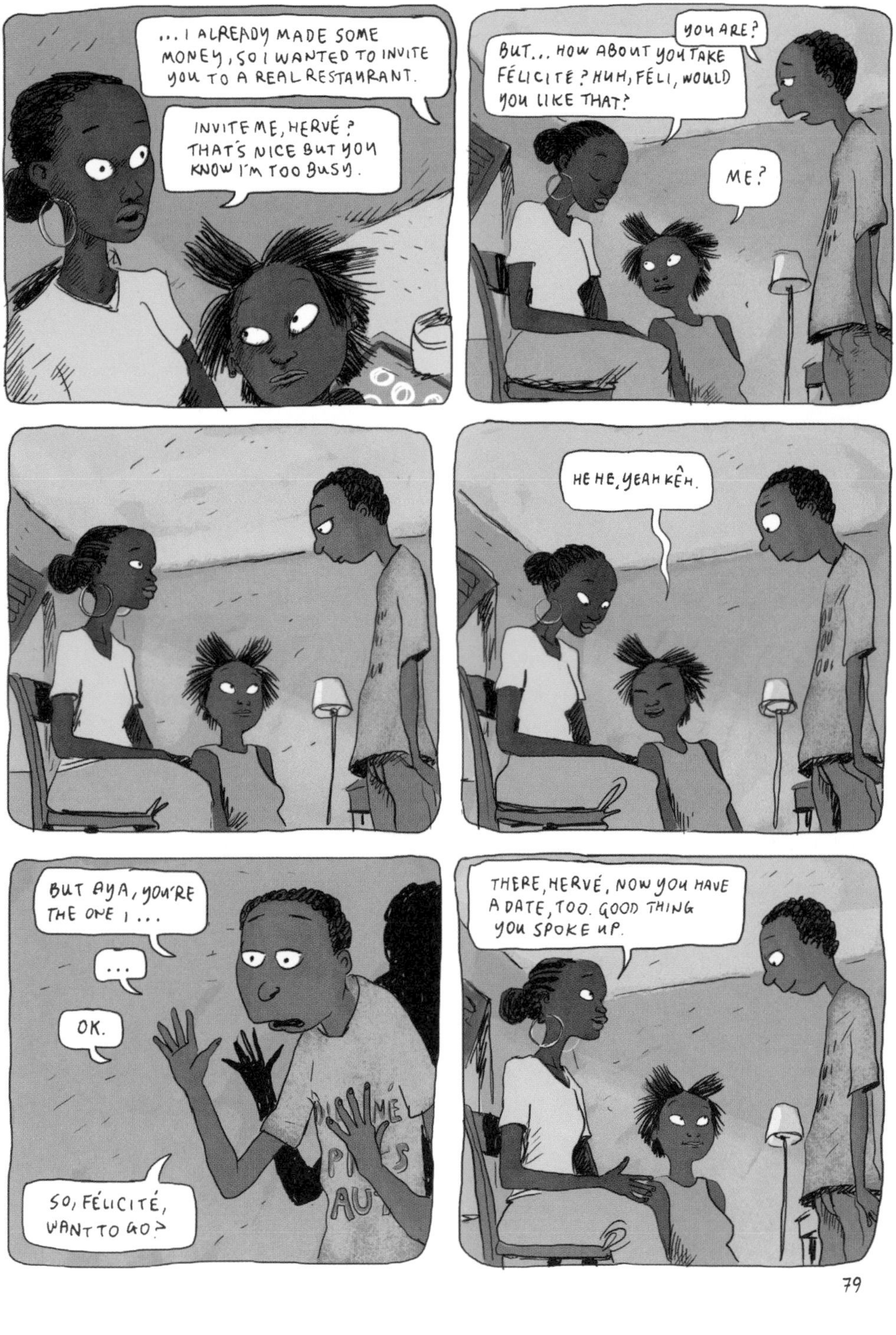

... I ALREADY MADE SOME MONEY, SO I WANTED TO INVITE YOU TO A REAL RESTAURANT.
INVITE ME, HERVÉ? THAT'S NICE BUT YOU KNOW I'M TOO BUSY.
BUT... HOW ABOUT YOU TAKE FÉLICITE? HUH, FÉLI, WOULD YOU LIKE THAT?
YOU ARE?
ME?
HE HE, YEAH KÊH.
BUT AYA, YOU'RE THE ONE I ...
...
OK.
SO, FÉLICITÉ, WANT TO GO?
THERE, HERVÉ, NOW YOU HAVE A DATE, TOO. GOOD THING YOU SPOKE UP.

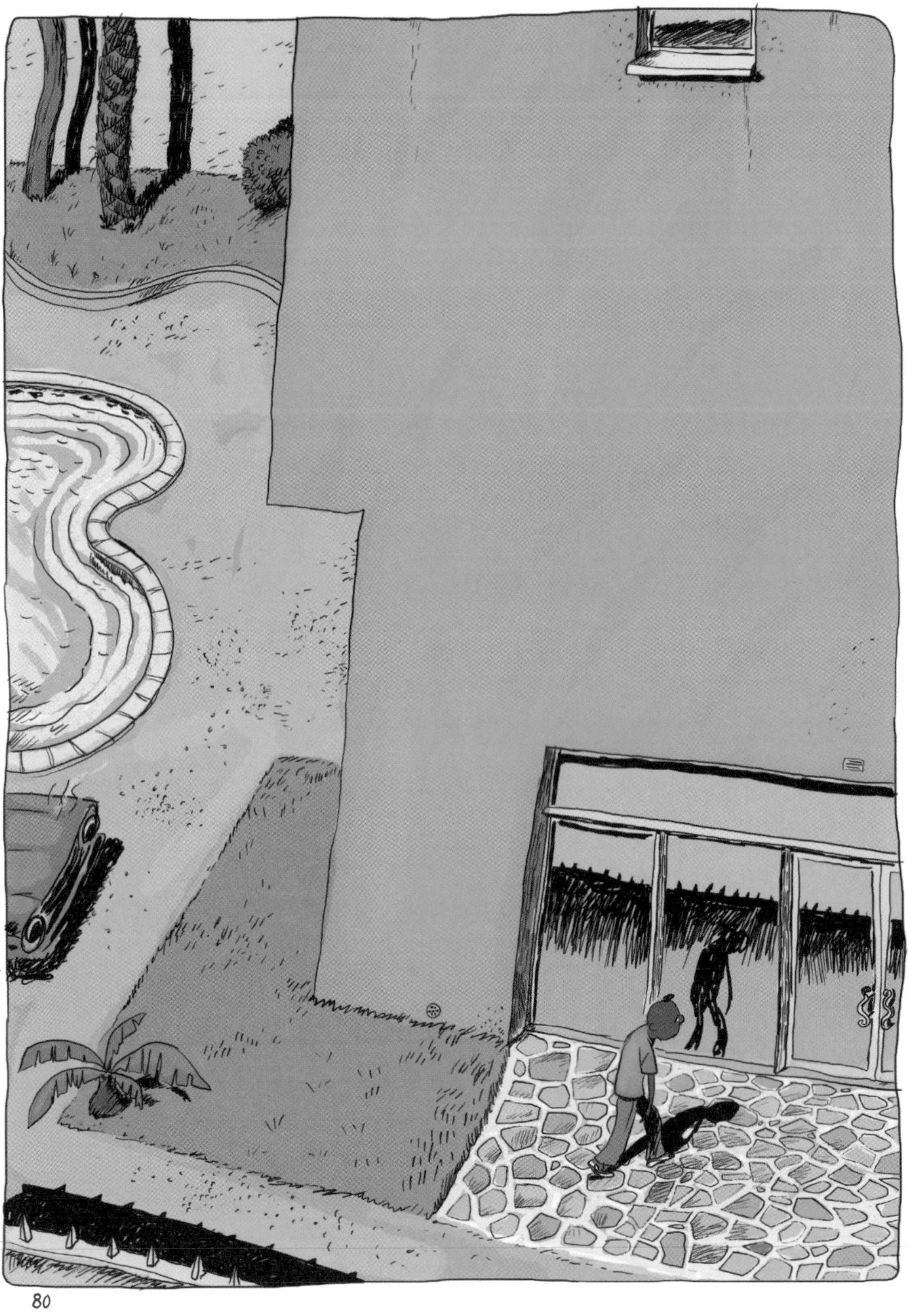

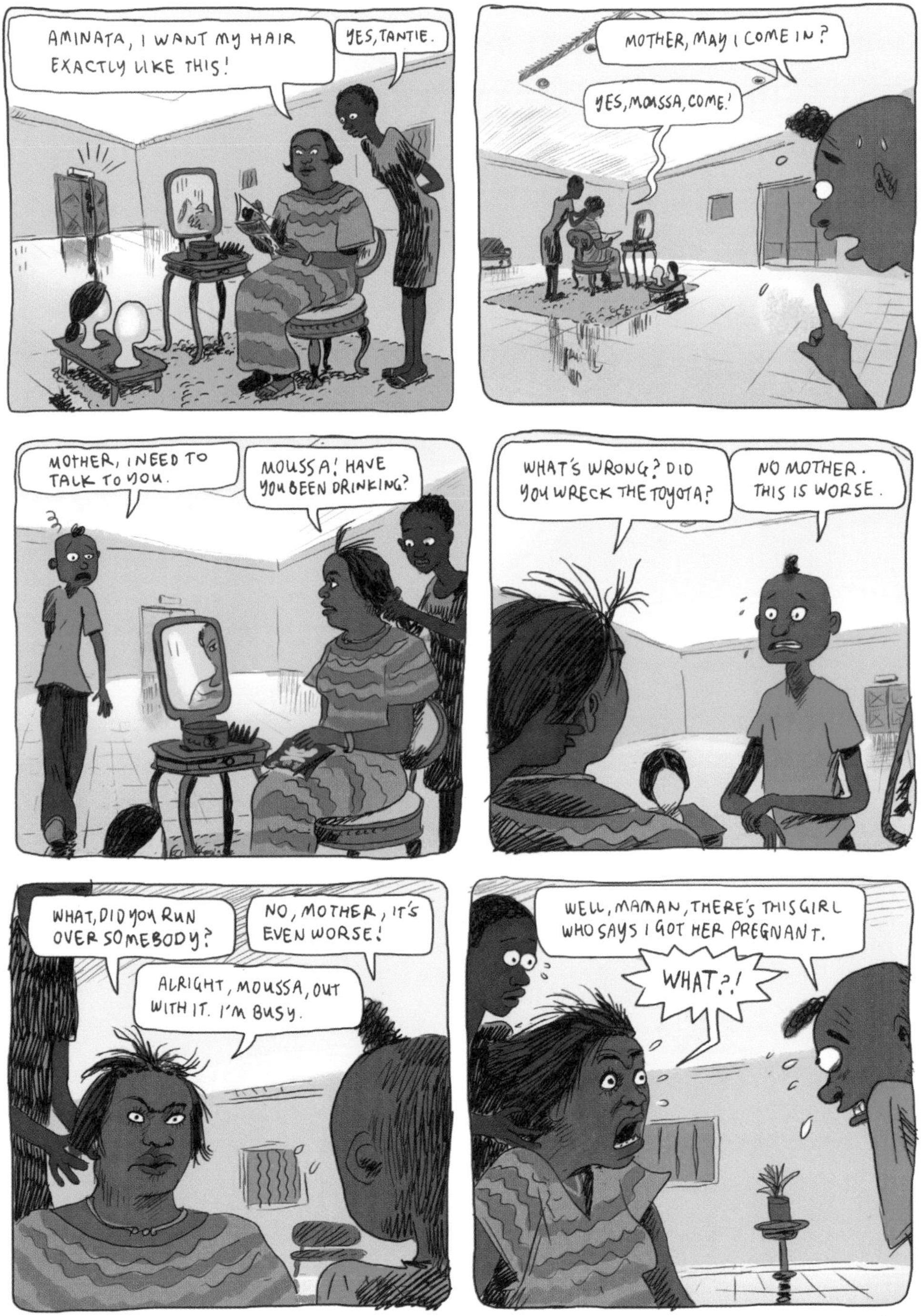
AMINATA, I WANT MY HAIR EXACTLY LIKE THIS!
YES, TANTIE.
MOTHER, MAY I COME IN?
YES, MOUSSA, COME!
MOTHER, I NEED TO TALK TO YOU.
MOUSSA! HAVE YOU BEEN DRINKING?
WHAT'S WRONG? DID YOU WRECK THE TOYOTA?
NO MOTHER. THIS IS WORSE.
WHAT, DID YOU RUN OVER SOMEBODY?
NO, MOTHER, IT'S EVEN WORSE!
ALRIGHT, MOUSSA, OUT WITH IT. I'M BUSY.
WELL, MAMAN, THERE'S THIS GIRL WHO SAYS I GOT HER PREGNANT.
WHAT?!

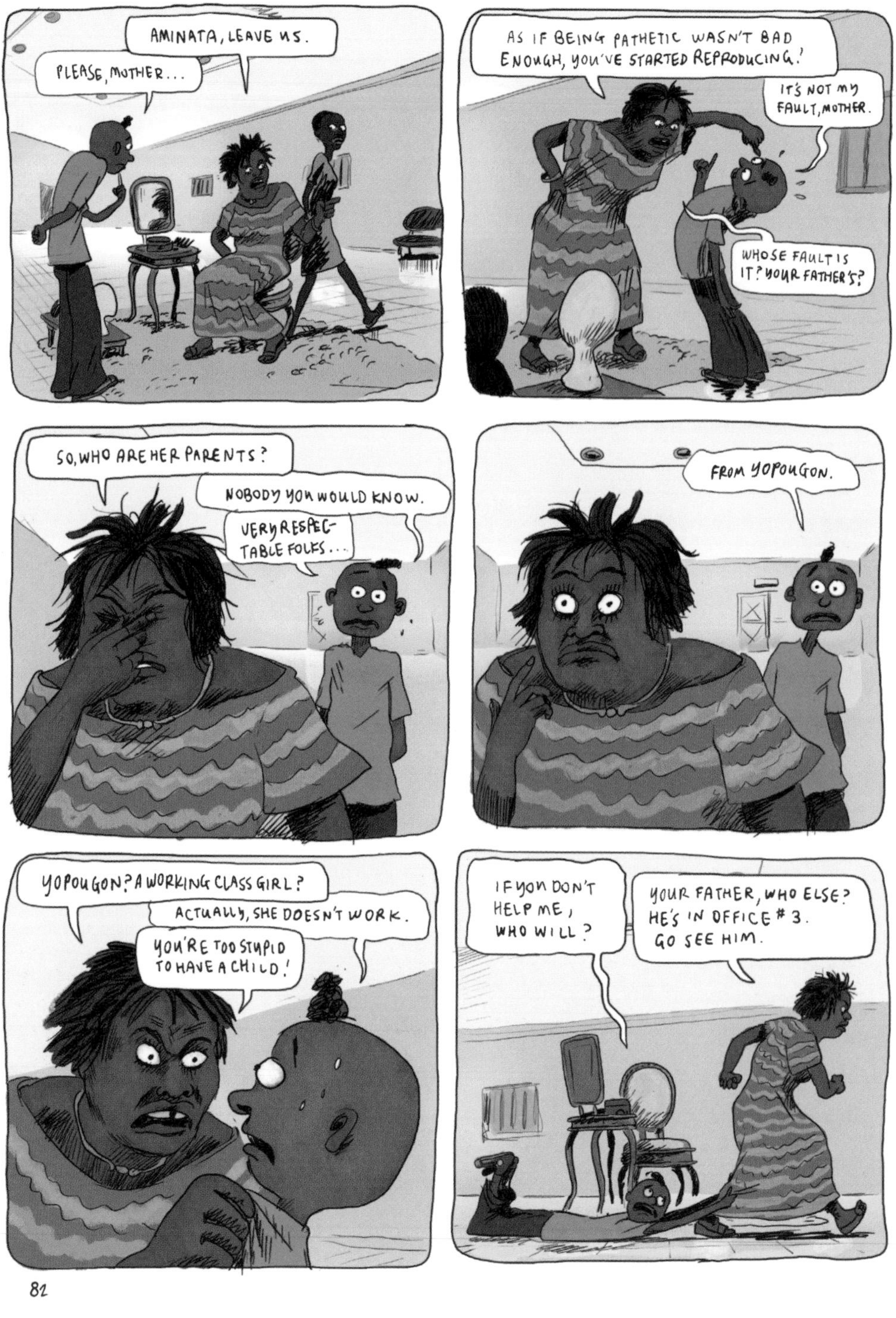
AMINATA, LEAVE US.
PLEASE, MOTHER...
AS IF BEING PATHETIC WASN'T BAD ENOUGH, YOU'VE STARTED REPRODUCING!
IT'S NOT MY FAULT, MOTHER.
WHOSE FAULT IS IT? YOUR FATHER'S?
SO, WHO ARE HER PARENTS?
NOBODY YOU WOULD KNOW.
VERY RESPECTABLE FOLKS...
FROM YOPOUGON.
YOPOUGON? A WORKING CLASS GIRL?
ACTUALLY, SHE DOESN'T WORK.
YOU'RE TOO STUPID TO HAVE A CHILD!
IF YOU DON'T HELP ME, WHO WILL?
YOUR FATHER, WHO ELSE? HE'S IN OFFICE # 3. GO SEE HIM.

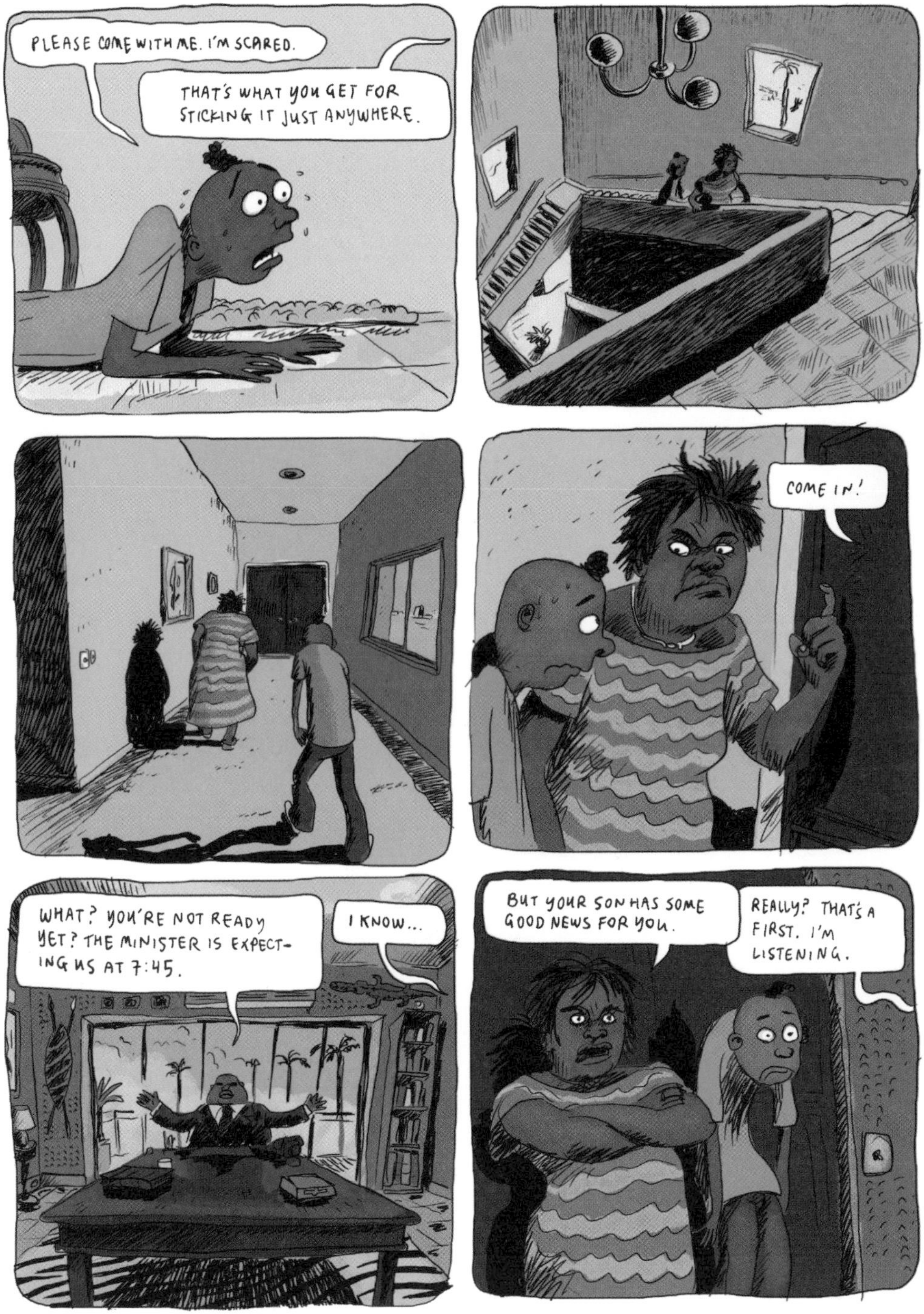
PLEASE COME WITH ME. I'M SCARED.
THAT'S WHAT YOU GET FOR STICKING IT JUST ANYWHERE.
COME IN!
WHAT? YOU'RE NOT READY YET? THE MINISTER IS EXPECTING US AT 7:45.
I KNOW...
BUT YOUR SON HAS SOME GOOD NEWS FOR YOU.
REALLY? THAT'S A FIRST. I'M LISTENING.

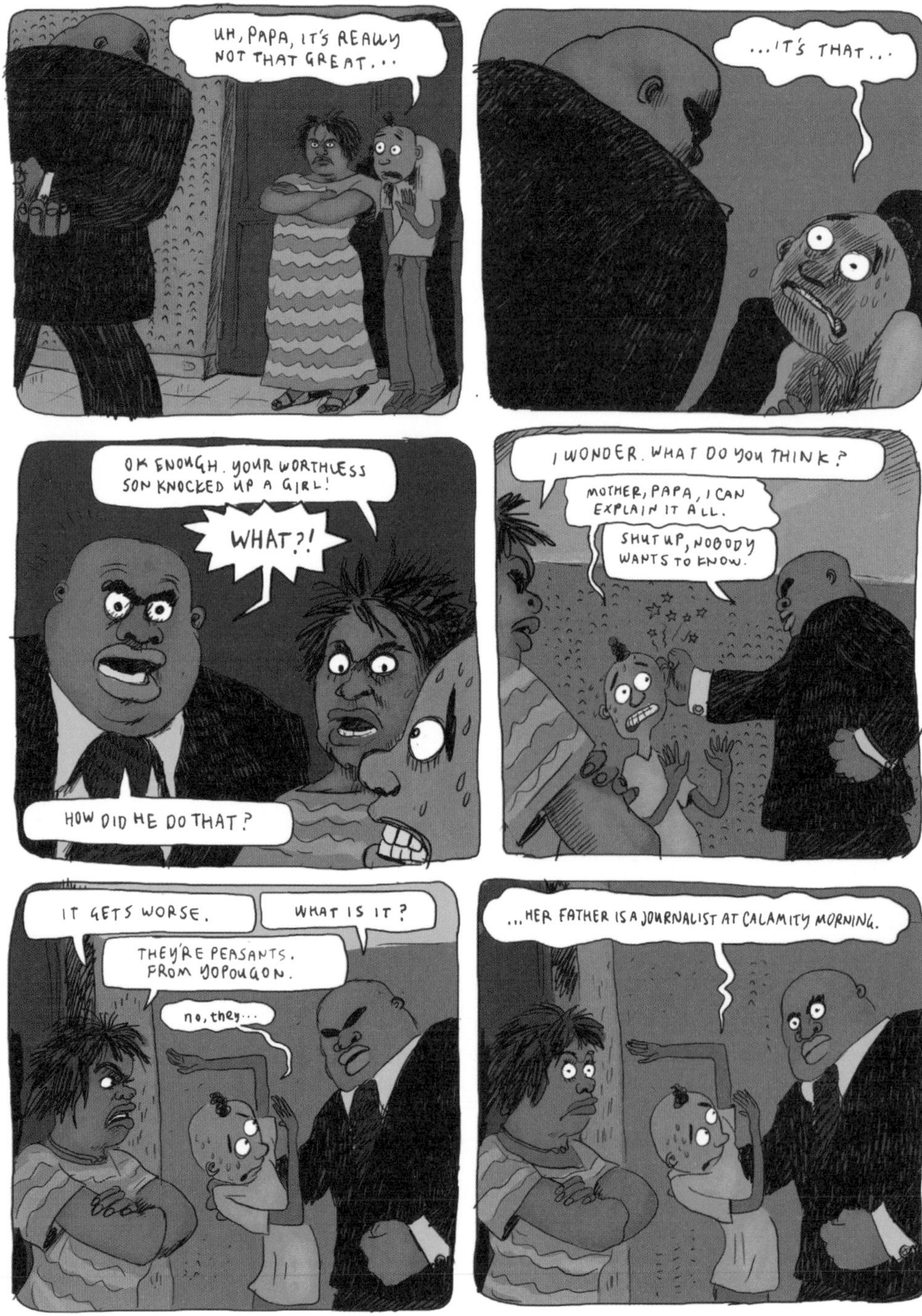
UH, PAPA, IT'S REALLY NOT THAT GREAT...
...IT'S THAT...
OK ENOUGH. YOUR WORTHLESS SON KNOCKED UP A GIRL!
WHAT?!
HOW DID HE DO THAT?
I WONDER. WHAT DO YOU THINK?
MOTHER, PAPA, I CAN EXPLAIN IT ALL.
SHUT UP, NOBODY WANTS TO KNOW.
IT GETS WORSE.
WHAT IS IT?
THEY'RE PEASANTS. FROM YOPOUGON.
no, they...
...HER FATHER IS A JOURNALIST AT CALAMITY MORNING.

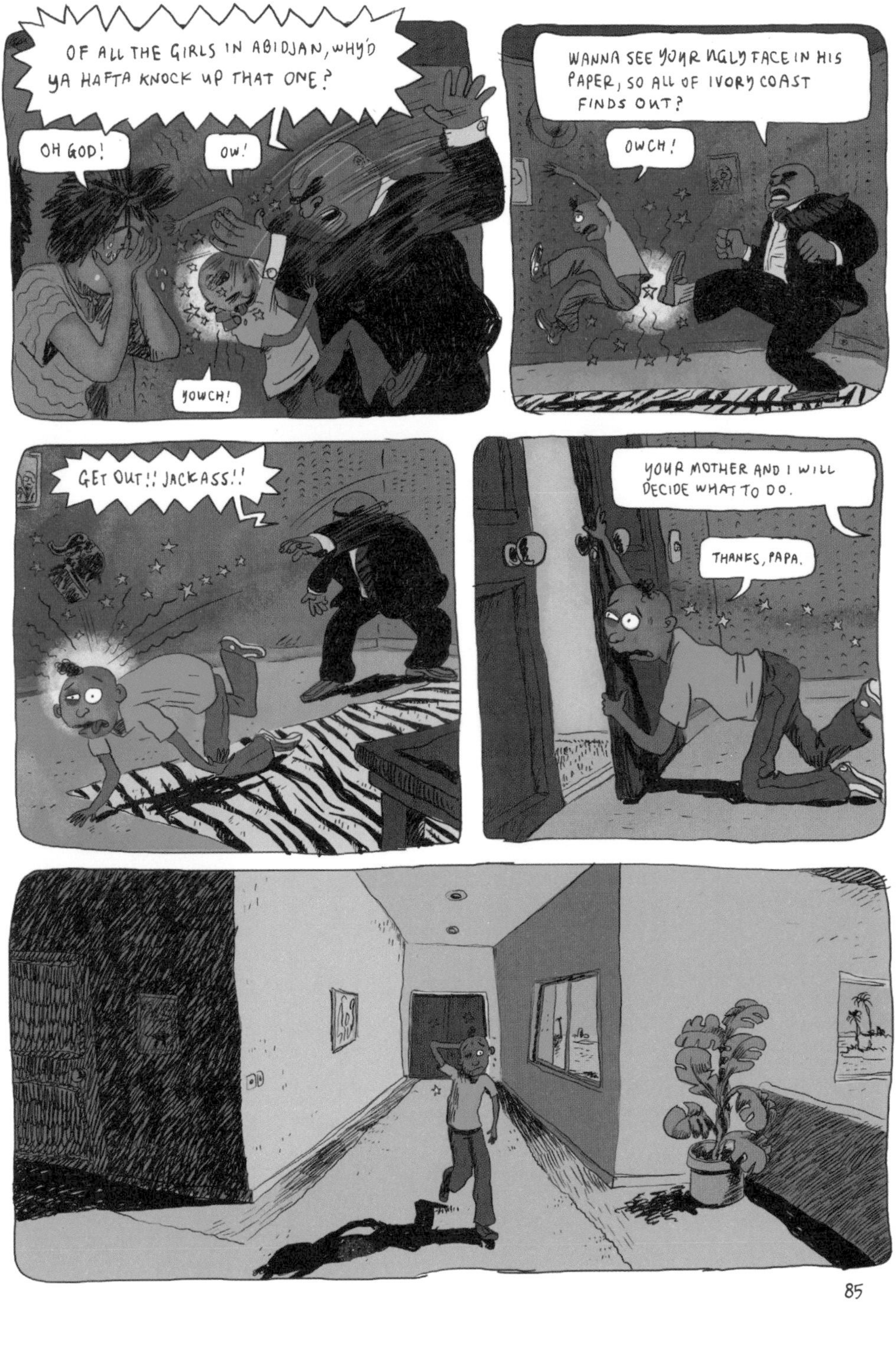
OF ALL THE GIRLS IN ABIDJAN, WHY'D YA HAFTA KNOCK UP THAT ONE?
OH GOD!
OW!
YOWCH!
WANNA SEE YOUR UGLY FACE IN HIS PAPER, SO ALL OF IVORY COAST FINDS OUT?
OWCH!
GET OUT!! JACKASS!!
YOUR MOTHER AND I WILL DECIDE WHAT TO DO.
THANKS, PAPA.

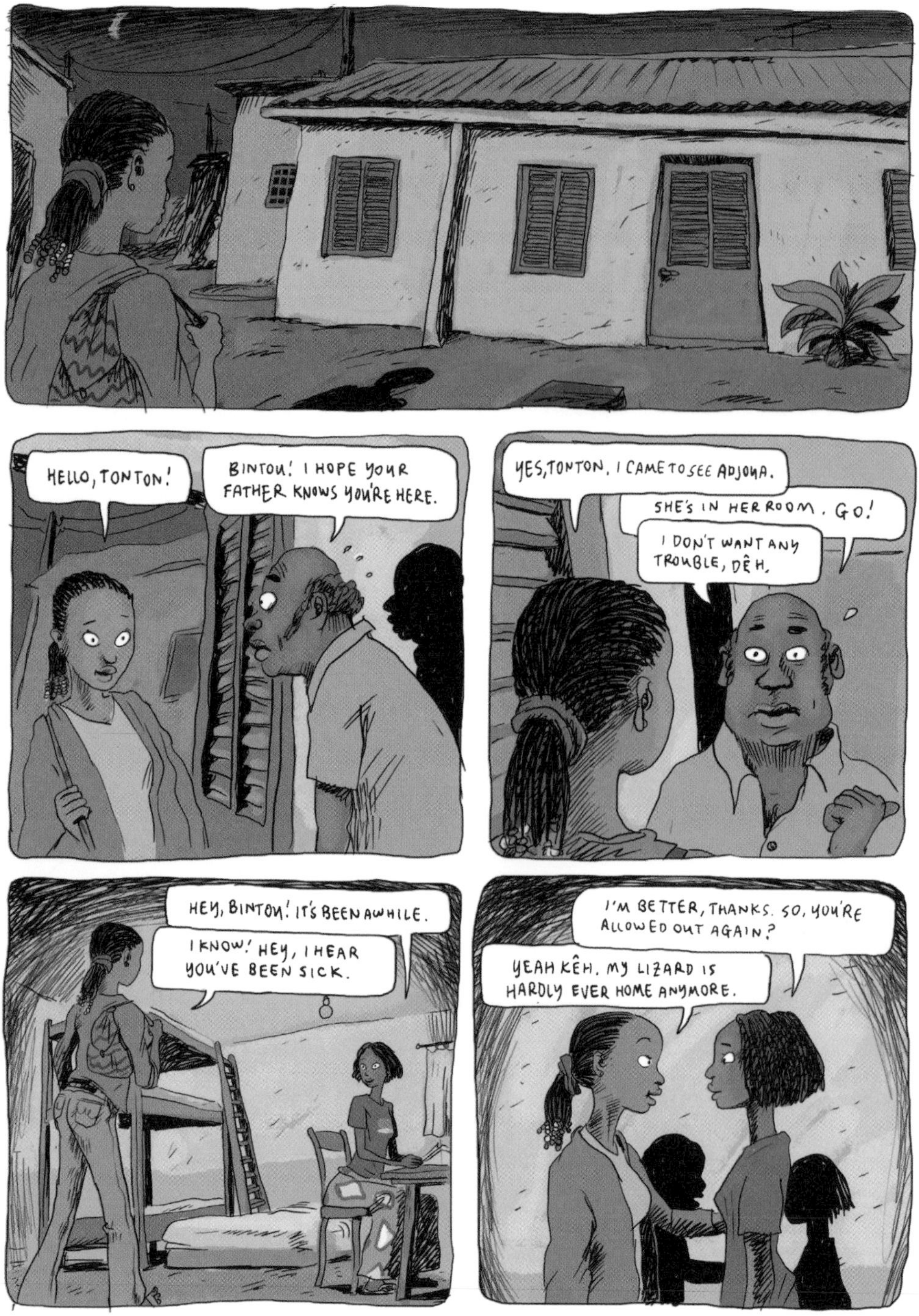
HELLO, TONTON!
BINTOU! I HOPE YOUR FATHER KNOWS YOU'RE HERE.
YES, TONTON. I CAME TO SEE ADJOUA.
SHE'S IN HER ROOM. GO!
I DON'T WANT ANY TROUBLE, DÊH.
HEY, BINTOU! IT'S BEEN AWHILE.
I KNOW! HEY, I HEAR YOU'VE BEEN SICK.
I'M BETTER, THANKS. SO, YOU'RE ALLOWED OUT AGAIN?
YEAH KÊH. MY LIZARD IS HARDLY EVER HOME ANYMORE.

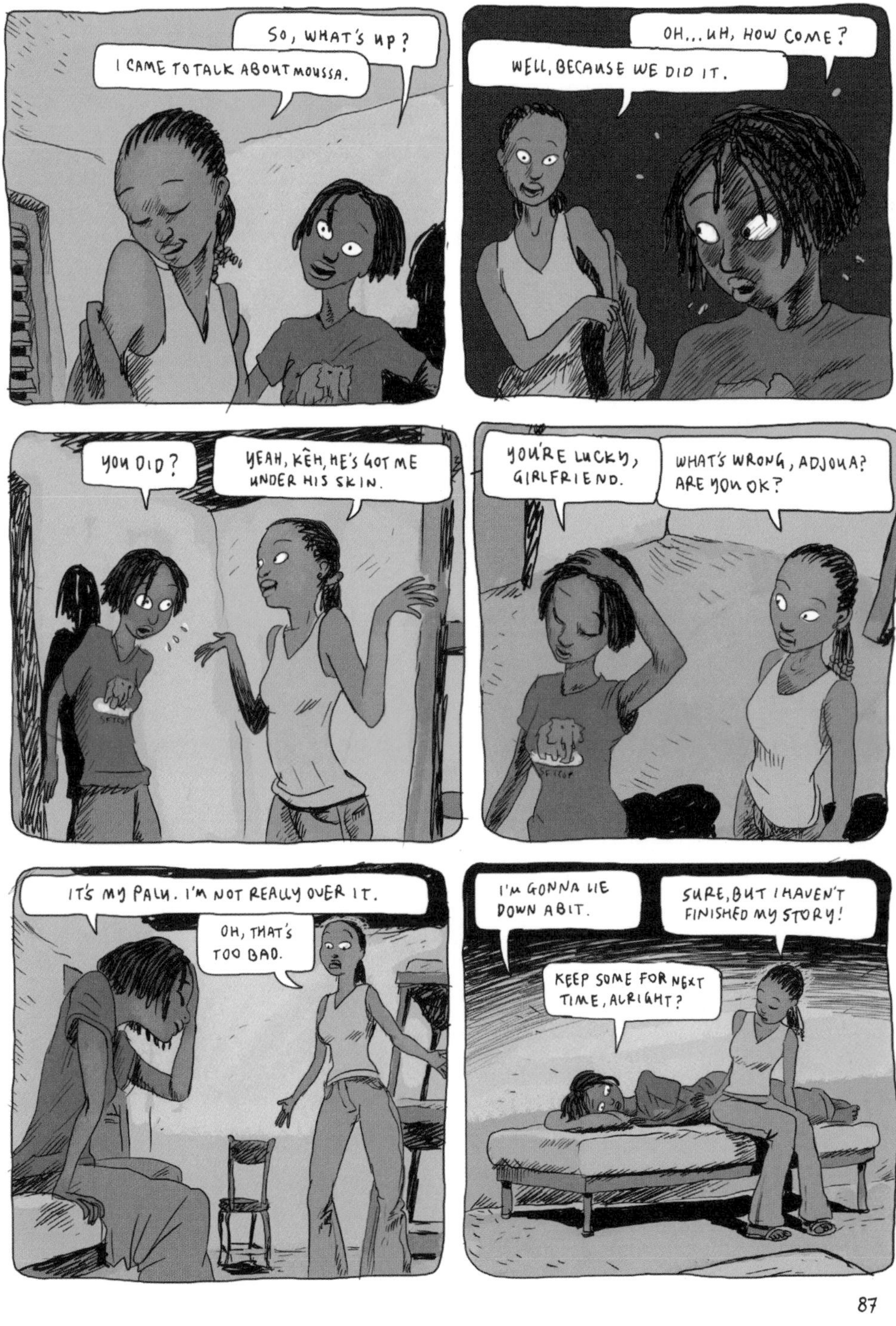
I CAME TO TALK ABOUT MOUSSA.
SO, WHAT'S UP?
WELL, BECAUSE WE DID IT.
OH... UH, HOW COME?
YOU DID?
YEAH, KÊH, HE'S GOT ME UNDER HIS SKIN.
YOU'RE LUCKY, GIRLFRIEND.
WHAT'S WRONG, ADJOUA? ARE YOU OK?
IT'S MY PALU. I'M NOT REALLY OVER IT.
OH, THAT'S TOO BAD.
I'M GONNA LIE DOWN A BIT.
SURE, BUT I HAVEN'T FINISHED MY STORY!
KEEP SOME FOR NEXT TIME, ALRIGHT?

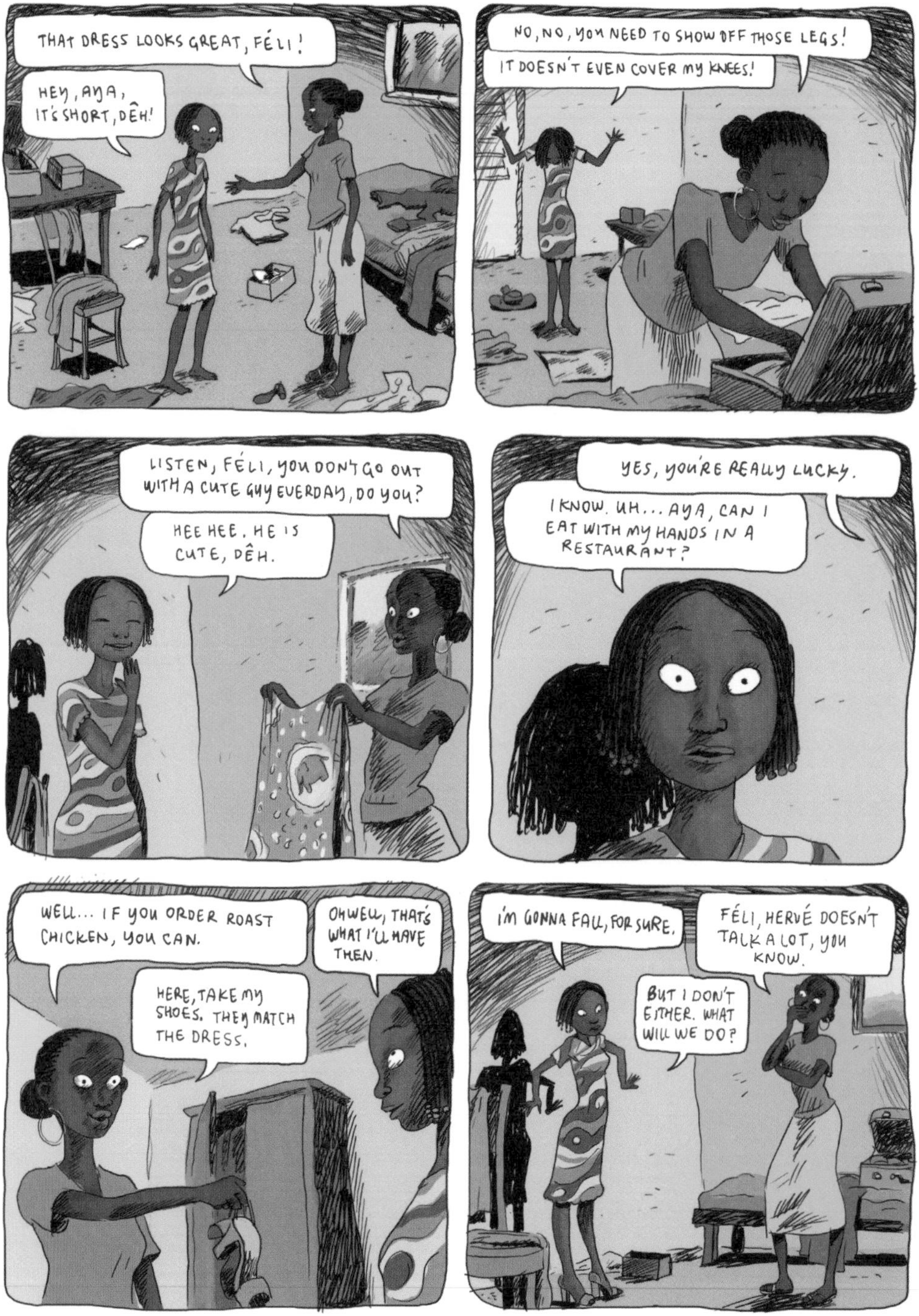
THAT DRESS LOOKS GREAT, FÉLI!
HEY, AYA, IT'S SHORT, DÊH!
NO, NO, YOU NEED TO SHOW OFF THOSE LEGS!
IT DOESN'T EVEN COVER MY KNEES!
LISTEN, FÉLI, YOU DON'T GO OUT WITH A CUTE GUY EVERDAY, DO YOU?
HEE HEE. HE IS CUTE, DÊH.
YES, YOU'RE REALLY LUCKY.
I KNOW. UH... AYA, CAN I EAT WITH MY HANDS IN A RESTAURANT?
WELL... IF YOU ORDER ROAST CHICKEN, YOU CAN.
OH WELL, THAT'S WHAT I'LL HAVE THEN.
HERE, TAKE MY SHOES. THEY MATCH THE DRESS.
I'M GONNA FALL, FOR SURE.
FÉLI, HERVÉ DOESN'T TALK A LOT, YOU KNOW.
BUT I DON'T EITHER. WHAT WILL WE DO?

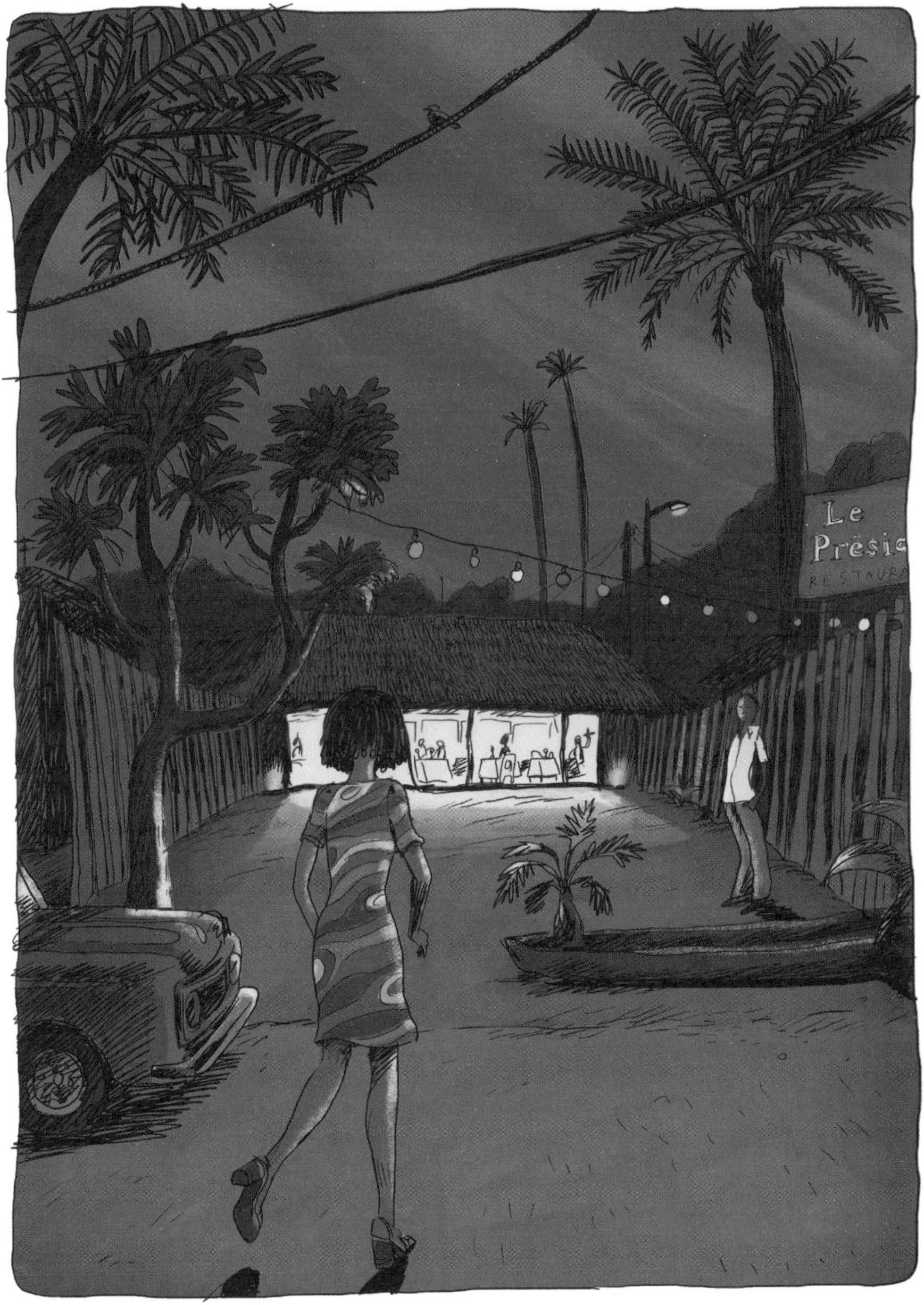
Le

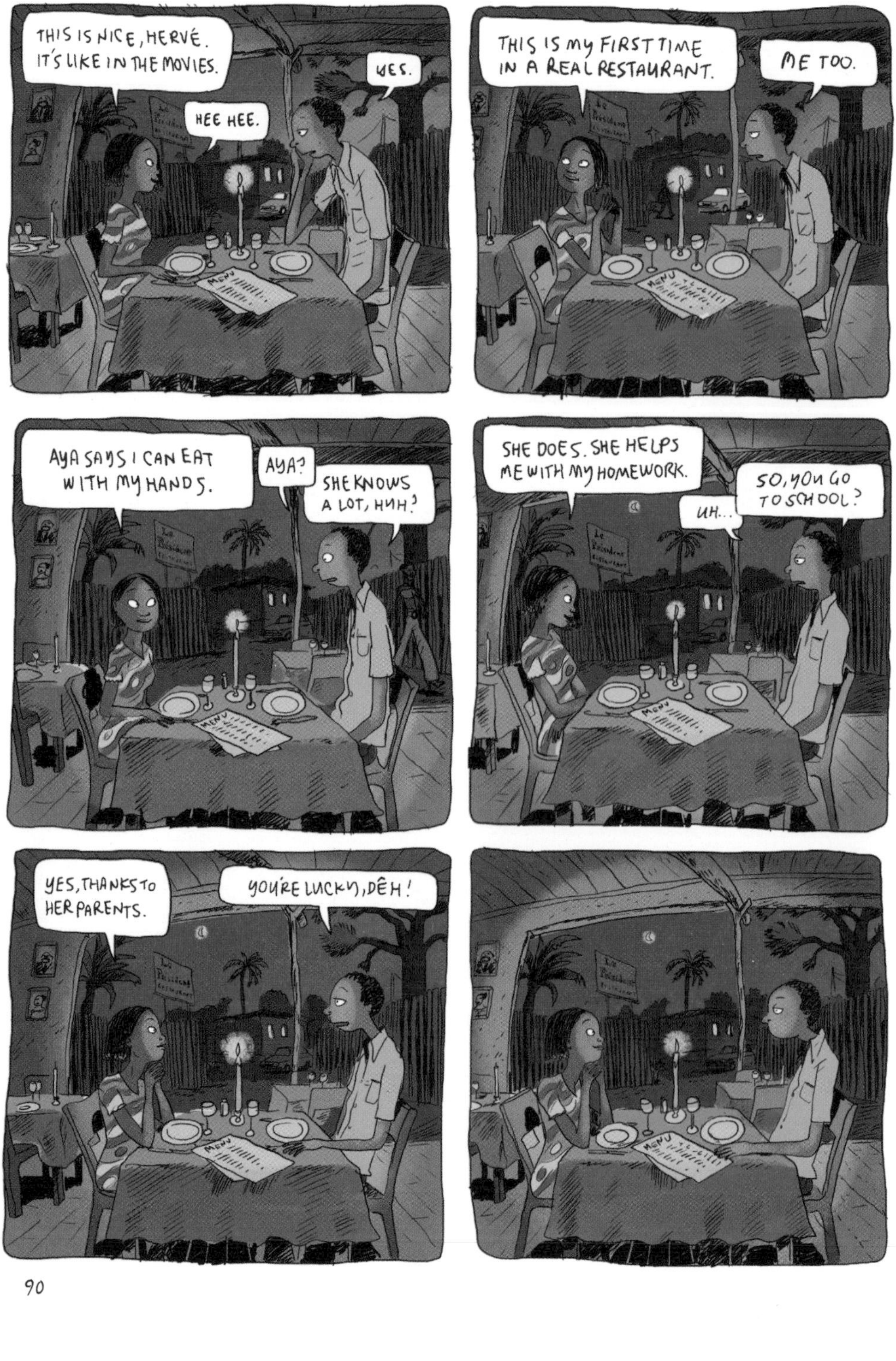
THIS IS NICE, HERVÉ. IT'S LIKE IN THE MOVIES.
HEE HEE.
YES.
THIS IS MY FIRST TIME IN A REAL RESTAURANT.
ME TOO.
AYA SAYS I CAN EAT WITH MY HANDS.
AYA?
SHE KNOWS A LOT, HUH?
SHE DOES. SHE HELPS ME WITH MY HOMEWORK.
SO, YOU GO TO SCHOOL?
UH...
YES, THANKS TO HER PARENTS.
YOU'RE LUCKY, DÊH!
MENU

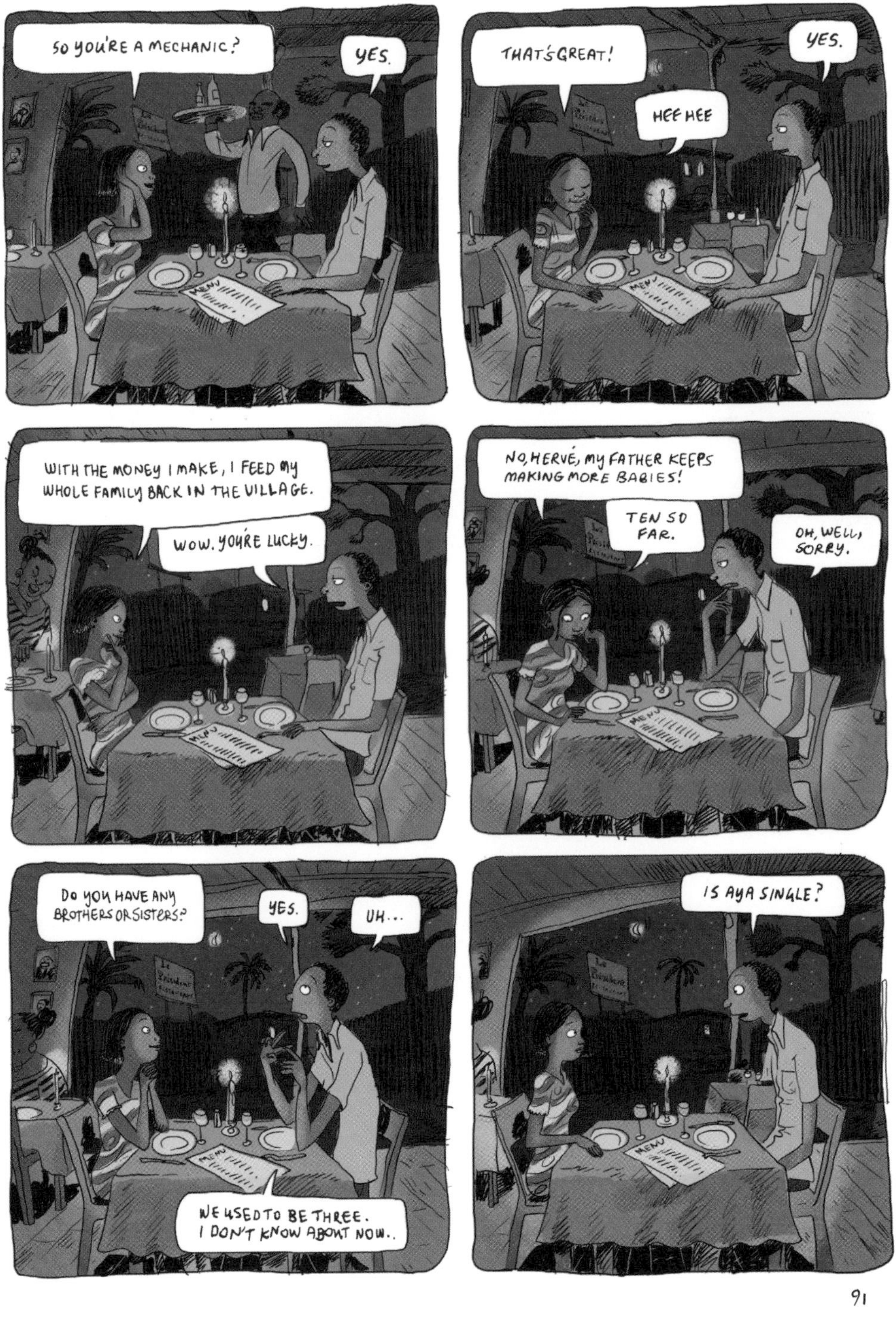
SO YOU'RE A MECHANIC?
YES.
THAT'S GREAT!
HEE HEE
YES.
WITH THE MONEY I MAKE, I FEED MY WHOLE FAMILY BACK IN THE VILLAGE.
WOW. YOU'RE LUCKY.
NO, HERVÉ, MY FATHER KEEPS MAKING MORE BABIES!
TEN SO FAR.
OH, WELL, SORRY.
DO YOU HAVE ANY BROTHERS OR SISTERS?
YES.
UH...
WE USED TO BE THREE. I DON'T KNOW ABOUT NOW..
IS AYA SINGLE?

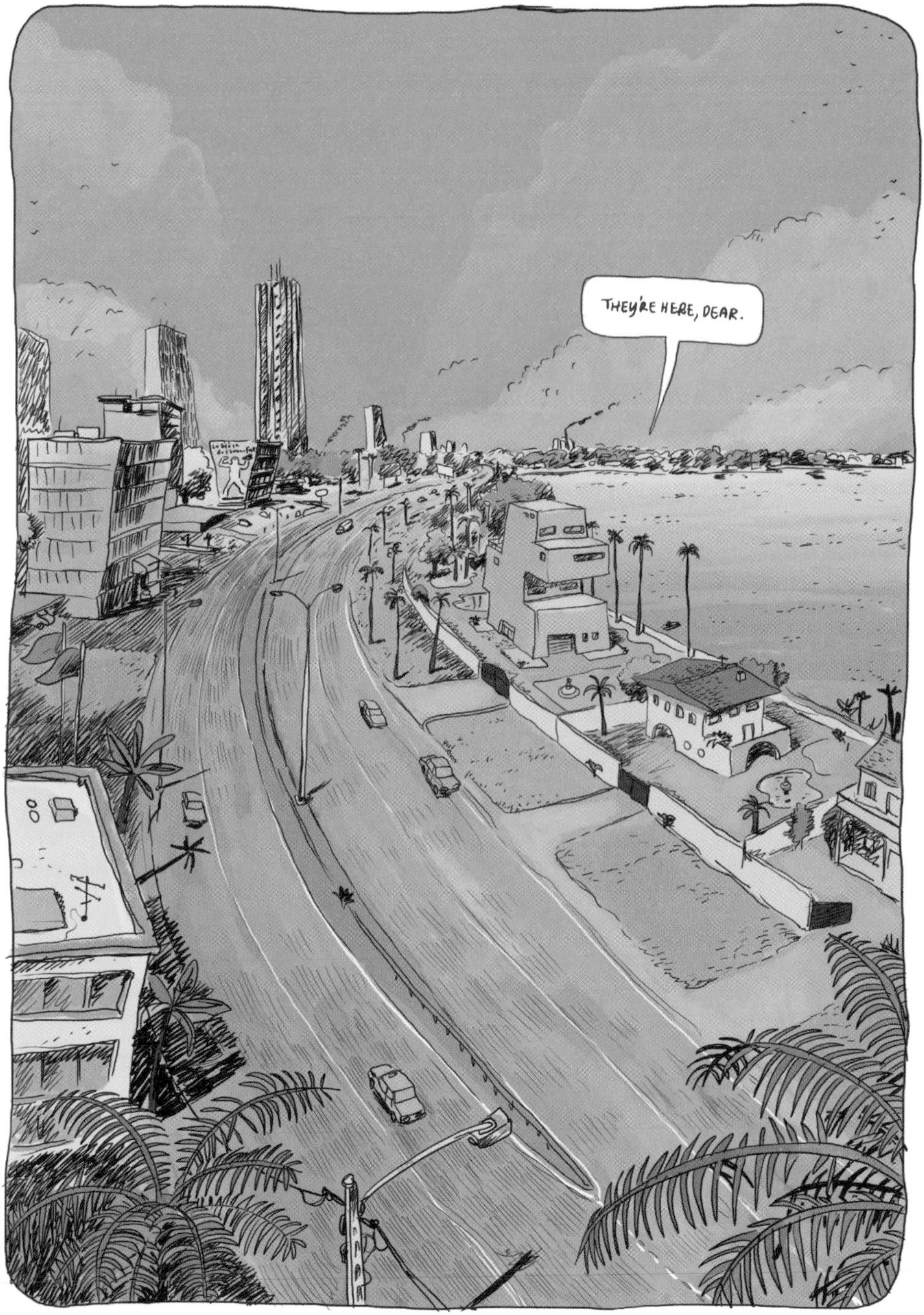
THEY'RE HERE, DEAR.

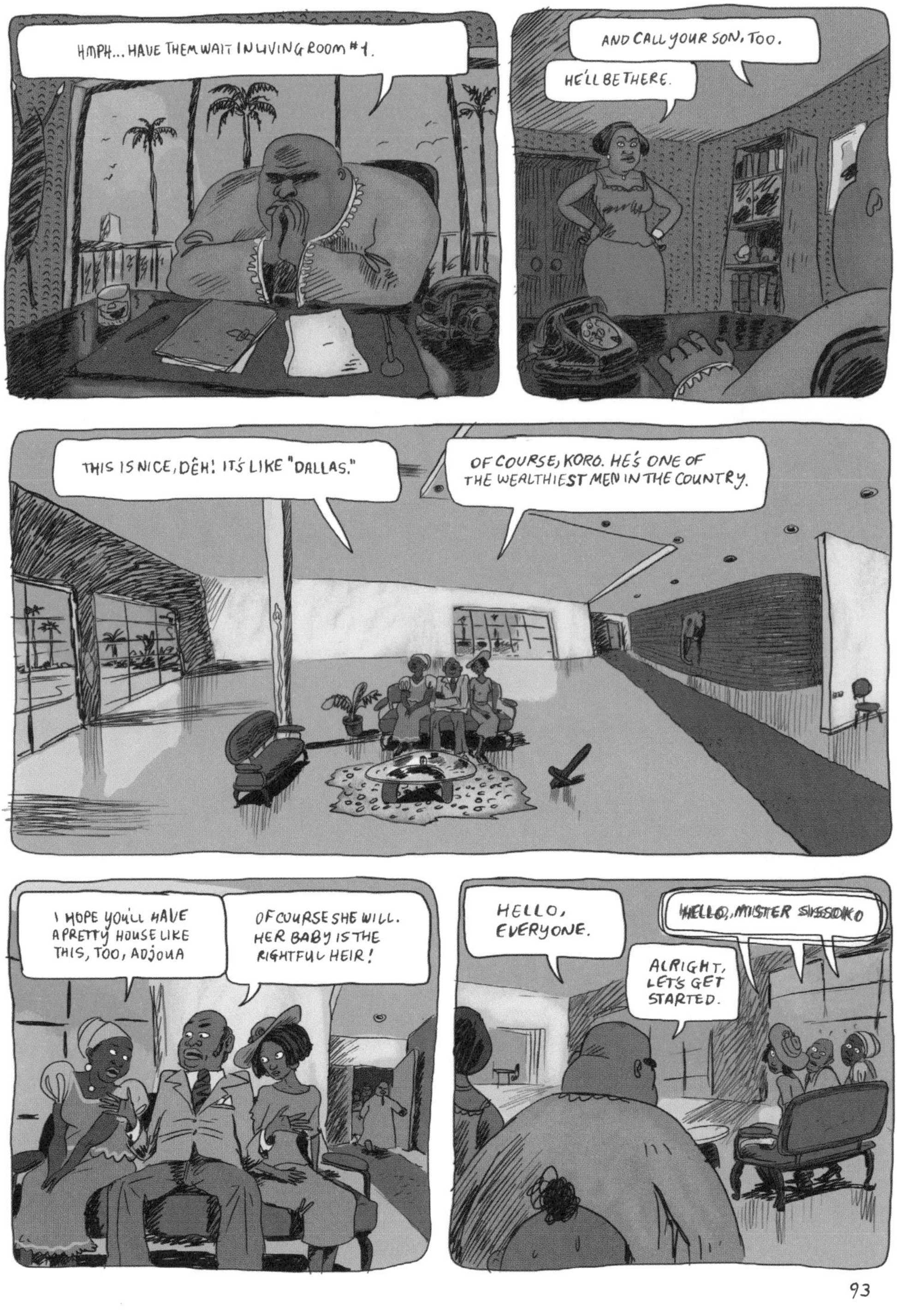
HMPH... HAVE THEM WAIT IN LIVING ROOM #1.
AND CALL YOUR SON, TOO.
HE'LL BE THERE.
THIS IS NICE, DÊH! IT'S LIKE "DALLAS."
OF COURSE, KORO. HE'S ONE OF THE WEALTHIEST MEN IN THE COUNTRY.
I HOPE YOU'LL HAVE A PRETTY HOUSE LIKE THIS, TOO, ADJOUA
OF COURSE SHE WILL. HER BABY IS THE RIGHTFUL HEIR!
HELLO, EVERYONE.
HELLO, MISTER SISSOKO
ALRIGHT, LET'S GET STARTED.

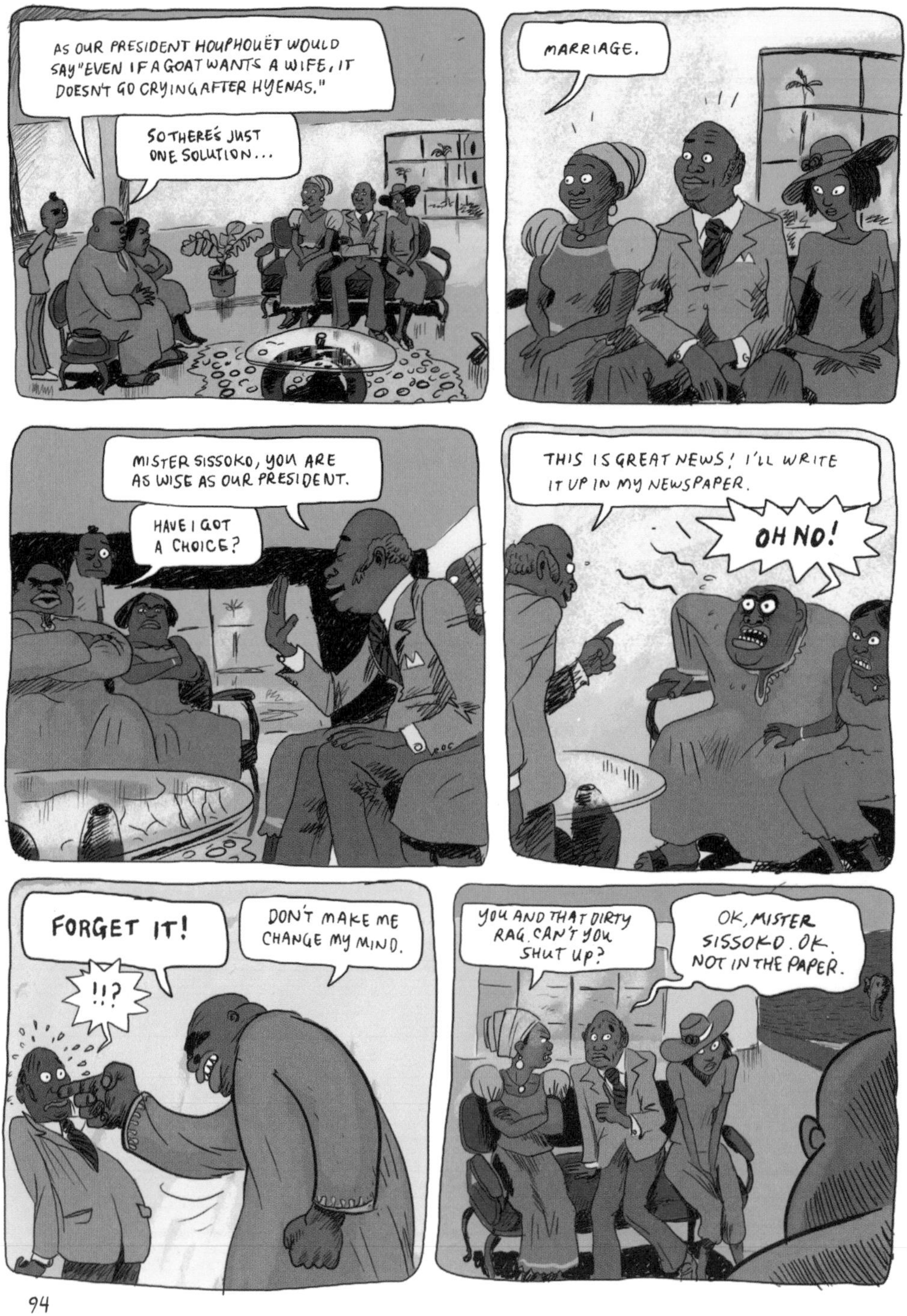
AS OUR PRESIDENT HOUPHOUËT WOULD SAY "EVEN IF A GOAT WANTS A WIFE, IT DOESN'T GO CRYING AFTER HYENAS."
SO THERE'S JUST ONE SOLUTION...
MARRIAGE.
MISTER SISSOKO, YOU ARE AS WISE AS OUR PRESIDENT.
HAVE I GOT A CHOICE?
THIS IS GREAT NEWS! I'LL WRITE IT UP IN MY NEWSPAPER.
OH NO!
FORGET IT!
DON'T MAKE ME CHANGE MY MIND.
!!?
YOU AND THAT DIRTY RAG. CAN'T YOU SHUT UP?
OK, MISTER SISSOKO. OK. NOT IN THE PAPER.

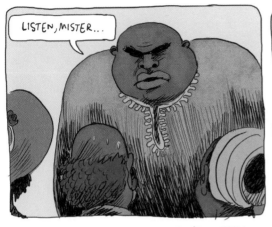

LISTEN, MISTER...

THE SOONER THE WEDDING THE LESS TALK THERE'LL BE AND THE BETTER I'LL FEEL, OK?

YES, MISTER SISSOKO.

...AND IN MY AGENDA, THE 22ND LOOKS PERFECT.

BUT...

THAT'S IN TWO WEEKS.

WE'RE NOT EVEN READY.

WELL, I AM! I'LL HANDLE EVERYTHING.

FINE, SO THAT'S THAT. I'VE GOT THINGS TO DO NOW. GOODBYE.

GOODBYE MISTER SISSOKO.

HE'S WORSE THAN J.R.

IT'S NORMAL, KORO. FOR HIM, TIME IS MONEY.

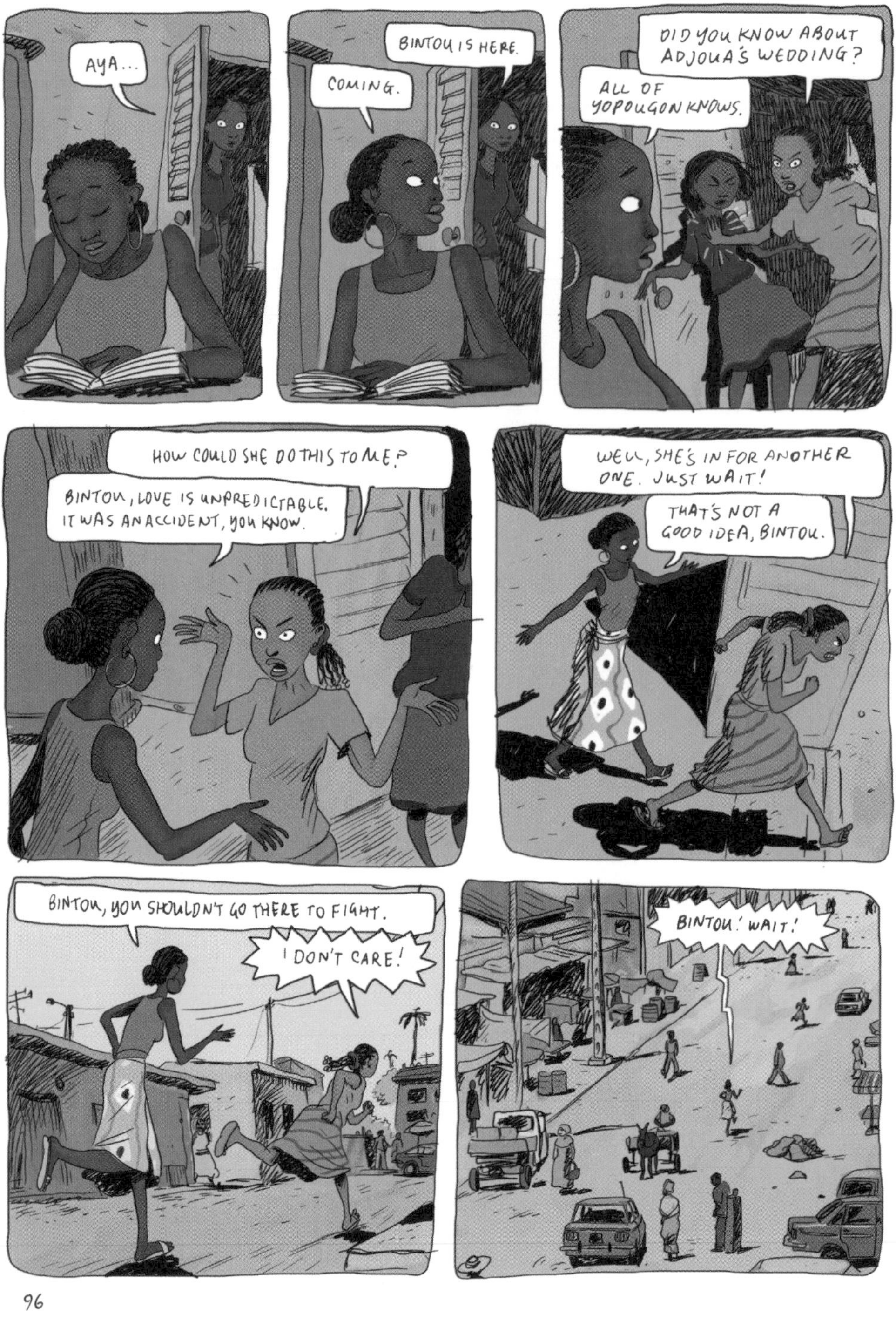
AYA...
BINTOU IS HERE.
COMING.
DID YOU KNOW ABOUT ADJOUA'S WEDDING?
ALL OF YOPOUGON KNOWS.
HOW COULD SHE DO THIS TO ME?
BINTOU, LOVE IS UNPREDICTABLE. IT WAS AN ACCIDENT, YOU KNOW.
WELL, SHE'S IN FOR ANOTHER ONE. JUST WAIT!
THAT'S NOT A GOOD IDEA, BINTOU.
BINTOU, YOU SHOULDN'T GO THERE TO FIGHT.
I DON'T CARE!
BINTOU! WAIT!

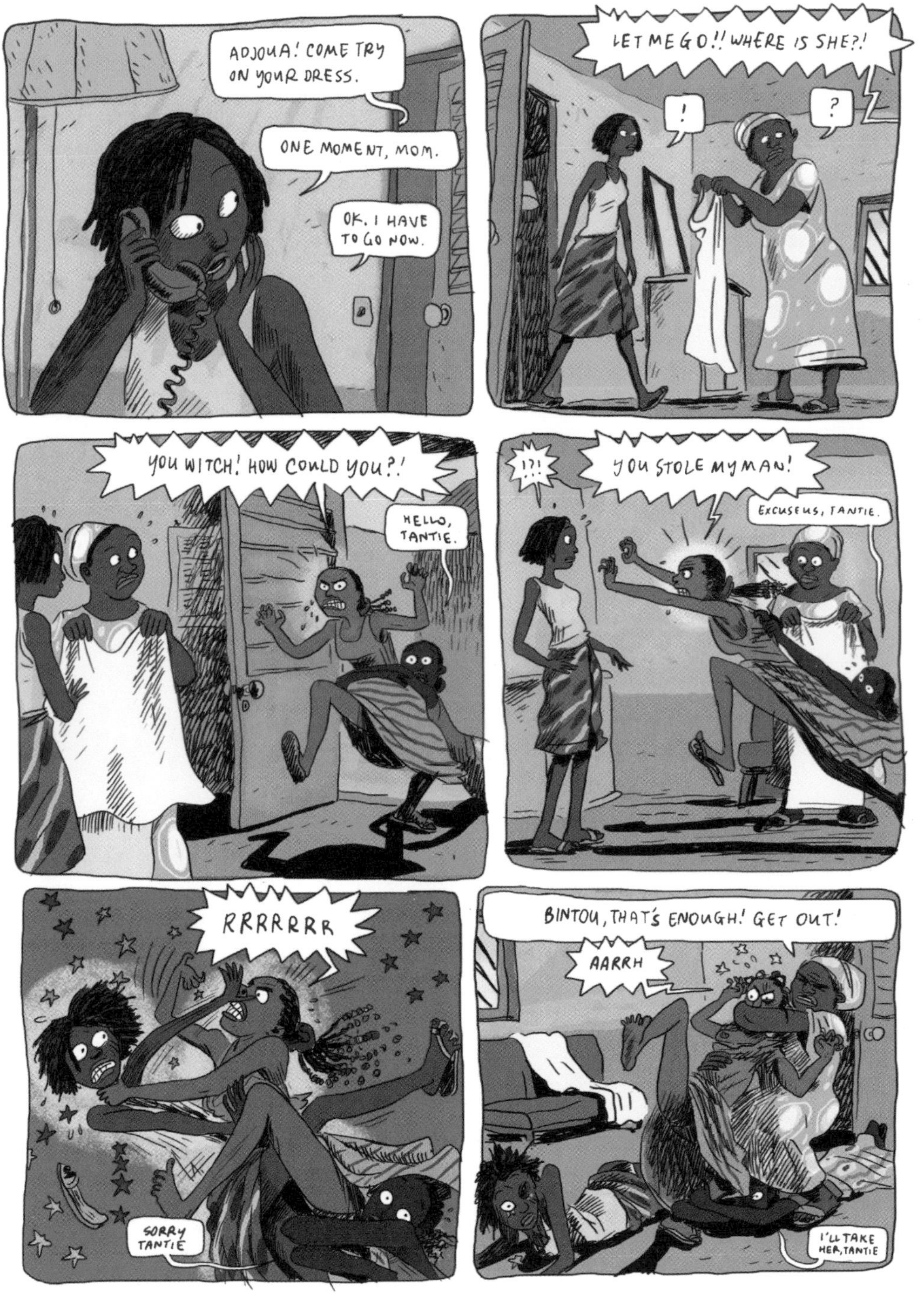
ADJOUA! COME TRY ON YOUR DRESS.
ONE MOMENT, MOM.
OK. I HAVE TO GO NOW.
LET ME GO!! WHERE IS SHE?!
!
?
YOU WITCH! HOW COULD YOU?!
HELLO, TANTIE.
!?!
YOU STOLE MY MAN!
EXCUSE US, TANTIE.
RRRRRRR
SORRY TANTIE
BINTOU, THAT'S ENOUGH! GET OUT!
AARRH
I'LL TAKE HER, TANTIE

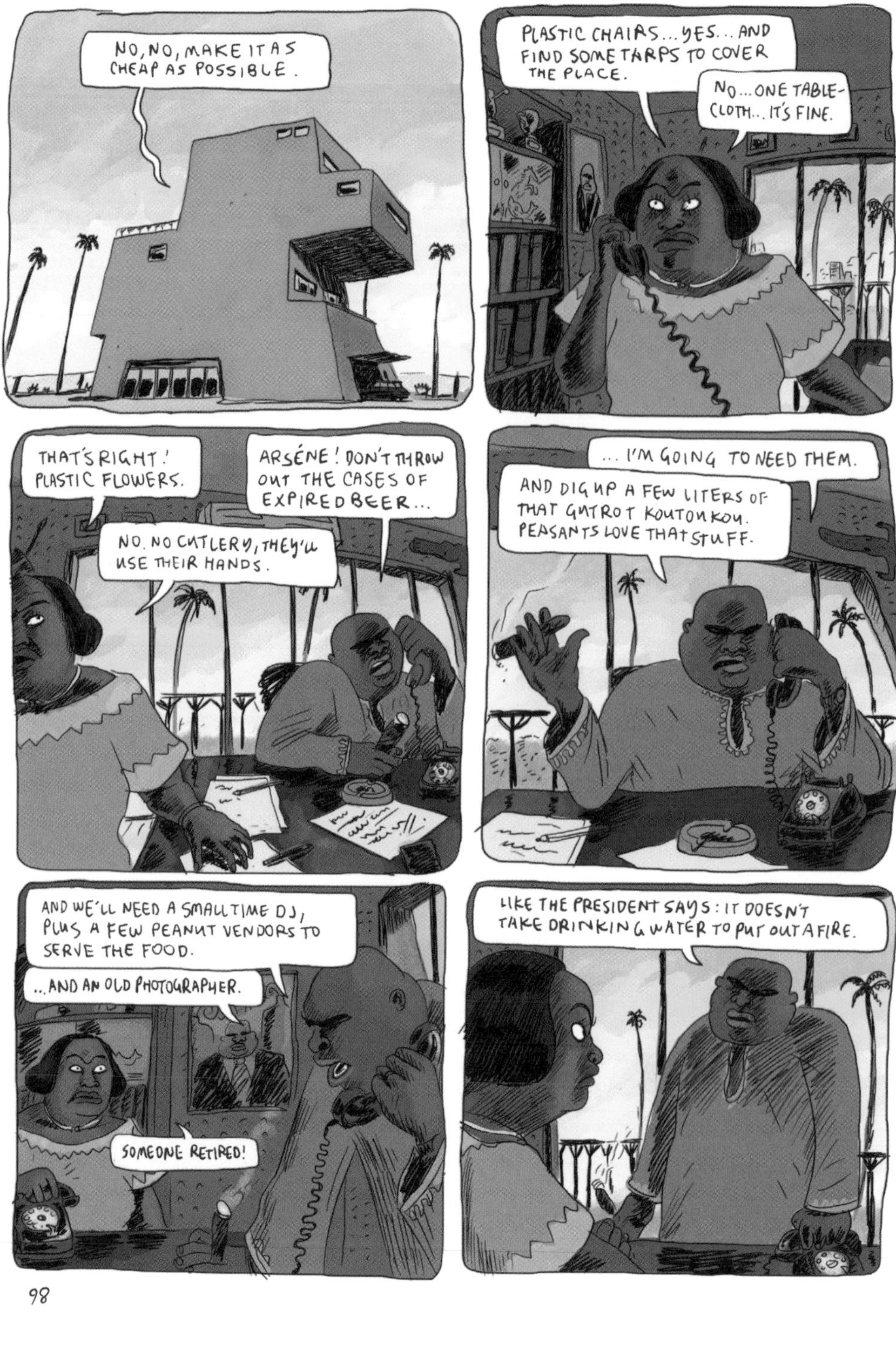
NO, NO, MAKE IT AS CHEAP AS POSSIBLE.
PLASTIC CHAIRS... YES... AND FIND SOME TARPS TO COVER THE PLACE.
NO... ONE TABLECLOTH... IT'S FINE.
THAT'S RIGHT! PLASTIC FLOWERS.
ARSÉNE! DON'T THROW OUT THE CASES OF EXPIRED BEER...
NO. NO CUTLERY, THEY'LL USE THEIR HANDS.
... I'M GOING TO NEED THEM.
AND DIG UP A FEW LITERS OF THAT GUTROT KOUTONKOU. PEASANTS LOVE THAT STUFF.
AND WE'LL NEED A SMALLTIME DJ, PLUS A FEW PEANUT VENDORS TO SERVE THE FOOD.
... AND AN OLD PHOTOGRAPHER.
SOMEONE RETIRED!
LIKE THE PRESIDENT SAYS: IT DOESN'T TAKE DRINKING WATER TO PUT OUT A FIRE.

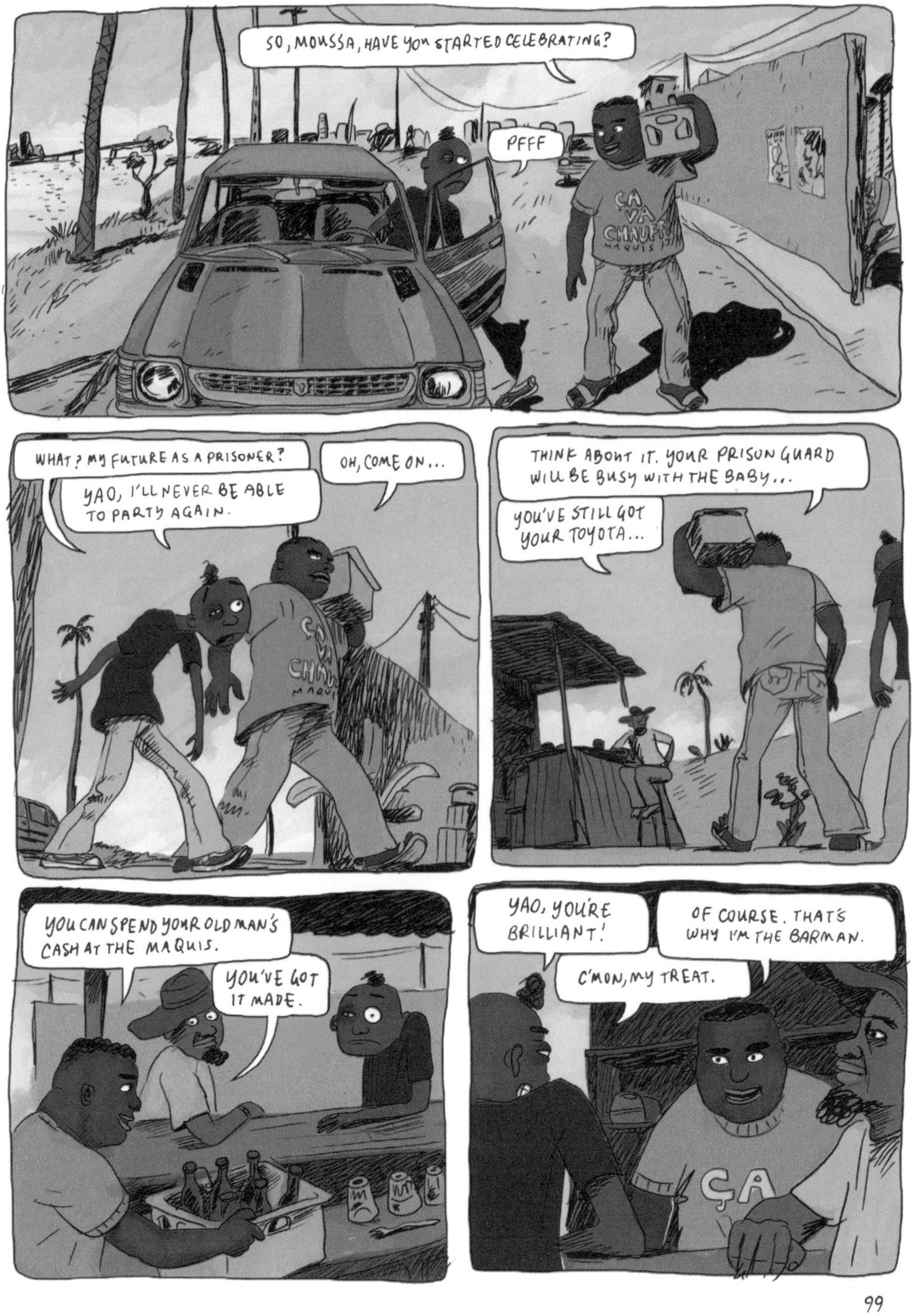
SO, MOUSSA, HAVE YOU STARTED CELEBRATING?
PFFF
ÇA VA CHAUFFE MAQUIS
WHAT? MY FUTURE AS A PRISONER?
YAO, I'LL NEVER BE ABLE TO PARTY AGAIN.
OH, COME ON...
THINK ABOUT IT. YOUR PRISON GUARD WILL BE BUSY WITH THE BABY...
YOU'VE STILL GOT YOUR TOYOTA...
YOU CAN SPEND YOUR OLD MAN'S CASH AT THE MAQUIS.
YOU'VE GOT IT MADE.
YAO, YOU'RE BRILLIANT!
OF COURSE. THAT'S WHY I'M THE BARMAN.
C'MON, MY TREAT.

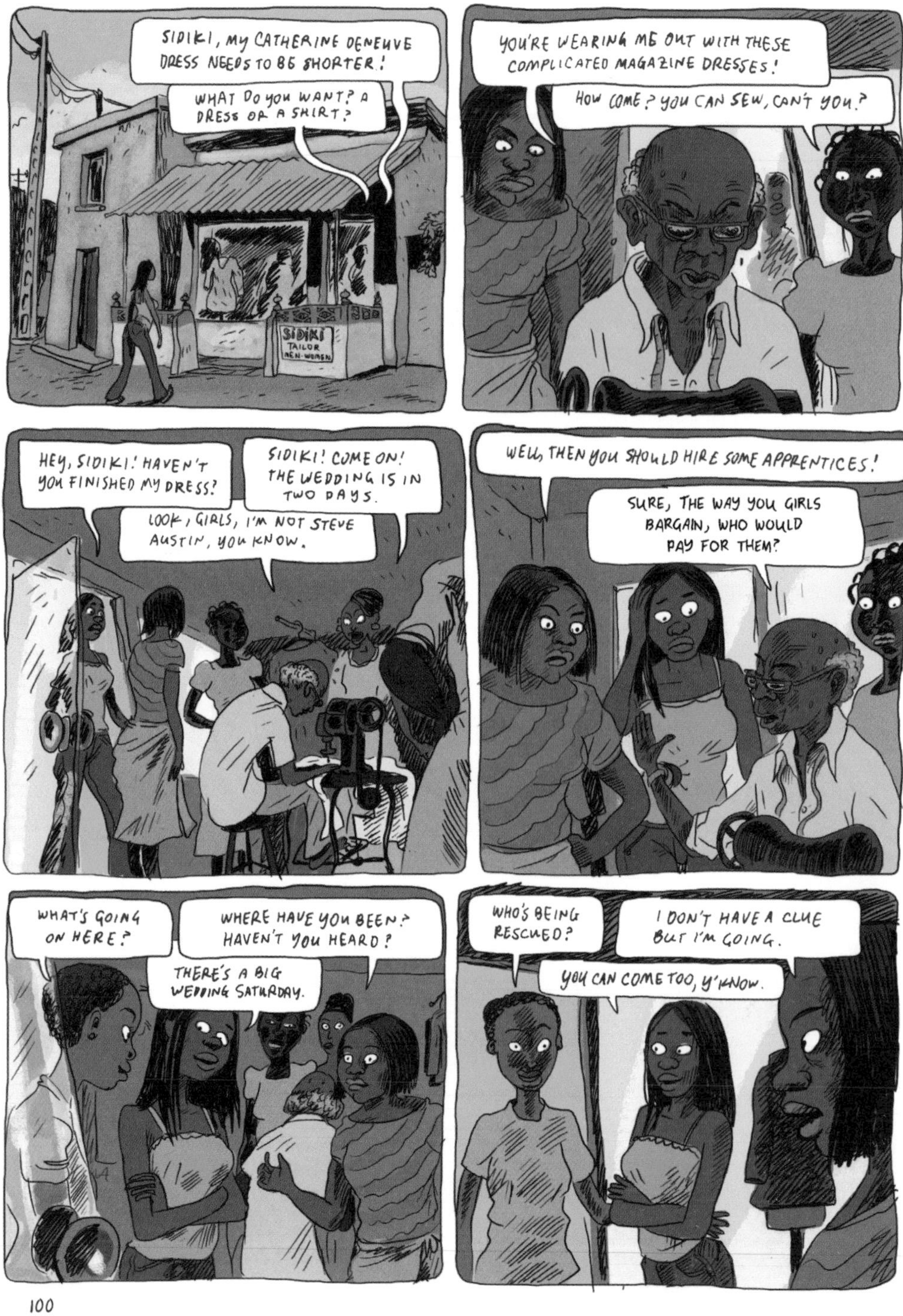
SIDIKI, MY CATHERINE DENEUVE DRESS NEEDS TO BE SHORTER!
WHAT DO YOU WANT? A DRESS OR A SHIRT?
SIDIKI
TAILOR
MEN-WOMEN
YOU'RE WEARING ME OUT WITH THESE COMPLICATED MAGAZINE DRESSES!
HOW COME? YOU CAN SEW, CAN'T YOU?
HEY, SIDIKI! HAVEN'T YOU FINISHED MY DRESS?
SIDIKI! COME ON! THE WEDDING IS IN TWO DAYS.
LOOK, GIRLS, I'M NOT STEVE AUSTIN, YOU KNOW.
WELL, THEN YOU SHOULD HIRE SOME APPRENTICES!
SURE, THE WAY YOU GIRLS BARGAIN, WHO WOULD PAY FOR THEM?
WHAT'S GOING ON HERE?
WHERE HAVE YOU BEEN? HAVEN'T YOU HEARD?
THERE'S A BIG WEDDING SATURDAY.
WHO'S BEING RESCUED?
I DON'T HAVE A CLUE BUT I'M GOING.
YOU CAN COME TOO, Y'KNOW.

And on Saturday the 22nd, despite everything, Yopougon got to see its biggest wedding ever, thanks to all the surprise guests who came.

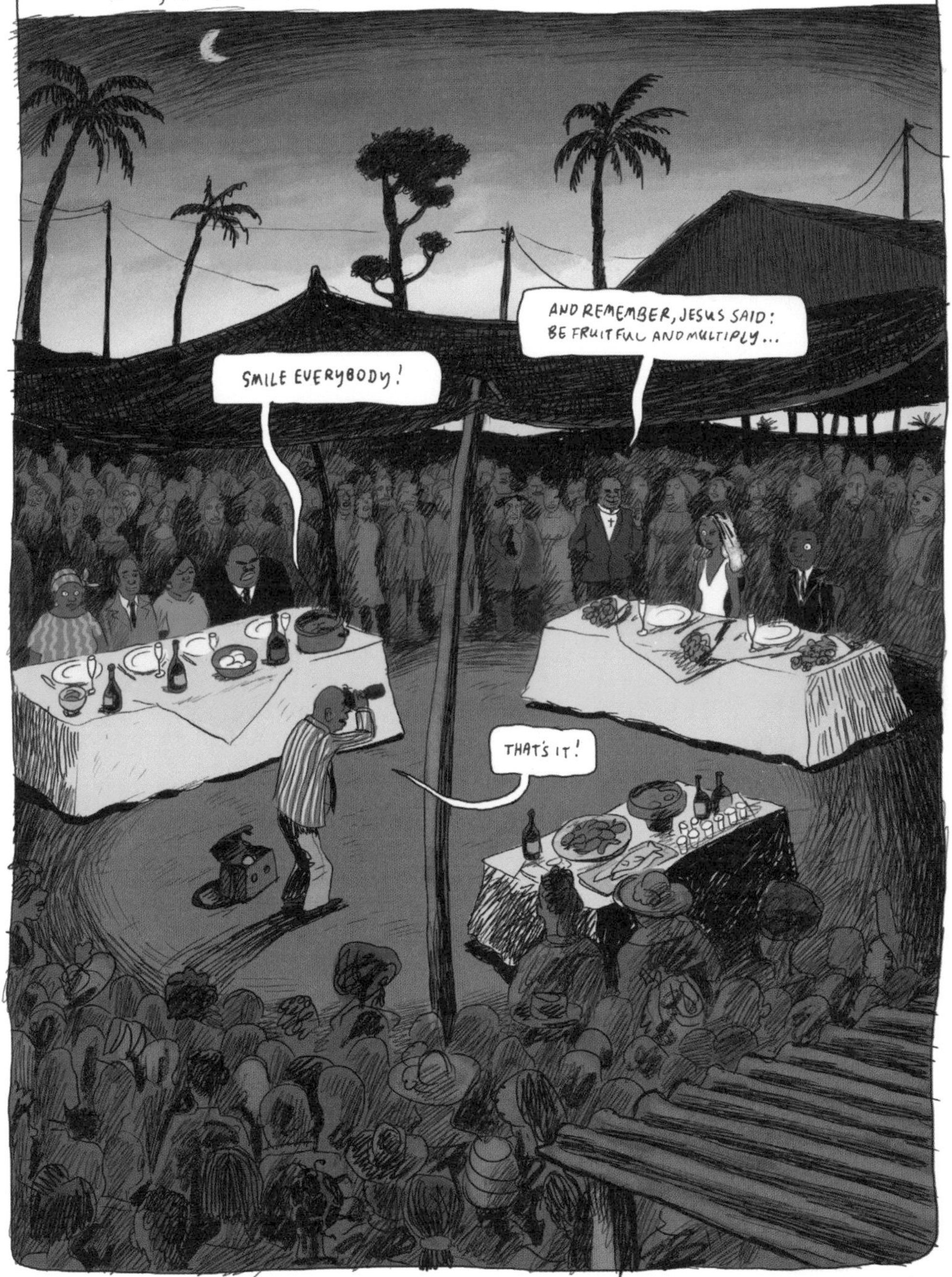
SMILE EVERYBODY!
AND REMEMBER, JESUS SAID: BE FRUITFUL AND MULTIPLY...
THAT'S IT!

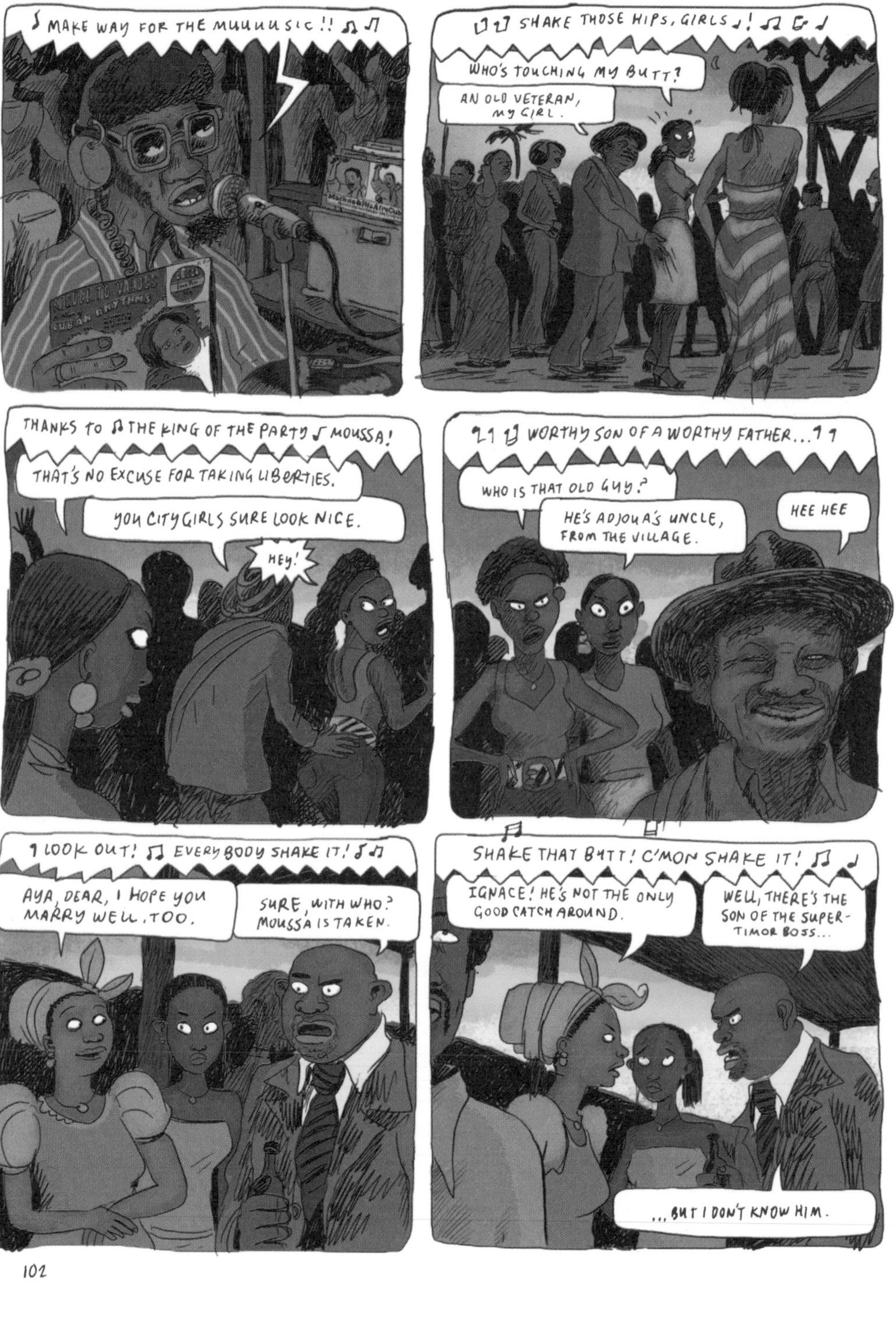
MAKE WAY FOR THE MUUUUSIC!!
CUBAN RHYTHMS
SHAKE THOSE HIPS, GIRLS!
WHO'S TOUCHING MY BUTT?
AN OLD VETERAN, MY GIRL.
THANKS TO THE KING OF THE PARTY MOUSSA!
THAT'S NO EXCUSE FOR TAKING LIBERTIES.
YOU CITY GIRLS SURE LOOK NICE.
HEY!
WORTHY SON OF A WORTHY FATHER...
WHO IS THAT OLD GUY?
HE'S ADJOUA'S UNCLE, FROM THE VILLAGE.
HEE HEE
LOOK OUT! EVERYBODY SHAKE IT!
AYA, DEAR, I HOPE YOU MARRY WELL, TOO.
SURE, WITH WHO? MOUSSA IS TAKEN.
SHAKE THAT BUTT! C'MON SHAKE IT!
IGNACE! HE'S NOT THE ONLY GOOD CATCH AROUND.
WELL, THERE'S THE SON OF THE SUPER-TIMOR BOSS...
...BUT I DON'T KNOW HIM.

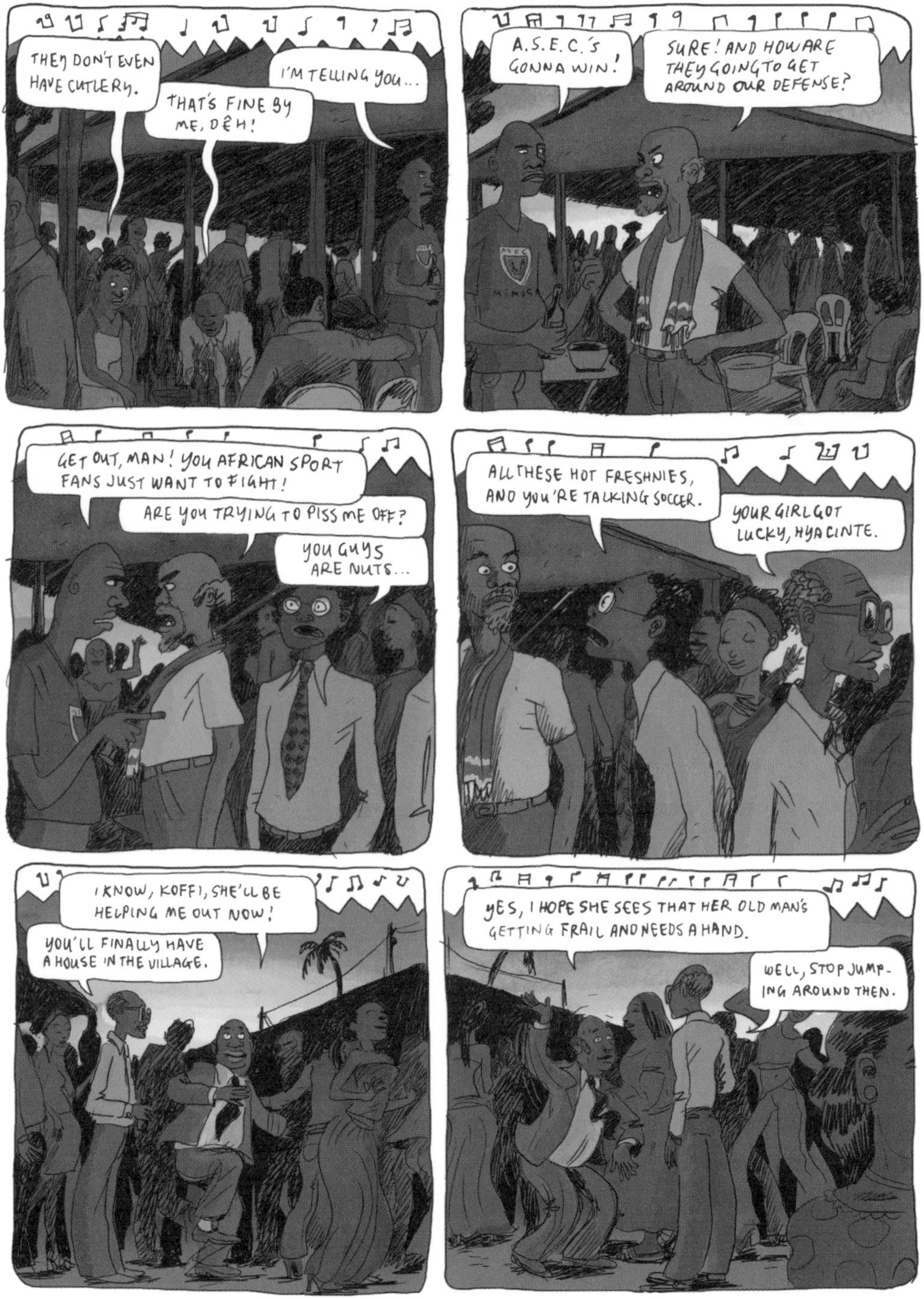
THEY DON'T EVEN HAVE CUTLERY.
THAT'S FINE BY ME, DÊH!
I'M TELLING YOU...
A.S.E.C.'S GONNA WIN!
SURE! AND HOW ARE THEY GOING TO GET AROUND OUR DEFENSE?
GET OUT, MAN! YOU AFRICAN SPORT FANS JUST WANT TO FIGHT!
ARE YOU TRYING TO PISS ME OFF?
YOU GUYS ARE NUTS...
ALL THESE HOT FRESHNIES, AND YOU'RE TALKING SOCCER.
YOUR GIRL GOT LUCKY, HYACINTE.
I KNOW, KOFFI, SHE'LL BE HELPING ME OUT NOW!
YOU'LL FINALLY HAVE A HOUSE IN THE VILLAGE.
YES, I HOPE SHE SEES THAT HER OLD MAN'S GETTING FRAIL AND NEEDS A HAND.
WELL, STOP JUMPING AROUND THEN.

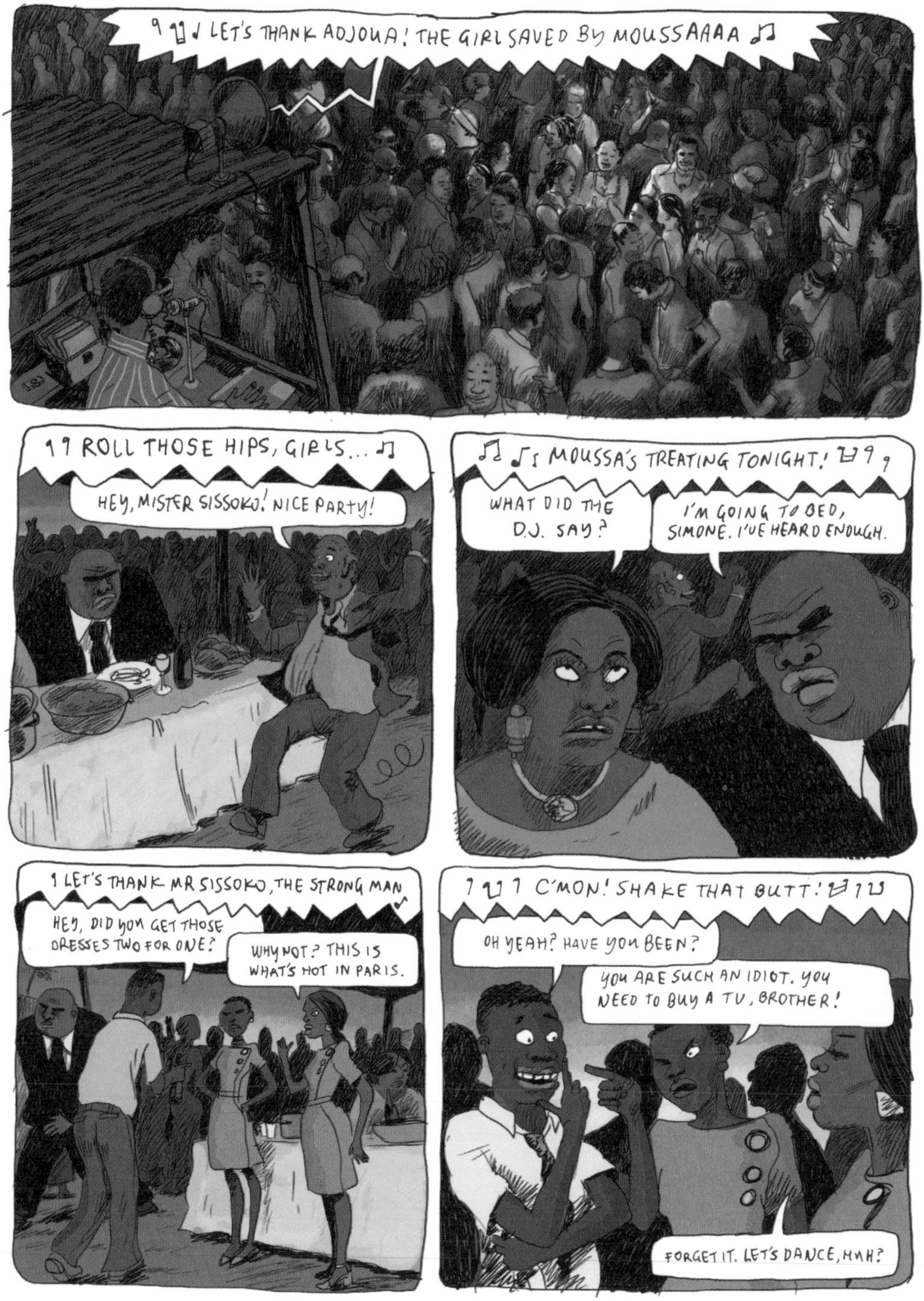
LET'S THANK ADJOUA! THE GIRL SAVED BY MOUSSAAAA
ROLL THOSE HIPS, GIRLS...
HEY, MISTER SISSOKO! NICE PARTY!
MOUSSA'S TREATING TONIGHT!
WHAT DID THE D.J. SAY?
I'M GOING TO BED, SIMONE. I'VE HEARD ENOUGH.
LET'S THANK MR SISSOKO, THE STRONG MAN
HEY, DID YOU GET THOSE DRESSES TWO FOR ONE?
WHY NOT? THIS IS WHAT'S HOT IN PARIS.
C'MON! SHAKE THAT BUTT!
OH YEAH? HAVE YOU BEEN?
YOU ARE SUCH AN IDIOT. YOU NEED TO BUY A TV, BROTHER!
FORGET IT. LET'S DANCE, HMH?

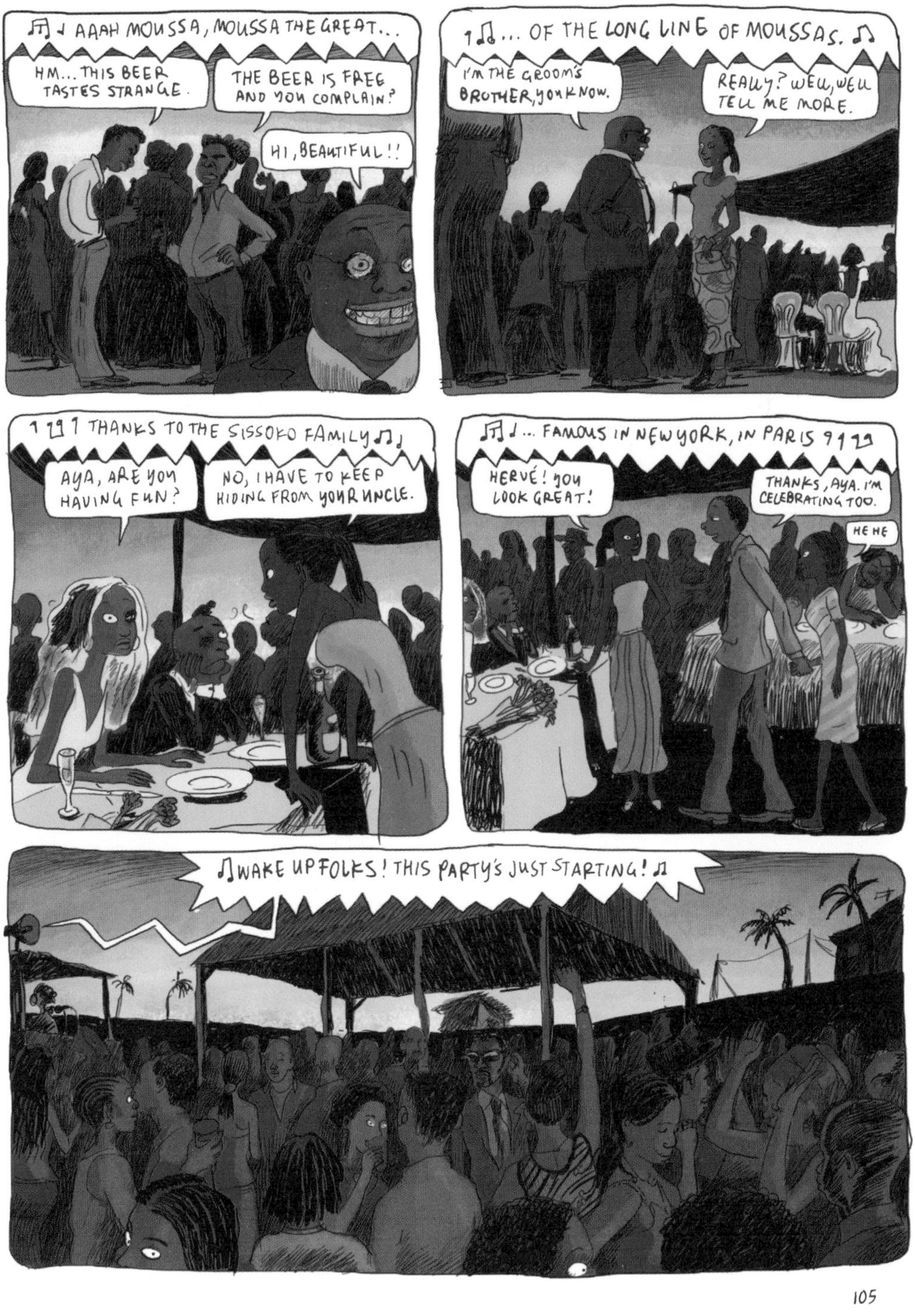
AAAH MOUSSA, MOUSSA THE GREAT...
HM... THIS BEER TASTES STRANGE.
THE BEER IS FREE AND YOU COMPLAIN?
HI, BEAUTIFUL!!
... OF THE LONG LINE OF MOUSSAS.
I'M THE GROOM'S BROTHER, YOU KNOW.
REALLY? WELL, WELL TELL ME MORE.
THANKS TO THE SISSOKO FAMILY
AYA, ARE YOU HAVING FUN?
NO, I HAVE TO KEEP HIDING FROM YOUR UNCLE.
... FAMOUS IN NEW YORK, IN PARIS
HERVÉ! YOU LOOK GREAT!
THANKS, AYA. I'M CELEBRATING TOO.
HE HE
WAKE UP FOLKS! THIS PARTY'S JUST STARTING!

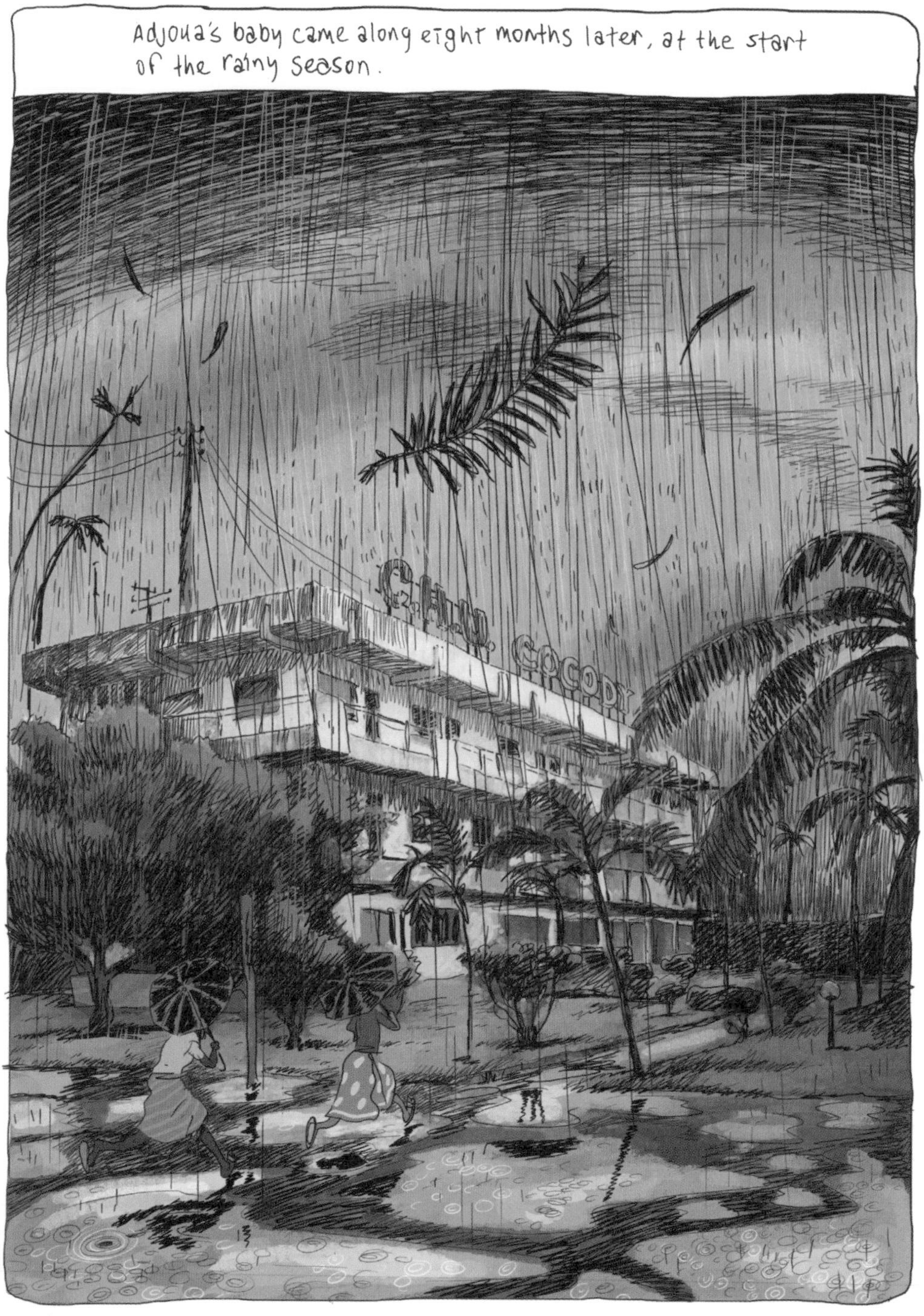
Adjoua's baby came along eight months later, at the start of the rainy season.
COCODY

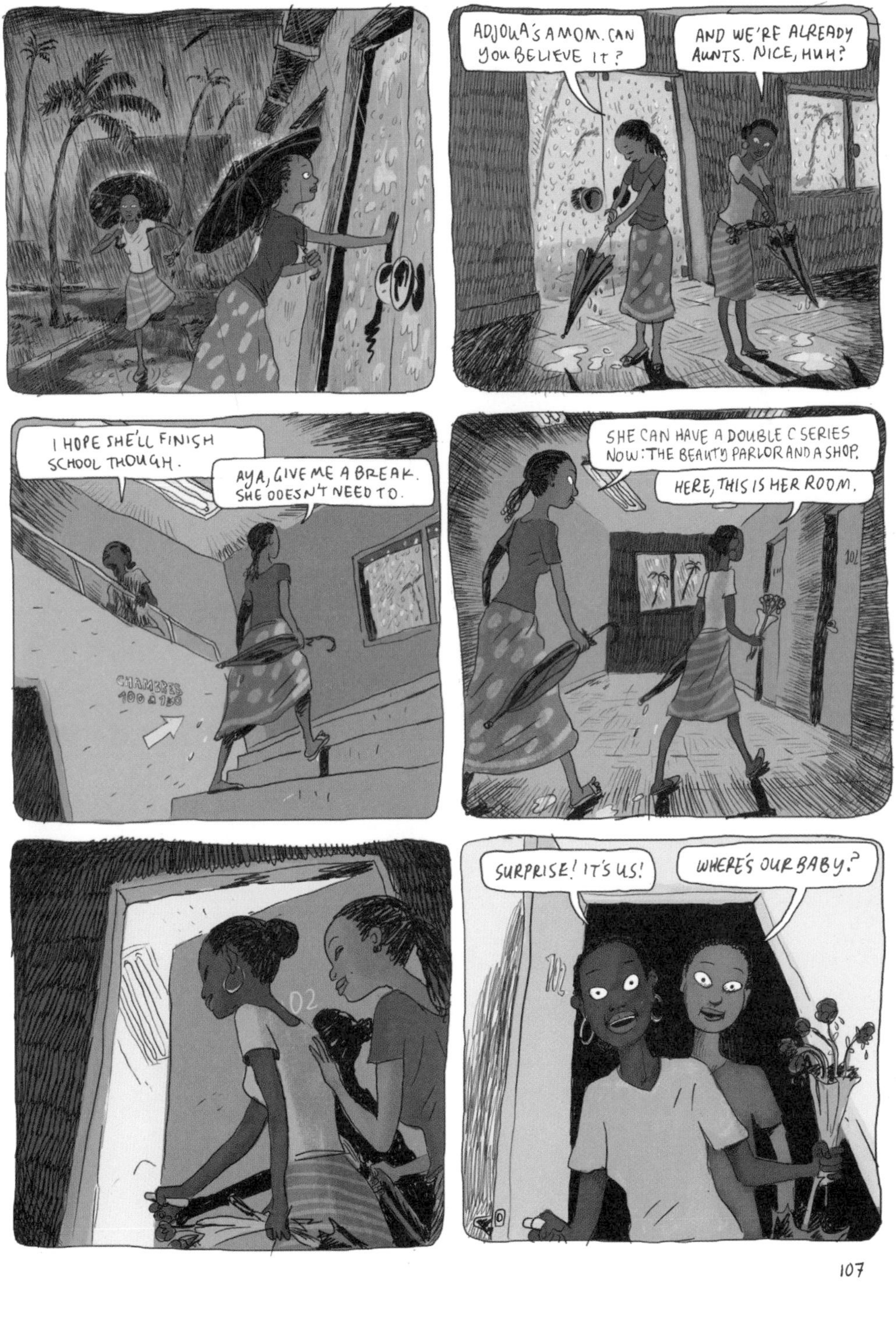
ADJOUA'S A MOM. CAN YOU BELIEVE IT?
AND WE'RE ALREADY AUNTS. NICE, HUH?
I HOPE SHE'LL FINISH SCHOOL THOUGH.
AYA, GIVE ME A BREAK. SHE DOESN'T NEED TO.
CHAMBRES 100 À 150
SHE CAN HAVE A DOUBLE C SERIES NOW: THE BEAUTY PARLOR AND A SHOP.
HERE, THIS IS HER ROOM.
102
SURPRISE! IT'S US!
WHERE'S OUR BABY?

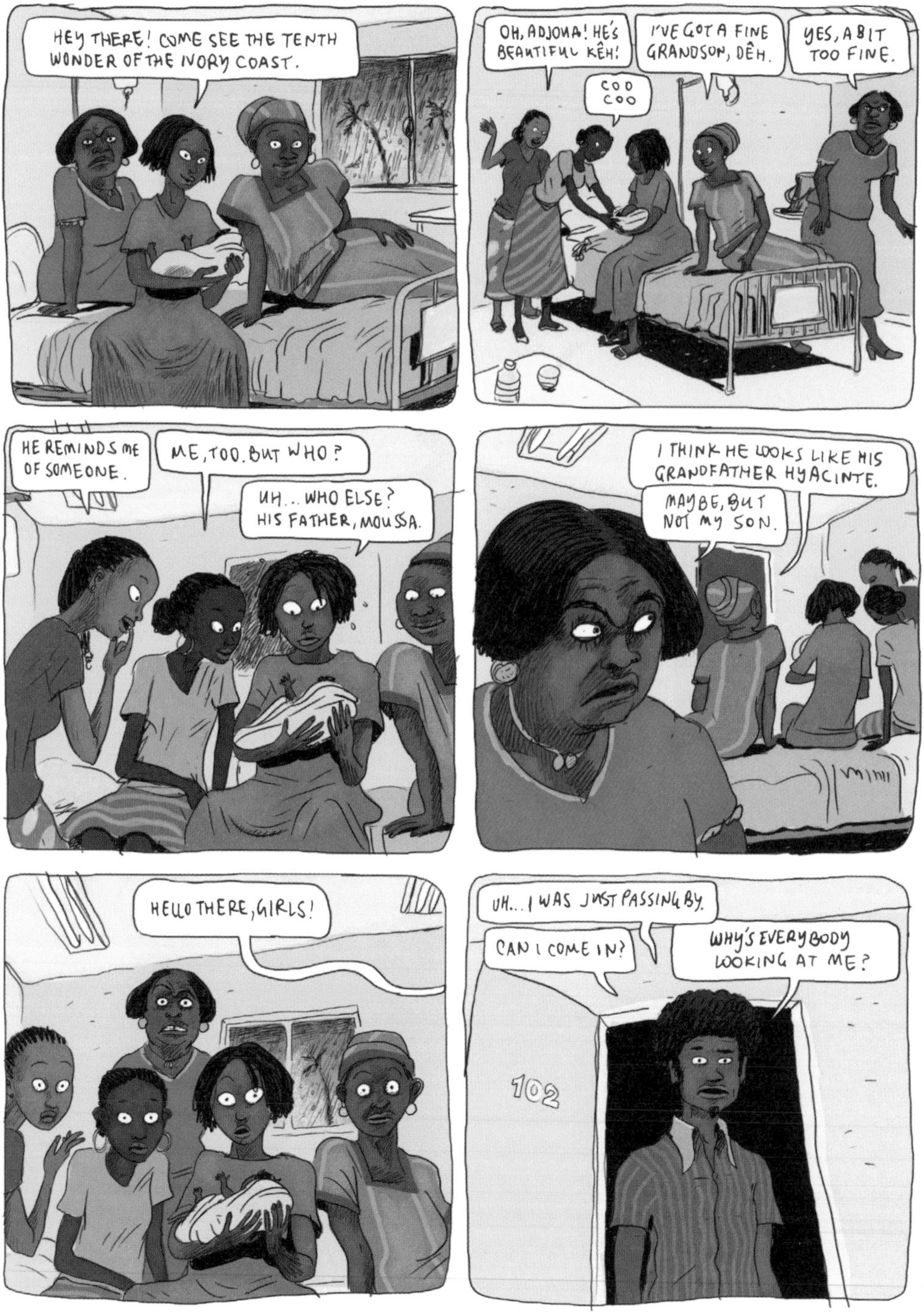
HEY THERE! COME SEE THE TENTH WONDER OF THE IVORY COAST.
OH, ADJOUA! HE'S BEAUTIFUL KÊH!
COO COO
I'VE GOT A FINE GRANDSON, DÊH.
YES, A BIT TOO FINE.
HE REMINDS ME OF SOMEONE.
ME, TOO. BUT WHO?
UH... WHO ELSE? HIS FATHER, MOUSSA.
I THINK HE LOOKS LIKE HIS GRANDFATHER HYACINTE.
MAYBE, BUT NOT MY SON.
HELLO THERE, GIRLS!
UH... I WAS JUST PASSING BY.
CAN I COME IN?
WHY'S EVERYBODY LOOKING AT ME?
102

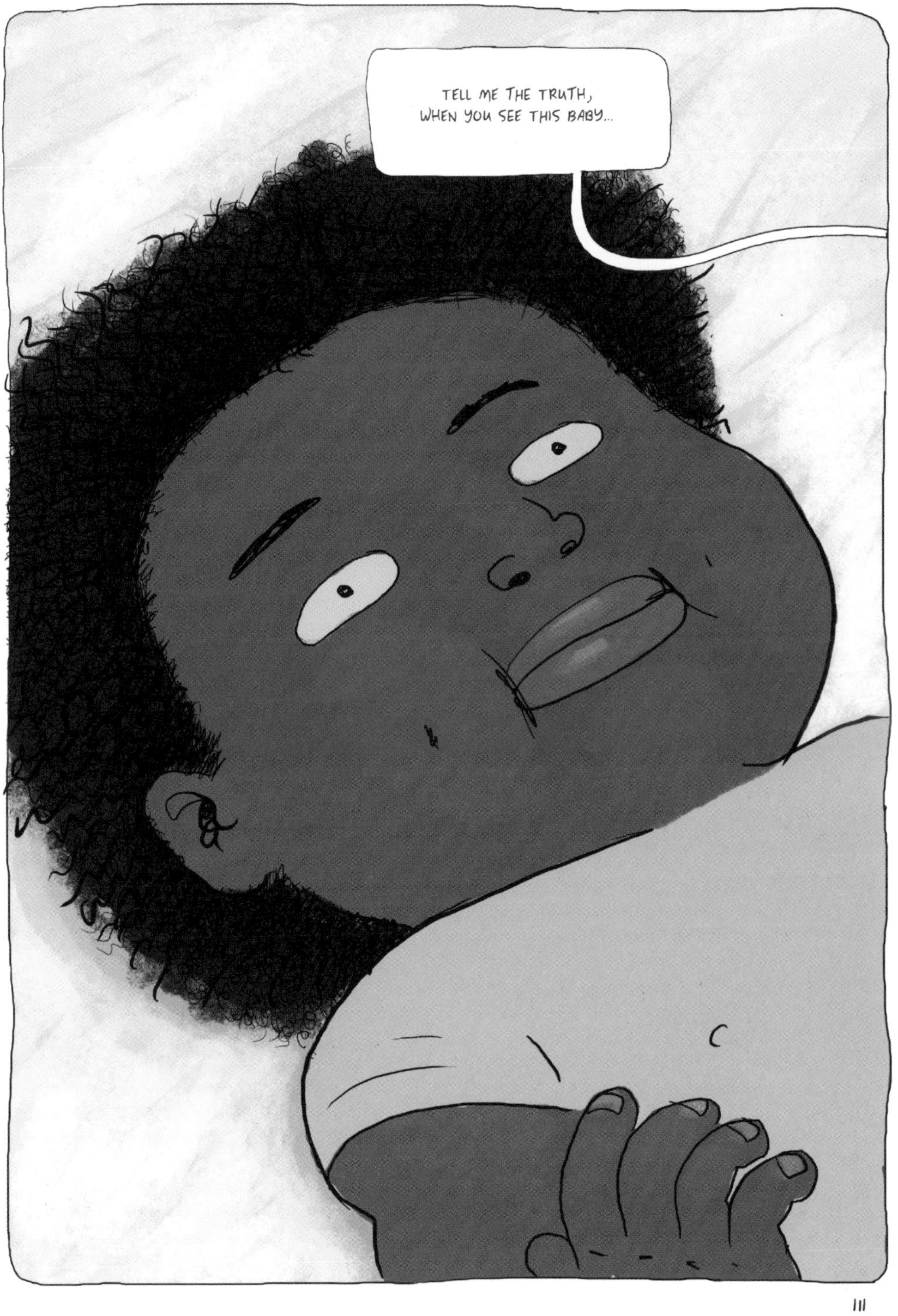
TELL ME THE TRUTH, WHEN YOU SEE THIS BABY...

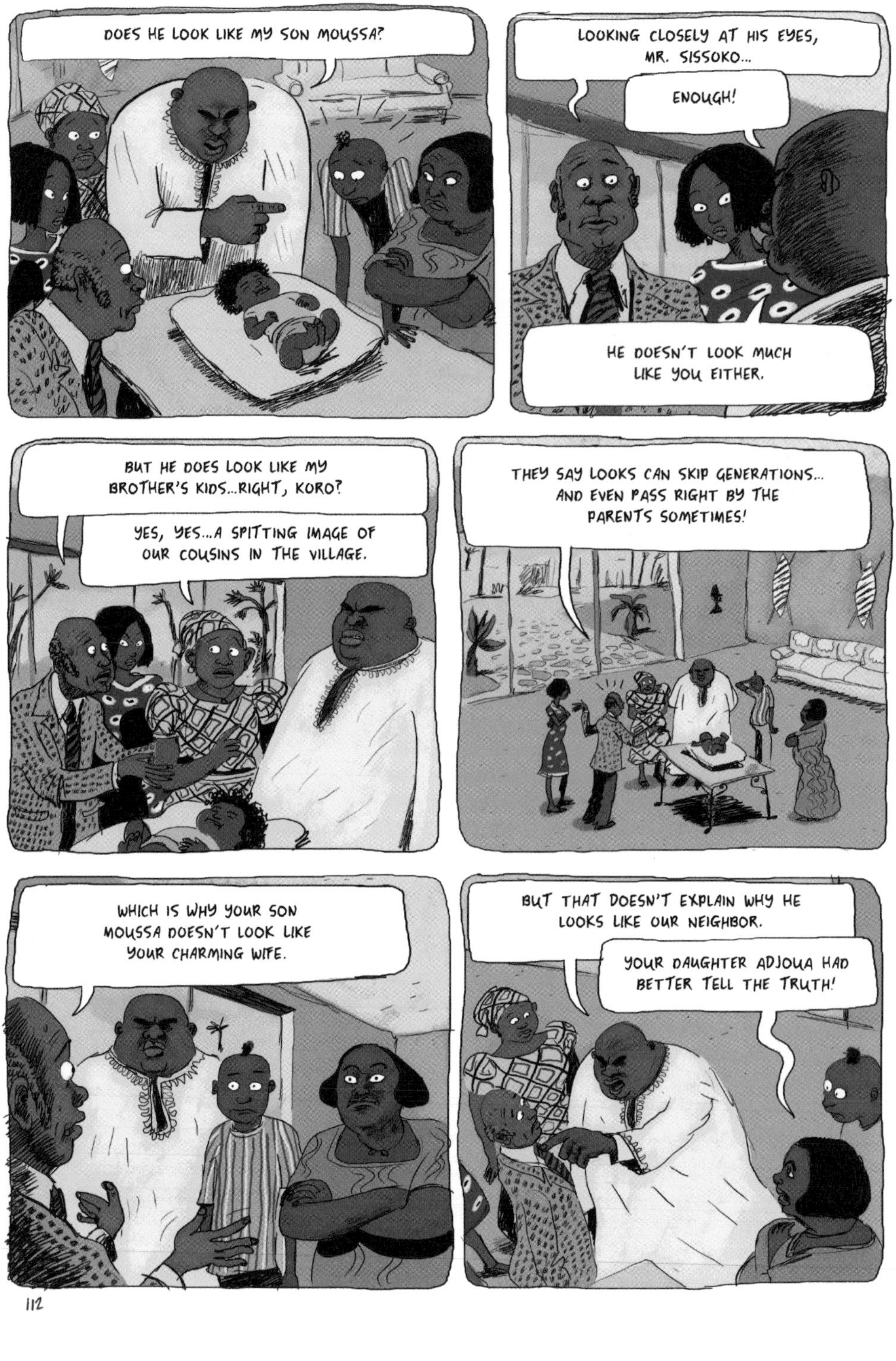
DOES HE LOOK LIKE MY SON MOUSSA?
LOOKING CLOSELY AT HIS EYES, MR. SISSOKO...
ENOUGH!
HE DOESN'T LOOK MUCH LIKE YOU EITHER.
BUT HE DOES LOOK LIKE MY BROTHER'S KIDS...RIGHT, KORO?
YES, YES...A SPITTING IMAGE OF OUR COUSINS IN THE VILLAGE.
THEY SAY LOOKS CAN SKIP GENERATIONS... AND EVEN PASS RIGHT BY THE PARENTS SOMETIMES!
WHICH IS WHY YOUR SON MOUSSA DOESN'T LOOK LIKE YOUR CHARMING WIFE.
BUT THAT DOESN'T EXPLAIN WHY HE LOOKS LIKE OUR NEIGHBOR.
YOUR DAUGHTER ADJOUA HAD BETTER TELL THE TRUTH!

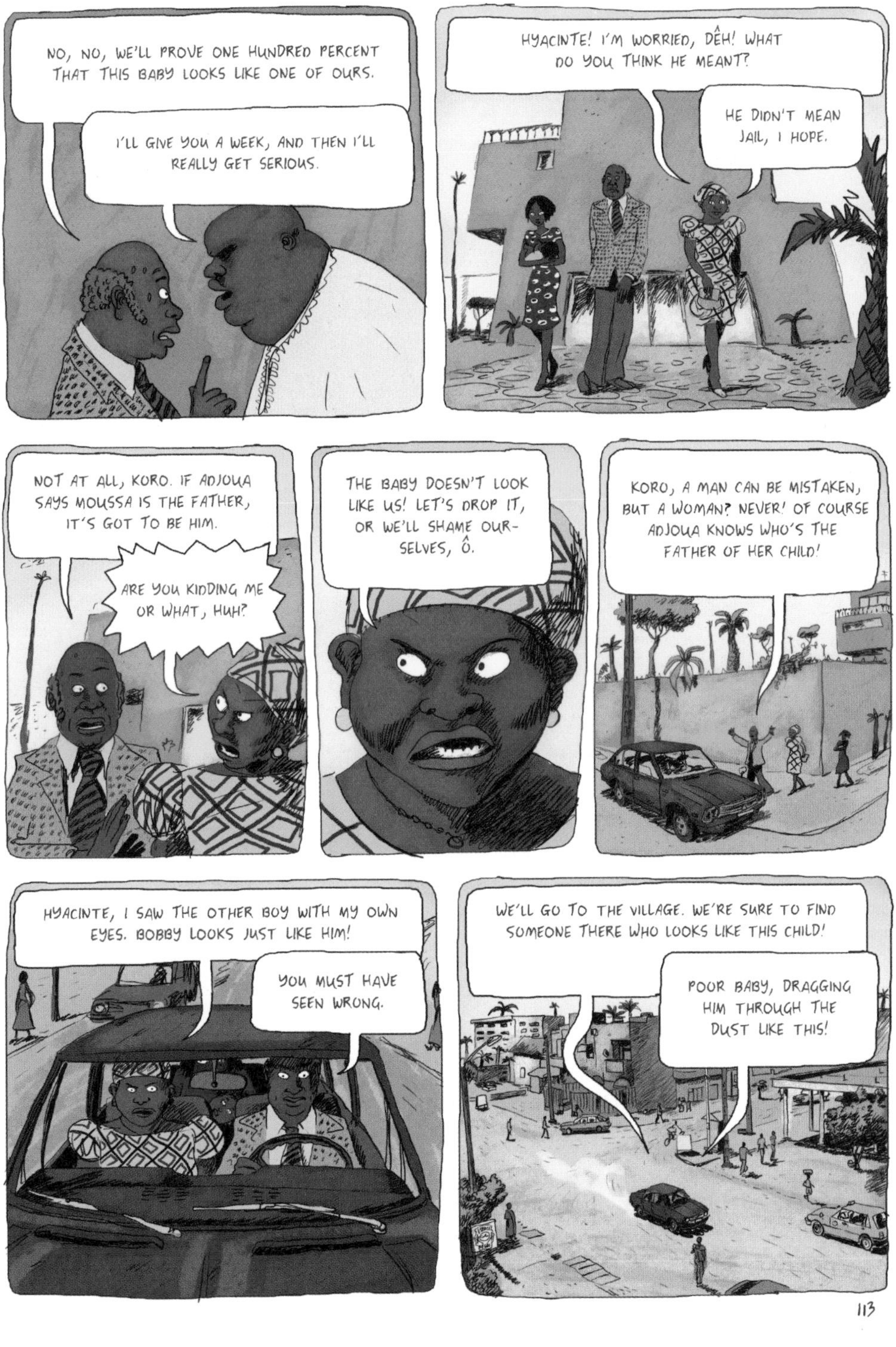
NO, NO, WE'LL PROVE ONE HUNDRED PERCENT THAT THIS BABY LOOKS LIKE ONE OF OURS.
I'LL GIVE YOU A WEEK, AND THEN I'LL REALLY GET SERIOUS.
HYACINTE! I'M WORRIED, DÊH! WHAT DO YOU THINK HE MEANT?
HE DIDN'T MEAN JAIL, I HOPE.
NOT AT ALL, KORO. IF ADJOUA SAYS MOUSSA IS THE FATHER, IT'S GOT TO BE HIM.
ARE YOU KIDDING ME OR WHAT, HUH?
THE BABY DOESN'T LOOK LIKE US! LET'S DROP IT, OR WE'LL SHAME OURSELVES, Ô.
KORO, A MAN CAN BE MISTAKEN, BUT A WOMAN? NEVER! OF COURSE ADJOUA KNOWS WHO'S THE FATHER OF HER CHILD!
HYACINTE, I SAW THE OTHER BOY WITH MY OWN EYES. BOBBY LOOKS JUST LIKE HIM!
YOU MUST HAVE SEEN WRONG.
WE'LL GO TO THE VILLAGE. WE'RE SURE TO FIND SOMEONE THERE WHO LOOKS LIKE THIS CHILD!
POOR BABY, DRAGGING HIM THROUGH THE DUST LIKE THIS!

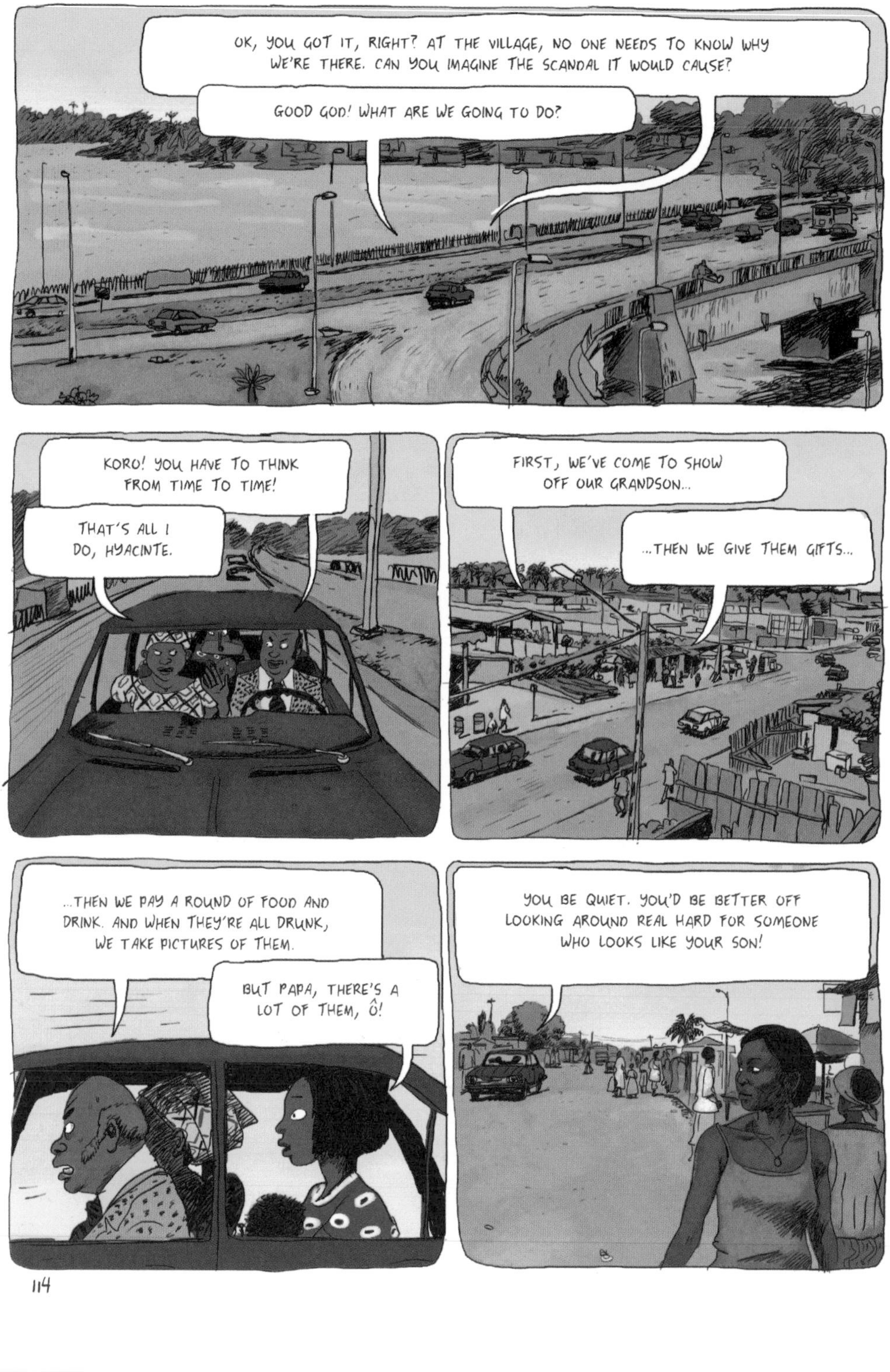
OK, YOU GOT IT, RIGHT? AT THE VILLAGE, NO ONE NEEDS TO KNOW WHY WE'RE THERE. CAN YOU IMAGINE THE SCANDAL IT WOULD CAUSE?
GOOD GOD! WHAT ARE WE GOING TO DO?
KORO! YOU HAVE TO THINK FROM TIME TO TIME!
THAT'S ALL I DO, HYACINTE.
FIRST, WE'VE COME TO SHOW OFF OUR GRANDSON...
...THEN WE GIVE THEM GIFTS...
...THEN WE PAY A ROUND OF FOOD AND DRINK. AND WHEN THEY'RE ALL DRUNK, WE TAKE PICTURES OF THEM.
BUT PAPA, THERE'S A LOT OF THEM, Ô!
YOU BE QUIET. YOU'D BE BETTER OFF LOOKING AROUND REAL HARD FOR SOMEONE WHO LOOKS LIKE YOUR SON!

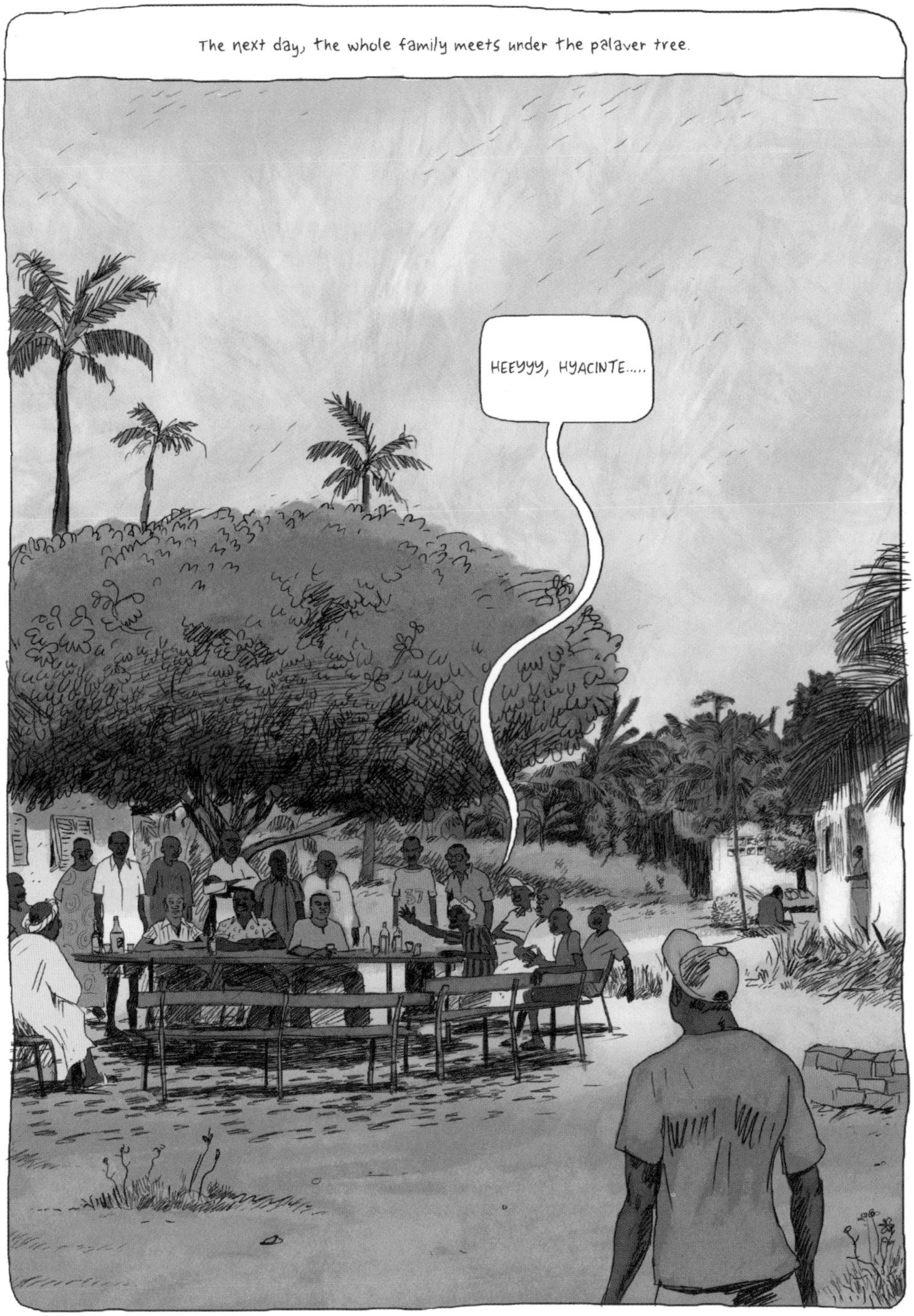
The next day, the whole family meets under the palaver tree.
HEEYYY, HYACINTE.....

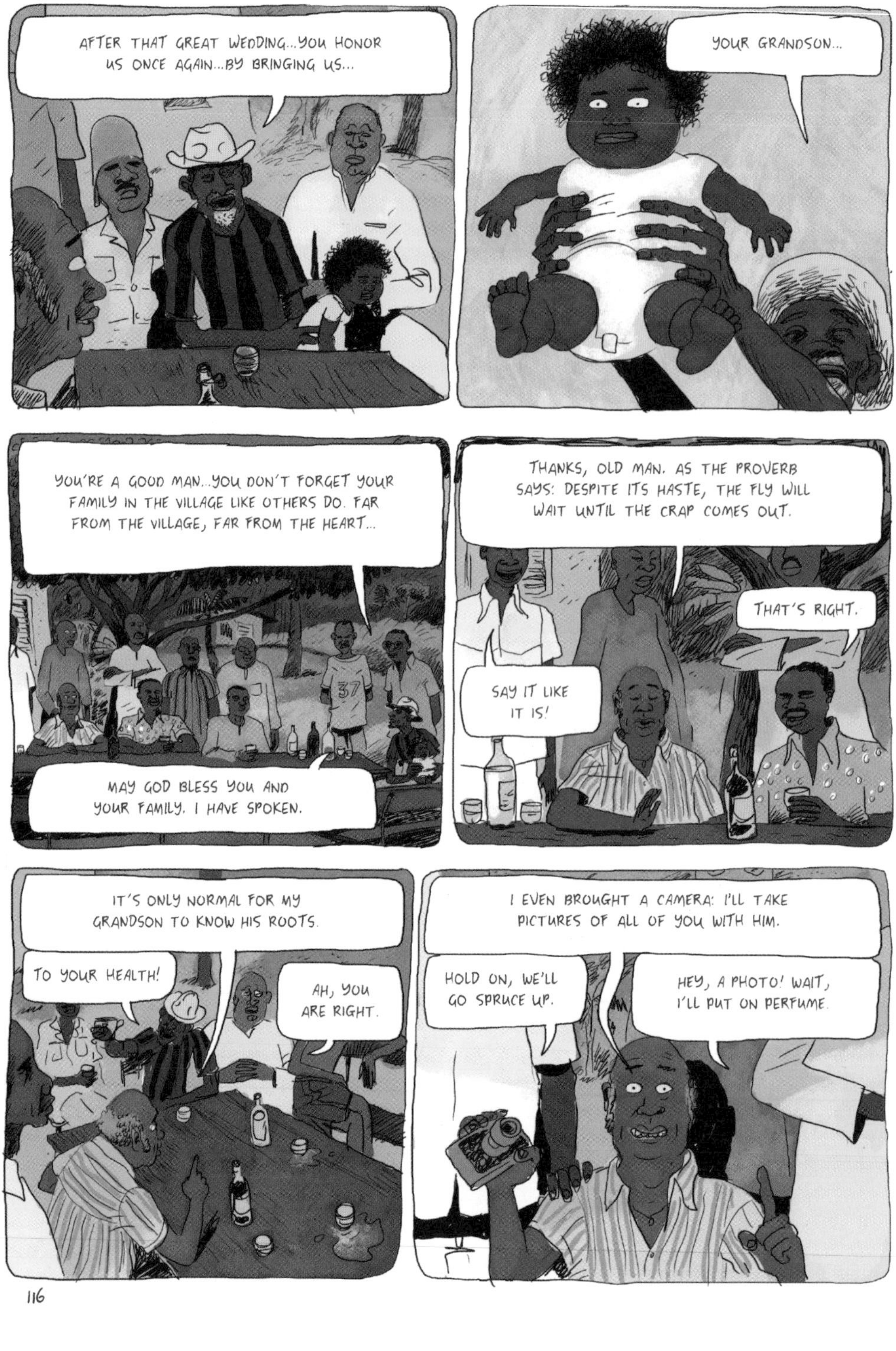
AFTER THAT GREAT WEDDING...YOU HONOR US ONCE AGAIN...BY BRINGING US...
YOUR GRANDSON...
YOU'RE A GOOD MAN...YOU DON'T FORGET YOUR FAMILY IN THE VILLAGE LIKE OTHERS DO. FAR FROM THE VILLAGE, FAR FROM THE HEART...
MAY GOD BLESS YOU AND YOUR FAMILY. I HAVE SPOKEN.
THANKS, OLD MAN. AS THE PROVERB SAYS: DESPITE ITS HASTE, THE FLY WILL WAIT UNTIL THE CRAP COMES OUT.
THAT'S RIGHT.
SAY IT LIKE IT IS!
IT'S ONLY NORMAL FOR MY GRANDSON TO KNOW HIS ROOTS.
TO YOUR HEALTH!
AH, YOU ARE RIGHT.
I EVEN BROUGHT A CAMERA: I'LL TAKE PICTURES OF ALL OF YOU WITH HIM.
HOLD ON, WE'LL GO SPRUCE UP.
HEY, A PHOTO! WAIT, I'LL PUT ON PERFUME.

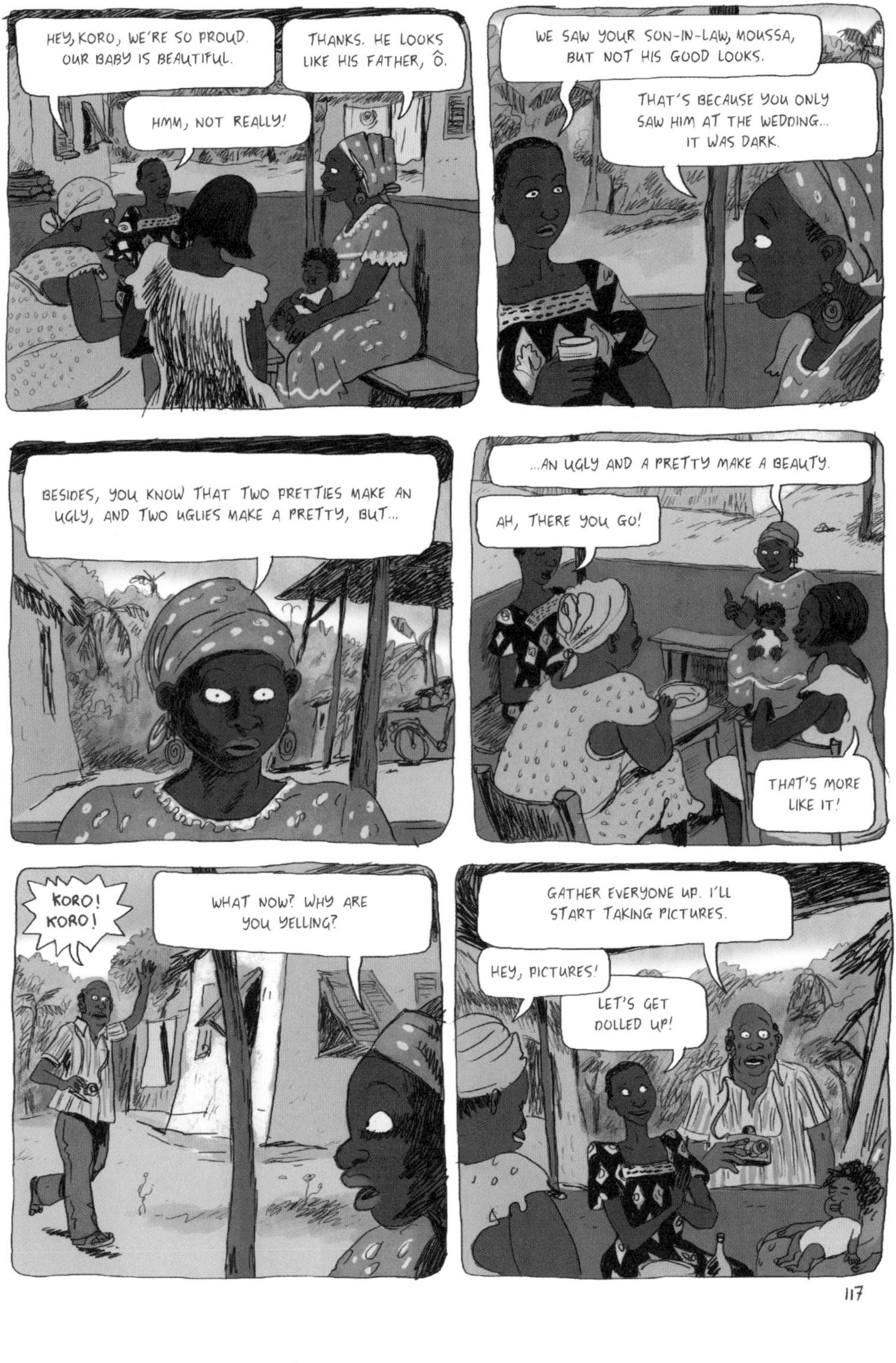
HEY, KORO, WE'RE SO PROUD. OUR BABY IS BEAUTIFUL.
THANKS. HE LOOKS LIKE HIS FATHER, Ô.
HMM, NOT REALLY!
WE SAW YOUR SON-IN-LAW, MOUSSA, BUT NOT HIS GOOD LOOKS.
THAT'S BECAUSE YOU ONLY SAW HIM AT THE WEDDING... IT WAS DARK.
BESIDES, YOU KNOW THAT TWO PRETTIES MAKE AN UGLY, AND TWO UGLIES MAKE A PRETTY, BUT...
...AN UGLY AND A PRETTY MAKE A BEAUTY.
AH, THERE YOU GO!
THAT'S MORE LIKE IT!
KORO! KORO!
WHAT NOW? WHY ARE YOU YELLING?
GATHER EVERYONE UP. I'LL START TAKING PICTURES.
HEY, PICTURES!
LET'S GET DOLLED UP!

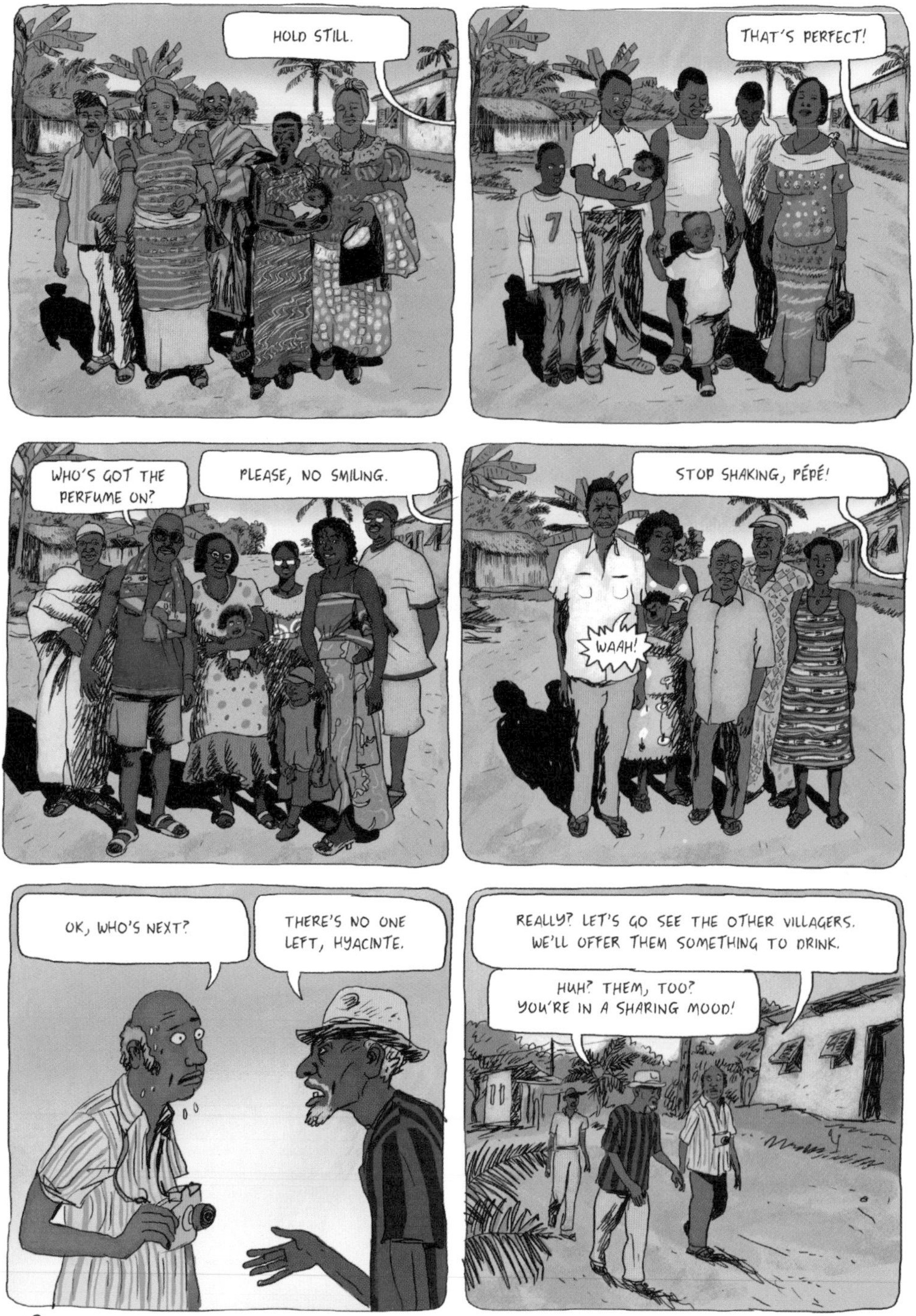
HOLD STILL.
THAT'S PERFECT!
WHO'S GOT THE PERFUME ON?
PLEASE, NO SMILING.
STOP SHAKING, PÉPÉ!
WAAH!
OK, WHO'S NEXT?
THERE'S NO ONE LEFT, HYACINTE.
REALLY? LET'S GO SEE THE OTHER VILLAGERS. WE'LL OFFER THEM SOMETHING TO DRINK.
HUH? THEM, TOO? YOU'RE IN A SHARING MOOD!

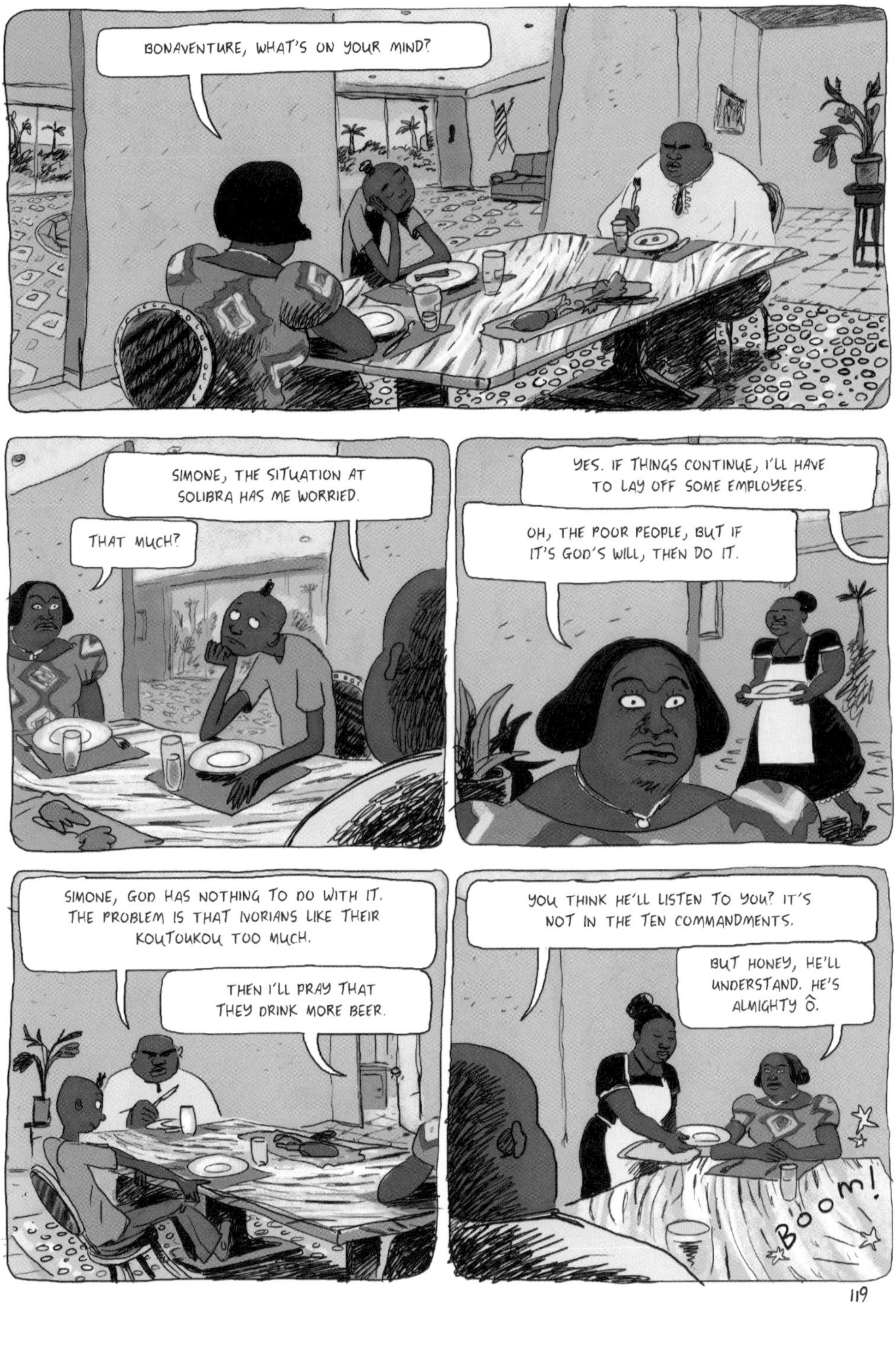
BONAVENTURE, WHAT'S ON YOUR MIND?
SIMONE, THE SITUATION AT SOLIBRA HAS ME WORRIED.
THAT MUCH?
YES. IF THINGS CONTINUE, I'LL HAVE TO LAY OFF SOME EMPLOYEES.
OH, THE POOR PEOPLE, BUT IF IT'S GOD'S WILL, THEN DO IT.
SIMONE, GOD HAS NOTHING TO DO WITH IT. THE PROBLEM IS THAT IVORIANS LIKE THEIR KOUTOUKOU TOO MUCH.
THEN I'LL PRAY THAT THEY DRINK MORE BEER.
YOU THINK HE'LL LISTEN TO YOU? IT'S NOT IN THE TEN COMMANDMENTS.
BUT HONEY, HE'LL UNDERSTAND. HE'S ALMIGHTY Ô.
Boom!

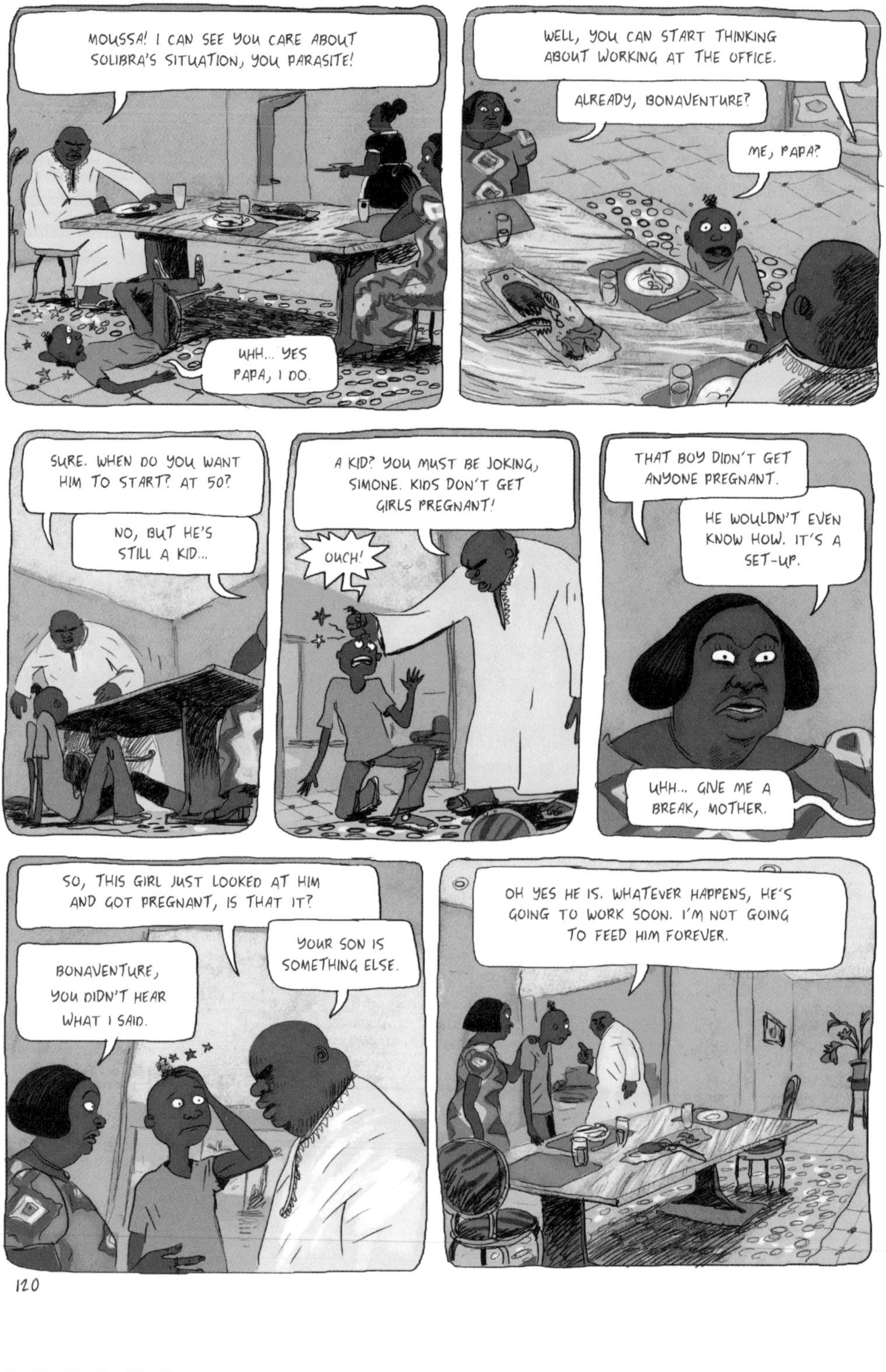
MOUSSA! I CAN SEE YOU CARE ABOUT SOLIBRA'S SITUATION, YOU PARASITE!
UHH... YES PAPA, I DO.
WELL, YOU CAN START THINKING ABOUT WORKING AT THE OFFICE.
ALREADY, BONAVENTURE?
ME, PAPA?
SURE. WHEN DO YOU WANT HIM TO START? AT 50?
NO, BUT HE'S STILL A KID...
A KID? YOU MUST BE JOKING, SIMONE. KIDS DON'T GET GIRLS PREGNANT!
OUCH!
THAT BOY DIDN'T GET ANYONE PREGNANT.
HE WOULDN'T EVEN KNOW HOW. IT'S A SET-UP.
UHH... GIVE ME A BREAK, MOTHER.
SO, THIS GIRL JUST LOOKED AT HIM AND GOT PREGNANT, IS THAT IT?
YOUR SON IS SOMETHING ELSE.
BONAVENTURE, YOU DIDN'T HEAR WHAT I SAID.
OH YES HE IS. WHATEVER HAPPENS, HE'S GOING TO WORK SOON. I'M NOT GOING TO FEED HIM FOREVER.

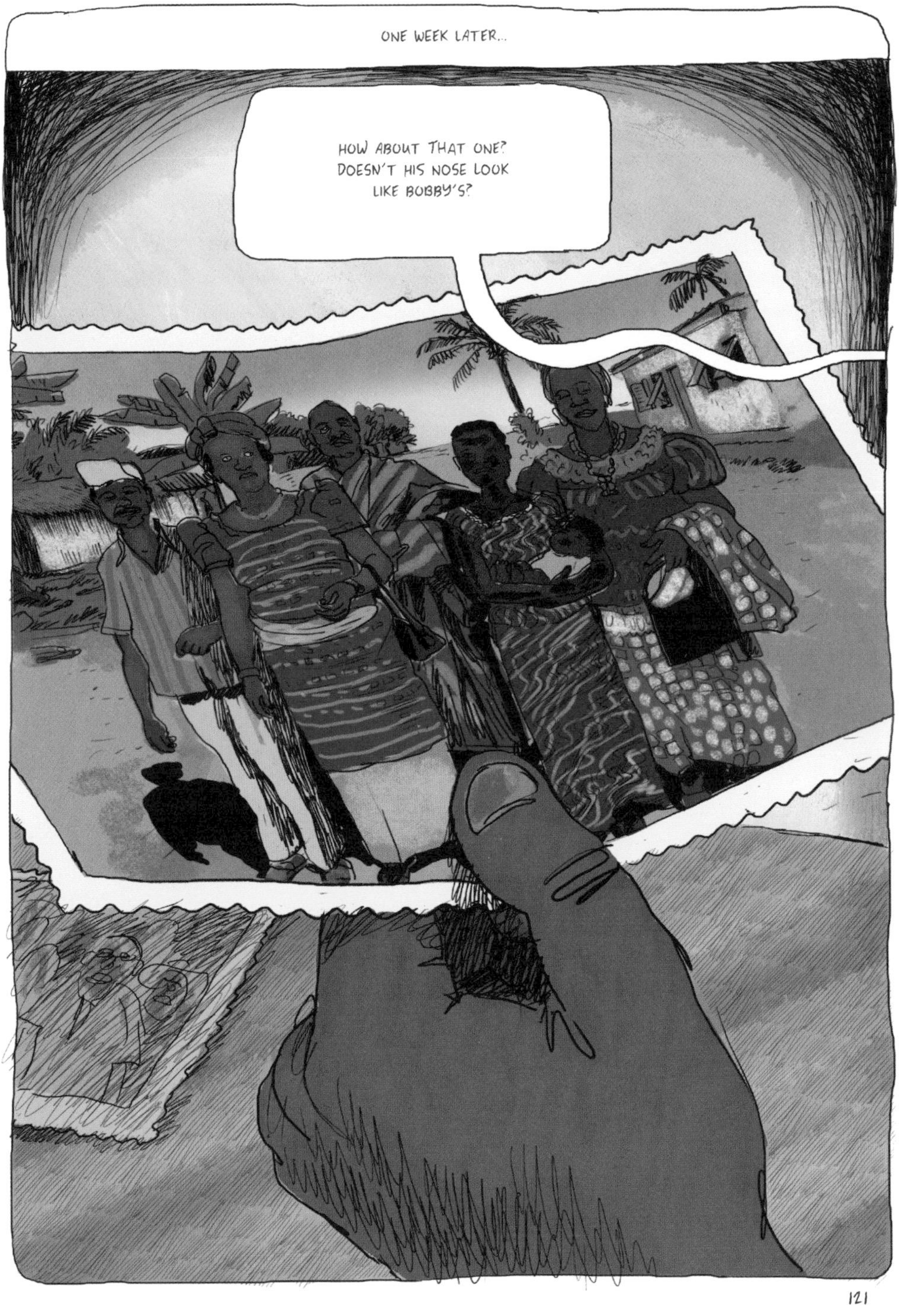
ONE WEEK LATER...
HOW ABOUT THAT ONE? DOESN'T HIS NOSE LOOK LIKE BOBBY'S?

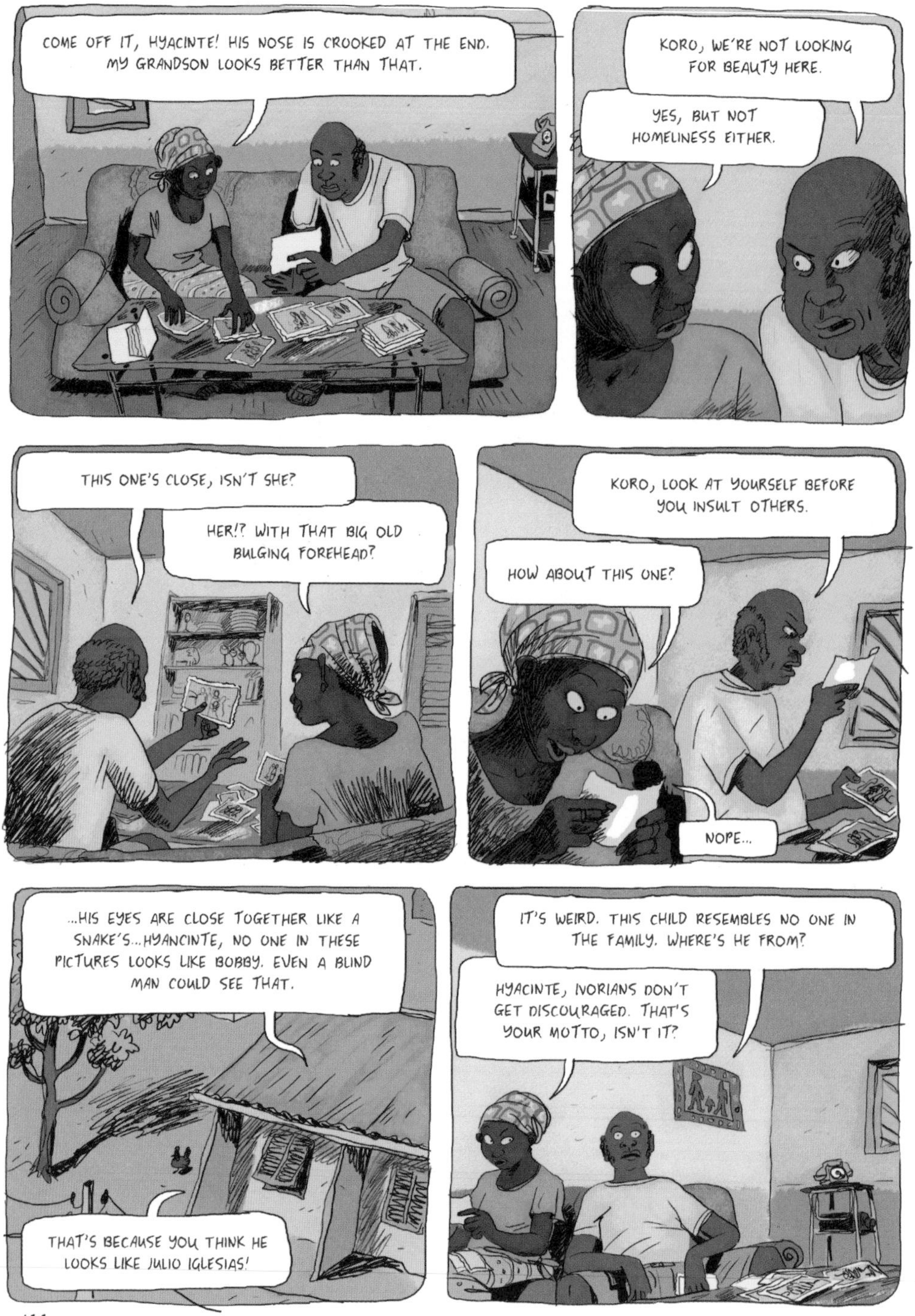
COME OFF IT, HYACINTE! HIS NOSE IS CROOKED AT THE END. MY GRANDSON LOOKS BETTER THAN THAT.
KORO, WE'RE NOT LOOKING FOR BEAUTY HERE.
YES, BUT NOT HOMELINESS EITHER.
THIS ONE'S CLOSE, ISN'T SHE?
HER!? WITH THAT BIG OLD BULGING FOREHEAD?
KORO, LOOK AT YOURSELF BEFORE YOU INSULT OTHERS.
HOW ABOUT THIS ONE?
NOPE...
...HIS EYES ARE CLOSE TOGETHER LIKE A SNAKE'S...HYANCINTE, NO ONE IN THESE PICTURES LOOKS LIKE BOBBY. EVEN A BLIND MAN COULD SEE THAT.
THAT'S BECAUSE YOU THINK HE LOOKS LIKE JULIO IGLESIAS!
IT'S WEIRD. THIS CHILD RESEMBLES NO ONE IN THE FAMILY. WHERE'S HE FROM?
HYACINTE, IVORIANS DON'T GET DISCOURAGED. THAT'S YOUR MOTTO, ISN'T IT?

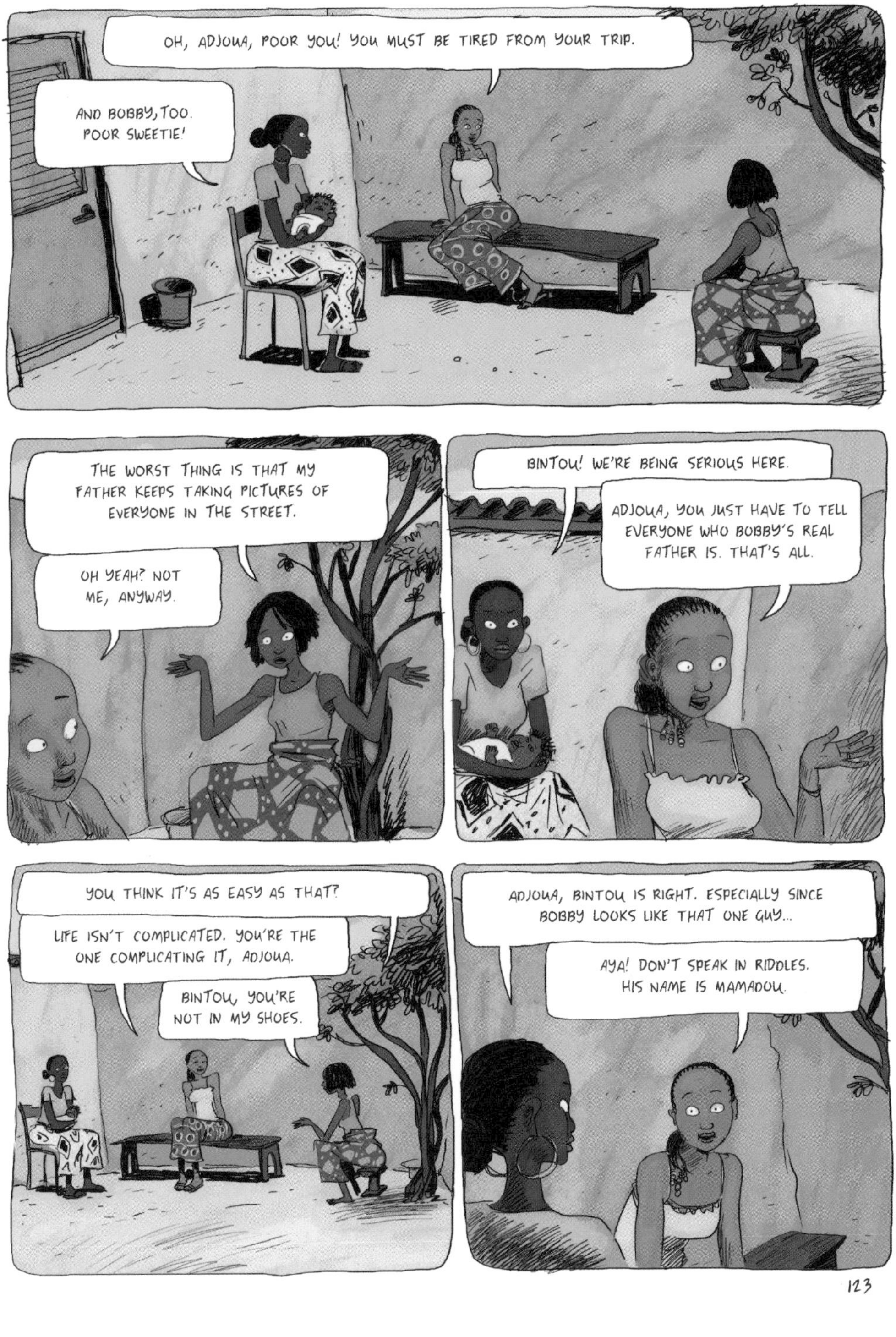
OH, ADJOUA, POOR YOU! YOU MUST BE TIRED FROM YOUR TRIP.
AND BOBBY, TOO. POOR SWEETIE!
THE WORST THING IS THAT MY FATHER KEEPS TAKING PICTURES OF EVERYONE IN THE STREET.
OH YEAH? NOT ME, ANYWAY.
BINTOU! WE'RE BEING SERIOUS HERE.
ADJOUA, YOU JUST HAVE TO TELL EVERYONE WHO BOBBY'S REAL FATHER IS. THAT'S ALL.
YOU THINK IT'S AS EASY AS THAT?
LIFE ISN'T COMPLICATED. YOU'RE THE ONE COMPLICATING IT, ADJOUA.
BINTOU, YOU'RE NOT IN MY SHOES.
ADJOUA, BINTOU IS RIGHT. ESPECIALLY SINCE BOBBY LOOKS LIKE THAT ONE GUY...
AYA! DON'T SPEAK IN RIDDLES. HIS NAME IS MAMADOU.

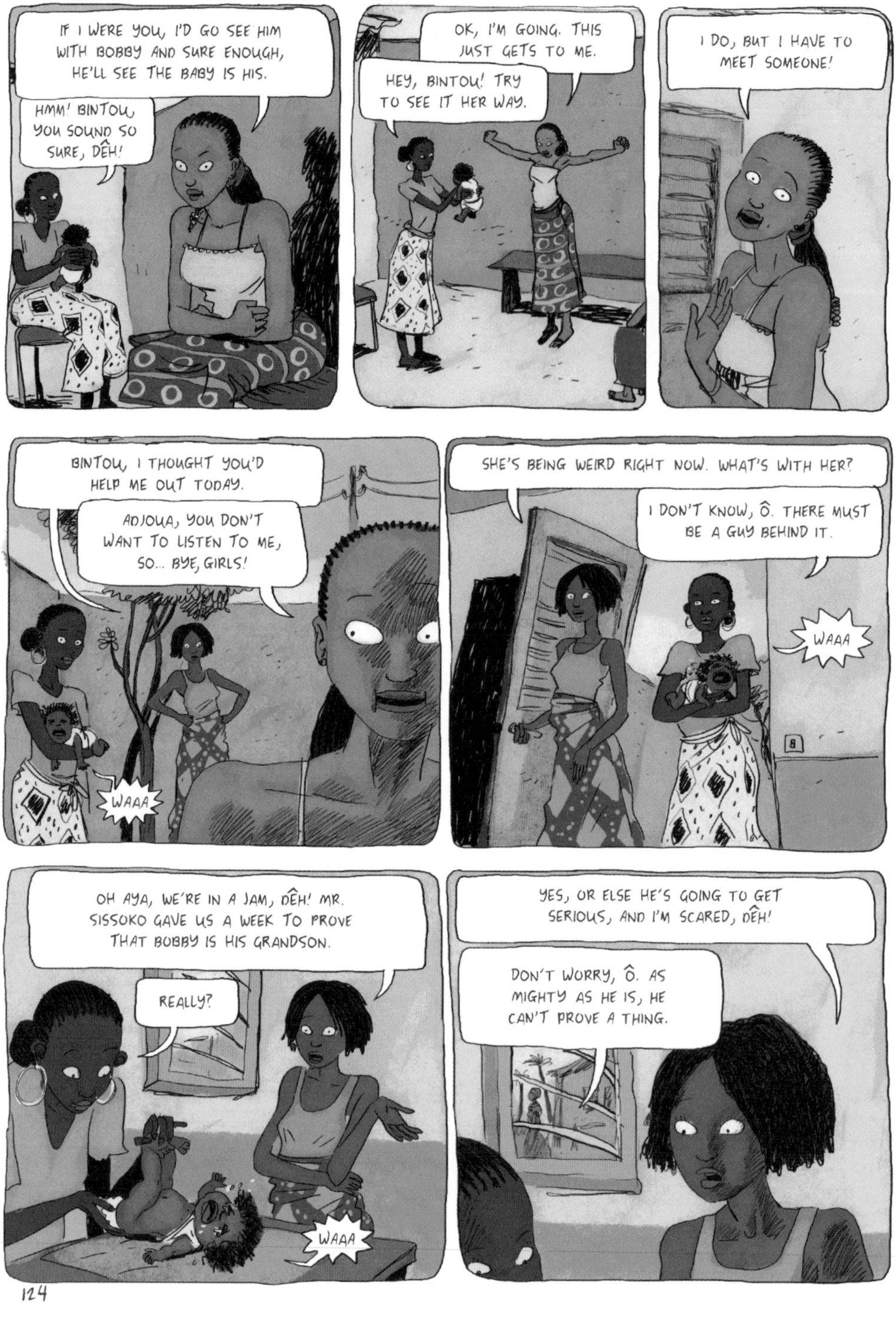
IF I WERE YOU, I'D GO SEE HIM WITH BOBBY AND SURE ENOUGH, HE'LL SEE THE BABY IS HIS.
HMM! BINTOU, YOU SOUND SO SURE, DÊH!
OK, I'M GOING. THIS JUST GETS TO ME.
HEY, BINTOU! TRY TO SEE IT HER WAY.
I DO, BUT I HAVE TO MEET SOMEONE!
BINTOU, I THOUGHT YOU'D HELP ME OUT TODAY.
ADJOUA, YOU DON'T WANT TO LISTEN TO ME, SO... BYE, GIRLS!
WAAA
SHE'S BEING WEIRD RIGHT NOW. WHAT'S WITH HER?
I DON'T KNOW, Ô. THERE MUST BE A GUY BEHIND IT.
WAAA
8
OH AYA, WE'RE IN A JAM, DÊH! MR. SISSOKO GAVE US A WEEK TO PROVE THAT BOBBY IS HIS GRANDSON.
REALLY?
WAAA
YES, OR ELSE HE'S GOING TO GET SERIOUS, AND I'M SCARED, DÊH!
DON'T WORRY, Ô. AS MIGHTY AS HE IS, HE CAN'T PROVE A THING.

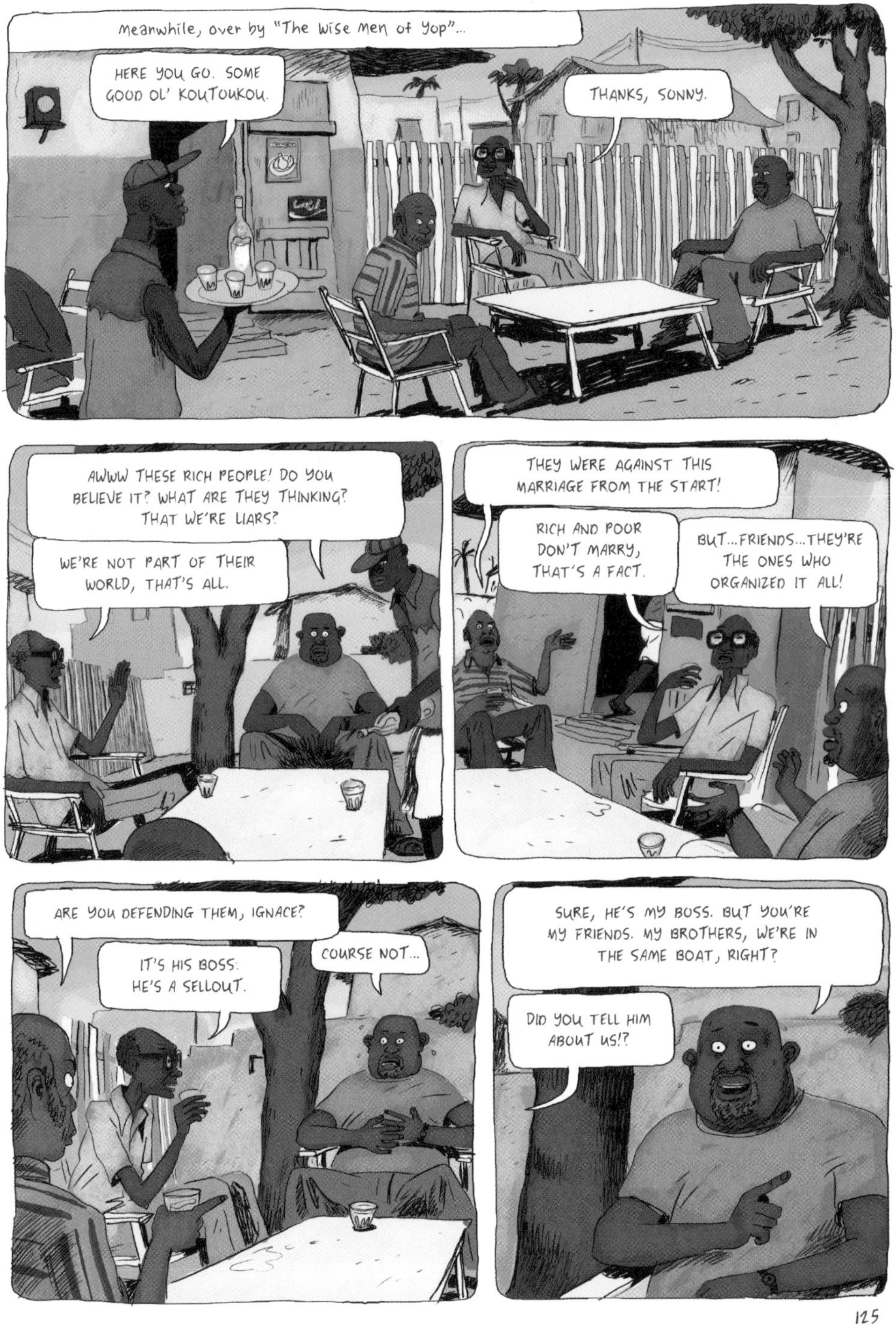
Meanwhile, over by "The Wise Men of Yop"...
HERE YOU GO. SOME GOOD OL' KOUTOUKOU.
THANKS, SONNY.
AWWW THESE RICH PEOPLE! DO YOU BELIEVE IT? WHAT ARE THEY THINKING? THAT WE'RE LIARS?
WE'RE NOT PART OF THEIR WORLD, THAT'S ALL.
THEY WERE AGAINST THIS MARRIAGE FROM THE START!
RICH AND POOR DON'T MARRY, THAT'S A FACT.
BUT...FRIENDS...THEY'RE THE ONES WHO ORGANIZED IT ALL!
ARE YOU DEFENDING THEM, IGNACE?
IT'S HIS BOSS: HE'S A SELLOUT.
COURSE NOT...
SURE, HE'S MY BOSS. BUT YOU'RE MY FRIENDS. MY BROTHERS, WE'RE IN THE SAME BOAT, RIGHT?
DID YOU TELL HIM ABOUT US!?

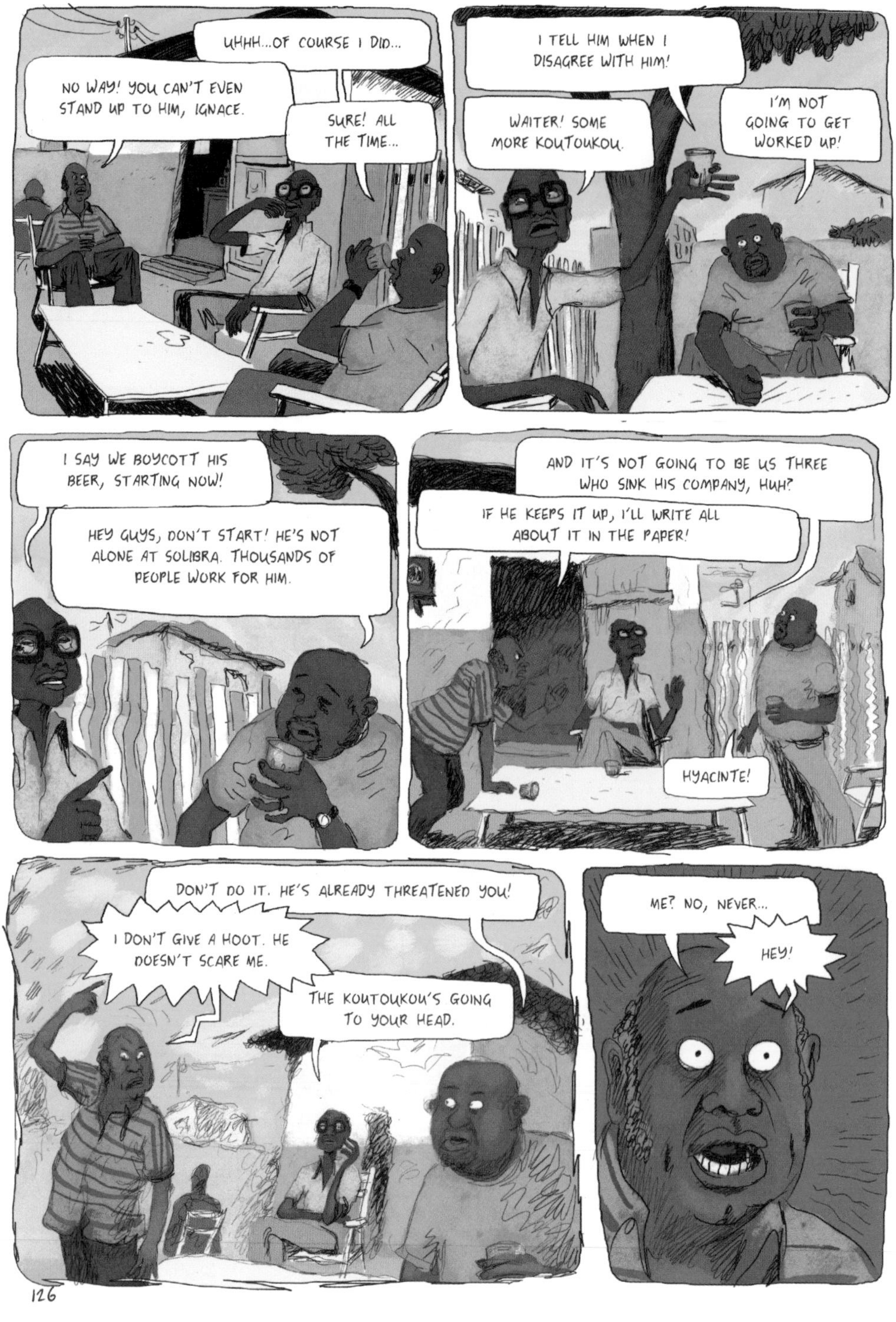
UHHH...OF COURSE I DID...
NO WAY! YOU CAN'T EVEN STAND UP TO HIM, IGNACE.
SURE! ALL THE TIME...
I TELL HIM WHEN I DISAGREE WITH HIM!
WAITER! SOME MORE KOUTOUKOU.
I'M NOT GOING TO GET WORKED UP!
I SAY WE BOYCOTT HIS BEER, STARTING NOW!
HEY GUYS, DON'T START! HE'S NOT ALONE AT SOLIBRA. THOUSANDS OF PEOPLE WORK FOR HIM.
AND IT'S NOT GOING TO BE US THREE WHO SINK HIS COMPANY, HUH?
IF HE KEEPS IT UP, I'LL WRITE ALL ABOUT IT IN THE PAPER!
HYACINTE!
DON'T DO IT. HE'S ALREADY THREATENED YOU!
I DON'T GIVE A HOOT. HE DOESN'T SCARE ME.
THE KOUTOUKOU'S GOING TO YOUR HEAD.
ME? NO, NEVER...
HEY!

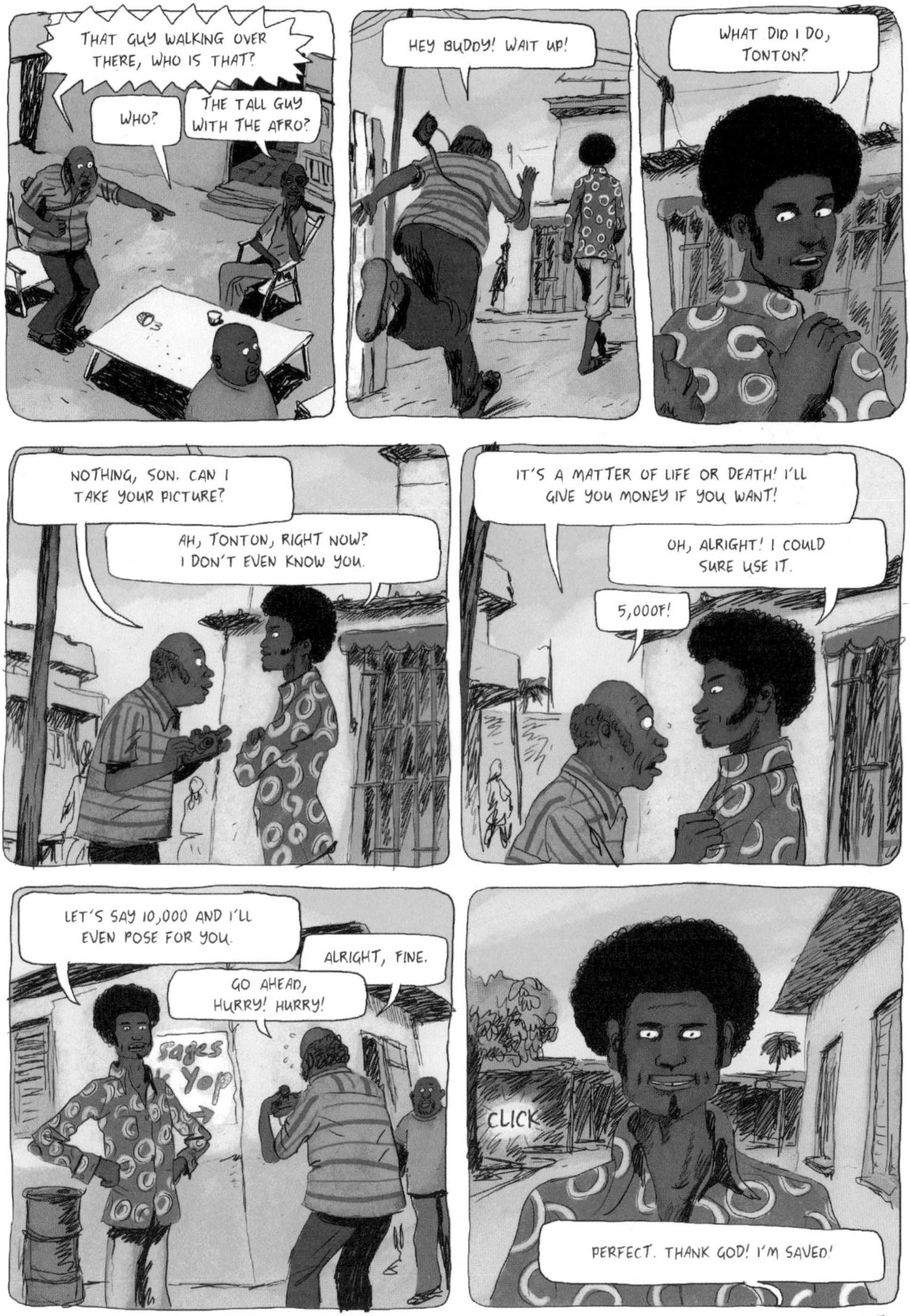
THAT GUY WALKING OVER THERE, WHO IS THAT?
WHO?
THE TALL GUY WITH THE AFRO?
HEY BUDDY! WAIT UP!
WHAT DID I DO, TONTON?
NOTHING, SON. CAN I TAKE YOUR PICTURE?
AH, TONTON, RIGHT NOW? I DON'T EVEN KNOW YOU.
IT'S A MATTER OF LIFE OR DEATH! I'LL GIVE YOU MONEY IF YOU WANT!
OH, ALRIGHT! I COULD SURE USE IT.
5,000F!
LET'S SAY 10,000 AND I'LL EVEN POSE FOR YOU.
ALRIGHT, FINE.
GO AHEAD, HURRY! HURRY!
CLICK
PERFECT. THANK GOD! I'M SAVED!

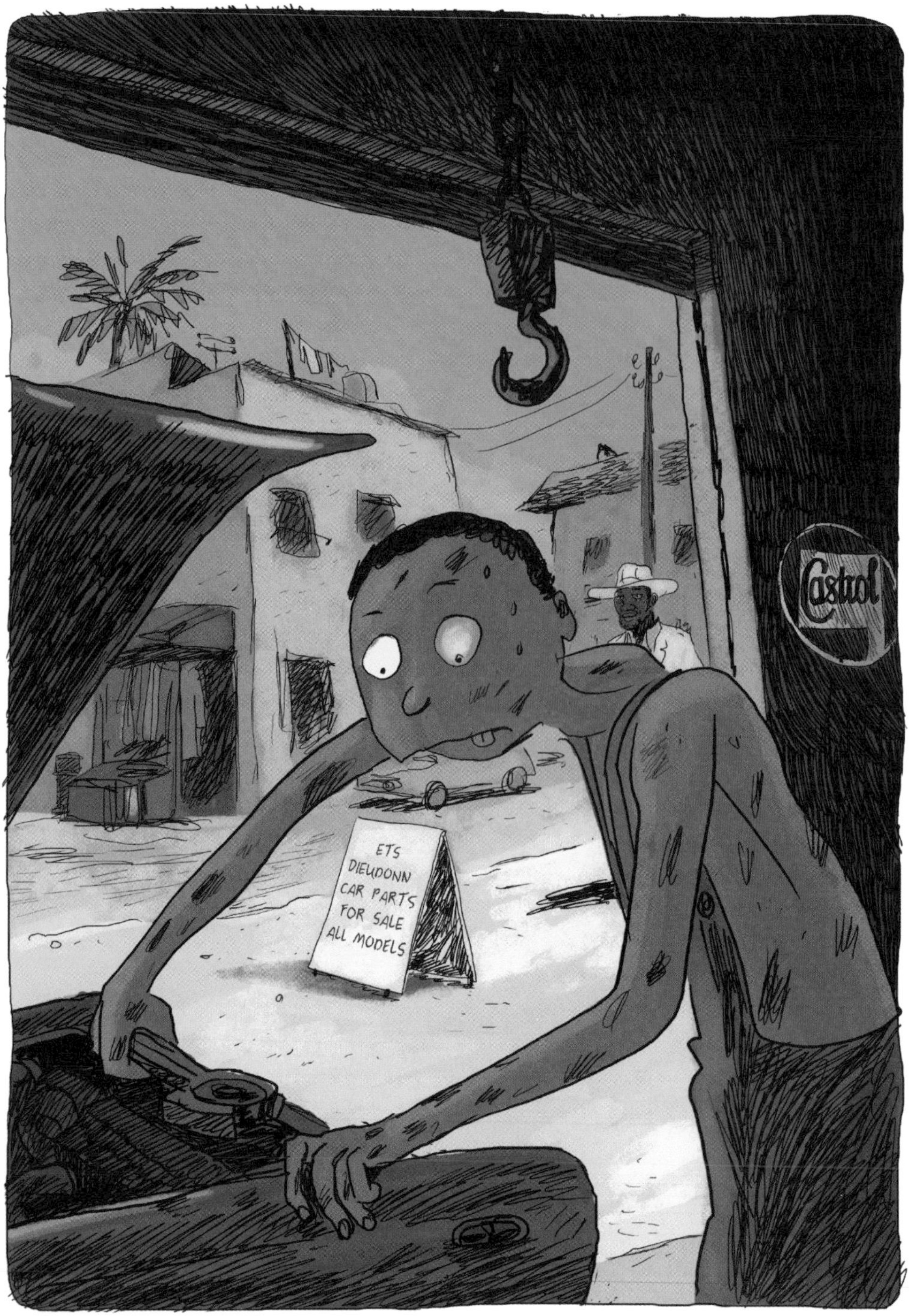
Castrol
ETS
DIEUDONN
CAR PARTS
FOR SALE
ALL MODELS

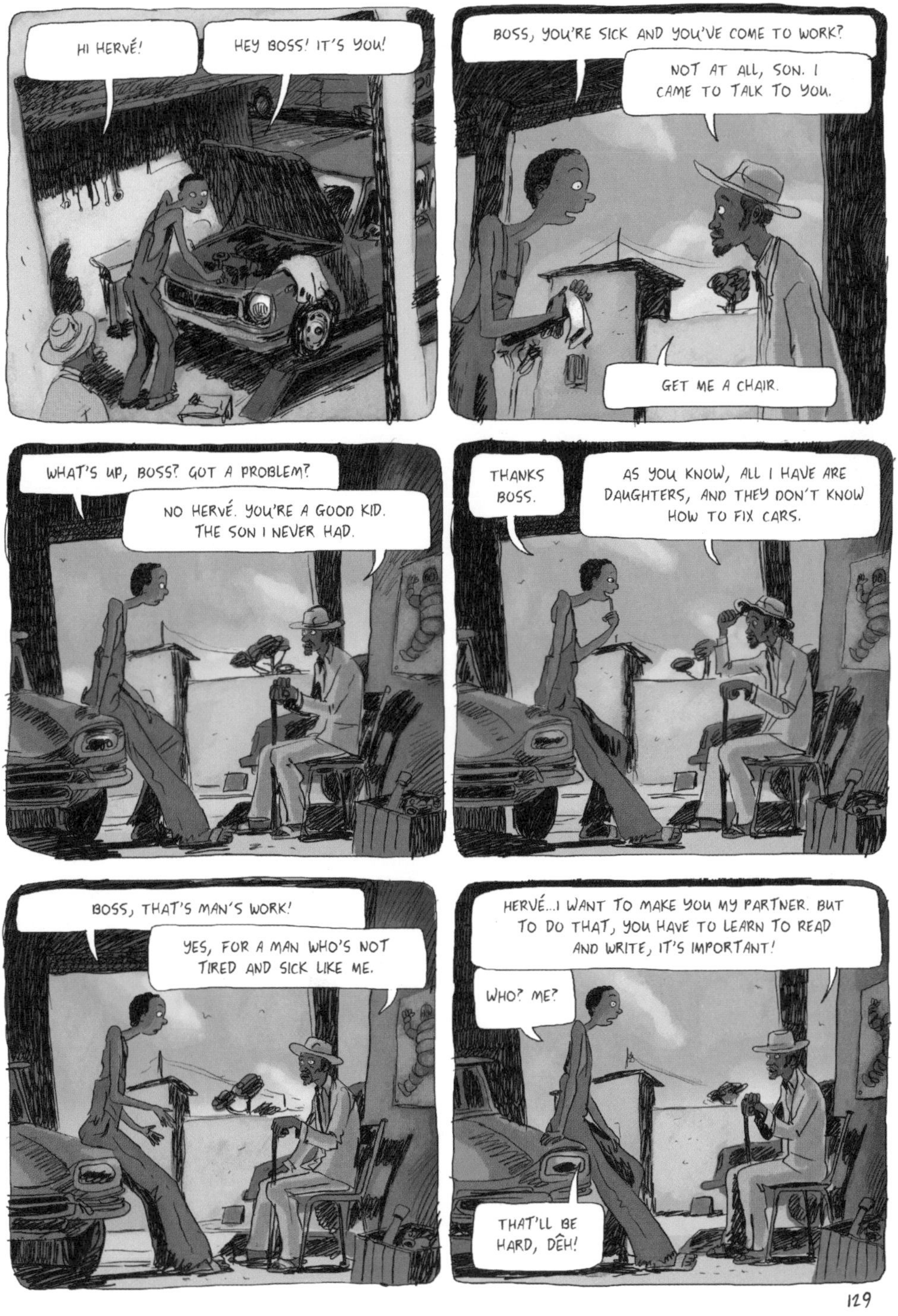
HI HERVÉ!
HEY BOSS! IT'S YOU!
BOSS, YOU'RE SICK AND YOU'VE COME TO WORK?
NOT AT ALL, SON. I CAME TO TALK TO YOU.
GET ME A CHAIR.
WHAT'S UP, BOSS? GOT A PROBLEM?
NO HERVÉ. YOU'RE A GOOD KID. THE SON I NEVER HAD.
THANKS BOSS.
AS YOU KNOW, ALL I HAVE ARE DAUGHTERS, AND THEY DON'T KNOW HOW TO FIX CARS.
BOSS, THAT'S MAN'S WORK!
YES, FOR A MAN WHO'S NOT TIRED AND SICK LIKE ME.
HERVÉ...I WANT TO MAKE YOU MY PARTNER. BUT TO DO THAT, YOU HAVE TO LEARN TO READ AND WRITE, IT'S IMPORTANT!
WHO? ME?
THAT'LL BE HARD, DÊH!

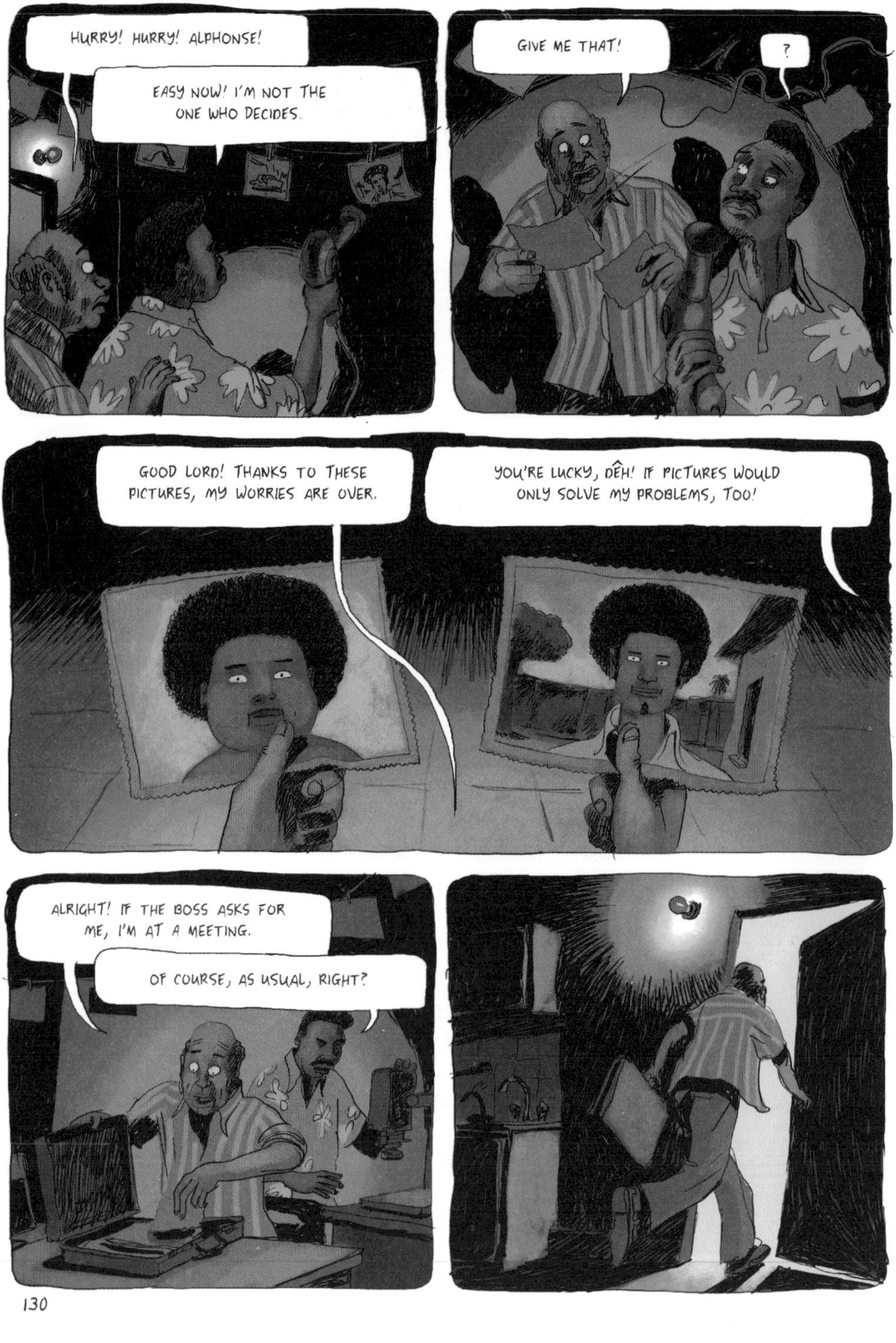
HURRY! HURRY! ALPHONSE!
EASY NOW! I'M NOT THE ONE WHO DECIDES.
GIVE ME THAT!
?
GOOD LORD! THANKS TO THESE PICTURES, MY WORRIES ARE OVER.
YOU'RE LUCKY, DÊH! IF PICTURES WOULD ONLY SOLVE MY PROBLEMS, TOO!
ALRIGHT! IF THE BOSS ASKS FOR ME, I'M AT A MEETING.
OF COURSE, AS USUAL, RIGHT?

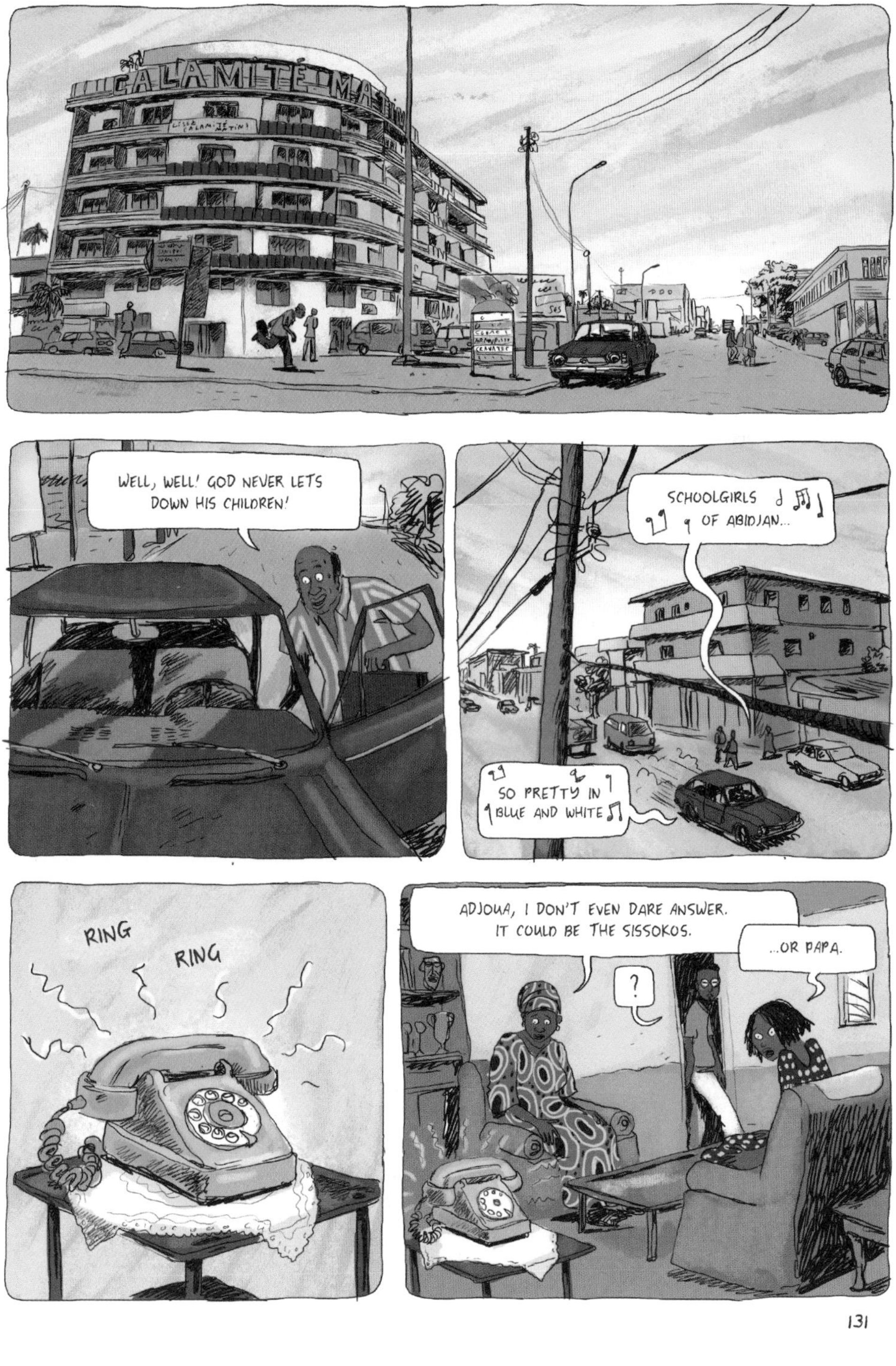
CALAMITÉ MATINI
WELL, WELL! GOD NEVER LETS DOWN HIS CHILDREN!
SCHOOLGIRLS OF ABIDJAN...
SO PRETTY IN BLUE AND WHITE
RING RING
ADJOUA, I DON'T EVEN DARE ANSWER. IT COULD BE THE SISSOKOS.
?
...OR PAPA.

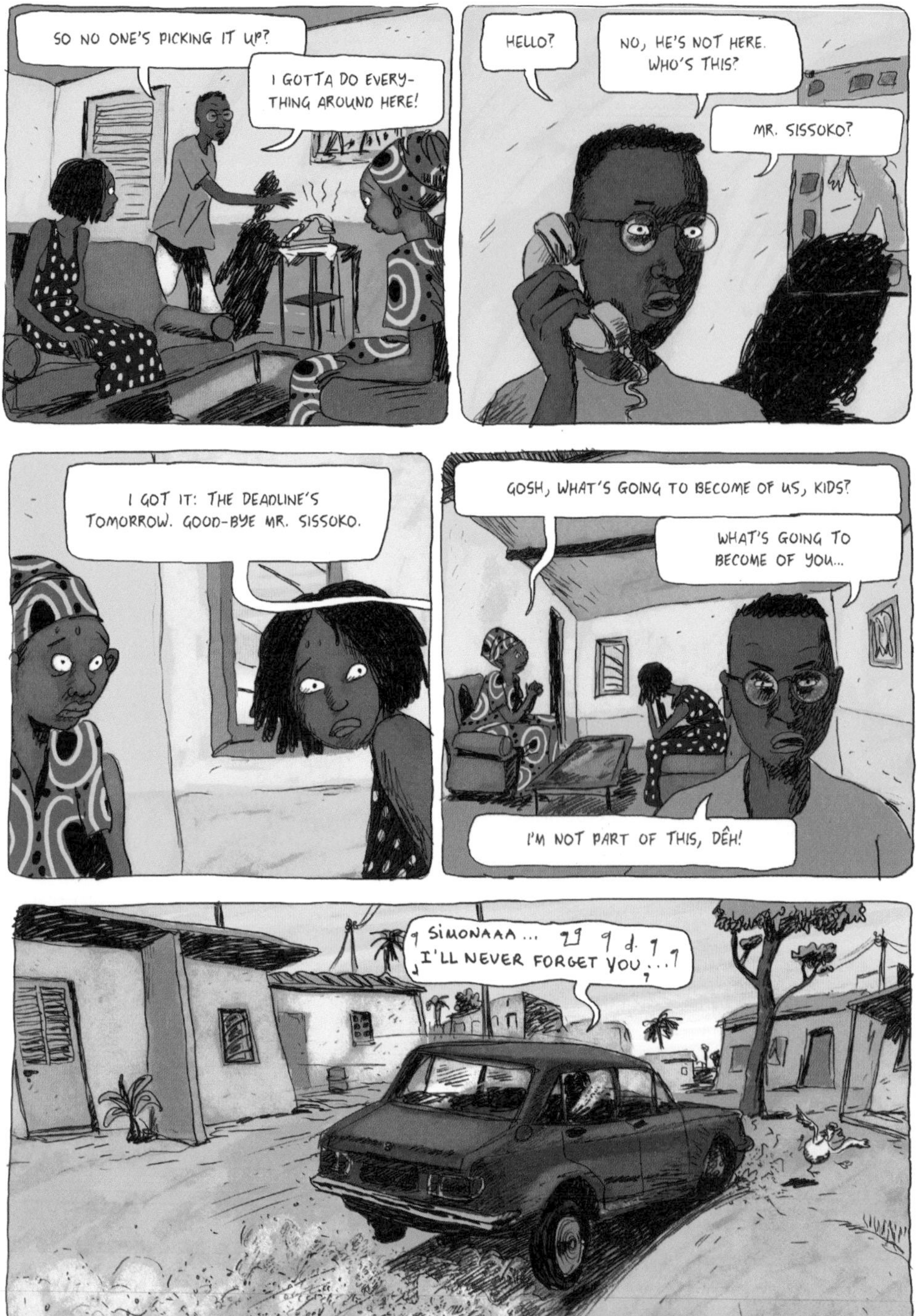
SO NO ONE'S PICKING IT UP?
I GOTTA DO EVERY-THING AROUND HERE!
HELLO?
NO, HE'S NOT HERE. WHO'S THIS?
MR. SISSOKO?
I GOT IT: THE DEADLINE'S TOMORROW. GOOD-BYE MR. SISSOKO.
GOSH, WHAT'S GOING TO BECOME OF US, KIDS?
WHAT'S GOING TO BECOME OF YOU...
I'M NOT PART OF THIS, DÊH!
SIMONAAA...
I'LL NEVER FORGET YOU...

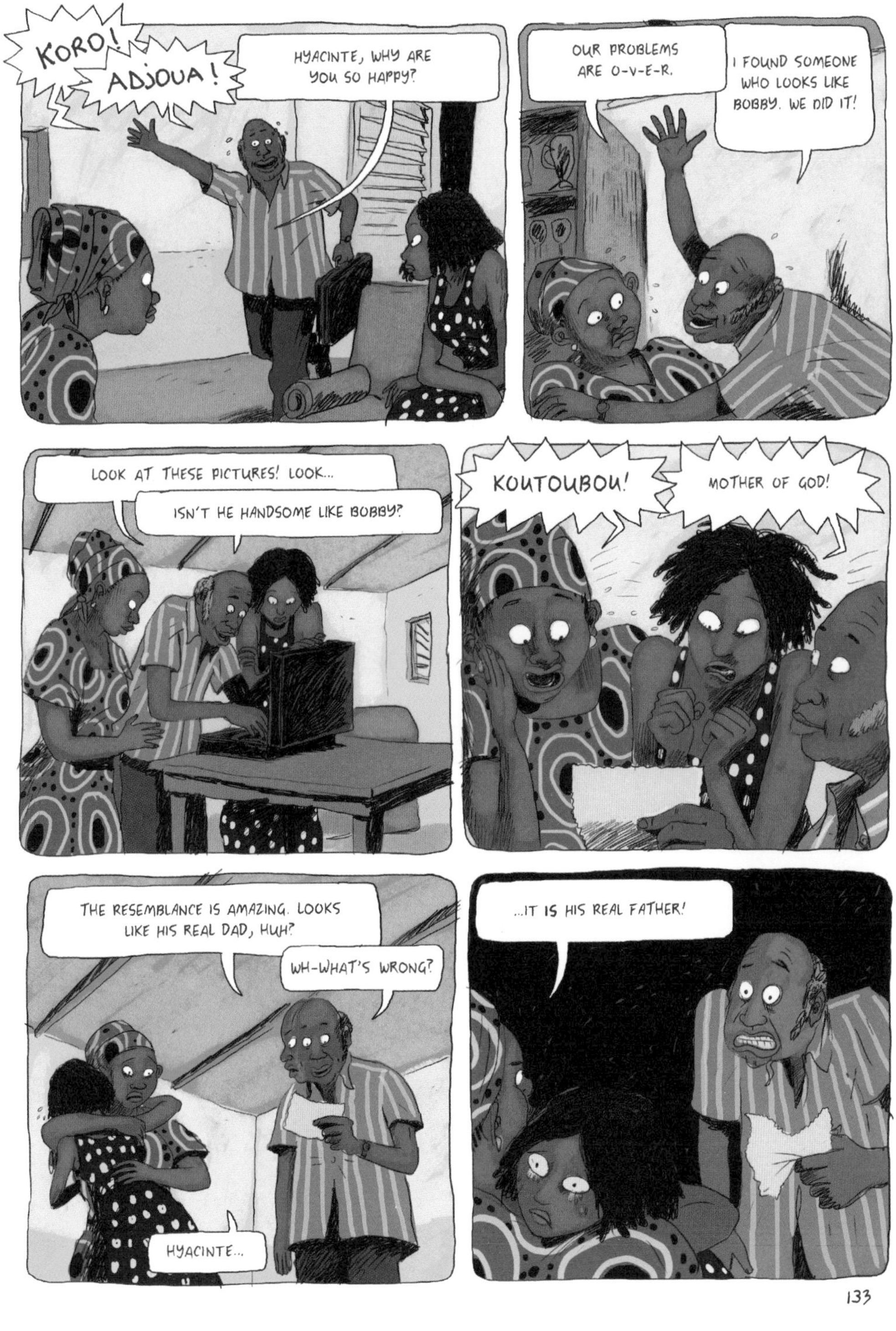

KORO!
ADJOUA!
HYACINTE, WHY ARE YOU SO HAPPY?
OUR PROBLEMS ARE O-V-E-R.
I FOUND SOMEONE WHO LOOKS LIKE BOBBY. WE DID IT!
LOOK AT THESE PICTURES! LOOK...
ISN'T HE HANDSOME LIKE BOBBY?
KOUTOUBOU!
MOTHER OF GOD!
THE RESEMBLANCE IS AMAZING. LOOKS LIKE HIS REAL DAD, HUH?
WH-WHAT'S WRONG?
HYACINTE...
...IT IS HIS REAL FATHER!

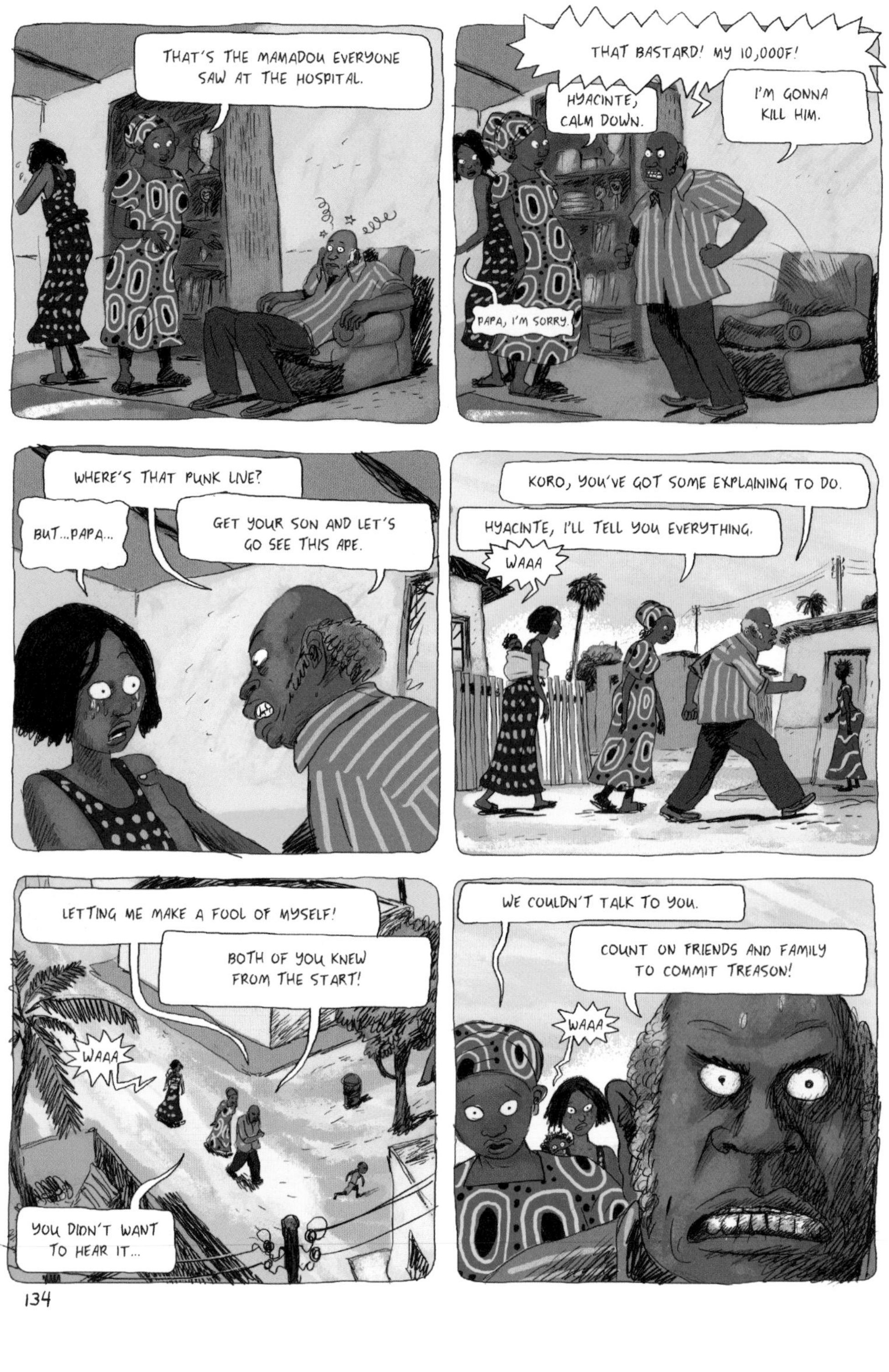
THAT'S THE MAMADOU EVERYONE SAW AT THE HOSPITAL.
THAT BASTARD! MY 10,000F!
HYACINTE, CALM DOWN.
I'M GONNA KILL HIM.
PAPA, I'M SORRY.
WHERE'S THAT PUNK LIVE?
BUT...PAPA...
GET YOUR SON AND LET'S GO SEE THIS APE.
KORO, YOU'VE GOT SOME EXPLAINING TO DO.
HYACINTE, I'LL TELL YOU EVERYTHING.
WAAA
LETTING ME MAKE A FOOL OF MYSELF!
BOTH OF YOU KNEW FROM THE START!
WAAA
YOU DIDN'T WANT TO HEAR IT...
WE COULDN'T TALK TO YOU.
COUNT ON FRIENDS AND FAMILY TO COMMIT TREASON!
WAAA

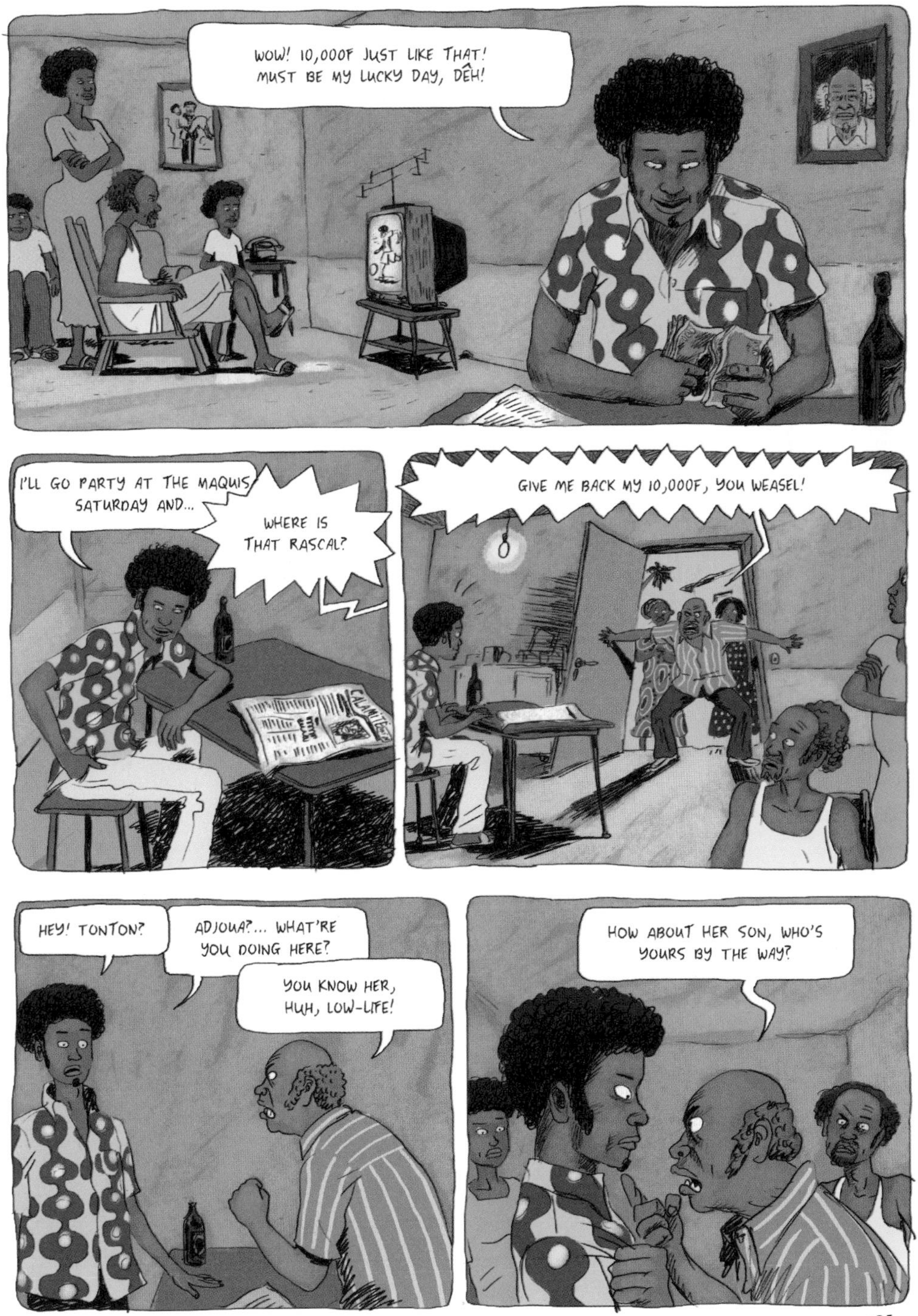
WOW! 10,000F JUST LIKE THAT! MUST BE MY LUCKY DAY, DÊH!
I'LL GO PARTY AT THE MAQUIS SATURDAY AND...
WHERE IS THAT RASCAL?
GIVE ME BACK MY 10,000F, YOU WEASEL!
HEY! TONTON?
ADJOUA?... WHAT'RE YOU DOING HERE?
YOU KNOW HER, HUH, LOW-LIFE!
HOW ABOUT HER SON, WHO'S YOURS BY THE WAY?

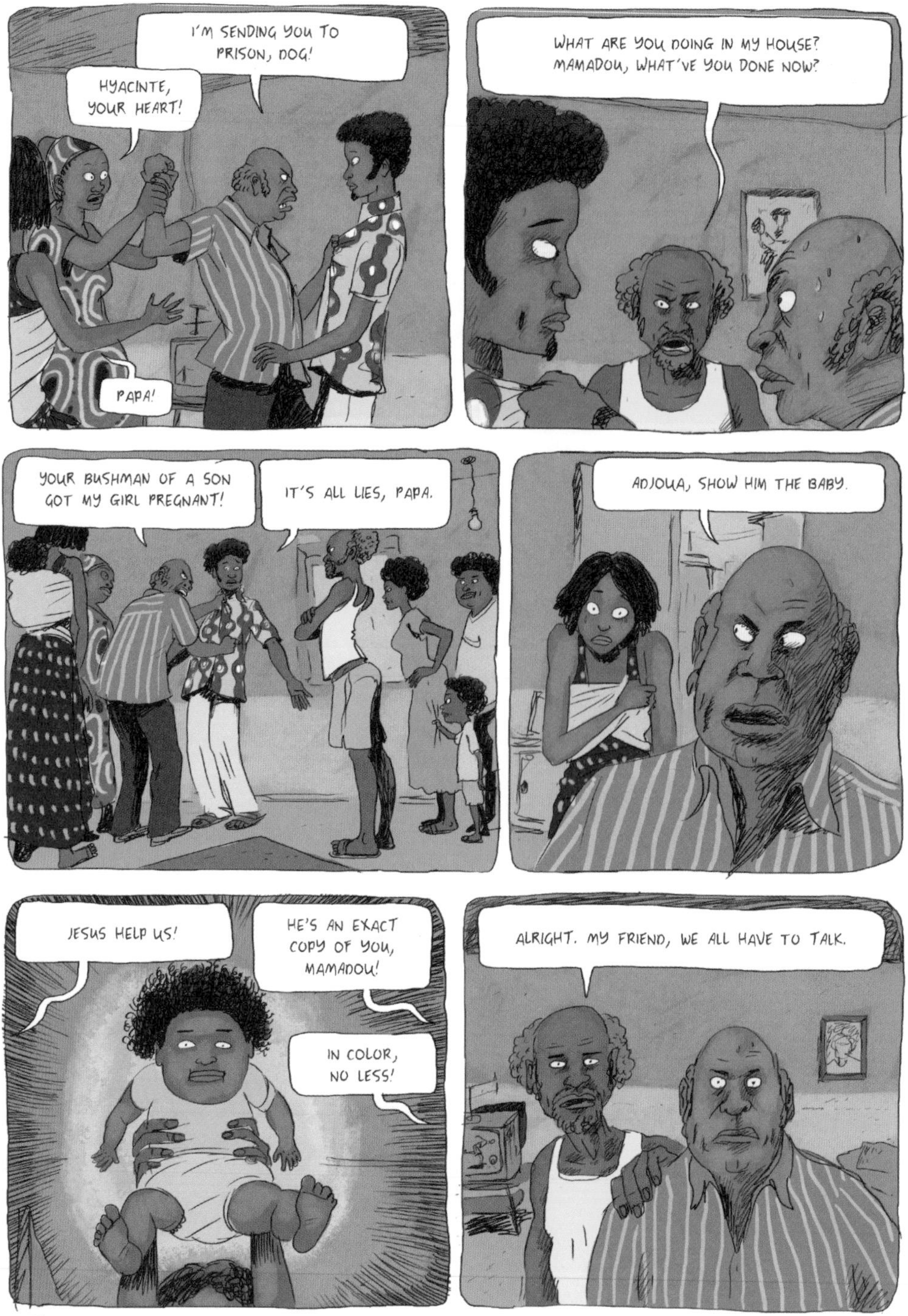
I'M SENDING YOU TO PRISON, DOG!
HYACINTE, YOUR HEART!
PAPA!
WHAT ARE YOU DOING IN MY HOUSE? MAMADOU, WHAT'VE YOU DONE NOW?
YOUR BUSHMAN OF A SON GOT MY GIRL PREGNANT!
IT'S ALL LIES, PAPA.
ADJOUA, SHOW HIM THE BABY.
JESUS HELP US!
HE'S AN EXACT COPY OF YOU, MAMADOU!
IN COLOR, NO LESS!
ALRIGHT. MY FRIEND, WE ALL HAVE TO TALK.

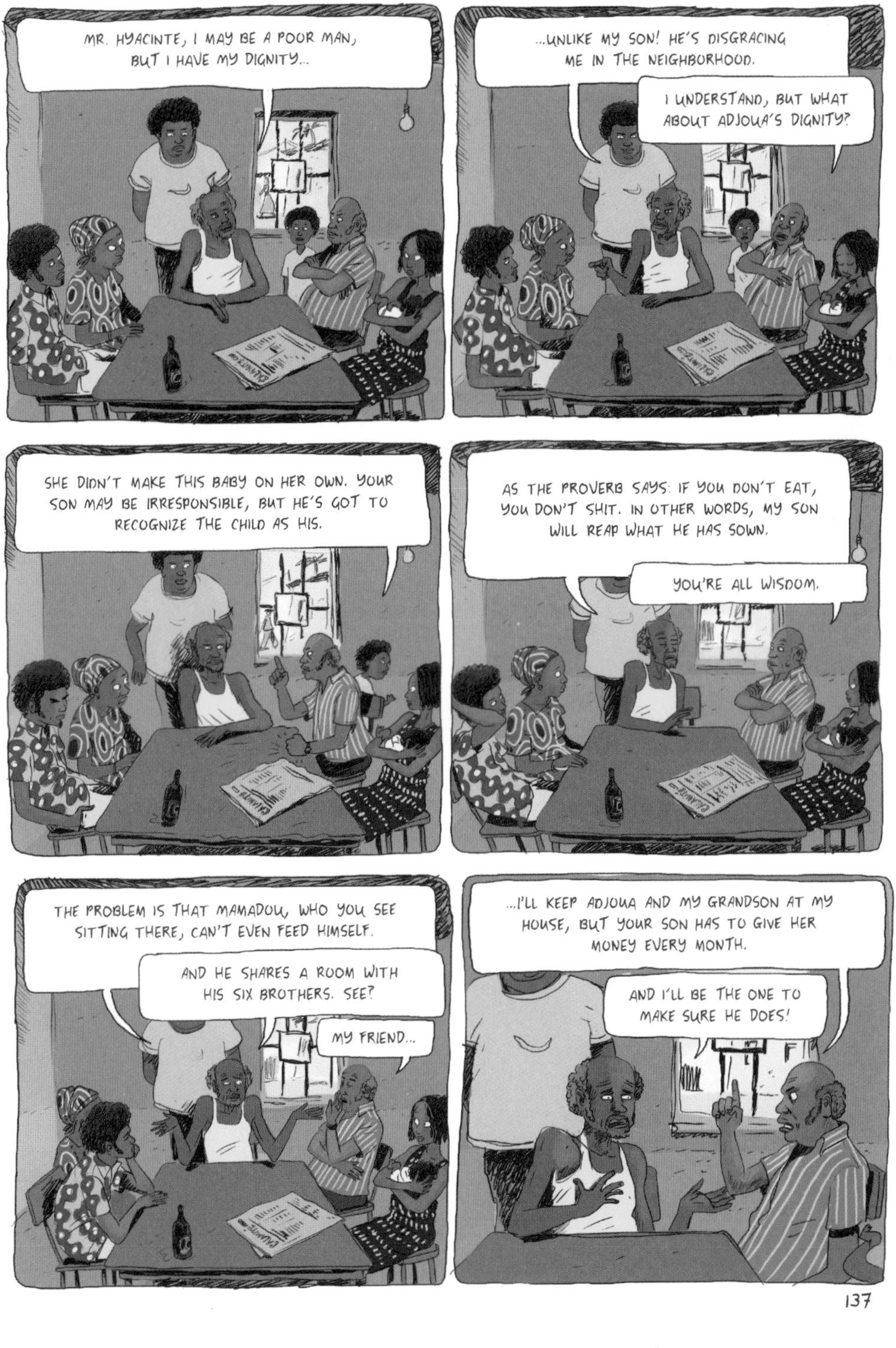
MR. HYACINTE, I MAY BE A POOR MAN, BUT I HAVE MY DIGNITY...
...UNLIKE MY SON! HE'S DISGRACING ME IN THE NEIGHBORHOOD.
I UNDERSTAND, BUT WHAT ABOUT ADJOUA'S DIGNITY?
SHE DIDN'T MAKE THIS BABY ON HER OWN. YOUR SON MAY BE IRRESPONSIBLE, BUT HE'S GOT TO RECOGNIZE THE CHILD AS HIS.
AS THE PROVERB SAYS: IF YOU DON'T EAT, YOU DON'T SHIT. IN OTHER WORDS, MY SON WILL REAP WHAT HE HAS SOWN.
YOU'RE ALL WISDOM.
THE PROBLEM IS THAT MAMADOU, WHO YOU SEE SITTING THERE, CAN'T EVEN FEED HIMSELF.
AND HE SHARES A ROOM WITH HIS SIX BROTHERS. SEE?
MY FRIEND...
...I'LL KEEP ADJOUA AND MY GRANDSON AT MY HOUSE, BUT YOUR SON HAS TO GIVE HER MONEY EVERY MONTH.
AND I'LL BE THE ONE TO MAKE SURE HE DOES!

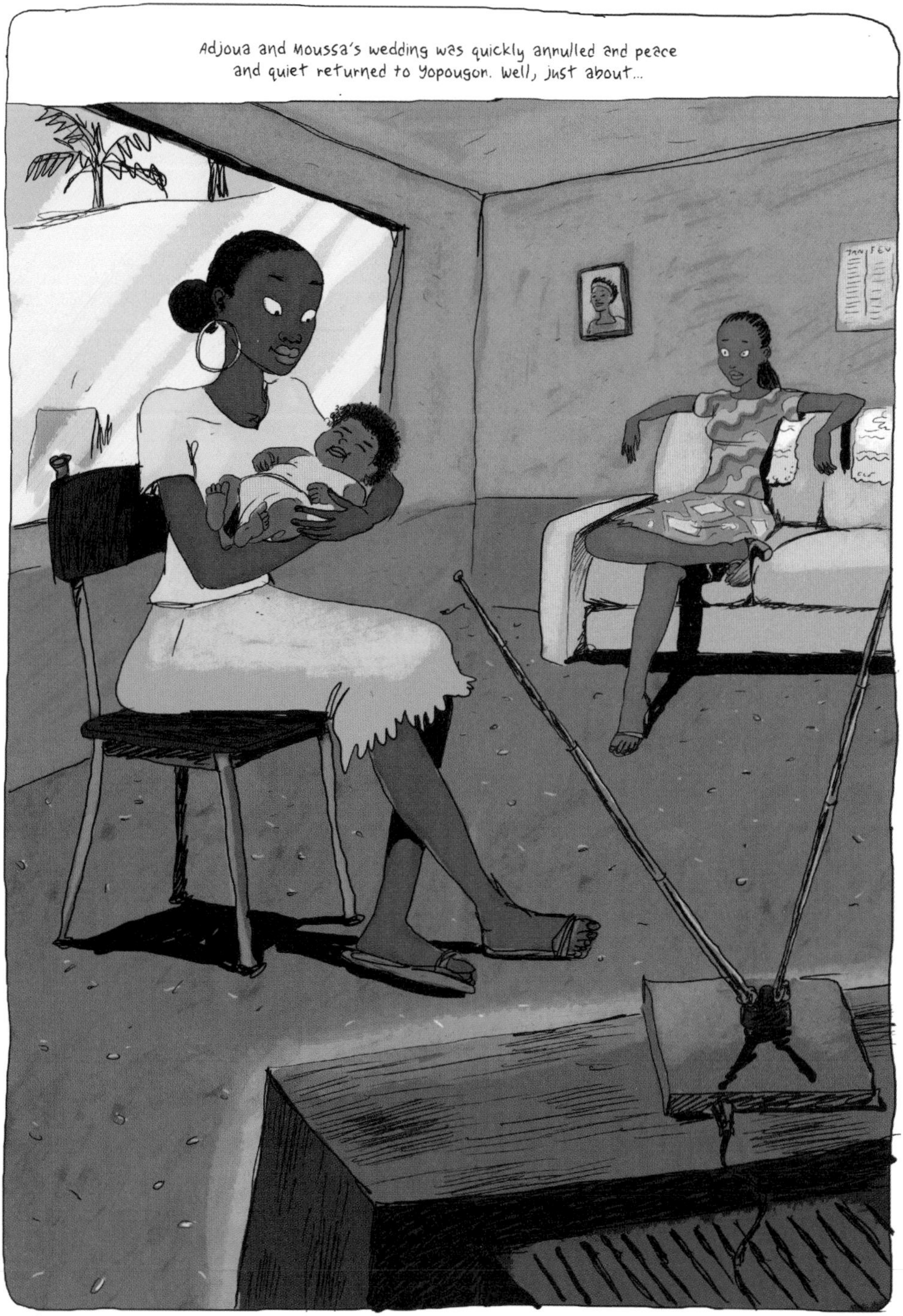
Adjoua and Moussa's wedding was quickly annulled and peace and quiet returned to Yopougon. Well, just about...

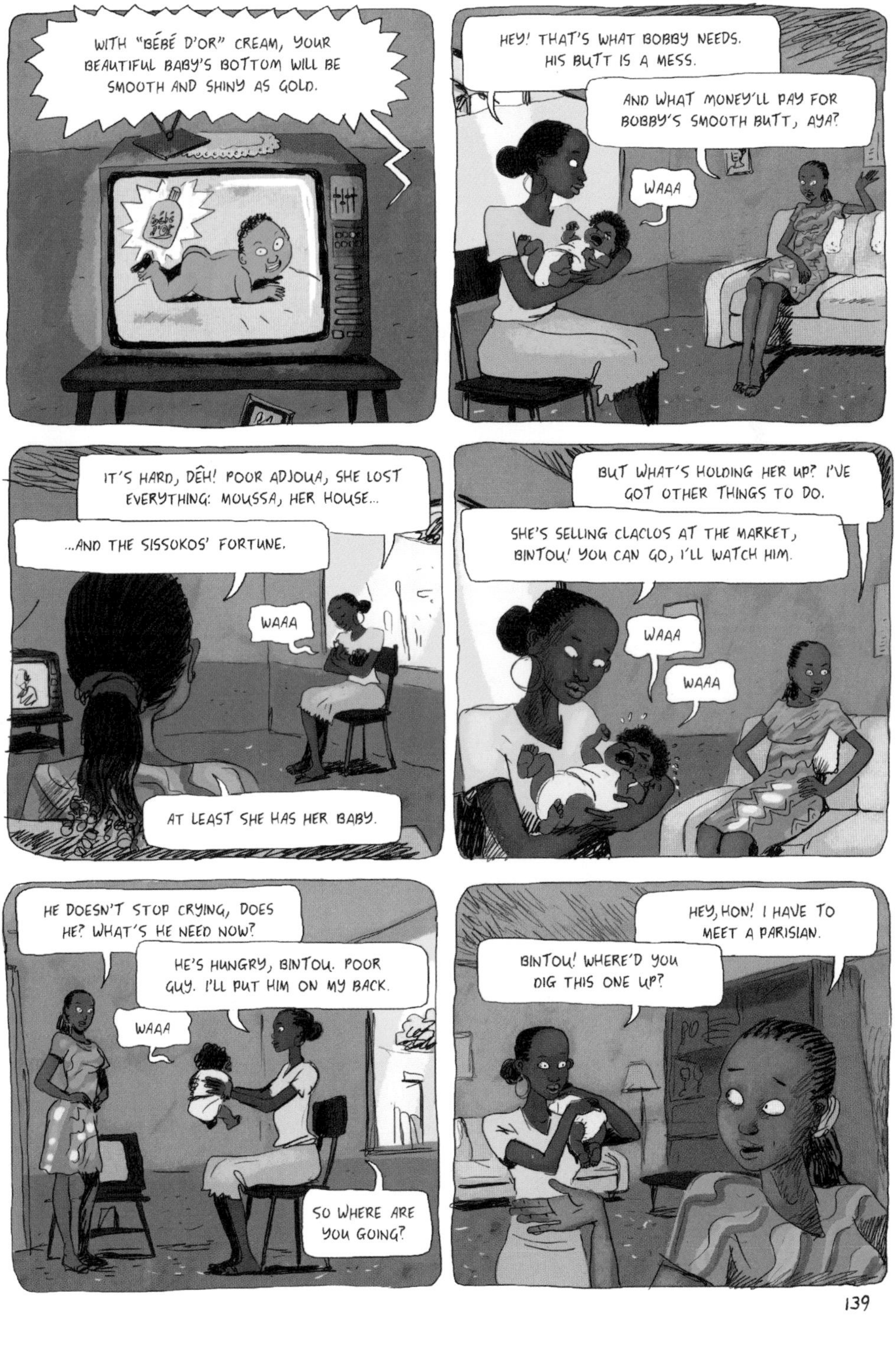
WITH "BÉBÉ D'OR" CREAM, YOUR BEAUTIFUL BABY'S BOTTOM WILL BE SMOOTH AND SHINY AS GOLD.
HEY! THAT'S WHAT BOBBY NEEDS. HIS BUTT IS A MESS.
AND WHAT MONEY'LL PAY FOR BOBBY'S SMOOTH BUTT, AYA?
WAAA
IT'S HARD, DÊH! POOR ADJOUA, SHE LOST EVERYTHING: MOUSSA, HER HOUSE...
...AND THE SISSOKOS' FORTUNE.
WAAA
AT LEAST SHE HAS HER BABY.
BUT WHAT'S HOLDING HER UP? I'VE GOT OTHER THINGS TO DO.
SHE'S SELLING CLACLOS AT THE MARKET, BINTOU! YOU CAN GO, I'LL WATCH HIM.
WAAA
WAAA
HE DOESN'T STOP CRYING, DOES HE? WHAT'S HE NEED NOW?
HE'S HUNGRY, BINTOU. POOR GUY. I'LL PUT HIM ON MY BACK.
WAAA
SO WHERE ARE YOU GOING?
HEY, HON! I HAVE TO MEET A PARISIAN.
BINTOU! WHERE'D YOU DIG THIS ONE UP?

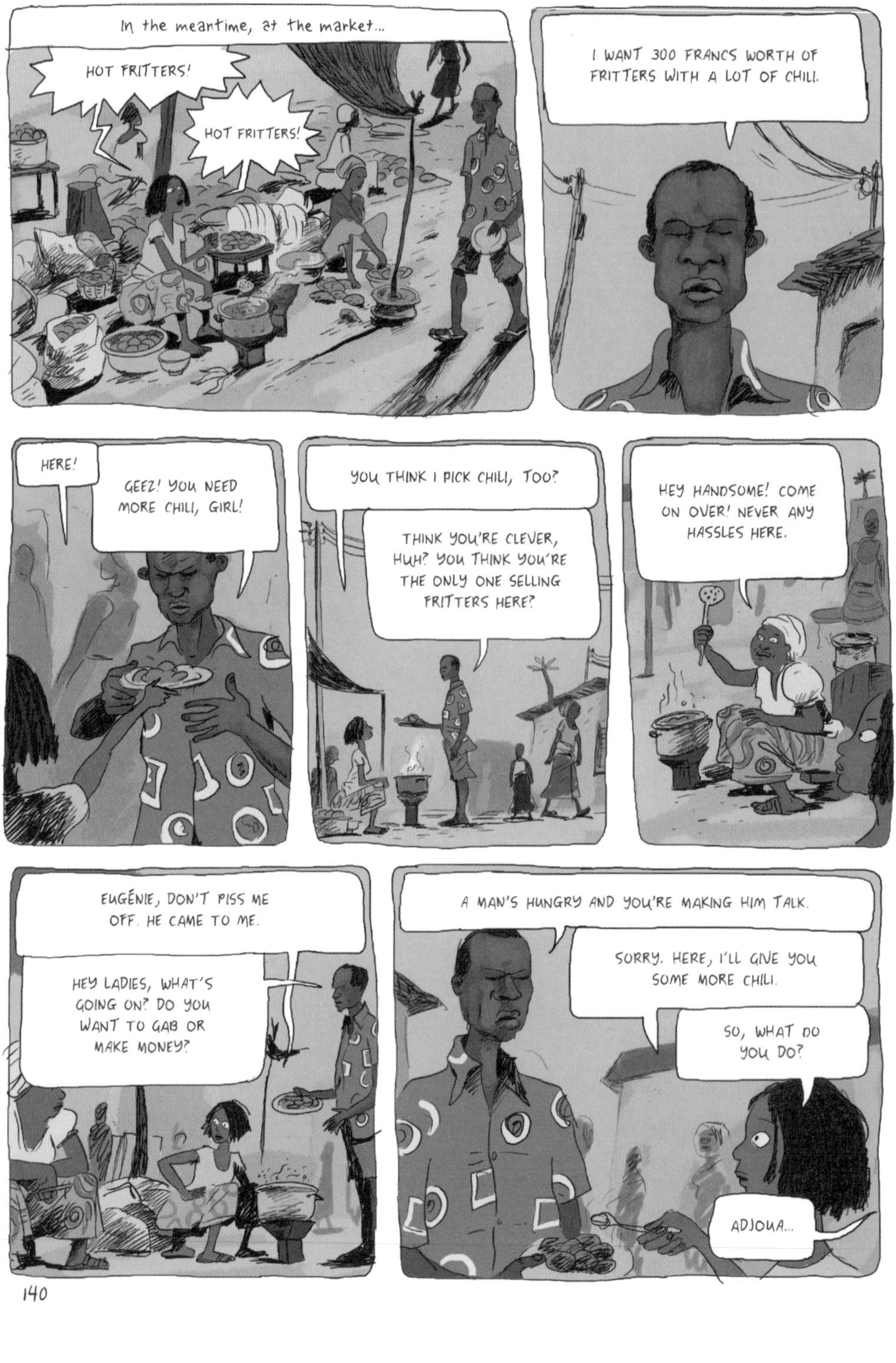
In the meantime, at the market...
HOT FRITTERS!
HOT FRITTERS!
I WANT 300 FRANCS WORTH OF FRITTERS WITH A LOT OF CHILI.
HERE!
GEEZ! YOU NEED MORE CHILI, GIRL!
YOU THINK I PICK CHILI, TOO?
THINK YOU'RE CLEVER, HUH? YOU THINK YOU'RE THE ONLY ONE SELLING FRITTERS HERE?
HEY HANDSOME! COME ON OVER! NEVER ANY HASSLES HERE.
EUGÉNIE, DON'T PISS ME OFF. HE CAME TO ME.
HEY LADIES, WHAT'S GOING ON? DO YOU WANT TO GAB OR MAKE MONEY?
A MAN'S HUNGRY AND YOU'RE MAKING HIM TALK.
SORRY. HERE, I'LL GIVE YOU SOME MORE CHILI.
SO, WHAT DO YOU DO?
ADJOUA...

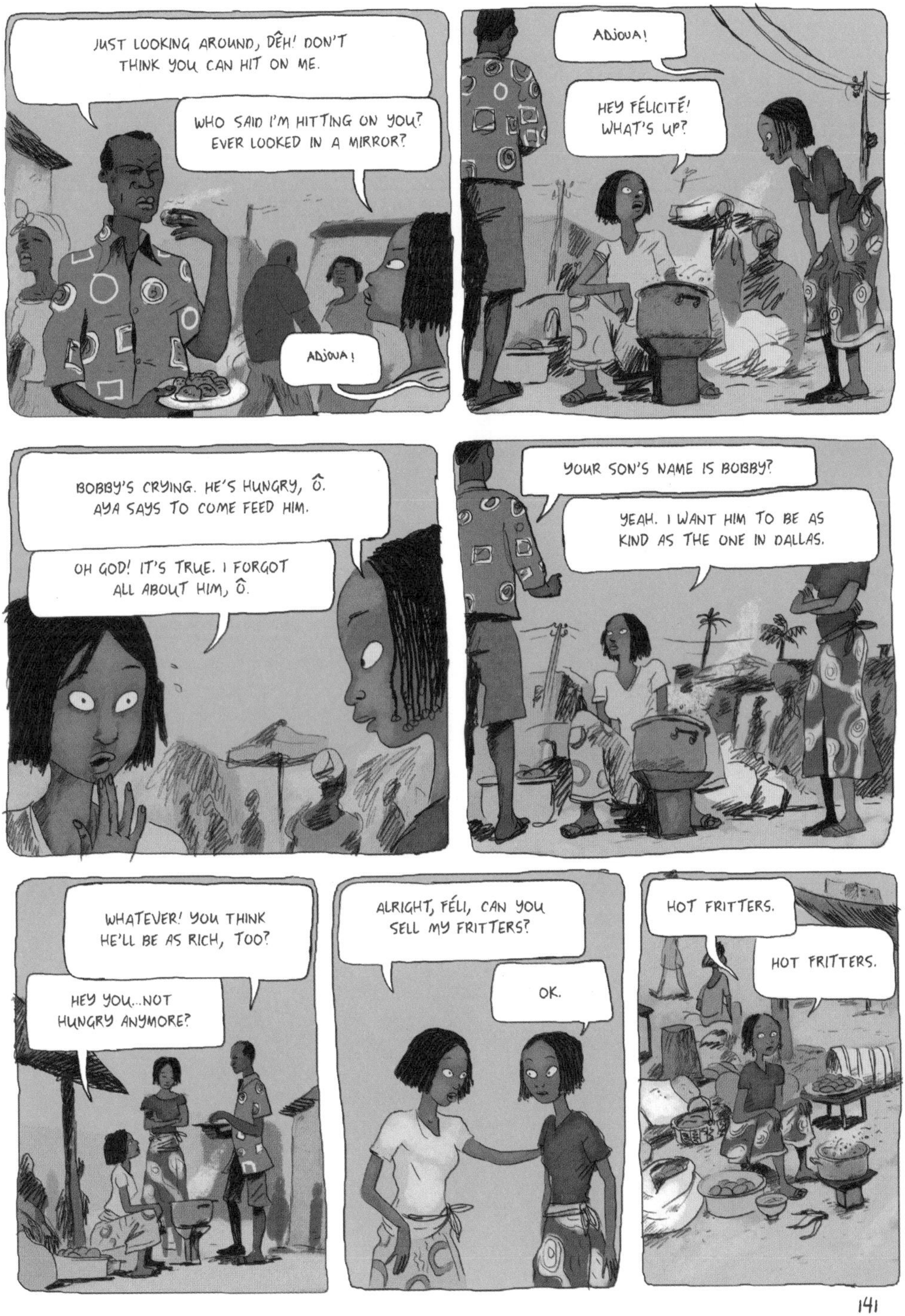

JUST LOOKING AROUND, DÊH! DON'T THINK YOU CAN HIT ON ME.
WHO SAID I'M HITTING ON YOU? EVER LOOKED IN A MIRROR?
ADJOUA!
ADJOUA!
HEY FÉLICITÉ! WHAT'S UP?
BOBBY'S CRYING. HE'S HUNGRY, Ô. AYA SAYS TO COME FEED HIM.
OH GOD! IT'S TRUE. I FORGOT ALL ABOUT HIM, Ô.
YOUR SON'S NAME IS BOBBY?
YEAH. I WANT HIM TO BE AS KIND AS THE ONE IN DALLAS.
WHATEVER! YOU THINK HE'LL BE AS RICH, TOO?
HEY YOU...NOT HUNGRY ANYMORE?
ALRIGHT, FÉLI, CAN YOU SELL MY FRITTERS?
OK.
HOT FRITTERS.
HOT FRITTERS.

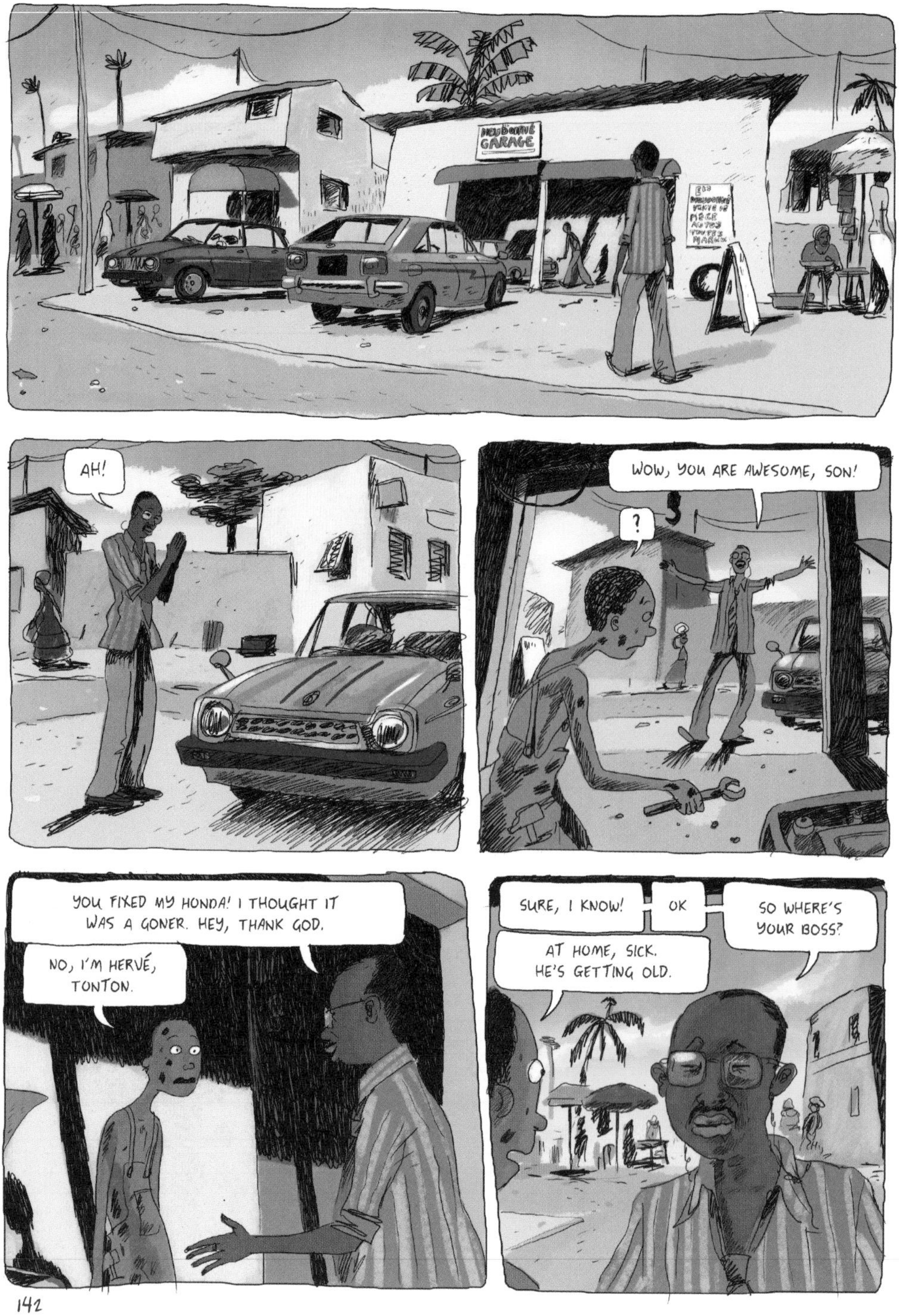
GARAGE
AH!
WOW, YOU ARE AWESOME, SON!
?
YOU FIXED MY HONDA! I THOUGHT IT WAS A GONER. HEY, THANK GOD.
NO, I'M HERVÉ, TONTON.
SURE, I KNOW!
OK
SO WHERE'S YOUR BOSS?
AT HOME, SICK. HE'S GETTING OLD.

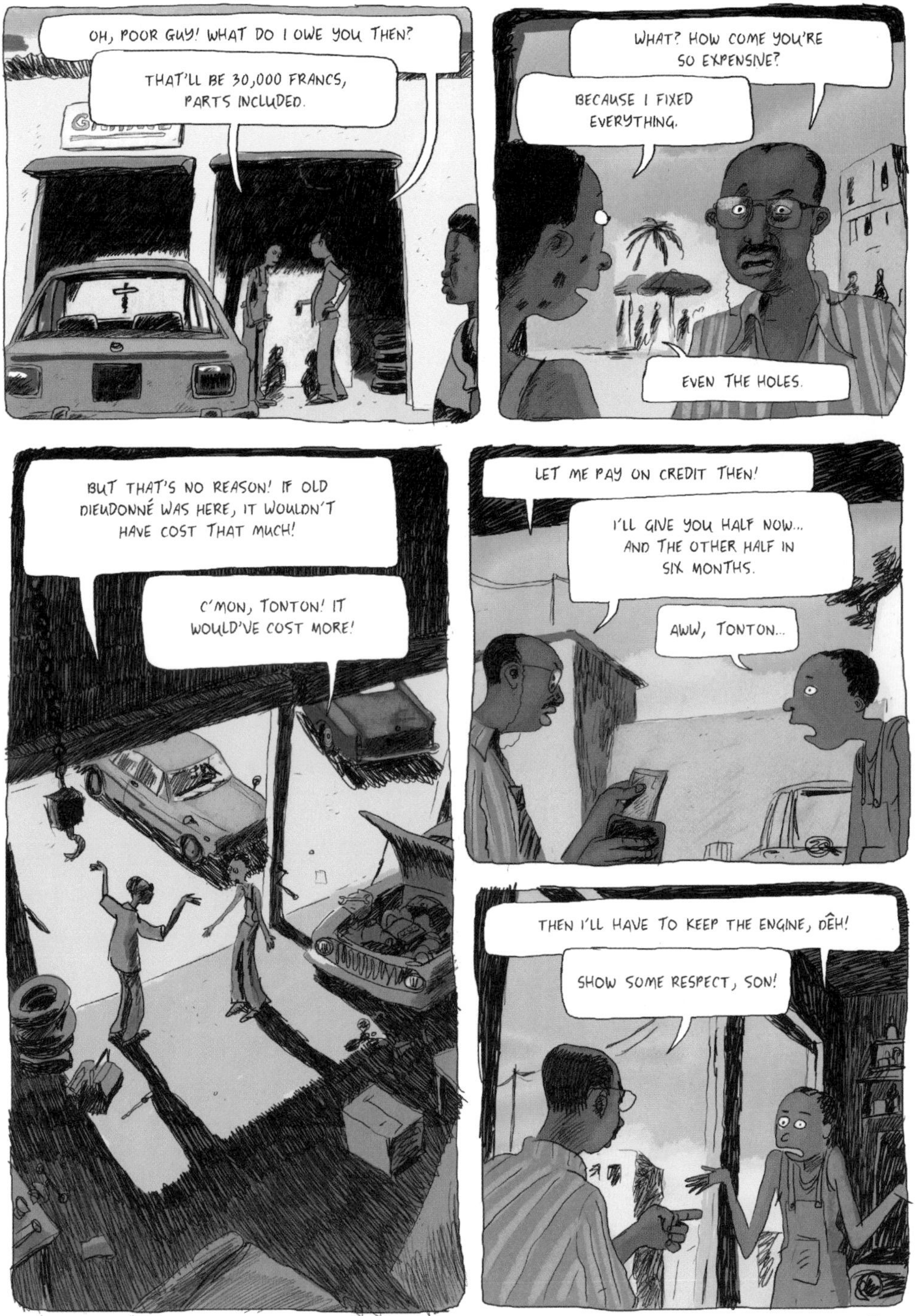
OH, POOR GUY! WHAT DO I OWE YOU THEN?
THAT'LL BE 30,000 FRANCS, PARTS INCLUDED.
WHAT? HOW COME YOU'RE SO EXPENSIVE?
BECAUSE I FIXED EVERYTHING.
EVEN THE HOLES.
BUT THAT'S NO REASON! IF OLD DIEUDONNÉ WAS HERE, IT WOULDN'T HAVE COST THAT MUCH!
C'MON, TONTON! IT WOULD'VE COST MORE!
LET ME PAY ON CREDIT THEN!
I'LL GIVE YOU HALF NOW... AND THE OTHER HALF IN SIX MONTHS.
AWW, TONTON...
THEN I'LL HAVE TO KEEP THE ENGINE, DÊH!
SHOW SOME RESPECT, SON!

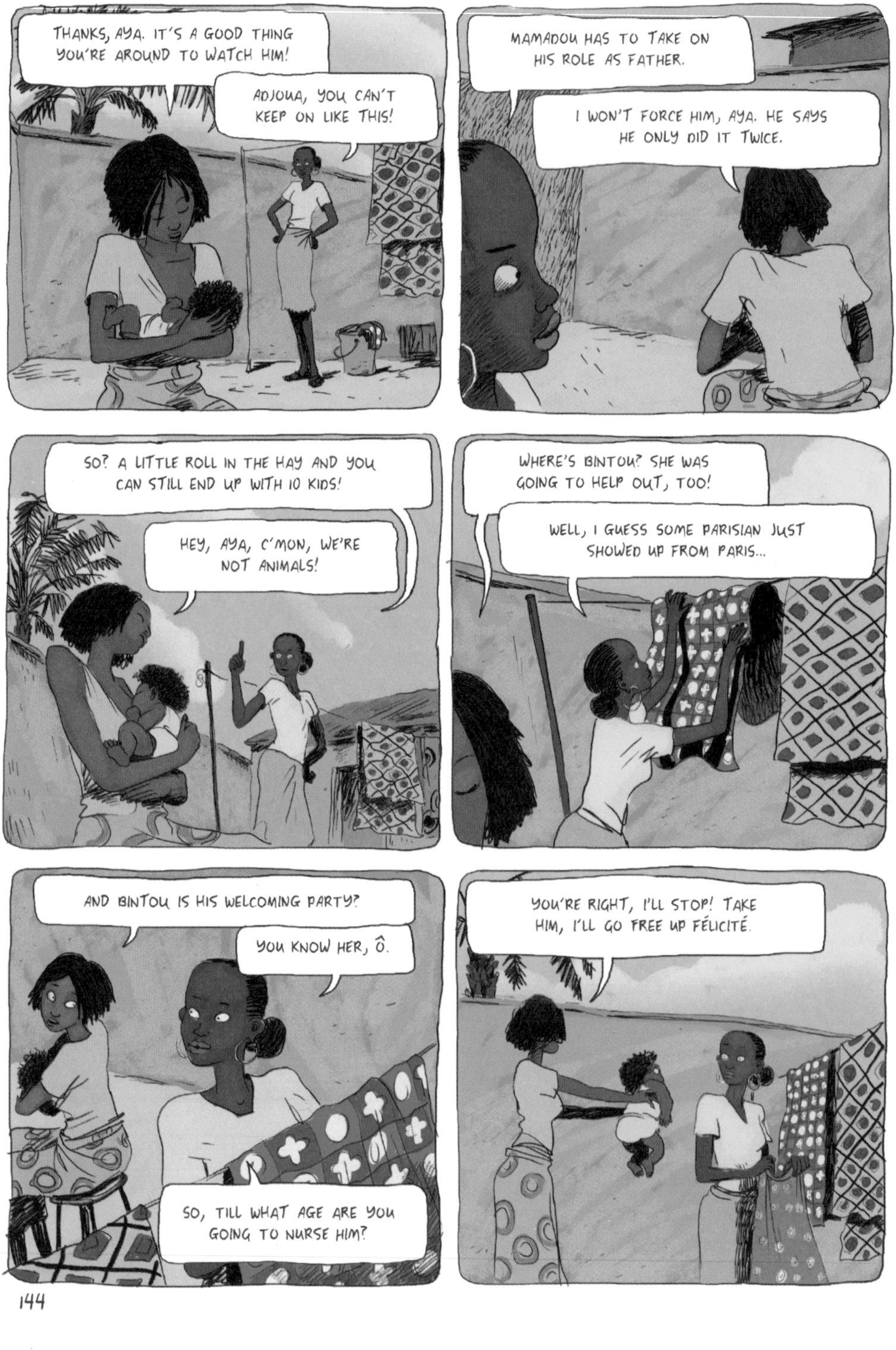
THANKS, AYA. IT'S A GOOD THING YOU'RE AROUND TO WATCH HIM!
ADJOUA, YOU CAN'T KEEP ON LIKE THIS!
MAMADOU HAS TO TAKE ON HIS ROLE AS FATHER.
I WON'T FORCE HIM, AYA. HE SAYS HE ONLY DID IT TWICE.
SO? A LITTLE ROLL IN THE HAY AND YOU CAN STILL END UP WITH 10 KIDS!
HEY, AYA, C'MON, WE'RE NOT ANIMALS!
WHERE'S BINTOU? SHE WAS GOING TO HELP OUT, TOO!
WELL, I GUESS SOME PARISIAN JUST SHOWED UP FROM PARIS...
AND BINTOU IS HIS WELCOMING PARTY?
YOU KNOW HER, Ô.
SO, TILL WHAT AGE ARE YOU GOING TO NURSE HIM?
YOU'RE RIGHT, I'LL STOP! TAKE HIM, I'LL GO FREE UP FÉLICITÉ.

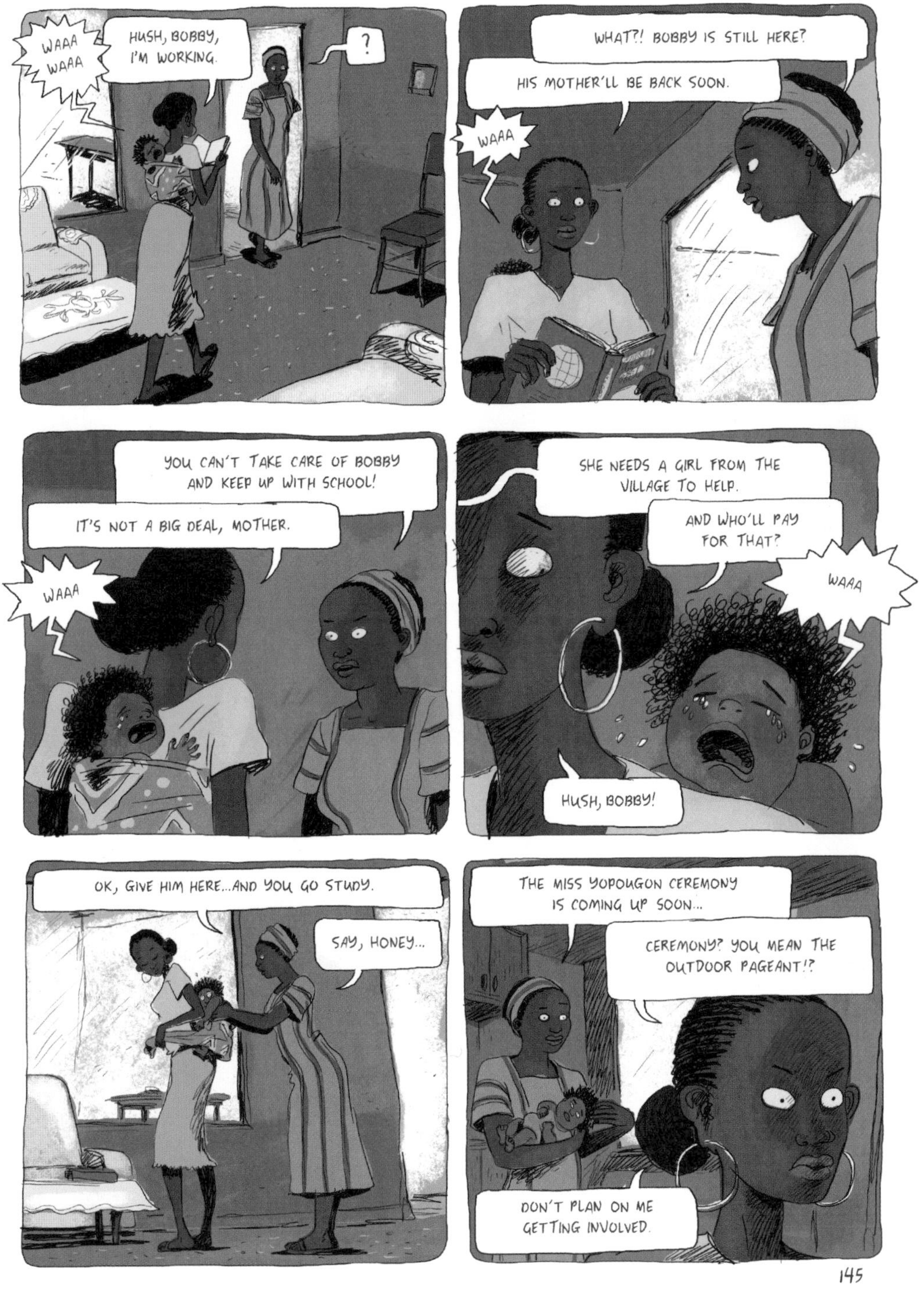

WAAA WAAA
HUSH, BOBBY, I'M WORKING.
?
WHAT?! BOBBY IS STILL HERE?
HIS MOTHER'LL BE BACK SOON.
WAAA
YOU CAN'T TAKE CARE OF BOBBY AND KEEP UP WITH SCHOOL!
IT'S NOT A BIG DEAL, MOTHER.
WAAA
SHE NEEDS A GIRL FROM THE VILLAGE TO HELP.
AND WHO'LL PAY FOR THAT?
WAAA
HUSH, BOBBY!
OK, GIVE HIM HERE...AND YOU GO STUDY.
SAY, HONEY...
THE MISS YOPOUGON CEREMONY IS COMING UP SOON...
CEREMONY? YOU MEAN THE OUTDOOR PAGEANT!?
DON'T PLAN ON ME GETTING INVOLVED.

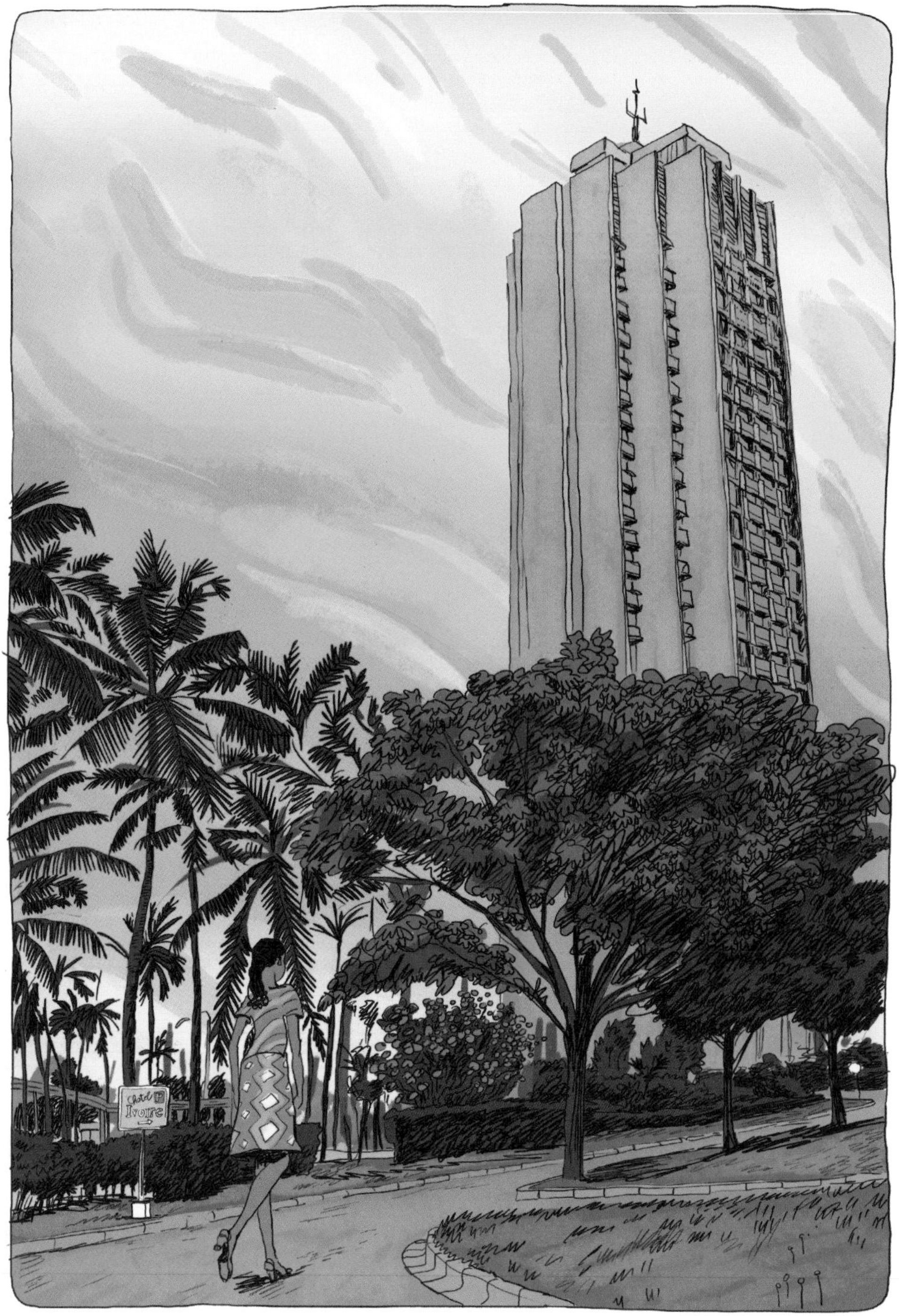
Hôtel P
Ivoire

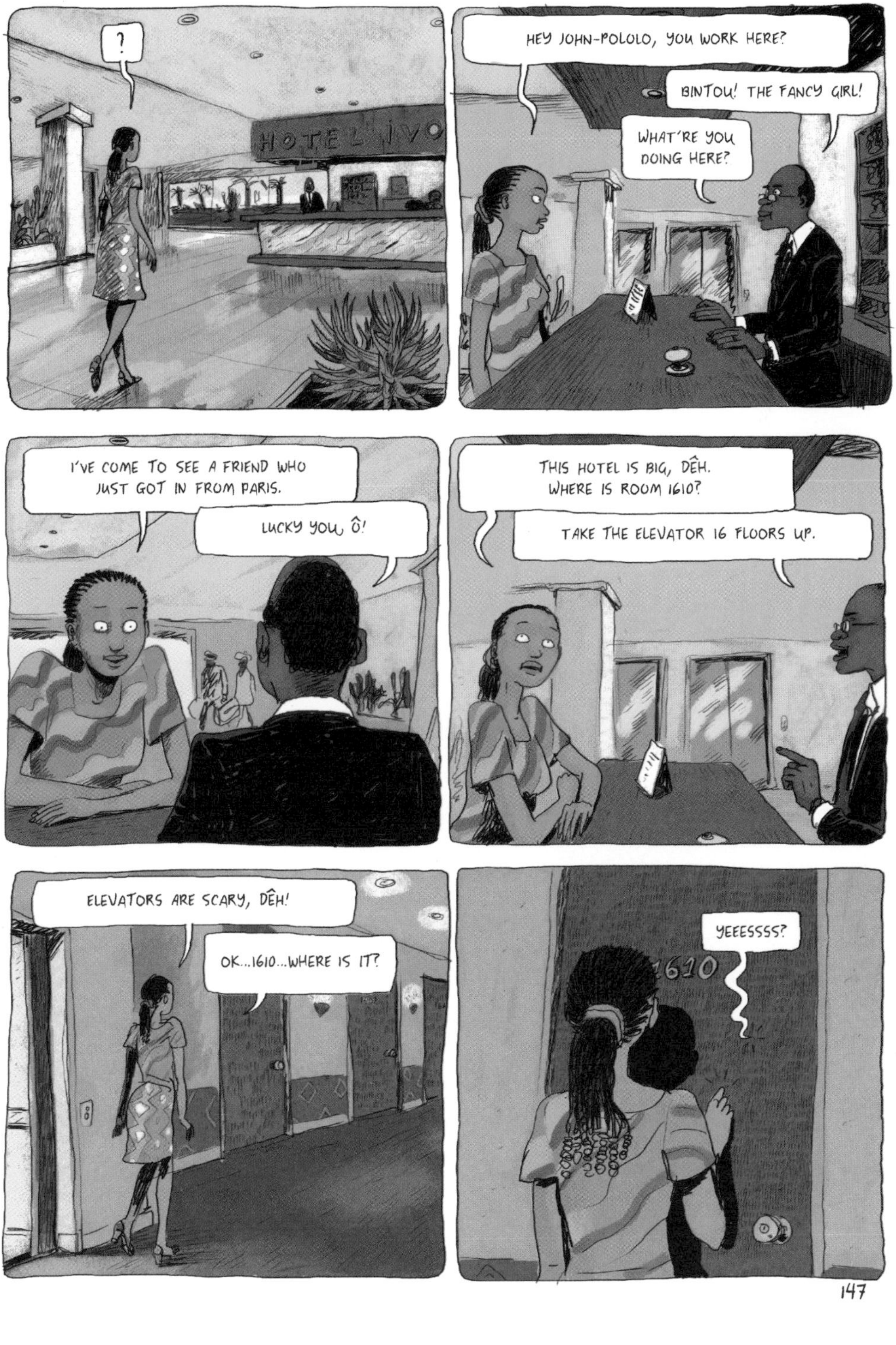
?
HEY JOHN-POLOLO, YOU WORK HERE?
BINTOU! THE FANCY GIRL!
WHAT'RE YOU DOING HERE?
I'VE COME TO SEE A FRIEND WHO JUST GOT IN FROM PARIS.
LUCKY YOU, Ô!
THIS HOTEL IS BIG, DÊH. WHERE IS ROOM 1610?
TAKE THE ELEVATOR 16 FLOORS UP.
ELEVATORS ARE SCARY, DÊH!
OK...1610...WHERE IS IT?
1610
YEEESSSS?

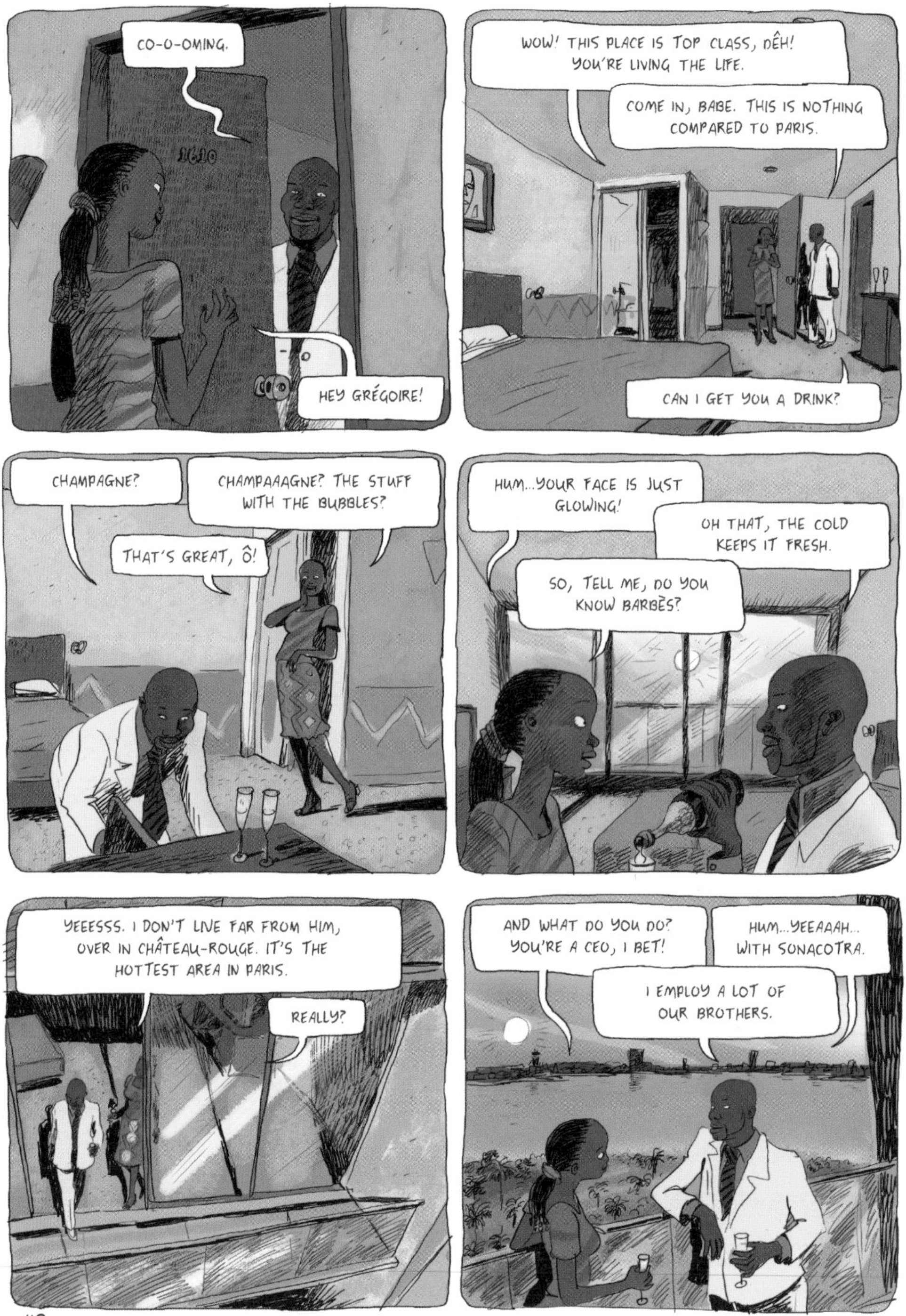
CO-O-OMING.
HEY GRÉGOIRE!
WOW! THIS PLACE IS TOP CLASS, DÊH! YOU'RE LIVING THE LIFE.
COME IN, BABE. THIS IS NOTHING COMPARED TO PARIS.
CAN I GET YOU A DRINK?
CHAMPAGNE?
CHAMPAAAGNE? THE STUFF WITH THE BUBBLES?
THAT'S GREAT, Ô!
HUM...YOUR FACE IS JUST GLOWING!
OH THAT, THE COLD KEEPS IT FRESH.
SO, TELL ME, DO YOU KNOW BARBÈS?
YEEESSS. I DON'T LIVE FAR FROM HIM, OVER IN CHÂTEAU-ROUGE. IT'S THE HOTTEST AREA IN PARIS.
REALLY?
AND WHAT DO YOU DO? YOU'RE A CEO, I BET!
HUM...YEEAAAH... WITH SONACOTRA.
I EMPLOY A LOT OF OUR BROTHERS.

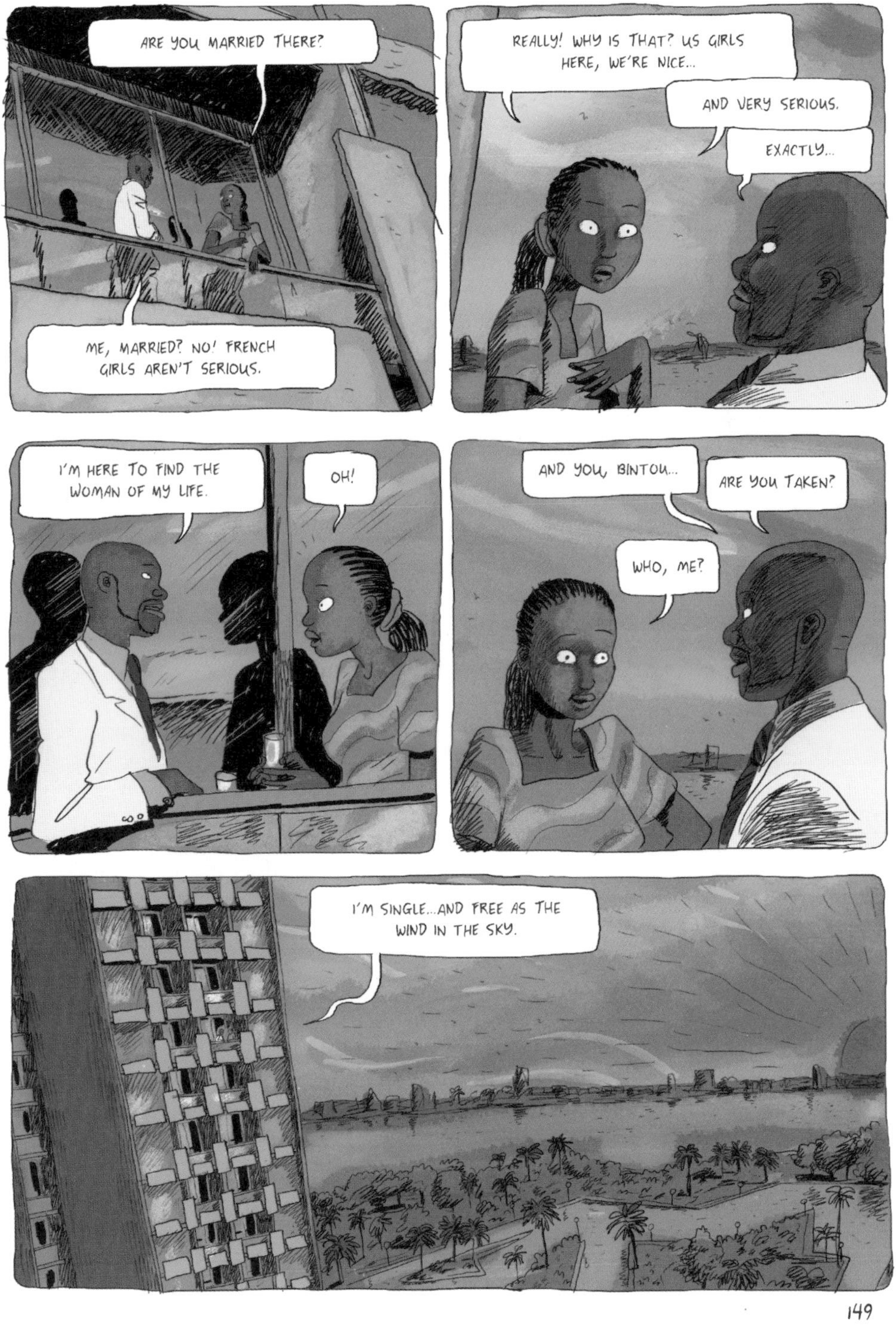
ARE YOU MARRIED THERE?
ME, MARRIED? NO! FRENCH GIRLS AREN'T SERIOUS.
REALLY! WHY IS THAT? US GIRLS HERE, WE'RE NICE...
AND VERY SERIOUS.
EXACTLY...
I'M HERE TO FIND THE WOMAN OF MY LIFE.
OH!
AND YOU, BINTOU...
ARE YOU TAKEN?
WHO, ME?
I'M SINGLE...AND FREE AS THE WIND IN THE SKY.

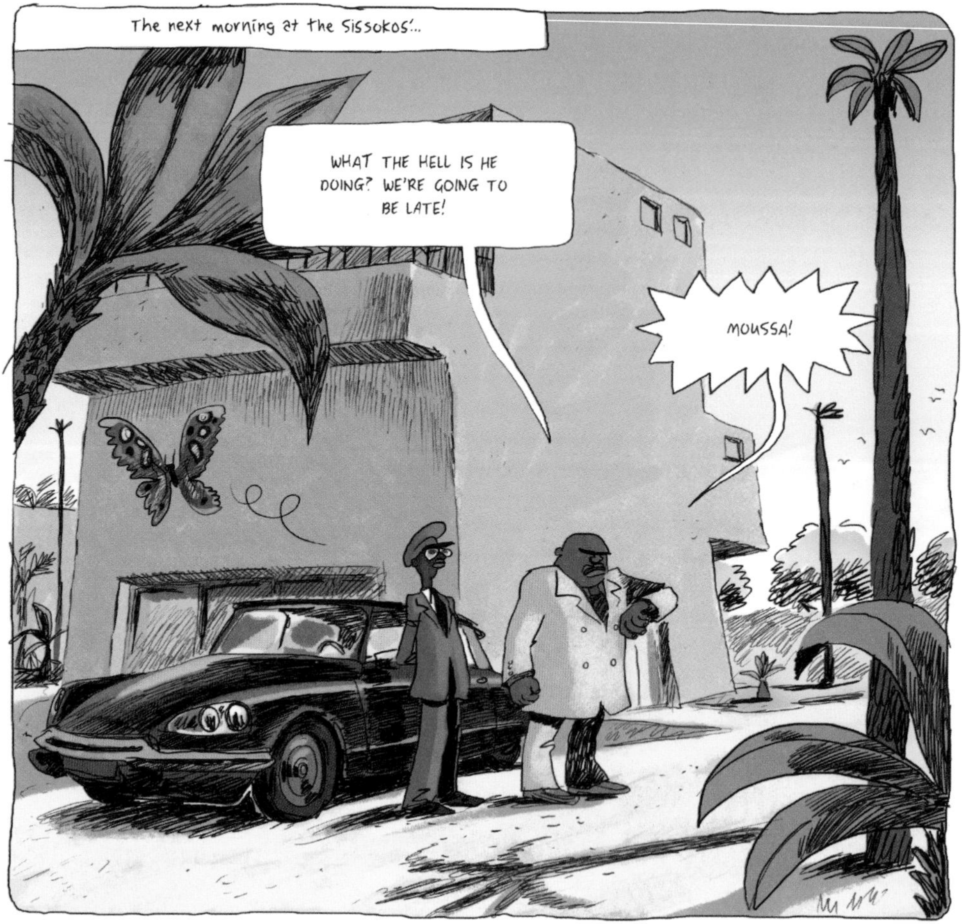
The next morning at the Sissokos'...
WHAT THE HELL IS HE DOING? WE'RE GOING TO BE LATE!
MOUSSA!

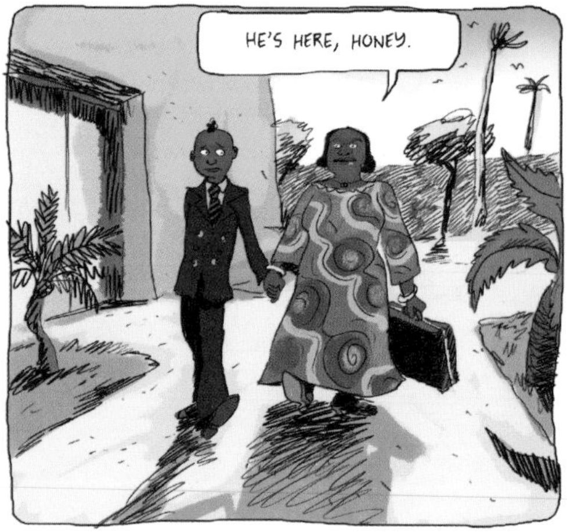
HE'S HERE, HONEY.

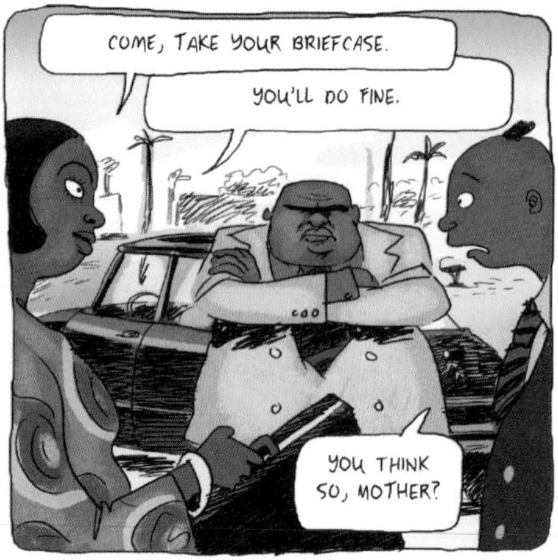
COME, TAKE YOUR BRIEFCASE.
YOU'LL DO FINE.
YOU THINK SO, MOTHER?

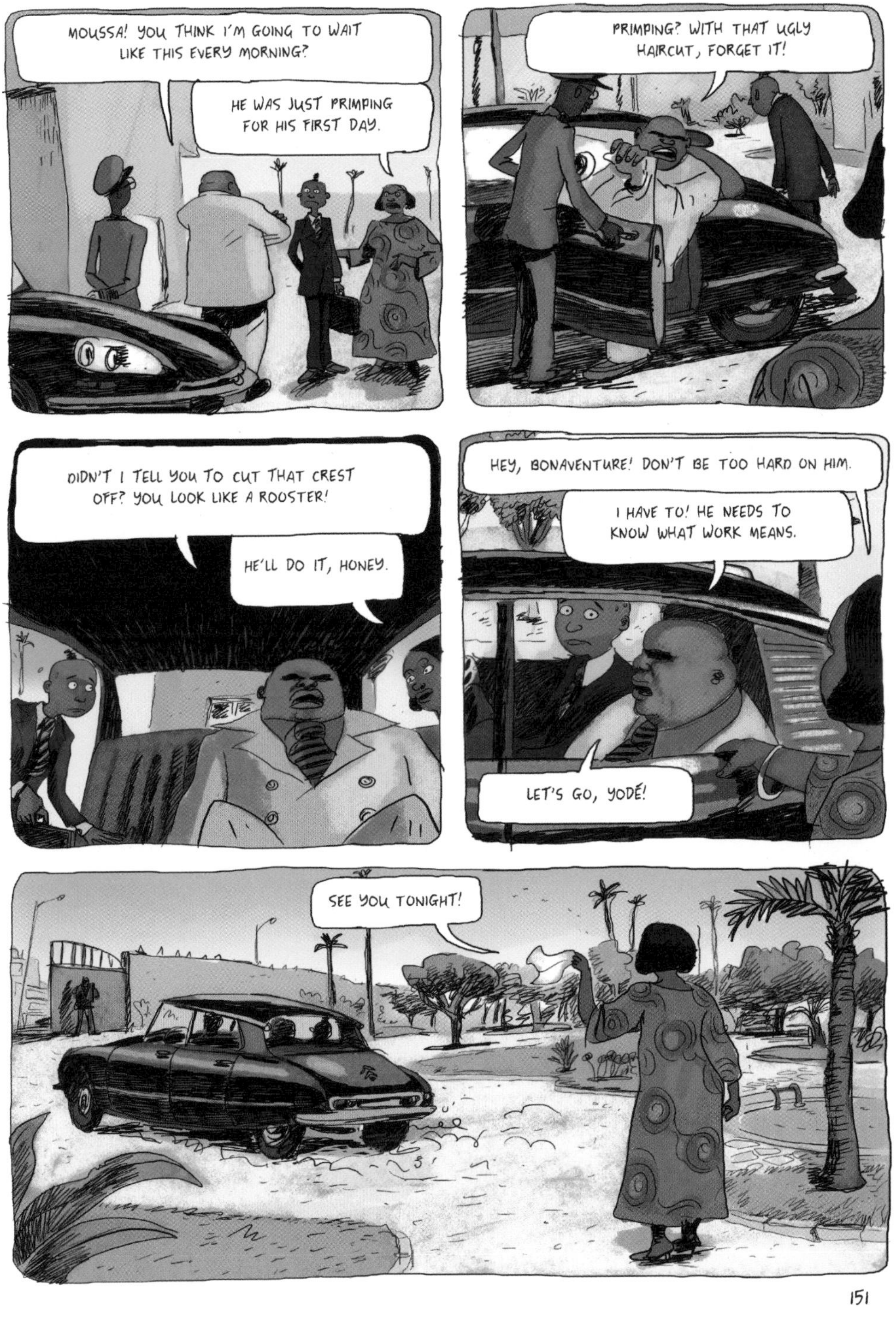
MOUSSA! YOU THINK I'M GOING TO WAIT LIKE THIS EVERY MORNING?
HE WAS JUST PRIMPING FOR HIS FIRST DAY.
PRIMPING? WITH THAT UGLY HAIRCUT, FORGET IT!
DIDN'T I TELL YOU TO CUT THAT CREST OFF? YOU LOOK LIKE A ROOSTER!
HE'LL DO IT, HONEY.
HEY, BONAVENTURE! DON'T BE TOO HARD ON HIM.
I HAVE TO! HE NEEDS TO KNOW WHAT WORK MEANS.
LET'S GO, YODÉ!
SEE YOU TONIGHT!

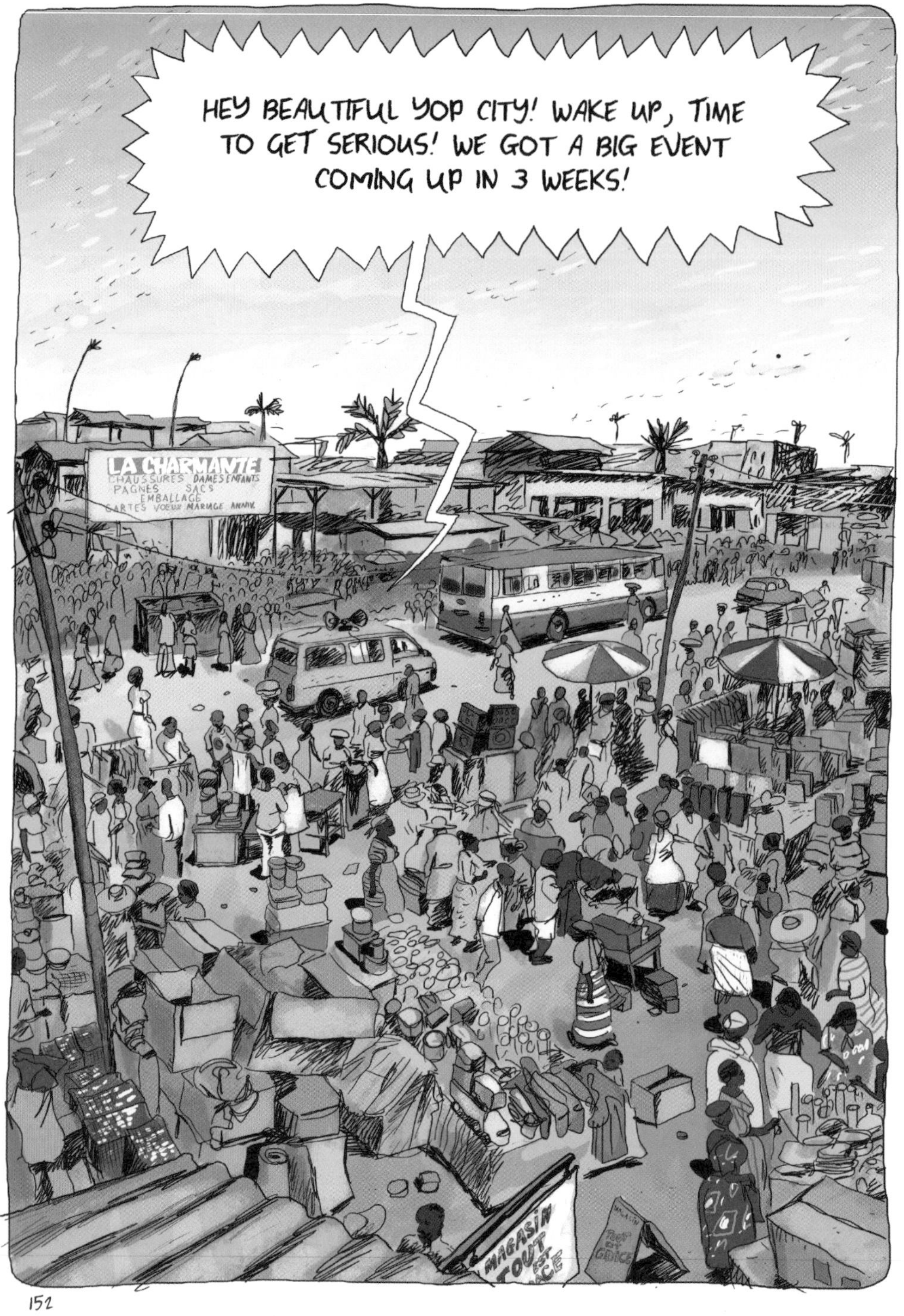
HEY BEAUTIFUL YOP CITY! WAKE UP, TIME TO GET SERIOUS! WE GOT A BIG EVENT COMING UP IN 3 WEEKS!
LA CHARMANTE
CHAUSSURES DAMES ENFANTS
PAGNES SACS
EMBALLAGE
CARTES VOEUX MARIAGE ANNIV.

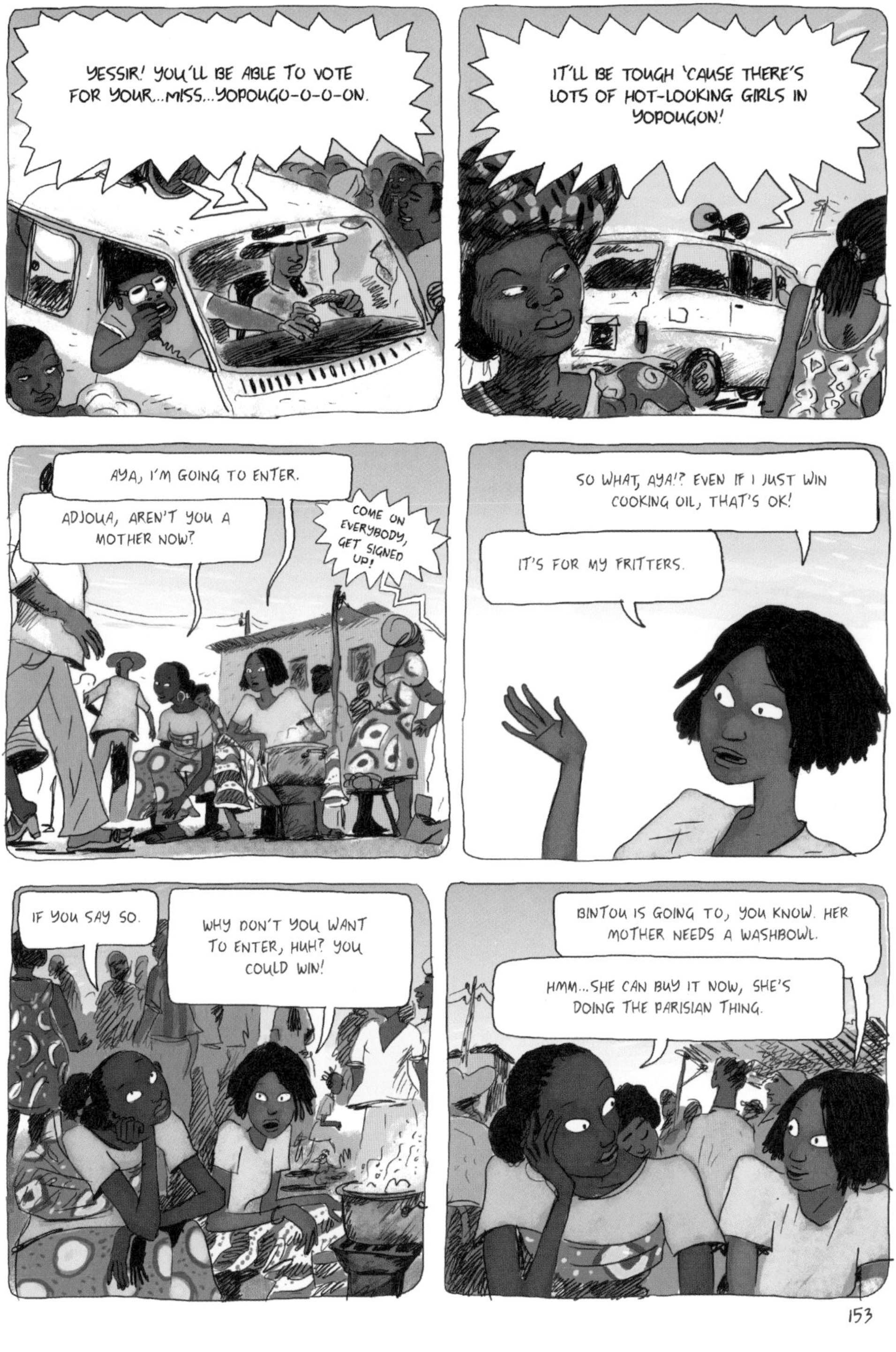
YESSIR! YOU'LL BE ABLE TO VOTE FOR YOUR...MISS...YOPOUGO-O-O-ON.
IT'LL BE TOUGH 'CAUSE THERE'S LOTS OF HOT-LOOKING GIRLS IN YOPOUGON!
AYA, I'M GOING TO ENTER.
ADJOUA, AREN'T YOU A MOTHER NOW?
COME ON EVERYBODY, GET SIGNED UP!
SO WHAT, AYA!? EVEN IF I JUST WIN COOKING OIL, THAT'S OK!
IT'S FOR MY FRITTERS.
IF YOU SAY SO.
WHY DON'T YOU WANT TO ENTER, HUH? YOU COULD WIN!
BINTOU IS GOING TO, YOU KNOW. HER MOTHER NEEDS A WASHBOWL.
HMM...SHE CAN BUY IT NOW, SHE'S DOING THE PARISIAN THING.

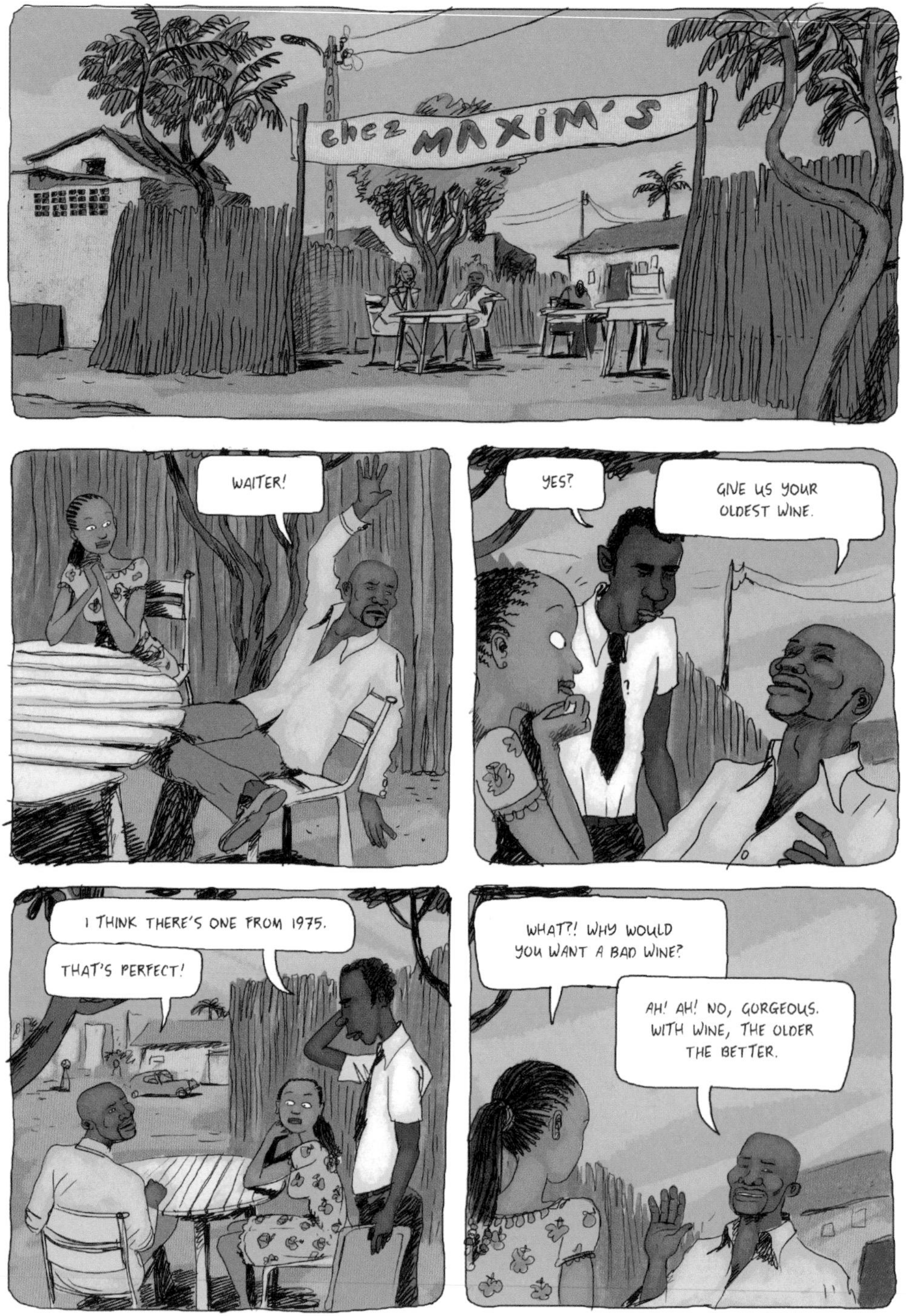
chez MAXIM'S
WAITER!
YES?
GIVE US YOUR OLDEST WINE.
I THINK THERE'S ONE FROM 1975.
THAT'S PERFECT!
WHAT?! WHY WOULD YOU WANT A BAD WINE?
AH! AH! NO, GORGEOUS. WITH WINE, THE OLDER THE BETTER.

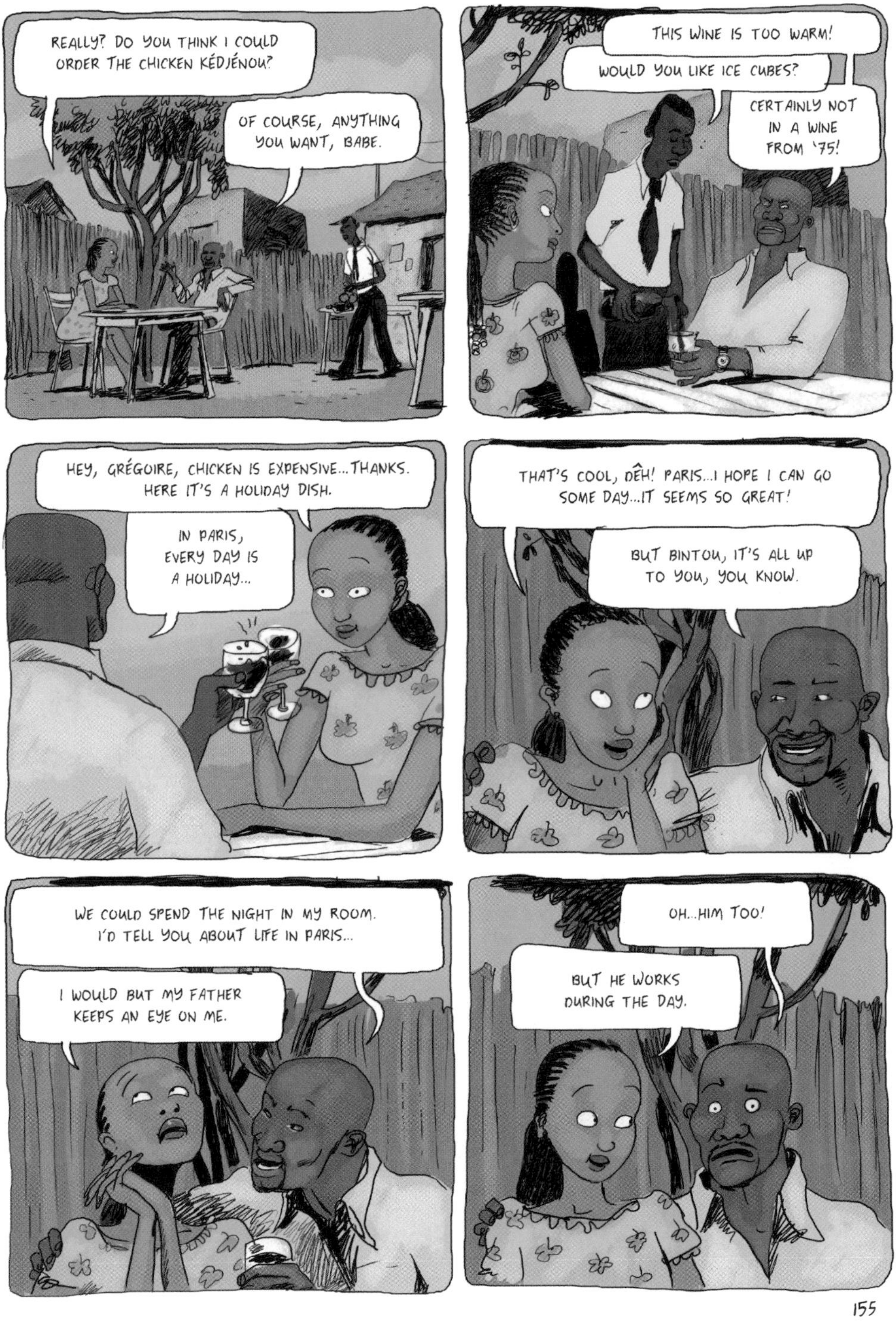
REALLY? DO YOU THINK I COULD ORDER THE CHICKEN KÉDJÉNOU?
OF COURSE, ANYTHING YOU WANT, BABE.
THIS WINE IS TOO WARM!
WOULD YOU LIKE ICE CUBES?
CERTAINLY NOT IN A WINE FROM '75!
HEY, GRÉGOIRE, CHICKEN IS EXPENSIVE... THANKS. HERE IT'S A HOLIDAY DISH.
IN PARIS, EVERY DAY IS A HOLIDAY...
THAT'S COOL, DÊH! PARIS... I HOPE I CAN GO SOME DAY... IT SEEMS SO GREAT!
BUT BINTOU, IT'S ALL UP TO YOU, YOU KNOW.
WE COULD SPEND THE NIGHT IN MY ROOM. I'D TELL YOU ABOUT LIFE IN PARIS...
I WOULD BUT MY FATHER KEEPS AN EYE ON ME.
OH... HIM TOO!
BUT HE WORKS DURING THE DAY.

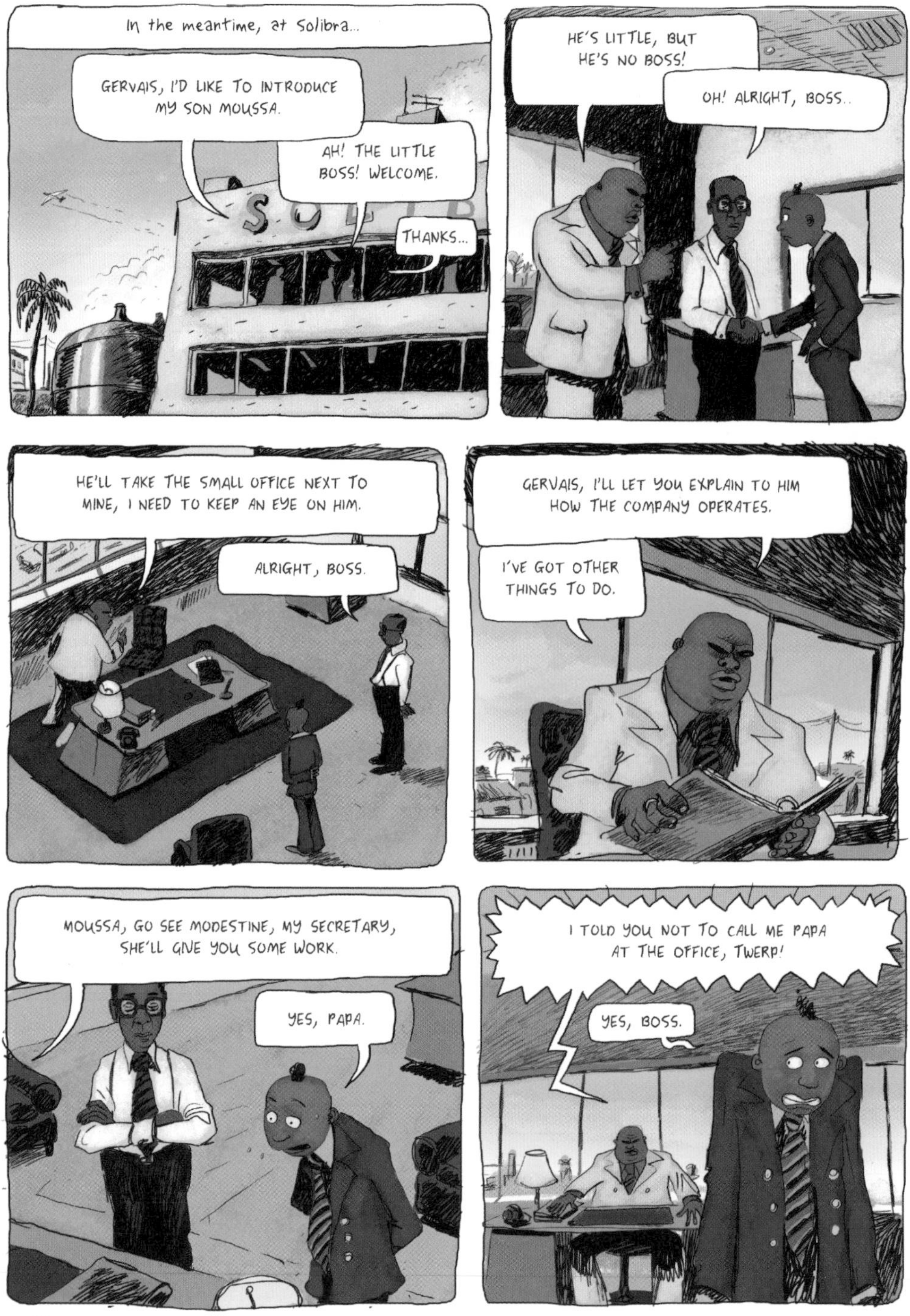
In the meantime, at Solibra...
GERVAIS, I'D LIKE TO INTRODUCE MY SON MOUSSA.
AH! THE LITTLE BOSS! WELCOME.
THANKS...
HE'S LITTLE, BUT HE'S NO BOSS!
OH! ALRIGHT, BOSS..
HE'LL TAKE THE SMALL OFFICE NEXT TO MINE, I NEED TO KEEP AN EYE ON HIM.
ALRIGHT, BOSS.
GERVAIS, I'LL LET YOU EXPLAIN TO HIM HOW THE COMPANY OPERATES.
I'VE GOT OTHER THINGS TO DO.
MOUSSA, GO SEE MODESTINE, MY SECRETARY, SHE'LL GIVE YOU SOME WORK.
YES, PAPA.
I TOLD YOU NOT TO CALL ME PAPA AT THE OFFICE, TWERP!
YES, BOSS.

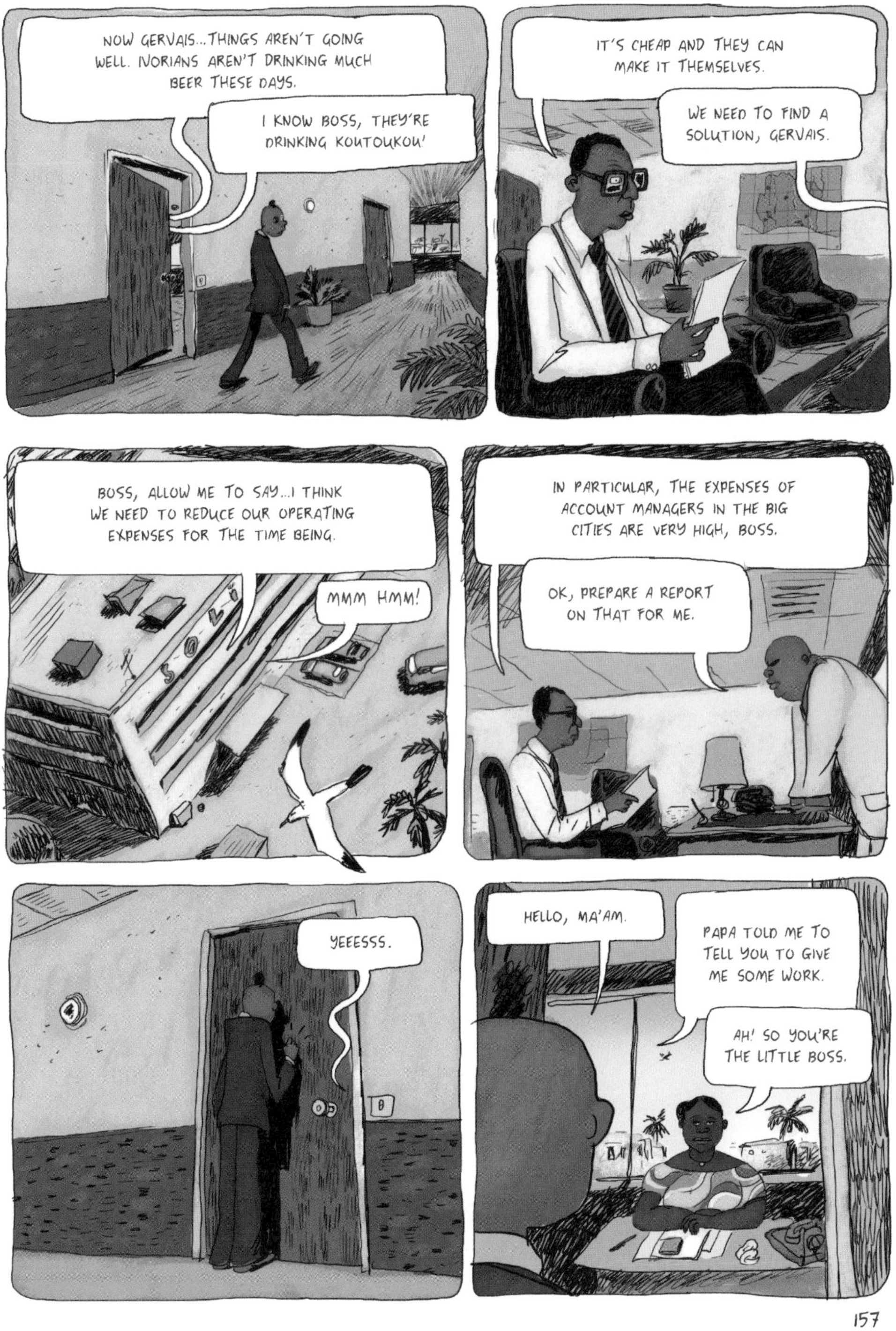
NOW GERVAIS...THINGS AREN'T GOING WELL. IVORIANS AREN'T DRINKING MUCH BEER THESE DAYS.
I KNOW BOSS, THEY'RE DRINKING KOUTOUKOU!
IT'S CHEAP AND THEY CAN MAKE IT THEMSELVES.
WE NEED TO FIND A SOLUTION, GERVAIS.
BOSS, ALLOW ME TO SAY...I THINK WE NEED TO REDUCE OUR OPERATING EXPENSES FOR THE TIME BEING.
MMM HMM!
IN PARTICULAR, THE EXPENSES OF ACCOUNT MANAGERS IN THE BIG CITIES ARE VERY HIGH, BOSS.
OK, PREPARE A REPORT ON THAT FOR ME.
YEEESSS.
HELLO, MA'AM.
PAPA TOLD ME TO TELL YOU TO GIVE ME SOME WORK.
AH! SO YOU'RE THE LITTLE BOSS.

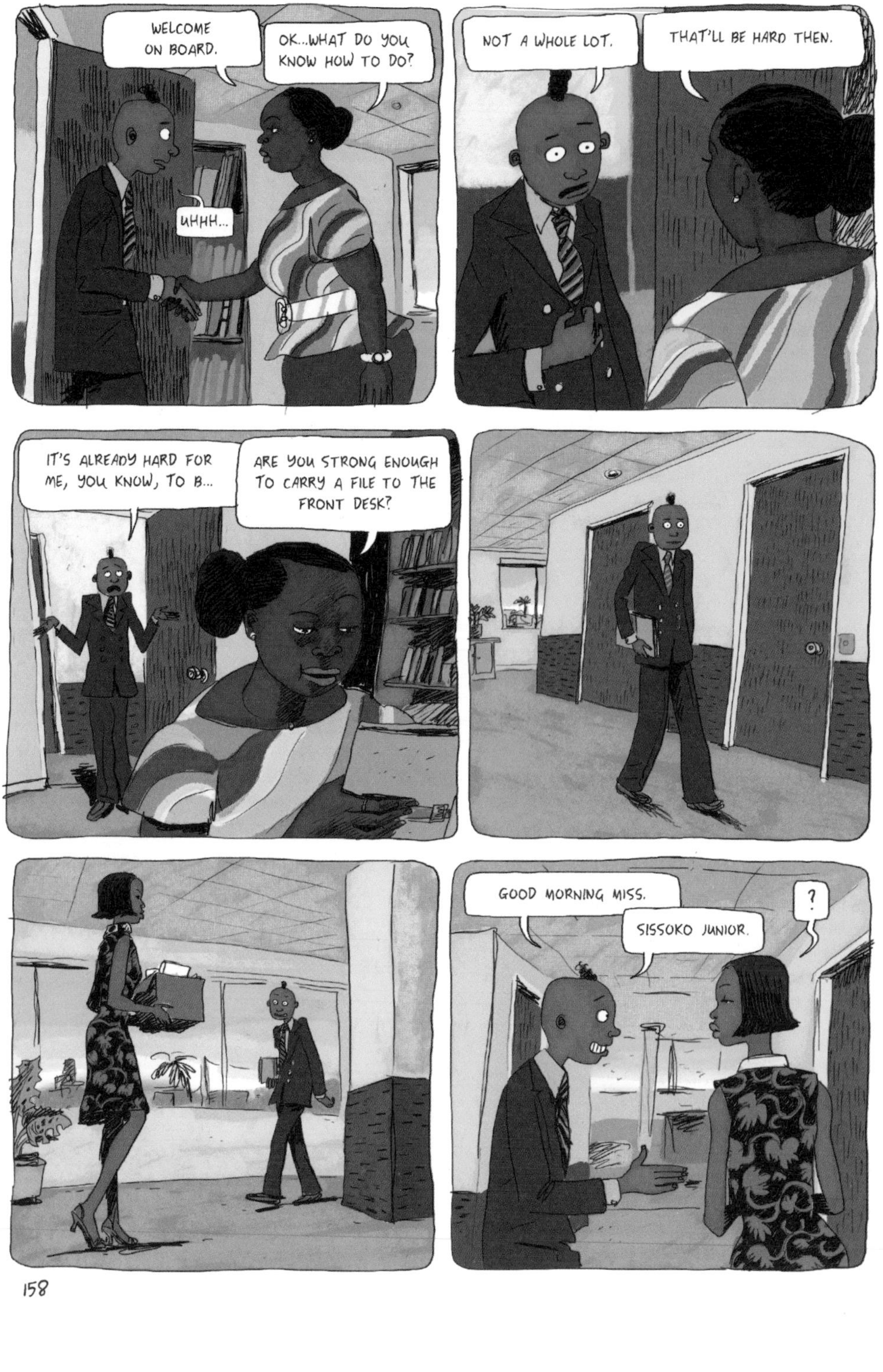
WELCOME
ON BOARD.
OK...WHAT DO YOU
KNOW HOW TO DO?
UHHH...
NOT A WHOLE LOT.
THAT'LL BE HARD THEN.
IT'S ALREADY HARD FOR
ME, YOU KNOW, TO B...
ARE YOU STRONG ENOUGH
TO CARRY A FILE TO THE
FRONT DESK?
GOOD MORNING MISS.
SISSOKO JUNIOR.
?

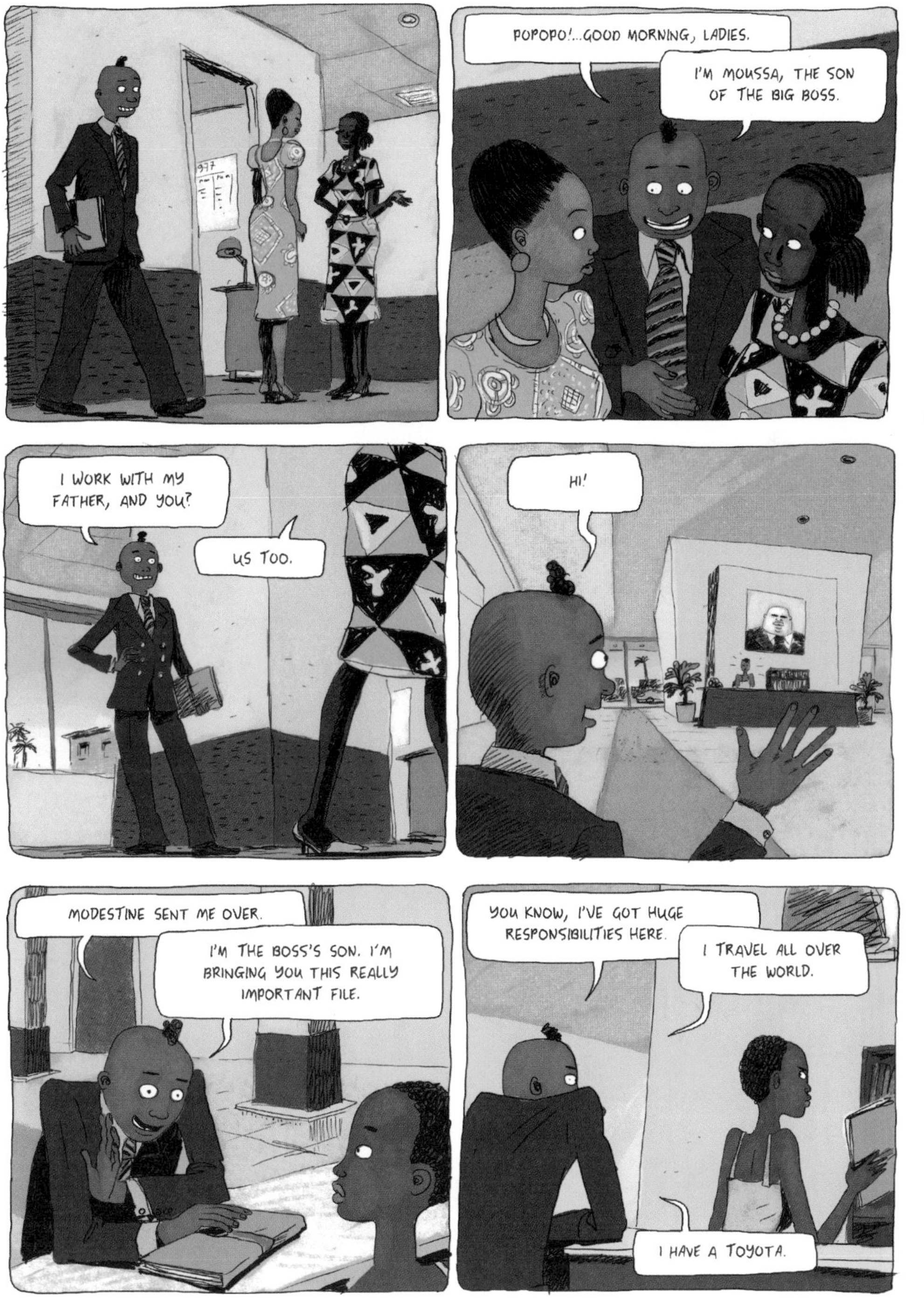
POPOPO!...GOOD MORNING, LADIES.
I'M MOUSSA, THE SON OF THE BIG BOSS.
I WORK WITH MY FATHER, AND YOU?
US TOO.
HI!
MODESTINE SENT ME OVER.
I'M THE BOSS'S SON. I'M BRINGING YOU THIS REALLY IMPORTANT FILE.
YOU KNOW, I'VE GOT HUGE RESPONSIBILITIES HERE.
I TRAVEL ALL OVER THE WORLD.
I HAVE A TOYOTA.

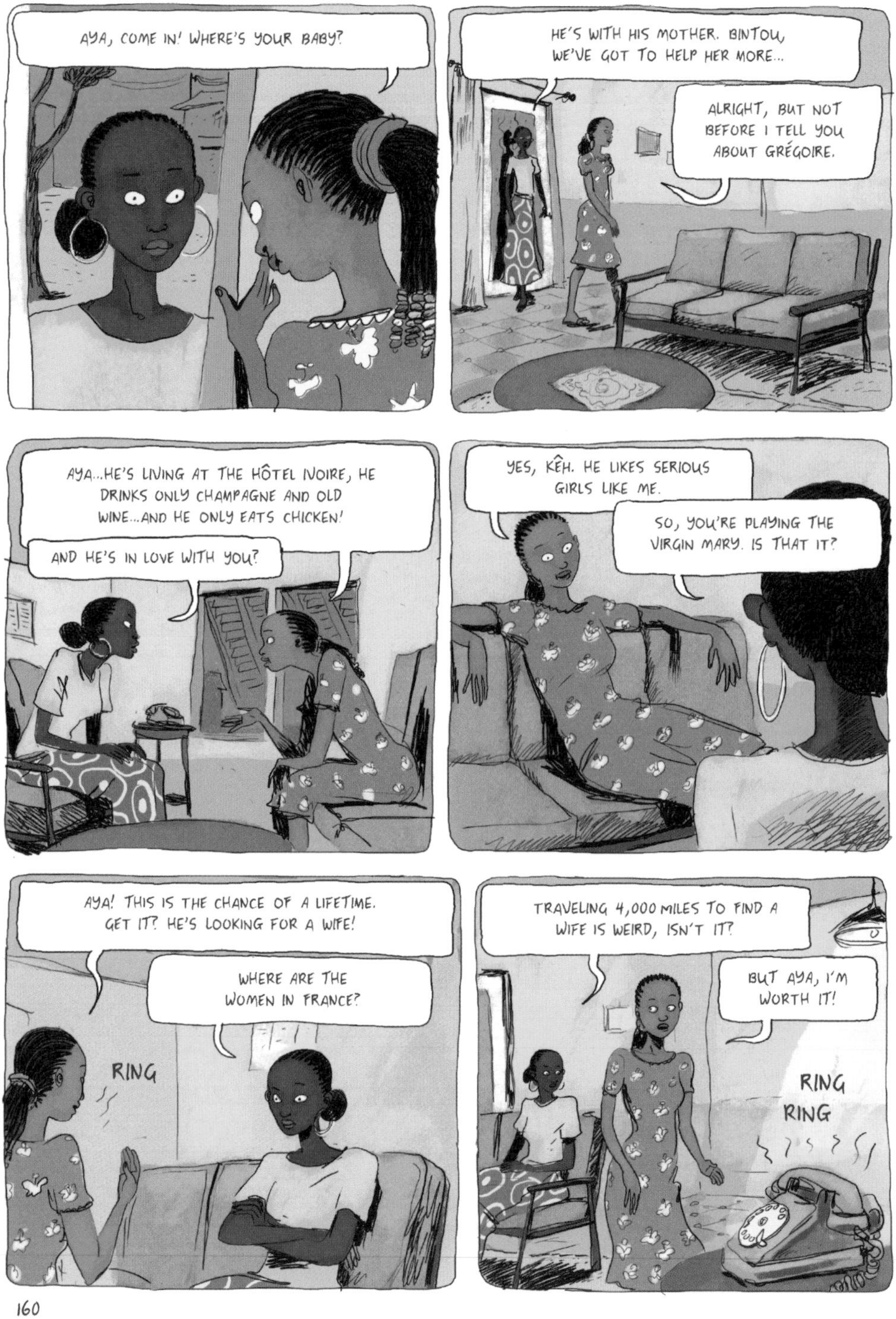
AYA, COME IN! WHERE'S YOUR BABY?
HE'S WITH HIS MOTHER. BINTOU, WE'VE GOT TO HELP HER MORE...
ALRIGHT, BUT NOT BEFORE I TELL YOU ABOUT GRÉGOIRE.
AYA...HE'S LIVING AT THE HÔTEL IVOIRE, HE DRINKS ONLY CHAMPAGNE AND OLD WINE...AND HE ONLY EATS CHICKEN!
AND HE'S IN LOVE WITH YOU?
YES, KÊH. HE LIKES SERIOUS GIRLS LIKE ME.
SO, YOU'RE PLAYING THE VIRGIN MARY. IS THAT IT?
AYA! THIS IS THE CHANCE OF A LIFETIME. GET IT? HE'S LOOKING FOR A WIFE!
WHERE ARE THE WOMEN IN FRANCE?
RING
TRAVELING 4,000 MILES TO FIND A WIFE IS WEIRD, ISN'T IT?
BUT AYA, I'M WORTH IT!
RING
RING

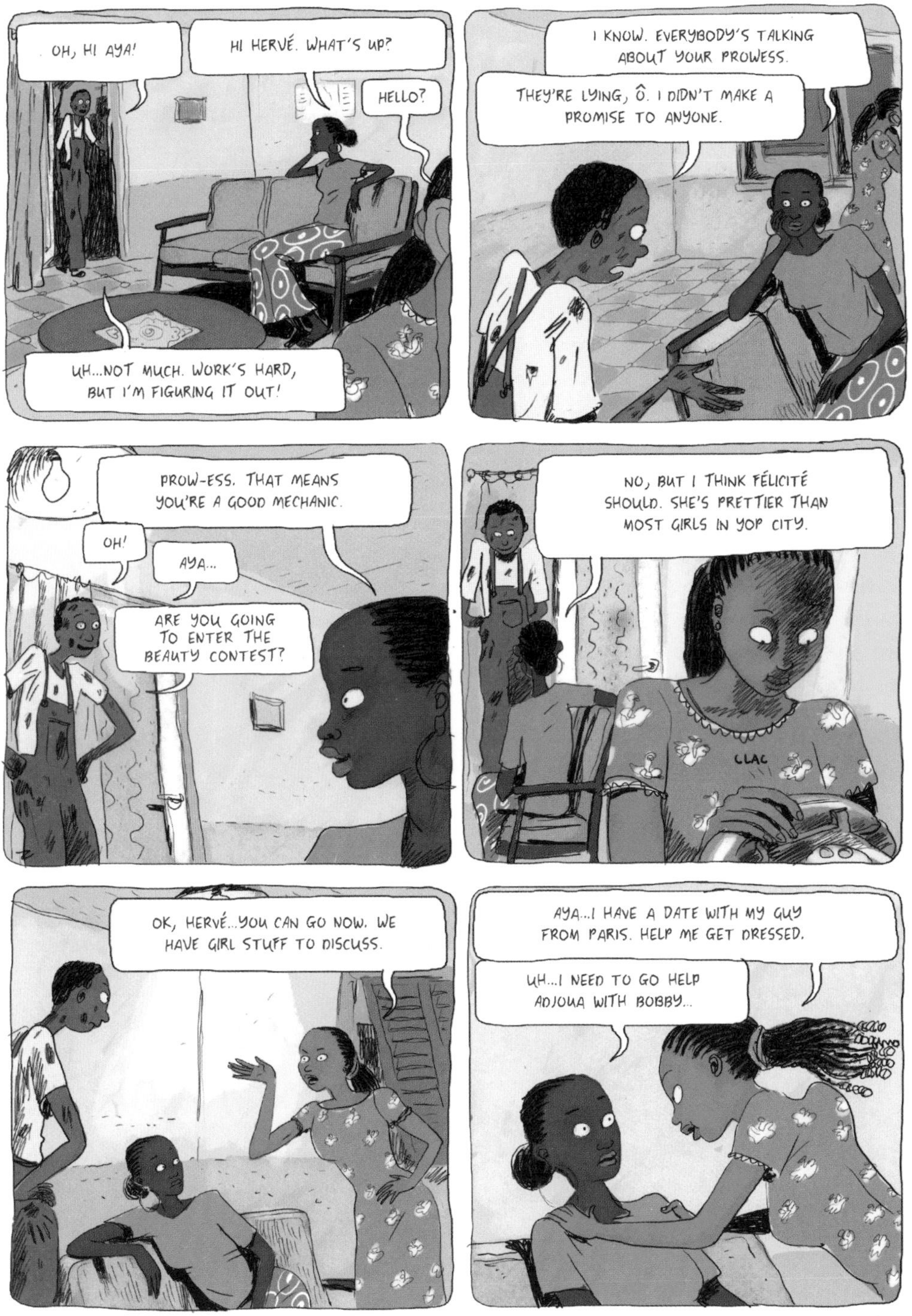
OH, HI AYA!
HI HERVÉ. WHAT'S UP?
HELLO?
UH...NOT MUCH. WORK'S HARD, BUT I'M FIGURING IT OUT!
I KNOW. EVERYBODY'S TALKING ABOUT YOUR PROWESS.
THEY'RE LYING, Ô. I DIDN'T MAKE A PROMISE TO ANYONE.
PROW-ESS. THAT MEANS YOU'RE A GOOD MECHANIC.
OH!
AYA...
ARE YOU GOING TO ENTER THE BEAUTY CONTEST?
NO, BUT I THINK FÉLICITÉ SHOULD. SHE'S PRETTIER THAN MOST GIRLS IN YOP CITY.
CLAC
OK, HERVÉ...YOU CAN GO NOW. WE HAVE GIRL STUFF TO DISCUSS.
AYA...I HAVE A DATE WITH MY GUY FROM PARIS. HELP ME GET DRESSED.
UH...I NEED TO GO HELP ADJOUA WITH BOBBY...

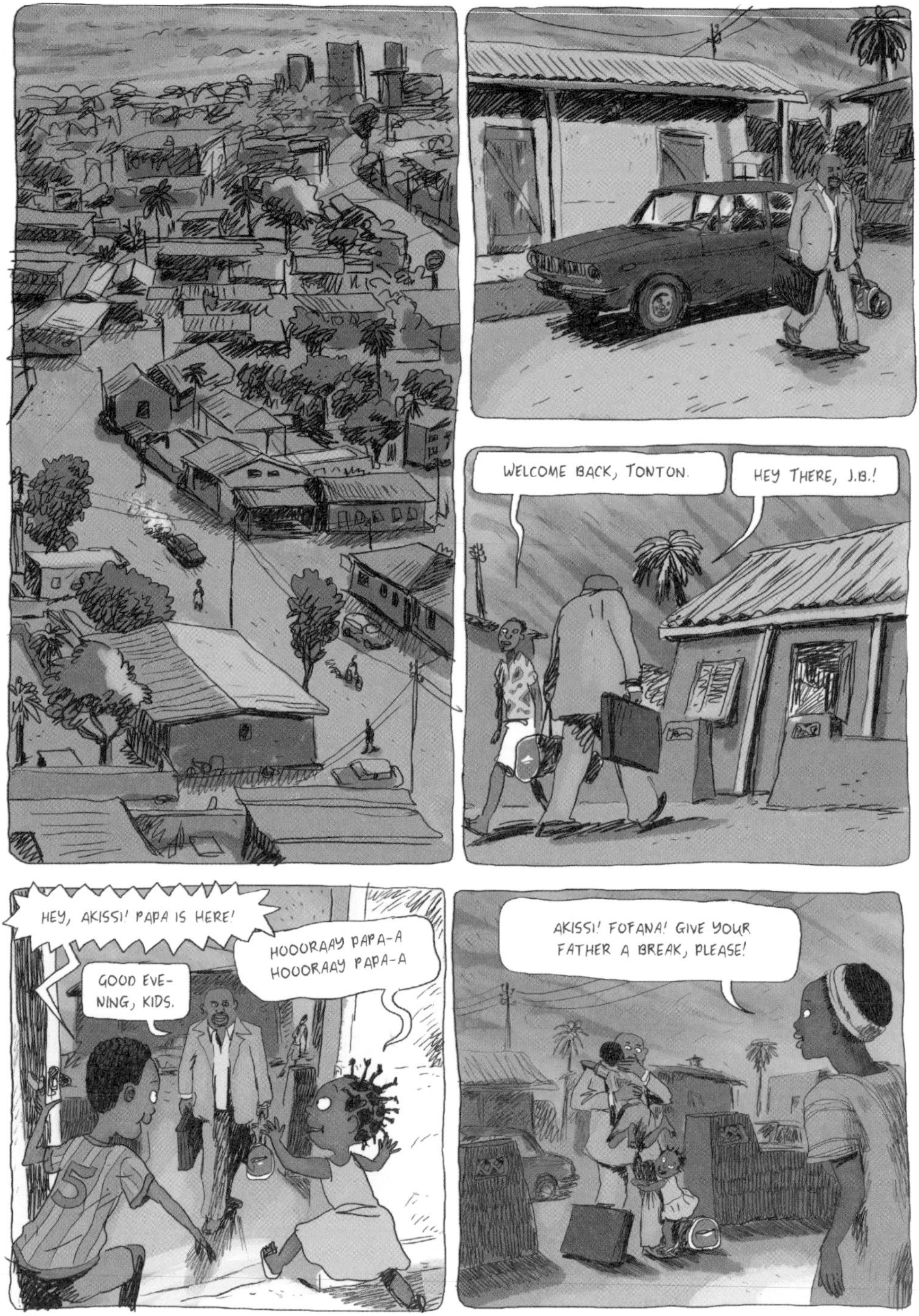
WELCOME BACK, TONTON.
HEY THERE, J.B.!
HEY, AKISSI! PAPA IS HERE!
GOOD EVENING, KIDS.
HOOORAAY PAPA-A HOOORAAY PAPA-A
AKISSI! FOFANA! GIVE YOUR FATHER A BREAK, PLEASE!

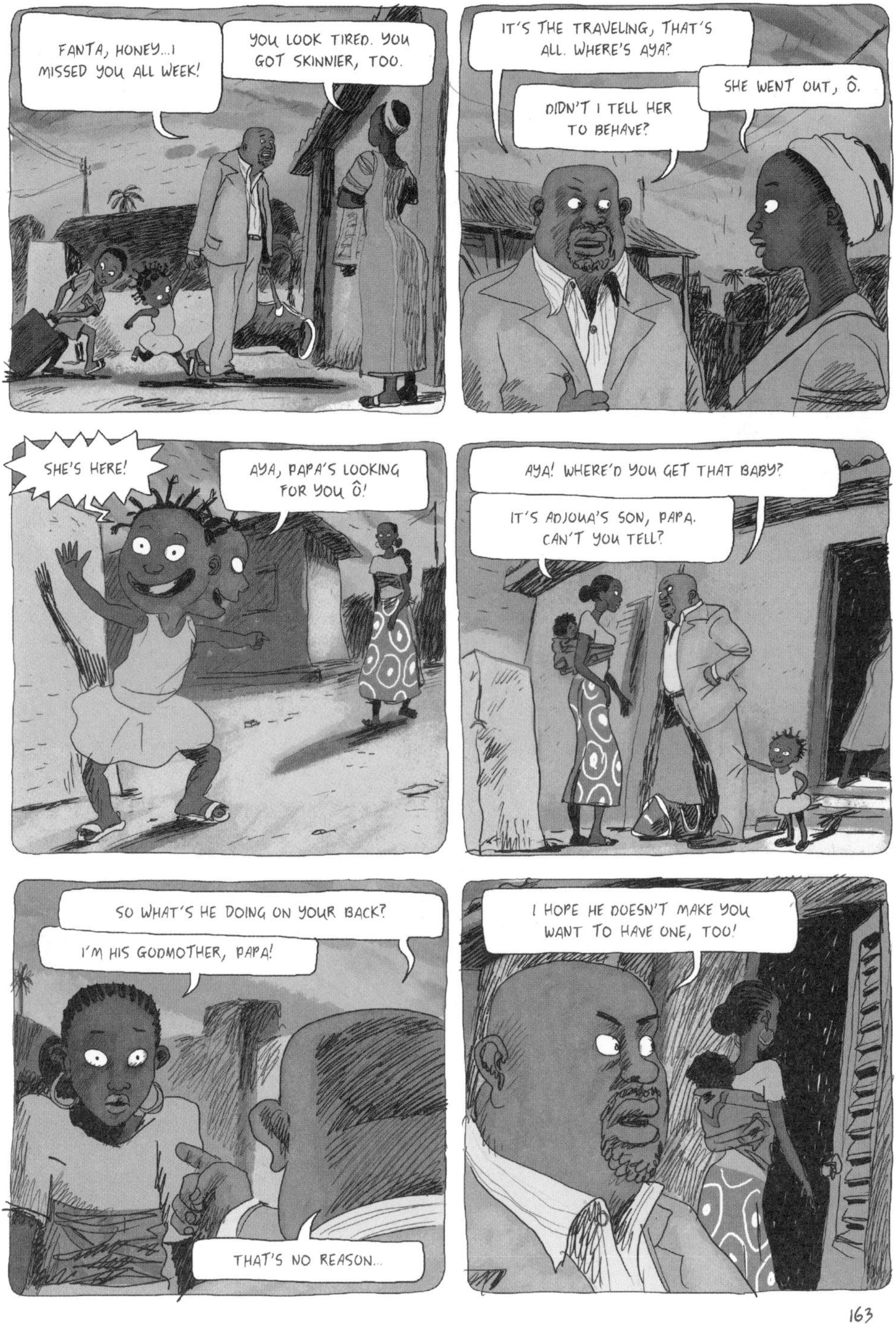
FANTA, HONEY...I MISSED YOU ALL WEEK!
YOU LOOK TIRED. YOU GOT SKINNIER, TOO.
IT'S THE TRAVELING, THAT'S ALL. WHERE'S AYA?
SHE WENT OUT, Ô.
DIDN'T I TELL HER TO BEHAVE?
SHE'S HERE!
AYA, PAPA'S LOOKING FOR YOU Ô!
AYA! WHERE'D YOU GET THAT BABY?
IT'S ADJOUA'S SON, PAPA. CAN'T YOU TELL?
SO WHAT'S HE DOING ON YOUR BACK?
I'M HIS GODMOTHER, PAPA!
THAT'S NO REASON...
I HOPE HE DOESN'T MAKE YOU WANT TO HAVE ONE, TOO!

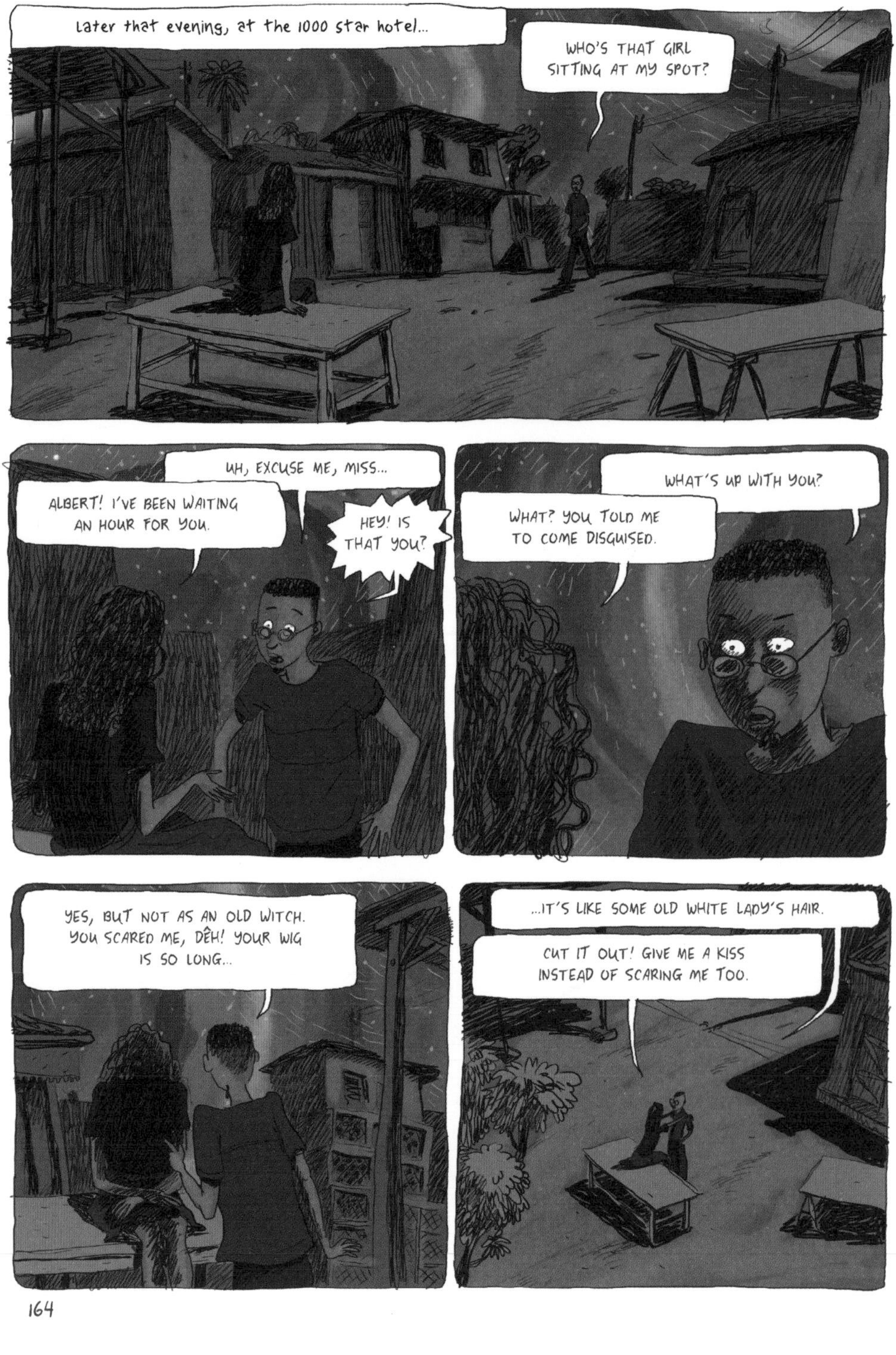
Later that evening, at the 1000 star hotel...
WHO'S THAT GIRL SITTING AT MY SPOT?
UH, EXCUSE ME, MISS...
ALBERT! I'VE BEEN WAITING AN HOUR FOR YOU.
HEY! IS THAT YOU?
WHAT'S UP WITH YOU?
WHAT? YOU TOLD ME TO COME DISGUISED.
YES, BUT NOT AS AN OLD WITCH. YOU SCARED ME, DÊH! YOUR WIG IS SO LONG...
...IT'S LIKE SOME OLD WHITE LADY'S HAIR.
CUT IT OUT! GIVE ME A KISS INSTEAD OF SCARING ME TOO.

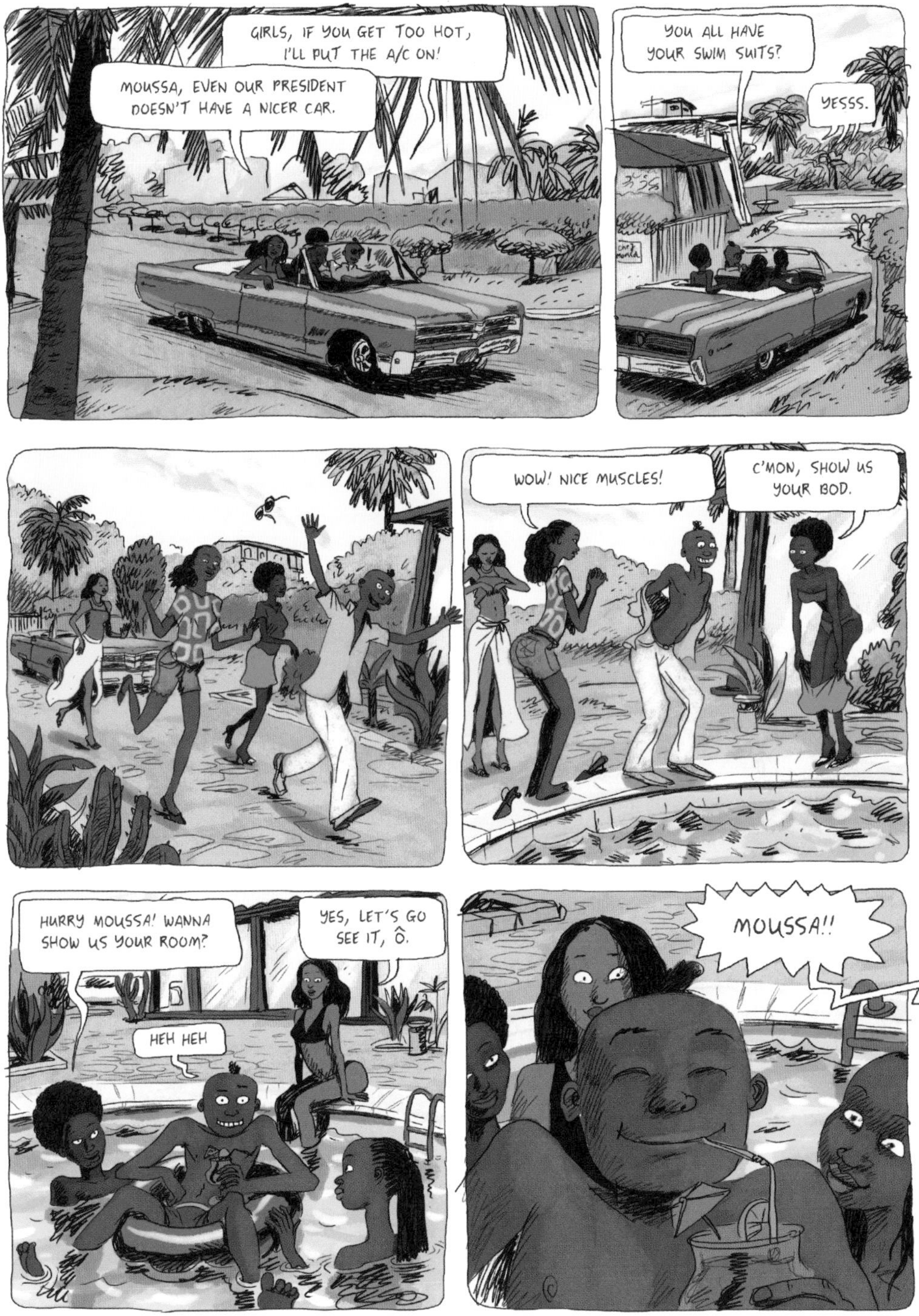
MOUSSA, EVEN OUR PRESIDENT DOESN'T HAVE A NICER CAR.
GIRLS, IF YOU GET TOO HOT, I'LL PUT THE A/C ON!
YOU ALL HAVE YOUR SWIM SUITS?
YESSS.
WOW! NICE MUSCLES!
C'MON, SHOW US YOUR BOD.
HURRY MOUSSA! WANNA SHOW US YOUR ROOM?
YES, LET'S GO SEE IT, Ô.
HEH HEH
MOUSSA!!

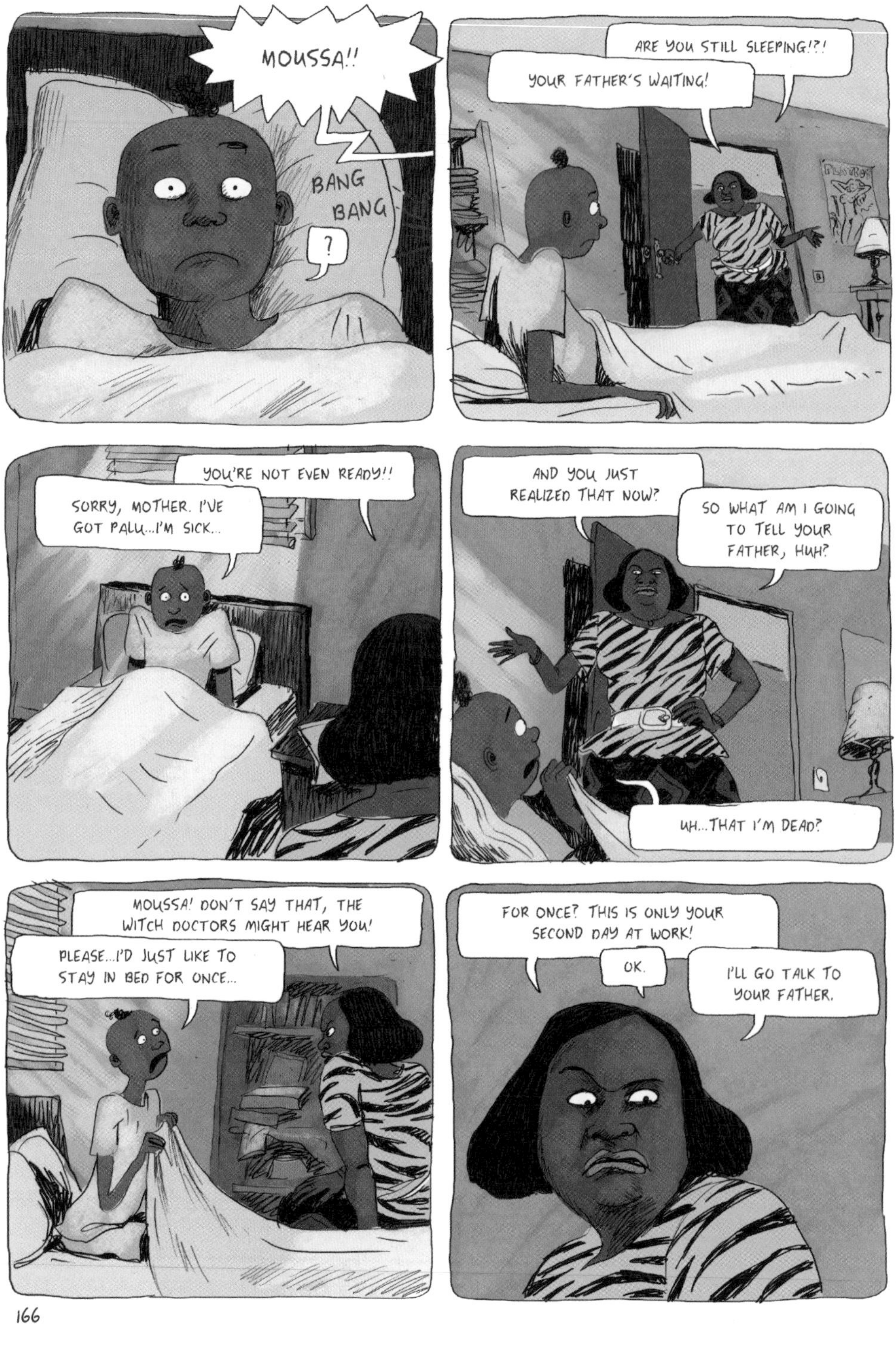
MOUSSA!!
BANG
BANG
?
ARE YOU STILL SLEEPING!?!
YOUR FATHER'S WAITING!
YOU'RE NOT EVEN READY!!
SORRY, MOTHER. I'VE GOT PALU...I'M SICK...
AND YOU JUST REALIZED THAT NOW?
SO WHAT AM I GOING TO TELL YOUR FATHER, HUH?
UH...THAT I'M DEAD?
MOUSSA! DON'T SAY THAT, THE WITCH DOCTORS MIGHT HEAR YOU!
PLEASE...I'D JUST LIKE TO STAY IN BED FOR ONCE...
FOR ONCE? THIS IS ONLY YOUR SECOND DAY AT WORK!
OK.
I'LL GO TALK TO YOUR FATHER.

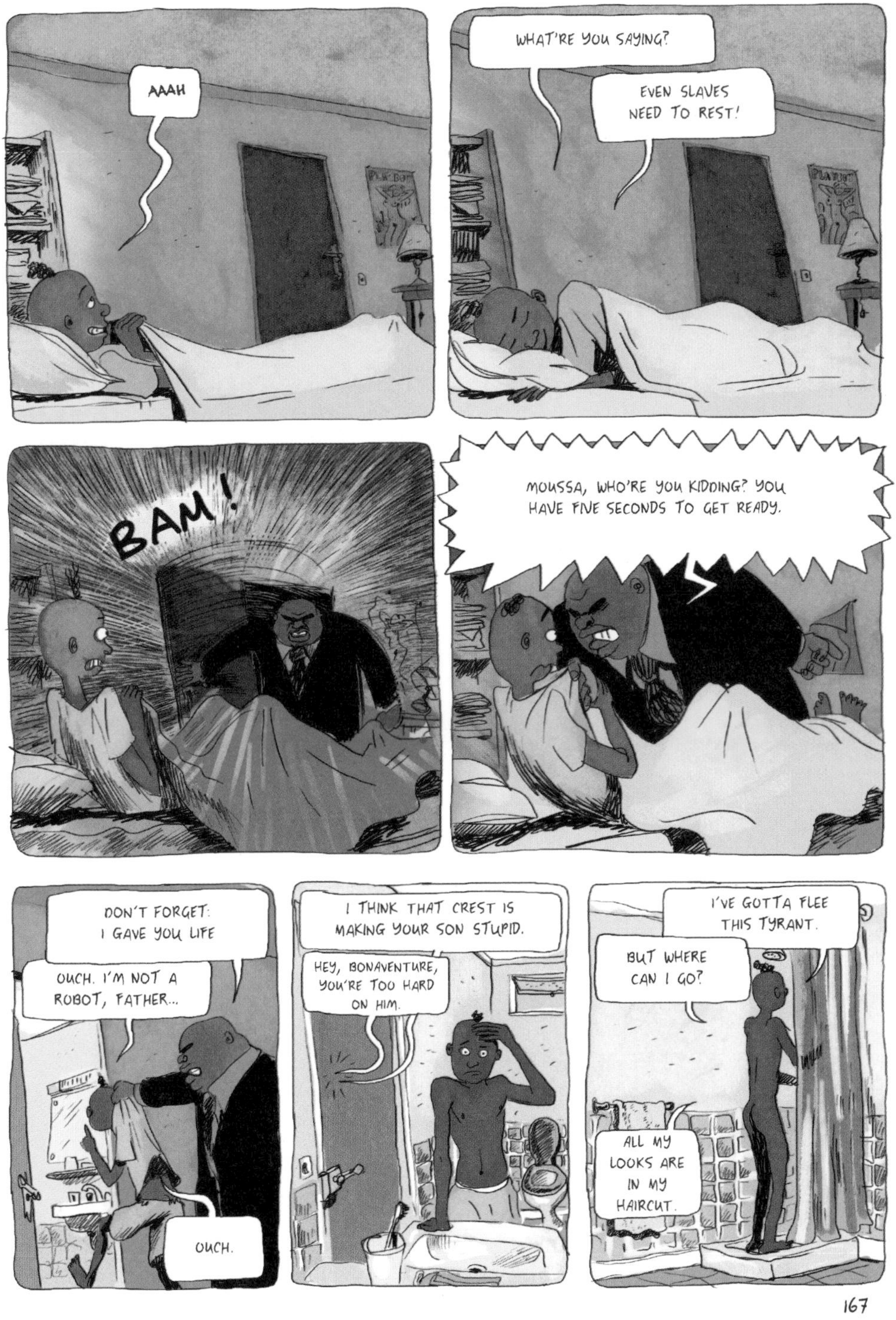
AAAH
WHAT'RE YOU SAYING?
EVEN SLAVES NEED TO REST!
BAM!
MOUSSA, WHO'RE YOU KIDDING? YOU HAVE FIVE SECONDS TO GET READY.
DON'T FORGET: I GAVE YOU LIFE
OUCH. I'M NOT A ROBOT, FATHER...
OUCH.
I THINK THAT CREST IS MAKING YOUR SON STUPID.
HEY, BONAVENTURE, YOU'RE TOO HARD ON HIM.
I'VE GOTTA FLEE THIS TYRANT.
BUT WHERE CAN I GO?
ALL MY LOOKS ARE IN MY HAIRCUT.

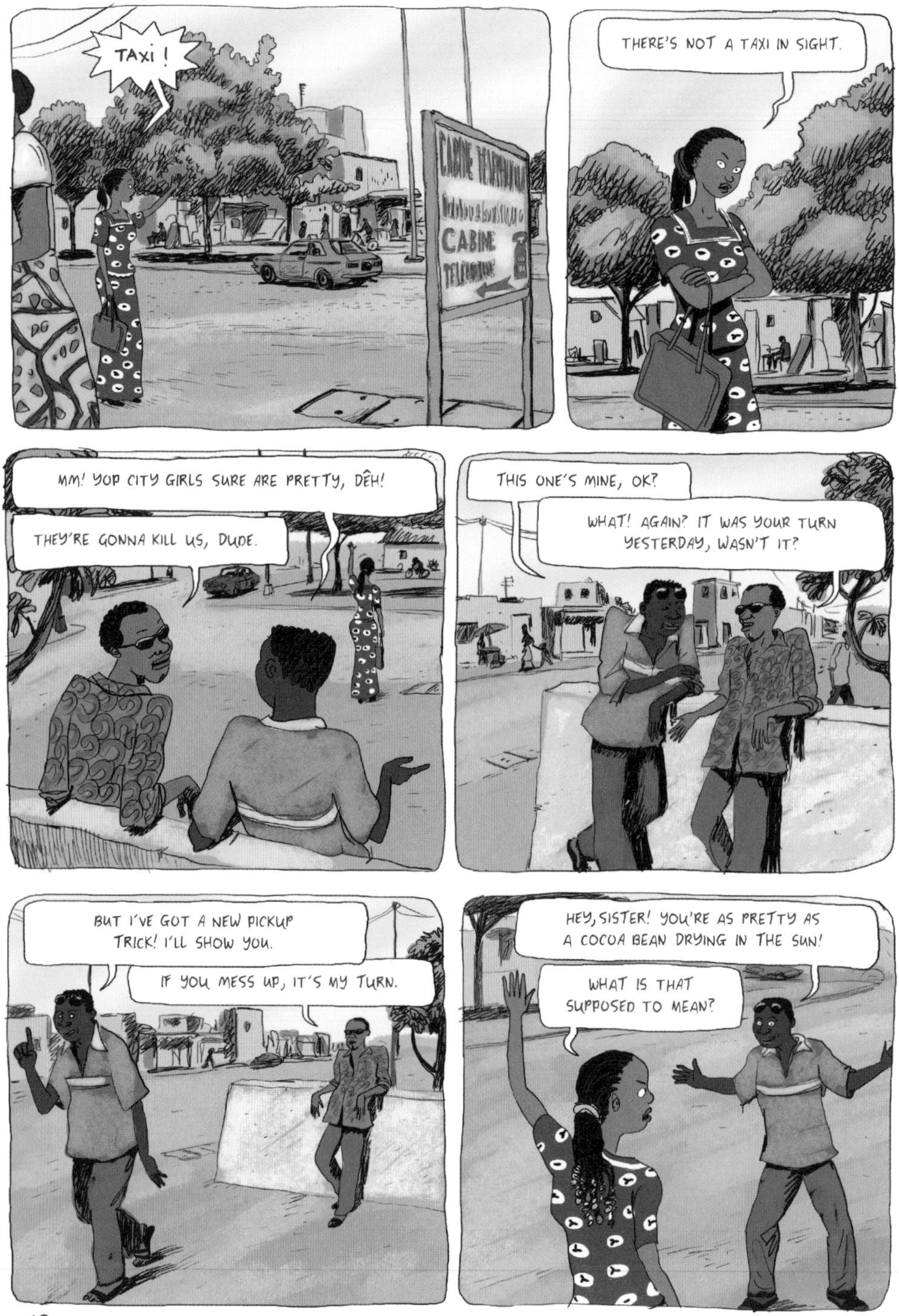
TAXI !
THERE'S NOT A TAXI IN SIGHT.
MM! YOP CITY GIRLS SURE ARE PRETTY, DÊH!
THEY'RE GONNA KILL US, DUDE.
THIS ONE'S MINE, OK?
WHAT! AGAIN? IT WAS YOUR TURN YESTERDAY, WASN'T IT?
BUT I'VE GOT A NEW PICKUP TRICK! I'LL SHOW YOU.
IF YOU MESS UP, IT'S MY TURN.
HEY, SISTER! YOU'RE AS PRETTY AS A COCOA BEAN DRYING IN THE SUN!
WHAT IS THAT SUPPOSED TO MEAN?

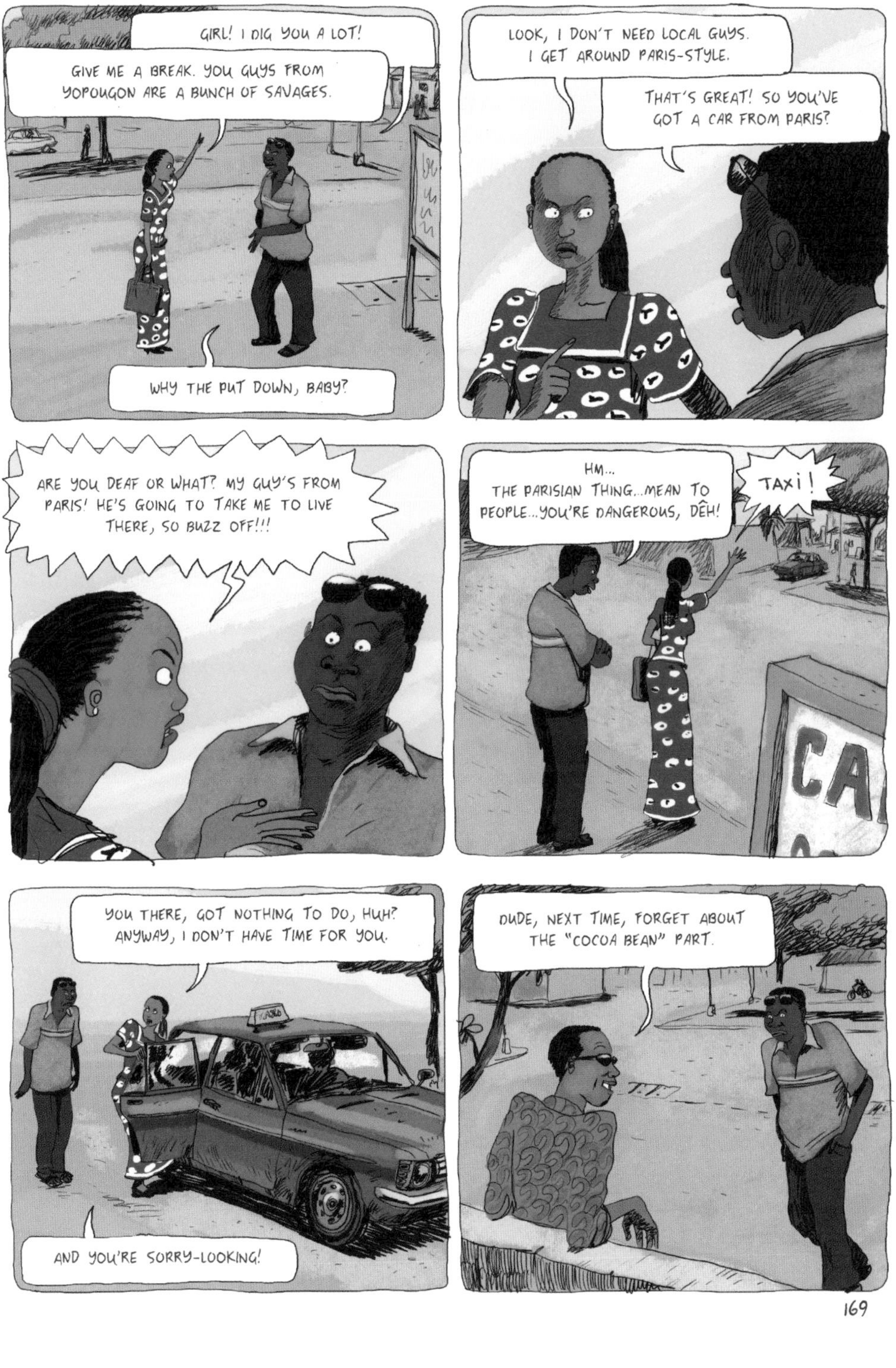
GIRL! I DIG YOU A LOT!
GIVE ME A BREAK. YOU GUYS FROM YOPOUGON ARE A BUNCH OF SAVAGES.
WHY THE PUT DOWN, BABY?
LOOK, I DON'T NEED LOCAL GUYS. I GET AROUND PARIS-STYLE.
THAT'S GREAT! SO YOU'VE GOT A CAR FROM PARIS?
ARE YOU DEAF OR WHAT? MY GUY'S FROM PARIS! HE'S GOING TO TAKE ME TO LIVE THERE, SO BUZZ OFF!!!
HM... THE PARISIAN THING...MEAN TO PEOPLE...YOU'RE DANGEROUS, DÊH!
TAXi!
YOU THERE, GOT NOTHING TO DO, HUH? ANYWAY, I DON'T HAVE TIME FOR YOU.
AND YOU'RE SORRY-LOOKING!
DUDE, NEXT TIME, FORGET ABOUT THE "COCOA BEAN" PART.

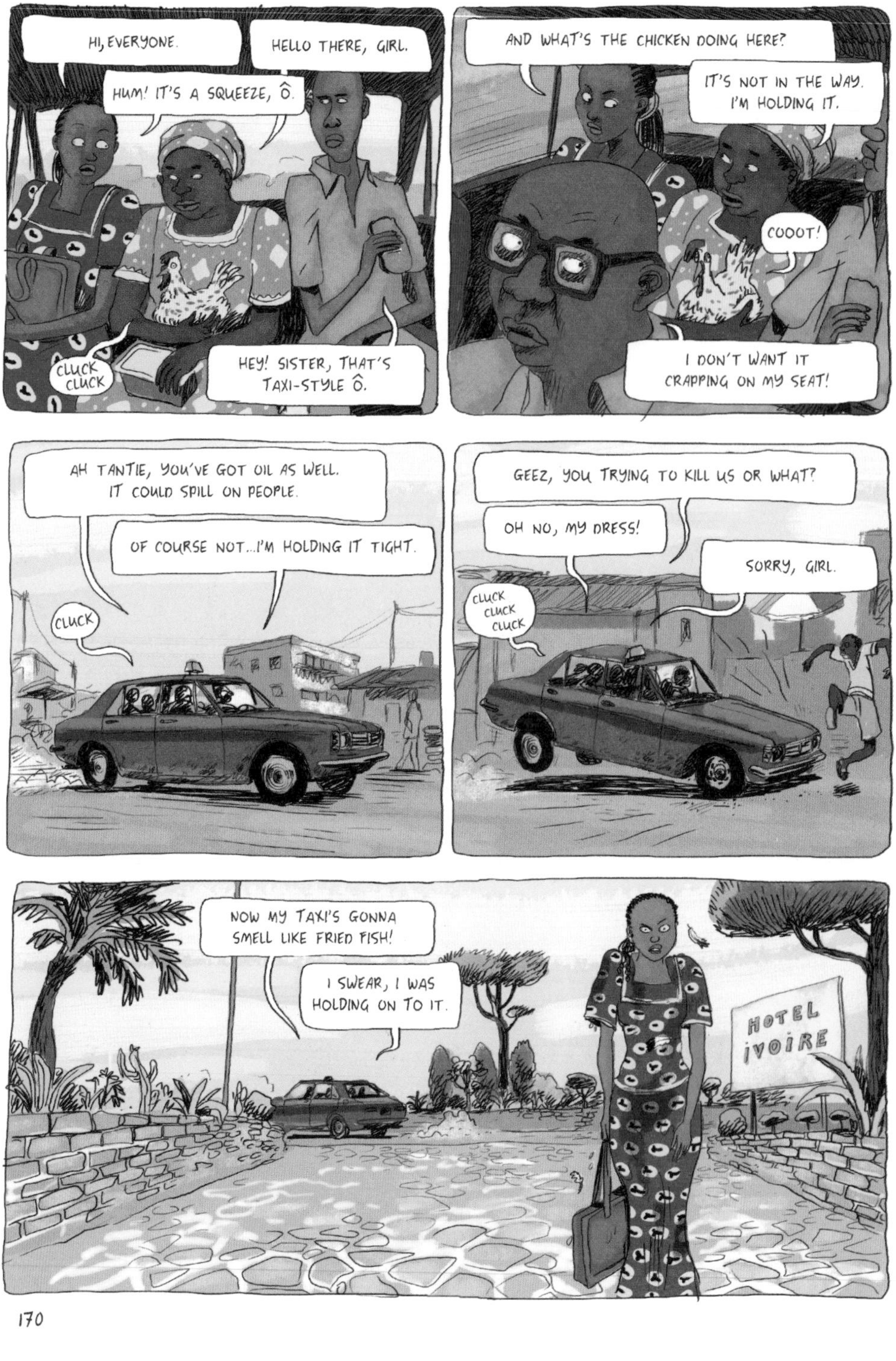
HI, EVERYONE.
HELLO THERE, GIRL.
HUM! IT'S A SQUEEZE, Ô.
CLUCK CLUCK
HEY! SISTER, THAT'S TAXI-STYLE Ô.
AND WHAT'S THE CHICKEN DOING HERE?
IT'S NOT IN THE WAY. I'M HOLDING IT.
COOOT!
I DON'T WANT IT CRAPPING ON MY SEAT!
AH TANTIE, YOU'VE GOT OIL AS WELL. IT COULD SPILL ON PEOPLE.
OF COURSE NOT...I'M HOLDING IT TIGHT.
CLUCK
GEEZ, YOU TRYING TO KILL US OR WHAT?
OH NO, MY DRESS!
SORRY, GIRL.
CLUCK CLUCK CLUCK
NOW MY TAXI'S GONNA SMELL LIKE FRIED FISH!
I SWEAR, I WAS HOLDING ON TO IT.
HOTEL IVOIRE

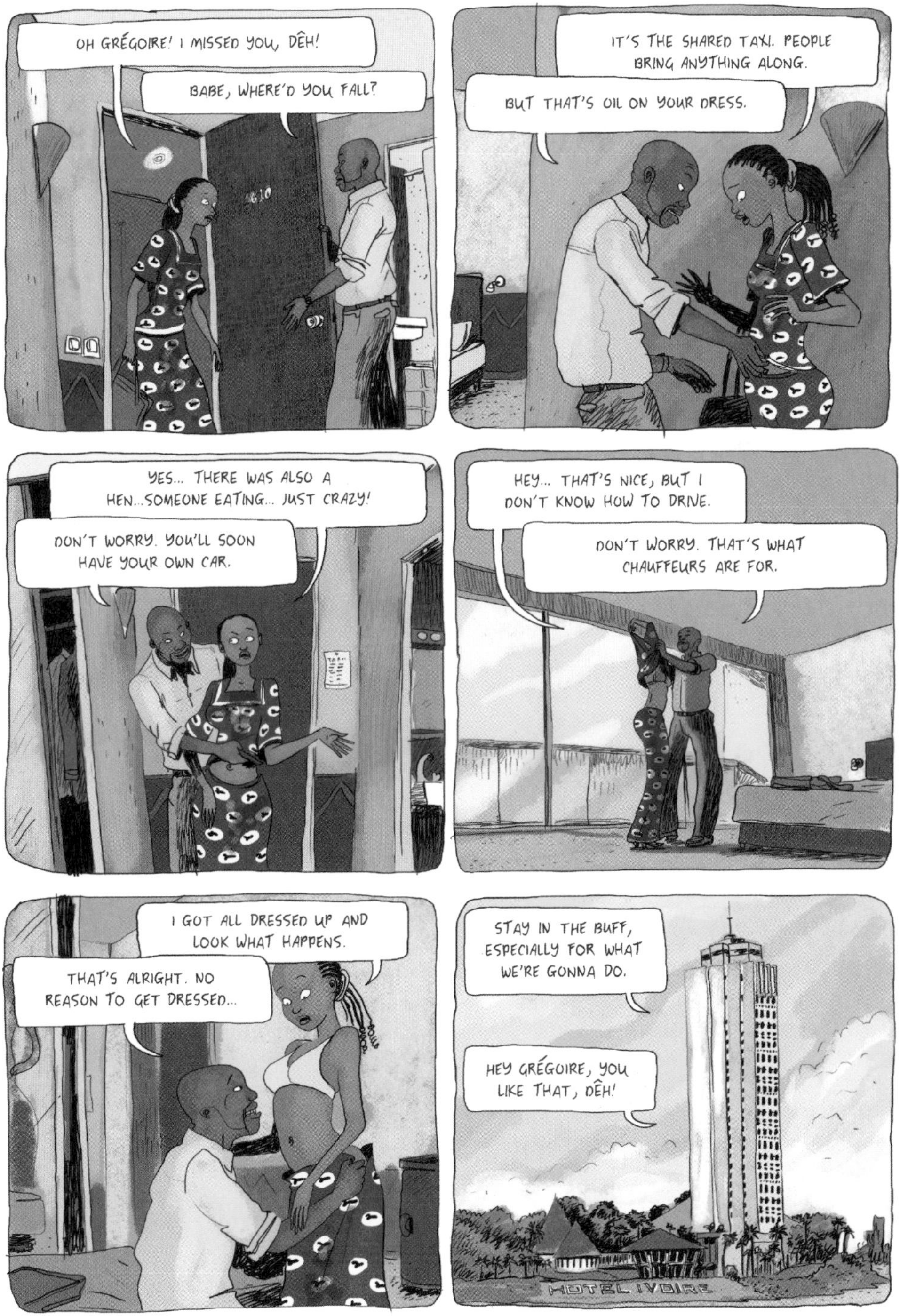
OH GRÉGOIRE! I MISSED YOU, DÊH!
BABE, WHERE'D YOU FALL?
IT'S THE SHARED TAXI. PEOPLE BRING ANYTHING ALONG.
BUT THAT'S OIL ON YOUR DRESS.
YES... THERE WAS ALSO A HEN...SOMEONE EATING... JUST CRAZY!
DON'T WORRY. YOU'LL SOON HAVE YOUR OWN CAR.
HEY... THAT'S NICE, BUT I DON'T KNOW HOW TO DRIVE.
DON'T WORRY. THAT'S WHAT CHAUFFEURS ARE FOR.
I GOT ALL DRESSED UP AND LOOK WHAT HAPPENS.
THAT'S ALRIGHT. NO REASON TO GET DRESSED...
STAY IN THE BUFF, ESPECIALLY FOR WHAT WE'RE GONNA DO.
HEY GRÉGOIRE, YOU LIKE THAT, DÊH!
HOTEL IVOIRE

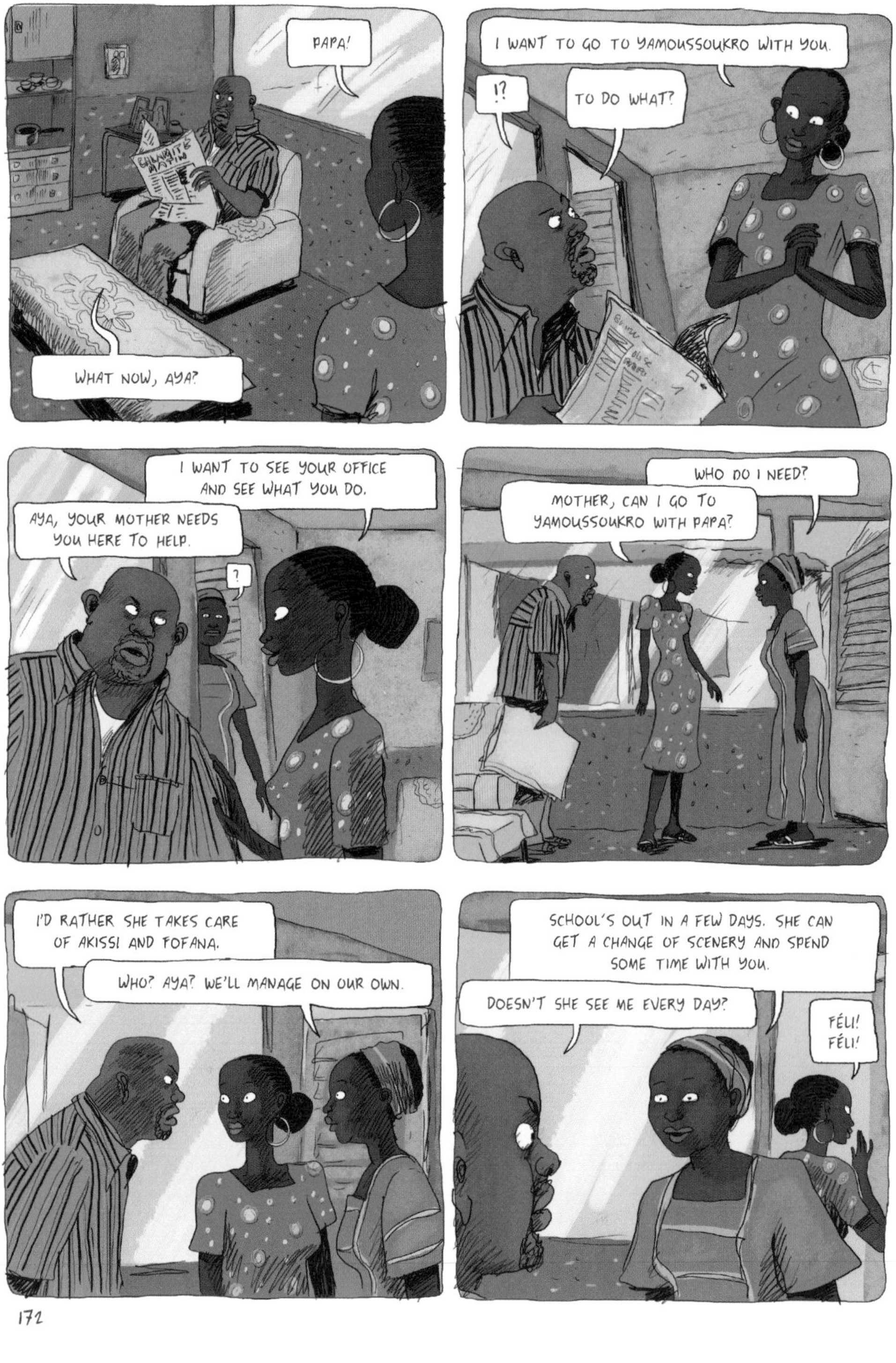
PAPA!
WHAT NOW, AYA?
I WANT TO GO TO YAMOUSSOUKRO WITH YOU.
!?
TO DO WHAT?
I WANT TO SEE YOUR OFFICE AND SEE WHAT YOU DO.
AYA, YOUR MOTHER NEEDS YOU HERE TO HELP.
?
WHO DO I NEED?
MOTHER, CAN I GO TO YAMOUSSOUKRO WITH PAPA?
I'D RATHER SHE TAKES CARE OF AKISSI AND FOFANA.
WHO? AYA? WE'LL MANAGE ON OUR OWN.
SCHOOL'S OUT IN A FEW DAYS. SHE CAN GET A CHANGE OF SCENERY AND SPEND SOME TIME WITH YOU.
DOESN'T SHE SEE ME EVERY DAY?
FÉLI! FÉLI!

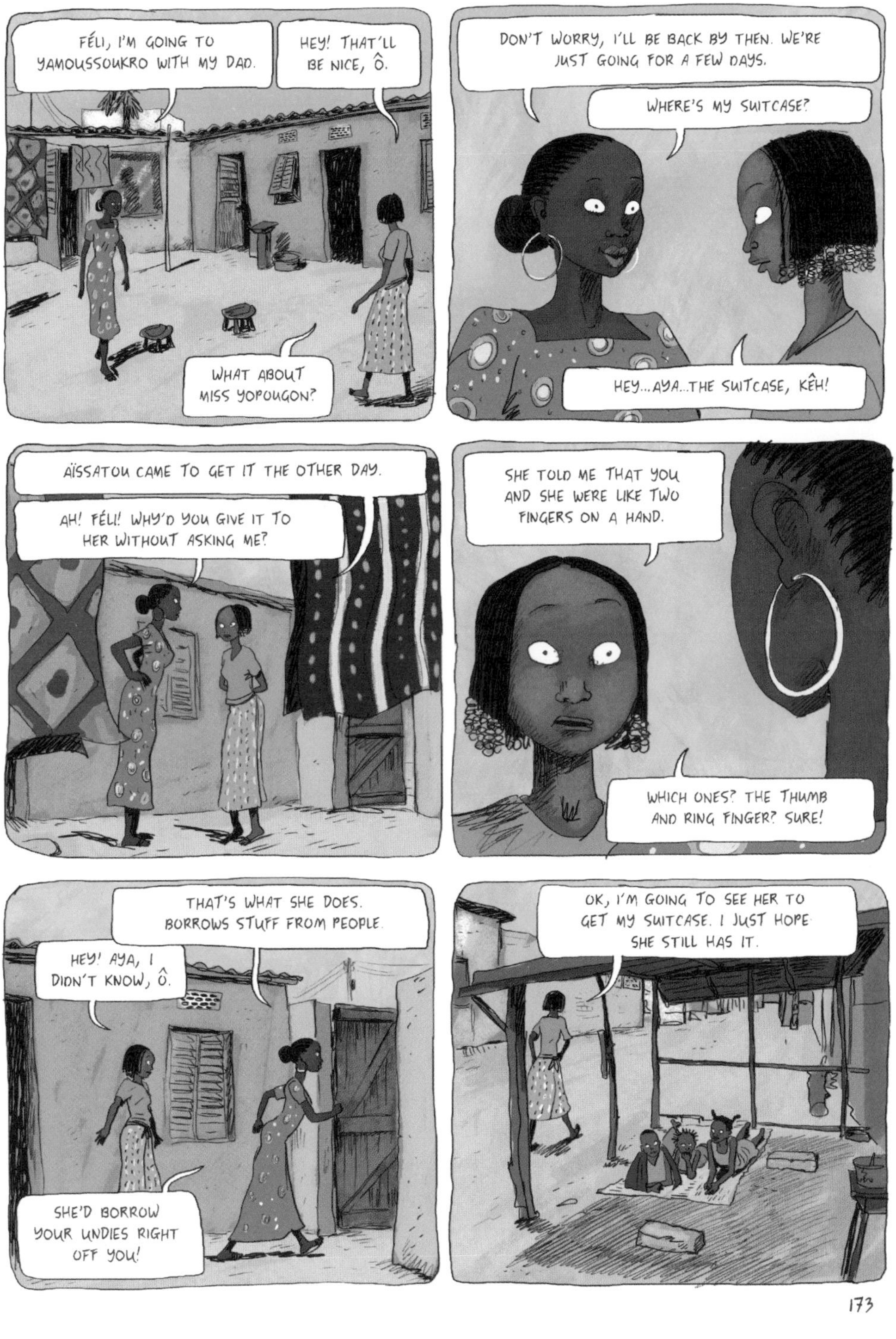
FÉLI, I'M GOING TO YAMOUSSOUKRO WITH MY DAD.
HEY! THAT'LL BE NICE, Ô.
WHAT ABOUT MISS YOPOUGON?
DON'T WORRY, I'LL BE BACK BY THEN. WE'RE JUST GOING FOR A FEW DAYS.
WHERE'S MY SUITCASE?
HEY...AYA...THE SUITCASE, KÊH!
AÏSSATOU CAME TO GET IT THE OTHER DAY.
AH! FÉLI! WHY'D YOU GIVE IT TO HER WITHOUT ASKING ME?
SHE TOLD ME THAT YOU AND SHE WERE LIKE TWO FINGERS ON A HAND.
WHICH ONES? THE THUMB AND RING FINGER? SURE!
THAT'S WHAT SHE DOES. BORROWS STUFF FROM PEOPLE.
HEY! AYA, I DIDN'T KNOW, Ô.
SHE'D BORROW YOUR UNDIES RIGHT OFF YOU!
OK, I'M GOING TO SEE HER TO GET MY SUITCASE. I JUST HOPE SHE STILL HAS IT.

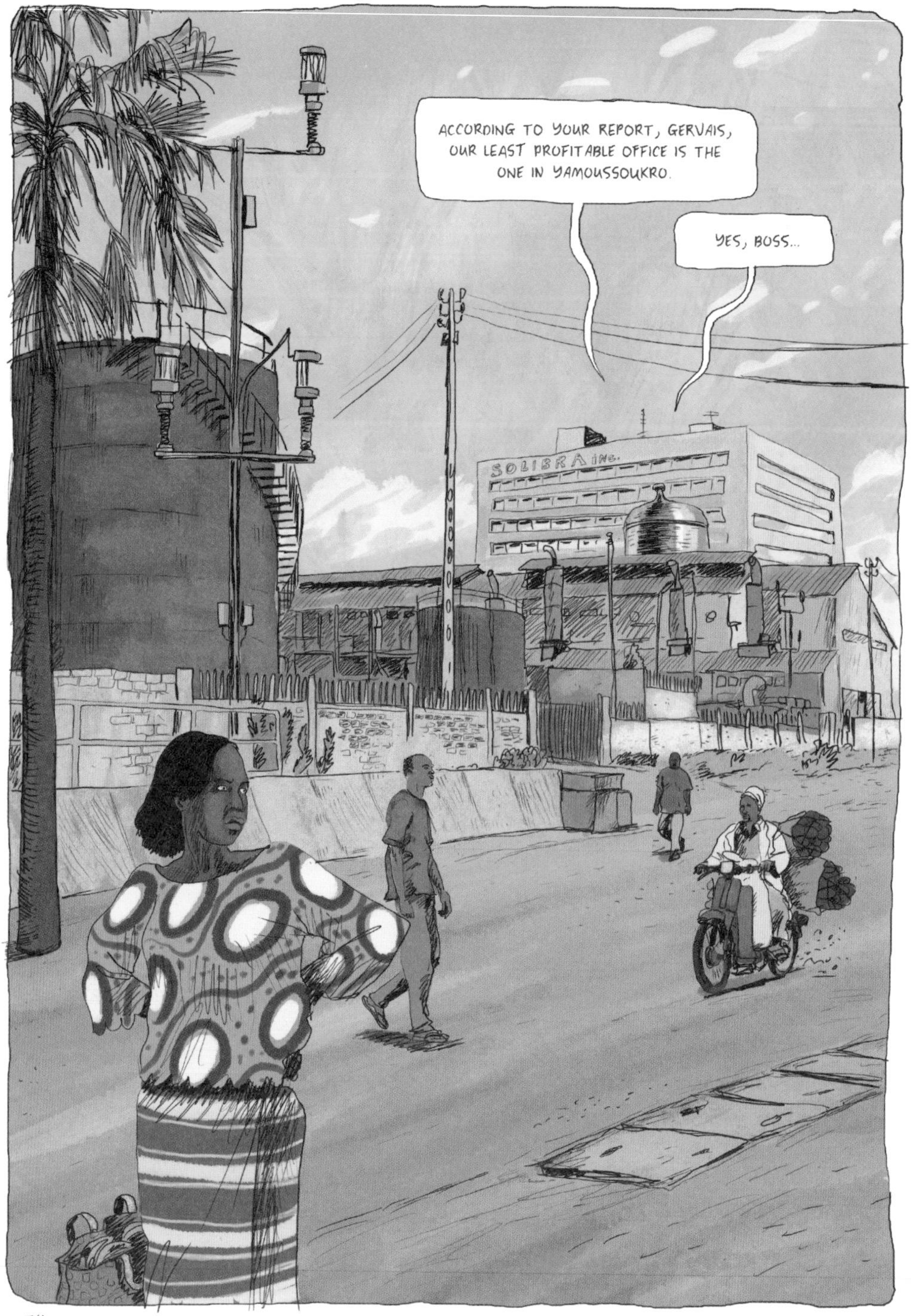
ACCORDING TO YOUR REPORT, GERVAIS, OUR LEAST PROFITABLE OFFICE IS THE ONE IN YAMOUSSOUKRO.
YES, BOSS...
SOLIBRA inc.

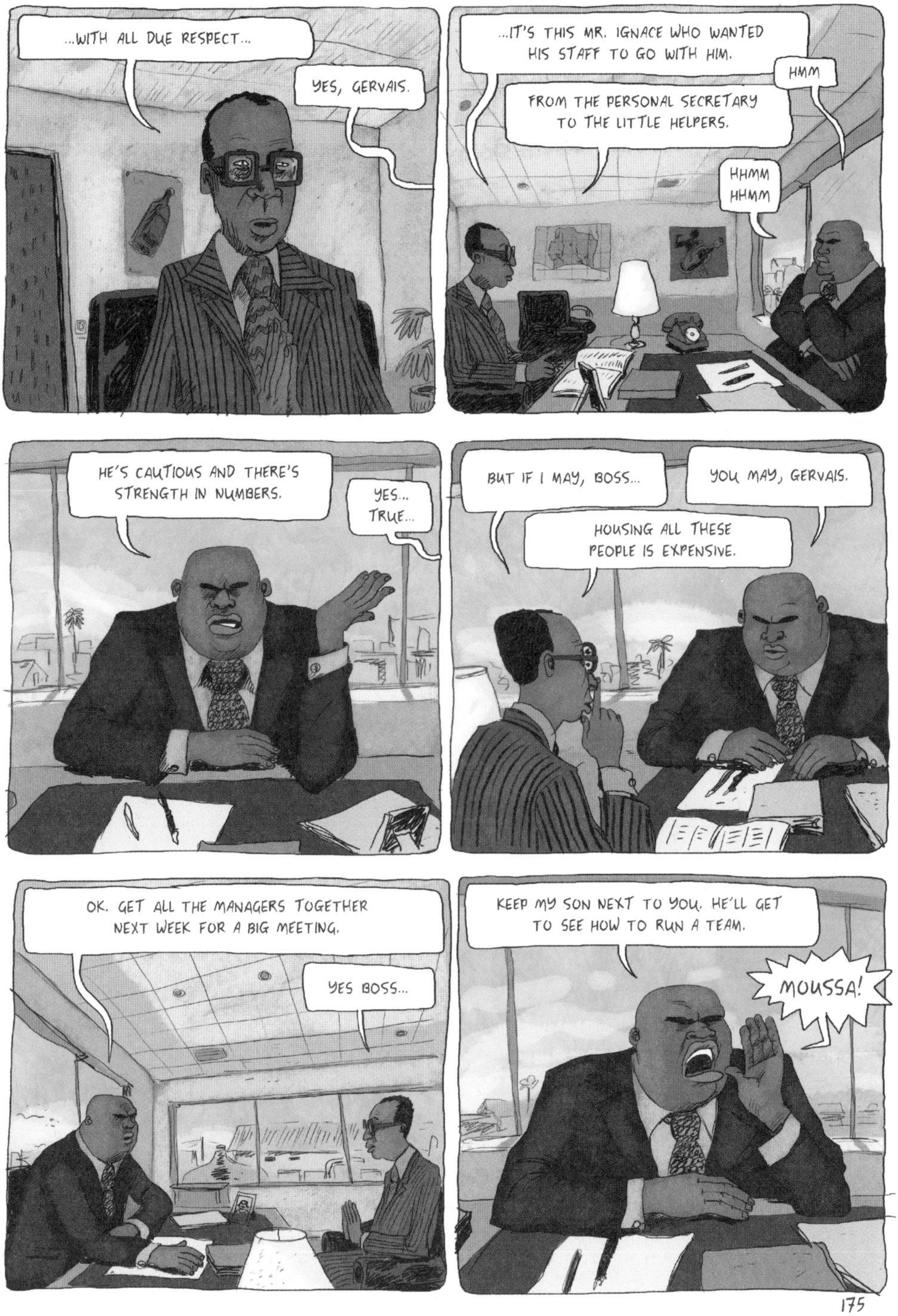
...WITH ALL DUE RESPECT...
YES, GERVAIS.
...IT'S THIS MR. IGNACE WHO WANTED HIS STAFF TO GO WITH HIM.
HMM
FROM THE PERSONAL SECRETARY TO THE LITTLE HELPERS.
HHMM HHMM
HE'S CAUTIOUS AND THERE'S STRENGTH IN NUMBERS.
YES... TRUE...
BUT IF I MAY, BOSS...
YOU MAY, GERVAIS.
HOUSING ALL THESE PEOPLE IS EXPENSIVE.
OK. GET ALL THE MANAGERS TOGETHER NEXT WEEK FOR A BIG MEETING.
YES BOSS...
KEEP MY SON NEXT TO YOU. HE'LL GET TO SEE HOW TO RUN A TEAM.
MOUSSA!

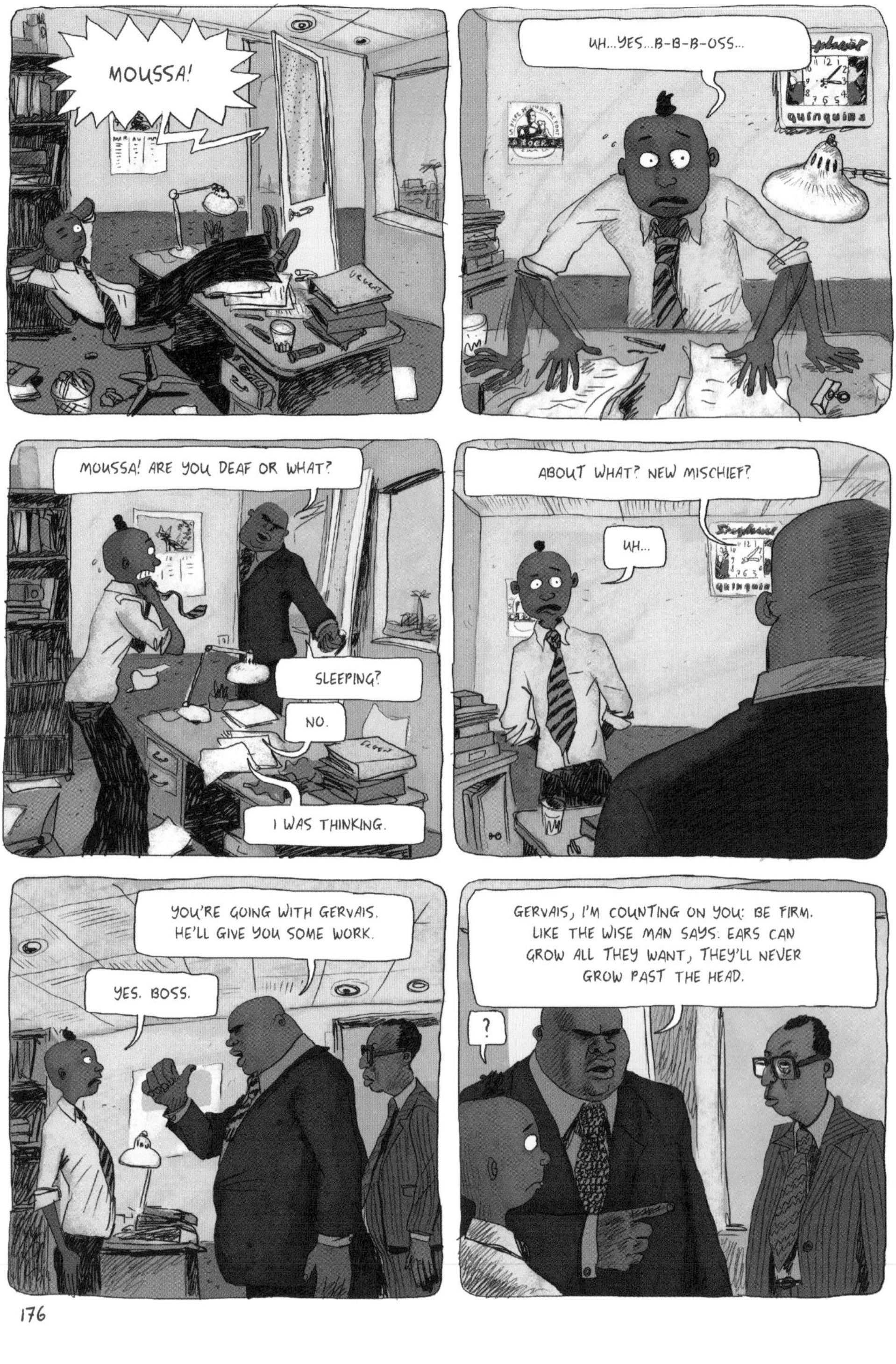
MOUSSA!
UH...YES...B-B-B-OSS...
MOUSSA! ARE YOU DEAF OR WHAT?
SLEEPING?
NO.
I WAS THINKING.
ABOUT WHAT? NEW MISCHIEF?
UH...
YOU'RE GOING WITH GERVAIS. HE'LL GIVE YOU SOME WORK.
YES. BOSS.
GERVAIS, I'M COUNTING ON YOU: BE FIRM. LIKE THE WISE MAN SAYS: EARS CAN GROW ALL THEY WANT, THEY'LL NEVER GROW PAST THE HEAD.
?

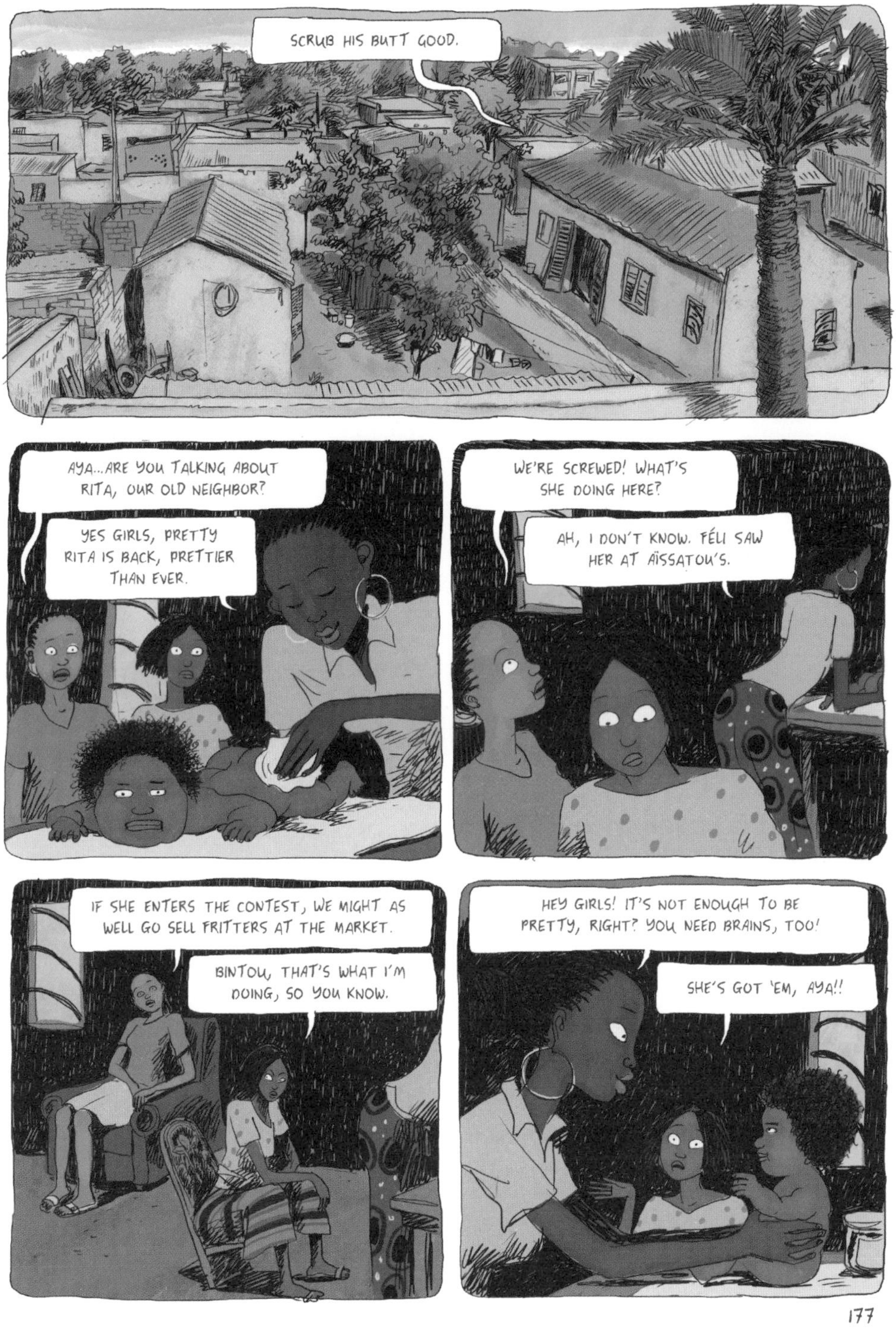
SCRUB HIS BUTT GOOD.
AYA...ARE YOU TALKING ABOUT RITA, OUR OLD NEIGHBOR?
YES GIRLS, PRETTY RITA IS BACK, PRETTIER THAN EVER.
WE'RE SCREWED! WHAT'S SHE DOING HERE?
AH, I DON'T KNOW. FÉLI SAW HER AT AÏSSATOU'S.
IF SHE ENTERS THE CONTEST, WE MIGHT AS WELL GO SELL FRITTERS AT THE MARKET.
BINTOU, THAT'S WHAT I'M DOING, SO YOU KNOW.
HEY GIRLS! IT'S NOT ENOUGH TO BE PRETTY, RIGHT? YOU NEED BRAINS, TOO!
SHE'S GOT 'EM, AYA!!

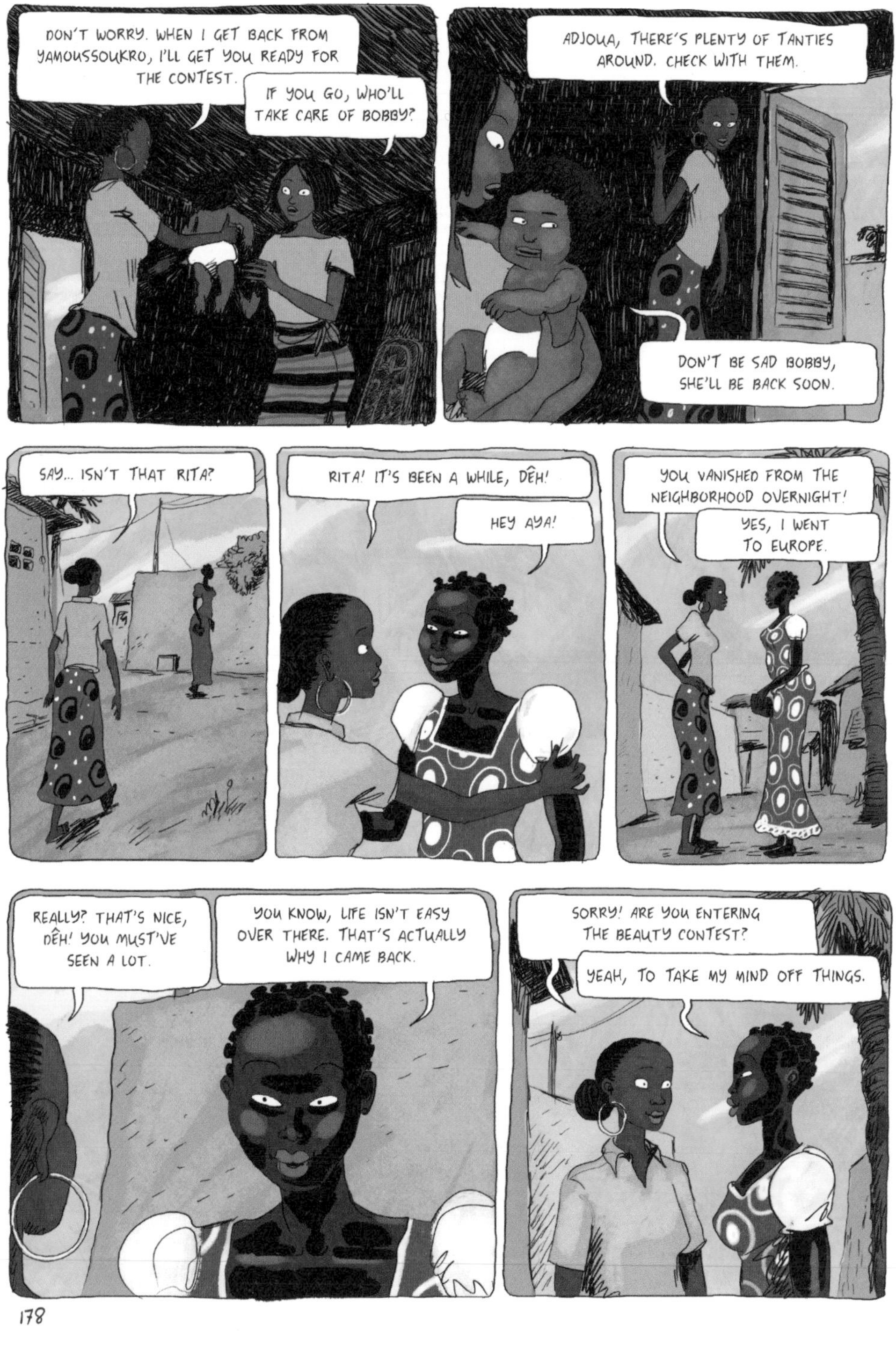
DON'T WORRY. WHEN I GET BACK FROM YAMOUSSOUKRO, I'LL GET YOU READY FOR THE CONTEST.
IF YOU GO, WHO'LL TAKE CARE OF BOBBY?
ADJOUA, THERE'S PLENTY OF TANTIES AROUND. CHECK WITH THEM.
DON'T BE SAD BOBBY, SHE'LL BE BACK SOON.
SAY... ISN'T THAT RITA?
RITA! IT'S BEEN A WHILE, DÊH!
HEY AYA!
YOU VANISHED FROM THE NEIGHBORHOOD OVERNIGHT!
YES, I WENT TO EUROPE.
REALLY? THAT'S NICE, DÊH! YOU MUST'VE SEEN A LOT.
YOU KNOW, LIFE ISN'T EASY OVER THERE. THAT'S ACTUALLY WHY I CAME BACK.
SORRY! ARE YOU ENTERING THE BEAUTY CONTEST?
YEAH, TO TAKE MY MIND OFF THINGS.

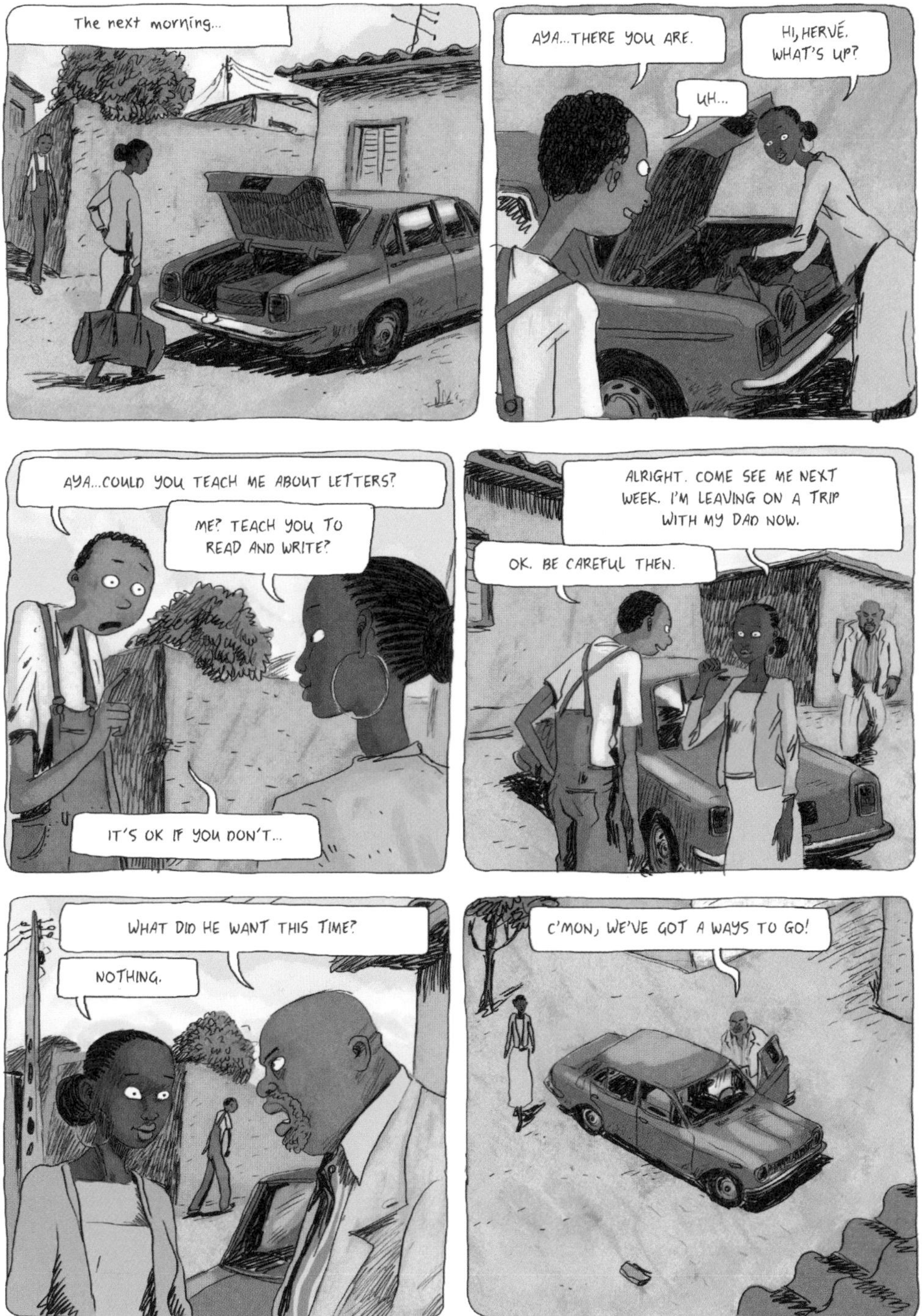
The next morning...
AYA...THERE YOU ARE.
HI, HERVÉ. WHAT'S UP?
UH...
AYA...COULD YOU TEACH ME ABOUT LETTERS?
ME? TEACH YOU TO READ AND WRITE?
IT'S OK IF YOU DON'T...
ALRIGHT. COME SEE ME NEXT WEEK. I'M LEAVING ON A TRIP WITH MY DAD NOW.
OK. BE CAREFUL THEN.
WHAT DID HE WANT THIS TIME?
NOTHING.
C'MON, WE'VE GOT A WAYS TO GO!

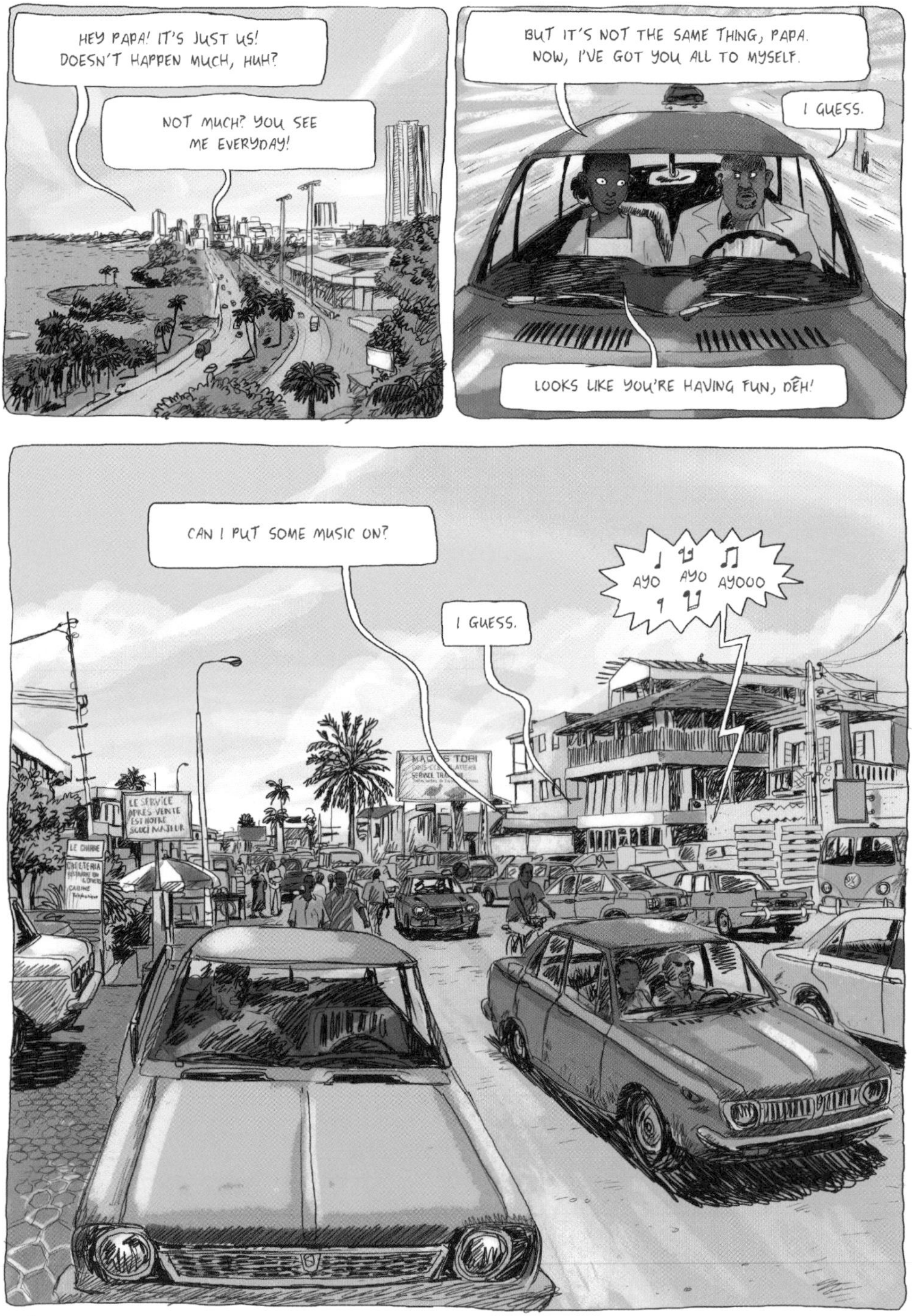

HEY PAPA! IT'S JUST US! DOESN'T HAPPEN MUCH, HUH?
NOT MUCH? YOU SEE ME EVERYDAY!
BUT IT'S NOT THE SAME THING, PAPA. NOW, I'VE GOT YOU ALL TO MYSELF.
I GUESS.
LOOKS LIKE YOU'RE HAVING FUN, DÊH!
CAN I PUT SOME MUSIC ON?
I GUESS.
AYO AYO AYOOO
LE SERVICE APRÈS-VENTE EST NOTRE SOUCI MAJEUR

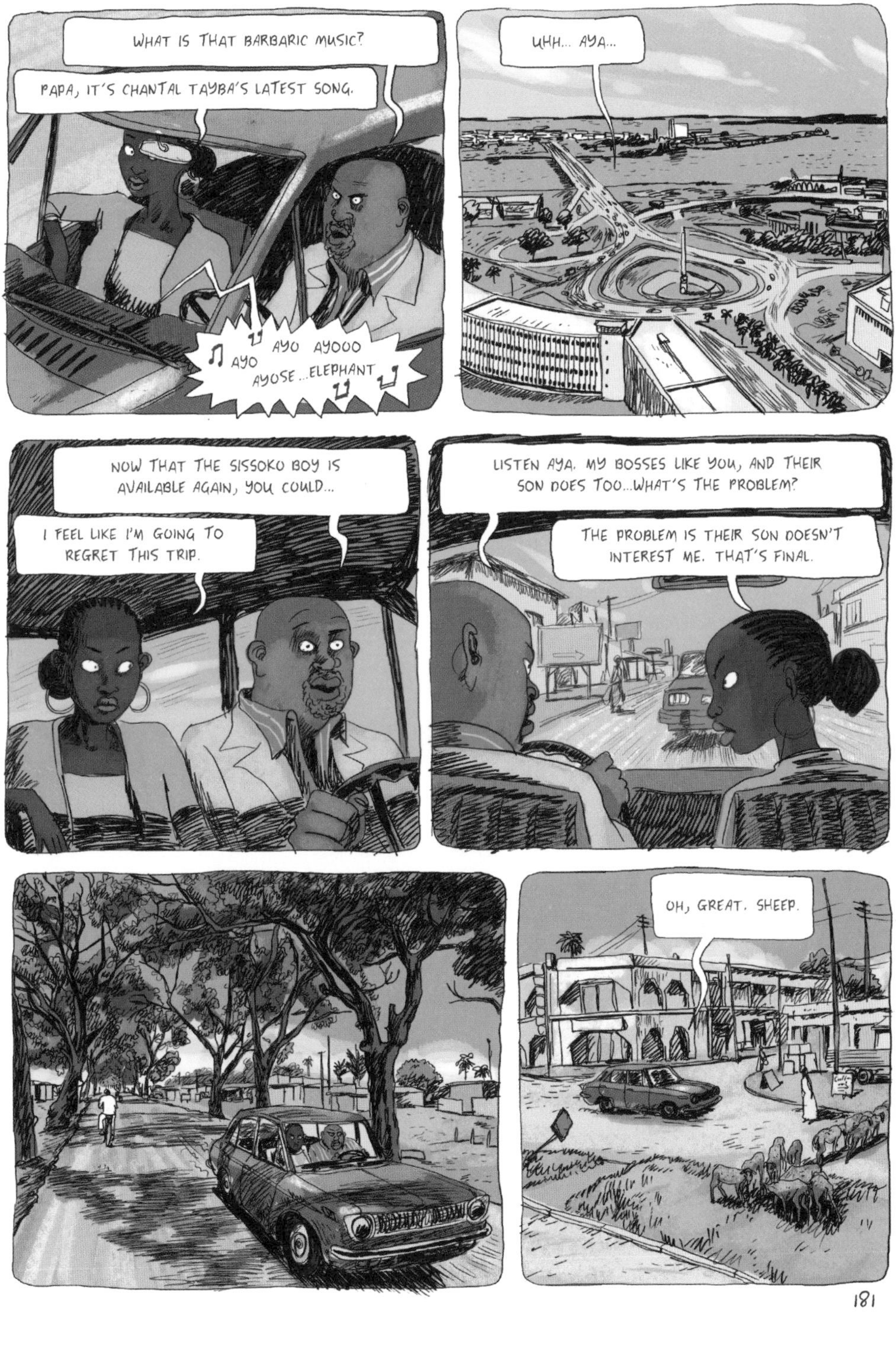
WHAT IS THAT BARBARIC MUSIC?
PAPA, IT'S CHANTAL TAYBA'S LATEST SONG.
AYO AYO AYOOO
AYOSE ...ELEPHANT
UHH... AYA...
NOW THAT THE SISSOKO BOY IS AVAILABLE AGAIN, YOU COULD...
I FEEL LIKE I'M GOING TO REGRET THIS TRIP.
LISTEN AYA. MY BOSSES LIKE YOU, AND THEIR SON DOES TOO...WHAT'S THE PROBLEM?
THE PROBLEM IS THEIR SON DOESN'T INTEREST ME. THAT'S FINAL.
OH, GREAT. SHEEP.

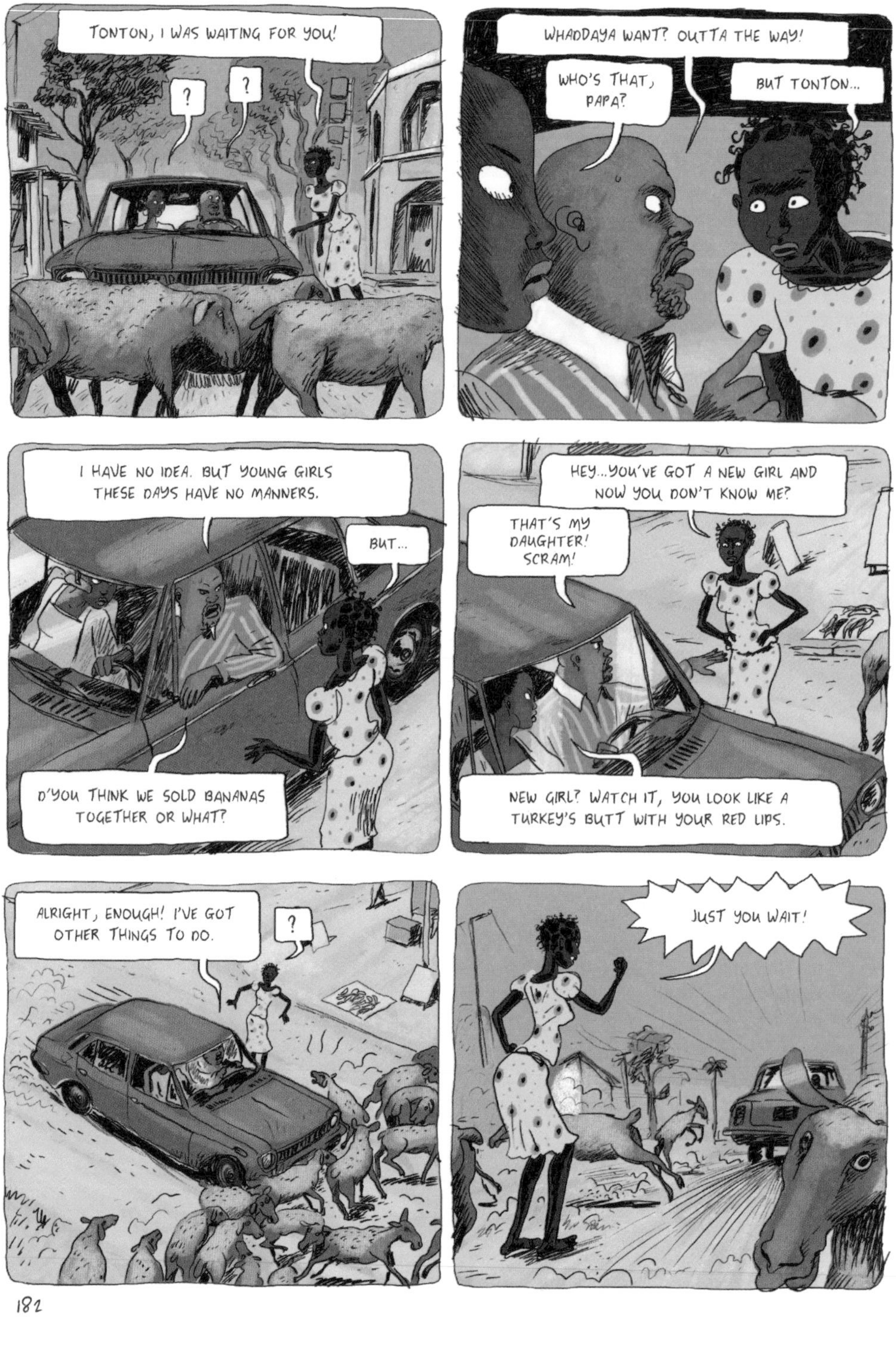
TONTON, I WAS WAITING FOR YOU!
?
?
WHADDAYA WANT? OUTTA THE WAY!
WHO'S THAT, PAPA?
BUT TONTON...
I HAVE NO IDEA. BUT YOUNG GIRLS THESE DAYS HAVE NO MANNERS.
BUT...
D'YOU THINK WE SOLD BANANAS TOGETHER OR WHAT?
HEY...YOU'VE GOT A NEW GIRL AND NOW YOU DON'T KNOW ME?
THAT'S MY DAUGHTER! SCRAM!
NEW GIRL? WATCH IT, YOU LOOK LIKE A TURKEY'S BUTT WITH YOUR RED LIPS.
ALRIGHT, ENOUGH! I'VE GOT OTHER THINGS TO DO.
?
JUST YOU WAIT!

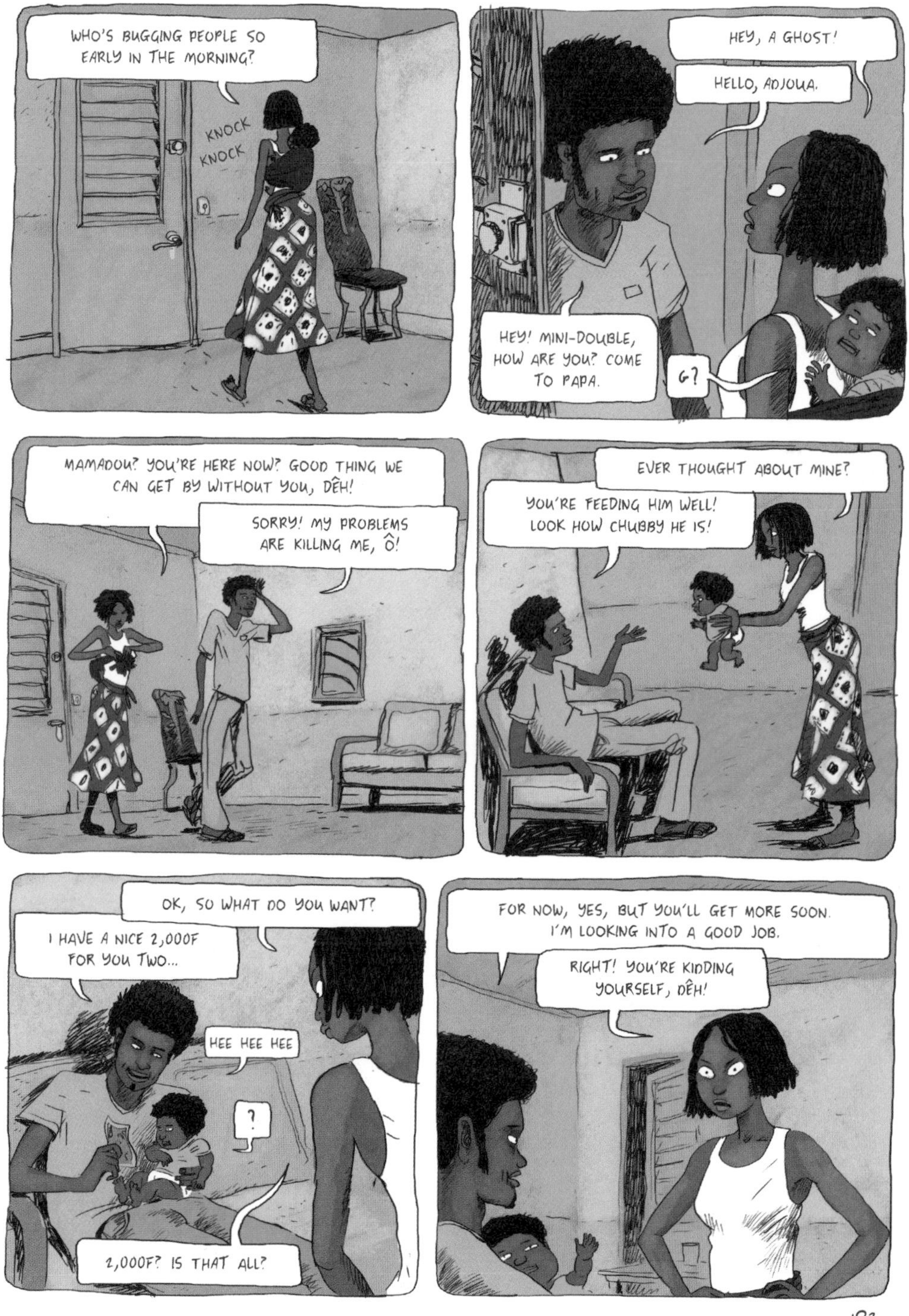
WHO'S BUGGING PEOPLE SO EARLY IN THE MORNING?
KNOCK KNOCK
HEY, A GHOST!
HELLO, ADJOUA.
HEY! MINI-DOUBLE, HOW ARE YOU? COME TO PAPA.
G?
MAMADOU? YOU'RE HERE NOW? GOOD THING WE CAN GET BY WITHOUT YOU, DÊH!
SORRY! MY PROBLEMS ARE KILLING ME, Ô!
EVER THOUGHT ABOUT MINE?
YOU'RE FEEDING HIM WELL! LOOK HOW CHUBBY HE IS!
OK, SO WHAT DO YOU WANT?
I HAVE A NICE 2,000F FOR YOU TWO...
HEE HEE HEE
?
2,000F? IS THAT ALL?
FOR NOW, YES, BUT YOU'LL GET MORE SOON. I'M LOOKING INTO A GOOD JOB.
RIGHT! YOU'RE KIDDING YOURSELF, DÊH!

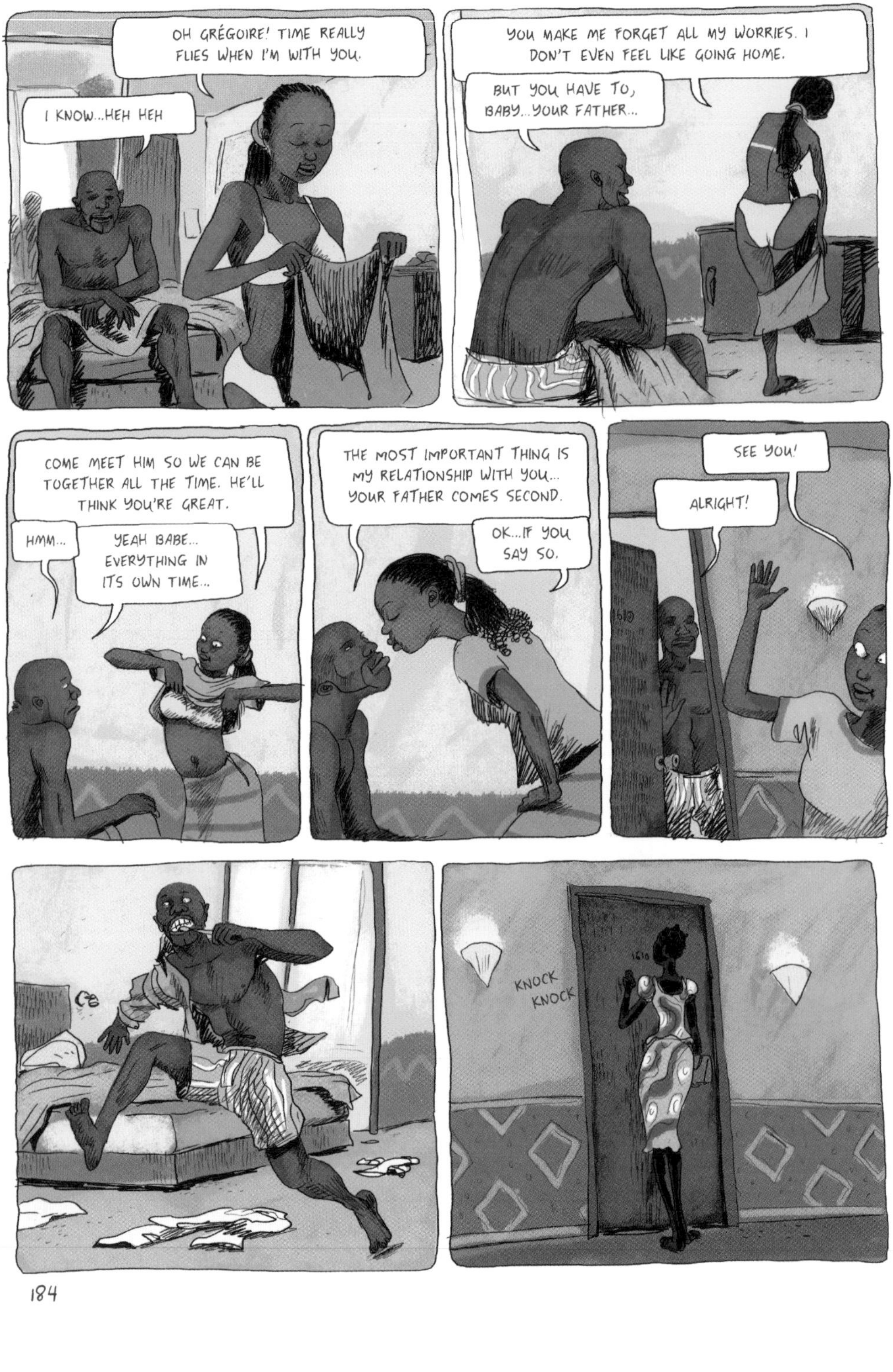
OH GRÉGOIRE! TIME REALLY FLIES WHEN I'M WITH YOU.
I KNOW...HEH HEH
YOU MAKE ME FORGET ALL MY WORRIES. I DON'T EVEN FEEL LIKE GOING HOME.
BUT YOU HAVE TO, BABY...YOUR FATHER...
COME MEET HIM SO WE CAN BE TOGETHER ALL THE TIME. HE'LL THINK YOU'RE GREAT.
HMM...
YEAH BABE... EVERYTHING IN ITS OWN TIME...
THE MOST IMPORTANT THING IS MY RELATIONSHIP WITH YOU... YOUR FATHER COMES SECOND.
OK...IF YOU SAY SO.
SEE YOU!
ALRIGHT!
1610
KNOCK KNOCK
1610

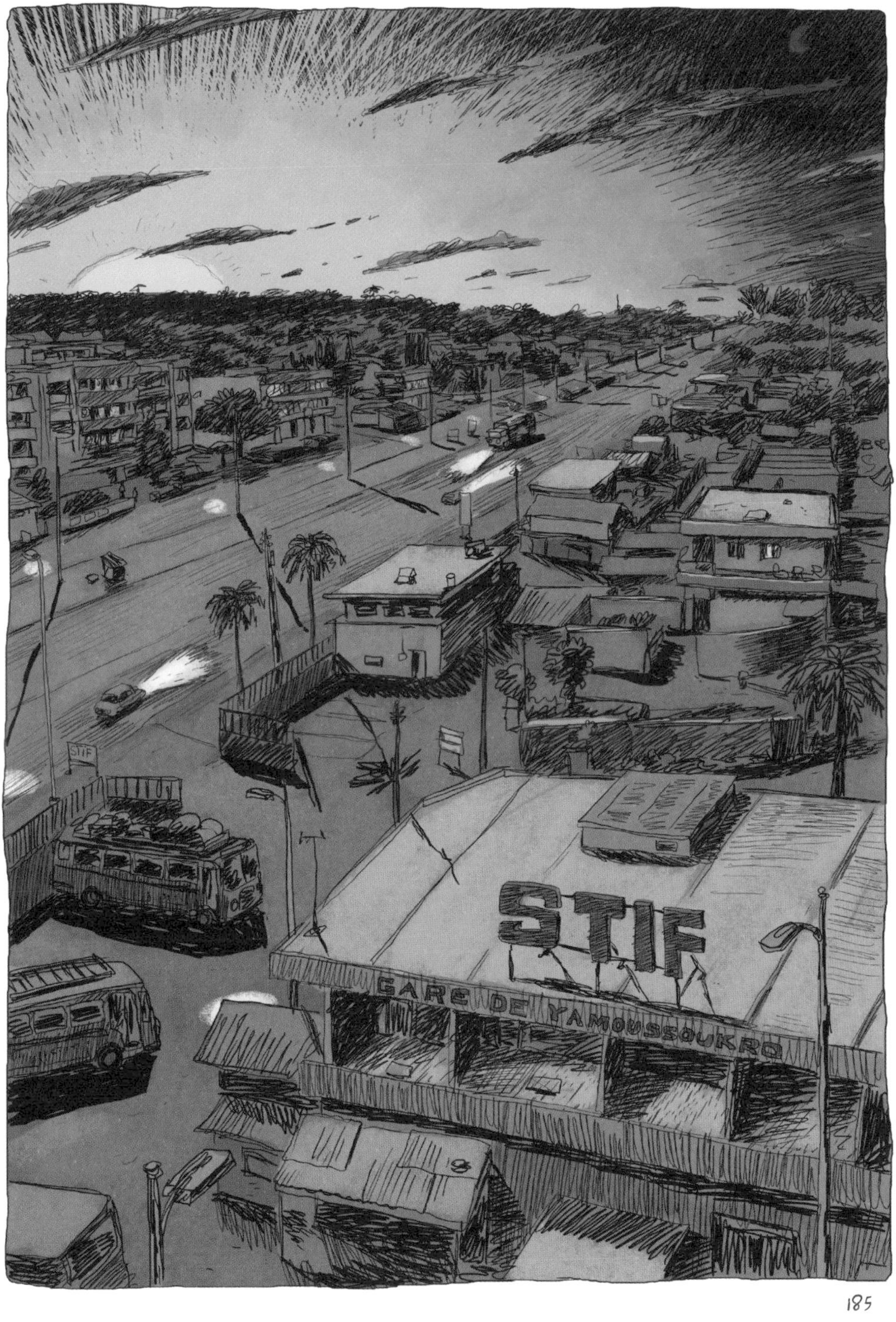
STIF
STIF
GARE DE YAMOUSSOUKRO

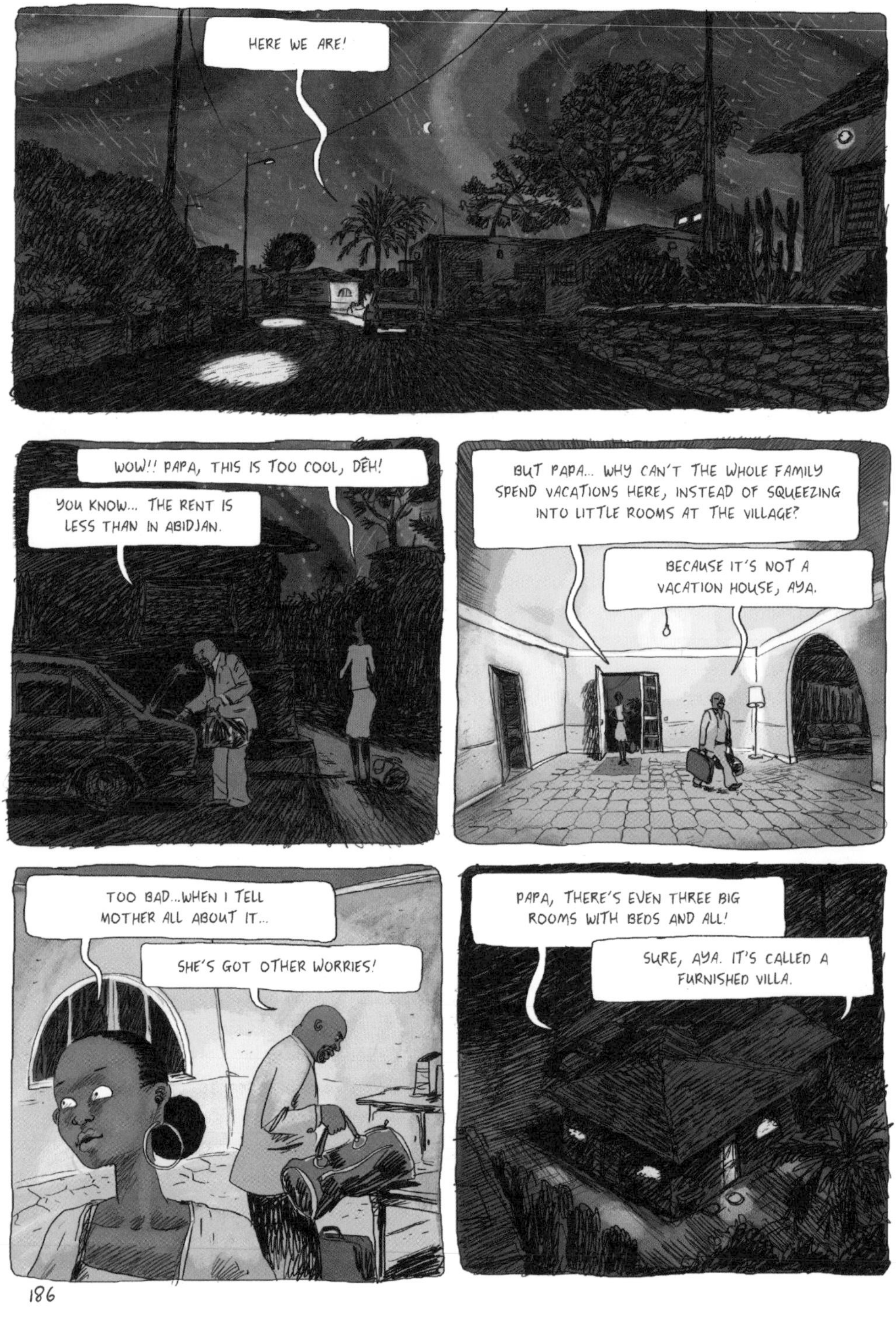
HERE WE ARE!
WOW!! PAPA, THIS IS TOO COOL, DÊH!
YOU KNOW... THE RENT IS LESS THAN IN ABIDJAN.
BUT PAPA... WHY CAN'T THE WHOLE FAMILY SPEND VACATIONS HERE, INSTEAD OF SQUEEZING INTO LITTLE ROOMS AT THE VILLAGE?
BECAUSE IT'S NOT A VACATION HOUSE, AYA.
TOO BAD...WHEN I TELL MOTHER ALL ABOUT IT...
SHE'S GOT OTHER WORRIES!
PAPA, THERE'S EVEN THREE BIG ROOMS WITH BEDS AND ALL!
SURE, AYA. IT'S CALLED A FURNISHED VILLA.

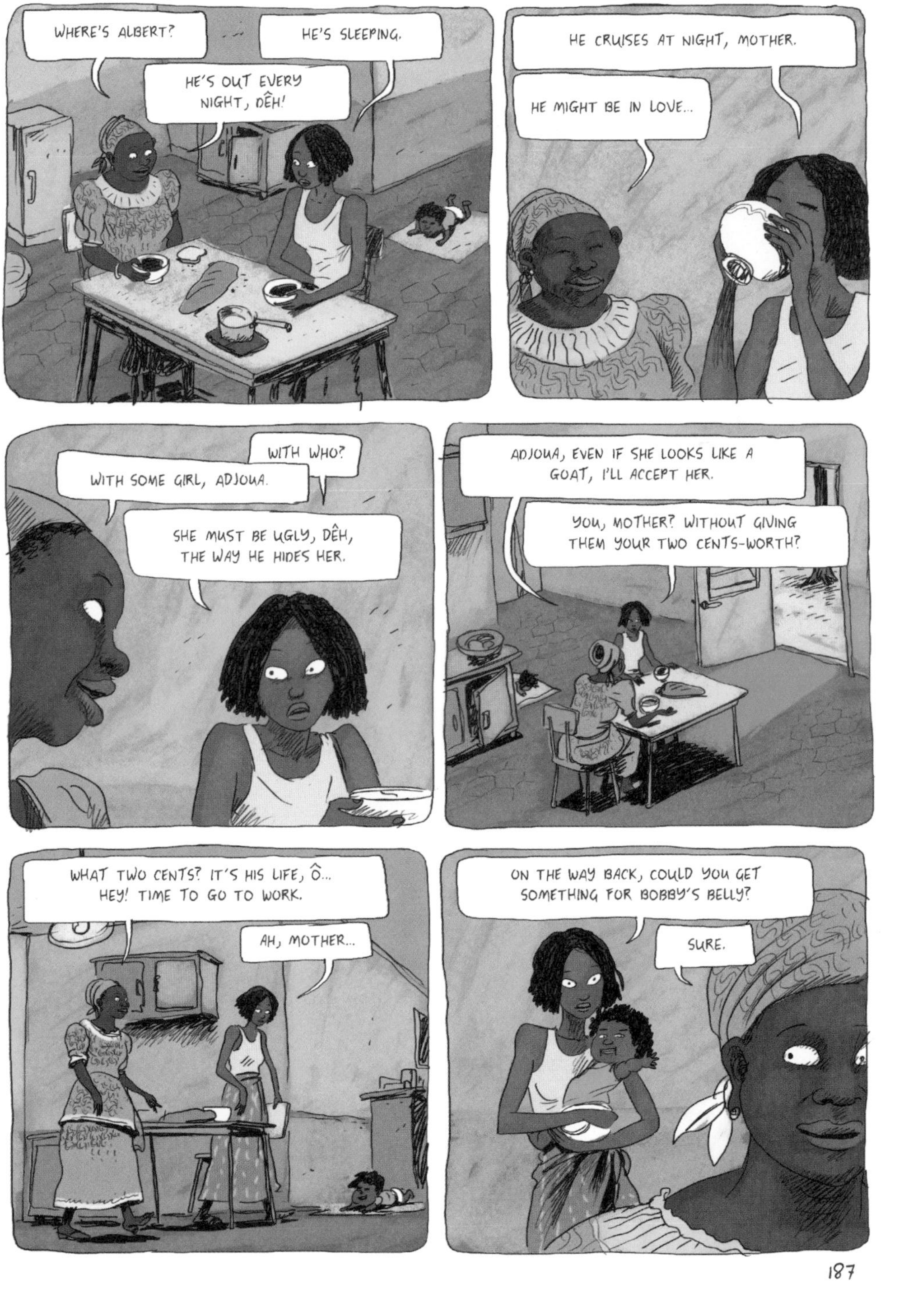
WHERE'S ALBERT?
HE'S SLEEPING.
HE'S OUT EVERY NIGHT, DÊH!
HE CRUISES AT NIGHT, MOTHER.
HE MIGHT BE IN LOVE...
WITH WHO?
WITH SOME GIRL, ADJOUA.
SHE MUST BE UGLY, DÊH, THE WAY HE HIDES HER.
ADJOUA, EVEN IF SHE LOOKS LIKE A GOAT, I'LL ACCEPT HER.
YOU, MOTHER? WITHOUT GIVING THEM YOUR TWO CENTS-WORTH?
WHAT TWO CENTS? IT'S HIS LIFE, Ô... HEY! TIME TO GO TO WORK.
AH, MOTHER...
ON THE WAY BACK, COULD YOU GET SOMETHING FOR BOBBY'S BELLY?
SURE.

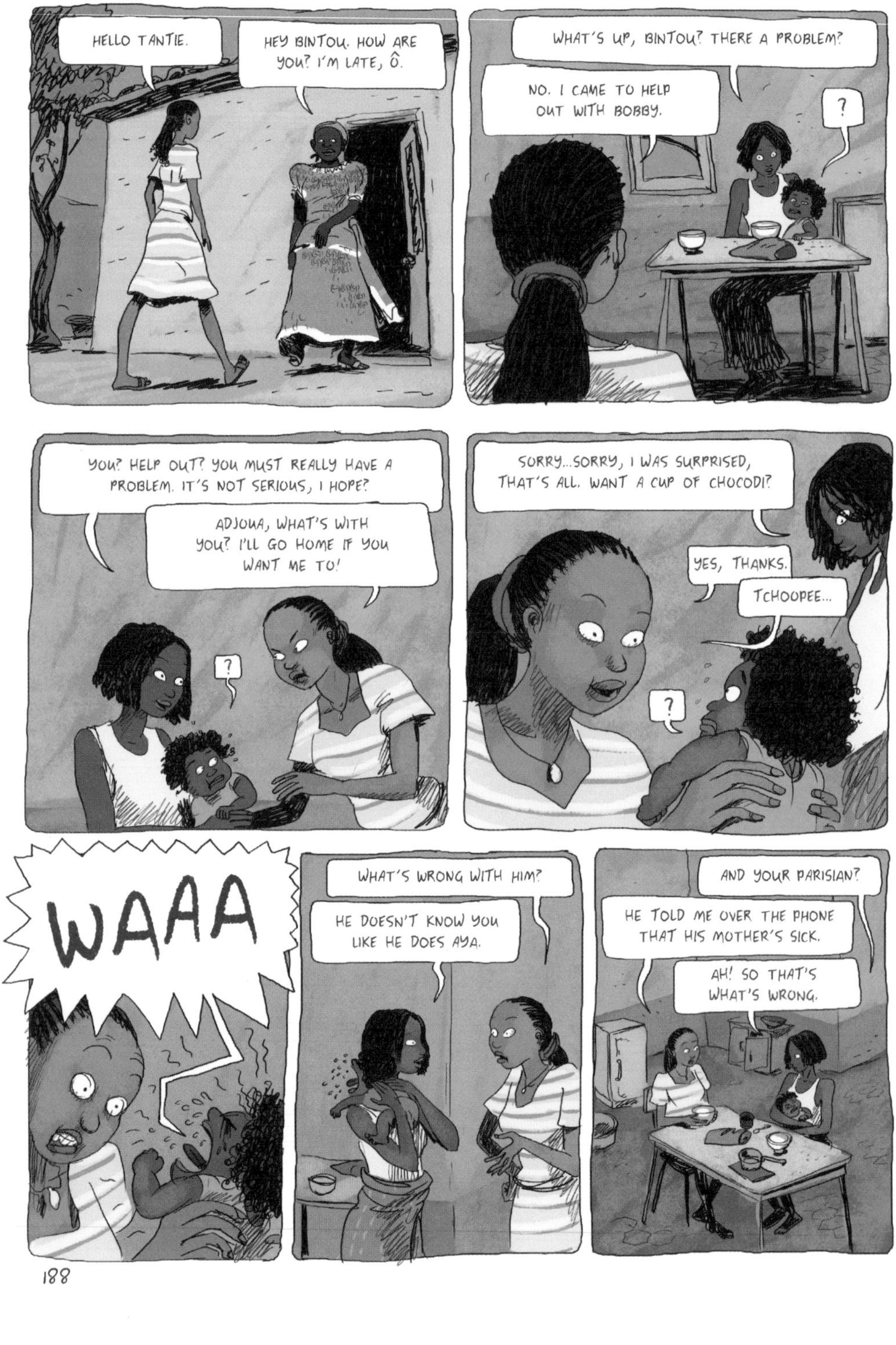
HELLO TANTIE.
HEY BINTOU. HOW ARE YOU? I'M LATE, Ô.
WHAT'S UP, BINTOU? THERE A PROBLEM?
NO. I CAME TO HELP OUT WITH BOBBY.
?
YOU? HELP OUT? YOU MUST REALLY HAVE A PROBLEM. IT'S NOT SERIOUS, I HOPE?
ADJOUA, WHAT'S WITH YOU? I'LL GO HOME IF YOU WANT ME TO!
?
SORRY...SORRY, I WAS SURPRISED, THAT'S ALL. WANT A CUP OF CHOCODI?
YES, THANKS.
TCHOOPEE...
?
WAAA
WHAT'S WRONG WITH HIM?
HE DOESN'T KNOW YOU LIKE HE DOES AYA.
AND YOUR PARISIAN?
HE TOLD ME OVER THE PHONE THAT HIS MOTHER'S SICK.
AH! SO THAT'S WHAT'S WRONG.

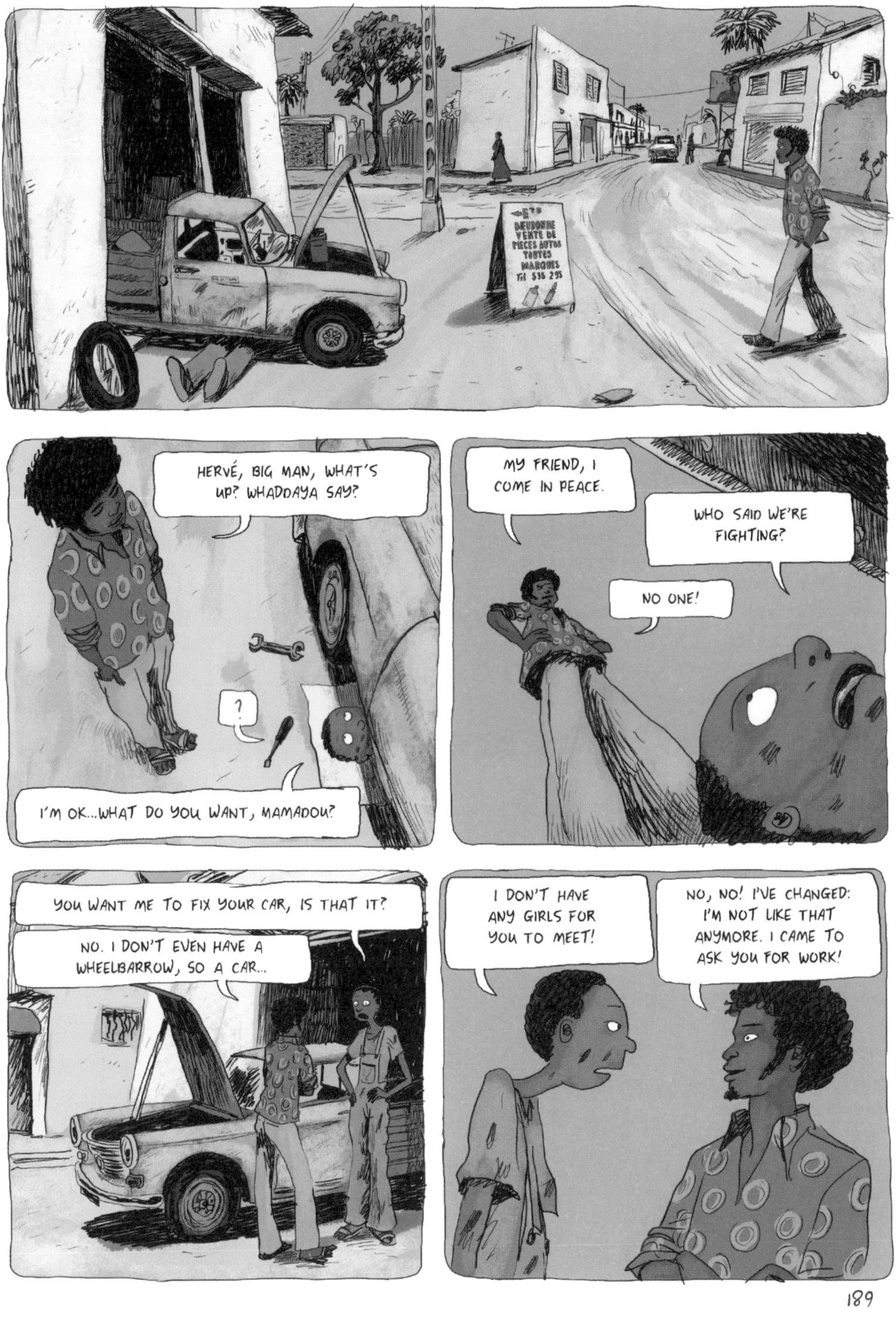

VENTE DE
PIECES AUTOS
MARQUES
Tél 535 295
HERVÉ, BIG MAN, WHAT'S UP? WHADDAYA SAY?
?
I'M OK...WHAT DO YOU WANT, MAMADOU?
MY FRIEND, I COME IN PEACE.
WHO SAID WE'RE FIGHTING?
NO ONE!
YOU WANT ME TO FIX YOUR CAR, IS THAT IT?
NO. I DON'T EVEN HAVE A WHEELBARROW, SO A CAR...
I DON'T HAVE ANY GIRLS FOR YOU TO MEET!
NO, NO! I'VE CHANGED: I'M NOT LIKE THAT ANYMORE. I CAME TO ASK YOU FOR WORK!

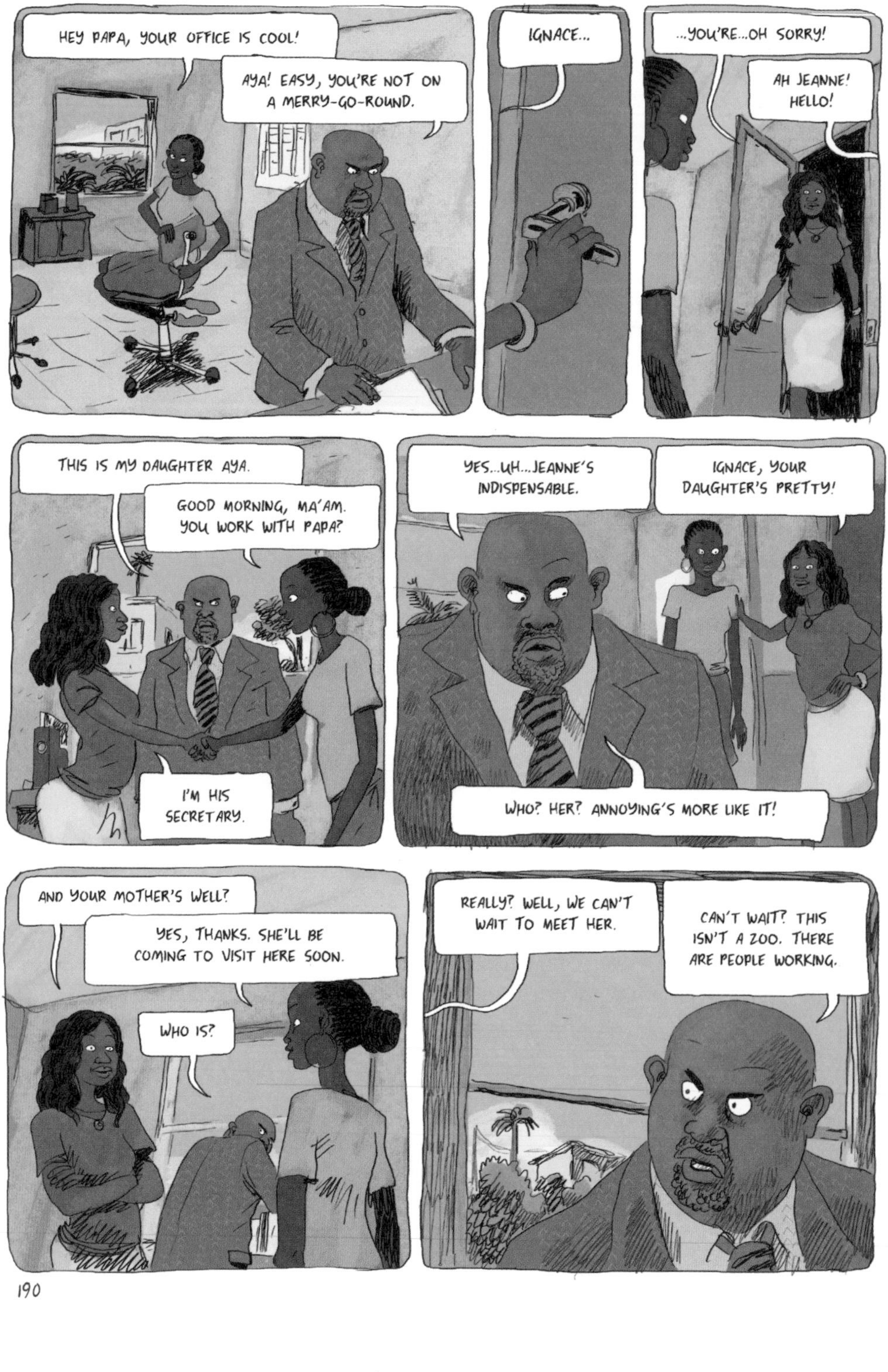
HEY PAPA, YOUR OFFICE IS COOL!
AYA! EASY, YOU'RE NOT ON A MERRY-GO-ROUND.
IGNACE...
...YOU'RE...OH SORRY!
AH JEANNE! HELLO!
THIS IS MY DAUGHTER AYA.
GOOD MORNING, MA'AM. YOU WORK WITH PAPA?
I'M HIS SECRETARY.
YES...UH...JEANNE'S INDISPENSABLE.
IGNACE, YOUR DAUGHTER'S PRETTY!
WHO? HER? ANNOYING'S MORE LIKE IT!
AND YOUR MOTHER'S WELL?
YES, THANKS. SHE'LL BE COMING TO VISIT HERE SOON.
WHO IS?
REALLY? WELL, WE CAN'T WAIT TO MEET HER.
CAN'T WAIT? THIS ISN'T A ZOO. THERE ARE PEOPLE WORKING.

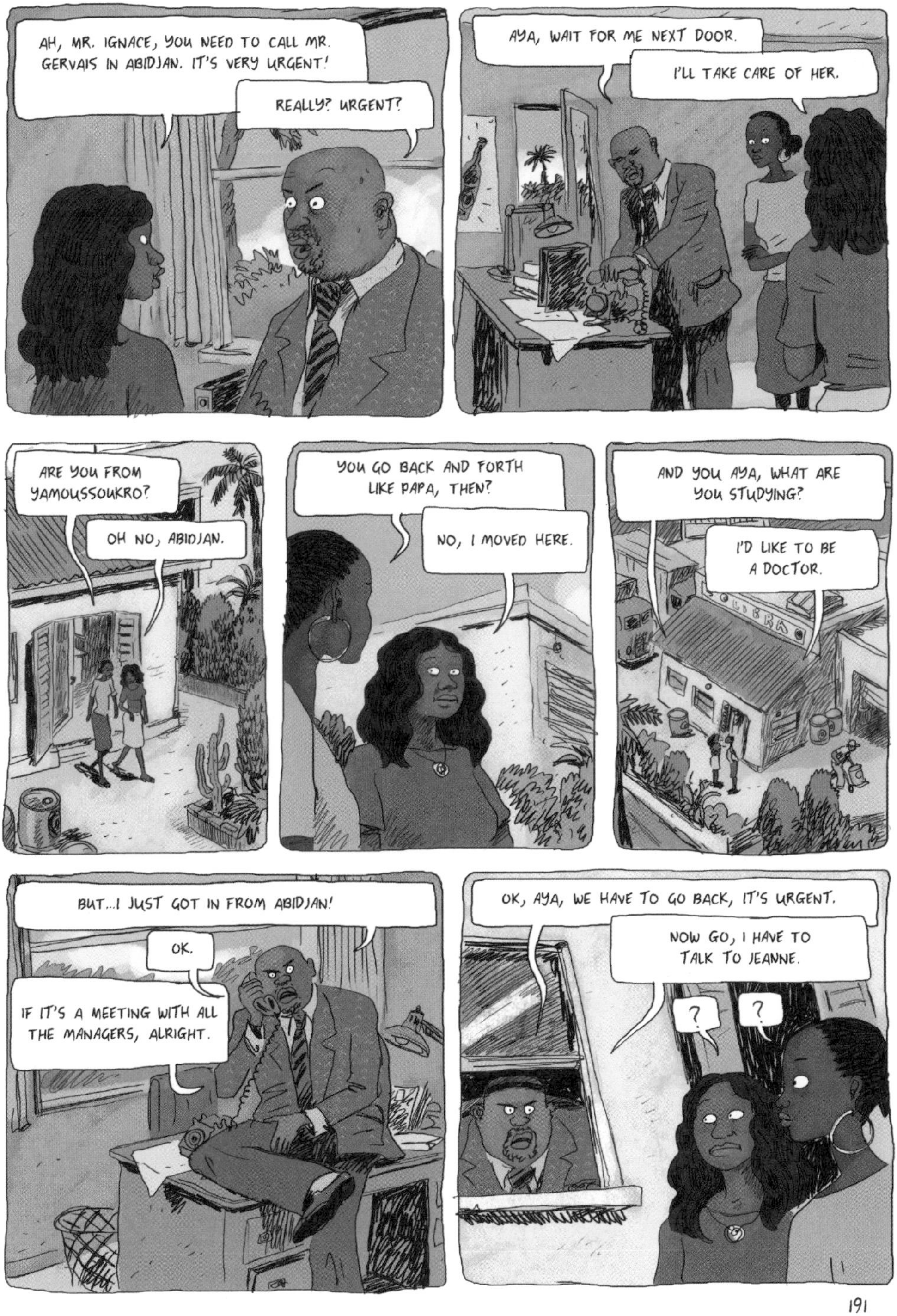
AH, MR. IGNACE, YOU NEED TO CALL MR. GERVAIS IN ABIDJAN. IT'S VERY URGENT!
REALLY? URGENT?
AYA, WAIT FOR ME NEXT DOOR.
I'LL TAKE CARE OF HER.
ARE YOU FROM YAMOUSSOUKRO?
OH NO, ABIDJAN.
YOU GO BACK AND FORTH LIKE PAPA, THEN?
NO, I MOVED HERE.
AND YOU AYA, WHAT ARE YOU STUDYING?
I'D LIKE TO BE A DOCTOR.
BUT... I JUST GOT IN FROM ABIDJAN!
OK.
IF IT'S A MEETING WITH ALL THE MANAGERS, ALRIGHT.
OK, AYA, WE HAVE TO GO BACK, IT'S URGENT.
NOW GO, I HAVE TO TALK TO JEANNE.
?
?

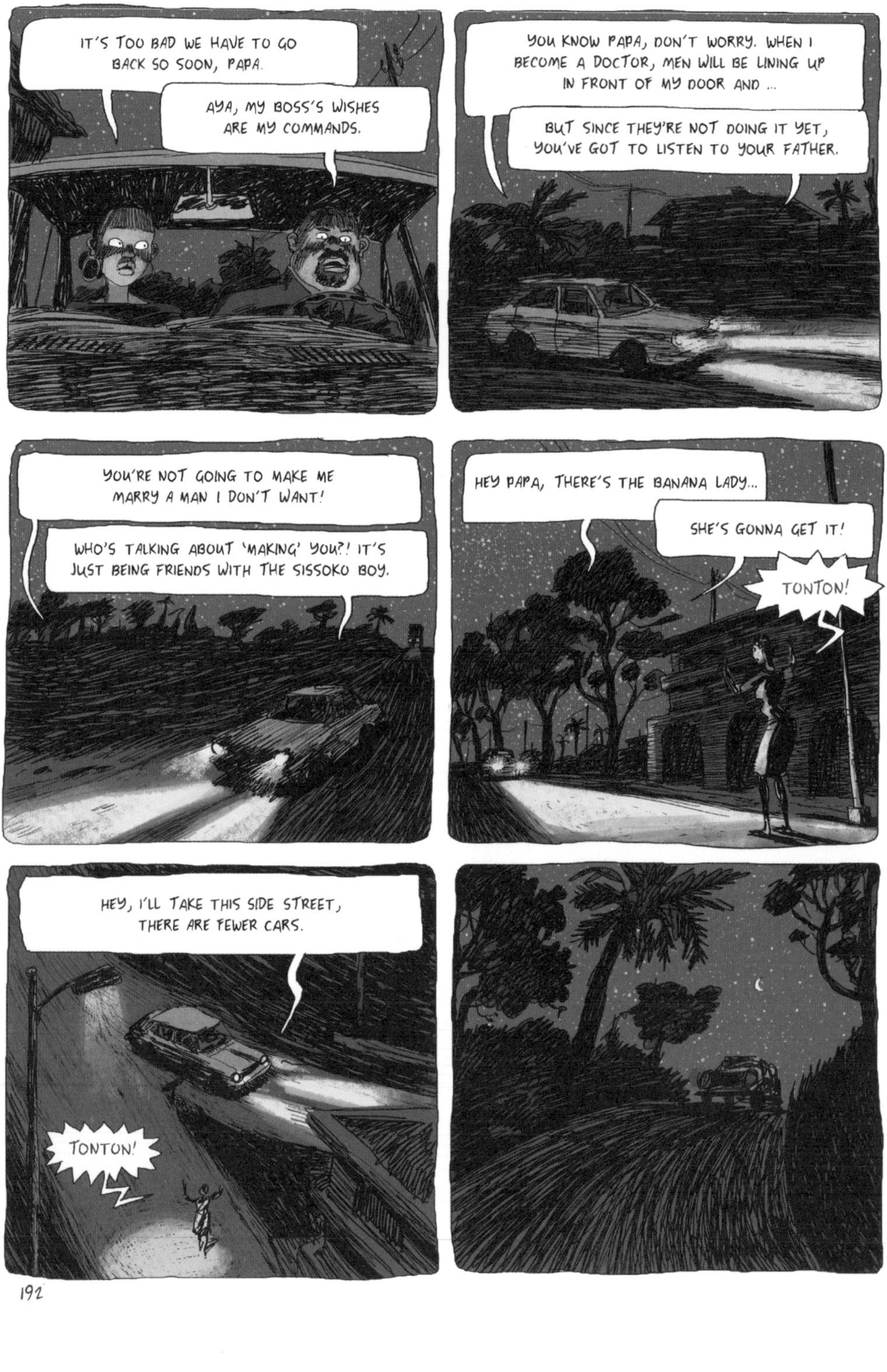
IT'S TOO BAD WE HAVE TO GO BACK SO SOON, PAPA.
AYA, MY BOSS'S WISHES ARE MY COMMANDS.
YOU KNOW PAPA, DON'T WORRY. WHEN I BECOME A DOCTOR, MEN WILL BE LINING UP IN FRONT OF MY DOOR AND ...
BUT SINCE THEY'RE NOT DOING IT YET, YOU'VE GOT TO LISTEN TO YOUR FATHER.
YOU'RE NOT GOING TO MAKE ME MARRY A MAN I DON'T WANT!
WHO'S TALKING ABOUT 'MAKING' YOU?! IT'S JUST BEING FRIENDS WITH THE SISSOKO BOY.
HEY PAPA, THERE'S THE BANANA LADY...
SHE'S GONNA GET IT!
TONTON!
HEY, I'LL TAKE THIS SIDE STREET, THERE ARE FEWER CARS.
TONTON!

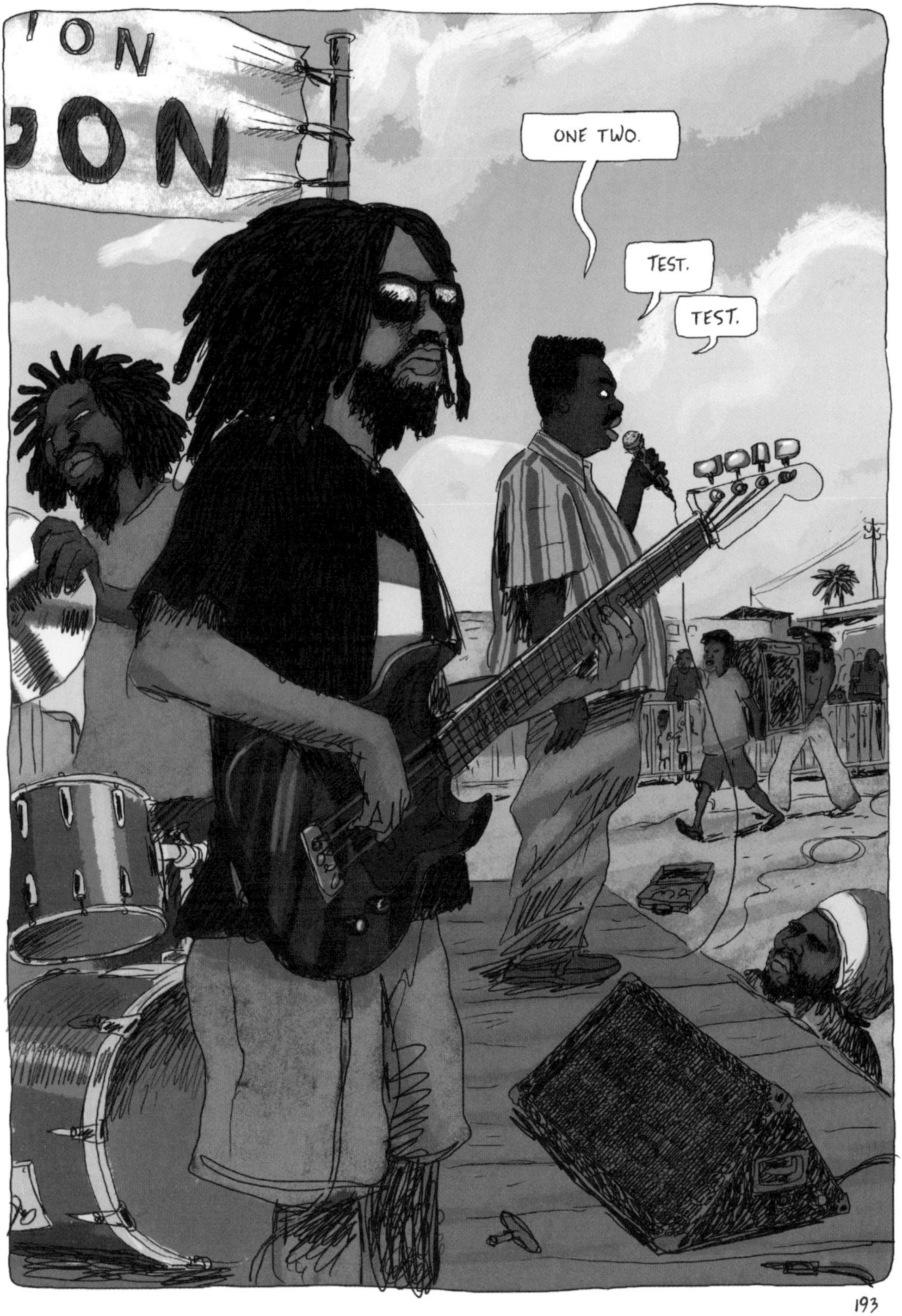
ION
GON
ONE TWO.
TEST.
TEST.

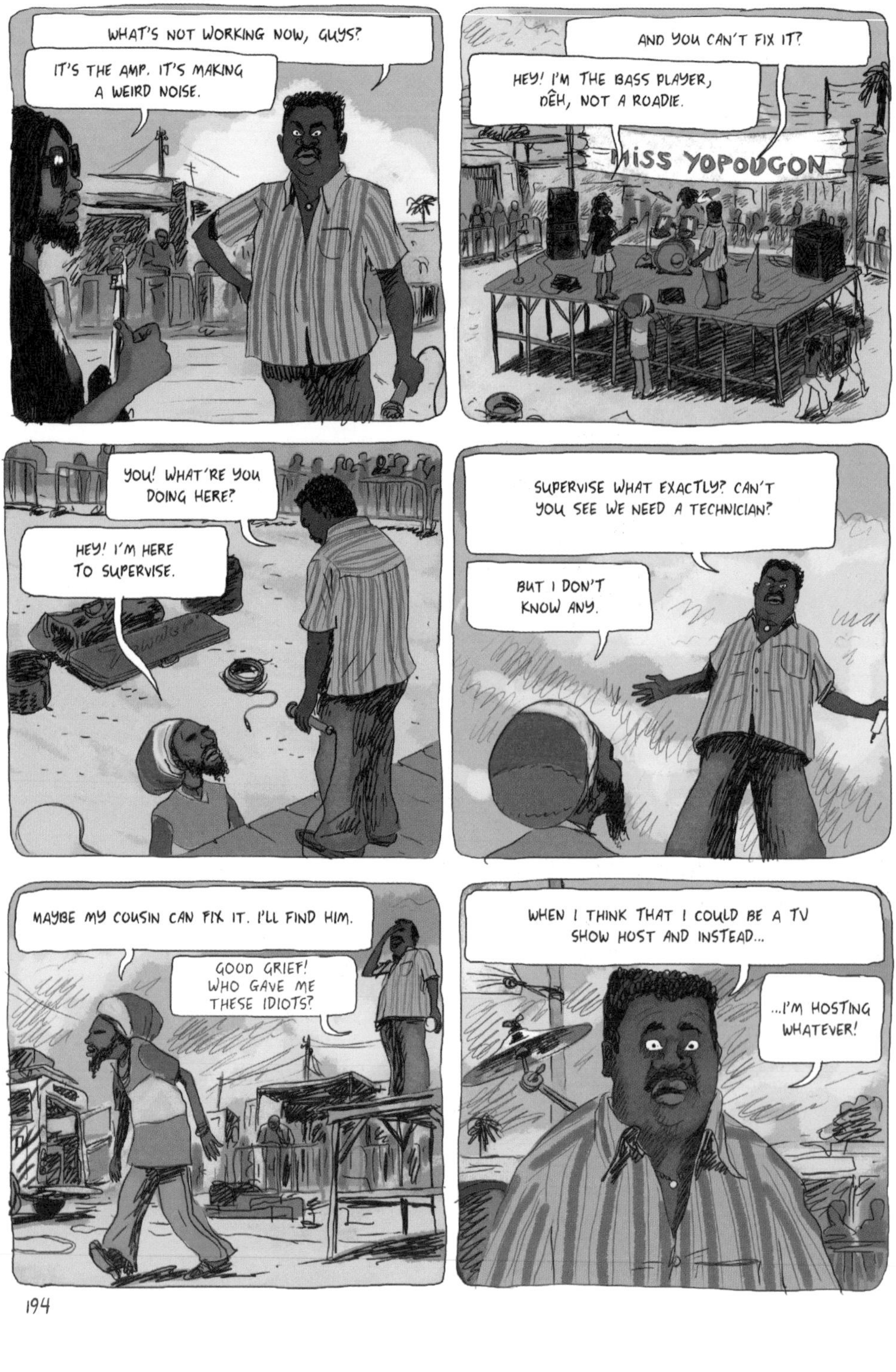
WHAT'S NOT WORKING NOW, GUYS?
IT'S THE AMP. IT'S MAKING A WEIRD NOISE.
AND YOU CAN'T FIX IT?
HEY! I'M THE BASS PLAYER, DÊH, NOT A ROADIE.
MISS YOPOUGON
YOU! WHAT'RE YOU DOING HERE?
HEY! I'M HERE TO SUPERVISE.
SUPERVISE WHAT EXACTLY? CAN'T YOU SEE WE NEED A TECHNICIAN?
BUT I DON'T KNOW ANY.
MAYBE MY COUSIN CAN FIX IT. I'LL FIND HIM.
GOOD GRIEF! WHO GAVE ME THESE IDIOTS?
WHEN I THINK THAT I COULD BE A TV SHOW HOST AND INSTEAD...
...I'M HOSTING WHATEVER!

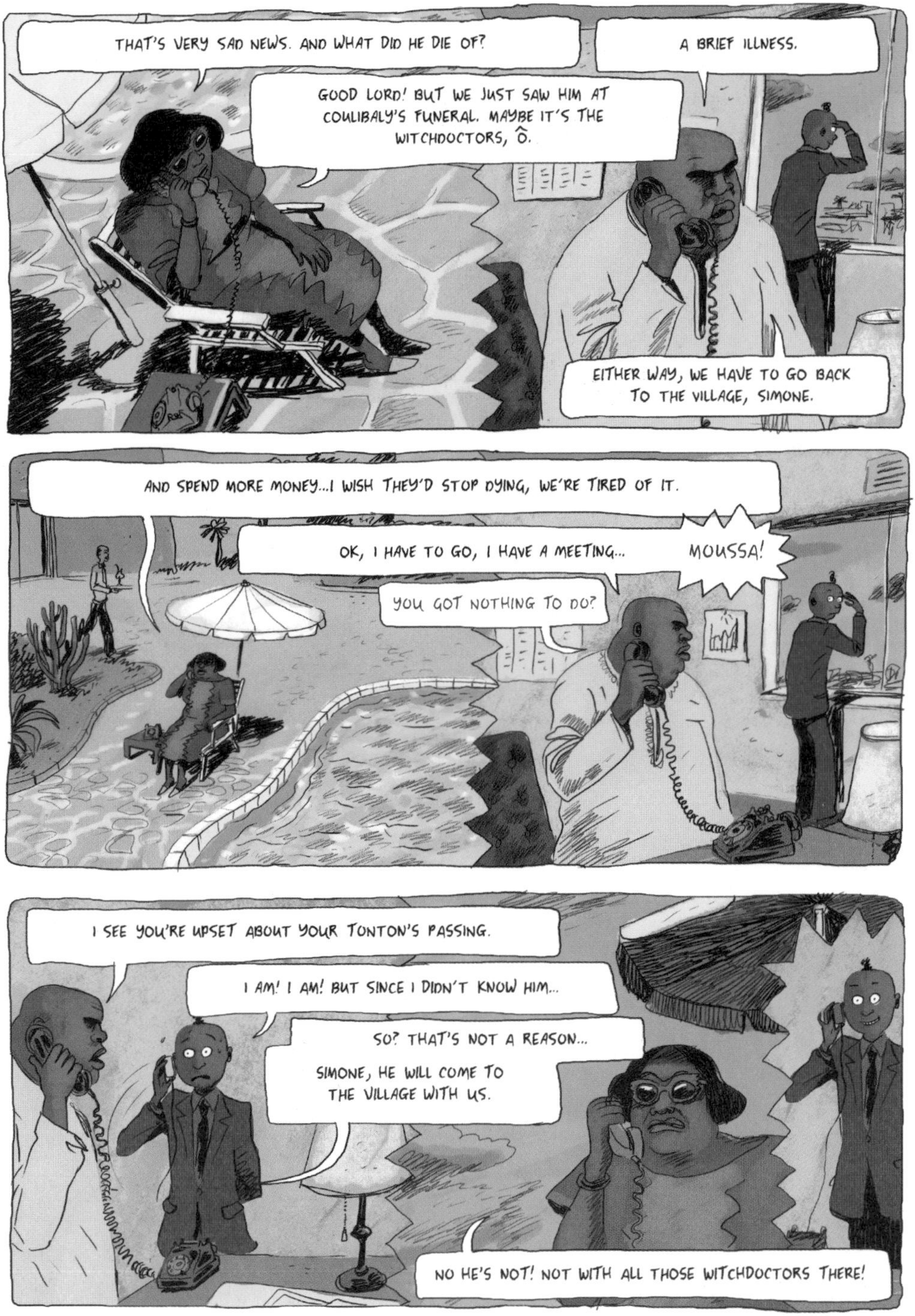

THAT'S VERY SAD NEWS. AND WHAT DID HE DIE OF?
A BRIEF ILLNESS.
GOOD LORD! BUT WE JUST SAW HIM AT COULIBALY'S FUNERAL. MAYBE IT'S THE WITCHDOCTORS, Ô.
EITHER WAY, WE HAVE TO GO BACK TO THE VILLAGE, SIMONE.
AND SPEND MORE MONEY...I WISH THEY'D STOP DYING, WE'RE TIRED OF IT.
OK, I HAVE TO GO, I HAVE A MEETING...
MOUSSA!
YOU GOT NOTHING TO DO?
I SEE YOU'RE UPSET ABOUT YOUR TONTON'S PASSING.
I AM! I AM! BUT SINCE I DIDN'T KNOW HIM...
SO? THAT'S NOT A REASON...
SIMONE, HE WILL COME TO THE VILLAGE WITH US.
NO HE'S NOT! NOT WITH ALL THOSE WITCHDOCTORS THERE!

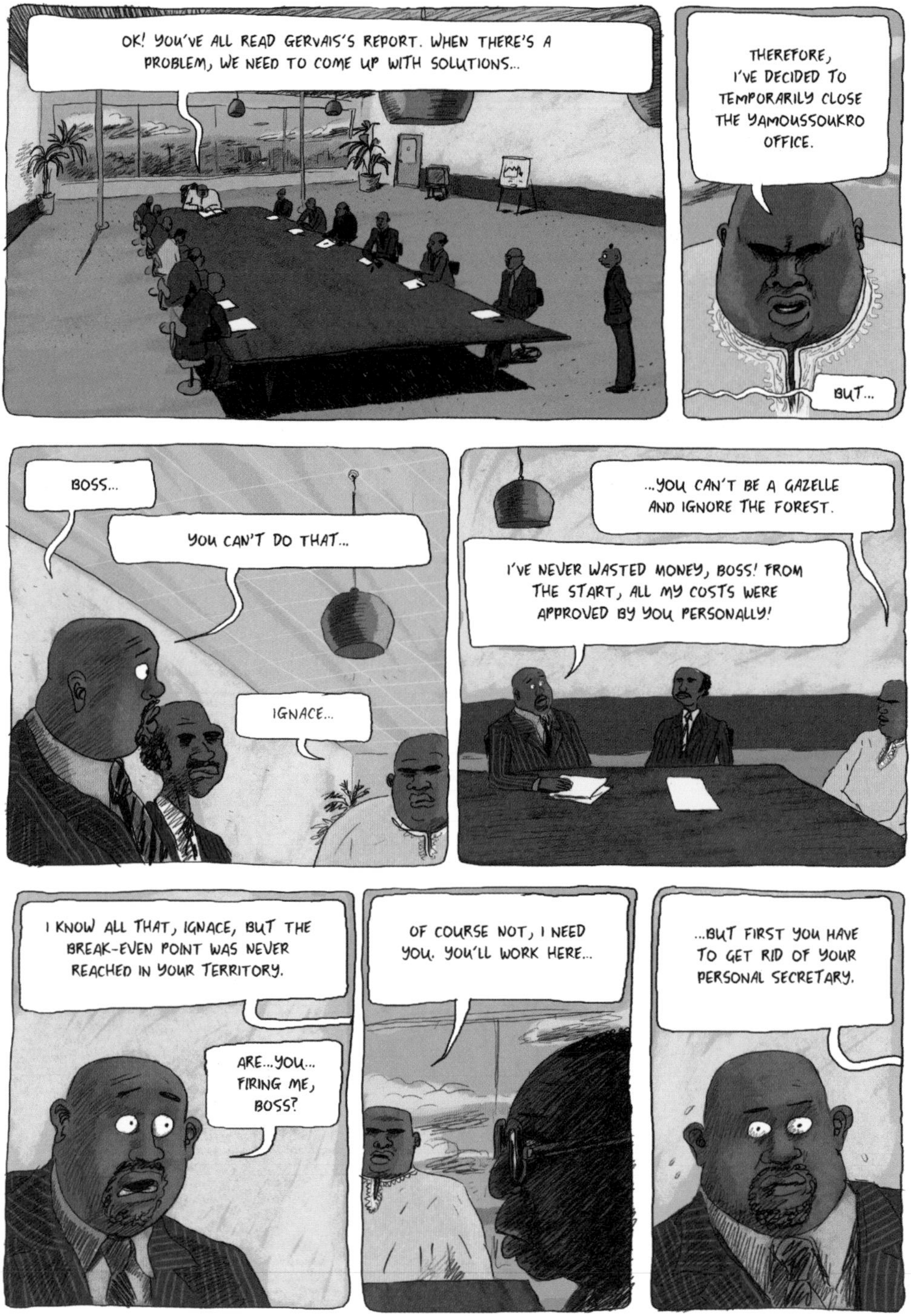
OK! YOU'VE ALL READ GERVAIS'S REPORT. WHEN THERE'S A PROBLEM, WE NEED TO COME UP WITH SOLUTIONS...
THEREFORE, I'VE DECIDED TO TEMPORARILY CLOSE THE YAMOUSSOUKRO OFFICE.
BUT...
BOSS...
YOU CAN'T DO THAT...
IGNACE...
...YOU CAN'T BE A GAZELLE AND IGNORE THE FOREST.
I'VE NEVER WASTED MONEY, BOSS! FROM THE START, ALL MY COSTS WERE APPROVED BY YOU PERSONALLY!
I KNOW ALL THAT, IGNACE, BUT THE BREAK-EVEN POINT WAS NEVER REACHED IN YOUR TERRITORY.
ARE...YOU... FIRING ME, BOSS?
OF COURSE NOT, I NEED YOU. YOU'LL WORK HERE...
...BUT FIRST YOU HAVE TO GET RID OF YOUR PERSONAL SECRETARY.

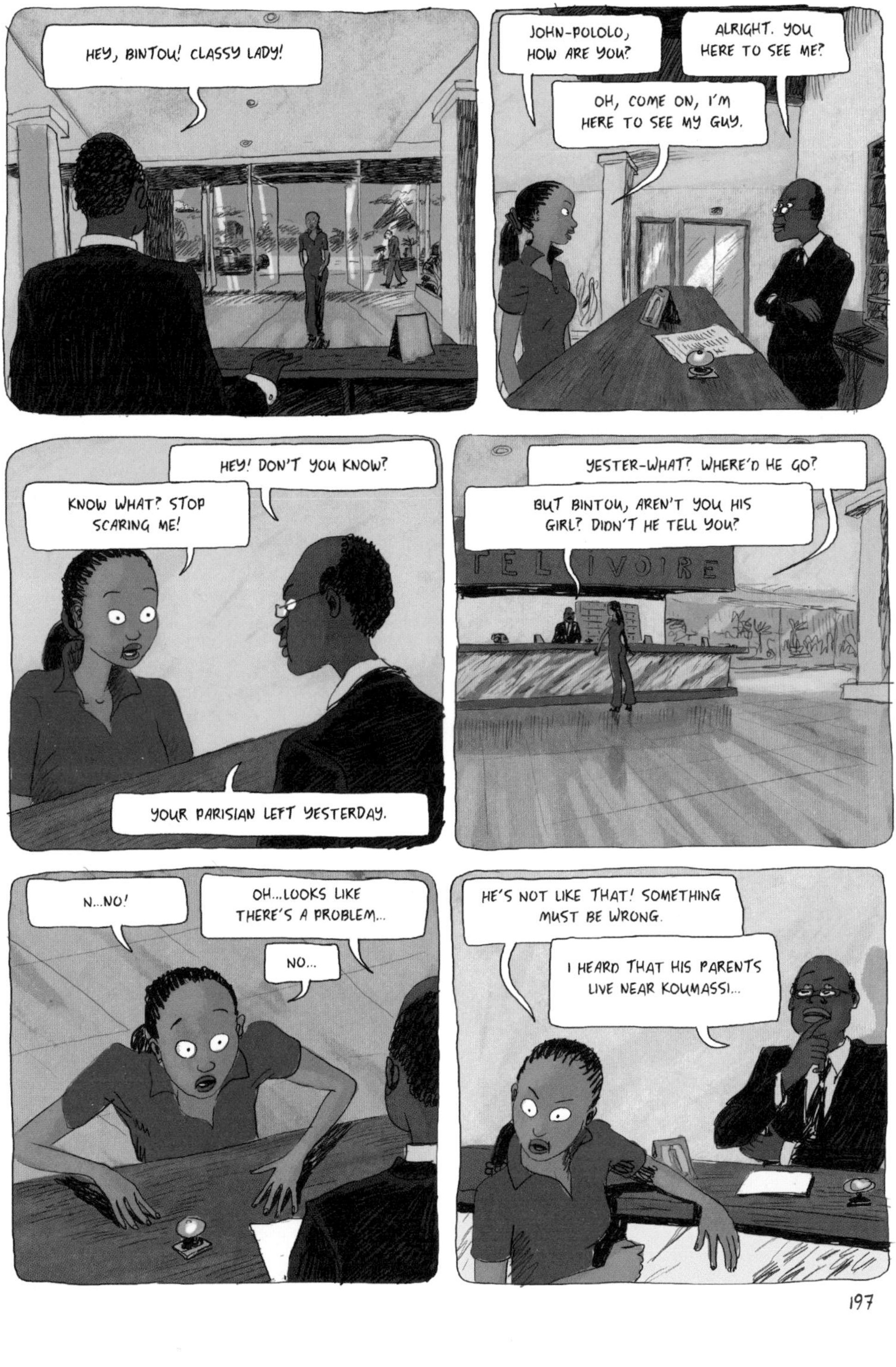
HEY, BINTOU! CLASSY LADY!
JOHN-POLOLO, HOW ARE YOU?
ALRIGHT. YOU HERE TO SEE ME?
OH, COME ON, I'M HERE TO SEE MY GUY.
HEY! DON'T YOU KNOW?
KNOW WHAT? STOP SCARING ME!
YOUR PARISIAN LEFT YESTERDAY.
YESTER-WHAT? WHERE'D HE GO?
BUT BINTOU, AREN'T YOU HIS GIRL? DIDN'T HE TELL YOU?
TEL IVOIRE
N...NO!
OH...LOOKS LIKE THERE'S A PROBLEM...
NO...
HE'S NOT LIKE THAT! SOMETHING MUST BE WRONG.
I HEARD THAT HIS PARENTS LIVE NEAR KOUMASSI...

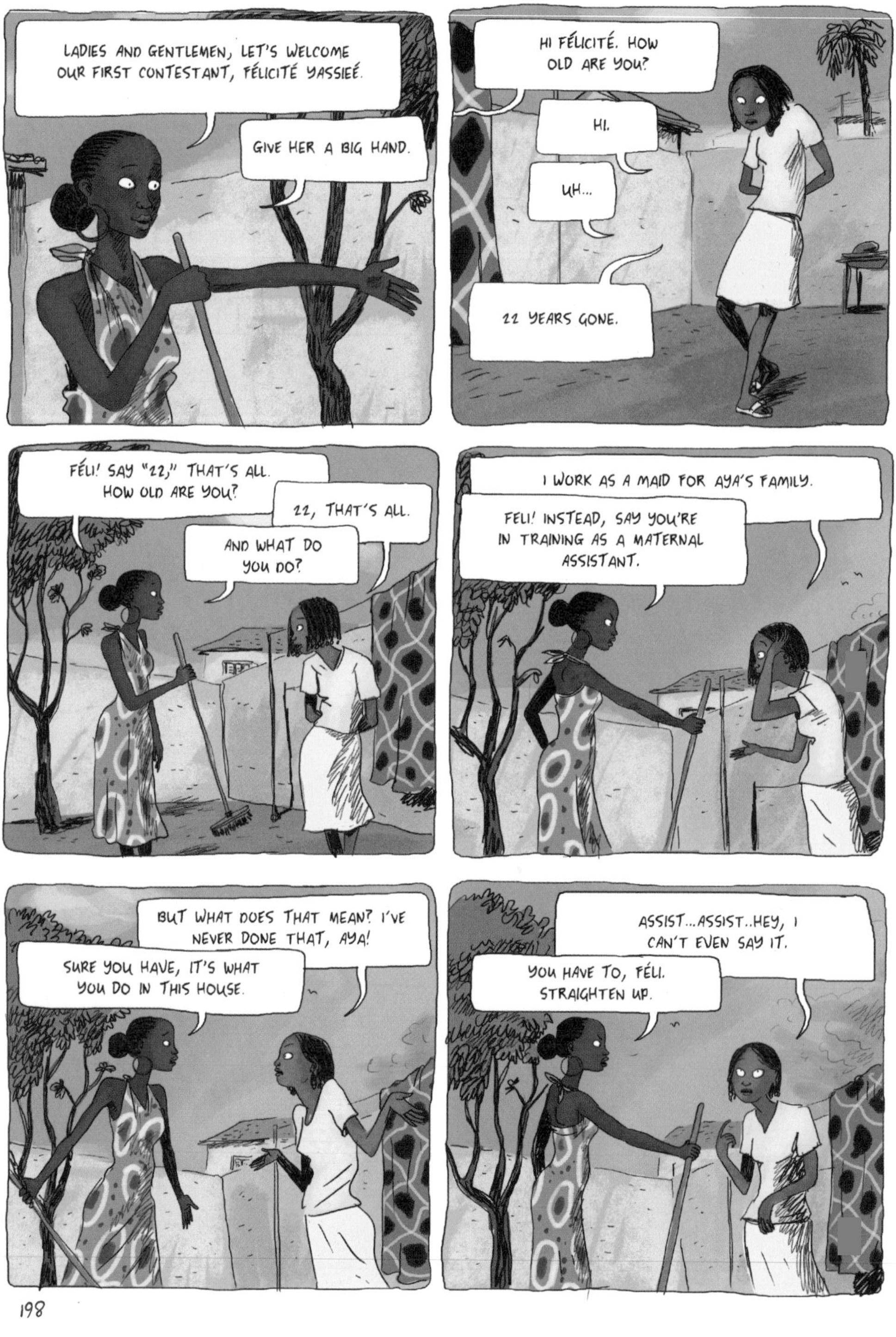
LADIES AND GENTLEMEN, LET'S WELCOME OUR FIRST CONTESTANT, FÉLICITÉ YASSIEÉ.
GIVE HER A BIG HAND.
HI FÉLICITÉ. HOW OLD ARE YOU?
HI.
UH...
22 YEARS GONE.
FÉLI! SAY "22," THAT'S ALL. HOW OLD ARE YOU?
22, THAT'S ALL.
AND WHAT DO YOU DO?
I WORK AS A MAID FOR AYA'S FAMILY.
FÉLI! INSTEAD, SAY YOU'RE IN TRAINING AS A MATERNAL ASSISTANT.
BUT WHAT DOES THAT MEAN? I'VE NEVER DONE THAT, AYA!
SURE YOU HAVE, IT'S WHAT YOU DO IN THIS HOUSE.
ASSIST...ASSIST..HEY, I CAN'T EVEN SAY IT.
YOU HAVE TO, FÉLI. STRAIGHTEN UP.

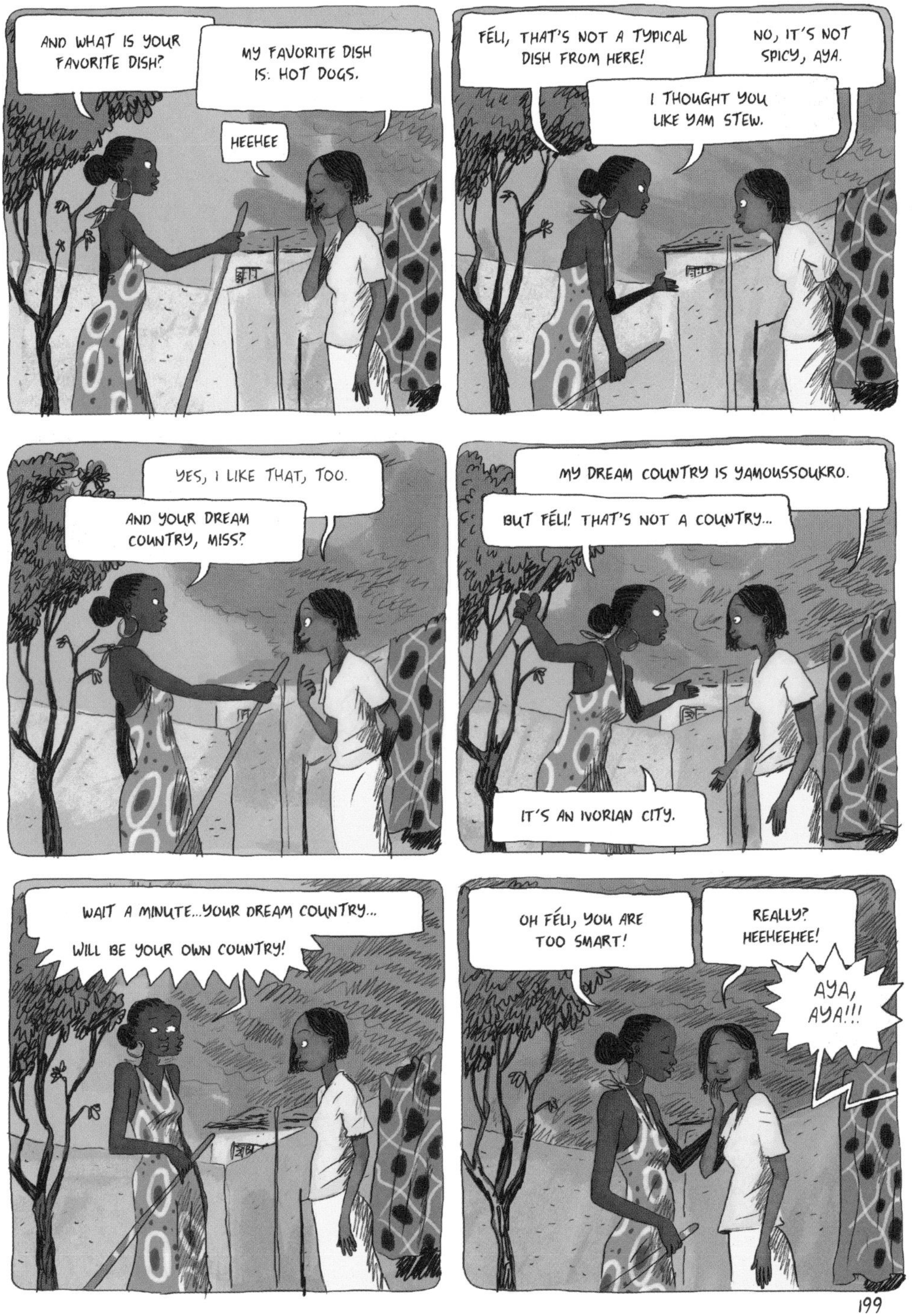
AND WHAT IS YOUR FAVORITE DISH?
MY FAVORITE DISH IS: HOT DOGS.
HEEHEE
FÉLI, THAT'S NOT A TYPICAL DISH FROM HERE!
NO, IT'S NOT SPICY, AYA.
I THOUGHT YOU LIKE YAM STEW.
YES, I LIKE THAT, TOO.
AND YOUR DREAM COUNTRY, MISS?
MY DREAM COUNTRY IS YAMOUSSOUKRO.
BUT FÉLI! THAT'S NOT A COUNTRY...
IT'S AN IVORIAN CITY.
WAIT A MINUTE...YOUR DREAM COUNTRY...
WILL BE YOUR OWN COUNTRY!
OH FÉLI, YOU ARE TOO SMART!
REALLY? HEEHEEHEE!
AYA, AYA!!!

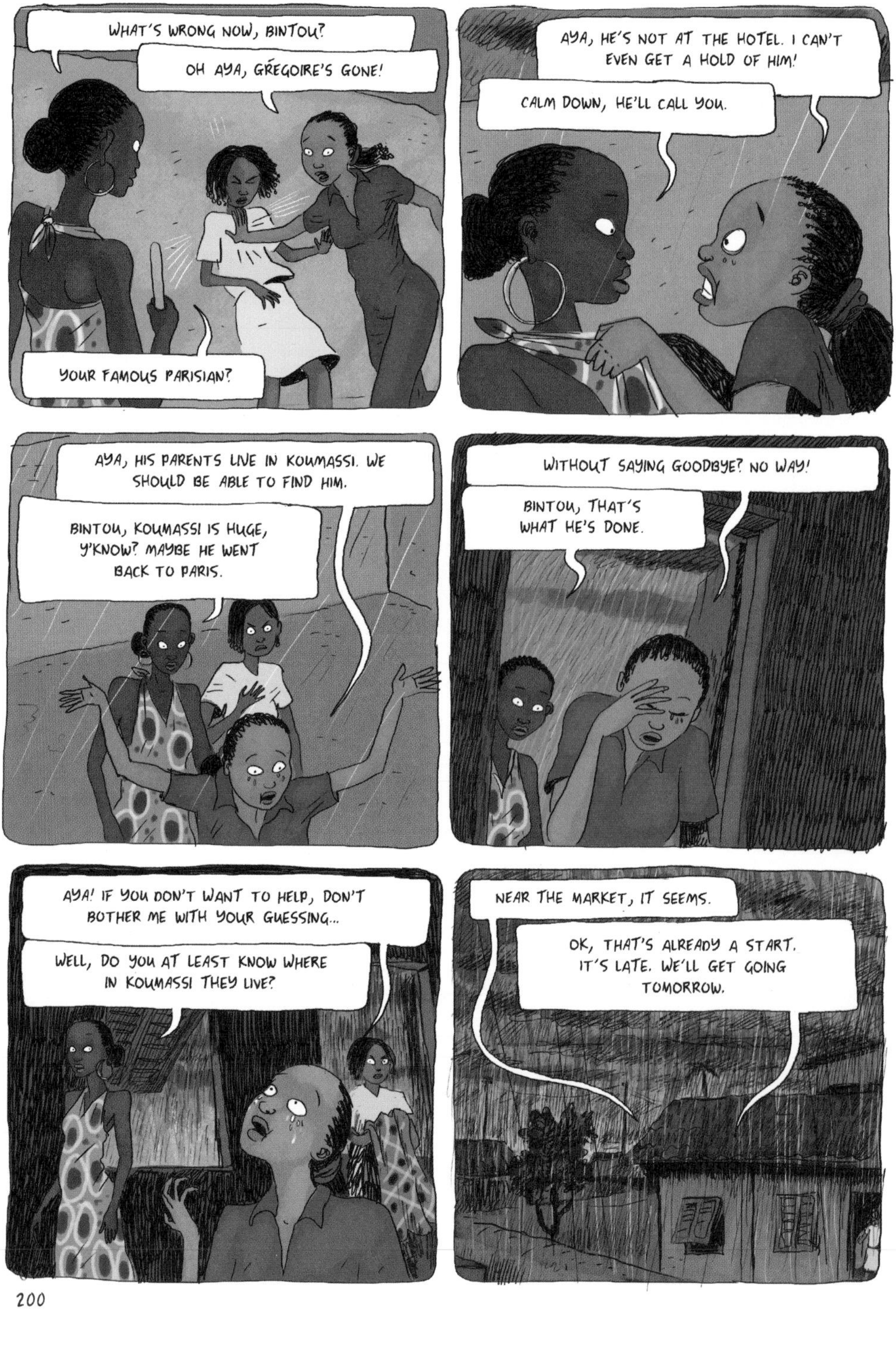
WHAT'S WRONG NOW, BINTOU?
OH AYA, GRÉGOIRE'S GONE!
YOUR FAMOUS PARISIAN?
AYA, HE'S NOT AT THE HOTEL. I CAN'T EVEN GET A HOLD OF HIM!
CALM DOWN, HE'LL CALL YOU.
AYA, HIS PARENTS LIVE IN KOUMASSI. WE SHOULD BE ABLE TO FIND HIM.
BINTOU, KOUMASSI IS HUGE, Y'KNOW? MAYBE HE WENT BACK TO PARIS.
WITHOUT SAYING GOODBYE? NO WAY!
BINTOU, THAT'S WHAT HE'S DONE.
AYA! IF YOU DON'T WANT TO HELP, DON'T BOTHER ME WITH YOUR GUESSING...
WELL, DO YOU AT LEAST KNOW WHERE IN KOUMASSI THEY LIVE?
NEAR THE MARKET, IT SEEMS.
OK, THAT'S ALREADY A START. IT'S LATE. WE'LL GET GOING TOMORROW.

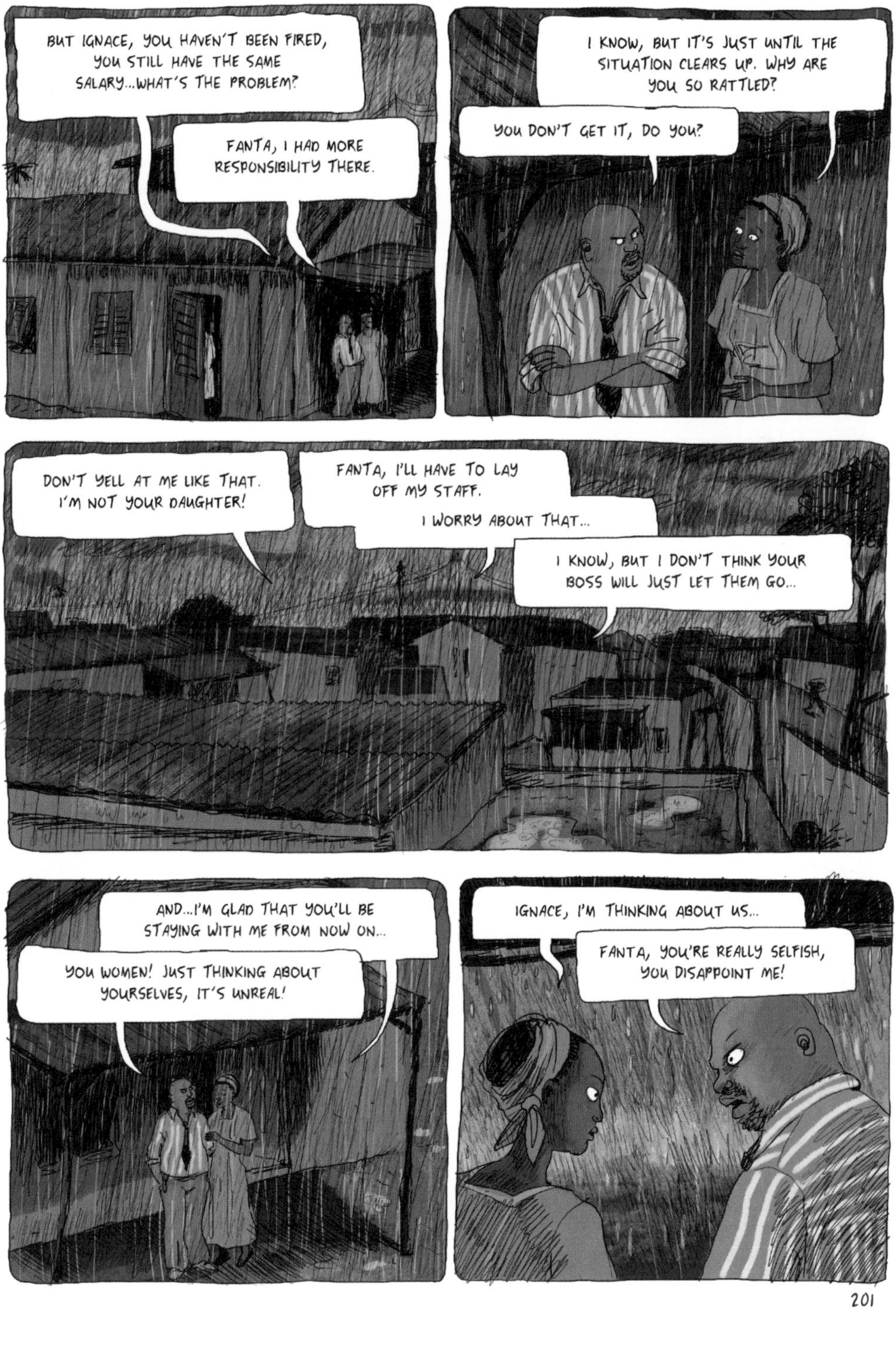
BUT IGNACE, YOU HAVEN'T BEEN FIRED, YOU STILL HAVE THE SAME SALARY...WHAT'S THE PROBLEM?
FANTA, I HAD MORE RESPONSIBILITY THERE.
I KNOW, BUT IT'S JUST UNTIL THE SITUATION CLEARS UP. WHY ARE YOU SO RATTLED?
YOU DON'T GET IT, DO YOU?
DON'T YELL AT ME LIKE THAT. I'M NOT YOUR DAUGHTER!
FANTA, I'LL HAVE TO LAY OFF MY STAFF.
I WORRY ABOUT THAT...
I KNOW, BUT I DON'T THINK YOUR BOSS WILL JUST LET THEM GO...
AND...I'M GLAD THAT YOU'LL BE STAYING WITH ME FROM NOW ON...
YOU WOMEN! JUST THINKING ABOUT YOURSELVES, IT'S UNREAL!
IGNACE, I'M THINKING ABOUT US...
FANTA, YOU'RE REALLY SELFISH, YOU DISAPPOINT ME!

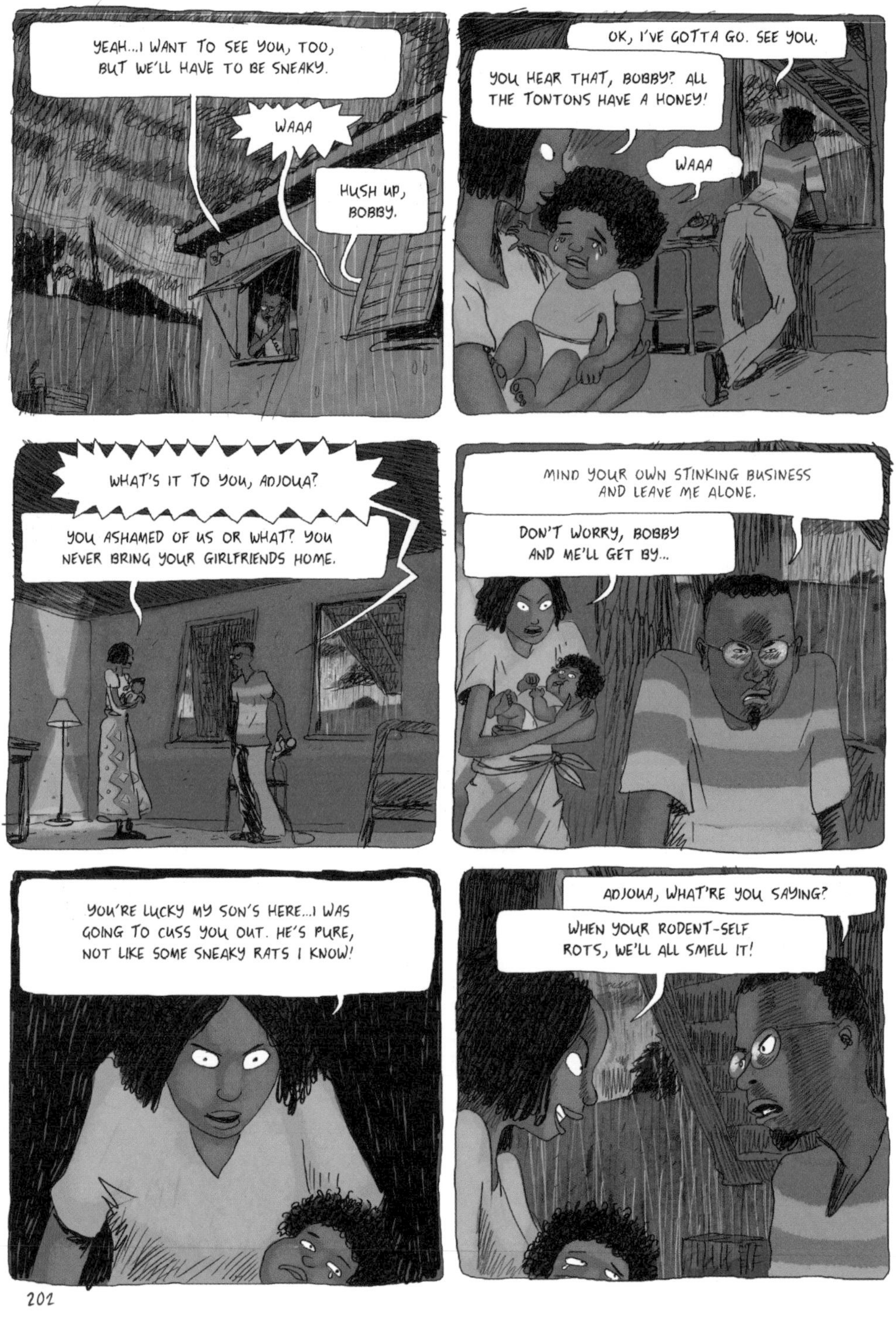
YEAH...I WANT TO SEE YOU, TOO, BUT WE'LL HAVE TO BE SNEAKY.
WAAA
HUSH UP, BOBBY.
OK, I'VE GOTTA GO. SEE YOU.
YOU HEAR THAT, BOBBY? ALL THE TONTONS HAVE A HONEY!
WAAA
WHAT'S IT TO YOU, ADJOUA?
YOU ASHAMED OF US OR WHAT? YOU NEVER BRING YOUR GIRLFRIENDS HOME.
MIND YOUR OWN STINKING BUSINESS AND LEAVE ME ALONE.
DON'T WORRY, BOBBY AND ME'LL GET BY...
YOU'RE LUCKY MY SON'S HERE...I WAS GOING TO CUSS YOU OUT. HE'S PURE, NOT LIKE SOME SNEAKY RATS I KNOW!
ADJOUA, WHAT'RE YOU SAYING?
WHEN YOUR RODENT-SELF ROTS, WE'LL ALL SMELL IT!

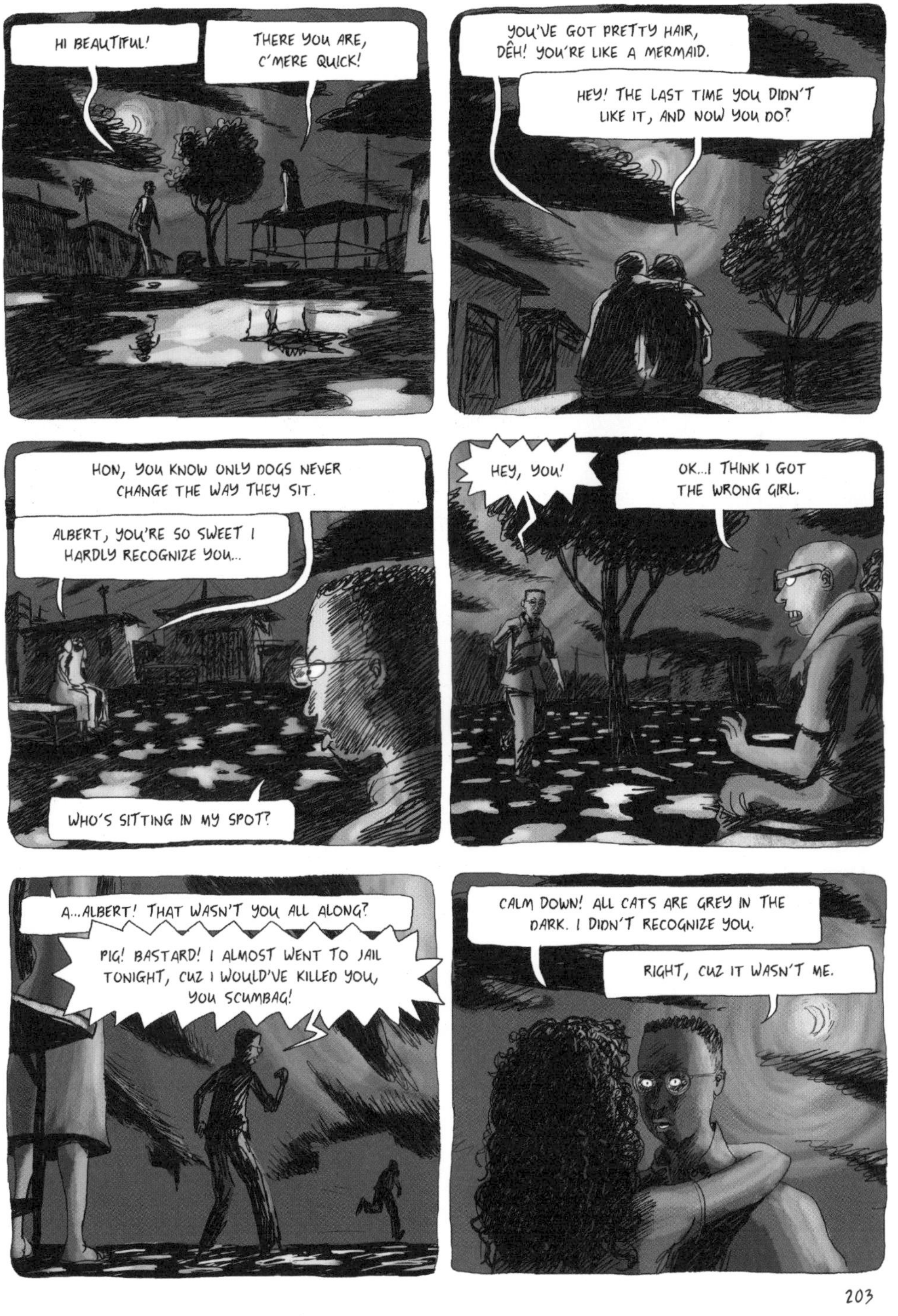
HI BEAUTIFUL!
THERE YOU ARE, C'MERE QUICK!
YOU'VE GOT PRETTY HAIR, DÊH! YOU'RE LIKE A MERMAID.
HEY! THE LAST TIME YOU DIDN'T LIKE IT, AND NOW YOU DO?
HON, YOU KNOW ONLY DOGS NEVER CHANGE THE WAY THEY SIT.
ALBERT, YOU'RE SO SWEET I HARDLY RECOGNIZE YOU...
WHO'S SITTING IN MY SPOT?
HEY, YOU!
OK...I THINK I GOT THE WRONG GIRL.
A...ALBERT! THAT WASN'T YOU ALL ALONG?
PIG! BASTARD! I ALMOST WENT TO JAIL TONIGHT, CUZ I WOULD'VE KILLED YOU, YOU SCUMBAG!
CALM DOWN! ALL CATS ARE GREY IN THE DARK. I DIDN'T RECOGNIZE YOU.
RIGHT, CUZ IT WASN'T ME.

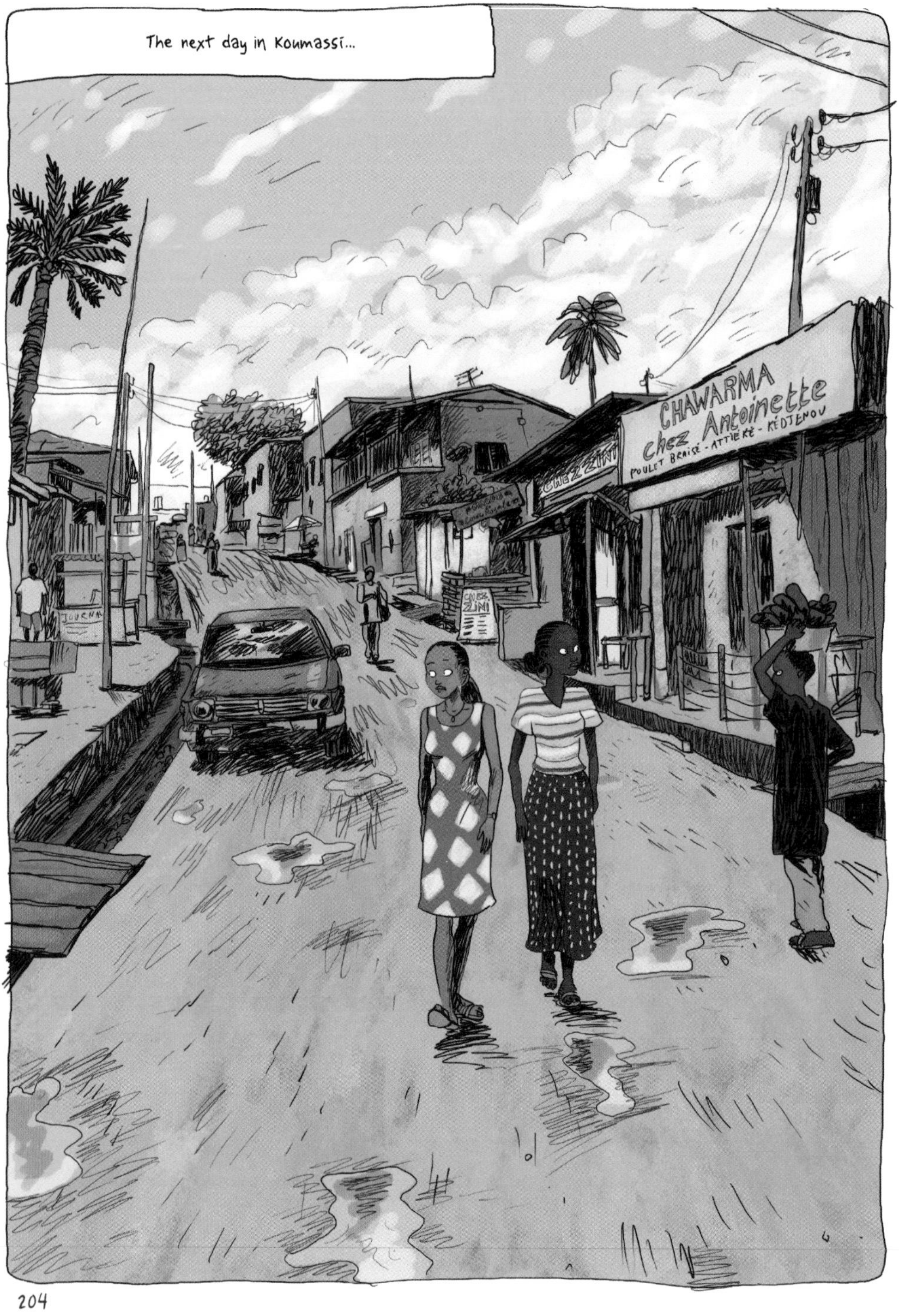
The next day in Koumassi...
CHAWARMA
chez Antoinette
POULET BRAISÉ - ATTIÉKÉ - KÉDJENOU
CHEZ ZINI
CHEZ ZINI

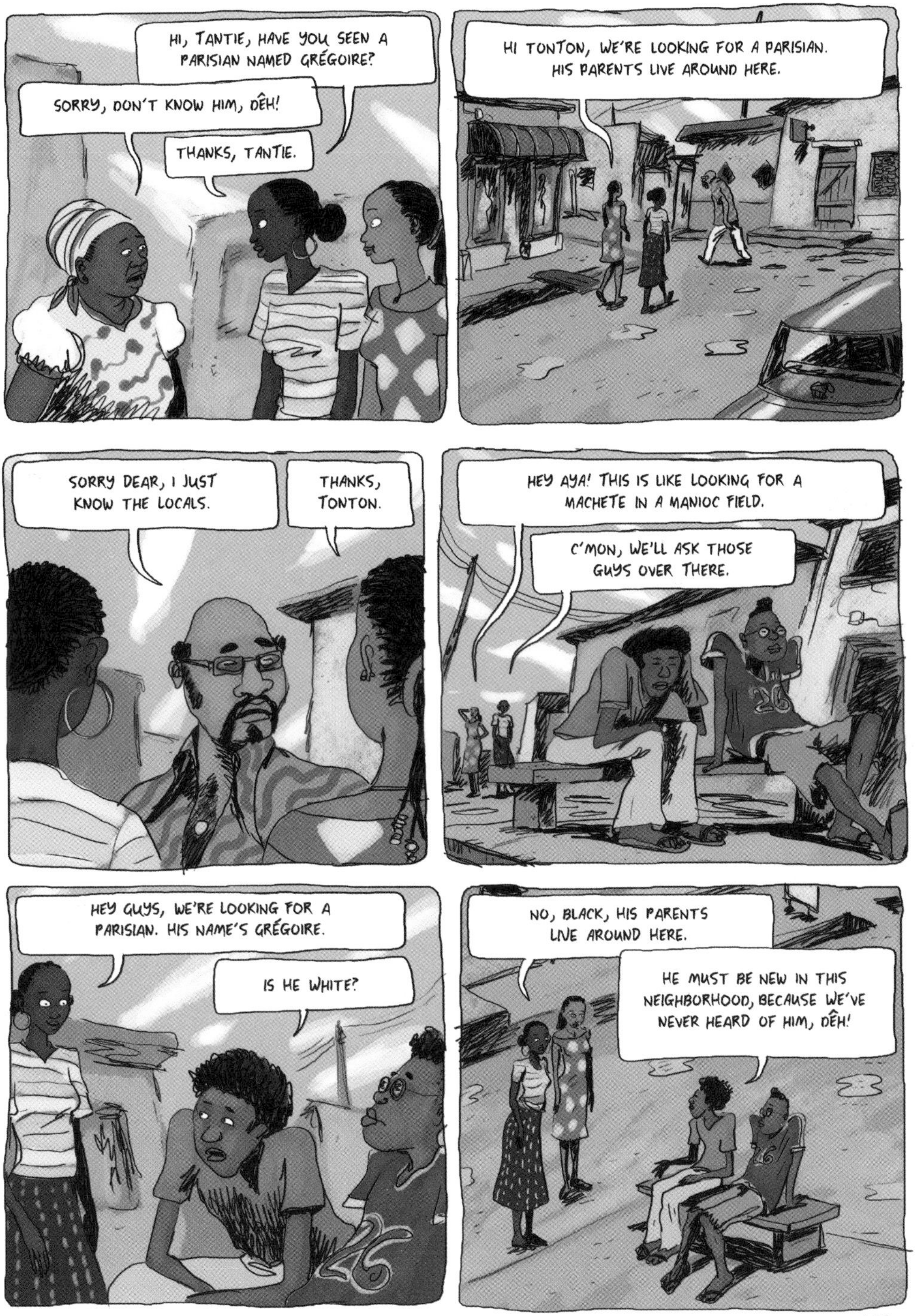
HI, TANTIE, HAVE YOU SEEN A PARISIAN NAMED GRÉGOIRE?
SORRY, DON'T KNOW HIM, DÊH!
THANKS, TANTIE.
HI TONTON, WE'RE LOOKING FOR A PARISIAN. HIS PARENTS LIVE AROUND HERE.
SORRY DEAR, I JUST KNOW THE LOCALS.
THANKS, TONTON.
HEY AYA! THIS IS LIKE LOOKING FOR A MACHETE IN A MANIOC FIELD.
C'MON, WE'LL ASK THOSE GUYS OVER THERE.
HEY GUYS, WE'RE LOOKING FOR A PARISIAN. HIS NAME'S GRÉGOIRE.
IS HE WHITE?
NO, BLACK, HIS PARENTS LIVE AROUND HERE.
HE MUST BE NEW IN THIS NEIGHBORHOOD, BECAUSE WE'VE NEVER HEARD OF HIM, DÊH!

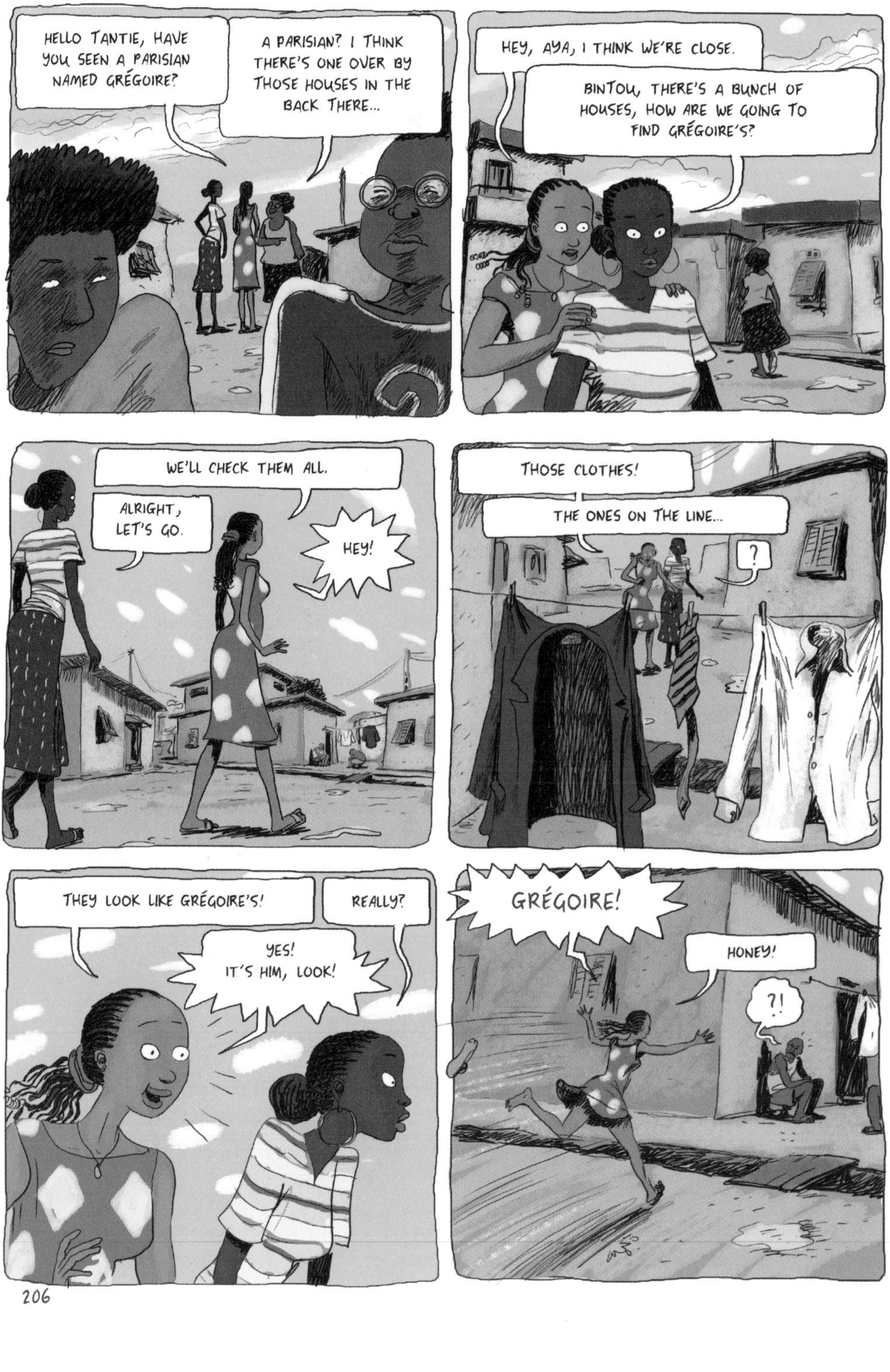

HELLO TANTIE, HAVE YOU SEEN A PARISIAN NAMED GRÉGOIRE?
A PARISIAN? I THINK THERE'S ONE OVER BY THOSE HOUSES IN THE BACK THERE...
HEY, AYA, I THINK WE'RE CLOSE.
BINTOU, THERE'S A BUNCH OF HOUSES, HOW ARE WE GOING TO FIND GRÉGOIRE'S?
WE'LL CHECK THEM ALL.
ALRIGHT, LET'S GO.
HEY!
THOSE CLOTHES!
THE ONES ON THE LINE...
?
THEY LOOK LIKE GRÉGOIRE'S!
REALLY?
YES! IT'S HIM, LOOK!
GRÉGOIRE!
HONEY!
?!

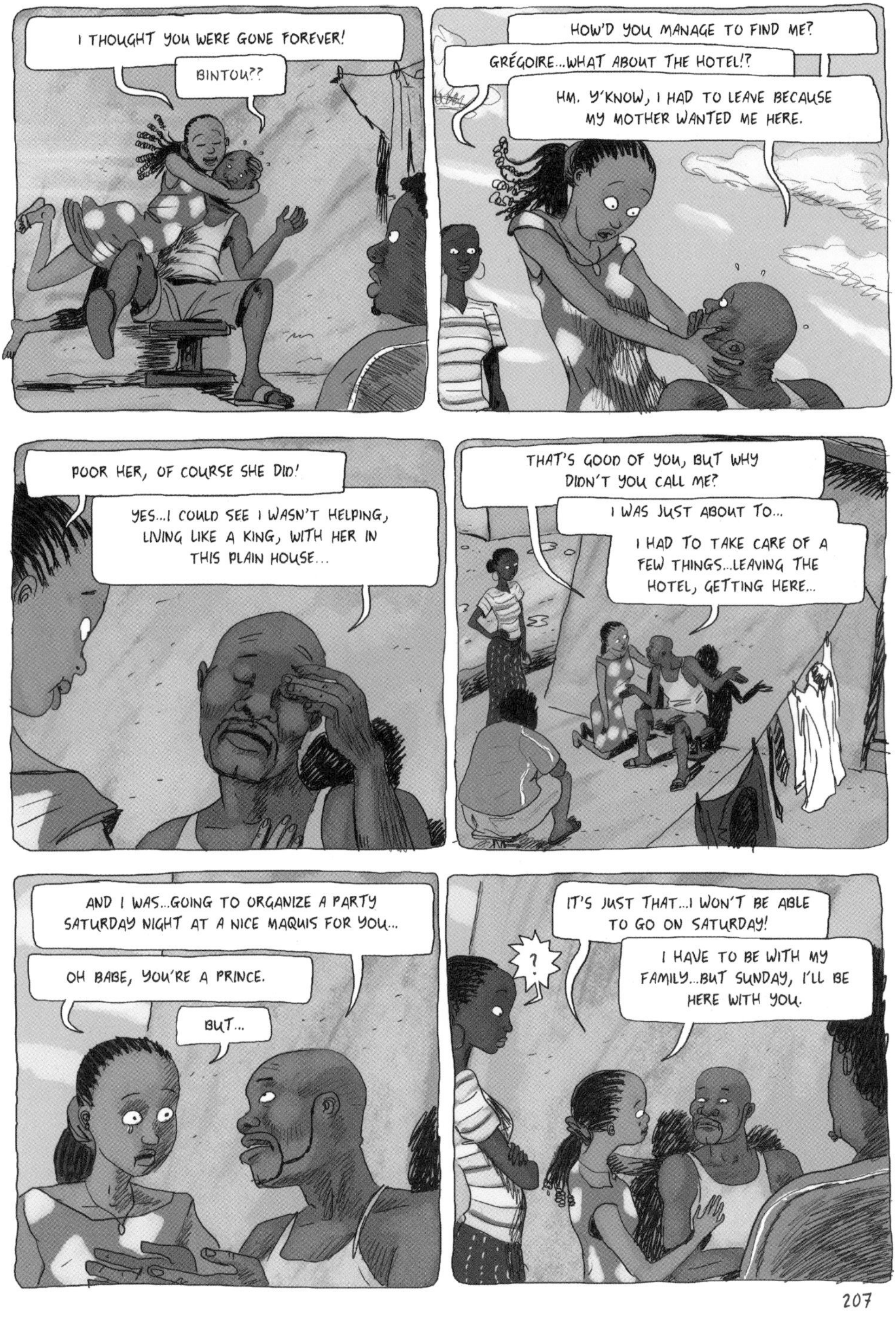
I THOUGHT YOU WERE GONE FOREVER!
BINTOU??
HOW'D YOU MANAGE TO FIND ME?
GRÉGOIRE...WHAT ABOUT THE HOTEL!?
HM. Y'KNOW, I HAD TO LEAVE BECAUSE MY MOTHER WANTED ME HERE.
POOR HER, OF COURSE SHE DID!
YES...I COULD SEE I WASN'T HELPING, LIVING LIKE A KING, WITH HER IN THIS PLAIN HOUSE...
THAT'S GOOD OF YOU, BUT WHY DIDN'T YOU CALL ME?
I WAS JUST ABOUT TO...
I HAD TO TAKE CARE OF A FEW THINGS...LEAVING THE HOTEL, GETTING HERE...
AND I WAS...GOING TO ORGANIZE A PARTY SATURDAY NIGHT AT A NICE MAQUIS FOR YOU...
OH BABE, YOU'RE A PRINCE.
BUT...
?
IT'S JUST THAT...I WON'T BE ABLE TO GO ON SATURDAY!
I HAVE TO BE WITH MY FAMILY...BUT SUNDAY, I'LL BE HERE WITH YOU.

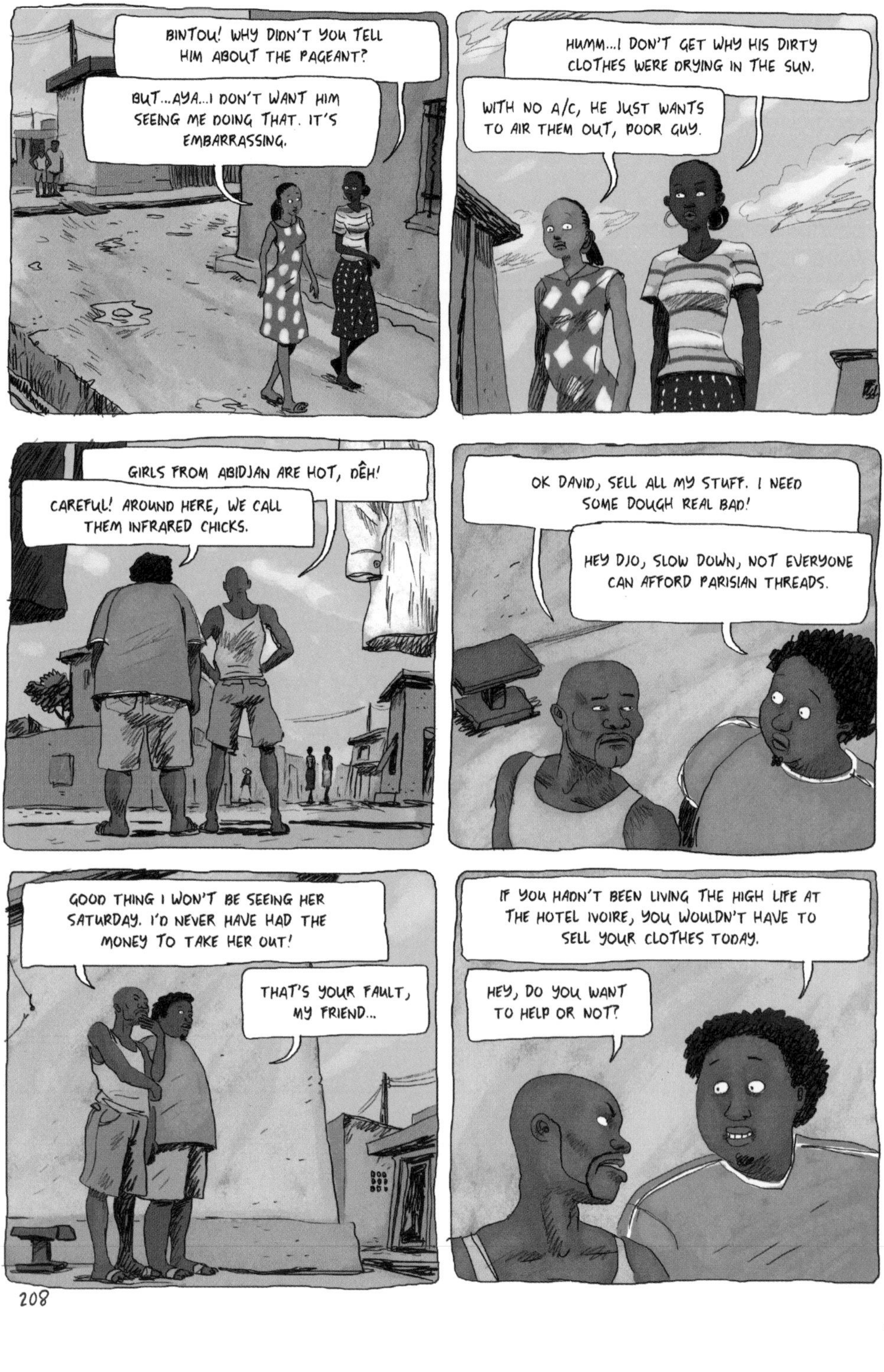
BINTOU! WHY DIDN'T YOU TELL HIM ABOUT THE PAGEANT?
BUT...AYA...I DON'T WANT HIM SEEING ME DOING THAT. IT'S EMBARRASSING.
HUMM...I DON'T GET WHY HIS DIRTY CLOTHES WERE DRYING IN THE SUN.
WITH NO A/C, HE JUST WANTS TO AIR THEM OUT, POOR GUY.
GIRLS FROM ABIDJAN ARE HOT, DÊH!
CAREFUL! AROUND HERE, WE CALL THEM INFRARED CHICKS.
OK DAVID, SELL ALL MY STUFF. I NEED SOME DOUGH REAL BAD!
HEY DJO, SLOW DOWN, NOT EVERYONE CAN AFFORD PARISIAN THREADS.
GOOD THING I WON'T BE SEEING HER SATURDAY. I'D NEVER HAVE HAD THE MONEY TO TAKE HER OUT!
THAT'S YOUR FAULT, MY FRIEND...
IF YOU HADN'T BEEN LIVING THE HIGH LIFE AT THE HOTEL IVOIRE, YOU WOULDN'T HAVE TO SELL YOUR CLOTHES TODAY.
HEY, DO YOU WANT TO HELP OR NOT?

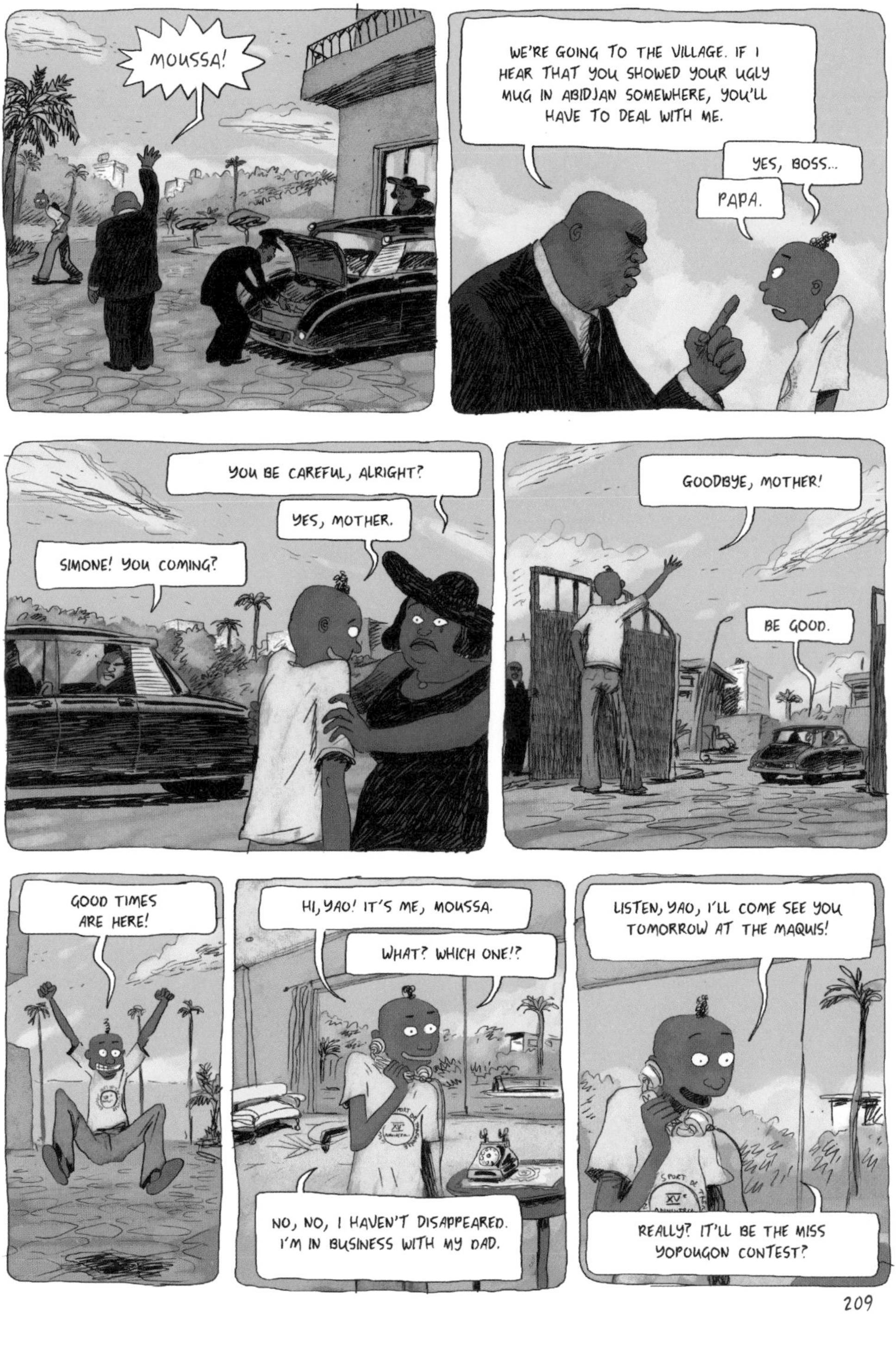
MOUSSA!
WE'RE GOING TO THE VILLAGE. IF I HEAR THAT YOU SHOWED YOUR UGLY MUG IN ABIDJAN SOMEWHERE, YOU'LL HAVE TO DEAL WITH ME.
YES, BOSS...
PAPA.
YOU BE CAREFUL, ALRIGHT?
YES, MOTHER.
SIMONE! YOU COMING?
GOODBYE, MOTHER!
BE GOOD.
GOOD TIMES ARE HERE!
HI, YAO! IT'S ME, MOUSSA.
WHAT? WHICH ONE!?
NO, NO, I HAVEN'T DISAPPEARED. I'M IN BUSINESS WITH MY DAD.
LISTEN, YAO, I'LL COME SEE YOU TOMORROW AT THE MAQUIS!
REALLY? IT'LL BE THE MISS YOPOUGON CONTEST?

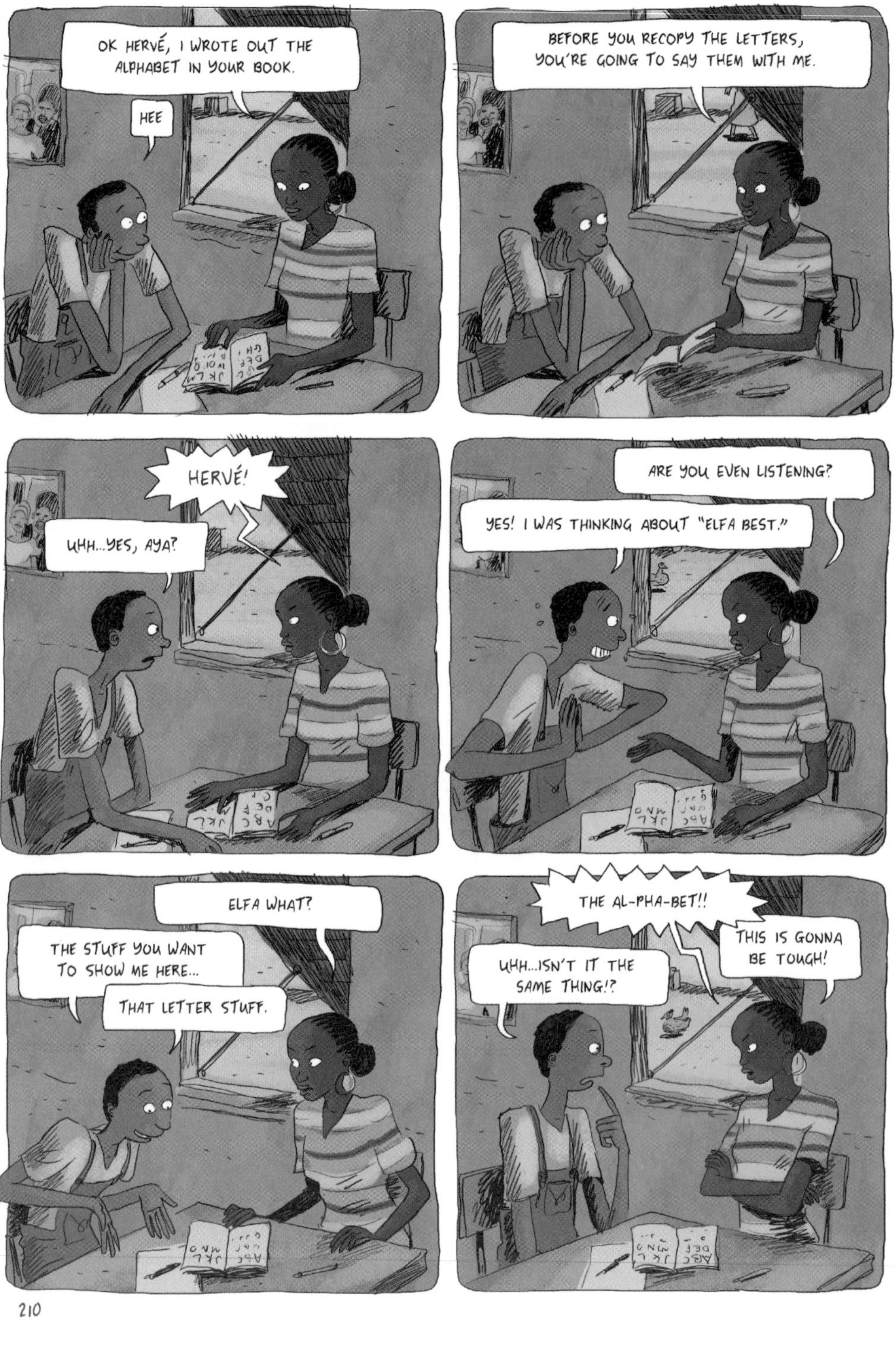
OK HERVÉ, I WROTE OUT THE ALPHABET IN YOUR BOOK.
HEE
BEFORE YOU RECOPY THE LETTERS, YOU'RE GOING TO SAY THEM WITH ME.
HERVÉ!
UHH...YES, AYA?
ARE YOU EVEN LISTENING?
YES! I WAS THINKING ABOUT "ELFA BEST."
ELFA WHAT?
THE STUFF YOU WANT TO SHOW ME HERE...
THAT LETTER STUFF.
THE AL-PHA-BET!!
UHH...ISN'T IT THE SAME THING!?
THIS IS GONNA BE TOUGH!

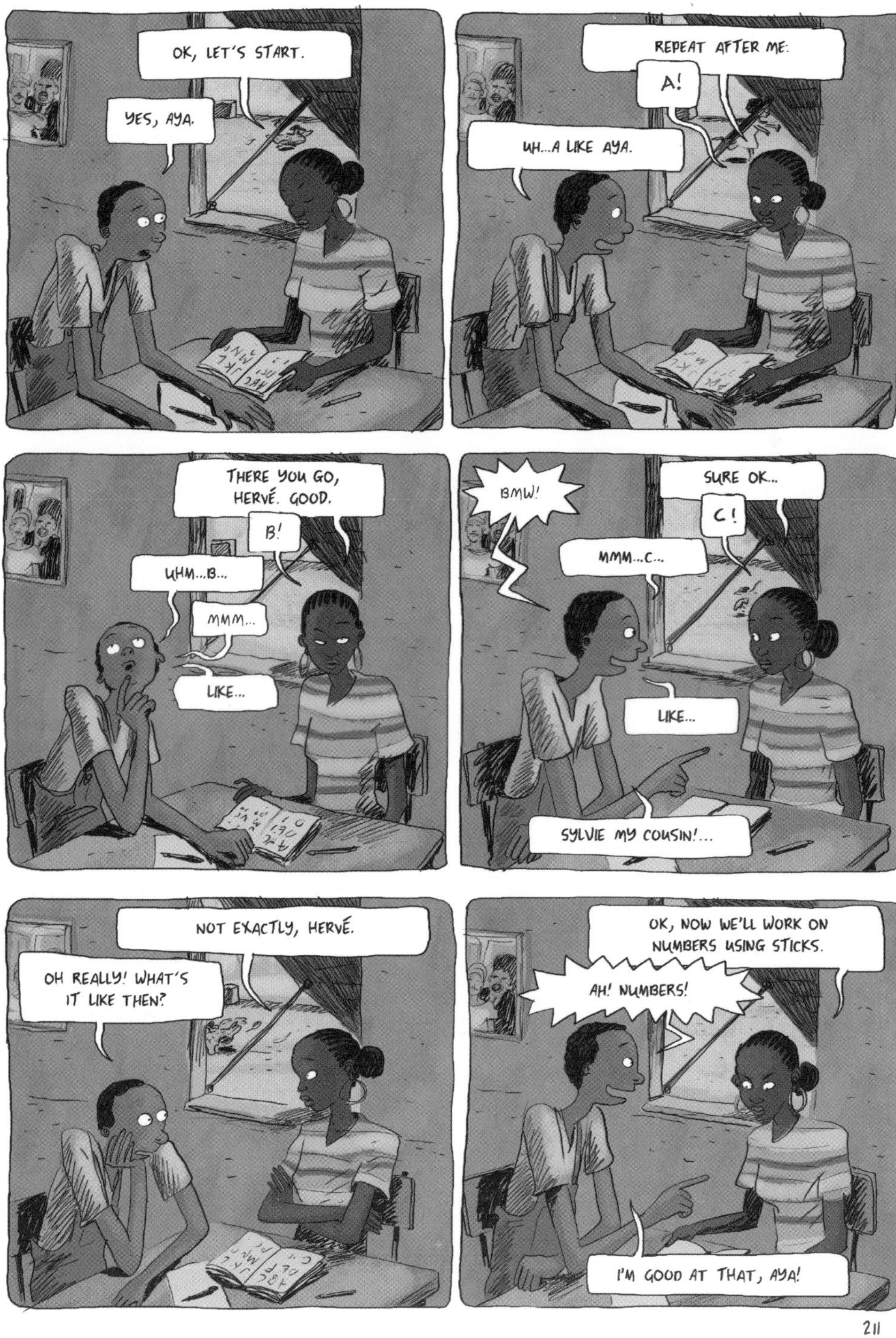
OK, LET'S START.
YES, AYA.
REPEAT AFTER ME:
A!
UH...A LIKE AYA.
THERE YOU GO, HERVÉ. GOOD.
B!
UHM...B...
MMM...
LIKE...
BMW!
SURE OK...
C!
MMM...C...
LIKE...
SYLVIE MY COUSIN!...
NOT EXACTLY, HERVÉ.
OH REALLY! WHAT'S IT LIKE THEN?
OK, NOW WE'LL WORK ON NUMBERS USING STICKS.
AH! NUMBERS!
I'M GOOD AT THAT, AYA!

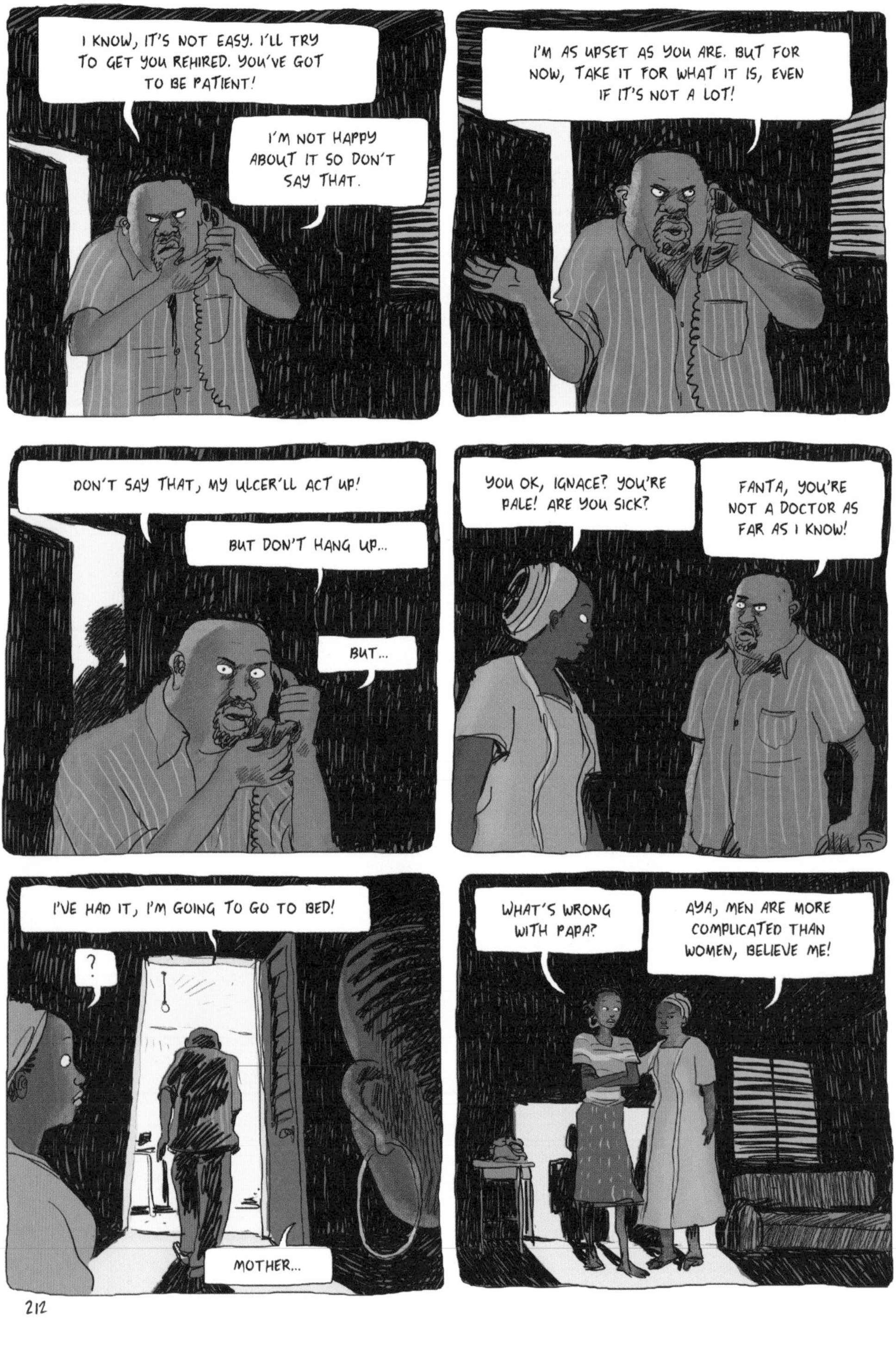
I KNOW, IT'S NOT EASY. I'LL TRY TO GET YOU REHIRED. YOU'VE GOT TO BE PATIENT!
I'M NOT HAPPY ABOUT IT SO DON'T SAY THAT.
I'M AS UPSET AS YOU ARE. BUT FOR NOW, TAKE IT FOR WHAT IT IS, EVEN IF IT'S NOT A LOT!
DON'T SAY THAT, MY ULCER'LL ACT UP!
BUT DON'T HANG UP...
BUT...
YOU OK, IGNACE? YOU'RE PALE! ARE YOU SICK?
FANTA, YOU'RE NOT A DOCTOR AS FAR AS I KNOW!
I'VE HAD IT, I'M GOING TO GO TO BED!
?
MOTHER...
WHAT'S WRONG WITH PAPA?
AYA, MEN ARE MORE COMPLICATED THAN WOMEN, BELIEVE ME!

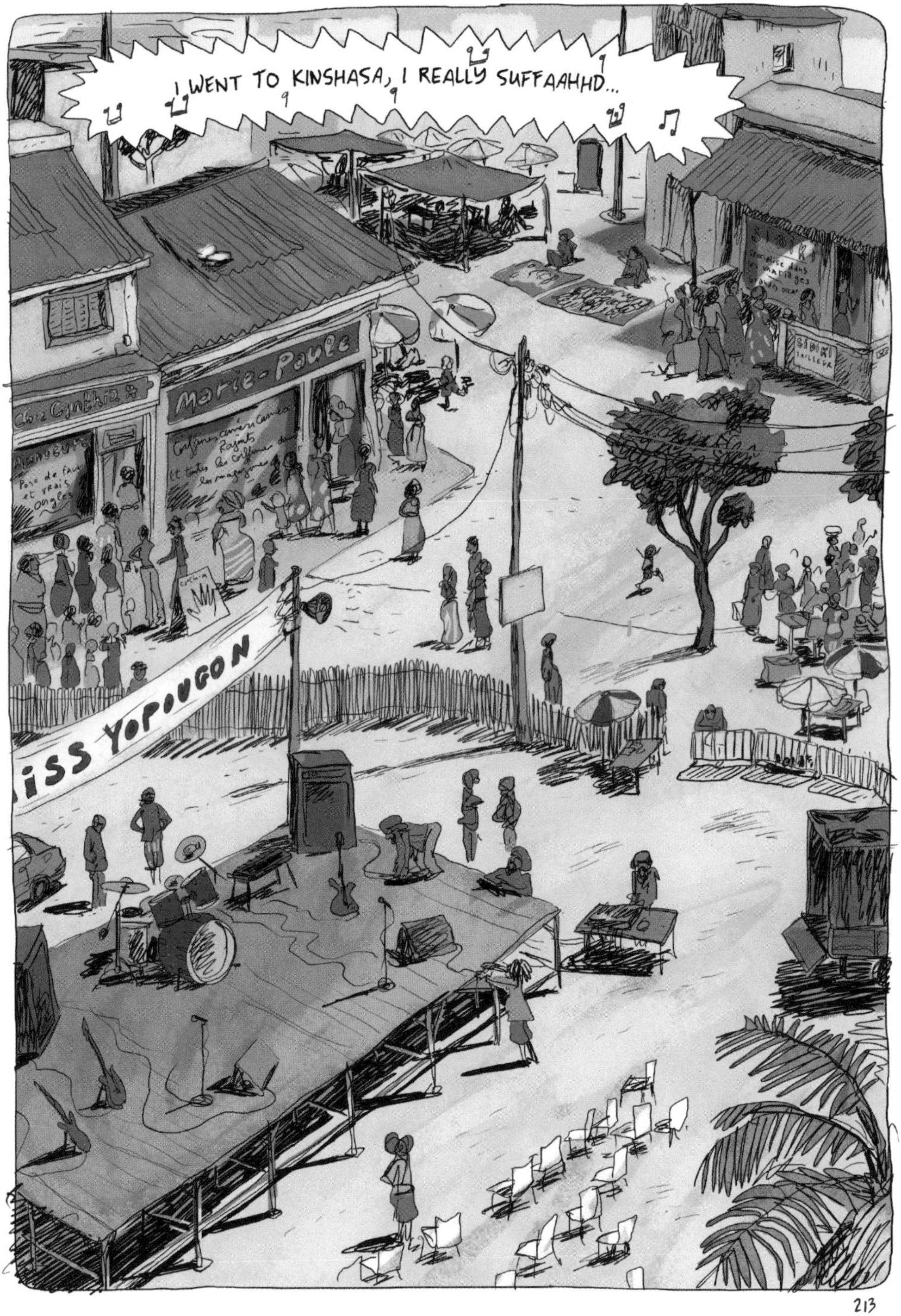
I WENT TO KINSHASA, I REALLY SUFFAAHHD...
Chez Cynthia
Pose de faux et vrais ongles
Marie-Paule
Rajouts
SIDIKI TAILLEUR
ISS YOPOUGON

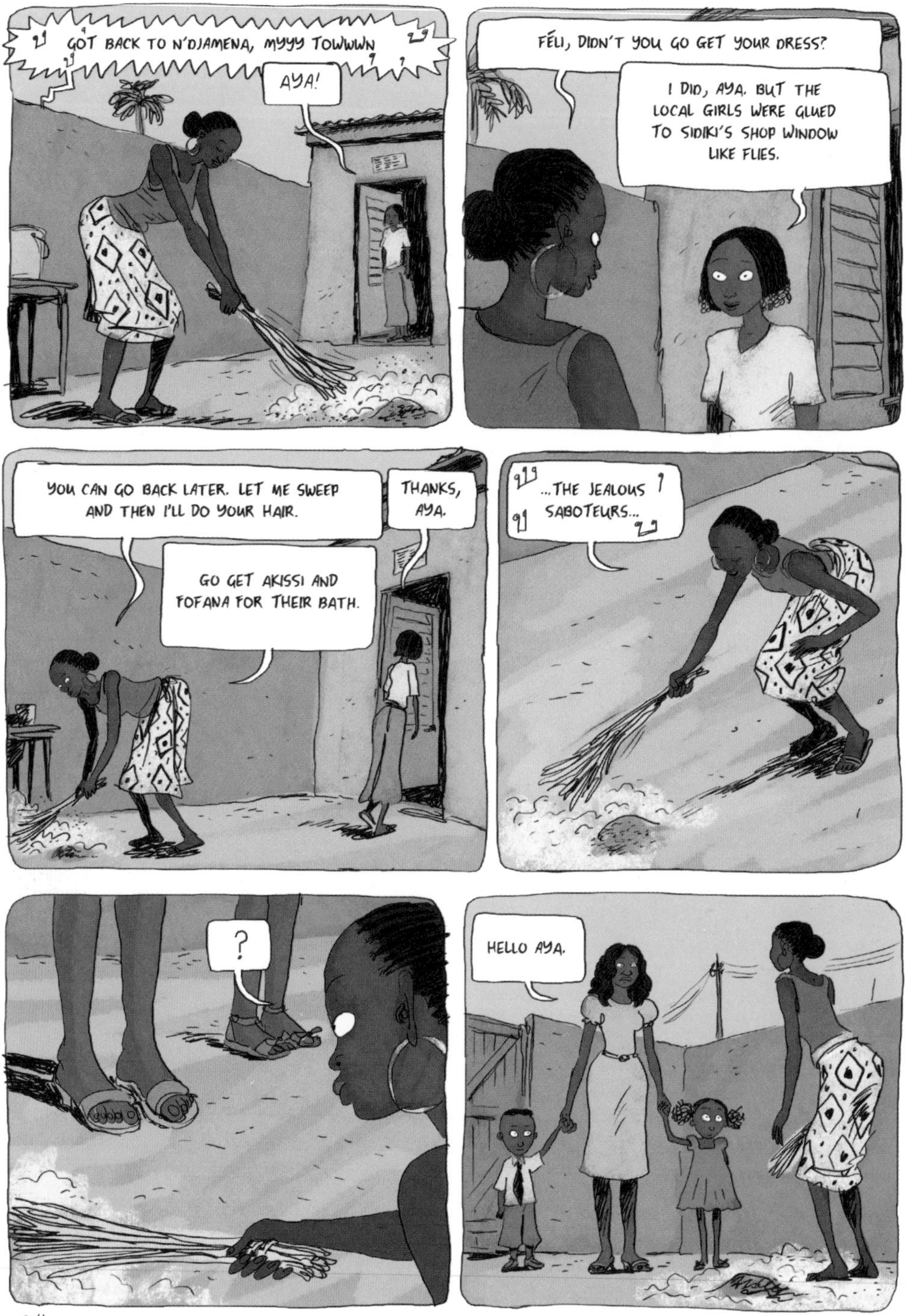
GOT BACK TO N'DJAMENA, MYYY TOWWWN
AYA!
FÉLI, DIDN'T YOU GO GET YOUR DRESS?
I DID, AYA. BUT THE LOCAL GIRLS WERE GLUED TO SIDIKI'S SHOP WINDOW LIKE FLIES.
YOU CAN GO BACK LATER. LET ME SWEEP AND THEN I'LL DO YOUR HAIR.
GO GET AKISSI AND FOFANA FOR THEIR BATH.
THANKS, AYA.
...THE JEALOUS SABOTEURS...
?
HELLO AYA.

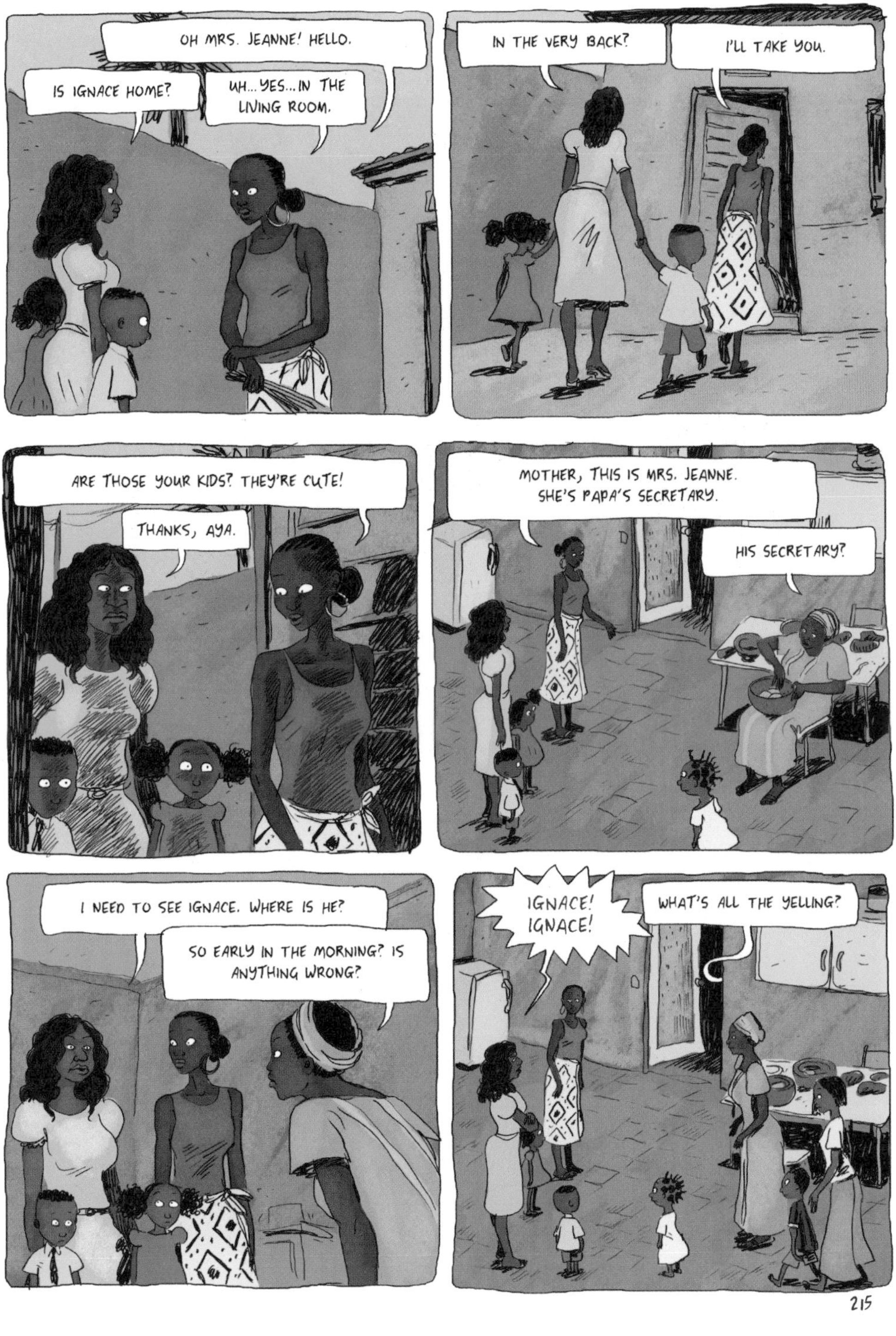
OH MRS. JEANNE! HELLO.
IS IGNACE HOME?
UH... YES... IN THE LIVING ROOM.
IN THE VERY BACK?
I'LL TAKE YOU.
ARE THOSE YOUR KIDS? THEY'RE CUTE!
THANKS, AYA.
MOTHER, THIS IS MRS. JEANNE. SHE'S PAPA'S SECRETARY.
HIS SECRETARY?
I NEED TO SEE IGNACE. WHERE IS HE?
SO EARLY IN THE MORNING? IS ANYTHING WRONG?
IGNACE! IGNACE!
WHAT'S ALL THE YELLING?

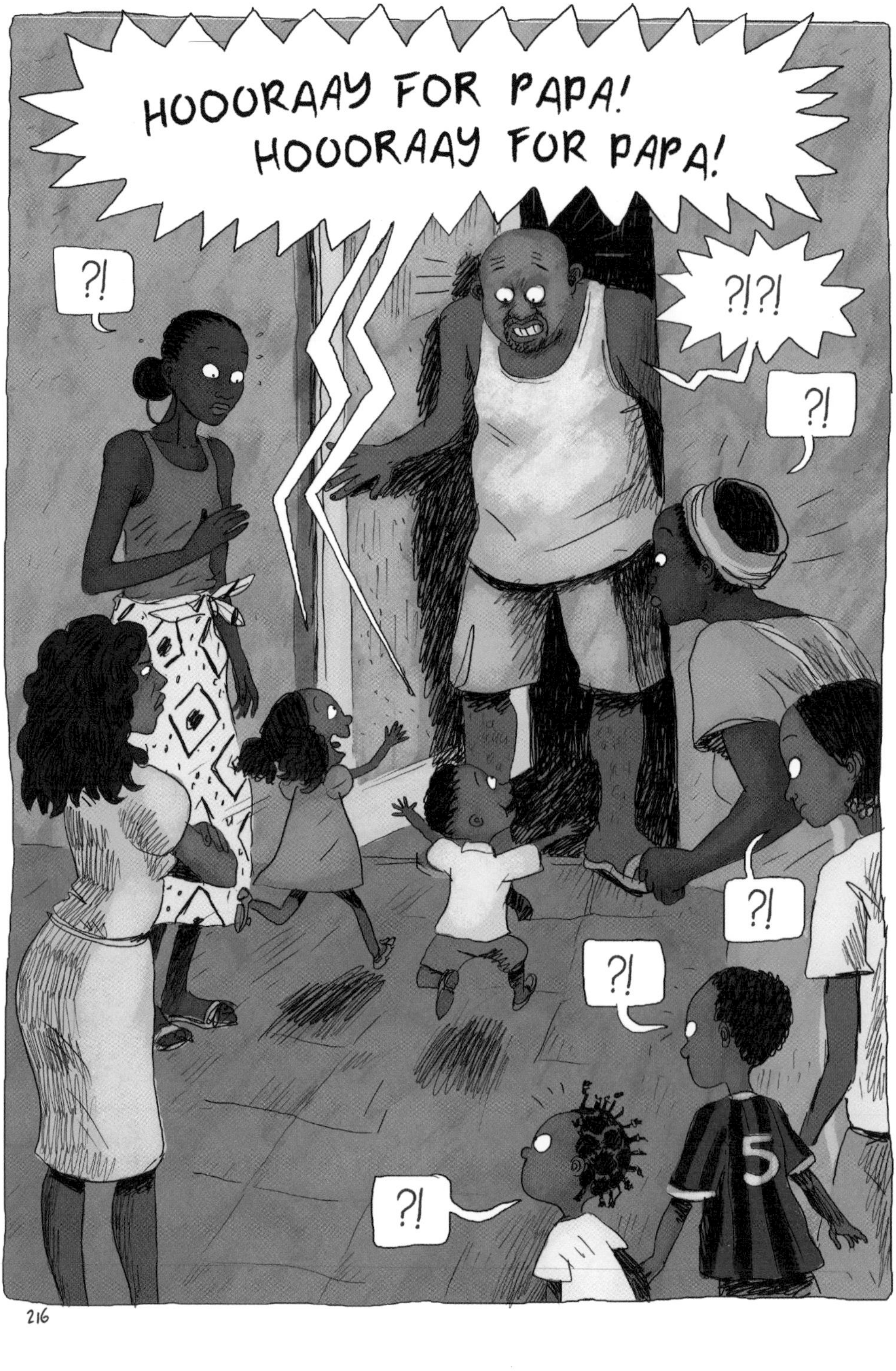
HOOORAAY FOR PAPA!
HOOORAAY FOR PAPA!
?!
?!?!
?!
?!
?!
?!

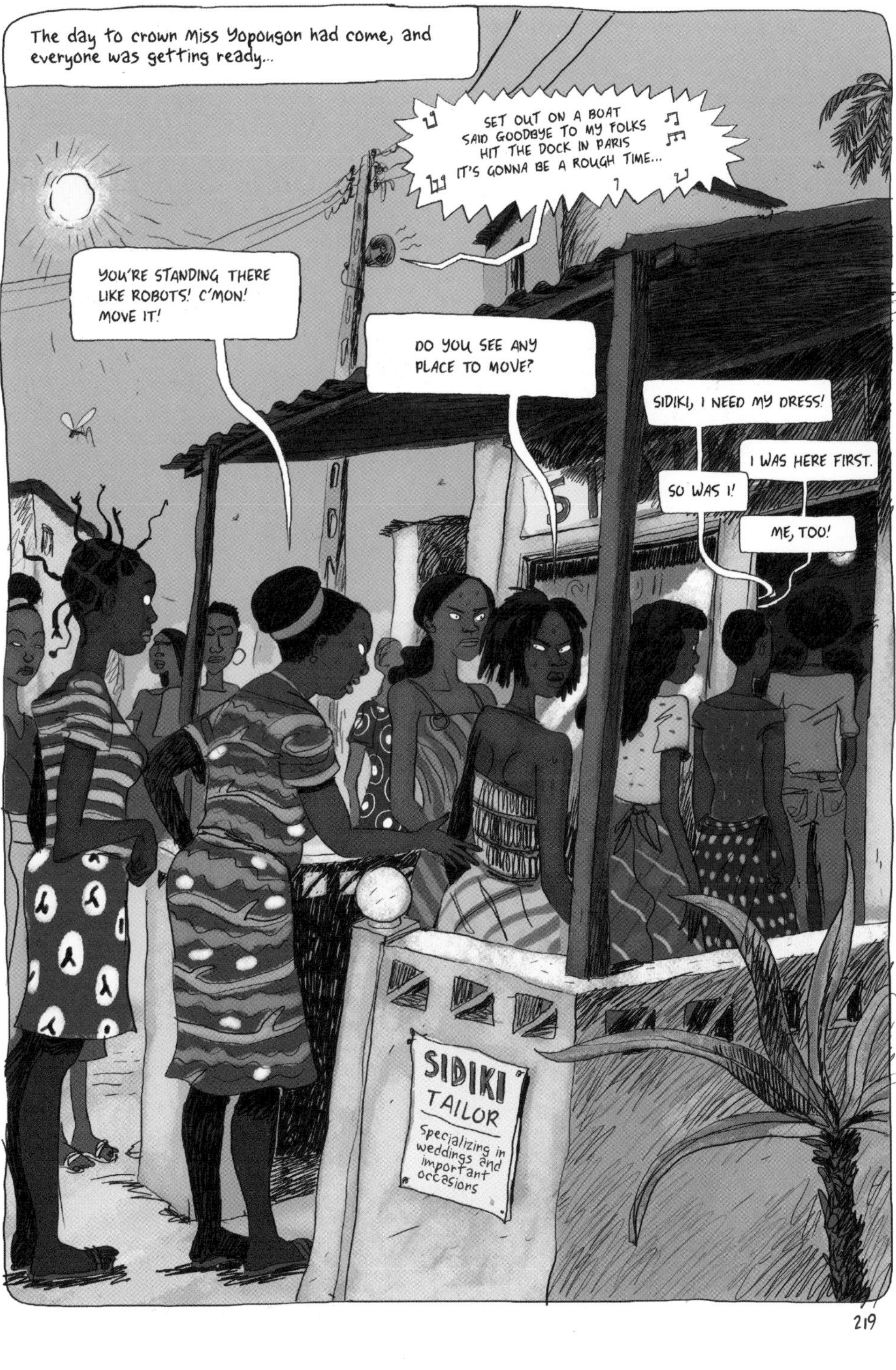
The day to crown Miss Yopougon had come, and everyone was getting ready...
SET OUT ON A BOAT
SAID GOODBYE TO MY FOLKS
HIT THE DOCK IN PARIS
IT'S GONNA BE A ROUGH TIME...
YOU'RE STANDING THERE LIKE ROBOTS! C'MON! MOVE IT!
DO YOU SEE ANY PLACE TO MOVE?
SIDIKI, I NEED MY DRESS!
I WAS HERE FIRST.
SO WAS I!
ME, TOO!
SIDIKI
TAILOR
Specializing in weddings and important occasions

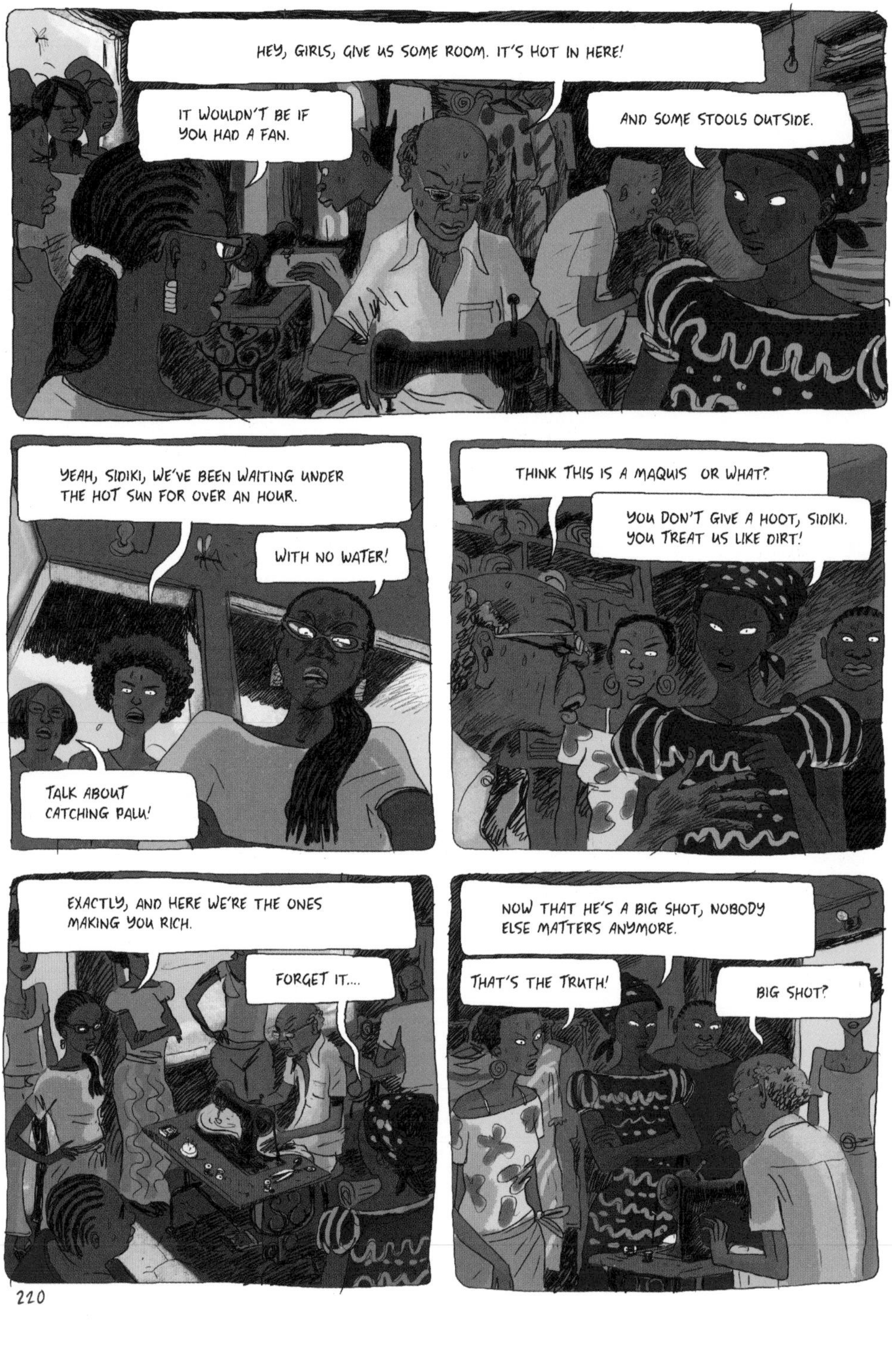
HEY, GIRLS, GIVE US SOME ROOM. IT'S HOT IN HERE!
IT WOULDN'T BE IF YOU HAD A FAN.
AND SOME STOOLS OUTSIDE.
YEAH, SIDIKI, WE'VE BEEN WAITING UNDER THE HOT SUN FOR OVER AN HOUR.
WITH NO WATER!
TALK ABOUT CATCHING PALU!
THINK THIS IS A MAQUIS OR WHAT?
YOU DON'T GIVE A HOOT, SIDIKI. YOU TREAT US LIKE DIRT!
EXACTLY, AND HERE WE'RE THE ONES MAKING YOU RICH.
FORGET IT....
NOW THAT HE'S A BIG SHOT, NOBODY ELSE MATTERS ANYMORE.
THAT'S THE TRUTH!
BIG SHOT?

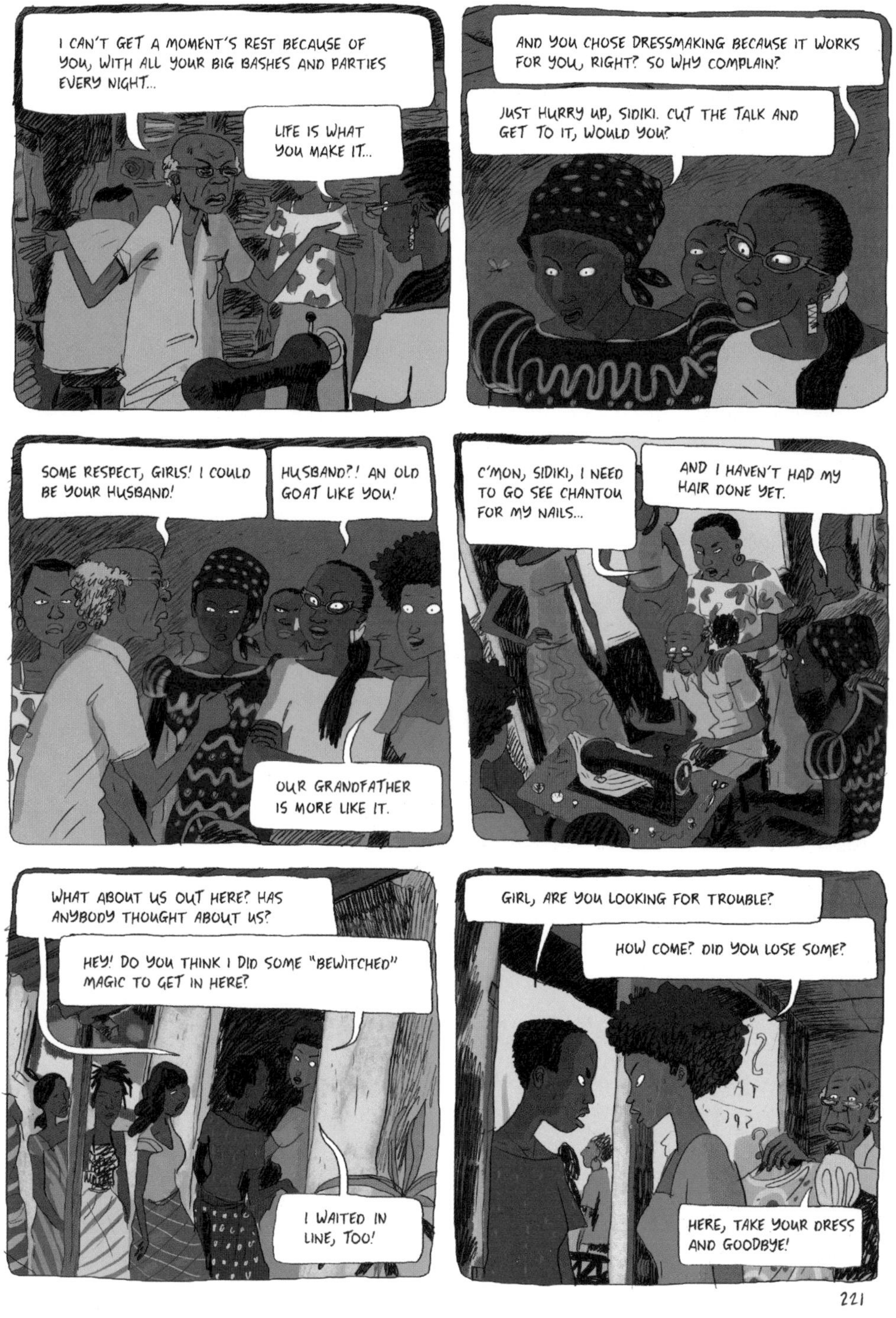
I CAN'T GET A MOMENT'S REST BECAUSE OF YOU, WITH ALL YOUR BIG BASHES AND PARTIES EVERY NIGHT...
LIFE IS WHAT YOU MAKE IT...
AND YOU CHOSE DRESSMAKING BECAUSE IT WORKS FOR YOU, RIGHT? SO WHY COMPLAIN?
JUST HURRY UP, SIDIKI. CUT THE TALK AND GET TO IT, WOULD YOU?
SOME RESPECT, GIRLS! I COULD BE YOUR HUSBAND!
HUSBAND?! AN OLD GOAT LIKE YOU!
OUR GRANDFATHER IS MORE LIKE IT.
C'MON, SIDIKI, I NEED TO GO SEE CHANTOU FOR MY NAILS...
AND I HAVEN'T HAD MY HAIR DONE YET.
WHAT ABOUT US OUT HERE? HAS ANYBODY THOUGHT ABOUT US?
HEY! DO YOU THINK I DID SOME "BEWITCHED" MAGIC TO GET IN HERE?
I WAITED IN LINE, TOO!
GIRL, ARE YOU LOOKING FOR TROUBLE?
HOW COME? DID YOU LOSE SOME?
HERE, TAKE YOUR DRESS AND GOODBYE!

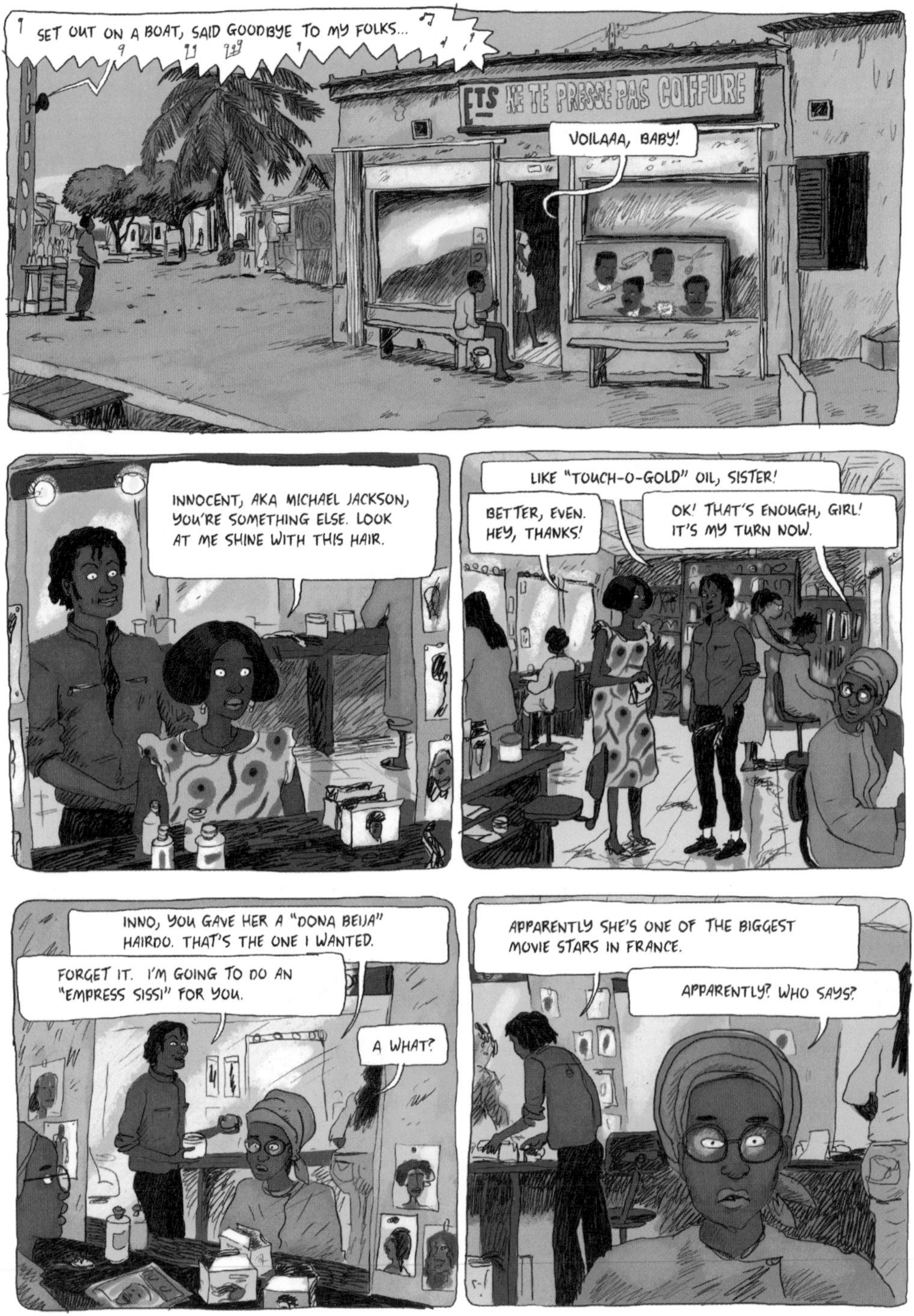
SET OUT ON A BOAT, SAID GOODBYE TO MY FOLKS...
ETS NE TE PRESSE PAS COIFFURE
VOILAAA, BABY!
INNOCENT, AKA MICHAEL JACKSON, YOU'RE SOMETHING ELSE. LOOK AT ME SHINE WITH THIS HAIR.
LIKE "TOUCH-O-GOLD" OIL, SISTER!
BETTER, EVEN. HEY, THANKS!
OK! THAT'S ENOUGH, GIRL! IT'S MY TURN NOW.
INNO, YOU GAVE HER A "DONA BEIJA" HAIRDO. THAT'S THE ONE I WANTED.
FORGET IT. I'M GOING TO DO AN "EMPRESS SISSI" FOR YOU.
A WHAT?
APPARENTLY SHE'S ONE OF THE BIGGEST MOVIE STARS IN FRANCE.
APPARENTLY? WHO SAYS?

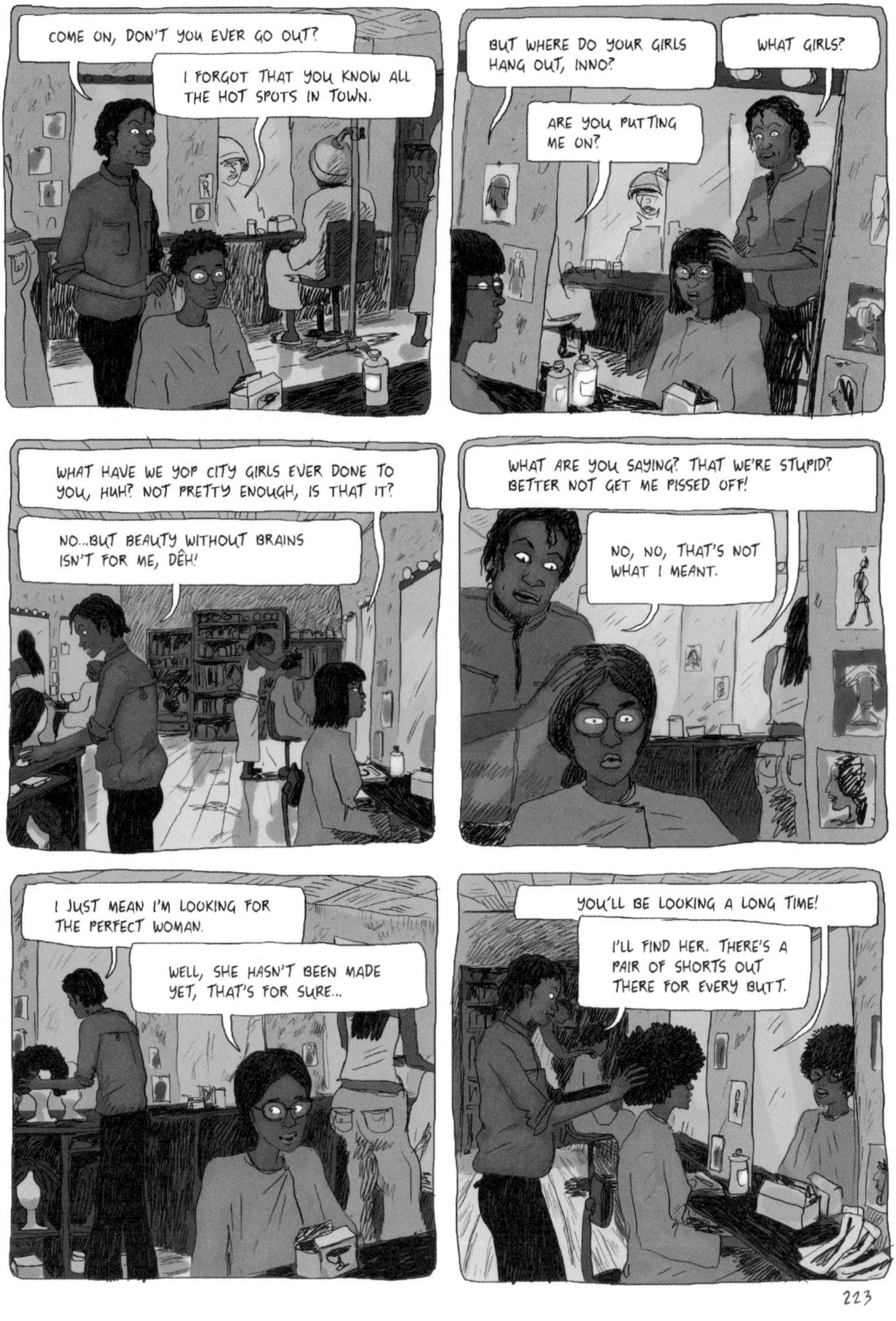
COME ON, DON'T YOU EVER GO OUT?
I FORGOT THAT YOU KNOW ALL THE HOT SPOTS IN TOWN.
BUT WHERE DO YOUR GIRLS HANG OUT, INNO?
WHAT GIRLS?
ARE YOU PUTTING ME ON?
WHAT HAVE WE YOP CITY GIRLS EVER DONE TO YOU, HUH? NOT PRETTY ENOUGH, IS THAT IT?
NO...BUT BEAUTY WITHOUT BRAINS ISN'T FOR ME, DÊH!
WHAT ARE YOU SAYING? THAT WE'RE STUPID? BETTER NOT GET ME PISSED OFF!
NO, NO, THAT'S NOT WHAT I MEANT.
I JUST MEAN I'M LOOKING FOR THE PERFECT WOMAN.
WELL, SHE HASN'T BEEN MADE YET, THAT'S FOR SURE...
YOU'LL BE LOOKING A LONG TIME!
I'LL FIND HER. THERE'S A PAIR OF SHORTS OUT THERE FOR EVERY BUTT.

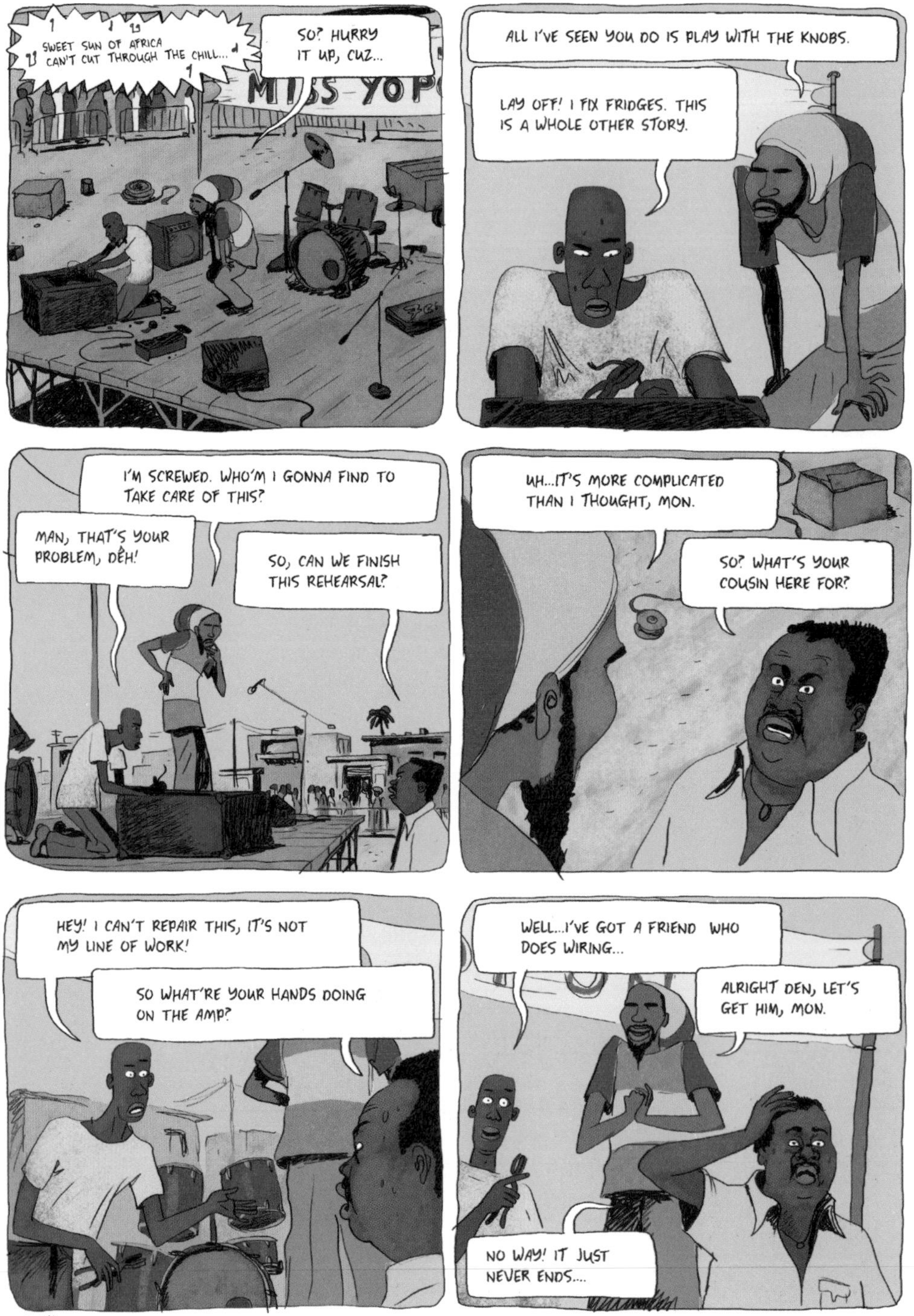
SWEET SUN OF AFRICA CAN'T CUT THROUGH THE CHILL...
SO? HURRY IT UP, CUZ...
ALL I'VE SEEN YOU DO IS PLAY WITH THE KNOBS.
LAY OFF! I FIX FRIDGES. THIS IS A WHOLE OTHER STORY.
I'M SCREWED. WHO'M I GONNA FIND TO TAKE CARE OF THIS?
MAN, THAT'S YOUR PROBLEM, DÈH!
SO, CAN WE FINISH THIS REHEARSAL?
UH...IT'S MORE COMPLICATED THAN I THOUGHT, MON.
SO? WHAT'S YOUR COUSIN HERE FOR?
HEY! I CAN'T REPAIR THIS, IT'S NOT MY LINE OF WORK!
SO WHAT'RE YOUR HANDS DOING ON THE AMP?
WELL...I'VE GOT A FRIEND WHO DOES WIRING...
ALRIGHT DEN, LET'S GET HIM, MON.
NO WAY! IT JUST NEVER ENDS....

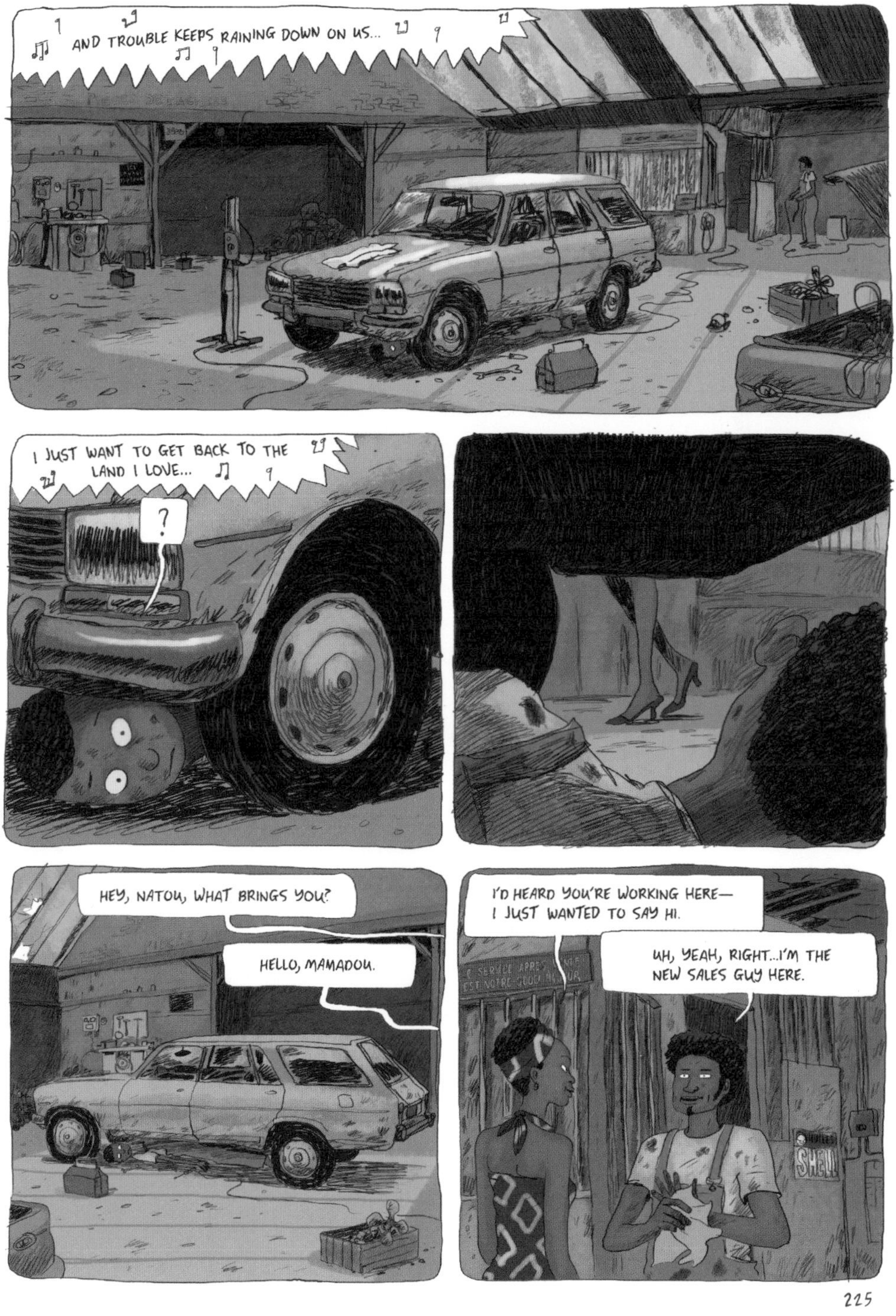
AND TROUBLE KEEPS RAINING DOWN ON US...
I JUST WANT TO GET BACK TO THE LAND I LOVE...
?
HEY, NATOU, WHAT BRINGS YOU?
HELLO, MAMADOU.
I'D HEARD YOU'RE WORKING HERE—I JUST WANTED TO SAY HI.
UH, YEAH, RIGHT...I'M THE NEW SALES GUY HERE.
SHELL

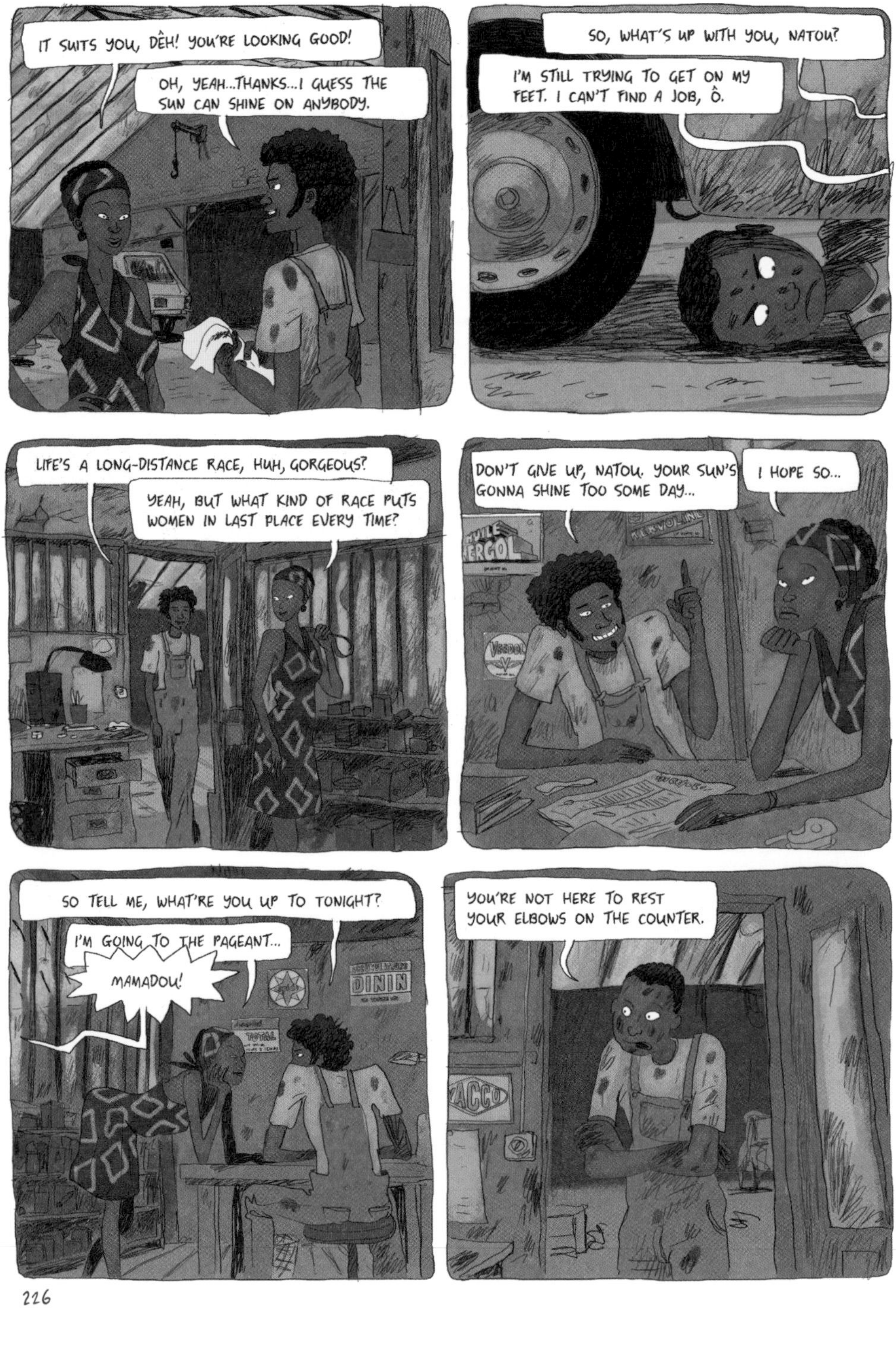
IT SUITS YOU, DÊH! YOU'RE LOOKING GOOD!
OH, YEAH...THANKS...I GUESS THE SUN CAN SHINE ON ANYBODY.
SO, WHAT'S UP WITH YOU, NATOU?
I'M STILL TRYING TO GET ON MY FEET. I CAN'T FIND A JOB, Ô.
LIFE'S A LONG-DISTANCE RACE, HUH, GORGEOUS?
YEAH, BUT WHAT KIND OF RACE PUTS WOMEN IN LAST PLACE EVERY TIME?
DON'T GIVE UP, NATOU. YOUR SUN'S GONNA SHINE TOO SOME DAY...
I HOPE SO...
SO TELL ME, WHAT'RE YOU UP TO TONIGHT?
I'M GOING TO THE PAGEANT...
MAMADOU!
DININ
TOTAL
YOU'RE NOT HERE TO REST YOUR ELBOWS ON THE COUNTER.
ZACCO

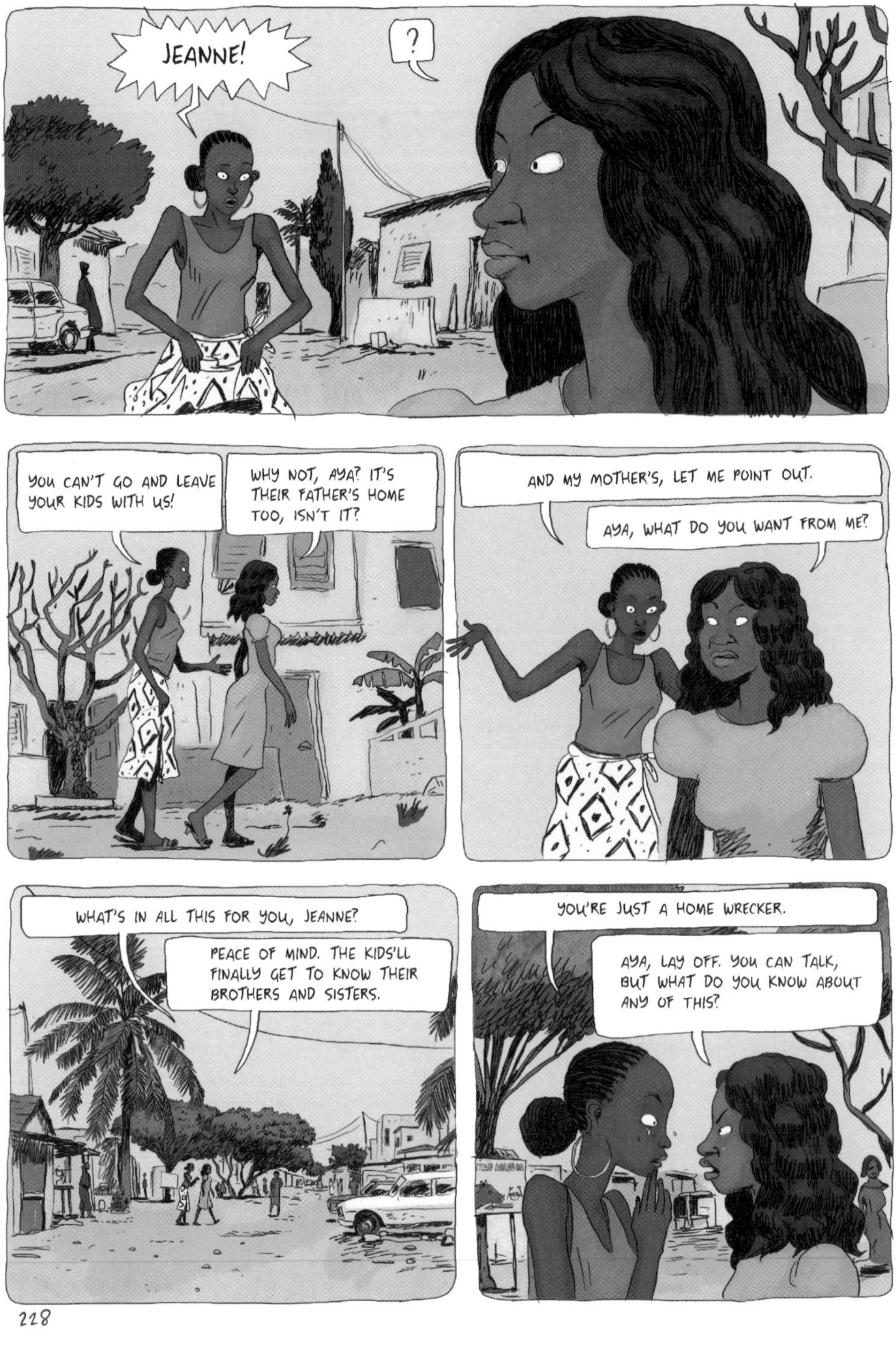
JEANNE!
?
YOU CAN'T GO AND LEAVE YOUR KIDS WITH US!
WHY NOT, AYA? IT'S THEIR FATHER'S HOME TOO, ISN'T IT?
AND MY MOTHER'S, LET ME POINT OUT.
AYA, WHAT DO YOU WANT FROM ME?
WHAT'S IN ALL THIS FOR YOU, JEANNE?
PEACE OF MIND. THE KIDS'LL FINALLY GET TO KNOW THEIR BROTHERS AND SISTERS.
YOU'RE JUST A HOME WRECKER.
AYA, LAY OFF. YOU CAN TALK, BUT WHAT DO YOU KNOW ABOUT ANY OF THIS?

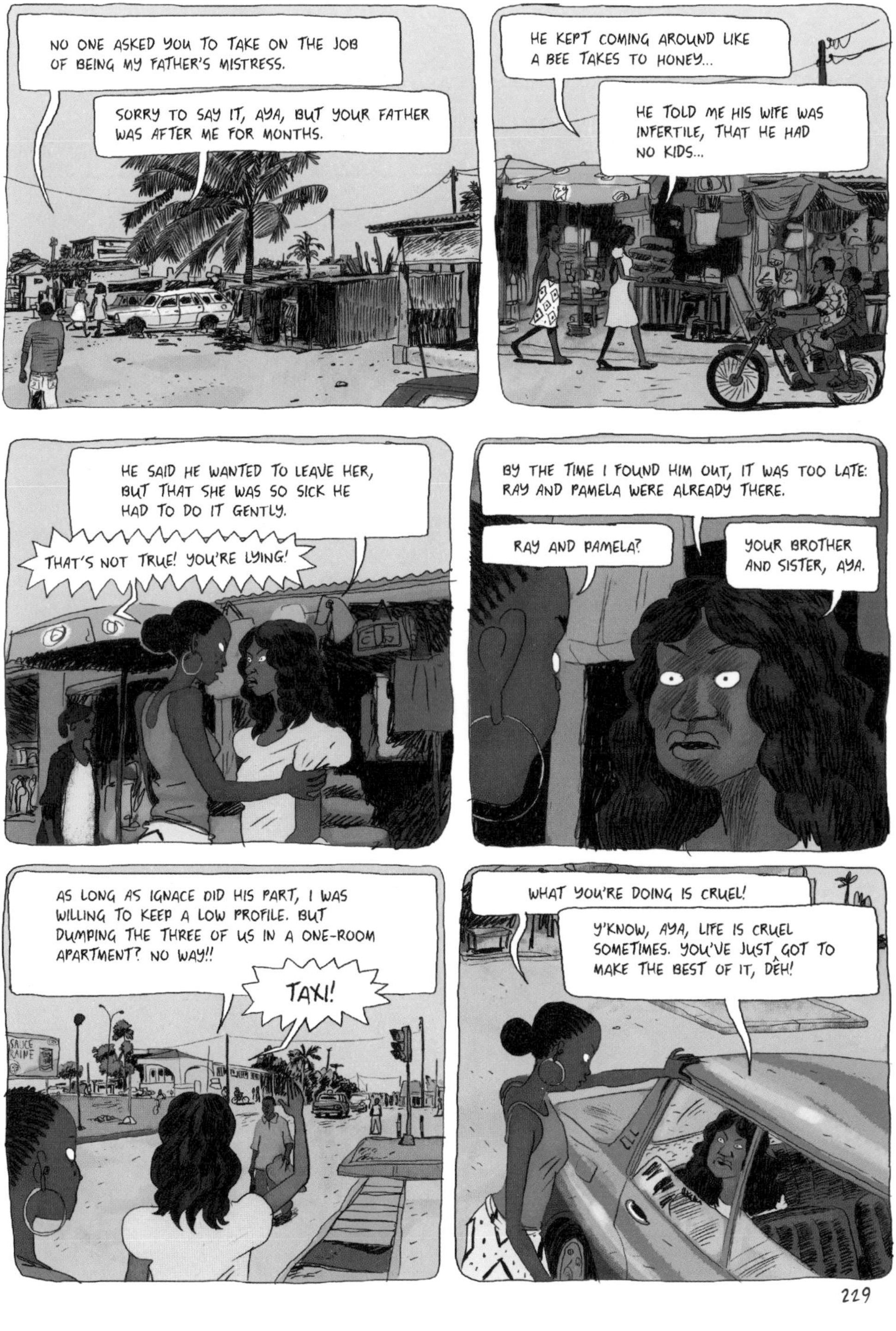

NO ONE ASKED YOU TO TAKE ON THE JOB OF BEING MY FATHER'S MISTRESS.
SORRY TO SAY IT, AYA, BUT YOUR FATHER WAS AFTER ME FOR MONTHS.
HE KEPT COMING AROUND LIKE A BEE TAKES TO HONEY...
HE TOLD ME HIS WIFE WAS INFERTILE, THAT HE HAD NO KIDS...
HE SAID HE WANTED TO LEAVE HER, BUT THAT SHE WAS SO SICK HE HAD TO DO IT GENTLY.
THAT'S NOT TRUE! YOU'RE LYING!
BY THE TIME I FOUND HIM OUT, IT WAS TOO LATE: RAY AND PAMELA WERE ALREADY THERE.
RAY AND PAMELA?
YOUR BROTHER AND SISTER, AYA.
AS LONG AS IGNACE DID HIS PART, I WAS WILLING TO KEEP A LOW PROFILE. BUT DUMPING THE THREE OF US IN A ONE-ROOM APARTMENT? NO WAY!!
TAXI!
WHAT YOU'RE DOING IS CRUEL!
Y'KNOW, AYA, LIFE IS CRUEL SOMETIMES. YOU'VE JUST GOT TO MAKE THE BEST OF IT, DÊH!

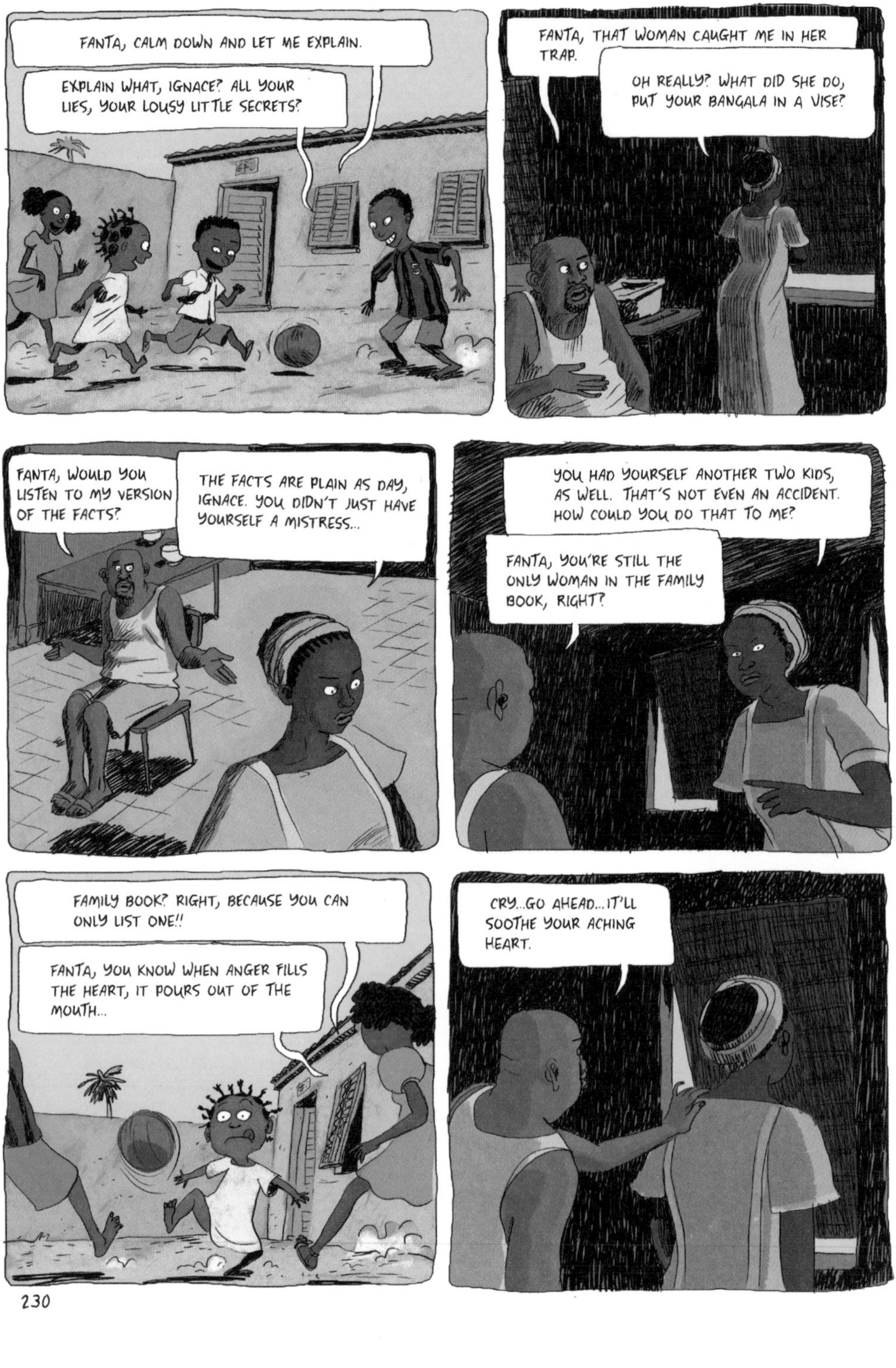
FANTA, CALM DOWN AND LET ME EXPLAIN.
EXPLAIN WHAT, IGNACE? ALL YOUR LIES, YOUR LOUSY LITTLE SECRETS?
FANTA, THAT WOMAN CAUGHT ME IN HER TRAP.
OH REALLY? WHAT DID SHE DO, PUT YOUR BANGALA IN A VISE?
FANTA, WOULD YOU LISTEN TO MY VERSION OF THE FACTS?
THE FACTS ARE PLAIN AS DAY, IGNACE. YOU DIDN'T JUST HAVE YOURSELF A MISTRESS...
YOU HAD YOURSELF ANOTHER TWO KIDS, AS WELL. THAT'S NOT EVEN AN ACCIDENT. HOW COULD YOU DO THAT TO ME?
FANTA, YOU'RE STILL THE ONLY WOMAN IN THE FAMILY BOOK, RIGHT?
FAMILY BOOK? RIGHT, BECAUSE YOU CAN ONLY LIST ONE!!
FANTA, YOU KNOW WHEN ANGER FILLS THE HEART, IT POURS OUT OF THE MOUTH...
CRY...GO AHEAD...IT'LL SOOTHE YOUR ACHING HEART.

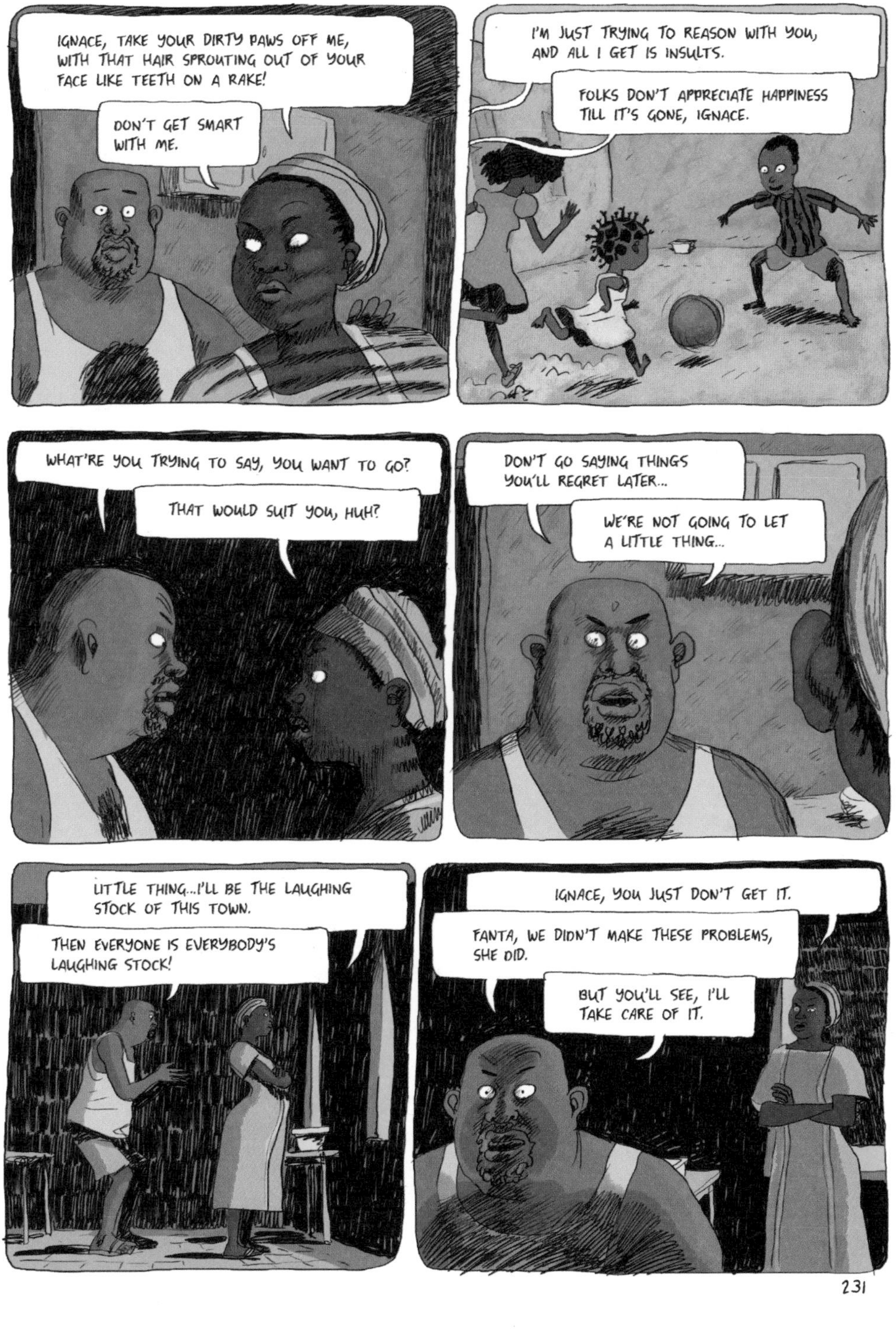
IGNACE, TAKE YOUR DIRTY PAWS OFF ME, WITH THAT HAIR SPROUTING OUT OF YOUR FACE LIKE TEETH ON A RAKE!
DON'T GET SMART WITH ME.
I'M JUST TRYING TO REASON WITH YOU, AND ALL I GET IS INSULTS.
FOLKS DON'T APPRECIATE HAPPINESS TILL IT'S GONE, IGNACE.
WHAT'RE YOU TRYING TO SAY, YOU WANT TO GO?
THAT WOULD SUIT YOU, HUH?
DON'T GO SAYING THINGS YOU'LL REGRET LATER...
WE'RE NOT GOING TO LET A LITTLE THING...
LITTLE THING...I'LL BE THE LAUGHING STOCK OF THIS TOWN.
THEN EVERYONE IS EVERYBODY'S LAUGHING STOCK!
IGNACE, YOU JUST DON'T GET IT.
FANTA, WE DIDN'T MAKE THESE PROBLEMS, SHE DID.
BUT YOU'LL SEE, I'LL TAKE CARE OF IT.

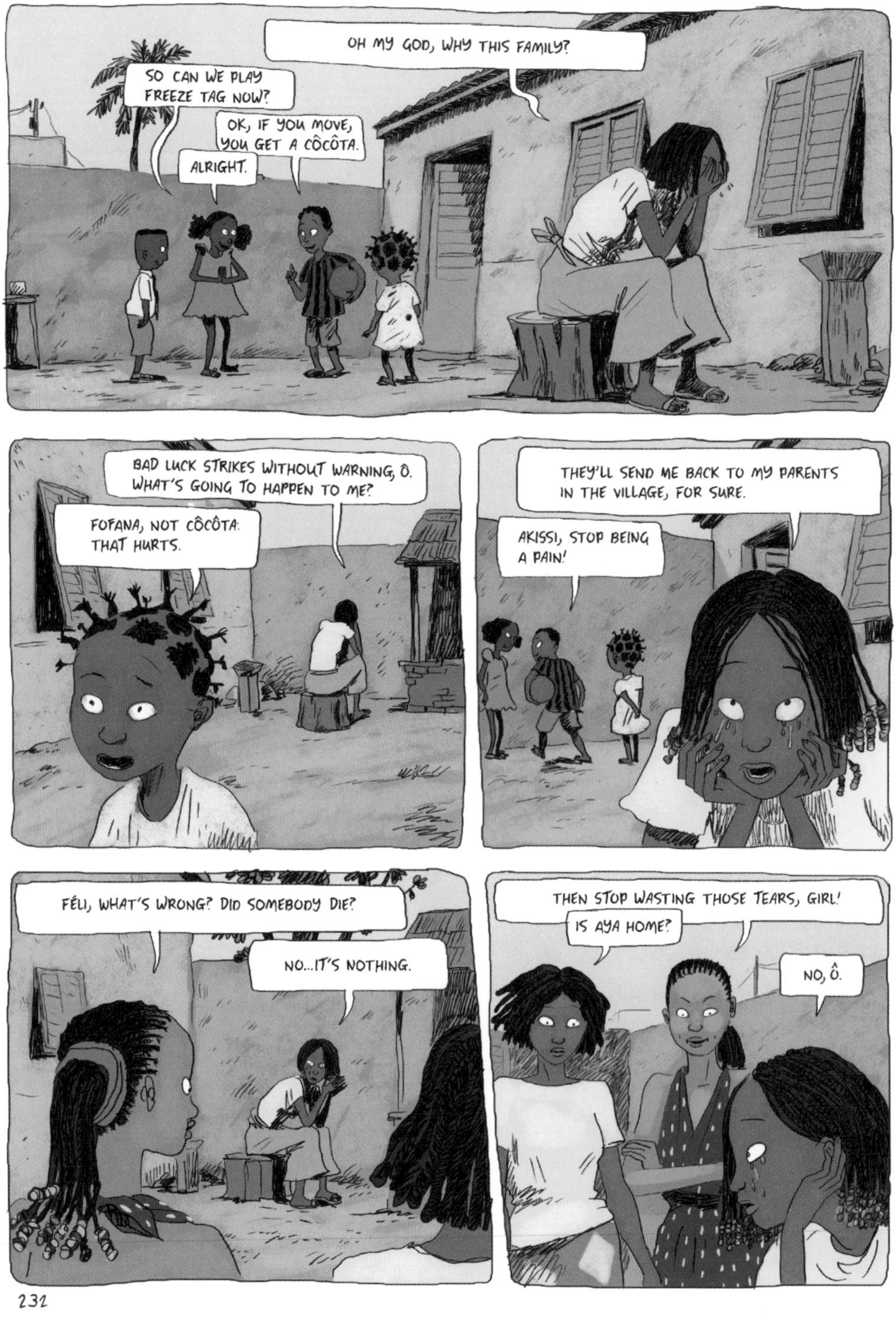
OH MY GOD, WHY THIS FAMILY?
SO CAN WE PLAY FREEZE TAG NOW?
ALRIGHT.
OK, IF YOU MOVE, YOU GET A CÔCÔTA.
BAD LUCK STRIKES WITHOUT WARNING, Ô. WHAT'S GOING TO HAPPEN TO ME?
FOFANA, NOT CÔCÔTA: THAT HURTS.
THEY'LL SEND ME BACK TO MY PARENTS IN THE VILLAGE, FOR SURE.
AKISSI, STOP BEING A PAIN!
FÉLI, WHAT'S WRONG? DID SOMEBODY DIE?
NO...IT'S NOTHING.
THEN STOP WASTING THOSE TEARS, GIRL!
IS AYA HOME?
NO, Ô.

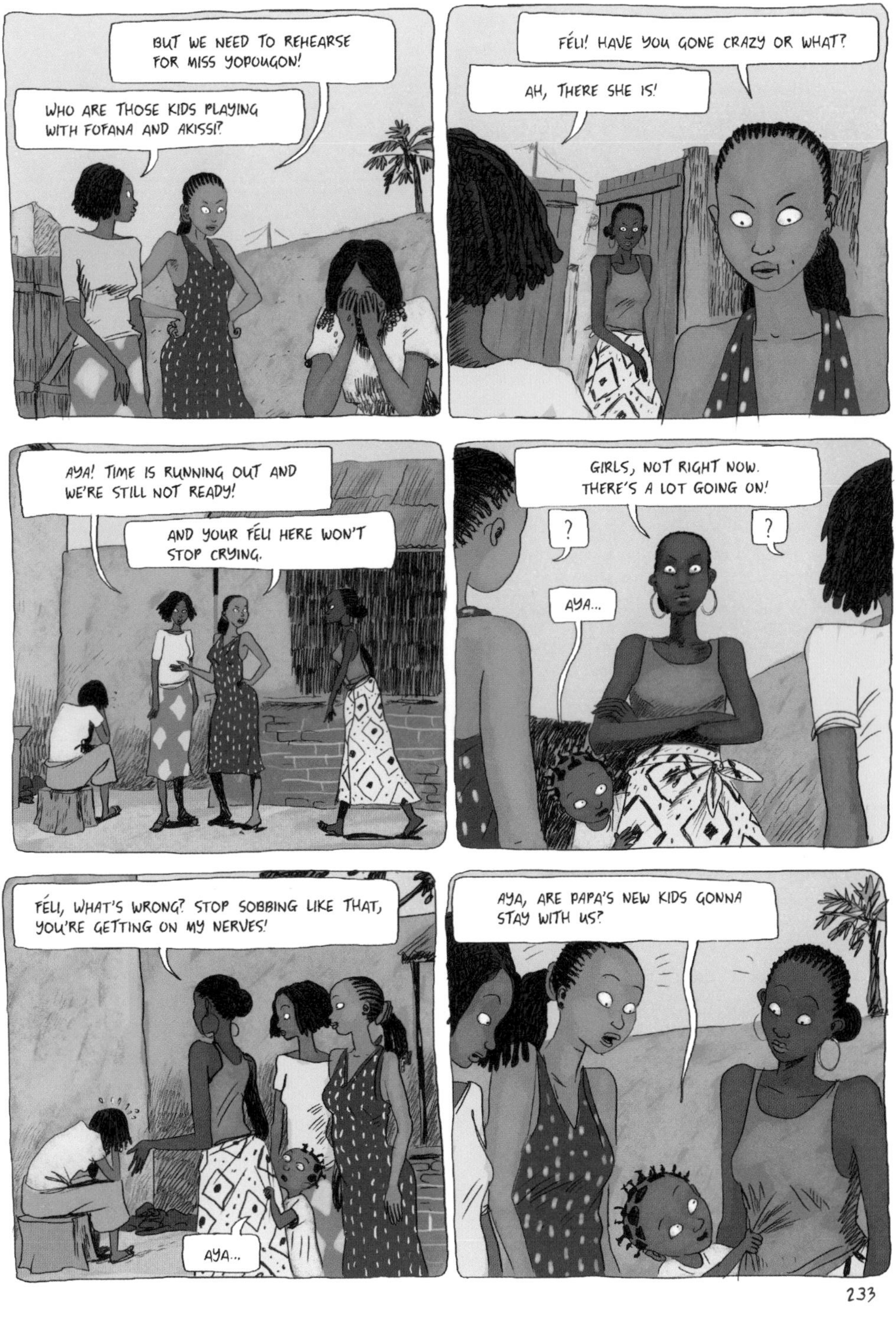
WHO ARE THOSE KIDS PLAYING WITH FOFANA AND AKISSI?
BUT WE NEED TO REHEARSE FOR MISS YOPOUGON!
FÉLI! HAVE YOU GONE CRAZY OR WHAT?
AH, THERE SHE IS!
AYA! TIME IS RUNNING OUT AND WE'RE STILL NOT READY!
AND YOUR FÉLI HERE WON'T STOP CRYING.
GIRLS, NOT RIGHT NOW. THERE'S A LOT GOING ON!
?
?
AYA...
FÉLI, WHAT'S WRONG? STOP SOBBING LIKE THAT, YOU'RE GETTING ON MY NERVES!
AYA...
AYA, ARE PAPA'S NEW KIDS GONNA STAY WITH US?

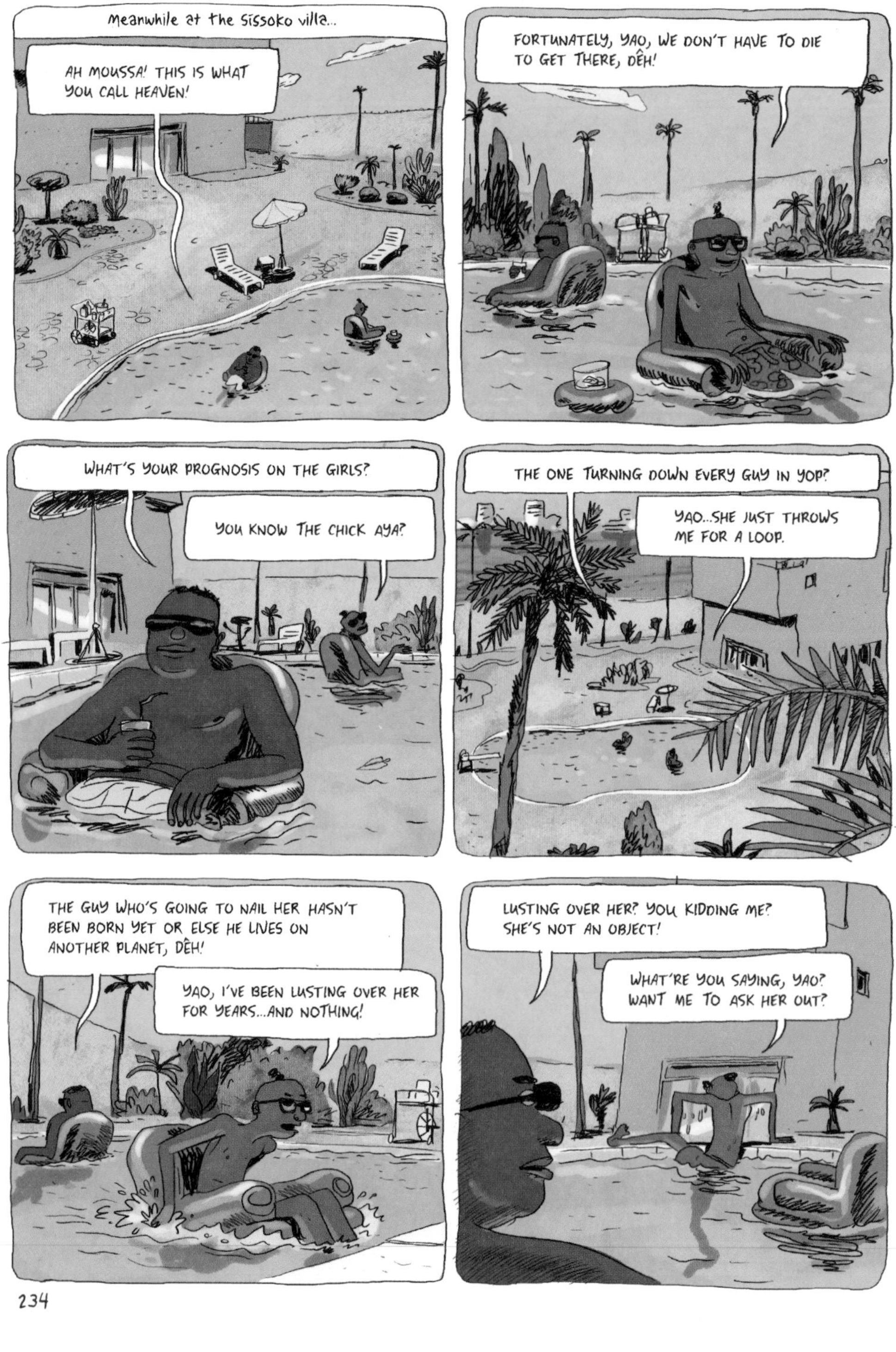
Meanwhile at the Sissoko villa...
AH MOUSSA! THIS IS WHAT YOU CALL HEAVEN!
FORTUNATELY, YAO, WE DON'T HAVE TO DIE TO GET THERE, DÊH!
WHAT'S YOUR PROGNOSIS ON THE GIRLS?
YOU KNOW THE CHICK AYA?
THE ONE TURNING DOWN EVERY GUY IN YOP?
YAO...SHE JUST THROWS ME FOR A LOOP.
THE GUY WHO'S GOING TO NAIL HER HASN'T BEEN BORN YET OR ELSE HE LIVES ON ANOTHER PLANET, DÊH!
YAO, I'VE BEEN LUSTING OVER HER FOR YEARS...AND NOTHING!
LUSTING OVER HER? YOU KIDDING ME? SHE'S NOT AN OBJECT!
WHAT'RE YOU SAYING, YAO? WANT ME TO ASK HER OUT?

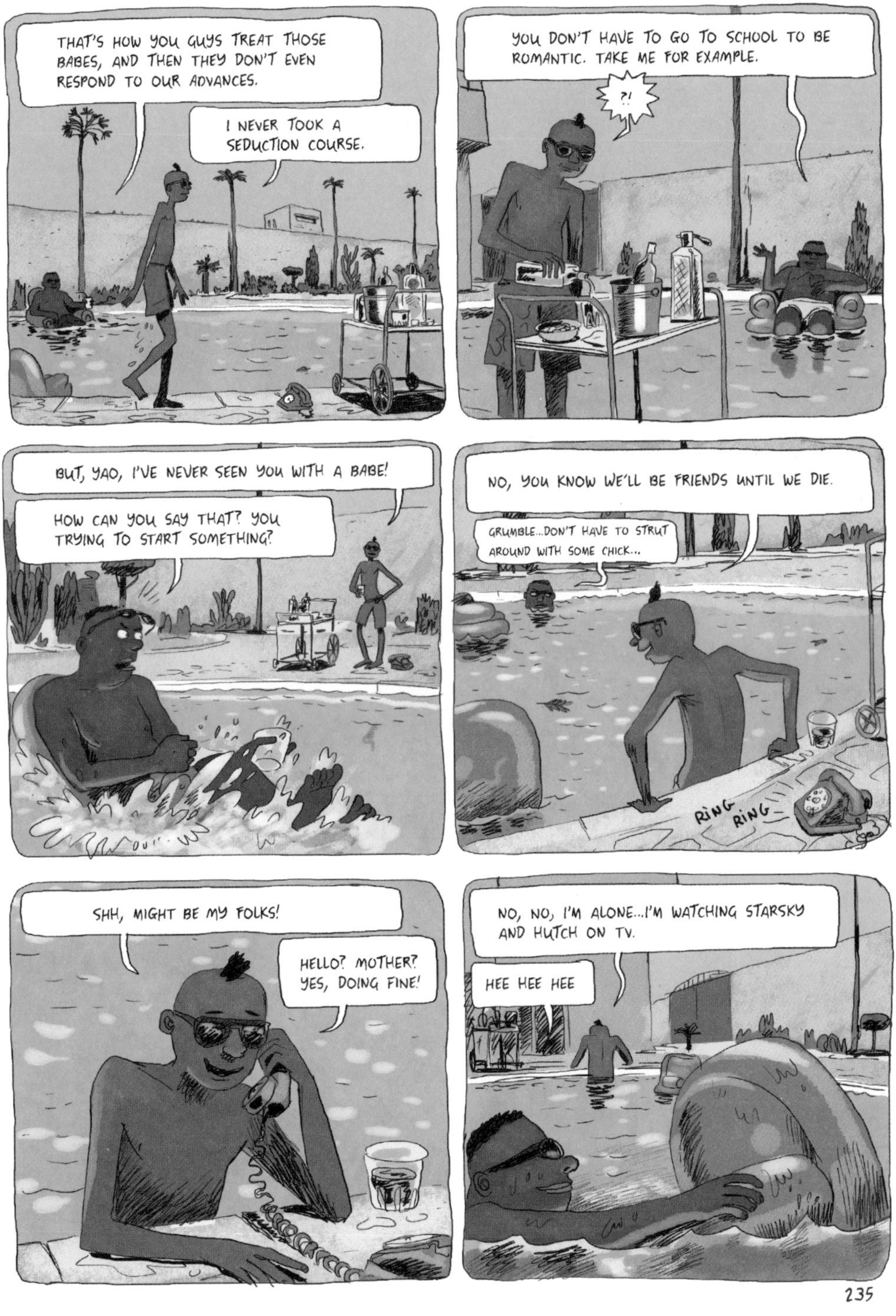
THAT'S HOW YOU GUYS TREAT THOSE BABES, AND THEN THEY DON'T EVEN RESPOND TO OUR ADVANCES.
I NEVER TOOK A SEDUCTION COURSE.
YOU DON'T HAVE TO GO TO SCHOOL TO BE ROMANTIC. TAKE ME FOR EXAMPLE.
?!
BUT, YAO, I'VE NEVER SEEN YOU WITH A BABE!
HOW CAN YOU SAY THAT? YOU TRYING TO START SOMETHING?
NO, YOU KNOW WE'LL BE FRIENDS UNTIL WE DIE.
GRUMBLE...DON'T HAVE TO STRUT AROUND WITH SOME CHICK...
RING RING
SHH, MIGHT BE MY FOLKS!
HELLO? MOTHER? YES, DOING FINE!
NO, NO, I'M ALONE...I'M WATCHING STARSKY AND HUTCH ON TV.
HEE HEE HEE

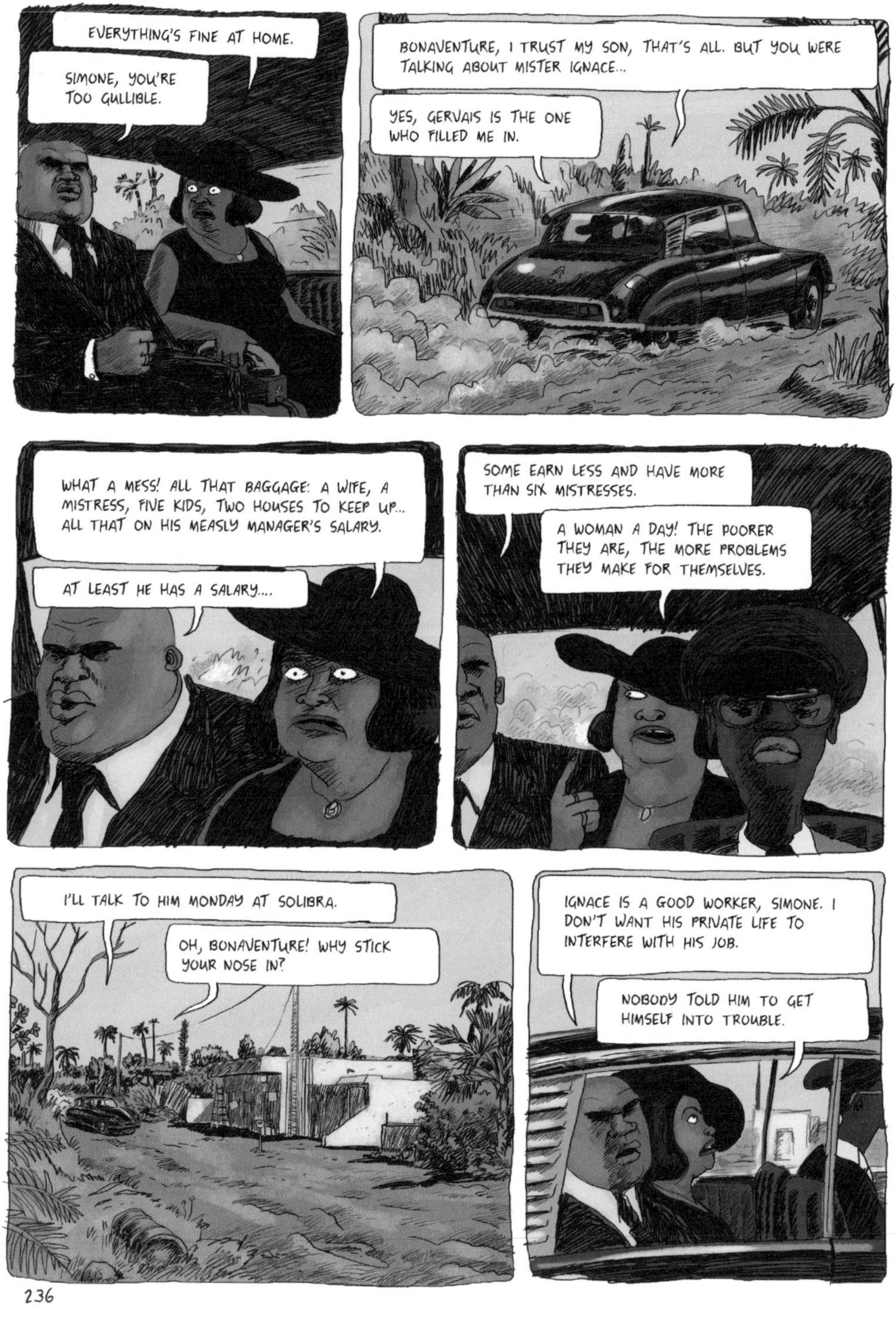
EVERYTHING'S FINE AT HOME.
SIMONE, YOU'RE TOO GULLIBLE.
BONAVENTURE, I TRUST MY SON, THAT'S ALL. BUT YOU WERE TALKING ABOUT MISTER IGNACE...
YES, GERVAIS IS THE ONE WHO FILLED ME IN.
WHAT A MESS! ALL THAT BAGGAGE: A WIFE, A MISTRESS, FIVE KIDS, TWO HOUSES TO KEEP UP... ALL THAT ON HIS MEASLY MANAGER'S SALARY.
AT LEAST HE HAS A SALARY....
SOME EARN LESS AND HAVE MORE THAN SIX MISTRESSES.
A WOMAN A DAY! THE POORER THEY ARE, THE MORE PROBLEMS THEY MAKE FOR THEMSELVES.
I'LL TALK TO HIM MONDAY AT SOLIBRA.
OH, BONAVENTURE! WHY STICK YOUR NOSE IN?
IGNACE IS A GOOD WORKER, SIMONE. I DON'T WANT HIS PRIVATE LIFE TO INTERFERE WITH HIS JOB.
NOBODY TOLD HIM TO GET HIMSELF INTO TROUBLE.

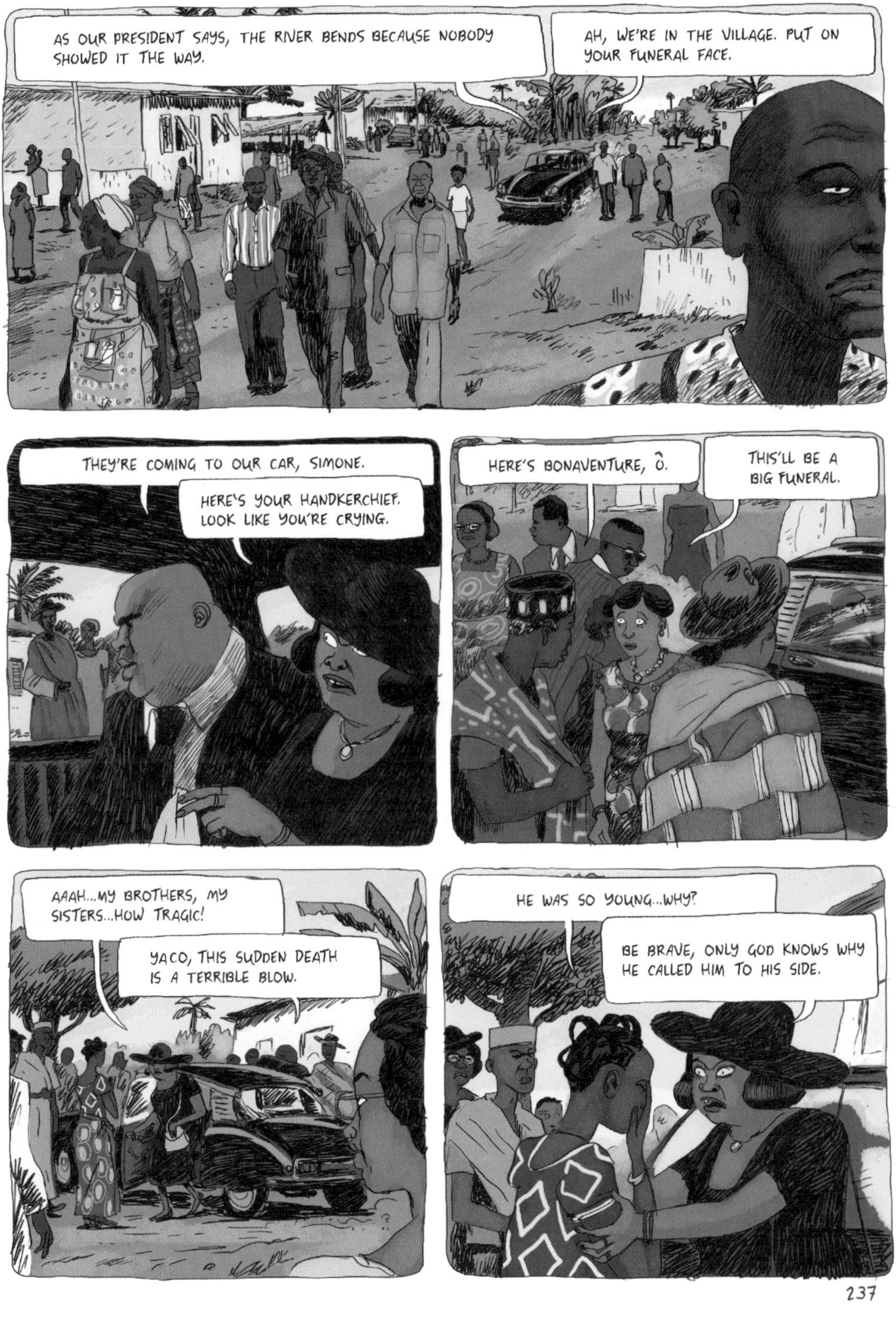
AS OUR PRESIDENT SAYS, THE RIVER BENDS BECAUSE NOBODY SHOWED IT THE WAY.
AH, WE'RE IN THE VILLAGE. PUT ON YOUR FUNERAL FACE.
THEY'RE COMING TO OUR CAR, SIMONE.
HERE'S YOUR HANDKERCHIEF. LOOK LIKE YOU'RE CRYING.
HERE'S BONAVENTURE, Ô.
THIS'LL BE A BIG FUNERAL.
AAAH...MY BROTHERS, MY SISTERS...HOW TRAGIC!
YACO, THIS SUDDEN DEATH IS A TERRIBLE BLOW.
HE WAS SO YOUNG...WHY?
BE BRAVE, ONLY GOD KNOWS WHY HE CALLED HIM TO HIS SIDE.

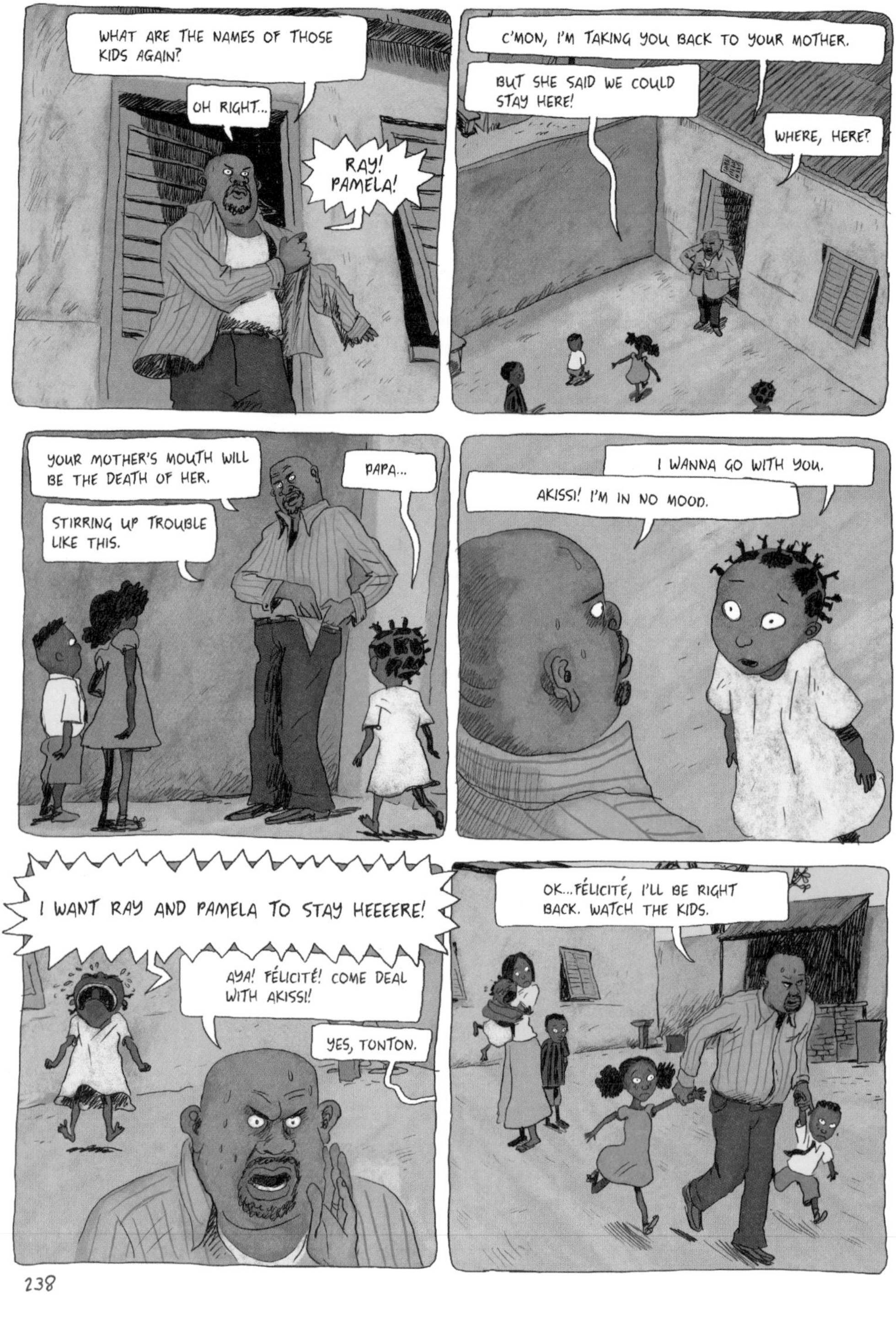
WHAT ARE THE NAMES OF THOSE KIDS AGAIN?
OH RIGHT...
RAY! PAMELA!
C'MON, I'M TAKING YOU BACK TO YOUR MOTHER.
BUT SHE SAID WE COULD STAY HERE!
WHERE, HERE?
YOUR MOTHER'S MOUTH WILL BE THE DEATH OF HER.
STIRRING UP TROUBLE LIKE THIS.
PAPA...
I WANNA GO WITH YOU.
AKISSI! I'M IN NO MOOD.
I WANT RAY AND PAMELA TO STAY HEEEERE!
AYA! FÉLICITÉ! COME DEAL WITH AKISSI!
YES, TONTON.
OK...FÉLICITÉ, I'LL BE RIGHT BACK. WATCH THE KIDS.

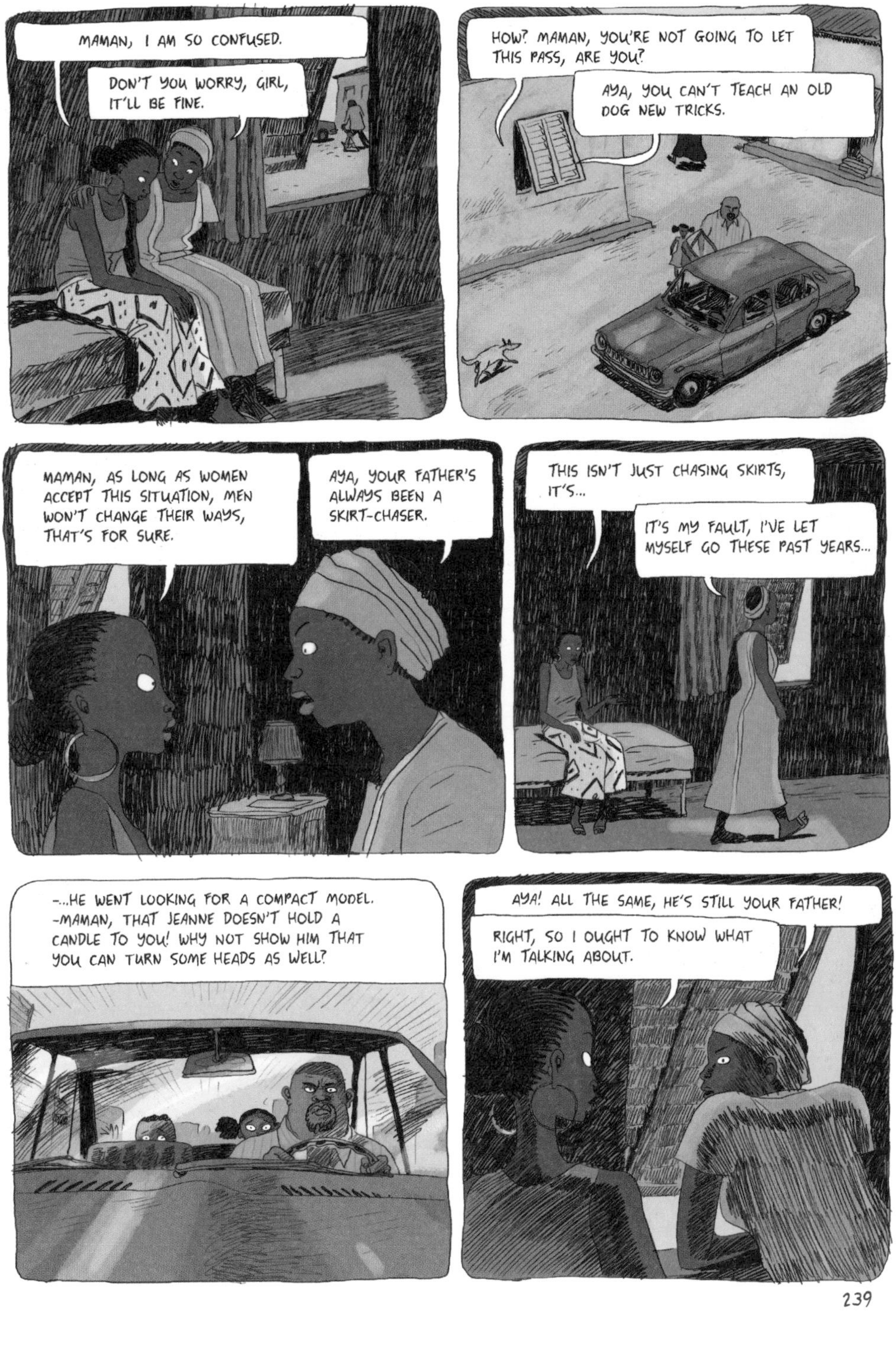
MAMAN, I AM SO CONFUSED.
DON'T YOU WORRY, GIRL, IT'LL BE FINE.
HOW? MAMAN, YOU'RE NOT GOING TO LET THIS PASS, ARE YOU?
AYA, YOU CAN'T TEACH AN OLD DOG NEW TRICKS.
MAMAN, AS LONG AS WOMEN ACCEPT THIS SITUATION, MEN WON'T CHANGE THEIR WAYS, THAT'S FOR SURE.
AYA, YOUR FATHER'S ALWAYS BEEN A SKIRT-CHASER.
THIS ISN'T JUST CHASING SKIRTS, IT'S...
IT'S MY FAULT, I'VE LET MYSELF GO THESE PAST YEARS...
-...HE WENT LOOKING FOR A COMPACT MODEL.
-MAMAN, THAT JEANNE DOESN'T HOLD A CANDLE TO YOU! WHY NOT SHOW HIM THAT YOU CAN TURN SOME HEADS AS WELL?
AYA! ALL THE SAME, HE'S STILL YOUR FATHER!
RIGHT, SO I OUGHT TO KNOW WHAT I'M TALKING ABOUT.

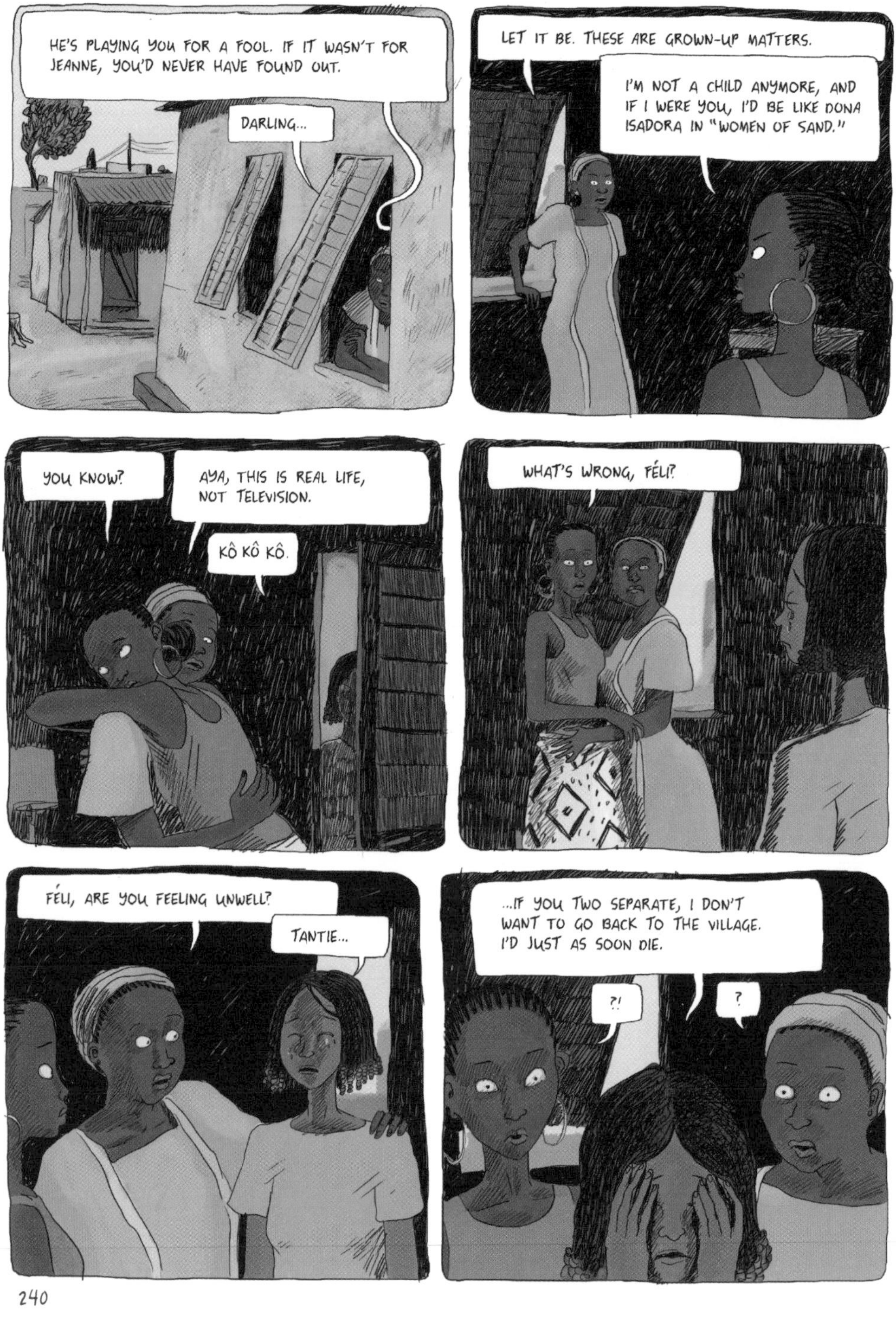
HE'S PLAYING YOU FOR A FOOL. IF IT WASN'T FOR JEANNE, YOU'D NEVER HAVE FOUND OUT.
DARLING...
LET IT BE. THESE ARE GROWN-UP MATTERS.
I'M NOT A CHILD ANYMORE, AND IF I WERE YOU, I'D BE LIKE DONA ISADORA IN "WOMEN OF SAND."
YOU KNOW?
AYA, THIS IS REAL LIFE, NOT TELEVISION.
KÔ KÔ KÔ.
WHAT'S WRONG, FÉLI?
FÉLI, ARE YOU FEELING UNWELL?
TANTIE...
...IF YOU TWO SEPARATE, I DON'T WANT TO GO BACK TO THE VILLAGE. I'D JUST AS SOON DIE.
?!
?

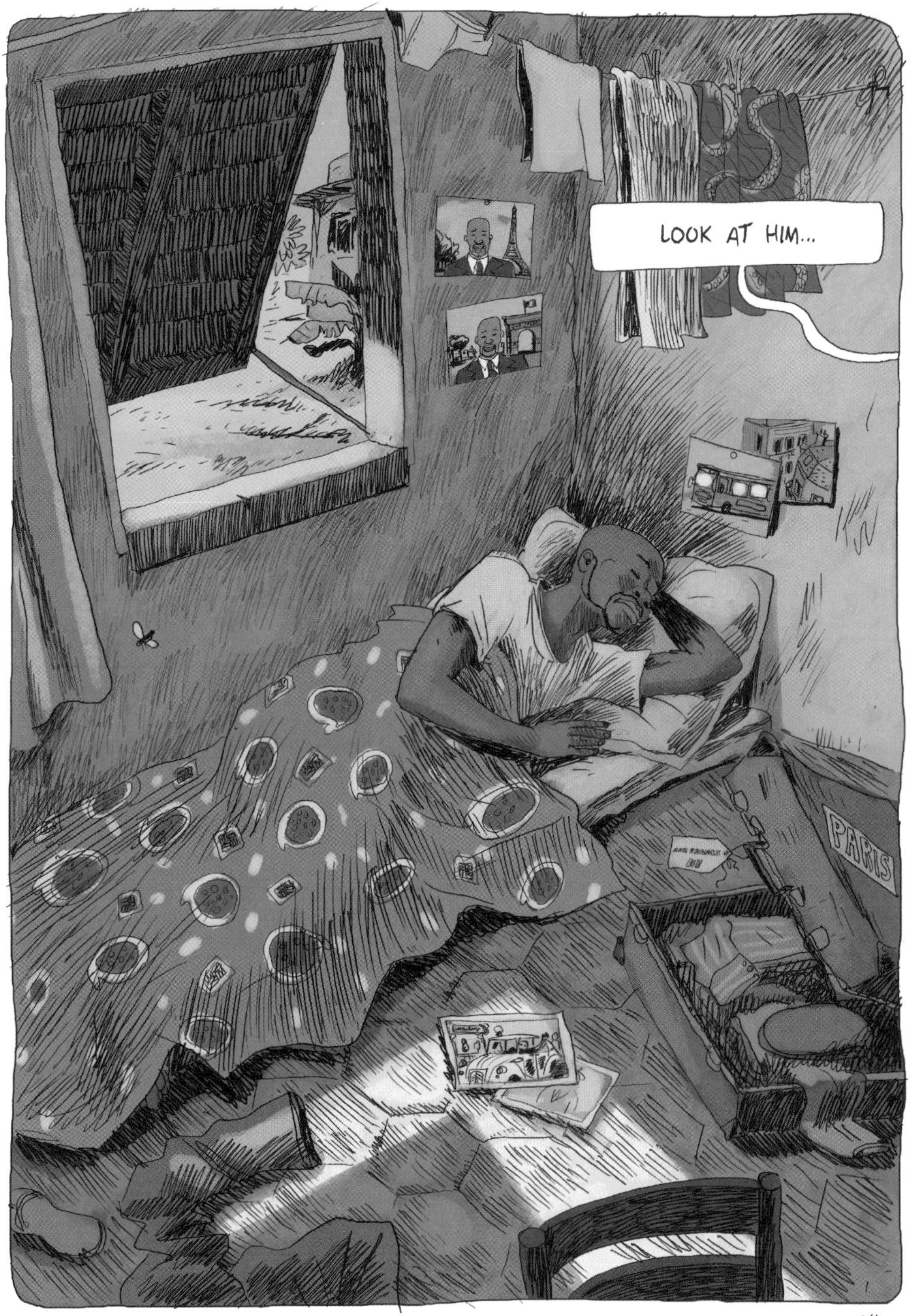
LOOK AT HIM...
PARIS

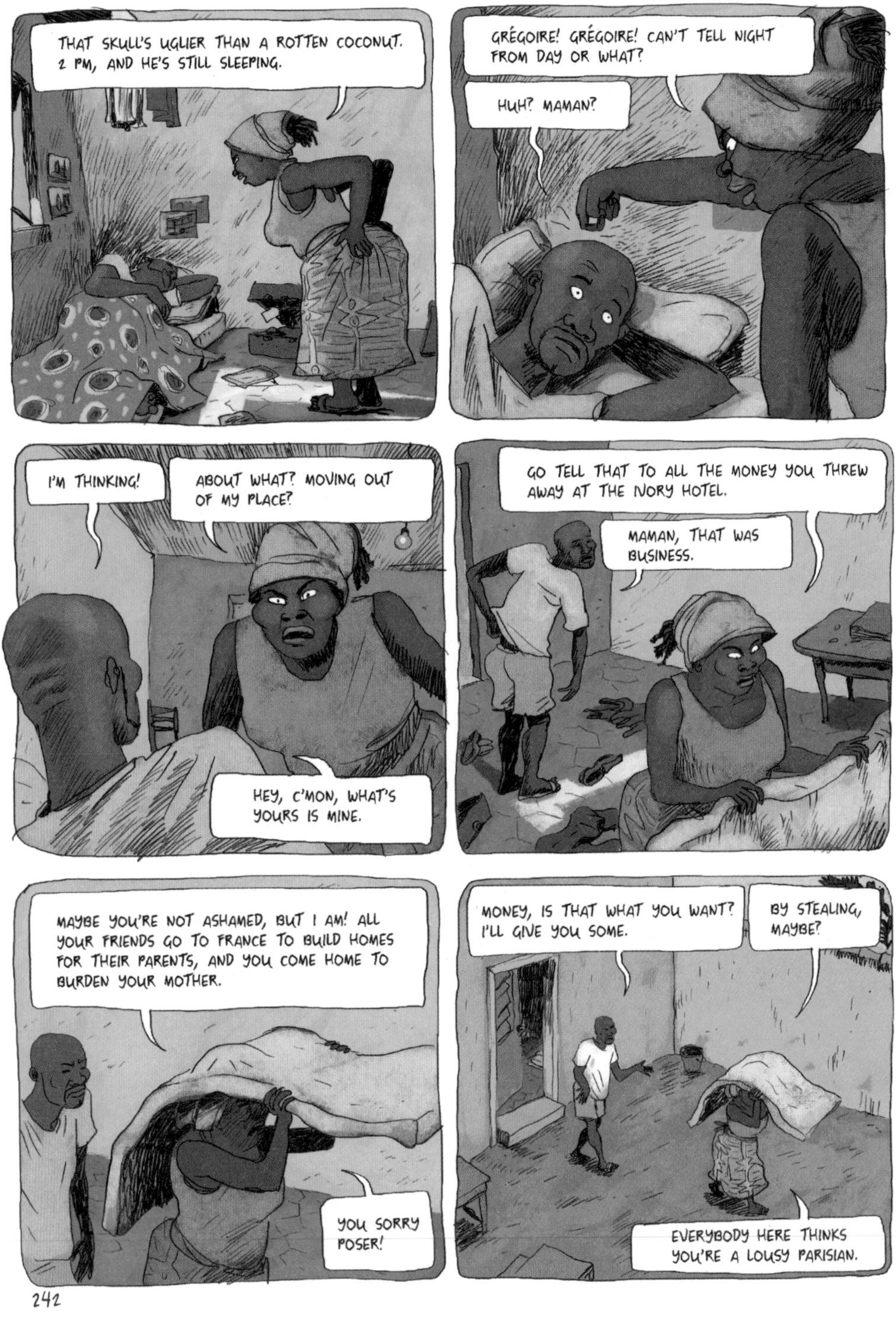
THAT SKULL'S UGLIER THAN A ROTTEN COCONUT. 2 PM, AND HE'S STILL SLEEPING.
GRÉGOIRE! GRÉGOIRE! CAN'T TELL NIGHT FROM DAY OR WHAT?
HUH? MAMAN?
I'M THINKING!
ABOUT WHAT? MOVING OUT OF MY PLACE?
HEY, C'MON, WHAT'S YOURS IS MINE.
GO TELL THAT TO ALL THE MONEY YOU THREW AWAY AT THE IVORY HOTEL.
MAMAN, THAT WAS BUSINESS.
MAYBE YOU'RE NOT ASHAMED, BUT I AM! ALL YOUR FRIENDS GO TO FRANCE TO BUILD HOMES FOR THEIR PARENTS, AND YOU COME HOME TO BURDEN YOUR MOTHER.
YOU SORRY POSER!
MONEY, IS THAT WHAT YOU WANT? I'LL GIVE YOU SOME.
BY STEALING, MAYBE?
EVERYBODY HERE THINKS YOU'RE A LOUSY PARISIAN.

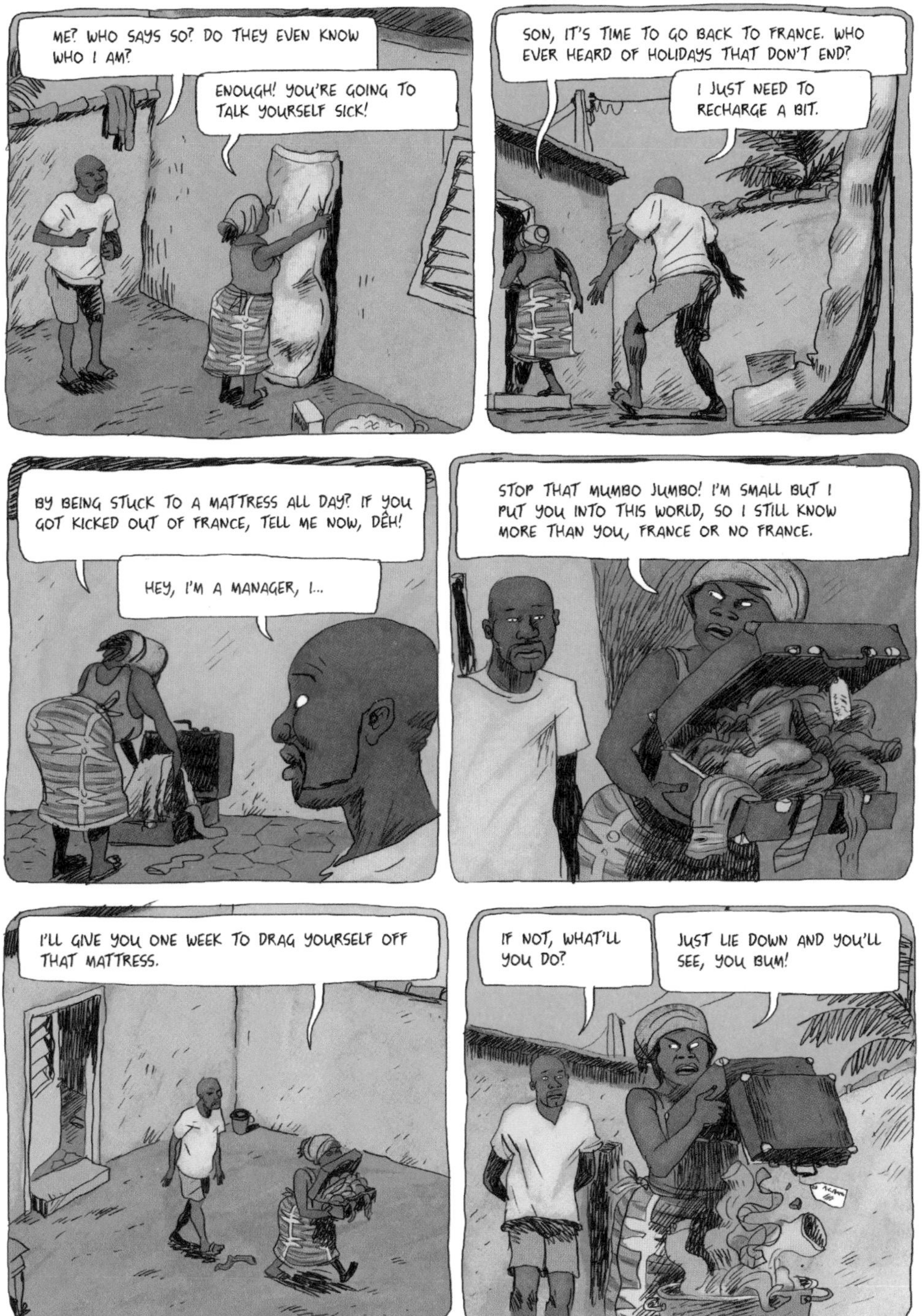
ME? WHO SAYS SO? DO THEY EVEN KNOW WHO I AM?
ENOUGH! YOU'RE GOING TO TALK YOURSELF SICK!
SON, IT'S TIME TO GO BACK TO FRANCE. WHO EVER HEARD OF HOLIDAYS THAT DON'T END?
I JUST NEED TO RECHARGE A BIT.
BY BEING STUCK TO A MATTRESS ALL DAY? IF YOU GOT KICKED OUT OF FRANCE, TELL ME NOW, DÊH!
HEY, I'M A MANAGER, I...
STOP THAT MUMBO JUMBO! I'M SMALL BUT I PUT YOU INTO THIS WORLD, SO I STILL KNOW MORE THAN YOU, FRANCE OR NO FRANCE.
I'LL GIVE YOU ONE WEEK TO DRAG YOURSELF OFF THAT MATTRESS.
IF NOT, WHAT'LL YOU DO?
JUST LIE DOWN AND YOU'LL SEE, YOU BUM!

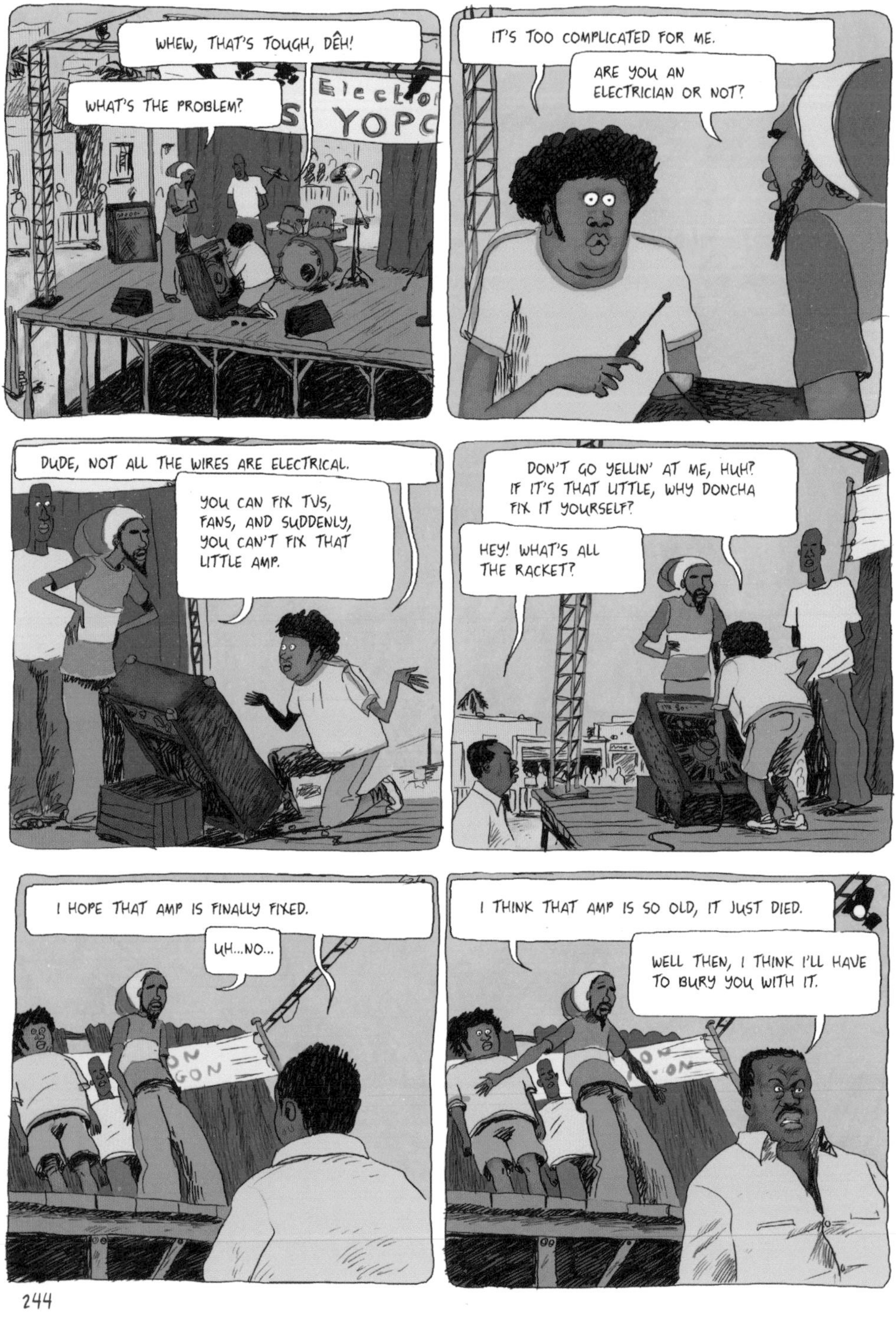

WHEW, THAT'S TOUGH, DÊH!
WHAT'S THE PROBLEM?
Election
YOPC
IT'S TOO COMPLICATED FOR ME.
ARE YOU AN ELECTRICIAN OR NOT?
DUDE, NOT ALL THE WIRES ARE ELECTRICAL.
YOU CAN FIX TVS, FANS, AND SUDDENLY, YOU CAN'T FIX THAT LITTLE AMP.
DON'T GO YELLIN' AT ME, HUH? IF IT'S THAT LITTLE, WHY DONCHA FIX IT YOURSELF?
HEY! WHAT'S ALL THE RACKET?
I HOPE THAT AMP IS FINALLY FIXED.
UH...NO...
I THINK THAT AMP IS SO OLD, IT JUST DIED.
WELL THEN, I THINK I'LL HAVE TO BURY YOU WITH IT.

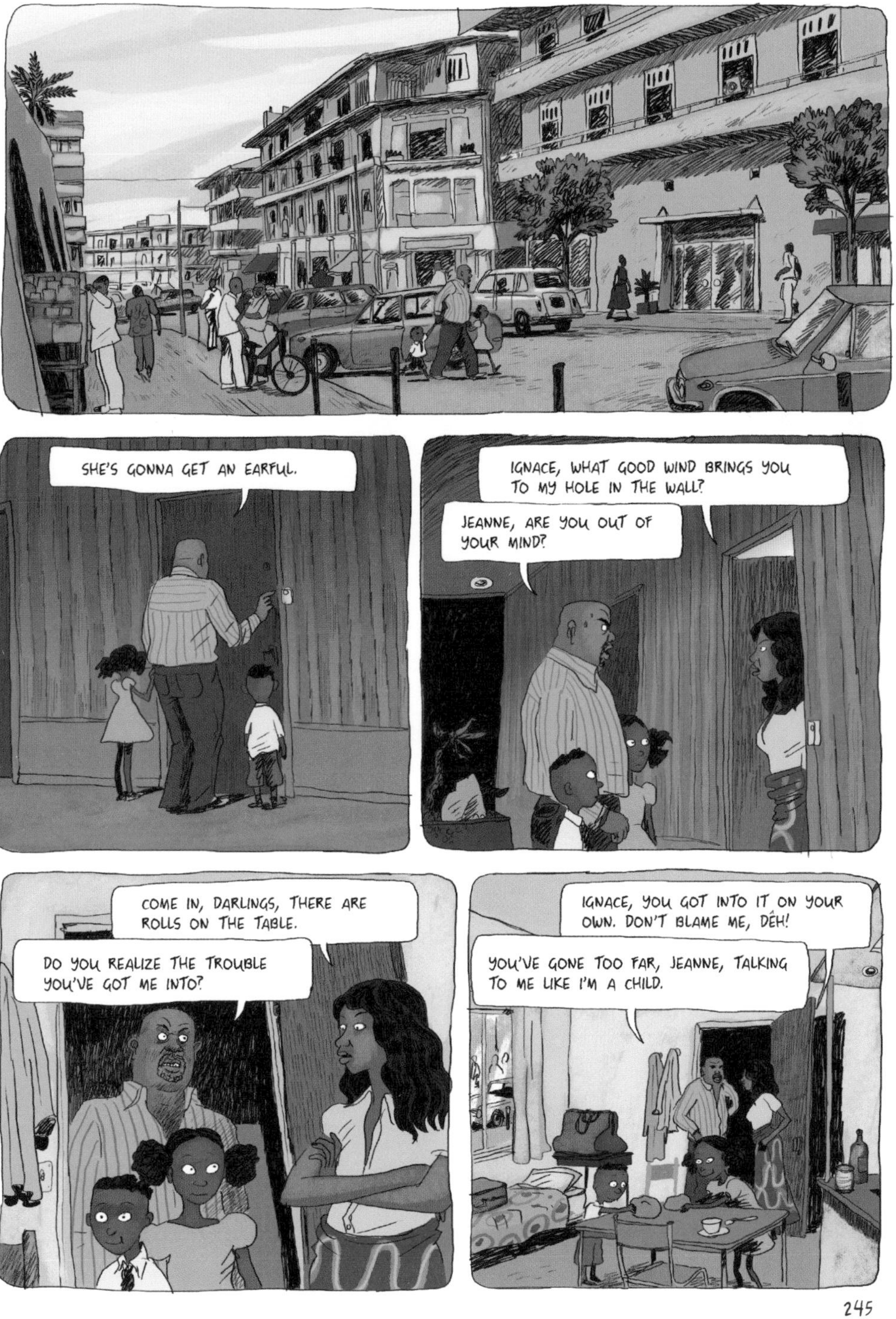
SHE'S GONNA GET AN EARFUL.
IGNACE, WHAT GOOD WIND BRINGS YOU TO MY HOLE IN THE WALL?
JEANNE, ARE YOU OUT OF YOUR MIND?
COME IN, DARLINGS, THERE ARE ROLLS ON THE TABLE.
DO YOU REALIZE THE TROUBLE YOU'VE GOT ME INTO?
IGNACE, YOU GOT INTO IT ON YOUR OWN. DON'T BLAME ME, DÉH!
YOU'VE GONE TOO FAR, JEANNE, TALKING TO ME LIKE I'M A CHILD.

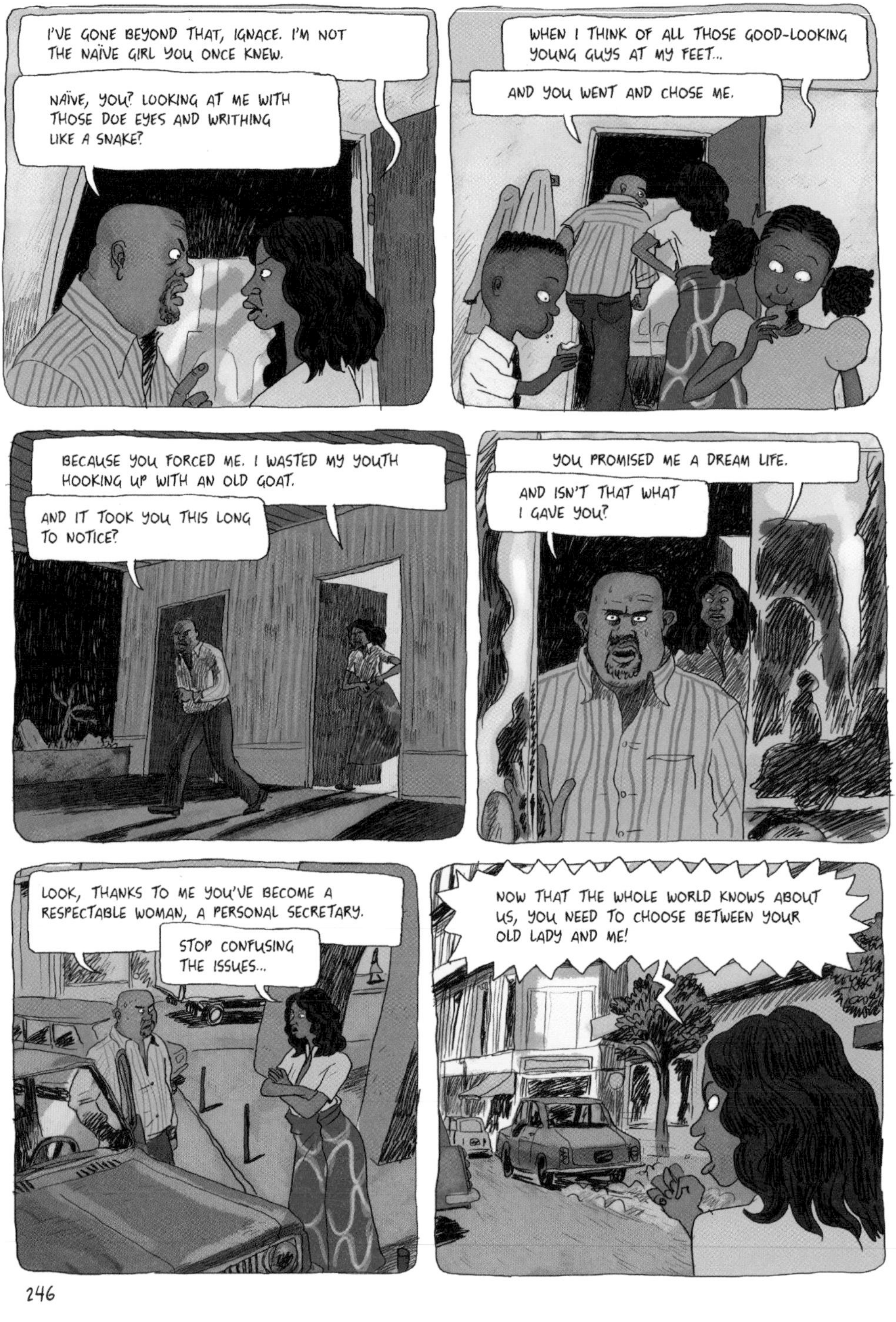
I'VE GONE BEYOND THAT, IGNACE. I'M NOT THE NAÏVE GIRL YOU ONCE KNEW.
NAÏVE, YOU? LOOKING AT ME WITH THOSE DOE EYES AND WRITHING LIKE A SNAKE?
WHEN I THINK OF ALL THOSE GOOD-LOOKING YOUNG GUYS AT MY FEET...
AND YOU WENT AND CHOSE ME.
BECAUSE YOU FORCED ME. I WASTED MY YOUTH HOOKING UP WITH AN OLD GOAT.
AND IT TOOK YOU THIS LONG TO NOTICE?
YOU PROMISED ME A DREAM LIFE.
AND ISN'T THAT WHAT I GAVE YOU?
LOOK, THANKS TO ME YOU'VE BECOME A RESPECTABLE WOMAN, A PERSONAL SECRETARY.
STOP CONFUSING THE ISSUES...
NOW THAT THE WHOLE WORLD KNOWS ABOUT US, YOU NEED TO CHOOSE BETWEEN YOUR OLD LADY AND ME!

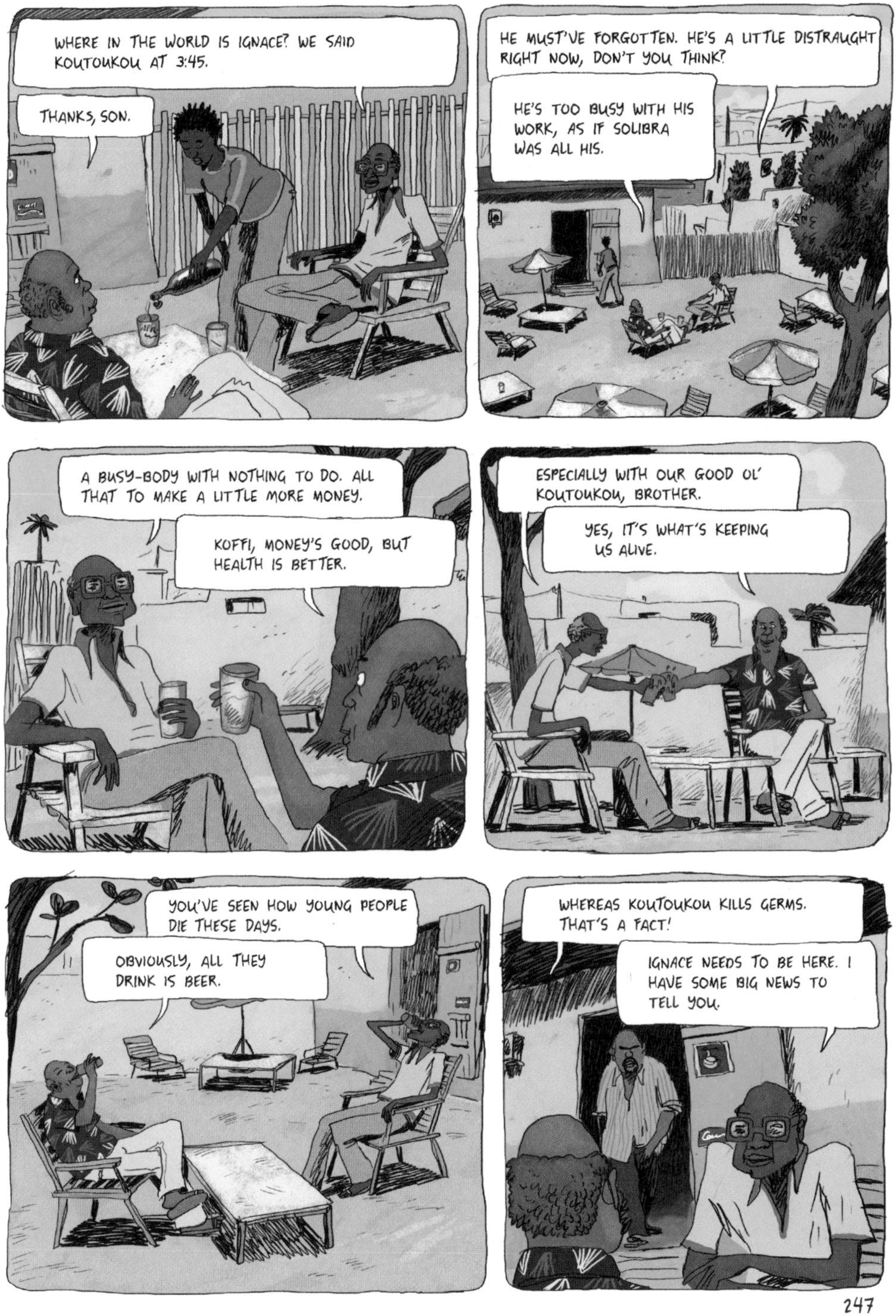
WHERE IN THE WORLD IS IGNACE? WE SAID KOUTOUKOU AT 3:45.
THANKS, SON.
HE MUST'VE FORGOTTEN. HE'S A LITTLE DISTRAUGHT RIGHT NOW, DON'T YOU THINK?
HE'S TOO BUSY WITH HIS WORK, AS IF SOLIBRA WAS ALL HIS.
A BUSY-BODY WITH NOTHING TO DO. ALL THAT TO MAKE A LITTLE MORE MONEY.
KOFFI, MONEY'S GOOD, BUT HEALTH IS BETTER.
ESPECIALLY WITH OUR GOOD OL' KOUTOUKOU, BROTHER.
YES, IT'S WHAT'S KEEPING US ALIVE.
YOU'VE SEEN HOW YOUNG PEOPLE DIE THESE DAYS.
OBVIOUSLY, ALL THEY DRINK IS BEER.
WHEREAS KOUTOUKOU KILLS GERMS. THAT'S A FACT!
IGNACE NEEDS TO BE HERE. I HAVE SOME BIG NEWS TO TELL YOU.

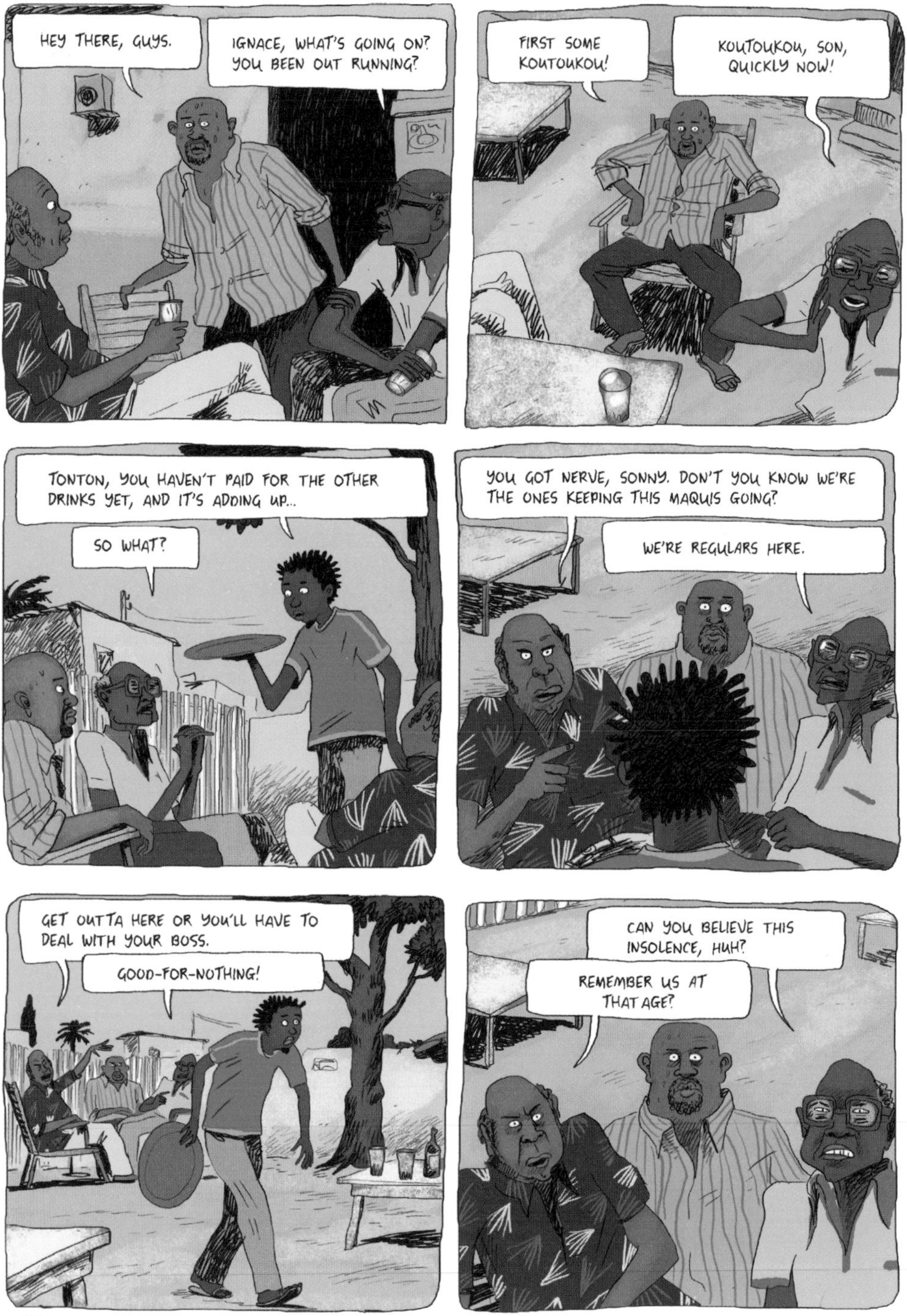
HEY THERE, GUYS.
IGNACE, WHAT'S GOING ON? YOU BEEN OUT RUNNING?
FIRST SOME KOUTOUKOU!
KOUTOUKOU, SON, QUICKLY NOW!
TONTON, YOU HAVEN'T PAID FOR THE OTHER DRINKS YET, AND IT'S ADDING UP...
SO WHAT?
YOU GOT NERVE, SONNY. DON'T YOU KNOW WE'RE THE ONES KEEPING THIS MAQUIS GOING?
WE'RE REGULARS HERE.
GET OUTTA HERE OR YOU'LL HAVE TO DEAL WITH YOUR BOSS.
GOOD-FOR-NOTHING!
CAN YOU BELIEVE THIS INSOLENCE, HUH?
REMEMBER US AT THAT AGE?

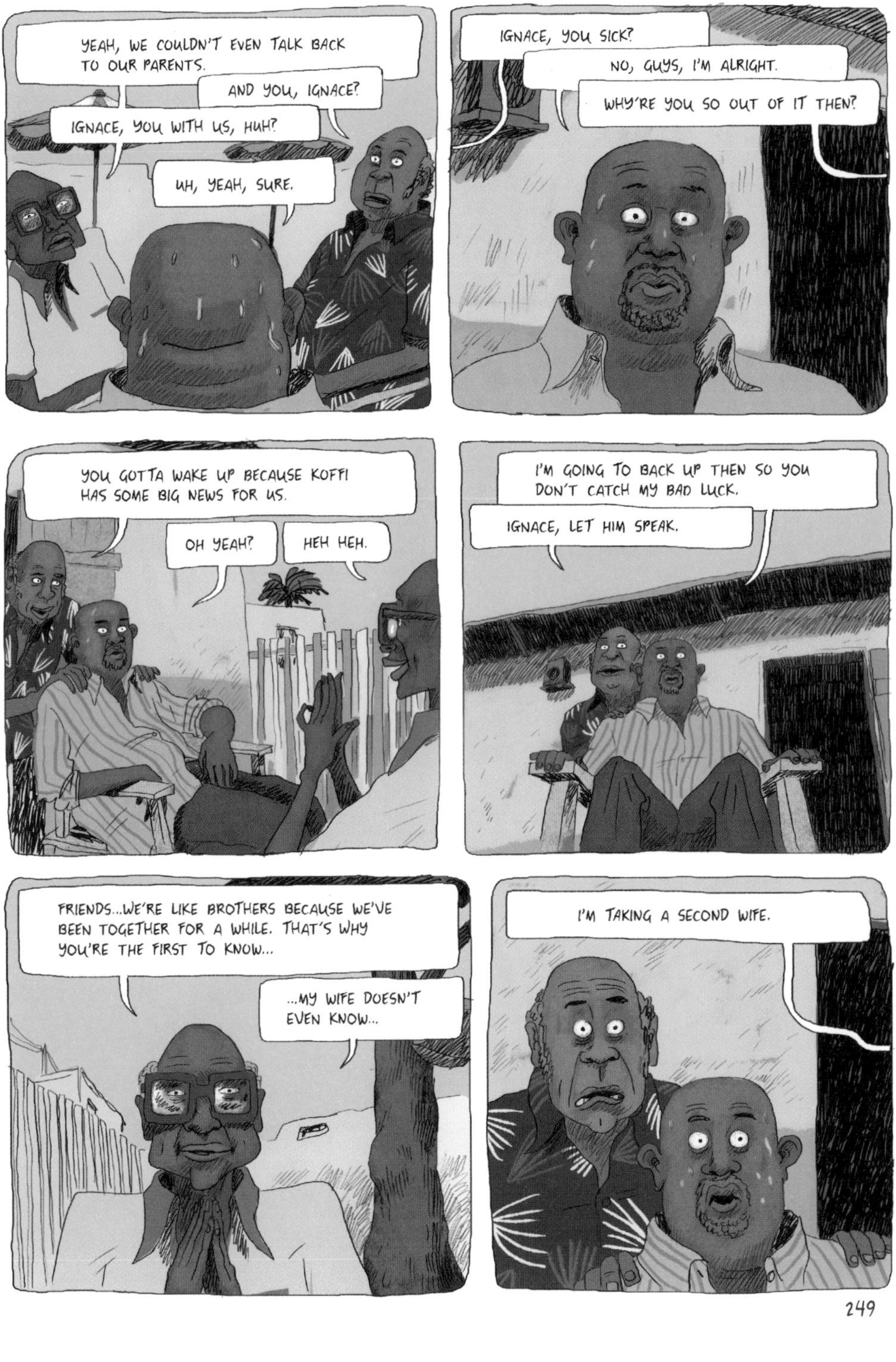
YEAH, WE COULDN'T EVEN TALK BACK TO OUR PARENTS.
AND YOU, IGNACE?
IGNACE, YOU WITH US, HUH?
UH, YEAH, SURE.
IGNACE, YOU SICK?
NO, GUYS, I'M ALRIGHT.
WHY'RE YOU SO OUT OF IT THEN?
YOU GOTTA WAKE UP BECAUSE KOFFI HAS SOME BIG NEWS FOR US.
OH YEAH?
HEH HEH.
I'M GOING TO BACK UP THEN SO YOU DON'T CATCH MY BAD LUCK.
IGNACE, LET HIM SPEAK.
FRIENDS...WE'RE LIKE BROTHERS BECAUSE WE'VE BEEN TOGETHER FOR A WHILE. THAT'S WHY YOU'RE THE FIRST TO KNOW...
...MY WIFE DOESN'T EVEN KNOW...
I'M TAKING A SECOND WIFE.

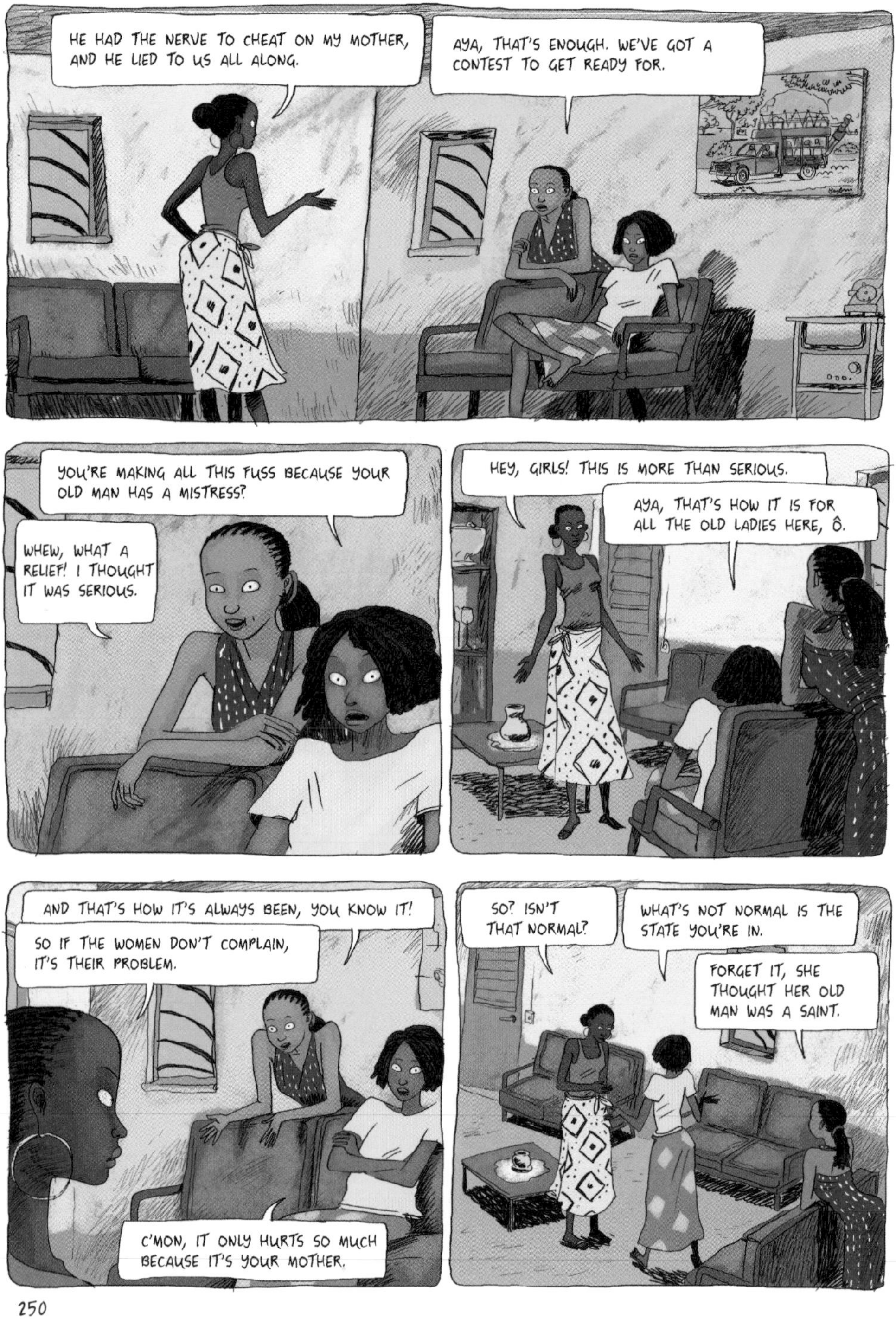
HE HAD THE NERVE TO CHEAT ON MY MOTHER, AND HE LIED TO US ALL ALONG.
AYA, THAT'S ENOUGH. WE'VE GOT A CONTEST TO GET READY FOR.
YOU'RE MAKING ALL THIS FUSS BECAUSE YOUR OLD MAN HAS A MISTRESS?
WHEW, WHAT A RELIEF! I THOUGHT IT WAS SERIOUS.
HEY, GIRLS! THIS IS MORE THAN SERIOUS.
AYA, THAT'S HOW IT IS FOR ALL THE OLD LADIES HERE, Ô.
AND THAT'S HOW IT'S ALWAYS BEEN, YOU KNOW IT!
SO IF THE WOMEN DON'T COMPLAIN, IT'S THEIR PROBLEM.
C'MON, IT ONLY HURTS SO MUCH BECAUSE IT'S YOUR MOTHER.
SO? ISN'T THAT NORMAL?
WHAT'S NOT NORMAL IS THE STATE YOU'RE IN.
FORGET IT, SHE THOUGHT HER OLD MAN WAS A SAINT.

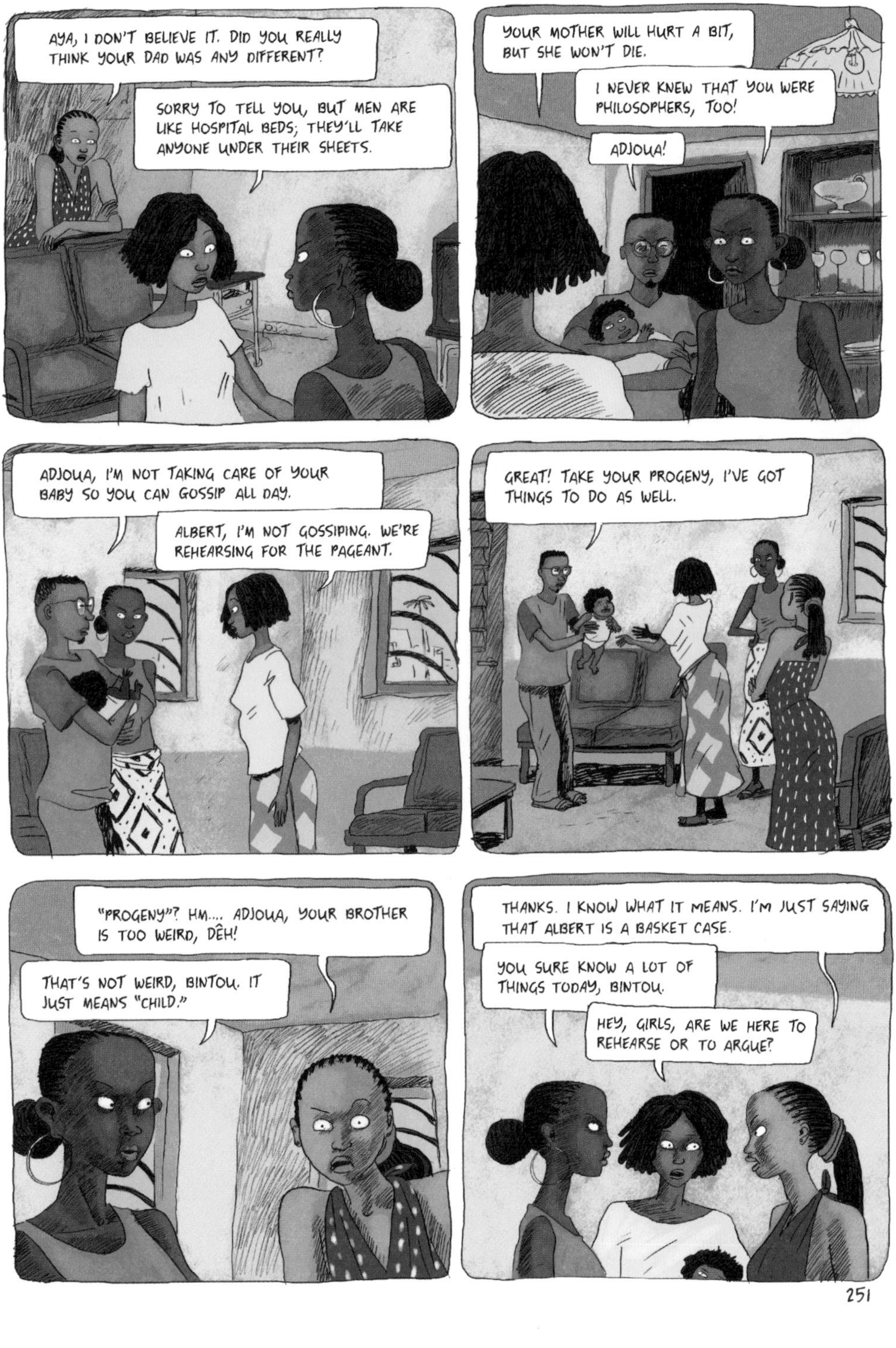
AYA, I DON'T BELIEVE IT. DID YOU REALLY THINK YOUR DAD WAS ANY DIFFERENT?
SORRY TO TELL YOU, BUT MEN ARE LIKE HOSPITAL BEDS; THEY'LL TAKE ANYONE UNDER THEIR SHEETS.
YOUR MOTHER WILL HURT A BIT, BUT SHE WON'T DIE.
I NEVER KNEW THAT YOU WERE PHILOSOPHERS, TOO!
ADJOUA!
ADJOUA, I'M NOT TAKING CARE OF YOUR BABY SO YOU CAN GOSSIP ALL DAY.
ALBERT, I'M NOT GOSSIPING. WE'RE REHEARSING FOR THE PAGEANT.
GREAT! TAKE YOUR PROGENY, I'VE GOT THINGS TO DO AS WELL.
"PROGENY"? HM.... ADJOUA, YOUR BROTHER IS TOO WEIRD, DÊH!
THAT'S NOT WEIRD, BINTOU. IT JUST MEANS "CHILD."
THANKS. I KNOW WHAT IT MEANS. I'M JUST SAYING THAT ALBERT IS A BASKET CASE.
YOU SURE KNOW A LOT OF THINGS TODAY, BINTOU.
HEY, GIRLS, ARE WE HERE TO REHEARSE OR TO ARGUE?

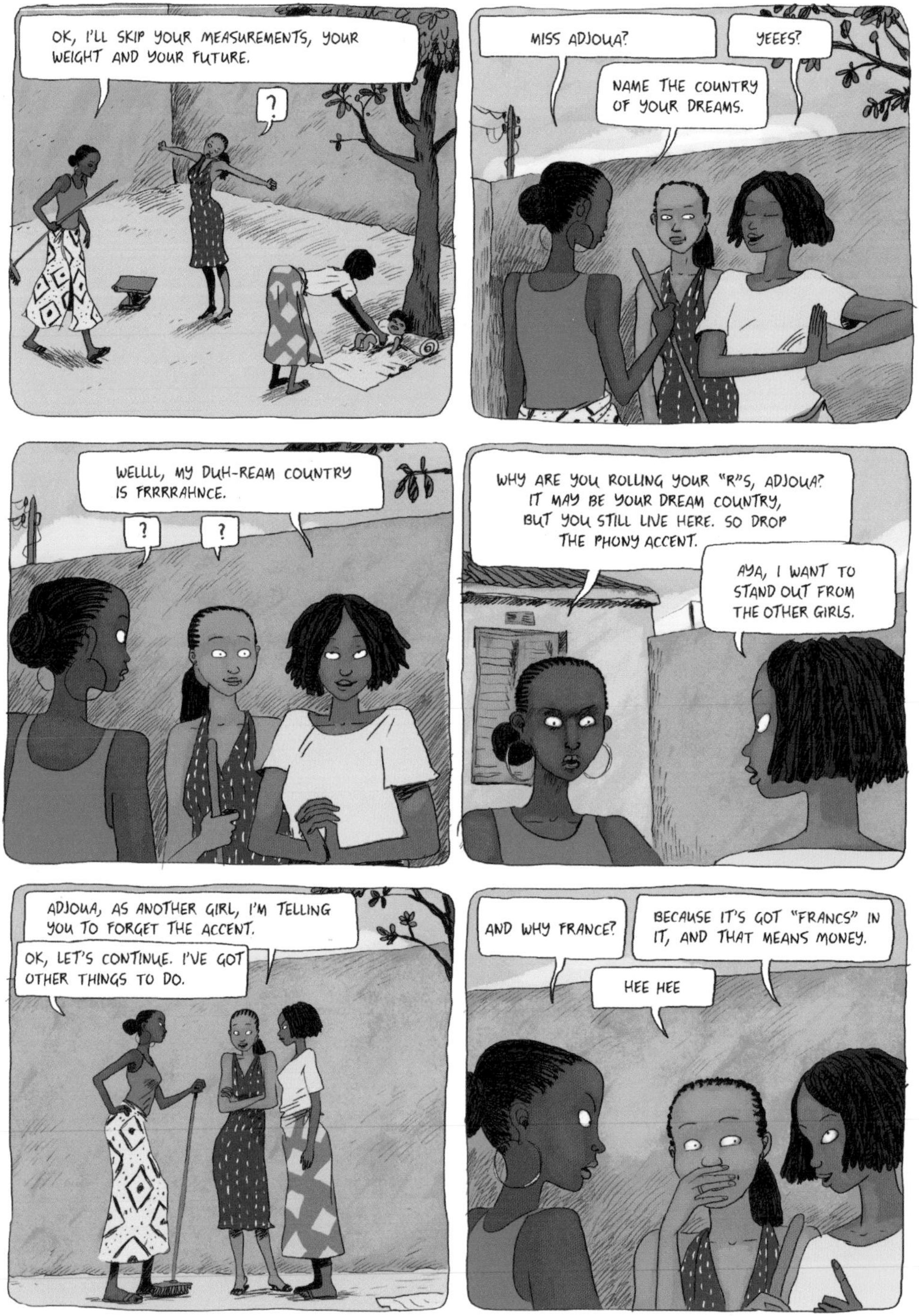
OK, I'LL SKIP YOUR MEASUREMENTS, YOUR WEIGHT AND YOUR FUTURE.
?
MISS ADJOUA?
YEEES?
NAME THE COUNTRY OF YOUR DREAMS.
WELLLL, MY DUH-REAM COUNTRY IS FRRRRAHNCE.
?
?
WHY ARE YOU ROLLING YOUR "R"S, ADJOUA? IT MAY BE YOUR DREAM COUNTRY, BUT YOU STILL LIVE HERE. SO DROP THE PHONY ACCENT.
AYA, I WANT TO STAND OUT FROM THE OTHER GIRLS.
ADJOUA, AS ANOTHER GIRL, I'M TELLING YOU TO FORGET THE ACCENT.
OK, LET'S CONTINUE. I'VE GOT OTHER THINGS TO DO.
AND WHY FRANCE?
BECAUSE IT'S GOT "FRANCS" IN IT, AND THAT MEANS MONEY.
HEE HEE

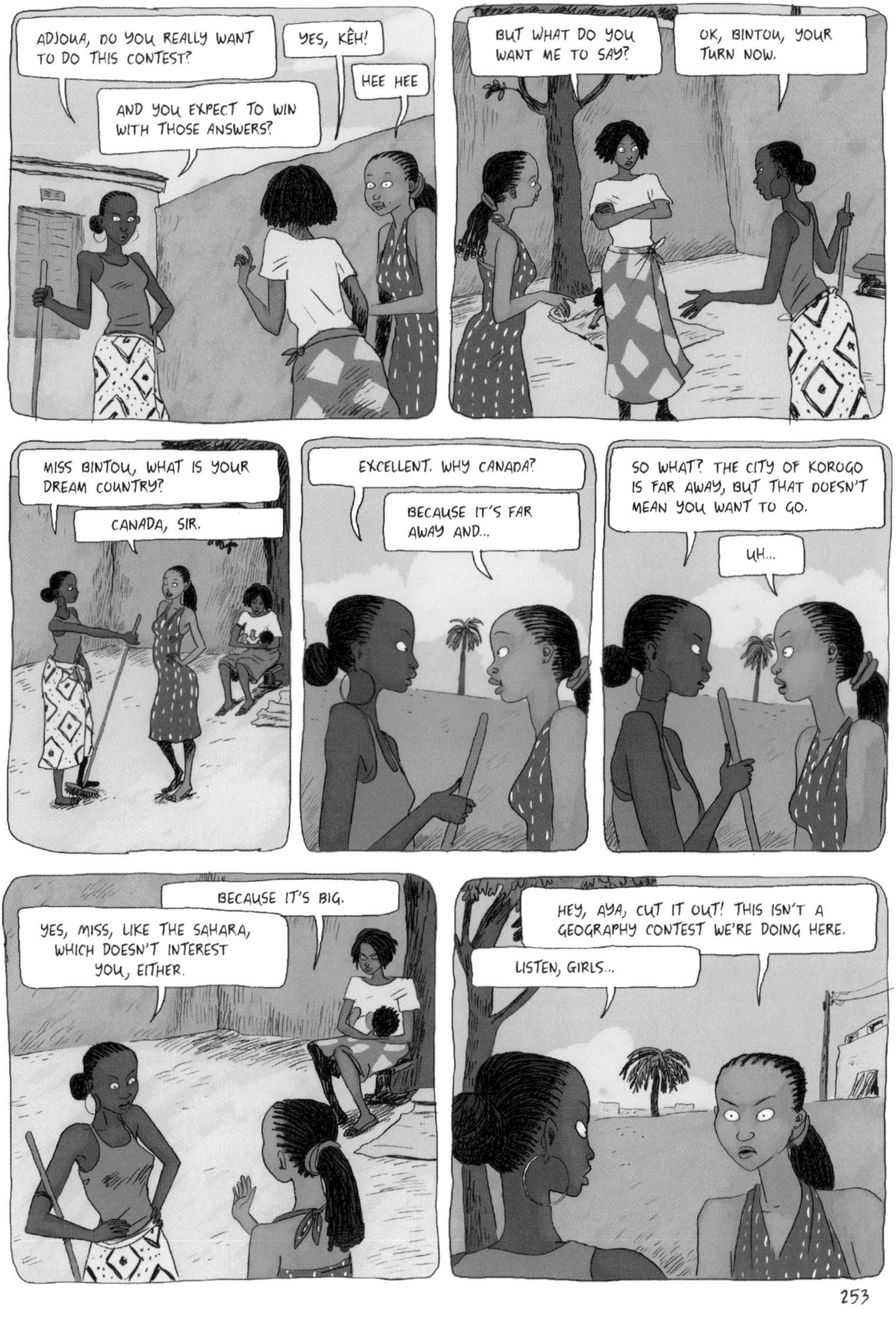
ADJOUA, DO YOU REALLY WANT TO DO THIS CONTEST?
AND YOU EXPECT TO WIN WITH THOSE ANSWERS?
YES, KÊH!
HEE HEE
BUT WHAT DO YOU WANT ME TO SAY?
OK, BINTOU, YOUR TURN NOW.
MISS BINTOU, WHAT IS YOUR DREAM COUNTRY?
CANADA, SIR.
EXCELLENT. WHY CANADA?
BECAUSE IT'S FAR AWAY AND...
SO WHAT? THE CITY OF KOROGO IS FAR AWAY, BUT THAT DOESN'T MEAN YOU WANT TO GO.
UH...
BECAUSE IT'S BIG.
YES, MISS, LIKE THE SAHARA, WHICH DOESN'T INTEREST YOU, EITHER.
HEY, AYA, CUT IT OUT! THIS ISN'T A GEOGRAPHY CONTEST WE'RE DOING HERE.
LISTEN, GIRLS...

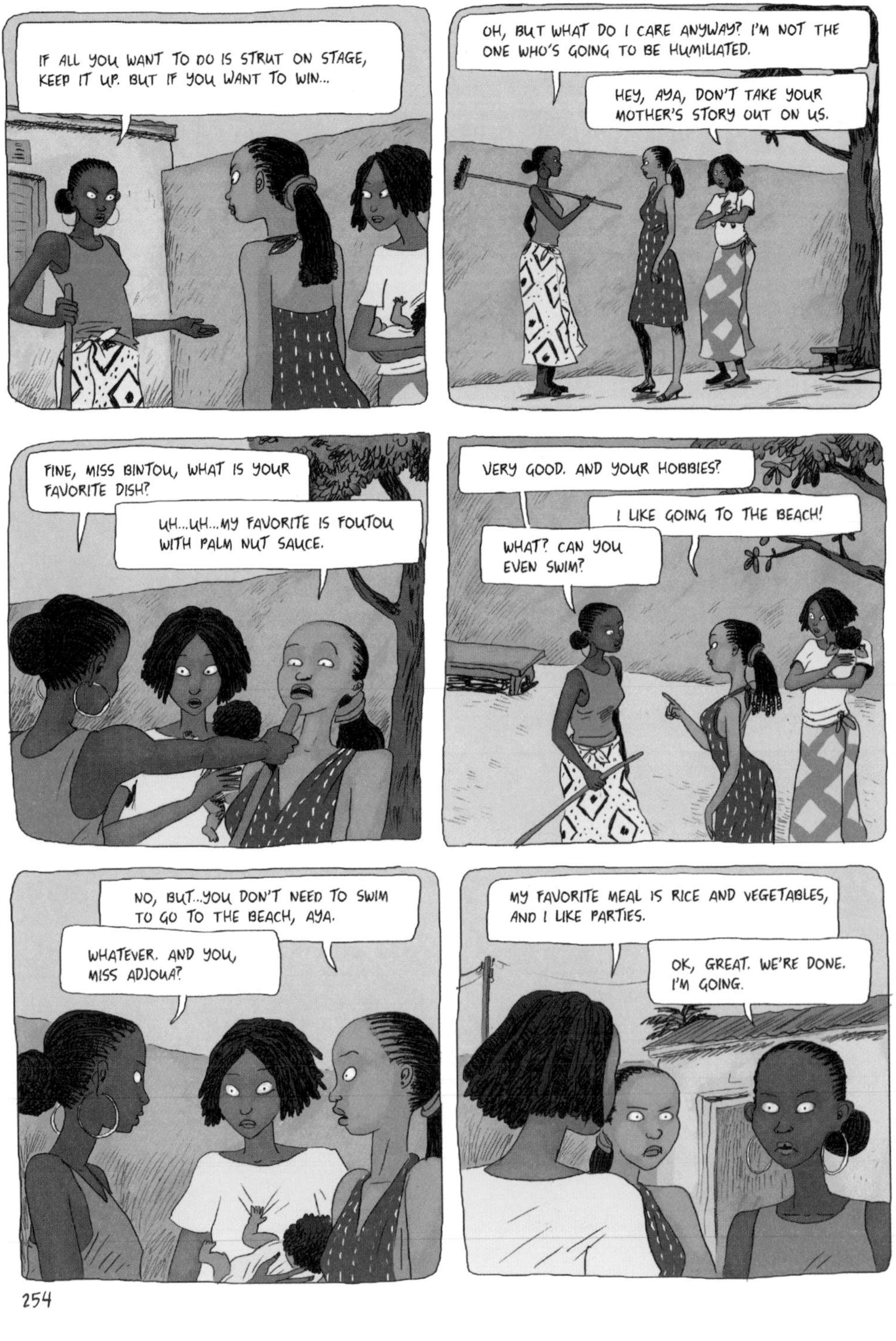
IF ALL YOU WANT TO DO IS STRUT ON STAGE, KEEP IT UP. BUT IF YOU WANT TO WIN...
OH, BUT WHAT DO I CARE ANYWAY? I'M NOT THE ONE WHO'S GOING TO BE HUMILIATED.
HEY, AYA, DON'T TAKE YOUR MOTHER'S STORY OUT ON US.
FINE, MISS BINTOU, WHAT IS YOUR FAVORITE DISH?
UH...UH...MY FAVORITE IS FOUTOU WITH PALM NUT SAUCE.
VERY GOOD. AND YOUR HOBBIES?
I LIKE GOING TO THE BEACH!
WHAT? CAN YOU EVEN SWIM?
NO, BUT...YOU DON'T NEED TO SWIM TO GO TO THE BEACH, AYA.
WHATEVER. AND YOU, MISS ADJOUA?
MY FAVORITE MEAL IS RICE AND VEGETABLES, AND I LIKE PARTIES.
OK, GREAT. WE'RE DONE. I'M GOING.

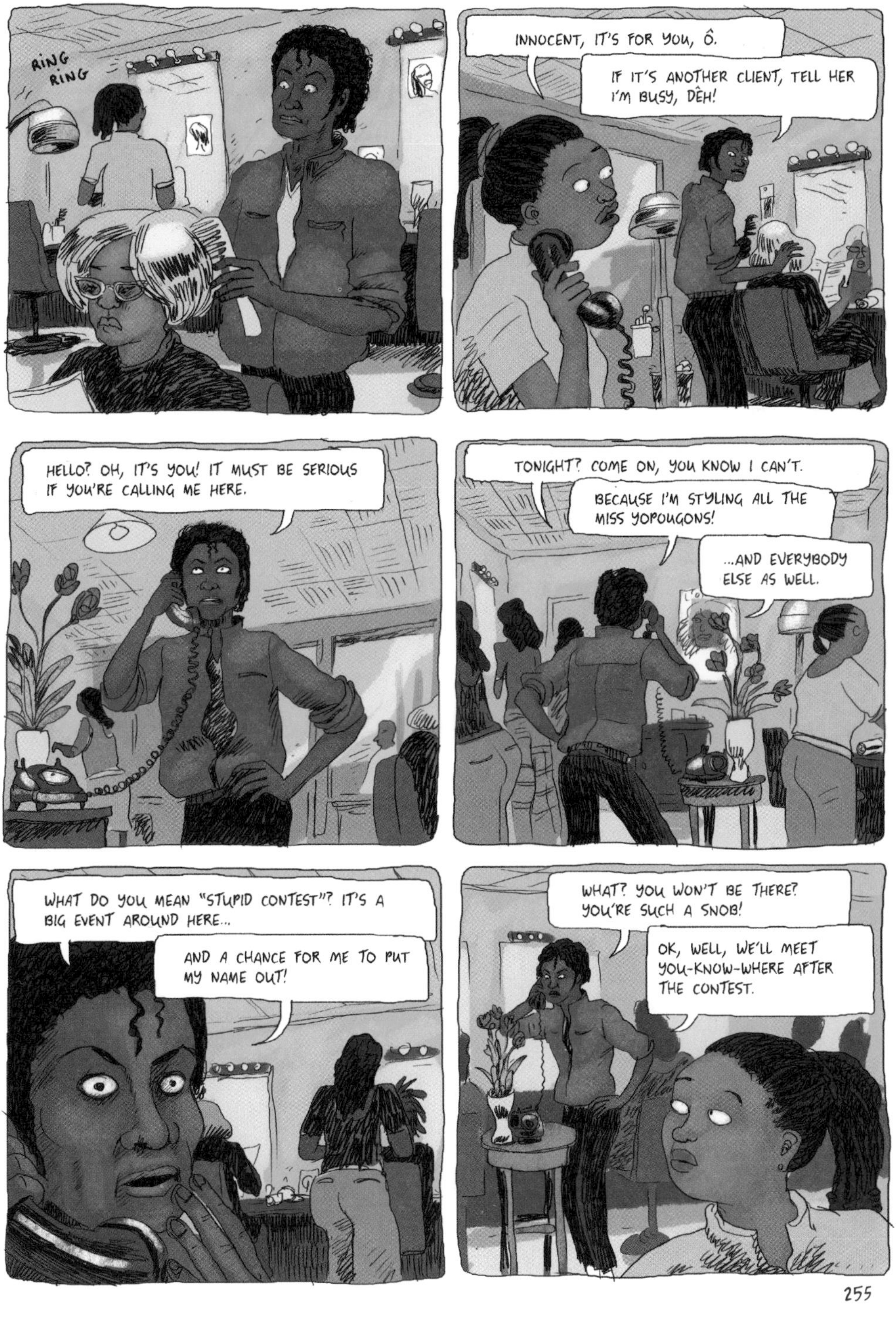
RING RING
INNOCENT, IT'S FOR YOU, Ô.
IF IT'S ANOTHER CLIENT, TELL HER I'M BUSY, DÊH!
HELLO? OH, IT'S YOU! IT MUST BE SERIOUS IF YOU'RE CALLING ME HERE.
TONIGHT? COME ON, YOU KNOW I CAN'T.
BECAUSE I'M STYLING ALL THE MISS YOPOUGONS!
...AND EVERYBODY ELSE AS WELL.
WHAT DO YOU MEAN "STUPID CONTEST"? IT'S A BIG EVENT AROUND HERE...
AND A CHANCE FOR ME TO PUT MY NAME OUT!
WHAT? YOU WON'T BE THERE? YOU'RE SUCH A SNOB!
OK, WELL, WE'LL MEET YOU-KNOW-WHERE AFTER THE CONTEST.

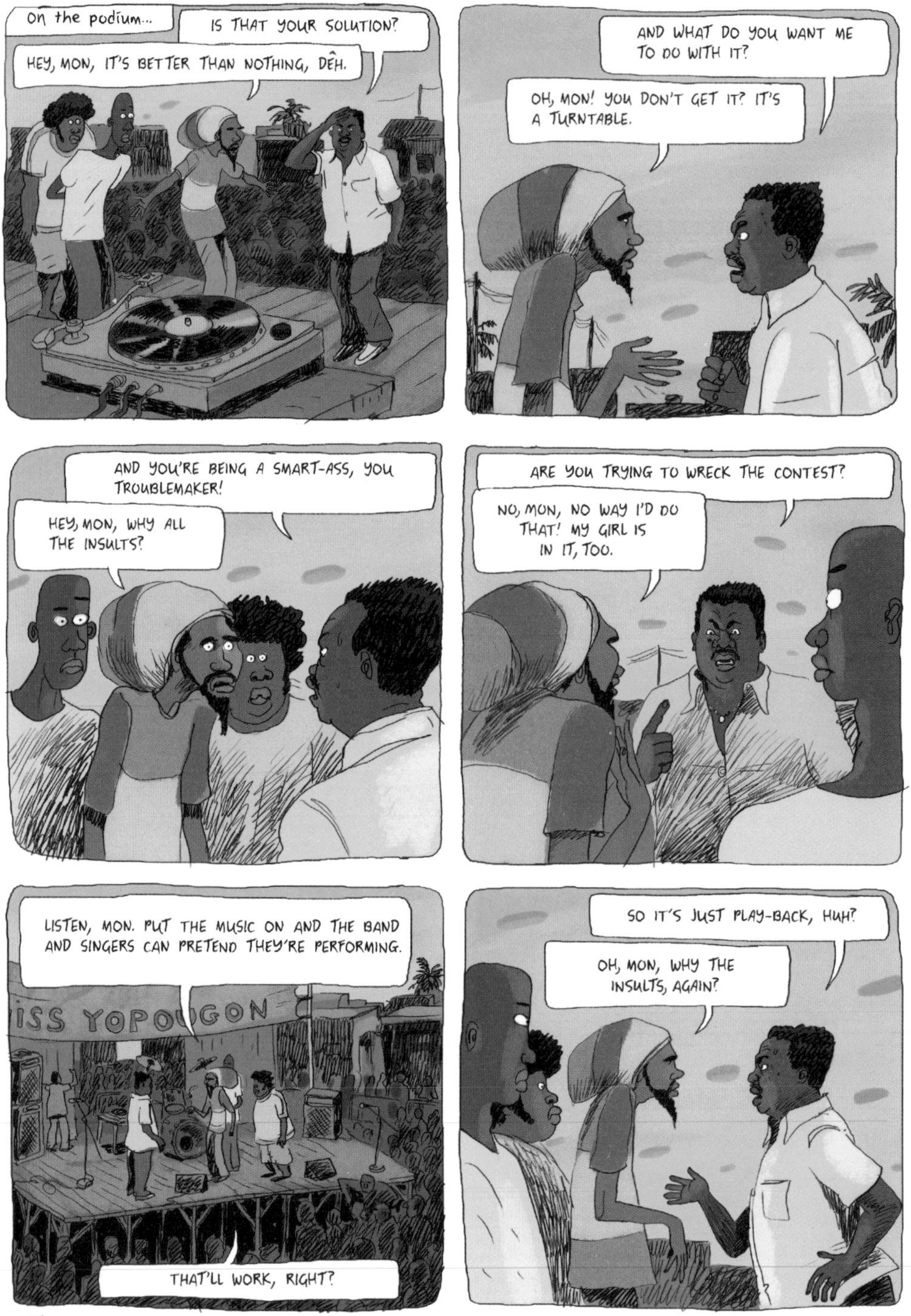
On the podium...
IS THAT YOUR SOLUTION?
HEY, MON, IT'S BETTER THAN NOTHING, DÊH.
AND WHAT DO YOU WANT ME TO DO WITH IT?
OH, MON! YOU DON'T GET IT? IT'S A TURNTABLE.
AND YOU'RE BEING A SMART-ASS, YOU TROUBLEMAKER!
HEY, MON, WHY ALL THE INSULTS?
ARE YOU TRYING TO WRECK THE CONTEST?
NO, MON, NO WAY I'D DO THAT! MY GIRL IS IN IT, TOO.
LISTEN, MON. PUT THE MUSIC ON AND THE BAND AND SINGERS CAN PRETEND THEY'RE PERFORMING.
ISS YOPOUGON
THAT'LL WORK, RIGHT?
SO IT'S JUST PLAY-BACK, HUH?
OH, MON, WHY THE INSULTS, AGAIN?

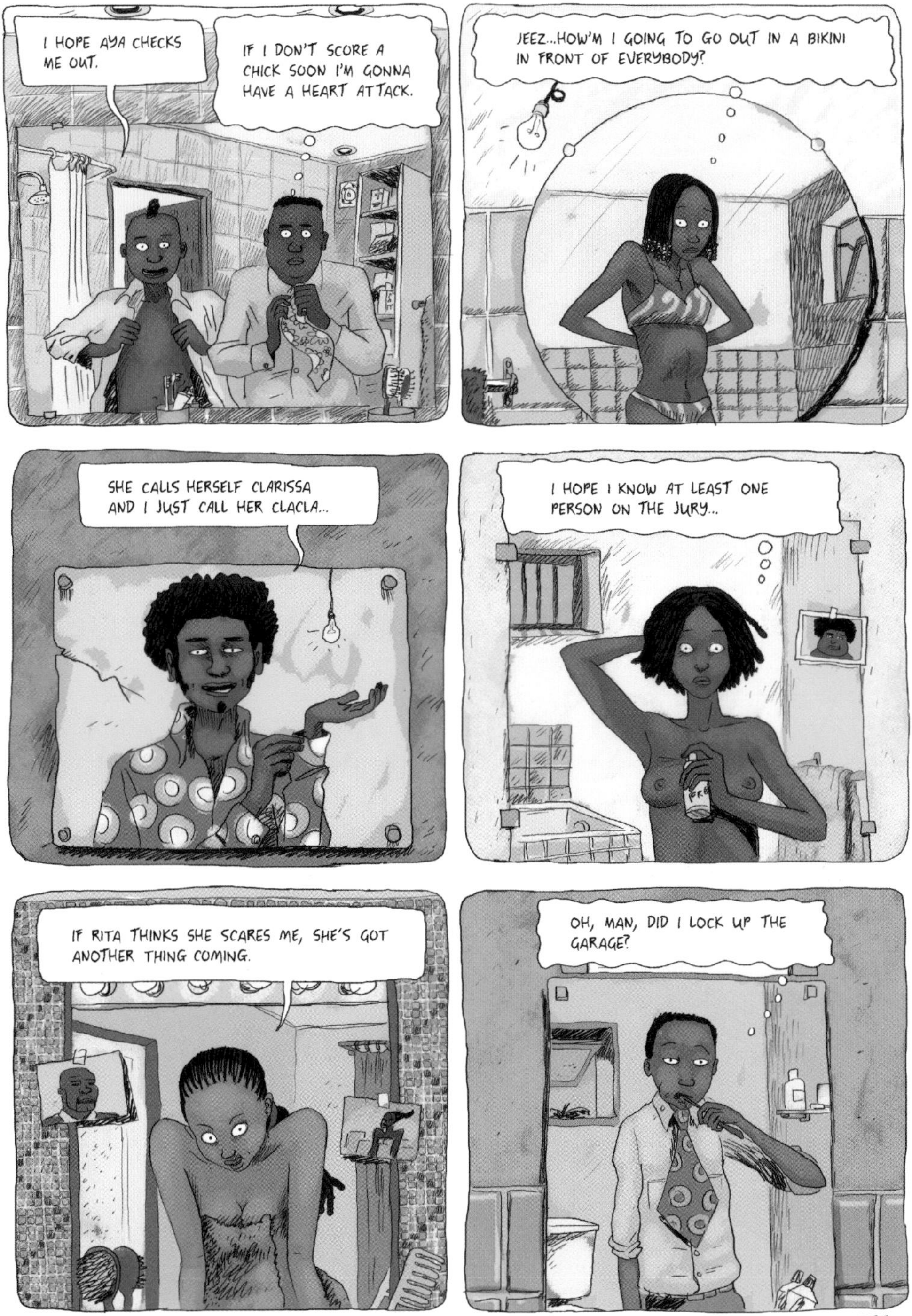
I HOPE AYA CHECKS ME OUT.
IF I DON'T SCORE A CHICK SOON I'M GONNA HAVE A HEART ATTACK.
JEEZ...HOW'M I GOING TO GO OUT IN A BIKINI IN FRONT OF EVERYBODY?
SHE CALLS HERSELF CLARISSA AND I JUST CALL HER CLACLA...
I HOPE I KNOW AT LEAST ONE PERSON ON THE JURY...
IF RITA THINKS SHE SCARES ME, SHE'S GOT ANOTHER THING COMING.
OH, MAN, DID I LOCK UP THE GARAGE?

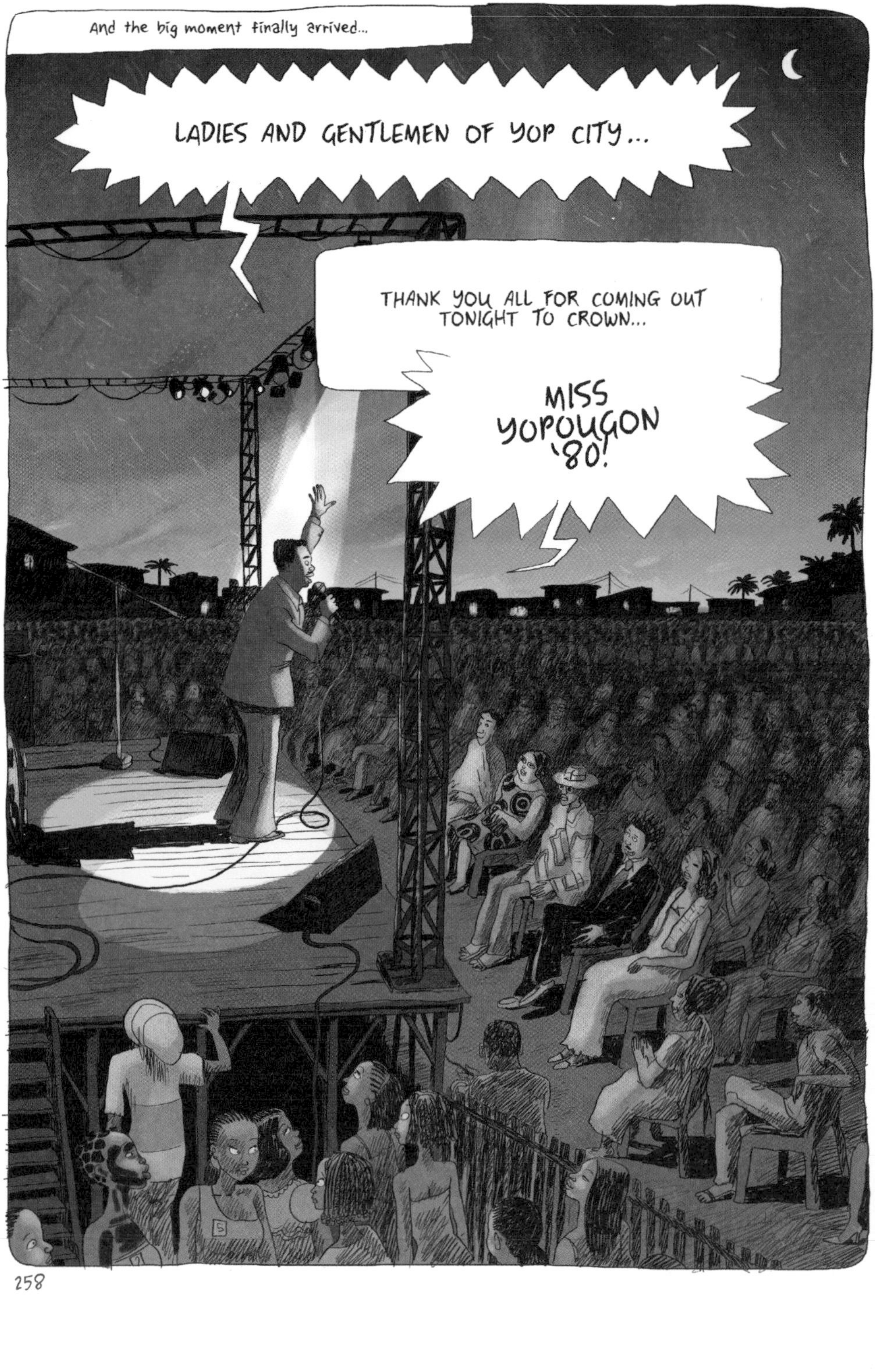
And the big moment finally arrived...
LADIES AND GENTLEMEN OF YOP CITY...
THANK YOU ALL FOR COMING OUT TONIGHT TO CROWN...
MISS YOPOUGON '80!

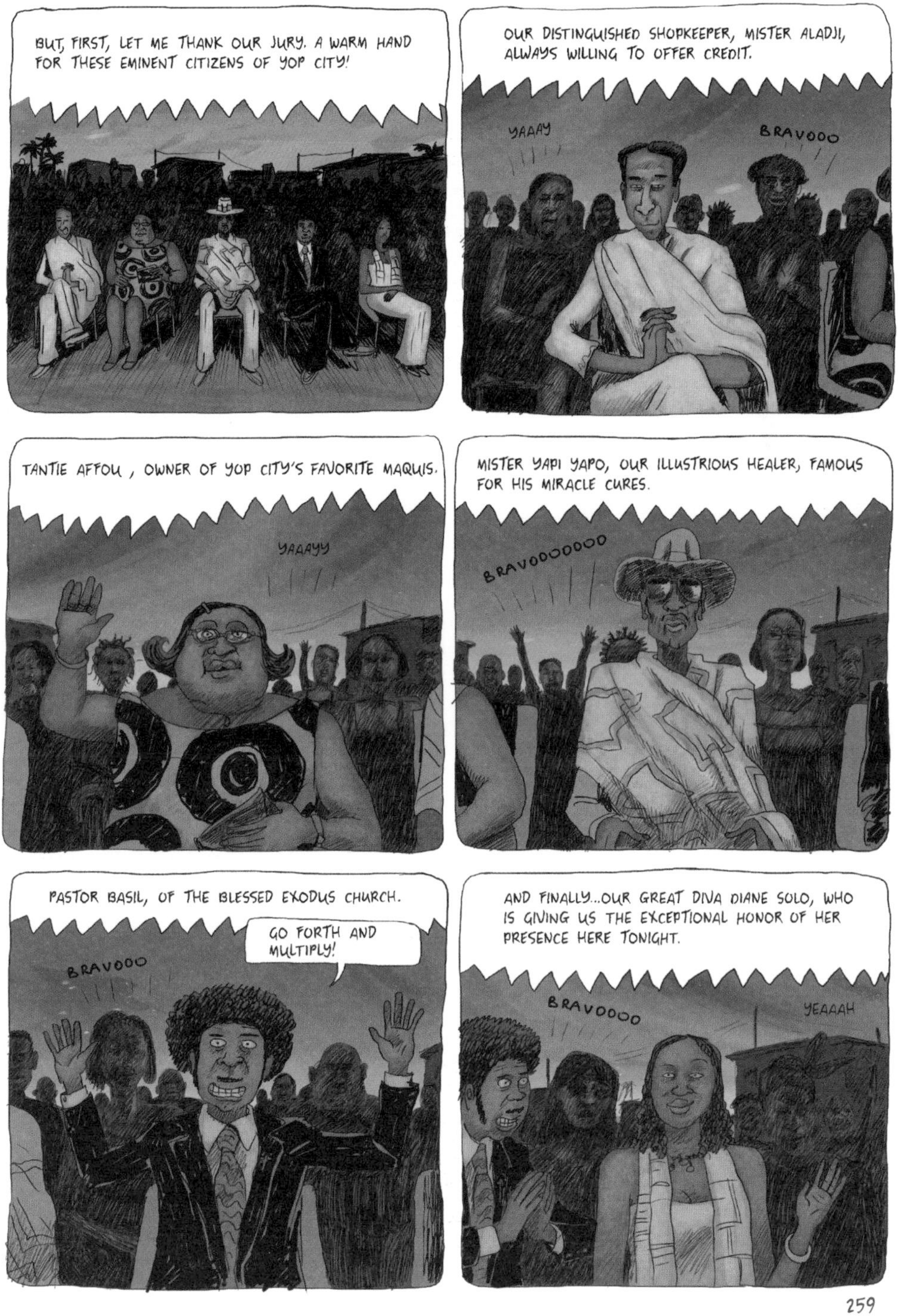
BUT, FIRST, LET ME THANK OUR JURY. A WARM HAND FOR THESE EMINENT CITIZENS OF YOP CITY!
OUR DISTINGUISHED SHOPKEEPER, MISTER ALADJI, ALWAYS WILLING TO OFFER CREDIT.
YAAAY
BRAVOOO
TANTIE AFFOU , OWNER OF YOP CITY'S FAVORITE MAQUIS.
YAAAYY
MISTER YAPI YAPO, OUR ILLUSTRIOUS HEALER, FAMOUS FOR HIS MIRACLE CURES.
BRAVOOOOOOOO
PASTOR BASIL, OF THE BLESSED EXODUS CHURCH.
GO FORTH AND MULTIPLY!
BRAVOOO
AND FINALLY...OUR GREAT DIVA DIANE SOLO, WHO IS GIVING US THE EXCEPTIONAL HONOR OF HER PRESENCE HERE TONIGHT.
BRAVOOOO
YEAAAH

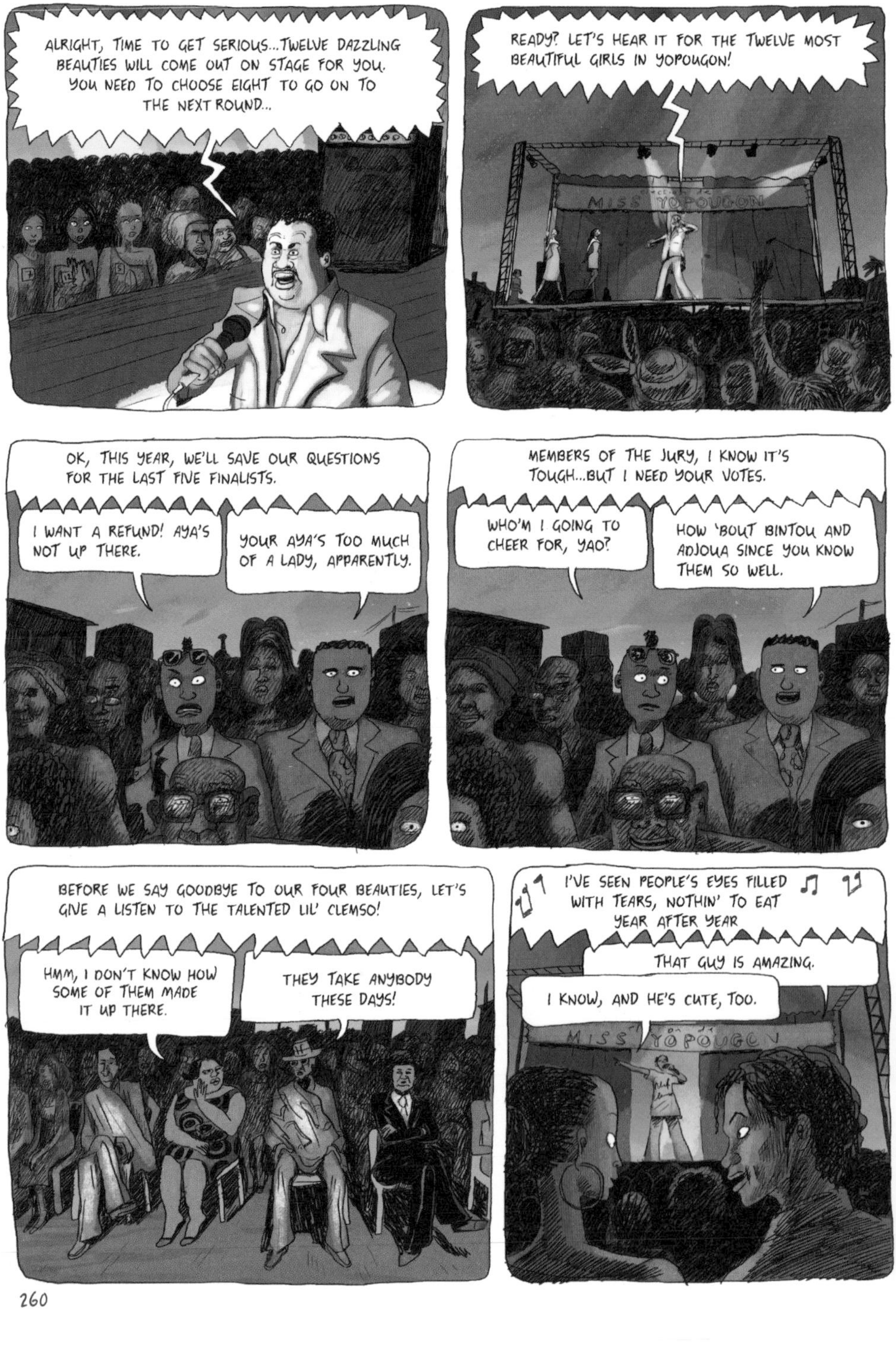
ALRIGHT, TIME TO GET SERIOUS...TWELVE DAZZLING BEAUTIES WILL COME OUT ON STAGE FOR YOU. YOU NEED TO CHOOSE EIGHT TO GO ON TO THE NEXT ROUND...
READY? LET'S HEAR IT FOR THE TWELVE MOST BEAUTIFUL GIRLS IN YOPOUGON!
MISS YOPOUGON
OK, THIS YEAR, WE'LL SAVE OUR QUESTIONS FOR THE LAST FIVE FINALISTS.
I WANT A REFUND! AYA'S NOT UP THERE.
YOUR AYA'S TOO MUCH OF A LADY, APPARENTLY.
MEMBERS OF THE JURY, I KNOW IT'S TOUGH...BUT I NEED YOUR VOTES.
WHO'M I GOING TO CHEER FOR, YAO?
HOW 'BOUT BINTOU AND ADJOUA SINCE YOU KNOW THEM SO WELL.
BEFORE WE SAY GOODBYE TO OUR FOUR BEAUTIES, LET'S GIVE A LISTEN TO THE TALENTED LIL' CLEMSO!
HMM, I DON'T KNOW HOW SOME OF THEM MADE IT UP THERE.
THEY TAKE ANYBODY THESE DAYS!
I'VE SEEN PEOPLE'S EYES FILLED WITH TEARS, NOTHIN' TO EAT YEAR AFTER YEAR
THAT GUY IS AMAZING.
I KNOW, AND HE'S CUTE, TOO.
MISS YOPOUGON

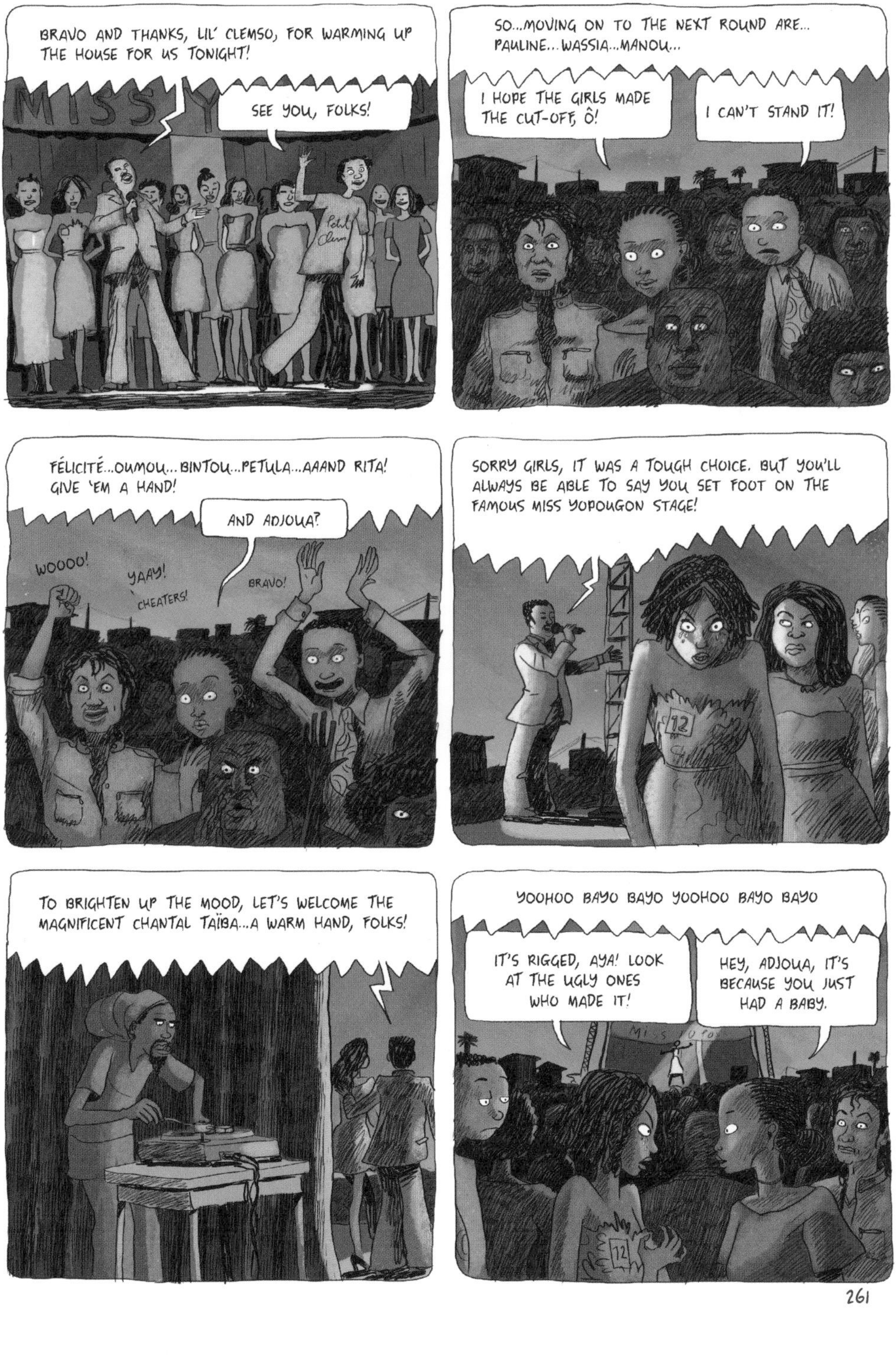
BRAVO AND THANKS, LIL' CLEMSO, FOR WARMING UP THE HOUSE FOR US TONIGHT!
SEE YOU, FOLKS!
MISS Y
SO...MOVING ON TO THE NEXT ROUND ARE... PAULINE...WASSIA...MANOU...
I HOPE THE GIRLS MADE THE CUT-OFF, Ô!
I CAN'T STAND IT!
FÉLICITÉ...OUMOU...BINTOU...PETULA...AAAND RITA! GIVE 'EM A HAND!
AND ADJOUA?
WOOOO!
YAAY!
CHEATERS!
BRAVO!
SORRY GIRLS, IT WAS A TOUGH CHOICE. BUT YOU'LL ALWAYS BE ABLE TO SAY YOU SET FOOT ON THE FAMOUS MISS YOPOUGON STAGE!
12
TO BRIGHTEN UP THE MOOD, LET'S WELCOME THE MAGNIFICENT CHANTAL TAÏBA...A WARM HAND, FOLKS!
YOOHOO BAYO BAYO YOOHOO BAYO BAYO
IT'S RIGGED, AYA! LOOK AT THE UGLY ONES WHO MADE IT!
HEY, ADJOUA, IT'S BECAUSE YOU JUST HAD A BABY.
12

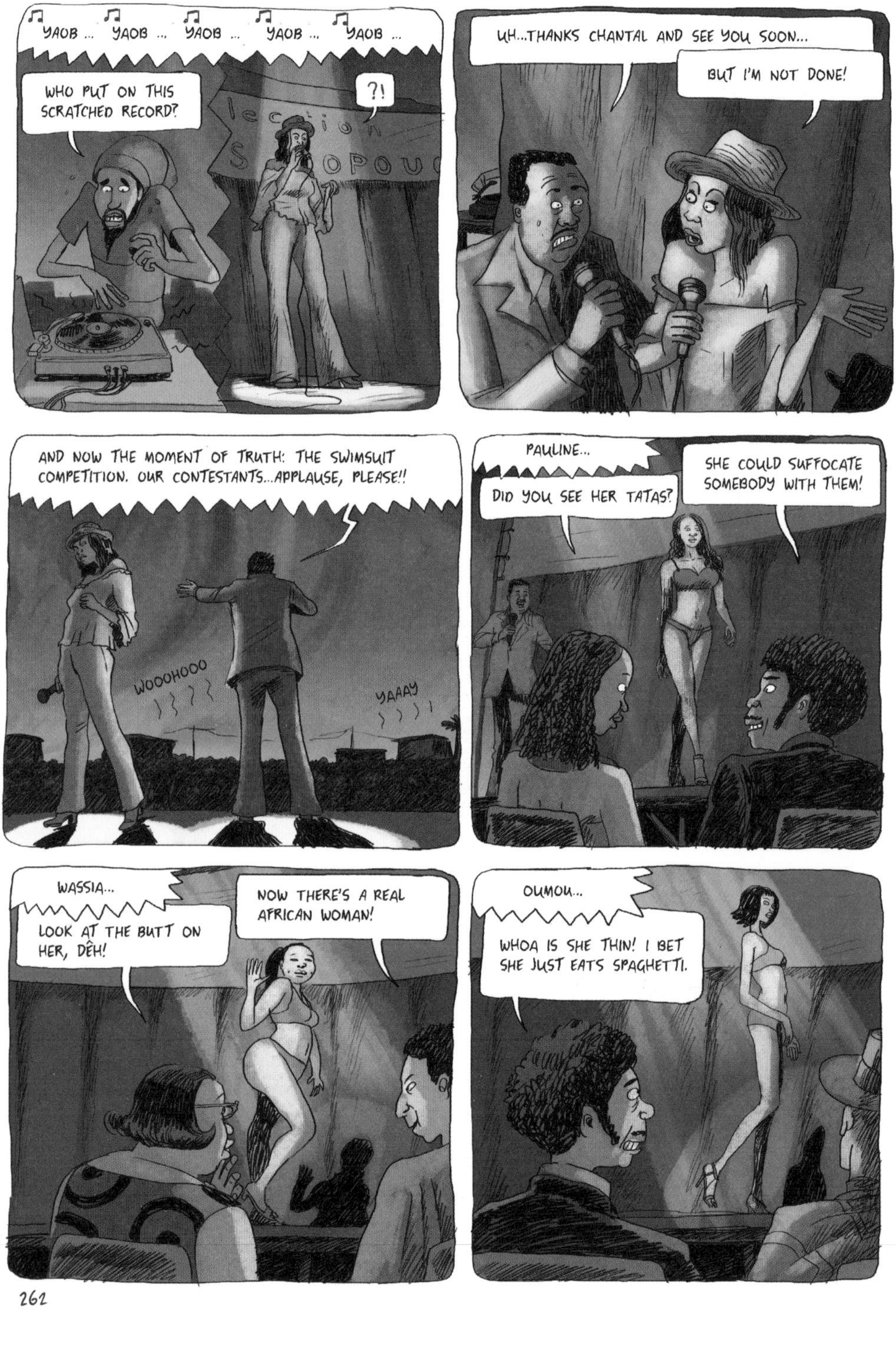
YAOB ... YAOB ... YAOB ... YAOB ... YAOB ...
WHO PUT ON THIS SCRATCHED RECORD?
?!
UH...THANKS CHANTAL AND SEE YOU SOON...
BUT I'M NOT DONE!
AND NOW THE MOMENT OF TRUTH: THE SWIMSUIT COMPETITION. OUR CONTESTANTS...APPLAUSE, PLEASE!!
WOOOHOOO
YAAAY
PAULINE...
DID YOU SEE HER TATAS?
SHE COULD SUFFOCATE SOMEBODY WITH THEM!
WASSIA...
LOOK AT THE BUTT ON HER, DÊH!
NOW THERE'S A REAL AFRICAN WOMAN!
OUMOU...
WHOA IS SHE THIN! I BET SHE JUST EATS SPAGHETTI.

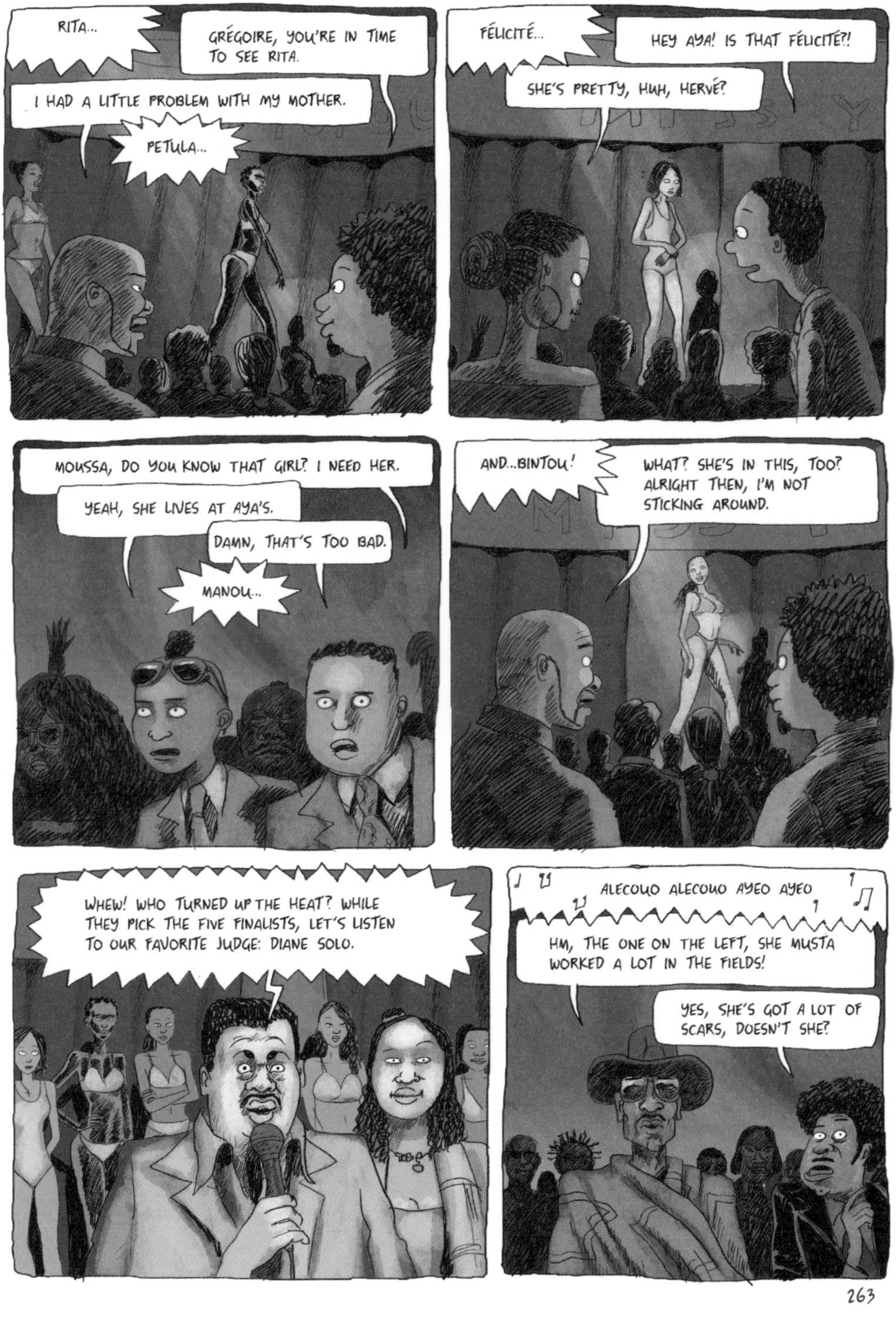
RITA...
GRÉGOIRE, YOU'RE IN TIME TO SEE RITA.
I HAD A LITTLE PROBLEM WITH MY MOTHER.
PETULA...
FÉLICITÉ...
HEY AYA! IS THAT FÉLICITÉ?!
SHE'S PRETTY, HUH, HERVÉ?
MOUSSA, DO YOU KNOW THAT GIRL? I NEED HER.
YEAH, SHE LIVES AT AYA'S.
DAMN, THAT'S TOO BAD.
MANOU...
AND...BINTOU!
WHAT? SHE'S IN THIS, TOO? ALRIGHT THEN, I'M NOT STICKING AROUND.
WHEW! WHO TURNED UP THE HEAT? WHILE THEY PICK THE FIVE FINALISTS, LET'S LISTEN TO OUR FAVORITE JUDGE: DIANE SOLO.
ALECOUO ALECOUO AYEO AYEO
HM, THE ONE ON THE LEFT, SHE MUSTA WORKED A LOT IN THE FIELDS!
YES, SHE'S GOT A LOT OF SCARS, DOESN'T SHE?

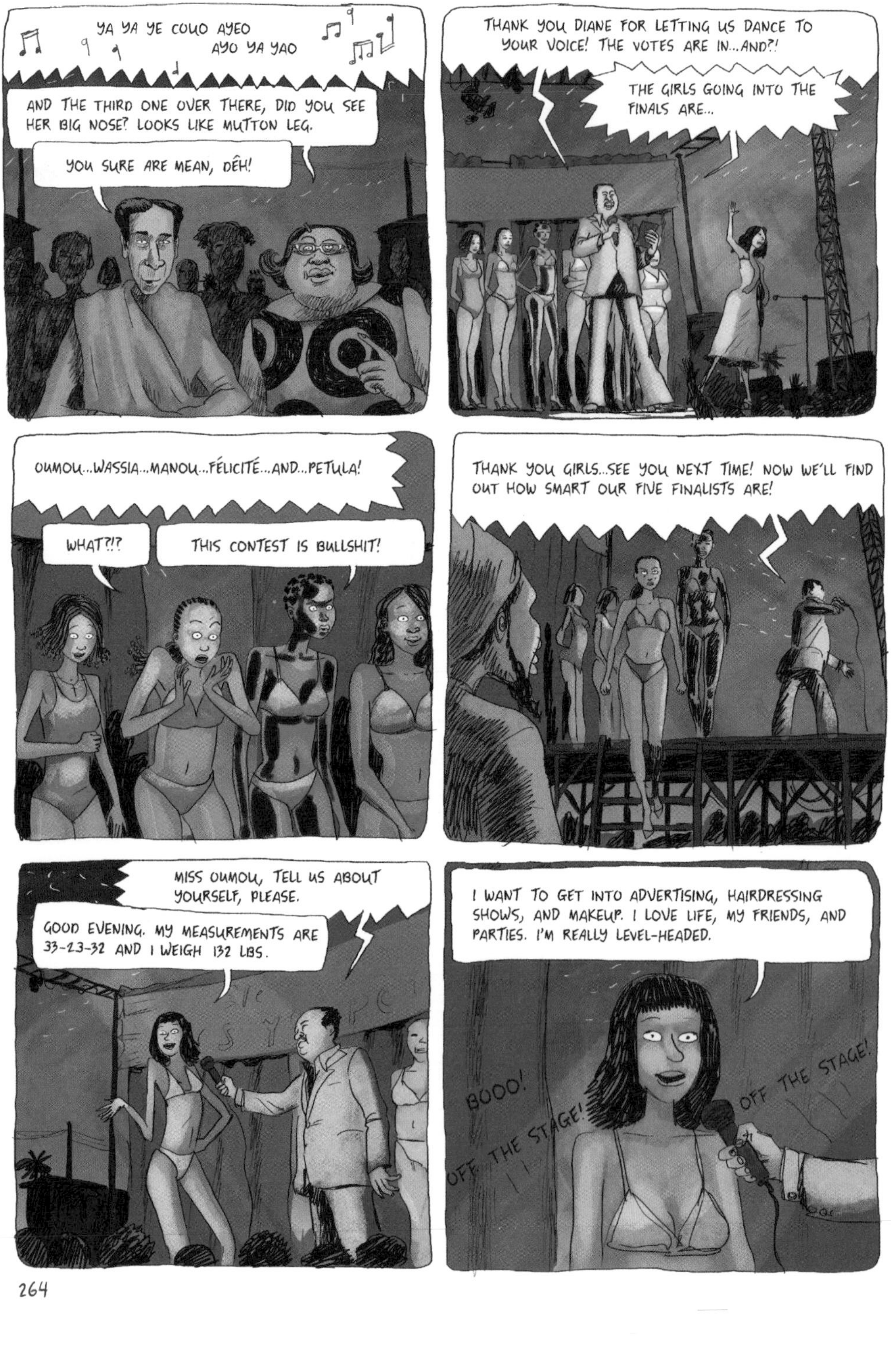

YA YA YE COUO AYEO
AYO YA YAO
AND THE THIRD ONE OVER THERE, DID YOU SEE HER BIG NOSE? LOOKS LIKE MUTTON LEG.
YOU SURE ARE MEAN, DÊH!
THANK YOU DIANE FOR LETTING US DANCE TO YOUR VOICE! THE VOTES ARE IN...AND?!
THE GIRLS GOING INTO THE FINALS ARE...
OUMOU...WASSIA...MANOU...FÉLICITÉ...AND...PETULA!
WHAT?!?
THIS CONTEST IS BULLSHIT!
THANK YOU GIRLS...SEE YOU NEXT TIME! NOW WE'LL FIND OUT HOW SMART OUR FIVE FINALISTS ARE!
MISS OUMOU, TELL US ABOUT YOURSELF, PLEASE.
GOOD EVENING. MY MEASUREMENTS ARE 33-23-32 AND I WEIGH 132 LBS.
I WANT TO GET INTO ADVERTISING, HAIRDRESSING SHOWS, AND MAKEUP. I LOVE LIFE, MY FRIENDS, AND PARTIES. I'M REALLY LEVEL-HEADED.
BOOO!
OFF THE STAGE!
OFF THE STAGE!

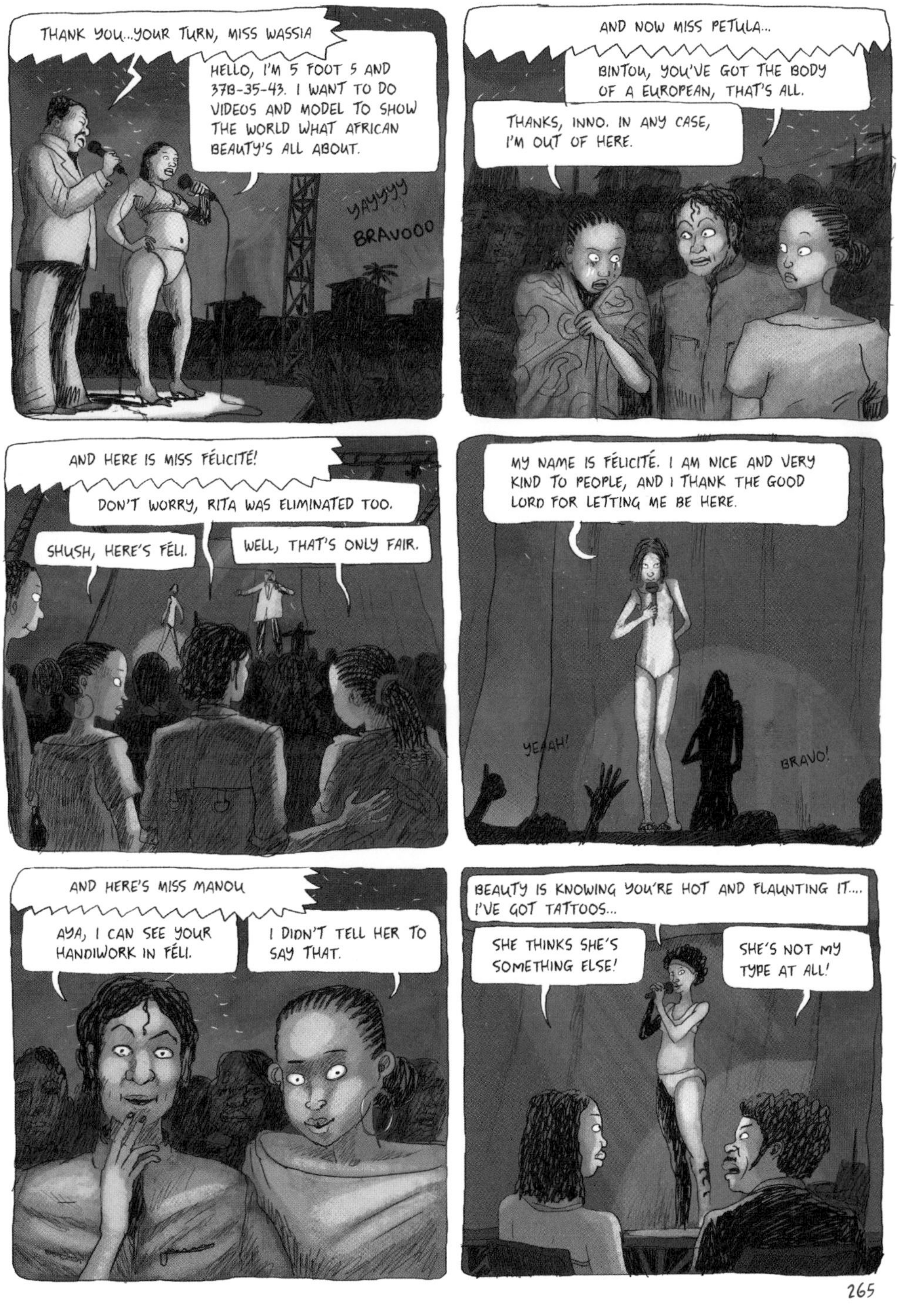
THANK YOU...YOUR TURN, MISS WASSIA
HELLO, I'M 5 FOOT 5 AND 37B-35-43. I WANT TO DO VIDEOS AND MODEL TO SHOW THE WORLD WHAT AFRICAN BEAUTY'S ALL ABOUT.
YAYYYY
BRAVOOO
AND NOW MISS PETULA...
BINTOU, YOU'VE GOT THE BODY OF A EUROPEAN, THAT'S ALL.
THANKS, INNO. IN ANY CASE, I'M OUT OF HERE.
AND HERE IS MISS FÉLICITÉ!
DON'T WORRY, RITA WAS ELIMINATED TOO.
SHUSH, HERE'S FÉLI.
WELL, THAT'S ONLY FAIR.
MY NAME IS FÉLICITÉ. I AM NICE AND VERY KIND TO PEOPLE, AND I THANK THE GOOD LORD FOR LETTING ME BE HERE.
YEAAH!
BRAVO!
AND HERE'S MISS MANOU
AYA, I CAN SEE YOUR HANDIWORK IN FÉLI.
I DIDN'T TELL HER TO SAY THAT.
BEAUTY IS KNOWING YOU'RE HOT AND FLAUNTING IT.... I'VE GOT TATTOOS...
SHE THINKS SHE'S SOMETHING ELSE!
SHE'S NOT MY TYPE AT ALL!

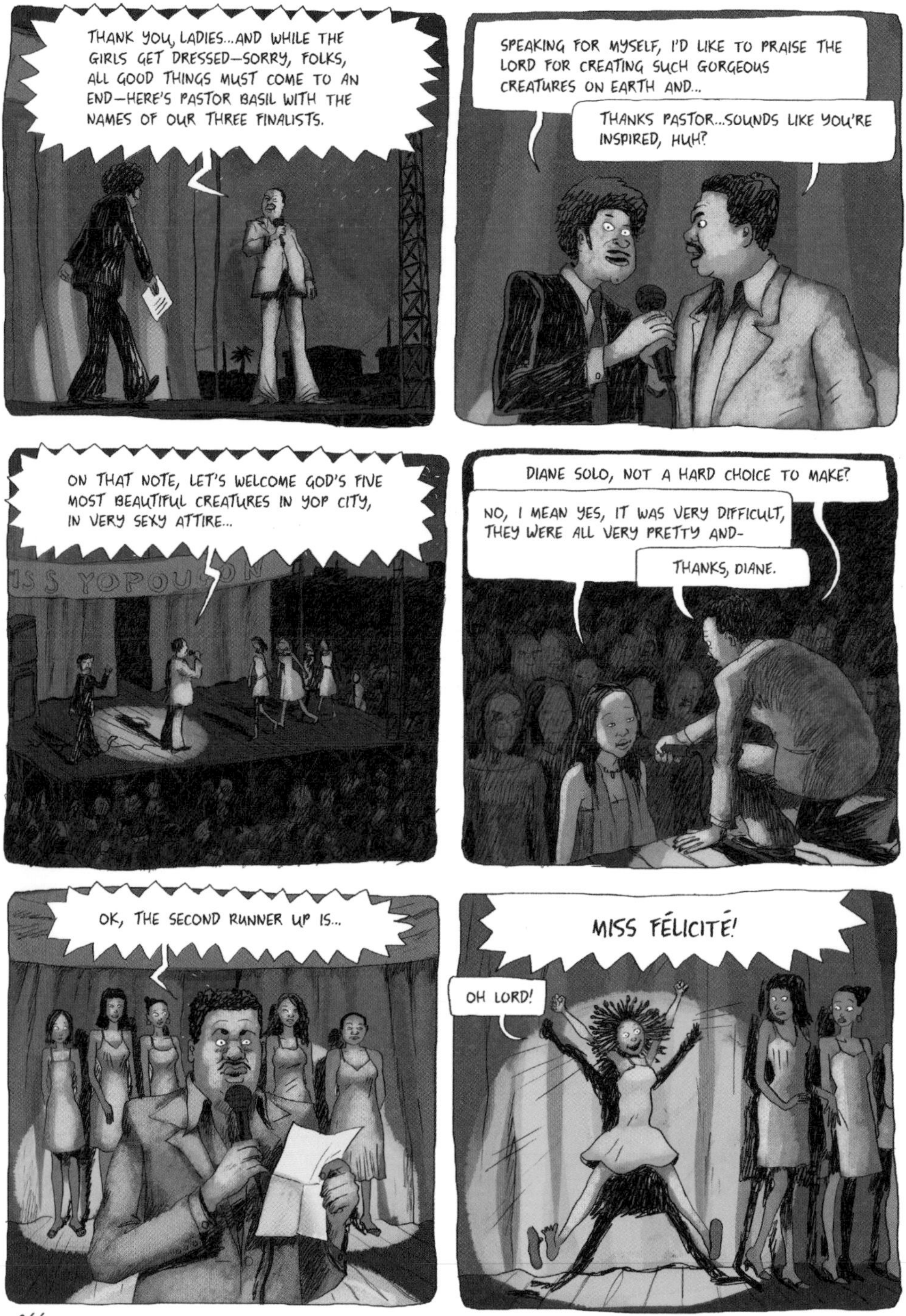
THANK YOU, LADIES...AND WHILE THE GIRLS GET DRESSED—SORRY, FOLKS, ALL GOOD THINGS MUST COME TO AN END—HERE'S PASTOR BASIL WITH THE NAMES OF OUR THREE FINALISTS.
SPEAKING FOR MYSELF, I'D LIKE TO PRAISE THE LORD FOR CREATING SUCH GORGEOUS CREATURES ON EARTH AND...
THANKS PASTOR...SOUNDS LIKE YOU'RE INSPIRED, HUH?
ON THAT NOTE, LET'S WELCOME GOD'S FIVE MOST BEAUTIFUL CREATURES IN YOP CITY, IN VERY SEXY ATTIRE...
DIANE SOLO, NOT A HARD CHOICE TO MAKE?
NO, I MEAN YES, IT WAS VERY DIFFICULT, THEY WERE ALL VERY PRETTY AND-
THANKS, DIANE.
OK, THE SECOND RUNNER UP IS...
MISS FÉLICITÉ!
OH LORD!

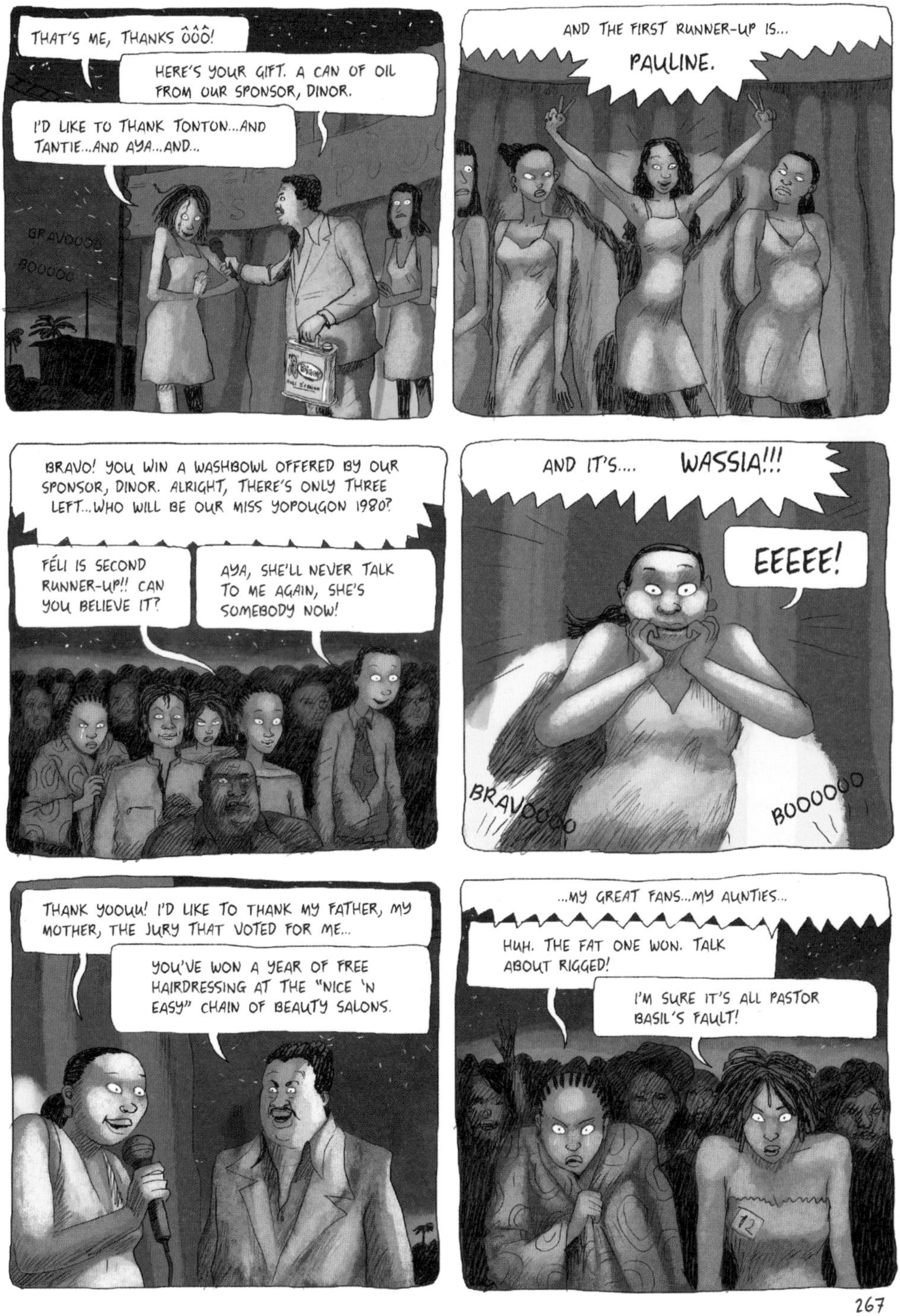
THAT'S ME, THANKS ÔÔÔ!
HERE'S YOUR GIFT. A CAN OF OIL FROM OUR SPONSOR, DINOR.
I'D LIKE TO THANK TONTON...AND TANTIE...AND AYA...AND...
BRAVOOOO
BOOOOO
AND THE FIRST RUNNER-UP IS...
PAULINE.
BRAVO! YOU WIN A WASHBOWL OFFERED BY OUR SPONSOR, DINOR. ALRIGHT, THERE'S ONLY THREE LEFT...WHO WILL BE OUR MISS YOPOUGON 1980?
FÉLI IS SECOND RUNNER-UP!! CAN YOU BELIEVE IT?
AYA, SHE'LL NEVER TALK TO ME AGAIN, SHE'S SOMEBODY NOW!
AND IT'S.... WASSIA!!!
EEEEE!
BRAVOOOO
BOOOOOO
THANK YOOUU! I'D LIKE TO THANK MY FATHER, MY MOTHER, THE JURY THAT VOTED FOR ME...
YOU'VE WON A YEAR OF FREE HAIRDRESSING AT THE "NICE 'N EASY" CHAIN OF BEAUTY SALONS.
...MY GREAT FANS...MY AUNTIES...
HUH. THE FAT ONE WON. TALK ABOUT RIGGED!
I'M SURE IT'S ALL PASTOR BASIL'S FAULT!
12

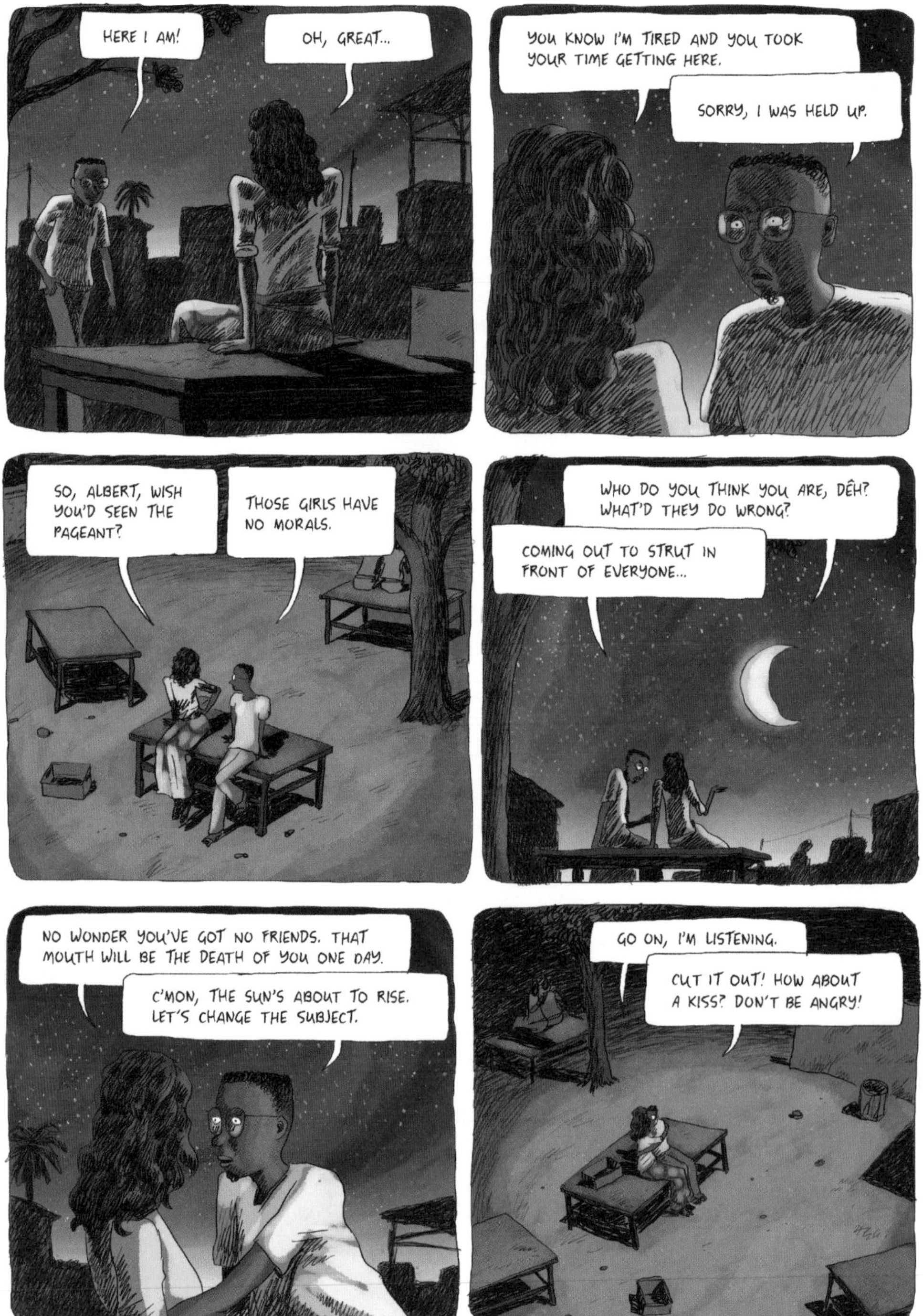
HERE I AM!
OH, GREAT...
YOU KNOW I'M TIRED AND YOU TOOK YOUR TIME GETTING HERE.
SORRY, I WAS HELD UP.
SO, ALBERT, WISH YOU'D SEEN THE PAGEANT?
THOSE GIRLS HAVE NO MORALS.
WHO DO YOU THINK YOU ARE, DÊH? WHAT'D THEY DO WRONG?
COMING OUT TO STRUT IN FRONT OF EVERYONE...
NO WONDER YOU'VE GOT NO FRIENDS. THAT MOUTH WILL BE THE DEATH OF YOU ONE DAY.
C'MON, THE SUN'S ABOUT TO RISE. LET'S CHANGE THE SUBJECT.
GO ON, I'M LISTENING.
CUT IT OUT! HOW ABOUT A KISS? DON'T BE ANGRY!

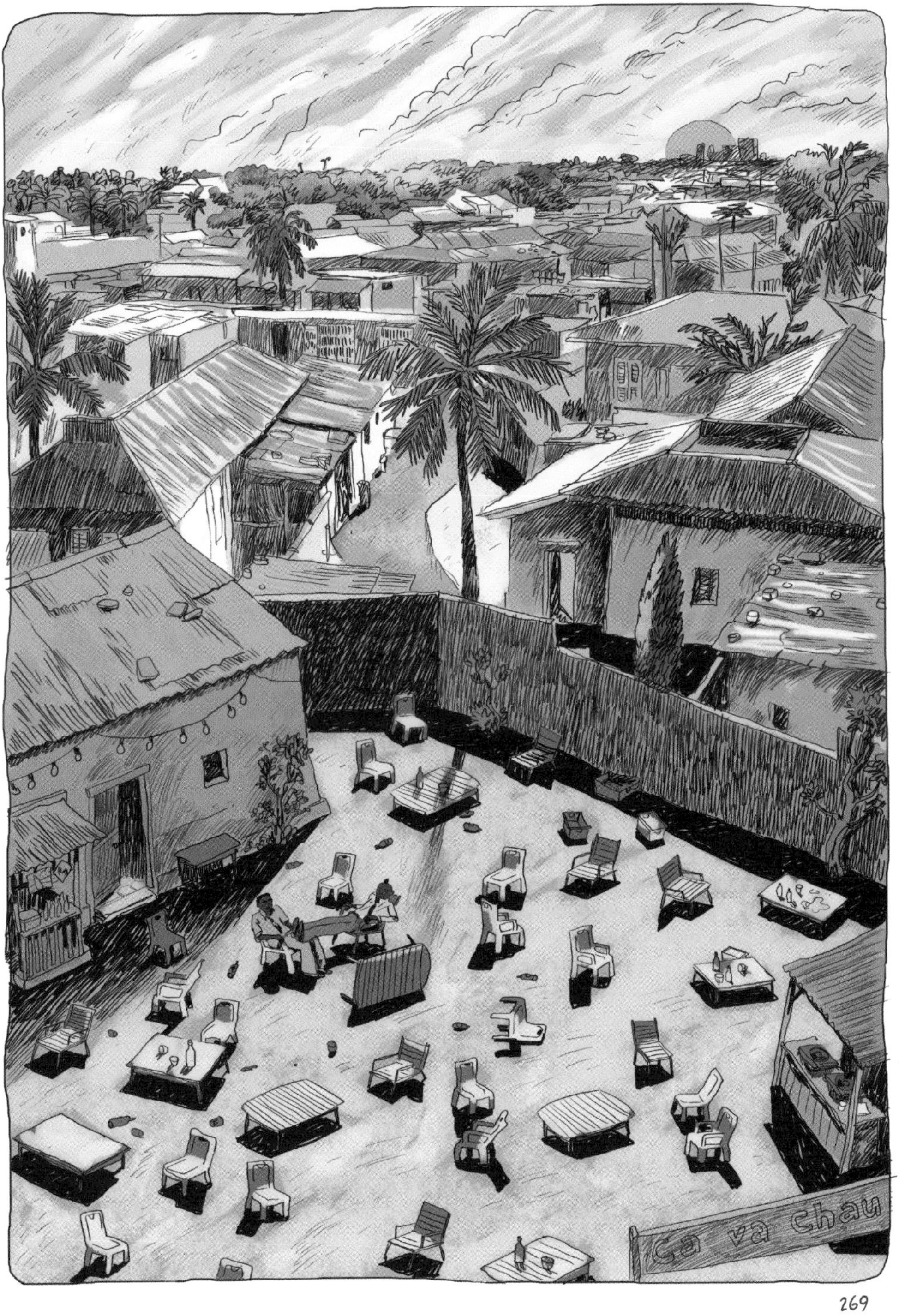
Ca va chau

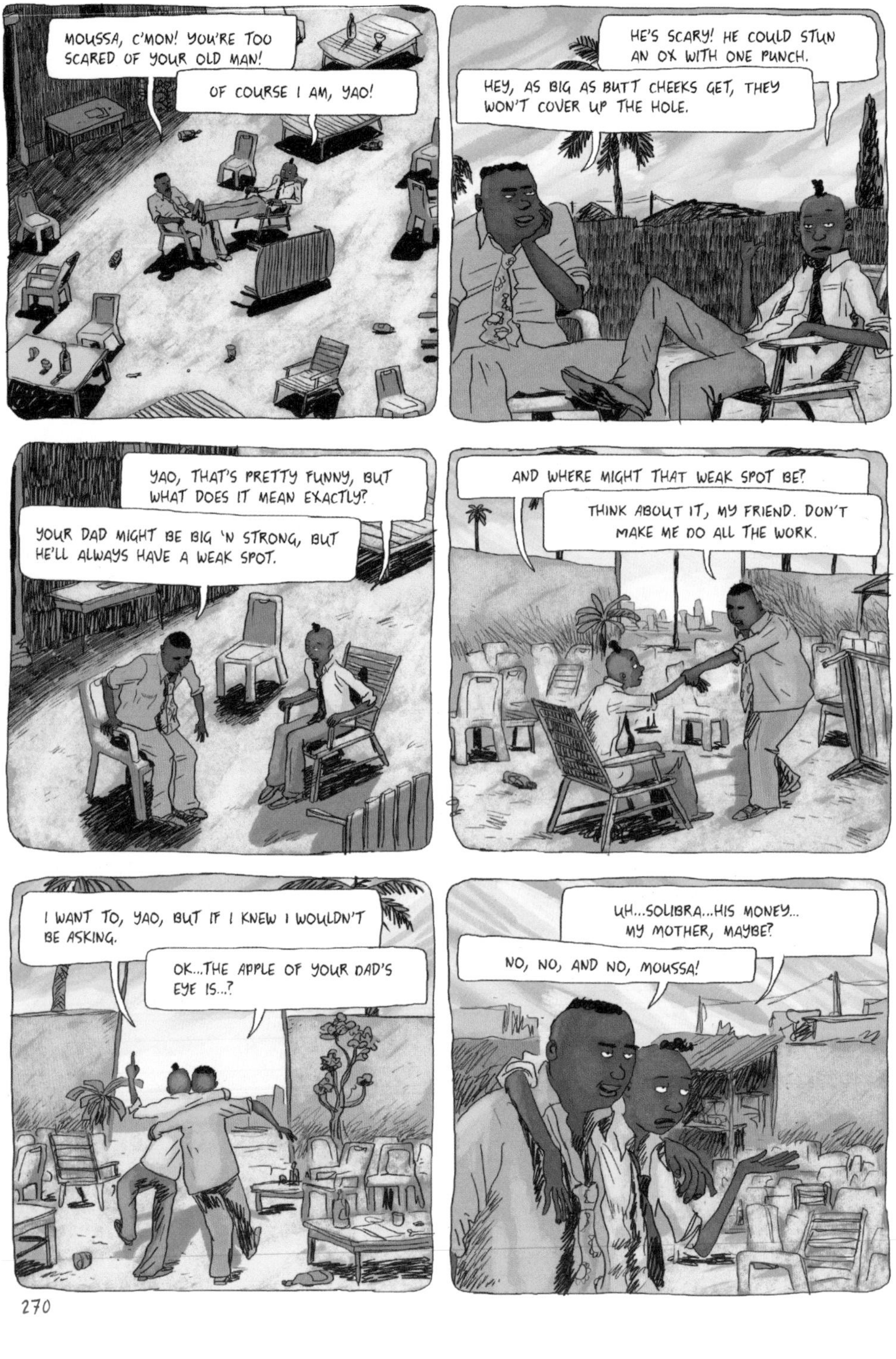

MOUSSA, C'MON! YOU'RE TOO SCARED OF YOUR OLD MAN!
OF COURSE I AM, YAO!
HE'S SCARY! HE COULD STUN AN OX WITH ONE PUNCH.
HEY, AS BIG AS BUTT CHEEKS GET, THEY WON'T COVER UP THE HOLE.
YAO, THAT'S PRETTY FUNNY, BUT WHAT DOES IT MEAN EXACTLY?
YOUR DAD MIGHT BE BIG 'N STRONG, BUT HE'LL ALWAYS HAVE A WEAK SPOT.
AND WHERE MIGHT THAT WEAK SPOT BE?
THINK ABOUT IT, MY FRIEND. DON'T MAKE ME DO ALL THE WORK.
I WANT TO, YAO, BUT IF I KNEW I WOULDN'T BE ASKING.
OK...THE APPLE OF YOUR DAD'S EYE IS...?
UH...SOLIBRA...HIS MONEY... MY MOTHER, MAYBE?
NO, NO, AND NO, MOUSSA!

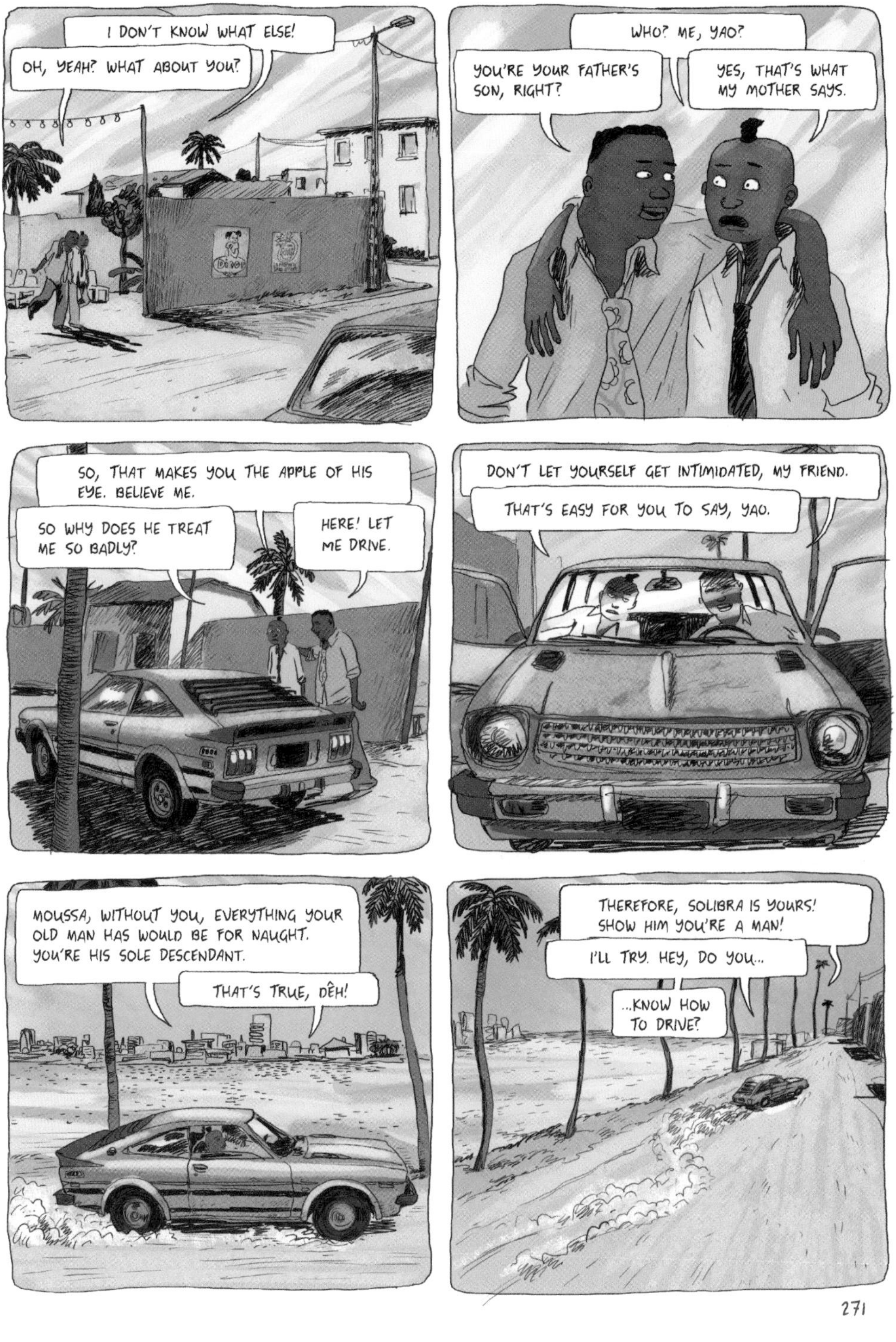
OH, YEAH? WHAT ABOUT YOU?
I DON'T KNOW WHAT ELSE!
YOU'RE YOUR FATHER'S SON, RIGHT?
WHO? ME, YAO?
YES, THAT'S WHAT MY MOTHER SAYS.
SO, THAT MAKES YOU THE APPLE OF HIS EYE. BELIEVE ME.
SO WHY DOES HE TREAT ME SO BADLY?
HERE! LET ME DRIVE.
DON'T LET YOURSELF GET INTIMIDATED, MY FRIEND.
THAT'S EASY FOR YOU TO SAY, YAO.
MOUSSA, WITHOUT YOU, EVERYTHING YOUR OLD MAN HAS WOULD BE FOR NAUGHT. YOU'RE HIS SOLE DESCENDANT.
THAT'S TRUE, DÊH!
THEREFORE, SOLIBRA IS YOURS! SHOW HIM YOU'RE A MAN!
I'LL TRY. HEY, DO YOU...
...KNOW HOW TO DRIVE?

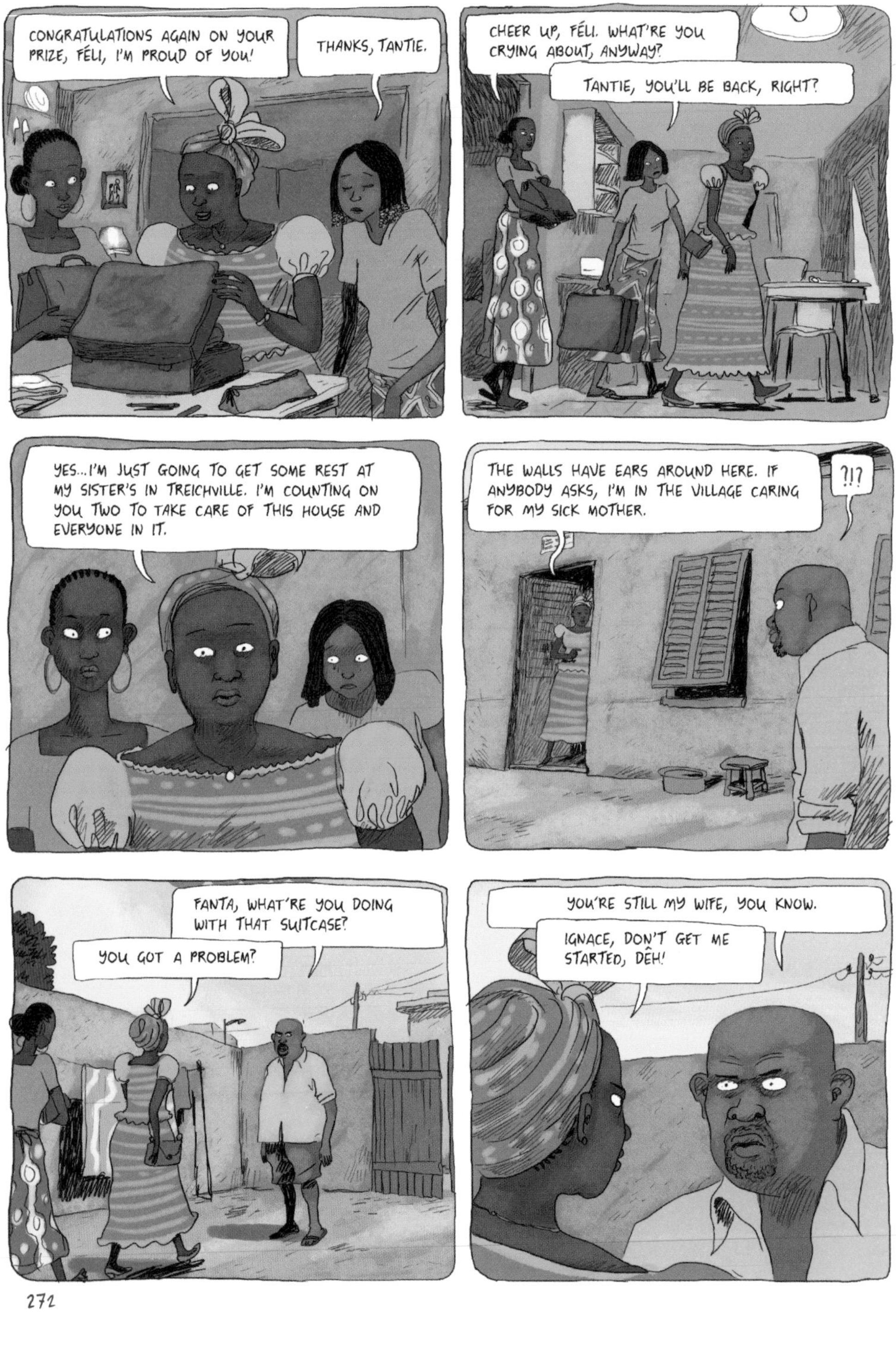
CONGRATULATIONS AGAIN ON YOUR PRIZE, FÉLI, I'M PROUD OF YOU!
THANKS, TANTIE.
CHEER UP, FÉLI. WHAT'RE YOU CRYING ABOUT, ANYWAY?
TANTIE, YOU'LL BE BACK, RIGHT?
YES...I'M JUST GOING TO GET SOME REST AT MY SISTER'S IN TREICHVILLE. I'M COUNTING ON YOU TWO TO TAKE CARE OF THIS HOUSE AND EVERYONE IN IT.
THE WALLS HAVE EARS AROUND HERE. IF ANYBODY ASKS, I'M IN THE VILLAGE CARING FOR MY SICK MOTHER.
?!?
FANTA, WHAT'RE YOU DOING WITH THAT SUITCASE?
YOU GOT A PROBLEM?
YOU'RE STILL MY WIFE, YOU KNOW.
IGNACE, DON'T GET ME STARTED, DÊH!

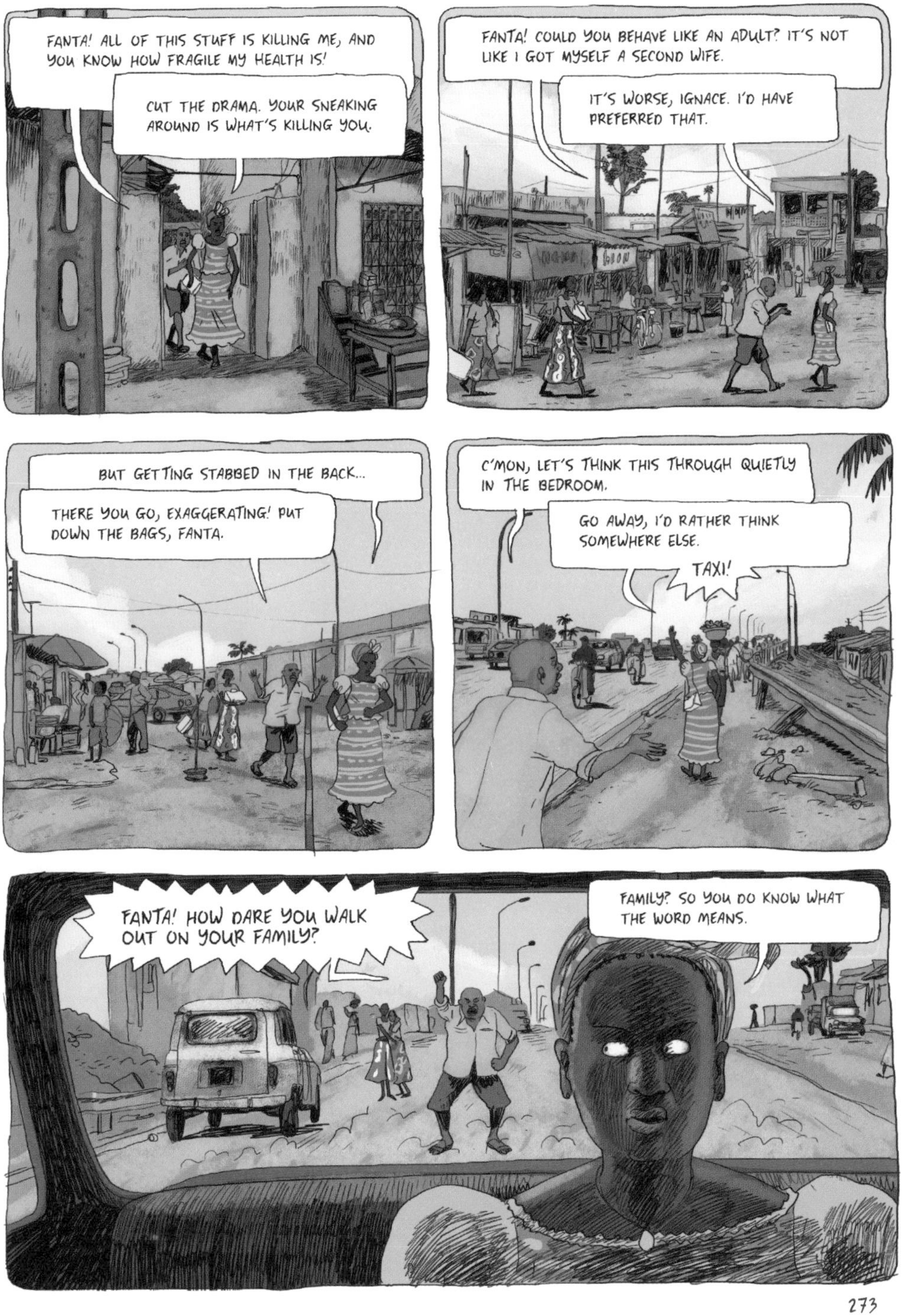
FANTA! ALL OF THIS STUFF IS KILLING ME, AND YOU KNOW HOW FRAGILE MY HEALTH IS!
CUT THE DRAMA. YOUR SNEAKING AROUND IS WHAT'S KILLING YOU.
FANTA! COULD YOU BEHAVE LIKE AN ADULT? IT'S NOT LIKE I GOT MYSELF A SECOND WIFE.
IT'S WORSE, IGNACE. I'D HAVE PREFERRED THAT.
BUT GETTING STABBED IN THE BACK...
THERE YOU GO, EXAGGERATING! PUT DOWN THE BAGS, FANTA.
C'MON, LET'S THINK THIS THROUGH QUIETLY IN THE BEDROOM.
GO AWAY, I'D RATHER THINK SOMEWHERE ELSE.
TAXI!
FANTA! HOW DARE YOU WALK OUT ON YOUR FAMILY?
FAMILY? SO YOU DO KNOW WHAT THE WORD MEANS.

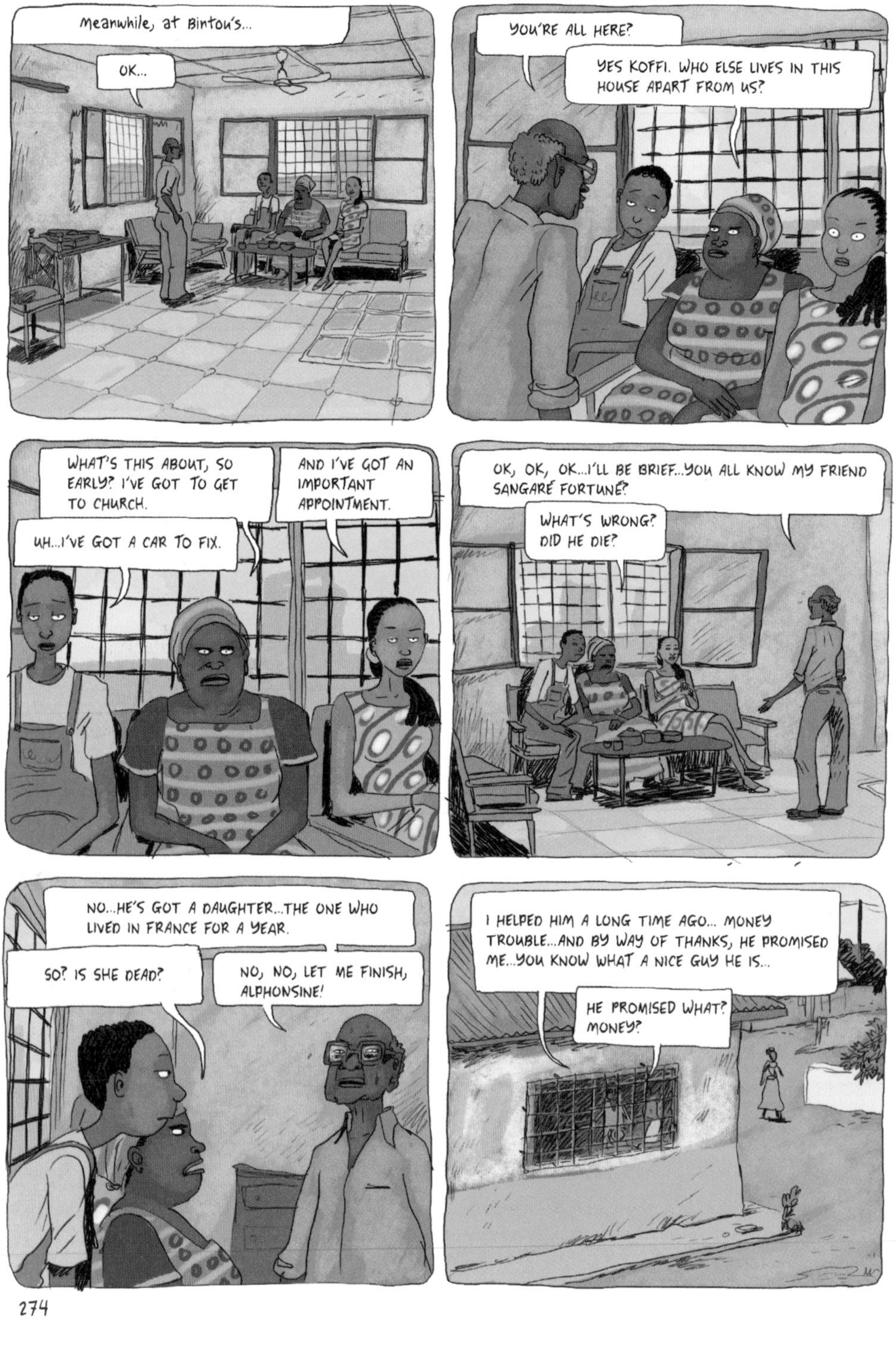
Meanwhile, at Bintou's...
OK...
YOU'RE ALL HERE?
YES KOFFI. WHO ELSE LIVES IN THIS HOUSE APART FROM US?
WHAT'S THIS ABOUT, SO EARLY? I'VE GOT TO GET TO CHURCH.
AND I'VE GOT AN IMPORTANT APPOINTMENT.
UH...I'VE GOT A CAR TO FIX.
OK, OK, OK...I'LL BE BRIEF...YOU ALL KNOW MY FRIEND SANGARÉ FORTUNÉ?
WHAT'S WRONG? DID HE DIE?
NO...HE'S GOT A DAUGHTER...THE ONE WHO LIVED IN FRANCE FOR A YEAR.
SO? IS SHE DEAD?
NO, NO, LET ME FINISH, ALPHONSINE!
I HELPED HIM A LONG TIME AGO... MONEY TROUBLE...AND BY WAY OF THANKS, HE PROMISED ME...YOU KNOW WHAT A NICE GUY HE IS...
HE PROMISED WHAT? MONEY?

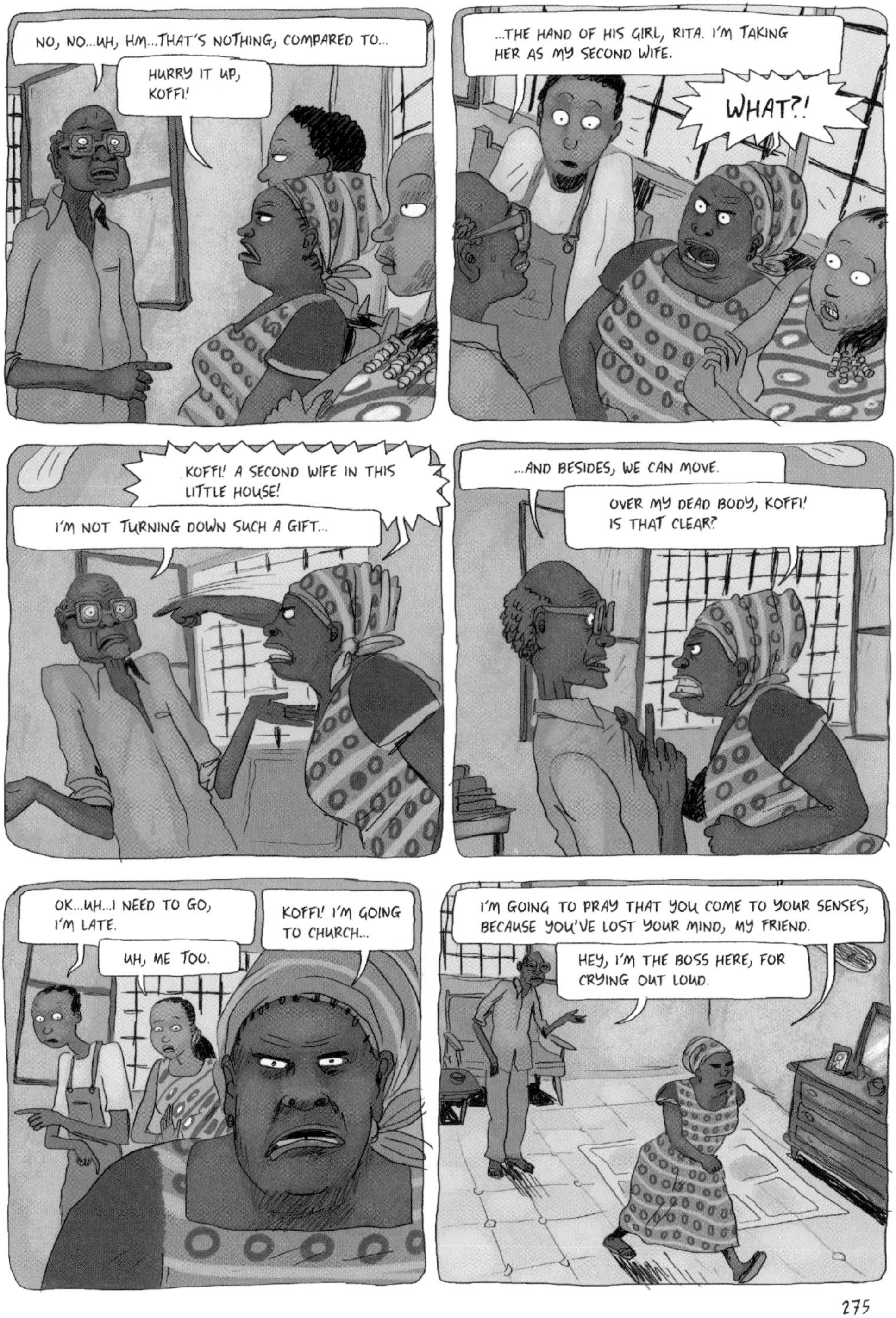
NO, NO...UH, HM...THAT'S NOTHING, COMPARED TO...
HURRY IT UP, KOFFI!
...THE HAND OF HIS GIRL, RITA. I'M TAKING HER AS MY SECOND WIFE.
WHAT?!
KOFFI! A SECOND WIFE IN THIS LITTLE HOUSE!
I'M NOT TURNING DOWN SUCH A GIFT...
...AND BESIDES, WE CAN MOVE.
OVER MY DEAD BODY, KOFFI! IS THAT CLEAR?
OK...UH...I NEED TO GO, I'M LATE.
UH, ME TOO.
KOFFI! I'M GOING TO CHURCH...
I'M GOING TO PRAY THAT YOU COME TO YOUR SENSES, BECAUSE YOU'VE LOST YOUR MIND, MY FRIEND.
HEY, I'M THE BOSS HERE, FOR CRYING OUT LOUD.

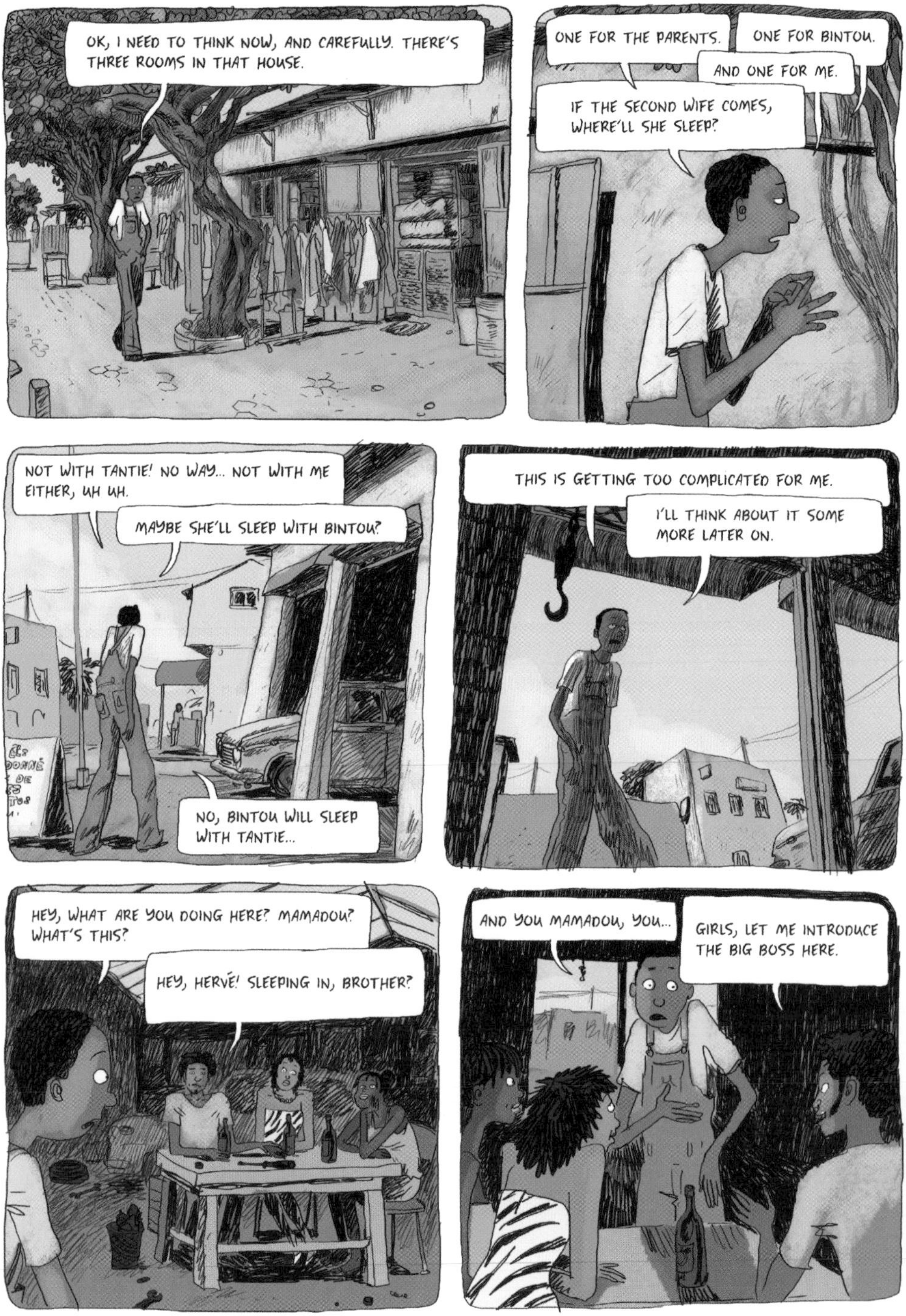
OK, I NEED TO THINK NOW, AND CAREFULLY. THERE'S THREE ROOMS IN THAT HOUSE.
ONE FOR THE PARENTS.
ONE FOR BINTOU.
AND ONE FOR ME.
IF THE SECOND WIFE COMES, WHERE'LL SHE SLEEP?
NOT WITH TANTIE! NO WAY... NOT WITH ME EITHER, UH UH.
MAYBE SHE'LL SLEEP WITH BINTOU?
NO, BINTOU WILL SLEEP WITH TANTIE...
THIS IS GETTING TOO COMPLICATED FOR ME.
I'LL THINK ABOUT IT SOME MORE LATER ON.
HEY, WHAT ARE YOU DOING HERE? MAMADOU? WHAT'S THIS?
HEY, HERVÉ! SLEEPING IN, BROTHER?
AND YOU MAMADOU, YOU...
GIRLS, LET ME INTRODUCE THE BIG BOSS HERE.

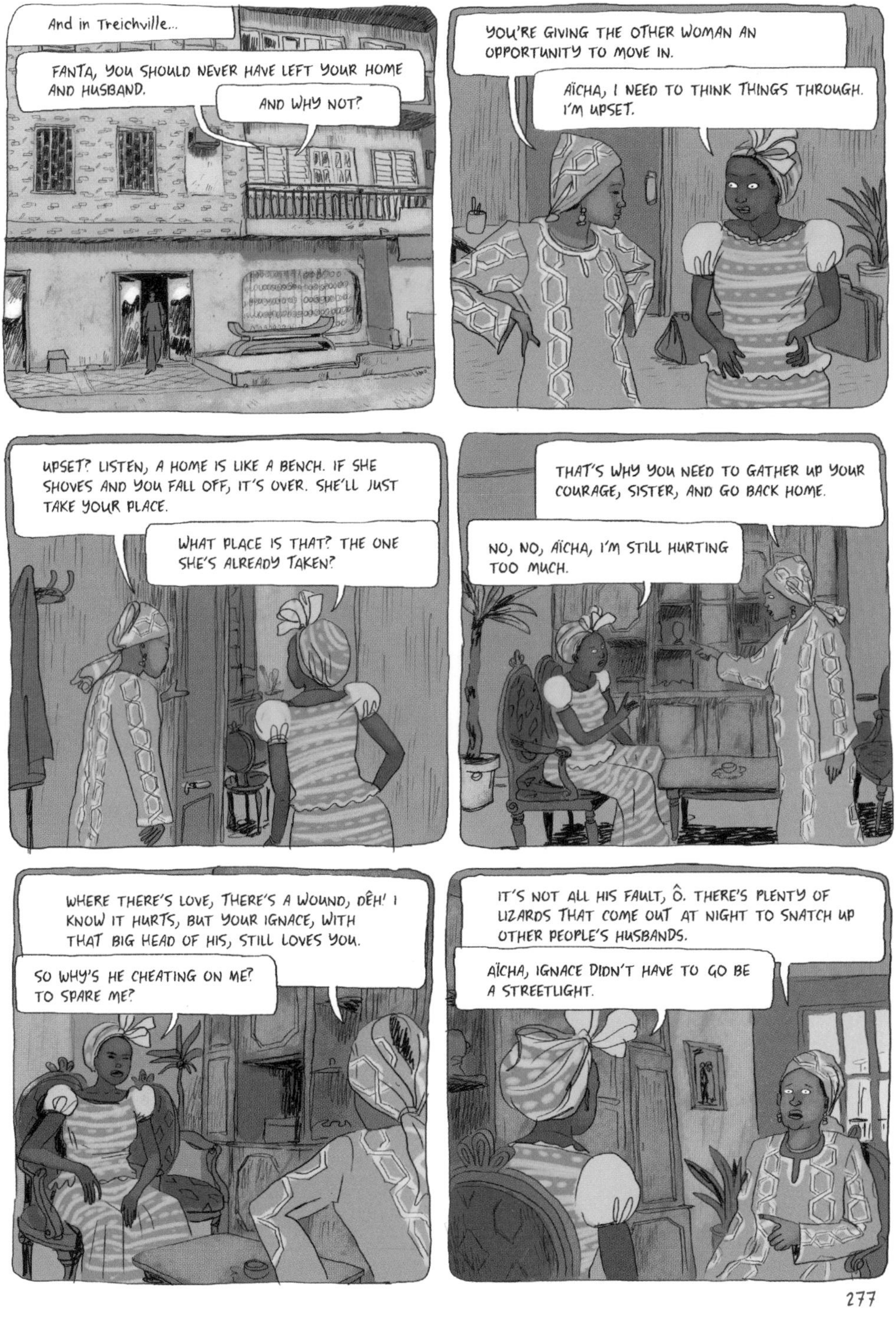
And in Treichville...
FANTA, YOU SHOULD NEVER HAVE LEFT YOUR HOME AND HUSBAND.
AND WHY NOT?
YOU'RE GIVING THE OTHER WOMAN AN OPPORTUNITY TO MOVE IN.
AÏCHA, I NEED TO THINK THINGS THROUGH. I'M UPSET.
UPSET? LISTEN, A HOME IS LIKE A BENCH. IF SHE SHOVES AND YOU FALL OFF, IT'S OVER. SHE'LL JUST TAKE YOUR PLACE.
WHAT PLACE IS THAT? THE ONE SHE'S ALREADY TAKEN?
THAT'S WHY YOU NEED TO GATHER UP YOUR COURAGE, SISTER, AND GO BACK HOME.
NO, NO, AÏCHA, I'M STILL HURTING TOO MUCH.
WHERE THERE'S LOVE, THERE'S A WOUND, DÊH! I KNOW IT HURTS, BUT YOUR IGNACE, WITH THAT BIG HEAD OF HIS, STILL LOVES YOU.
SO WHY'S HE CHEATING ON ME? TO SPARE ME?
IT'S NOT ALL HIS FAULT, Ô. THERE'S PLENTY OF LIZARDS THAT COME OUT AT NIGHT TO SNATCH UP OTHER PEOPLE'S HUSBANDS.
AÏCHA, IGNACE DIDN'T HAVE TO GO BE A STREETLIGHT.

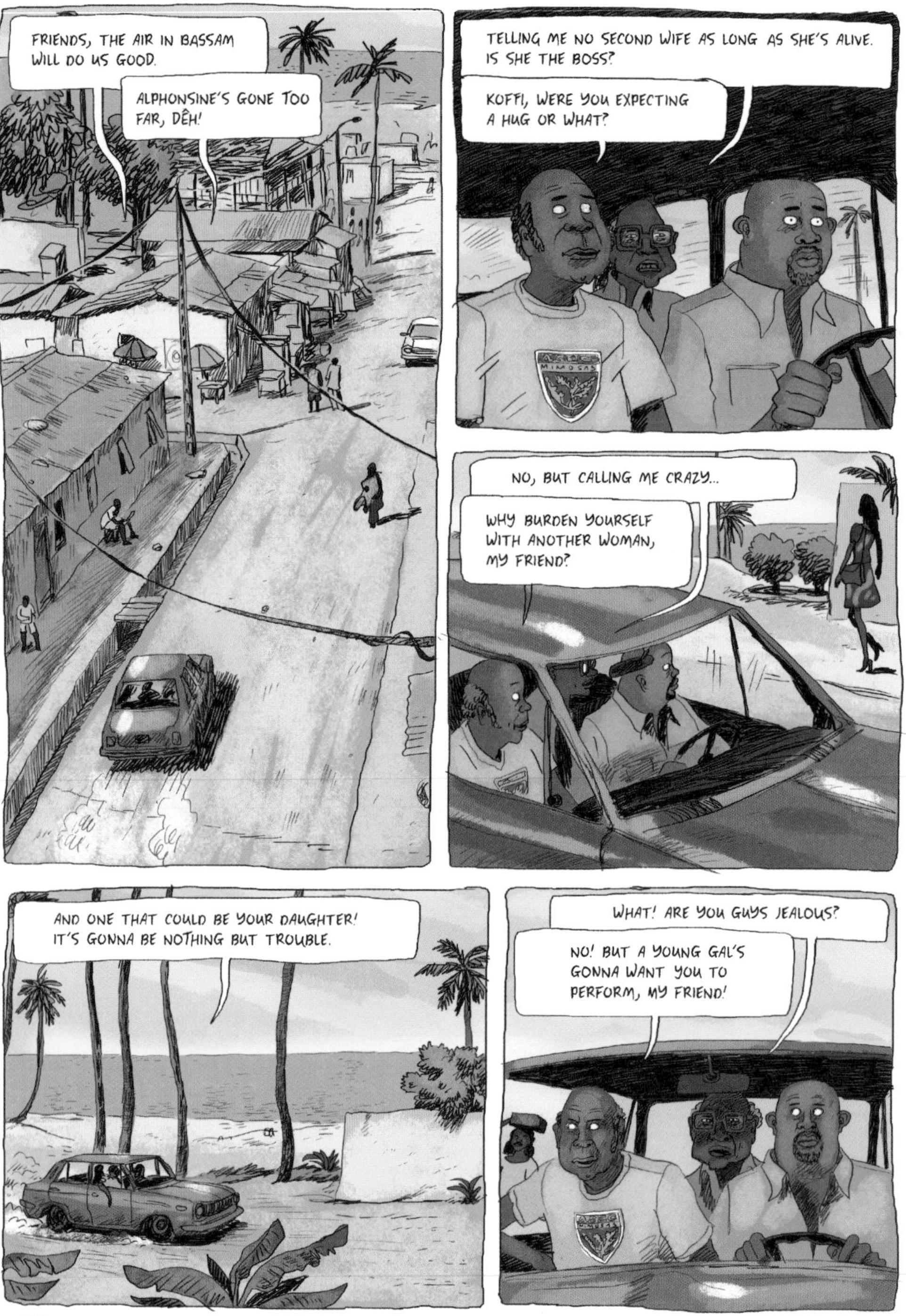
FRIENDS, THE AIR IN BASSAM WILL DO US GOOD.
ALPHONSINE'S GONE TOO FAR, DÊH!
TELLING ME NO SECOND WIFE AS LONG AS SHE'S ALIVE. IS SHE THE BOSS?
KOFFI, WERE YOU EXPECTING A HUG OR WHAT?
NO, BUT CALLING ME CRAZY...
WHY BURDEN YOURSELF WITH ANOTHER WOMAN, MY FRIEND?
AND ONE THAT COULD BE YOUR DAUGHTER! IT'S GONNA BE NOTHING BUT TROUBLE.
WHAT! ARE YOU GUYS JEALOUS?
NO! BUT A YOUNG GAL'S GONNA WANT YOU TO PERFORM, MY FRIEND!

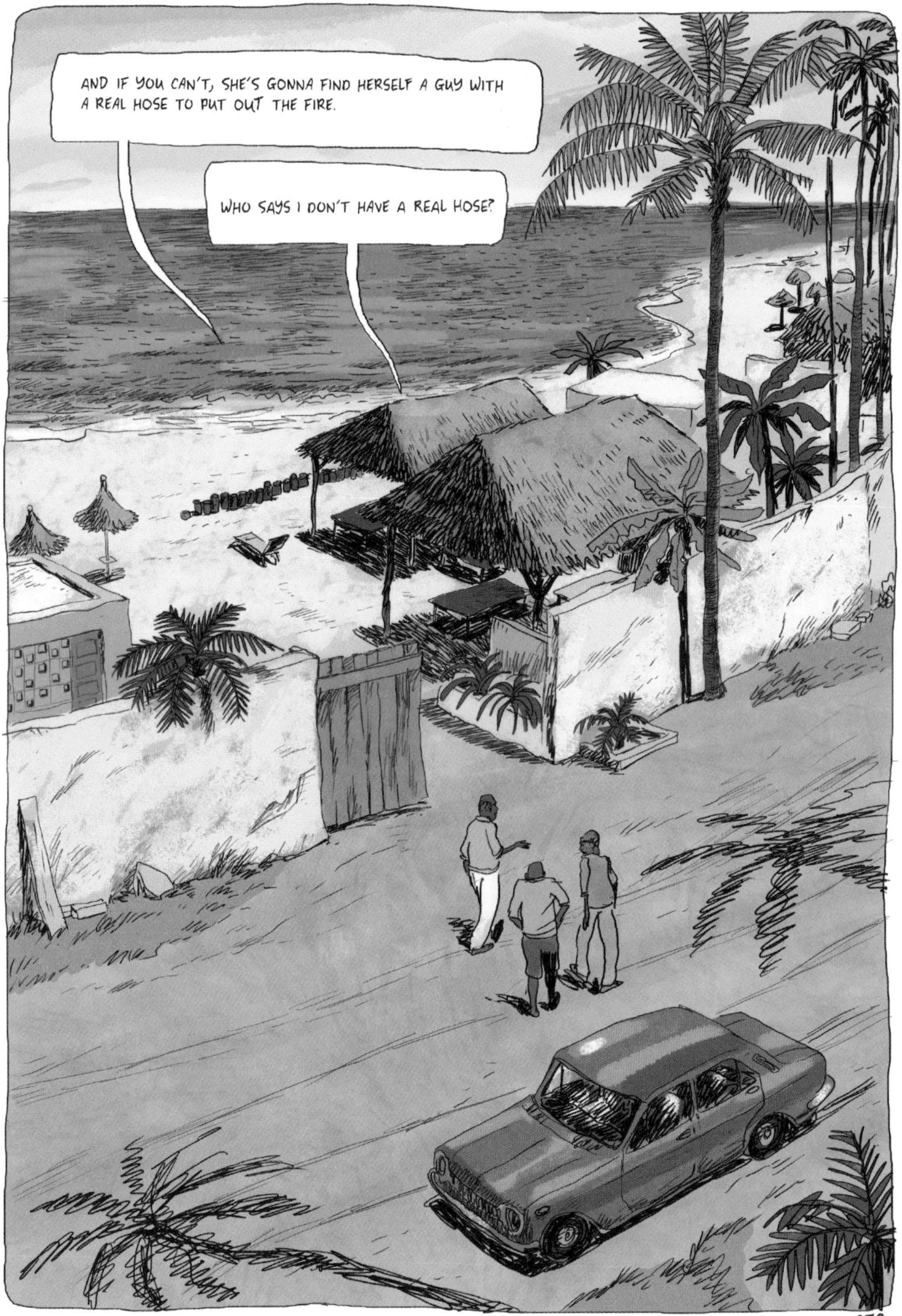
AND IF YOU CAN'T, SHE'S GONNA FIND HERSELF A GUY WITH A REAL HOSE TO PUT OUT THE FIRE.
WHO SAYS I DON'T HAVE A REAL HOSE?

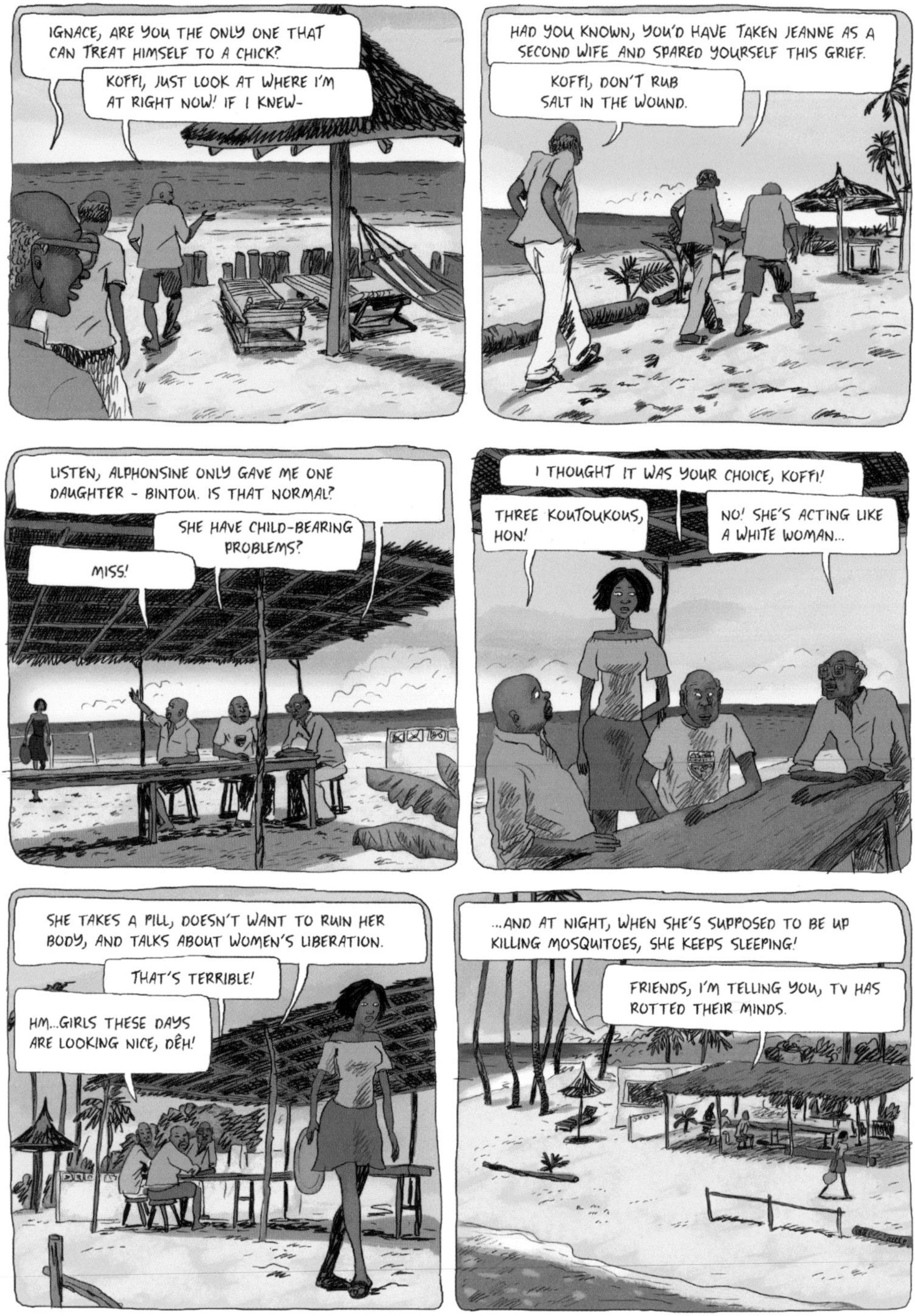
IGNACE, ARE YOU THE ONLY ONE THAT CAN TREAT HIMSELF TO A CHICK?
KOFFI, JUST LOOK AT WHERE I'M AT RIGHT NOW! IF I KNEW-
HAD YOU KNOWN, YOU'D HAVE TAKEN JEANNE AS A SECOND WIFE AND SPARED YOURSELF THIS GRIEF.
KOFFI, DON'T RUB SALT IN THE WOUND.
LISTEN, ALPHONSINE ONLY GAVE ME ONE DAUGHTER - BINTOU. IS THAT NORMAL?
SHE HAVE CHILD-BEARING PROBLEMS?
MISS!
I THOUGHT IT WAS YOUR CHOICE, KOFFI!
THREE KOUTOUKOUS, HON!
NO! SHE'S ACTING LIKE A WHITE WOMAN...
SHE TAKES A PILL, DOESN'T WANT TO RUIN HER BODY, AND TALKS ABOUT WOMEN'S LIBERATION.
THAT'S TERRIBLE!
HM...GIRLS THESE DAYS ARE LOOKING NICE, DÊH!
...AND AT NIGHT, WHEN SHE'S SUPPOSED TO BE UP KILLING MOSQUITOES, SHE KEEPS SLEEPING!
FRIENDS, I'M TELLING YOU, TV HAS ROTTED THEIR MINDS.

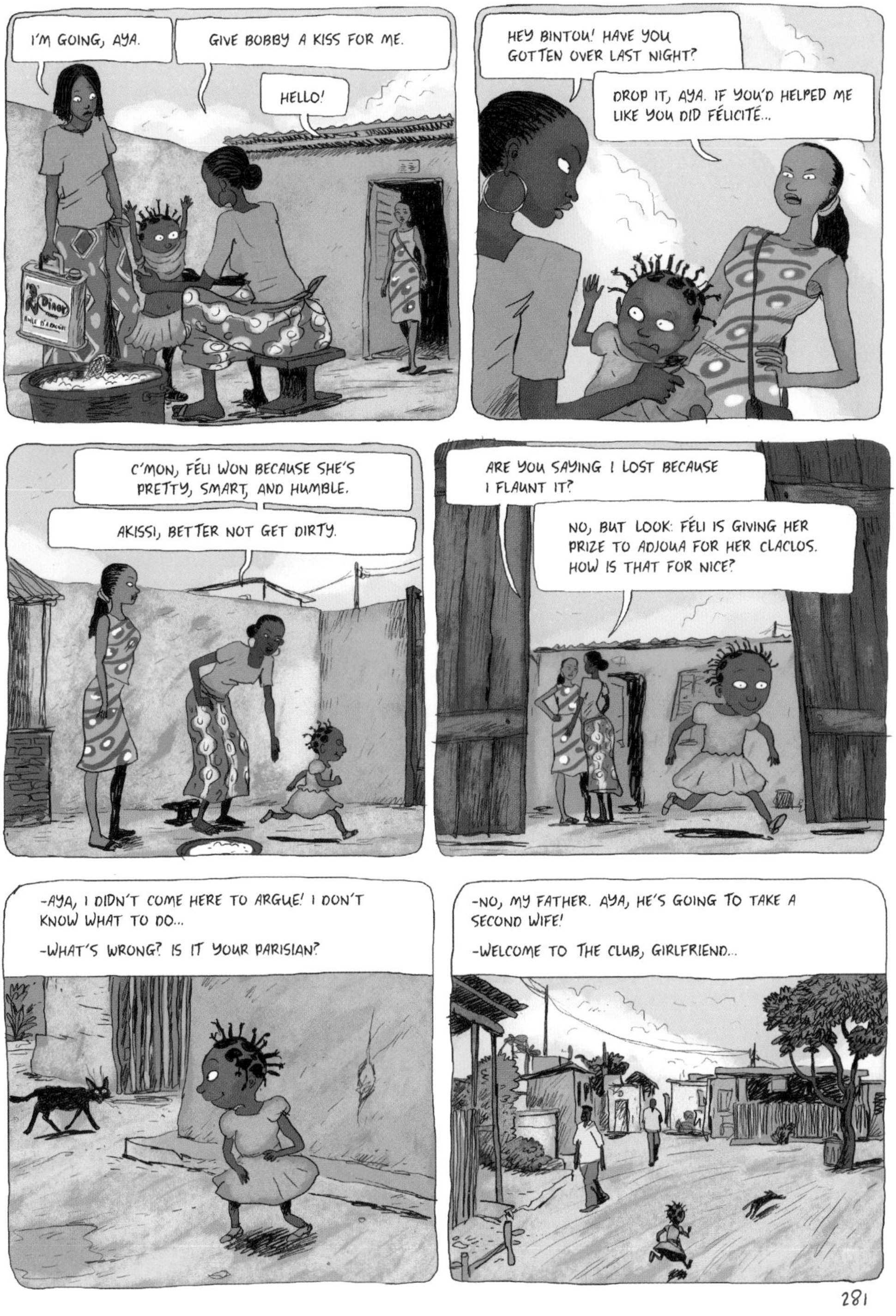
I'M GOING, AYA.
GIVE BOBBY A KISS FOR ME.
HELLO!
HEY BINTOU! HAVE YOU GOTTEN OVER LAST NIGHT?
DROP IT, AYA. IF YOU'D HELPED ME LIKE YOU DID FÉLICITÉ...
C'MON, FÉLI WON BECAUSE SHE'S PRETTY, SMART, AND HUMBLE.
AKISSI, BETTER NOT GET DIRTY.
ARE YOU SAYING I LOST BECAUSE I FLAUNT IT?
NO, BUT LOOK: FÉLI IS GIVING HER PRIZE TO ADJOUA FOR HER CLACLOS. HOW IS THAT FOR NICE?
-AYA, I DIDN'T COME HERE TO ARGUE! I DON'T KNOW WHAT TO DO...
-WHAT'S WRONG? IS IT YOUR PARISIAN?
-NO, MY FATHER. AYA, HE'S GOING TO TAKE A SECOND WIFE!
-WELCOME TO THE CLUB, GIRLFRIEND...

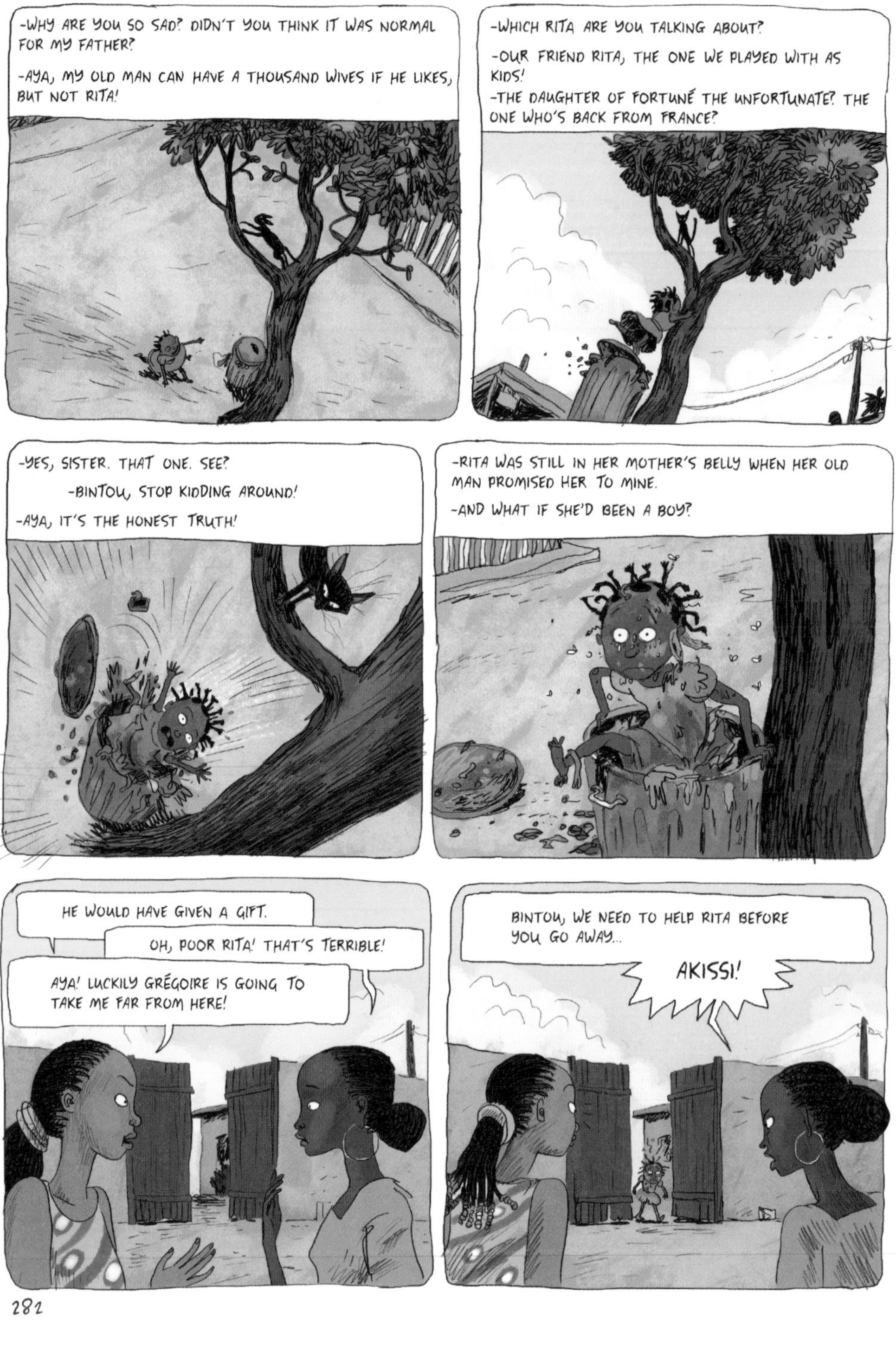
-WHY ARE YOU SO SAD? DIDN'T YOU THINK IT WAS NORMAL FOR MY FATHER?
-AYA, MY OLD MAN CAN HAVE A THOUSAND WIVES IF HE LIKES, BUT NOT RITA!
-WHICH RITA ARE YOU TALKING ABOUT?
-OUR FRIEND RITA, THE ONE WE PLAYED WITH AS KIDS!
-THE DAUGHTER OF FORTUNÉ THE UNFORTUNATE? THE ONE WHO'S BACK FROM FRANCE?
-YES, SISTER. THAT ONE. SEE?
-BINTOU, STOP KIDDING AROUND!
-AYA, IT'S THE HONEST TRUTH!
-RITA WAS STILL IN HER MOTHER'S BELLY WHEN HER OLD MAN PROMISED HER TO MINE.
-AND WHAT IF SHE'D BEEN A BOY?
HE WOULD HAVE GIVEN A GIFT.
OH, POOR RITA! THAT'S TERRIBLE!
AYA! LUCKILY GRÉGOIRE IS GOING TO TAKE ME FAR FROM HERE!
BINTOU, WE NEED TO HELP RITA BEFORE YOU GO AWAY...
AKISSI!

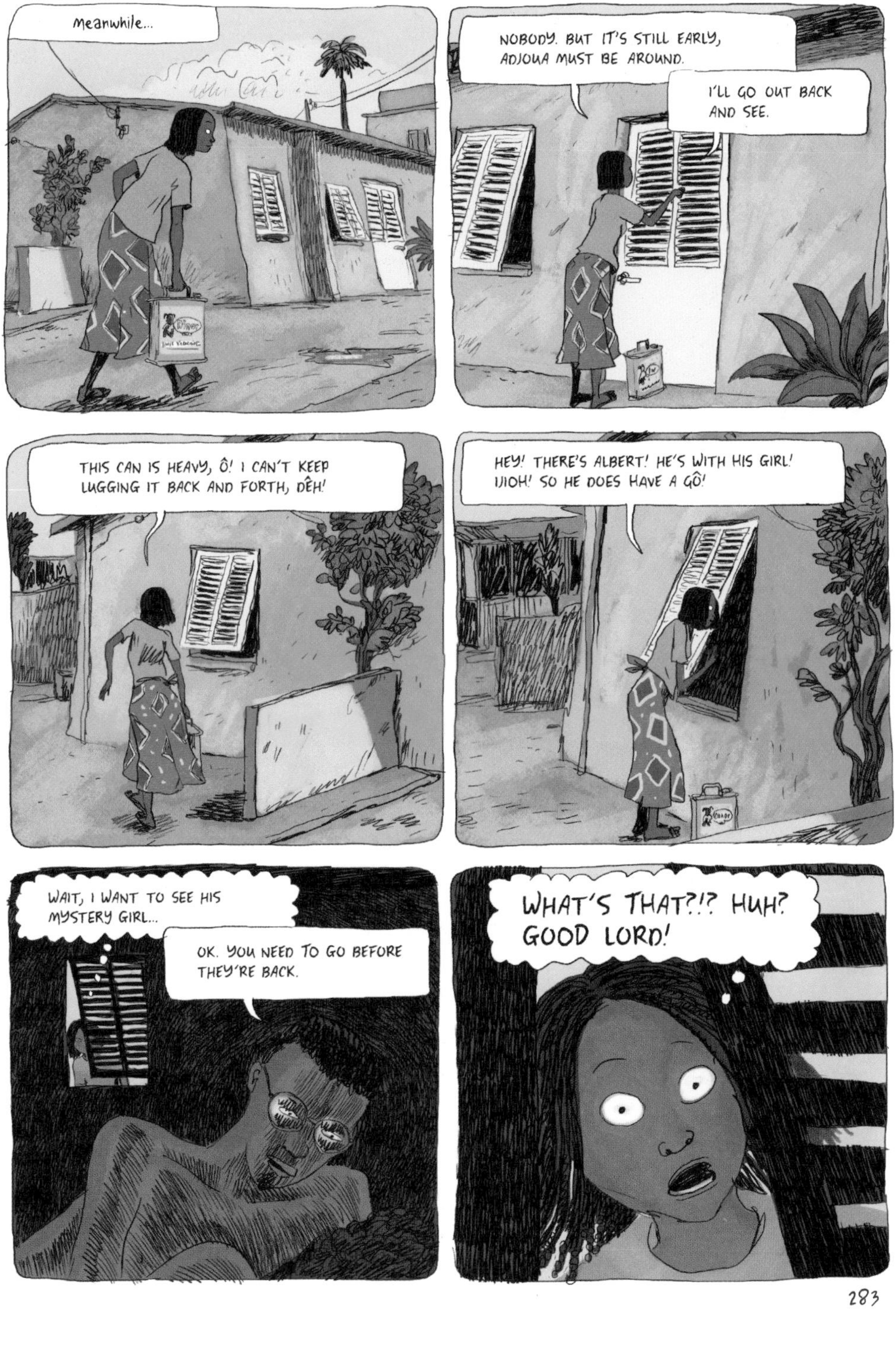
Meanwhile...
NOBODY. BUT IT'S STILL EARLY, ADJOUA MUST BE AROUND.
I'LL GO OUT BACK AND SEE.
THIS CAN IS HEAVY, Ô! I CAN'T KEEP LUGGING IT BACK AND FORTH, DÊH!
HEY! THERE'S ALBERT! HE'S WITH HIS GIRL! IJIOH! SO HE DOES HAVE A GÔ!
WAIT, I WANT TO SEE HIS MYSTERY GIRL...
OK. YOU NEED TO GO BEFORE THEY'RE BACK.
WHAT'S THAT?!? HUH? GOOD LORD!

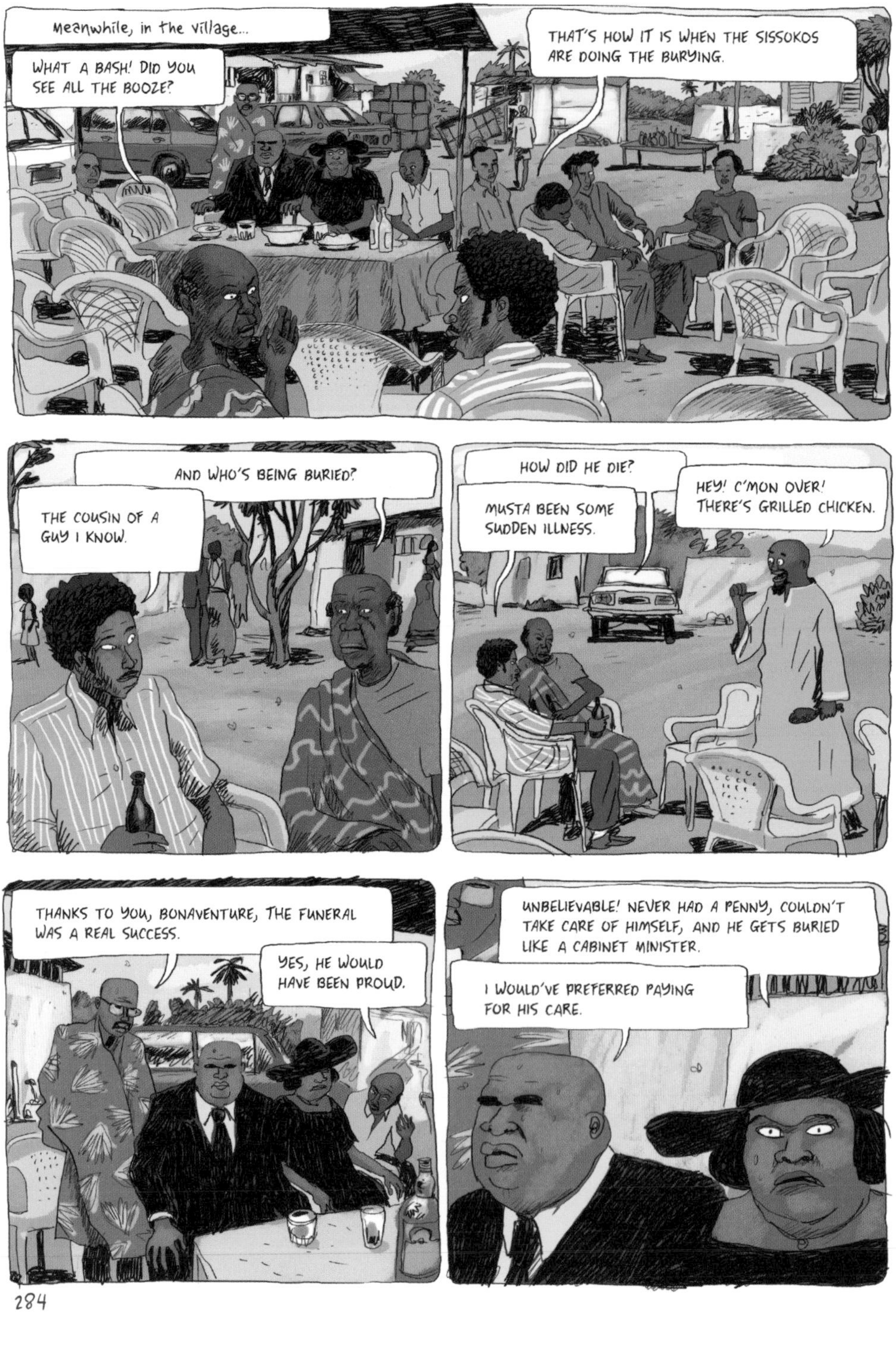
Meanwhile, in the village...
WHAT A BASH! DID YOU SEE ALL THE BOOZE?
THAT'S HOW IT IS WHEN THE SISSOKOS ARE DOING THE BURYING.
AND WHO'S BEING BURIED?
THE COUSIN OF A GUY I KNOW.
HOW DID HE DIE?
MUSTA BEEN SOME SUDDEN ILLNESS.
HEY! C'MON OVER! THERE'S GRILLED CHICKEN.
THANKS TO YOU, BONAVENTURE, THE FUNERAL WAS A REAL SUCCESS.
YES, HE WOULD HAVE BEEN PROUD.
UNBELIEVABLE! NEVER HAD A PENNY, COULDN'T TAKE CARE OF HIMSELF, AND HE GETS BURIED LIKE A CABINET MINISTER.
I WOULD'VE PREFERRED PAYING FOR HIS CARE.

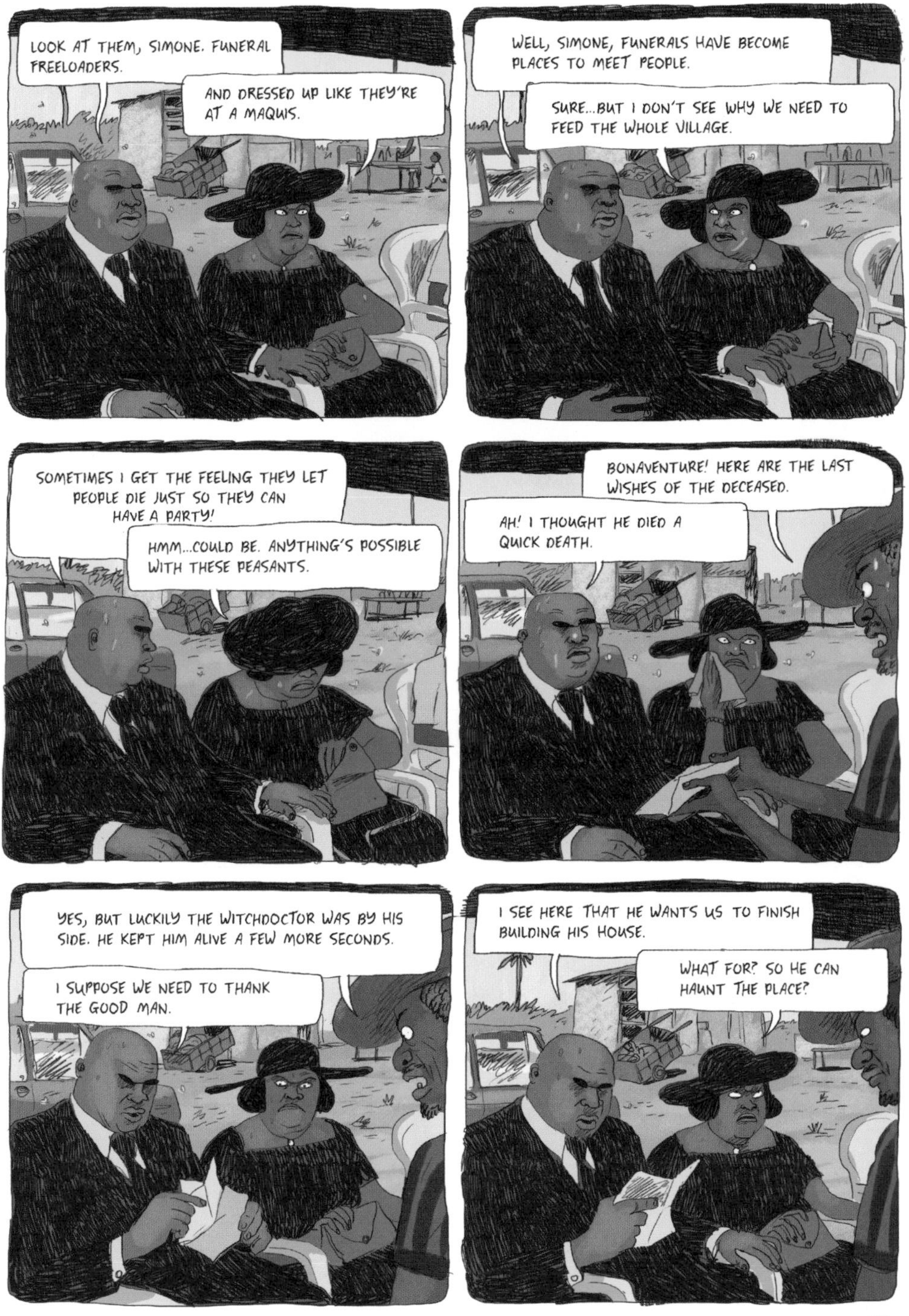
LOOK AT THEM, SIMONE. FUNERAL FREELOADERS.
AND DRESSED UP LIKE THEY'RE AT A MAQUIS.
WELL, SIMONE, FUNERALS HAVE BECOME PLACES TO MEET PEOPLE.
SURE...BUT I DON'T SEE WHY WE NEED TO FEED THE WHOLE VILLAGE.
SOMETIMES I GET THE FEELING THEY LET PEOPLE DIE JUST SO THEY CAN HAVE A PARTY!
HMM...COULD BE. ANYTHING'S POSSIBLE WITH THESE PEASANTS.
BONAVENTURE! HERE ARE THE LAST WISHES OF THE DECEASED.
AH! I THOUGHT HE DIED A QUICK DEATH.
YES, BUT LUCKILY THE WITCHDOCTOR WAS BY HIS SIDE. HE KEPT HIM ALIVE A FEW MORE SECONDS.
I SUPPOSE WE NEED TO THANK THE GOOD MAN.
I SEE HERE THAT HE WANTS US TO FINISH BUILDING HIS HOUSE.
WHAT FOR? SO HE CAN HAUNT THE PLACE?

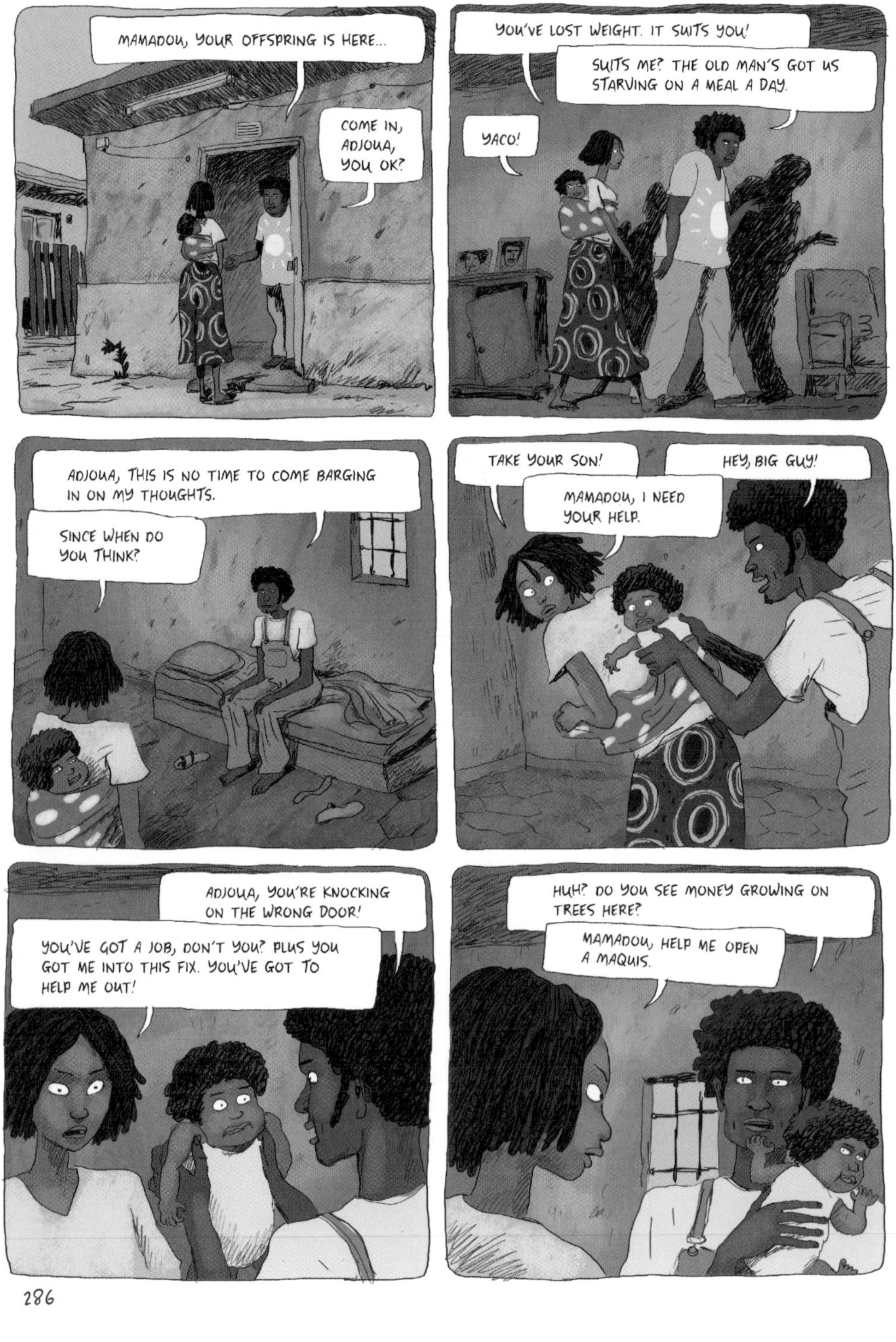
MAMADOU, YOUR OFFSPRING IS HERE...
COME IN, ADJOUA, YOU OK?
YOU'VE LOST WEIGHT. IT SUITS YOU!
SUITS ME? THE OLD MAN'S GOT US STARVING ON A MEAL A DAY.
YACO!
ADJOUA, THIS IS NO TIME TO COME BARGING IN ON MY THOUGHTS.
SINCE WHEN DO YOU THINK?
TAKE YOUR SON!
HEY, BIG GUY!
MAMADOU, I NEED YOUR HELP.
ADJOUA, YOU'RE KNOCKING ON THE WRONG DOOR!
YOU'VE GOT A JOB, DON'T YOU? PLUS YOU GOT ME INTO THIS FIX. YOU'VE GOT TO HELP ME OUT!
HUH? DO YOU SEE MONEY GROWING ON TREES HERE?
MAMADOU, HELP ME OPEN A MAQUIS.

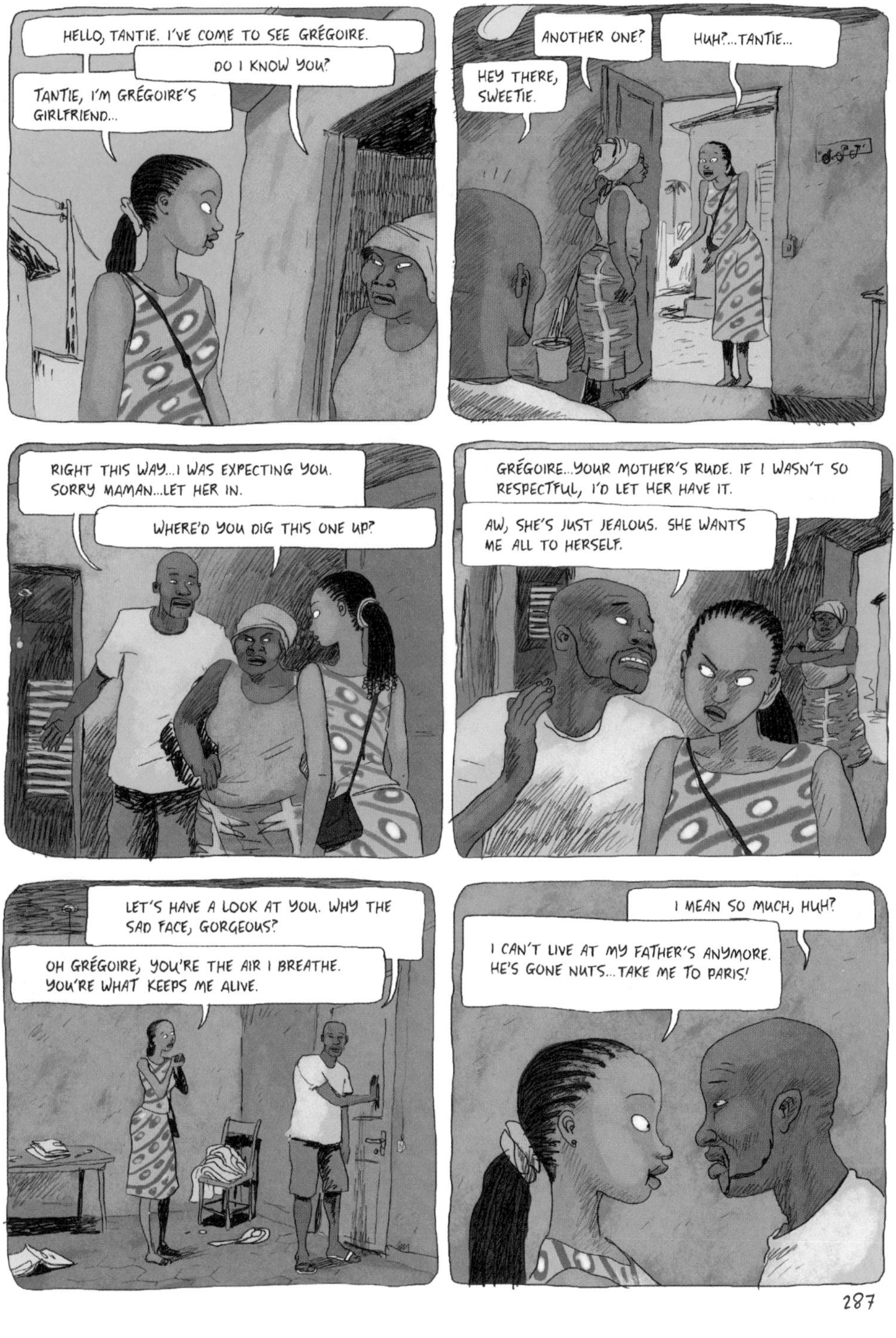
HELLO, TANTIE. I'VE COME TO SEE GRÉGOIRE.
DO I KNOW YOU?
TANTIE, I'M GRÉGOIRE'S GIRLFRIEND...
HEY THERE, SWEETIE.
ANOTHER ONE?
HUH?...TANTIE...
RIGHT THIS WAY...I WAS EXPECTING YOU. SORRY MAMAN...LET HER IN.
WHERE'D YOU DIG THIS ONE UP?
GRÉGOIRE...YOUR MOTHER'S RUDE. IF I WASN'T SO RESPECTFUL, I'D LET HER HAVE IT.
AW, SHE'S JUST JEALOUS. SHE WANTS ME ALL TO HERSELF.
LET'S HAVE A LOOK AT YOU. WHY THE SAD FACE, GORGEOUS?
OH GRÉGOIRE, YOU'RE THE AIR I BREATHE. YOU'RE WHAT KEEPS ME ALIVE.
I MEAN SO MUCH, HUH?
I CAN'T LIVE AT MY FATHER'S ANYMORE. HE'S GONE NUTS...TAKE ME TO PARIS!

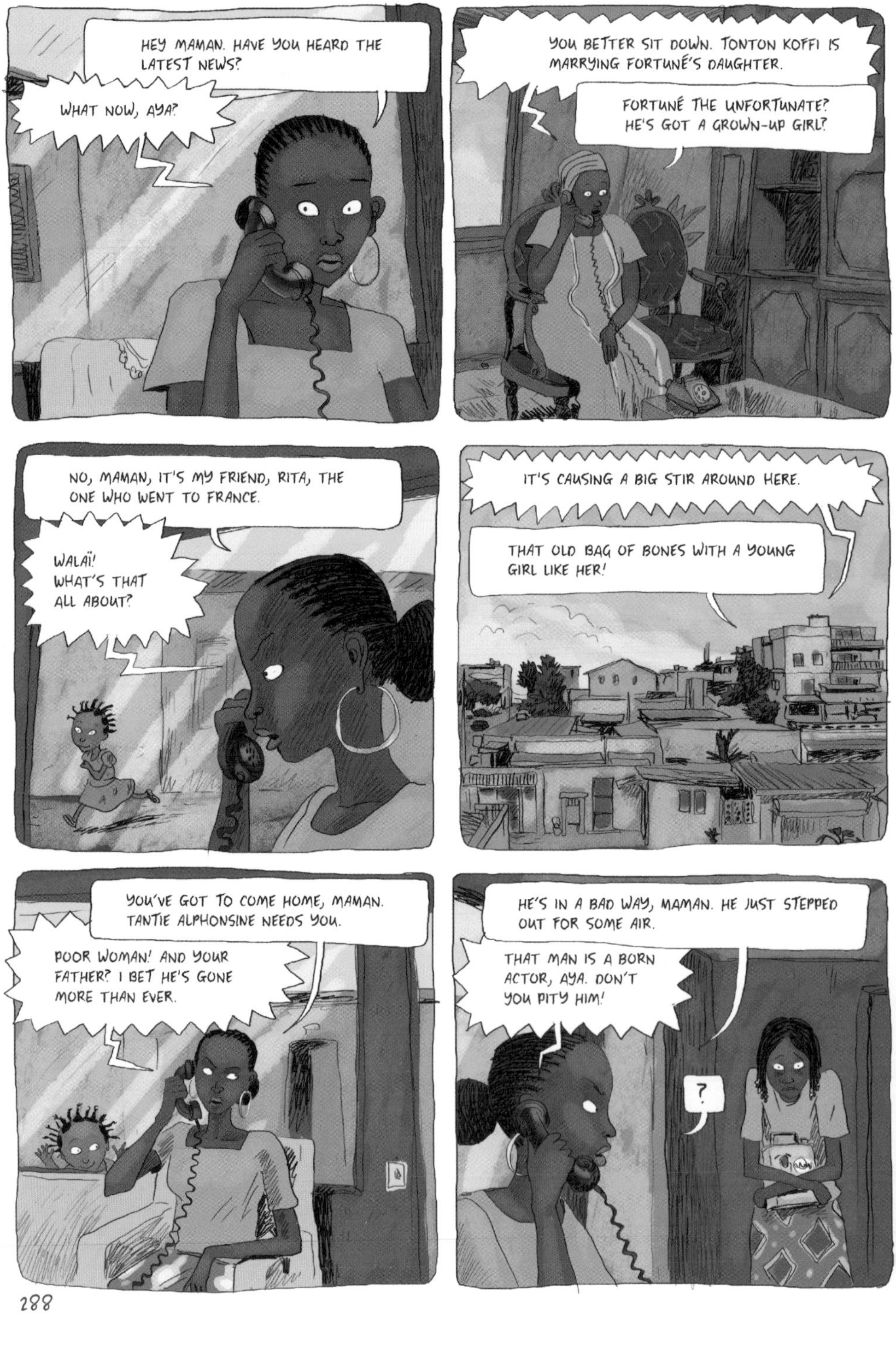
HEY MAMAN. HAVE YOU HEARD THE LATEST NEWS?
WHAT NOW, AYA?
YOU BETTER SIT DOWN. TONTON KOFFI IS MARRYING FORTUNÉ'S DAUGHTER.
FORTUNÉ THE UNFORTUNATE? HE'S GOT A GROWN-UP GIRL?
NO, MAMAN, IT'S MY FRIEND, RITA, THE ONE WHO WENT TO FRANCE.
WALAÏ! WHAT'S THAT ALL ABOUT?
IT'S CAUSING A BIG STIR AROUND HERE.
THAT OLD BAG OF BONES WITH A YOUNG GIRL LIKE HER!
YOU'VE GOT TO COME HOME, MAMAN. TANTIE ALPHONSINE NEEDS YOU.
POOR WOMAN! AND YOUR FATHER? I BET HE'S GONE MORE THAN EVER.
HE'S IN A BAD WAY, MAMAN. HE JUST STEPPED OUT FOR SOME AIR.
THAT MAN IS A BORN ACTOR, AYA. DON'T YOU PITY HIM!
?

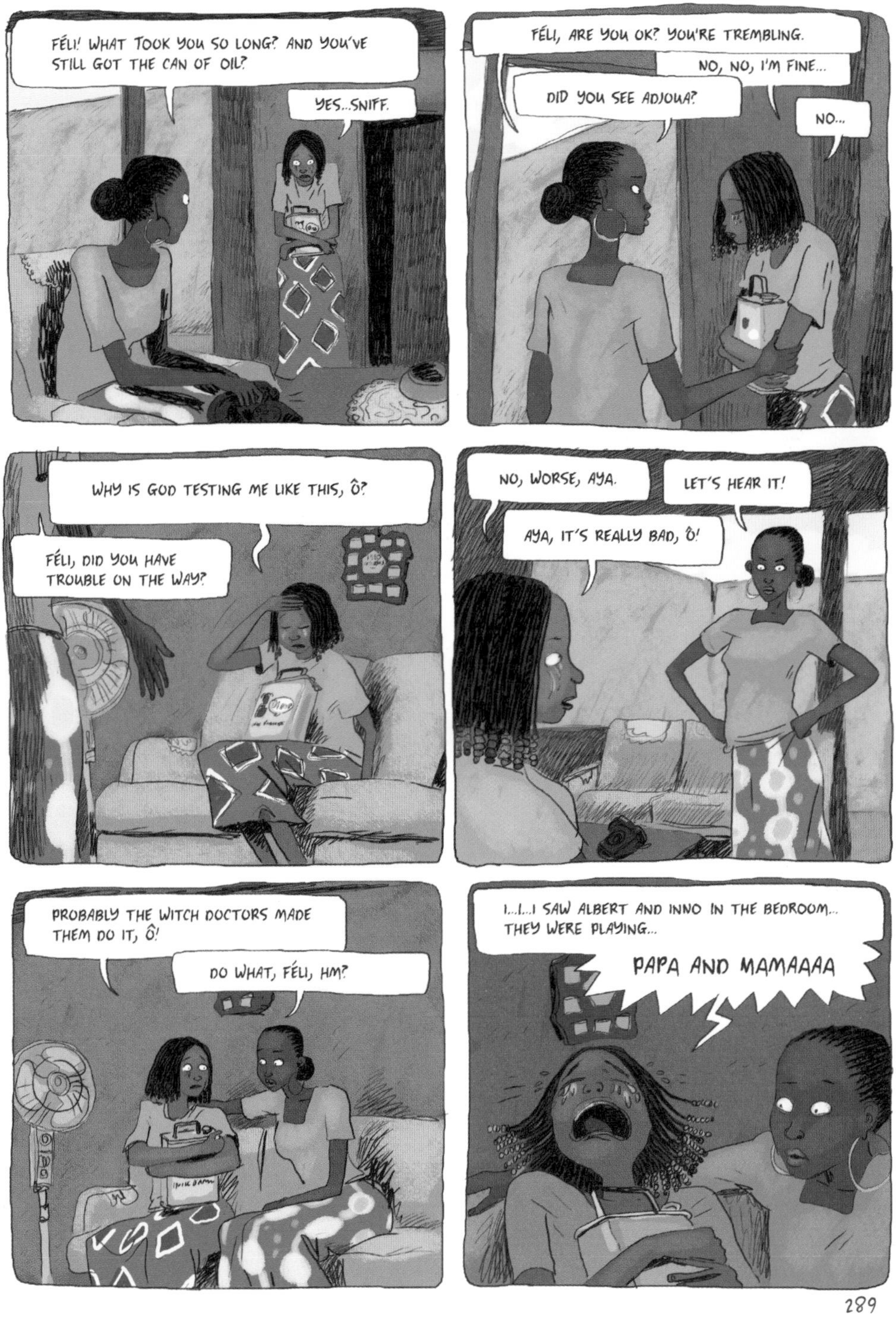
FÉLI! WHAT TOOK YOU SO LONG? AND YOU'VE STILL GOT THE CAN OF OIL?
YES...SNIFF.
FÉLI, ARE YOU OK? YOU'RE TREMBLING.
NO, NO, I'M FINE...
DID YOU SEE ADJOUA?
NO...
WHY IS GOD TESTING ME LIKE THIS, Ô?
FÉLI, DID YOU HAVE TROUBLE ON THE WAY?
NO, WORSE, AYA.
LET'S HEAR IT!
AYA, IT'S REALLY BAD, Ô!
PROBABLY THE WITCH DOCTORS MADE THEM DO IT, Ô!
DO WHAT, FÉLI, HM?
I...I...I SAW ALBERT AND INNO IN THE BEDROOM... THEY WERE PLAYING...
PAPA AND MAMAAAA

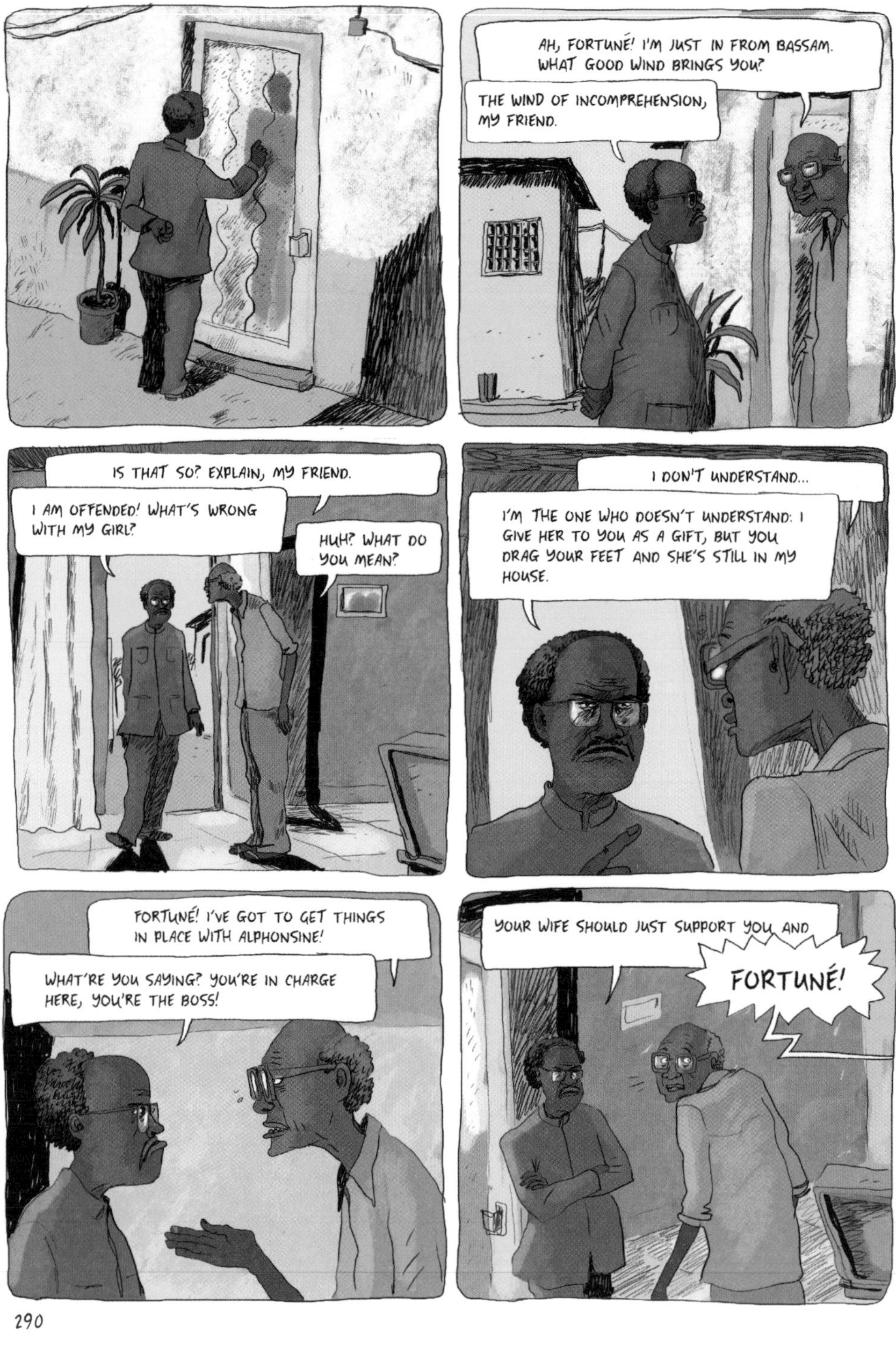
AH, FORTUNÉ! I'M JUST IN FROM BASSAM. WHAT GOOD WIND BRINGS YOU?
THE WIND OF INCOMPREHENSION, MY FRIEND.
IS THAT SO? EXPLAIN, MY FRIEND.
I AM OFFENDED! WHAT'S WRONG WITH MY GIRL?
HUH? WHAT DO YOU MEAN?
I DON'T UNDERSTAND...
I'M THE ONE WHO DOESN'T UNDERSTAND: I GIVE HER TO YOU AS A GIFT, BUT YOU DRAG YOUR FEET AND SHE'S STILL IN MY HOUSE.
FORTUNÉ! I'VE GOT TO GET THINGS IN PLACE WITH ALPHONSINE!
WHAT'RE YOU SAYING? YOU'RE IN CHARGE HERE, YOU'RE THE BOSS!
YOUR WIFE SHOULD JUST SUPPORT YOU AND
FORTUNÉ!

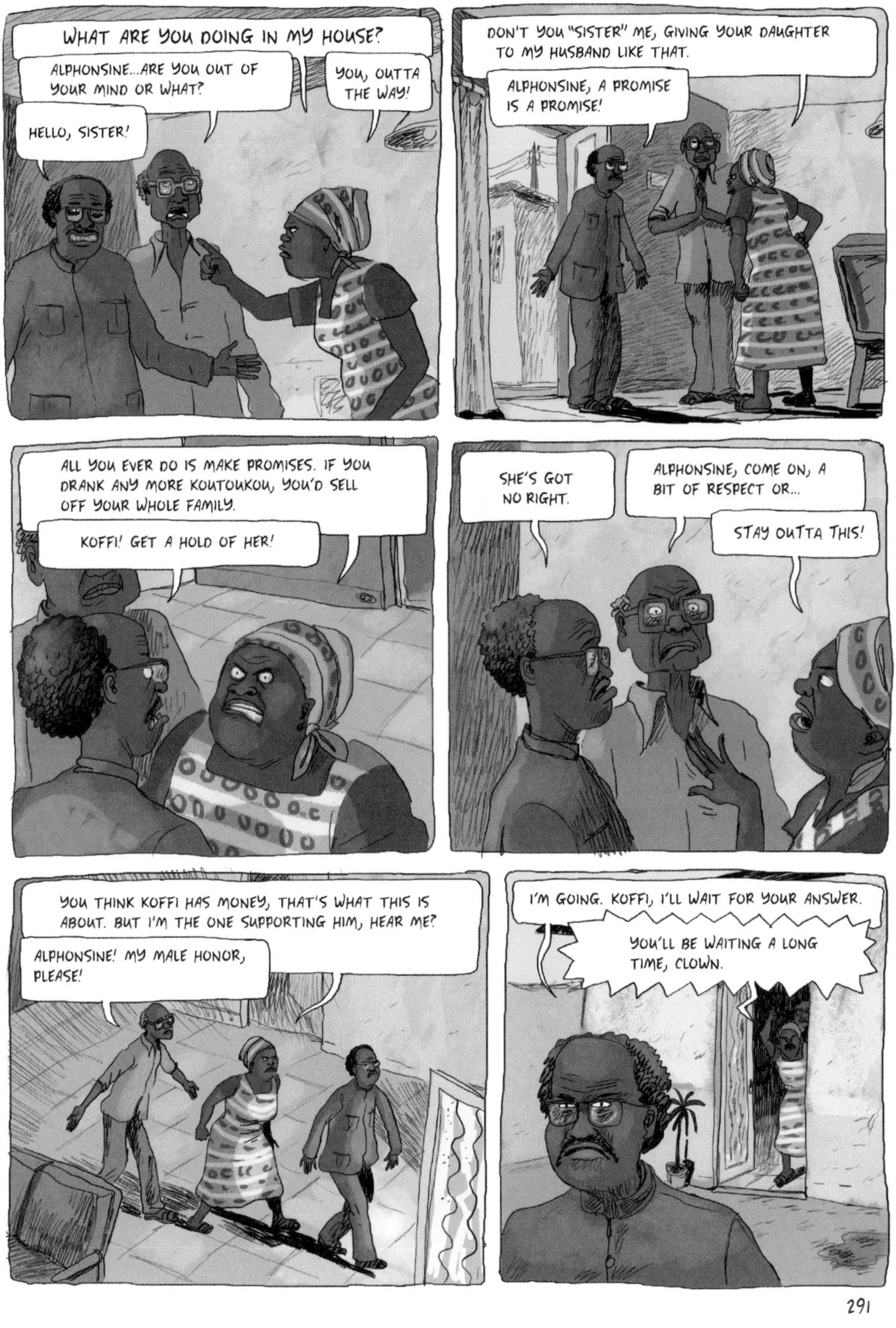
WHAT ARE YOU DOING IN MY HOUSE?
ALPHONSINE...ARE YOU OUT OF YOUR MIND OR WHAT?
YOU, OUTTA THE WAY!
HELLO, SISTER!
DON'T YOU "SISTER" ME, GIVING YOUR DAUGHTER TO MY HUSBAND LIKE THAT.
ALPHONSINE, A PROMISE IS A PROMISE!
ALL YOU EVER DO IS MAKE PROMISES. IF YOU DRANK ANY MORE KOUTOUKOU, YOU'D SELL OFF YOUR WHOLE FAMILY.
KOFFI! GET A HOLD OF HER!
SHE'S GOT NO RIGHT.
ALPHONSINE, COME ON, A BIT OF RESPECT OR...
STAY OUTTA THIS!
YOU THINK KOFFI HAS MONEY, THAT'S WHAT THIS IS ABOUT. BUT I'M THE ONE SUPPORTING HIM, HEAR ME?
ALPHONSINE! MY MALE HONOR, PLEASE!
I'M GOING. KOFFI, I'LL WAIT FOR YOUR ANSWER.
YOU'LL BE WAITING A LONG TIME, CLOWN.

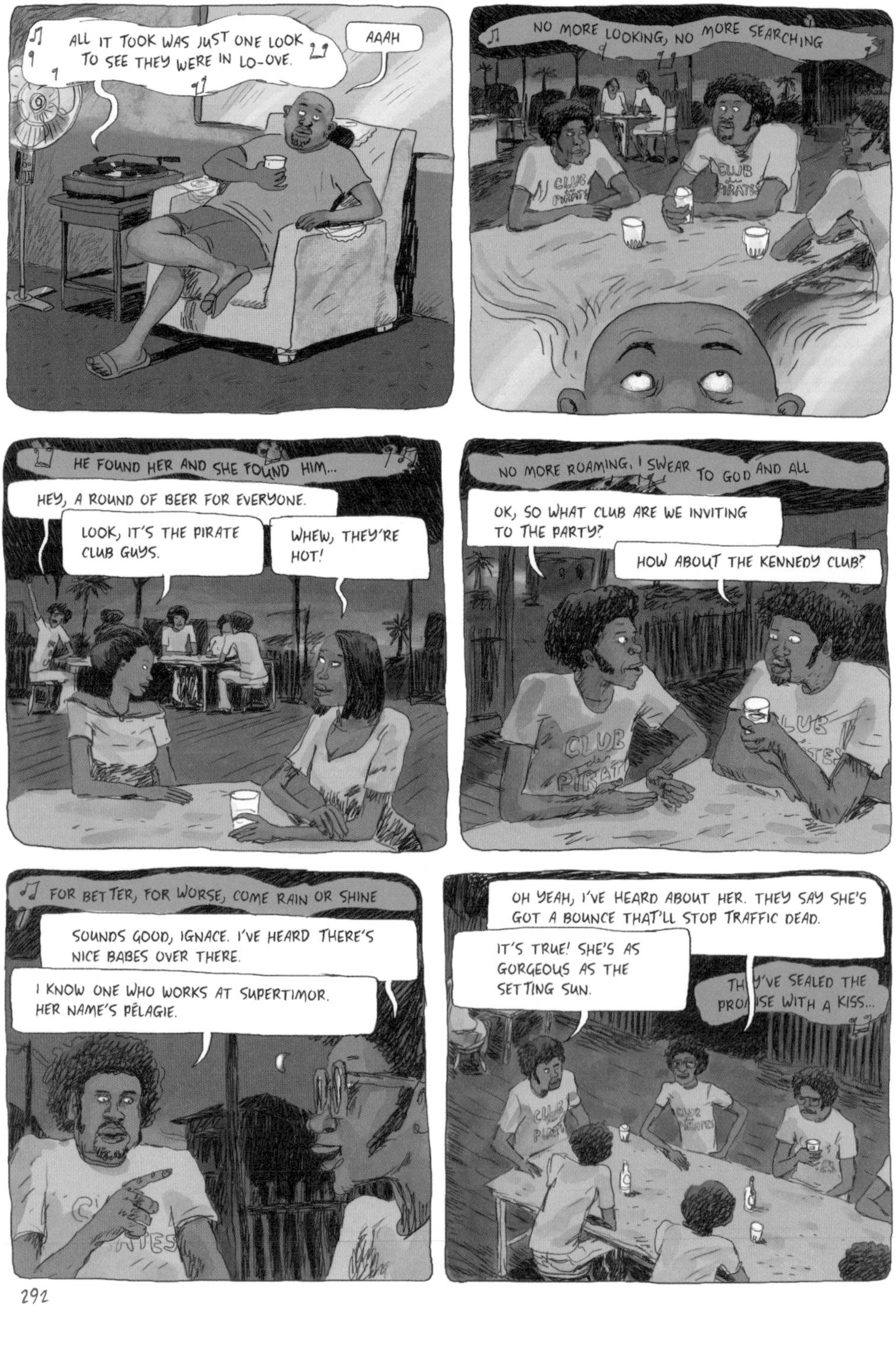
ALL IT TOOK WAS JUST ONE LOOK TO SEE THEY WERE IN LO-OVE.
AAAH
NO MORE LOOKING, NO MORE SEARCHING
HE FOUND HER AND SHE FOUND HIM...
HEY, A ROUND OF BEER FOR EVERYONE.
LOOK, IT'S THE PIRATE CLUB GUYS.
WHEW, THEY'RE HOT!
NO MORE ROAMING, I SWEAR TO GOD AND ALL
OK, SO WHAT CLUB ARE WE INVITING TO THE PARTY?
HOW ABOUT THE KENNEDY CLUB?
CLUB PIRATES
FOR BETTER, FOR WORSE, COME RAIN OR SHINE
SOUNDS GOOD, IGNACE. I'VE HEARD THERE'S NICE BABES OVER THERE.
I KNOW ONE WHO WORKS AT SUPERTIMOR. HER NAME'S PÉLAGIE.
OH YEAH, I'VE HEARD ABOUT HER. THEY SAY SHE'S GOT A BOUNCE THAT'LL STOP TRAFFIC DEAD.
IT'S TRUE! SHE'S AS GORGEOUS AS THE SETTING SUN.
THEY'VE SEALED THE PROMISE WITH A KISS...

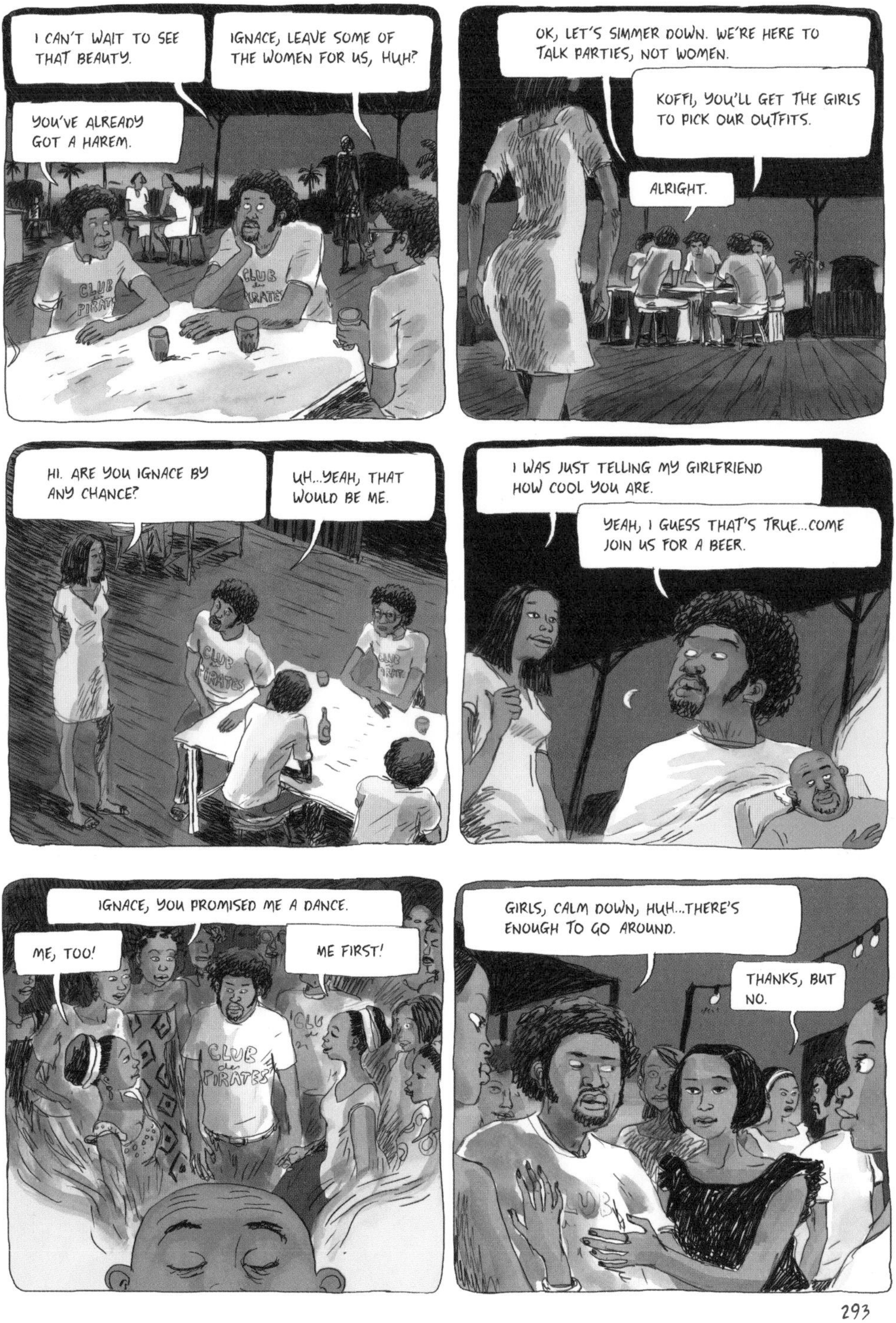
I CAN'T WAIT TO SEE THAT BEAUTY.
IGNACE, LEAVE SOME OF THE WOMEN FOR US, HUH?
YOU'VE ALREADY GOT A HAREM.
CLUB des PIRATES
OK, LET'S SIMMER DOWN. WE'RE HERE TO TALK PARTIES, NOT WOMEN.
KOFFI, YOU'LL GET THE GIRLS TO PICK OUR OUTFITS.
ALRIGHT.
HI. ARE YOU IGNACE BY ANY CHANCE?
UH...YEAH, THAT WOULD BE ME.
I WAS JUST TELLING MY GIRLFRIEND HOW COOL YOU ARE.
YEAH, I GUESS THAT'S TRUE...COME JOIN US FOR A BEER.
IGNACE, YOU PROMISED ME A DANCE.
ME, TOO!
ME FIRST!
GIRLS, CALM DOWN, HUH...THERE'S ENOUGH TO GO AROUND.
THANKS, BUT NO.

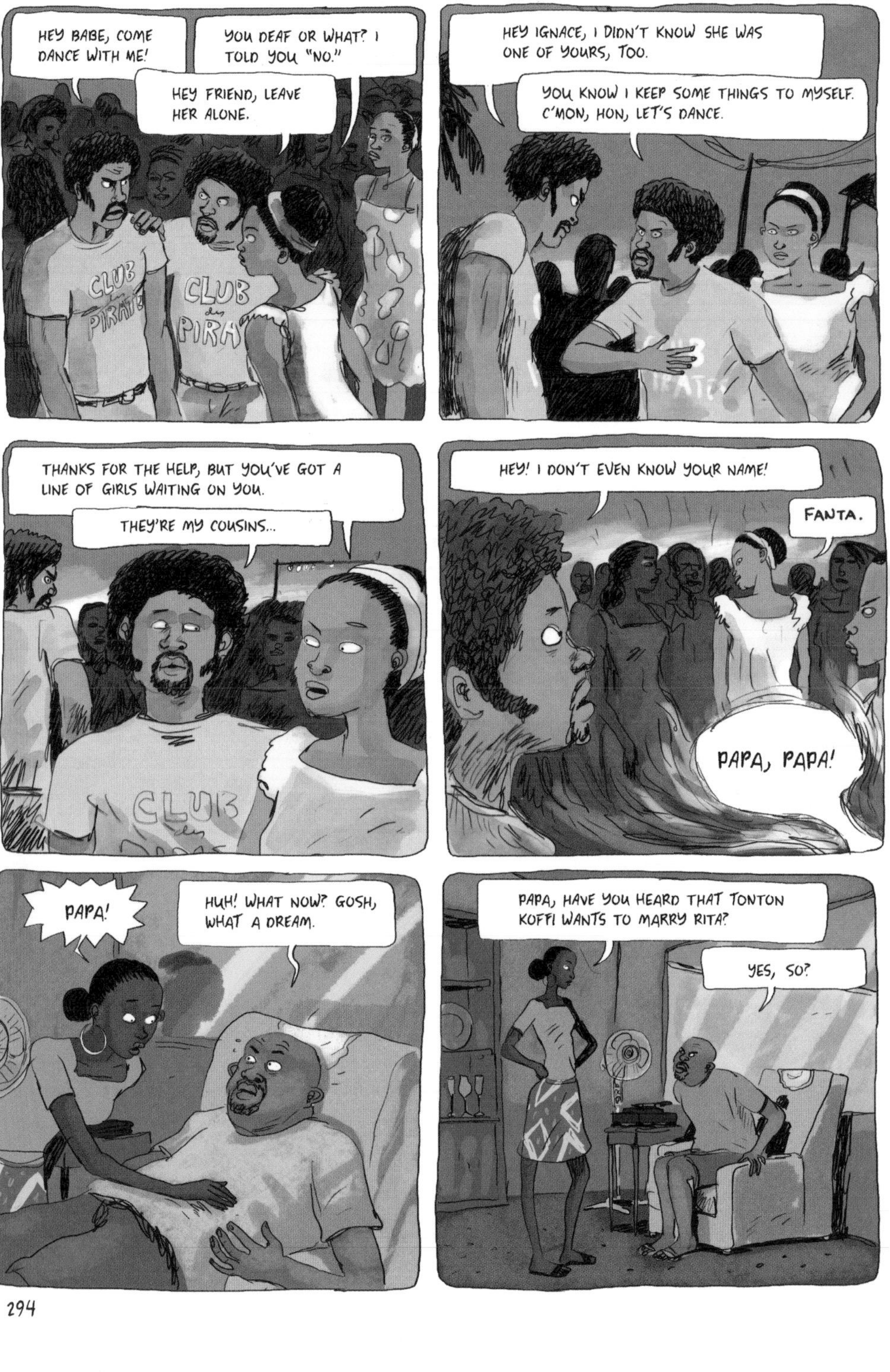
HEY BABE, COME DANCE WITH ME!
YOU DEAF OR WHAT? I TOLD YOU "NO."
HEY FRIEND, LEAVE HER ALONE.
CLUB des PIRATES
HEY IGNACE, I DIDN'T KNOW SHE WAS ONE OF YOURS, TOO.
YOU KNOW I KEEP SOME THINGS TO MYSELF. C'MON, HON, LET'S DANCE.
THANKS FOR THE HELP, BUT YOU'VE GOT A LINE OF GIRLS WAITING ON YOU.
THEY'RE MY COUSINS...
HEY! I DON'T EVEN KNOW YOUR NAME!
FANTA.
PAPA, PAPA!
PAPA!
HUH! WHAT NOW? GOSH, WHAT A DREAM.
PAPA, HAVE YOU HEARD THAT TONTON KOFFI WANTS TO MARRY RITA?
YES, SO?

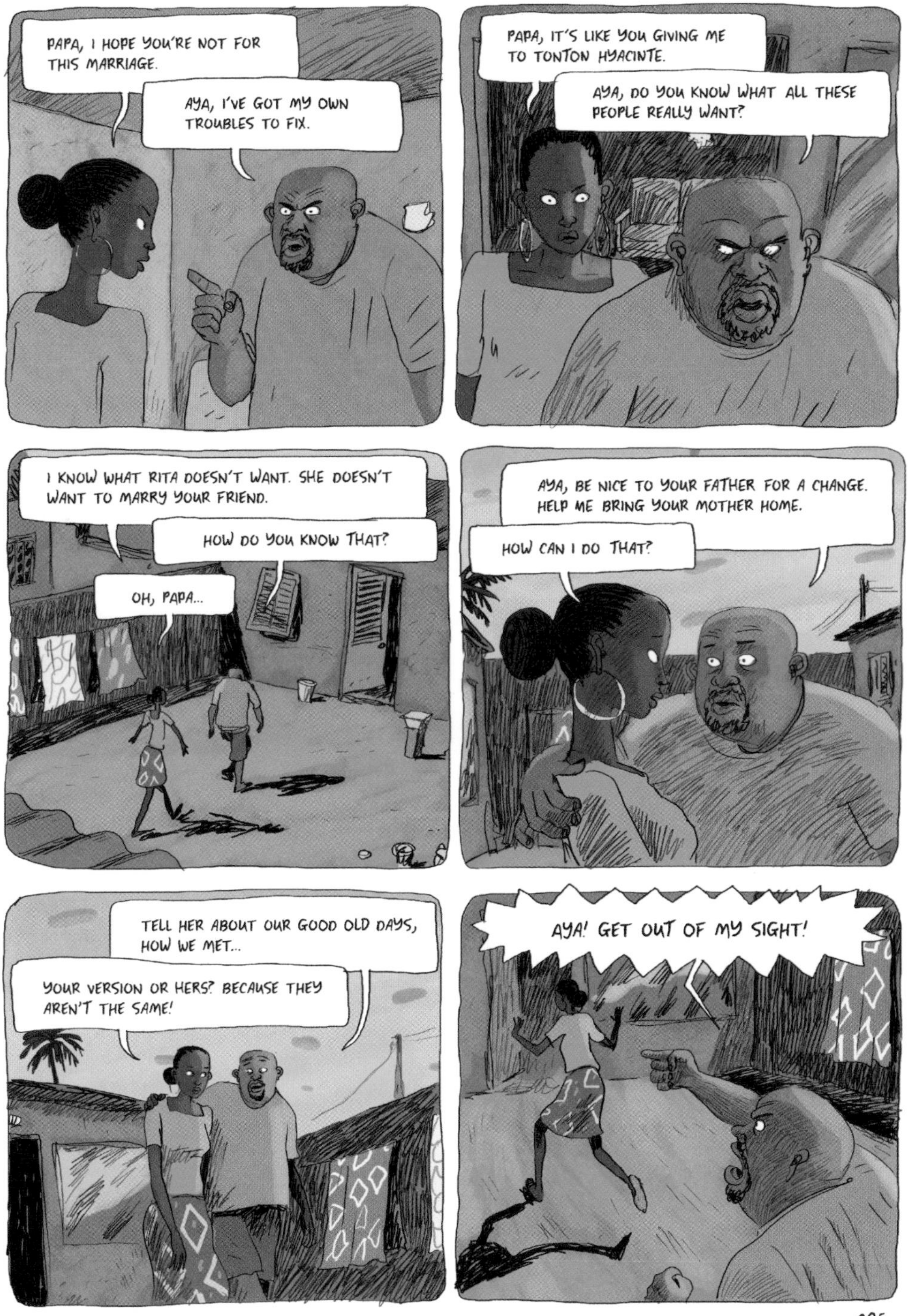
PAPA, I HOPE YOU'RE NOT FOR THIS MARRIAGE.
AYA, I'VE GOT MY OWN TROUBLES TO FIX.
PAPA, IT'S LIKE YOU GIVING ME TO TONTON HYACINTE.
AYA, DO YOU KNOW WHAT ALL THESE PEOPLE REALLY WANT?
I KNOW WHAT RITA DOESN'T WANT. SHE DOESN'T WANT TO MARRY YOUR FRIEND.
HOW DO YOU KNOW THAT?
OH, PAPA...
AYA, BE NICE TO YOUR FATHER FOR A CHANGE. HELP ME BRING YOUR MOTHER HOME.
HOW CAN I DO THAT?
TELL HER ABOUT OUR GOOD OLD DAYS, HOW WE MET...
YOUR VERSION OR HERS? BECAUSE THEY AREN'T THE SAME!
AYA! GET OUT OF MY SIGHT!

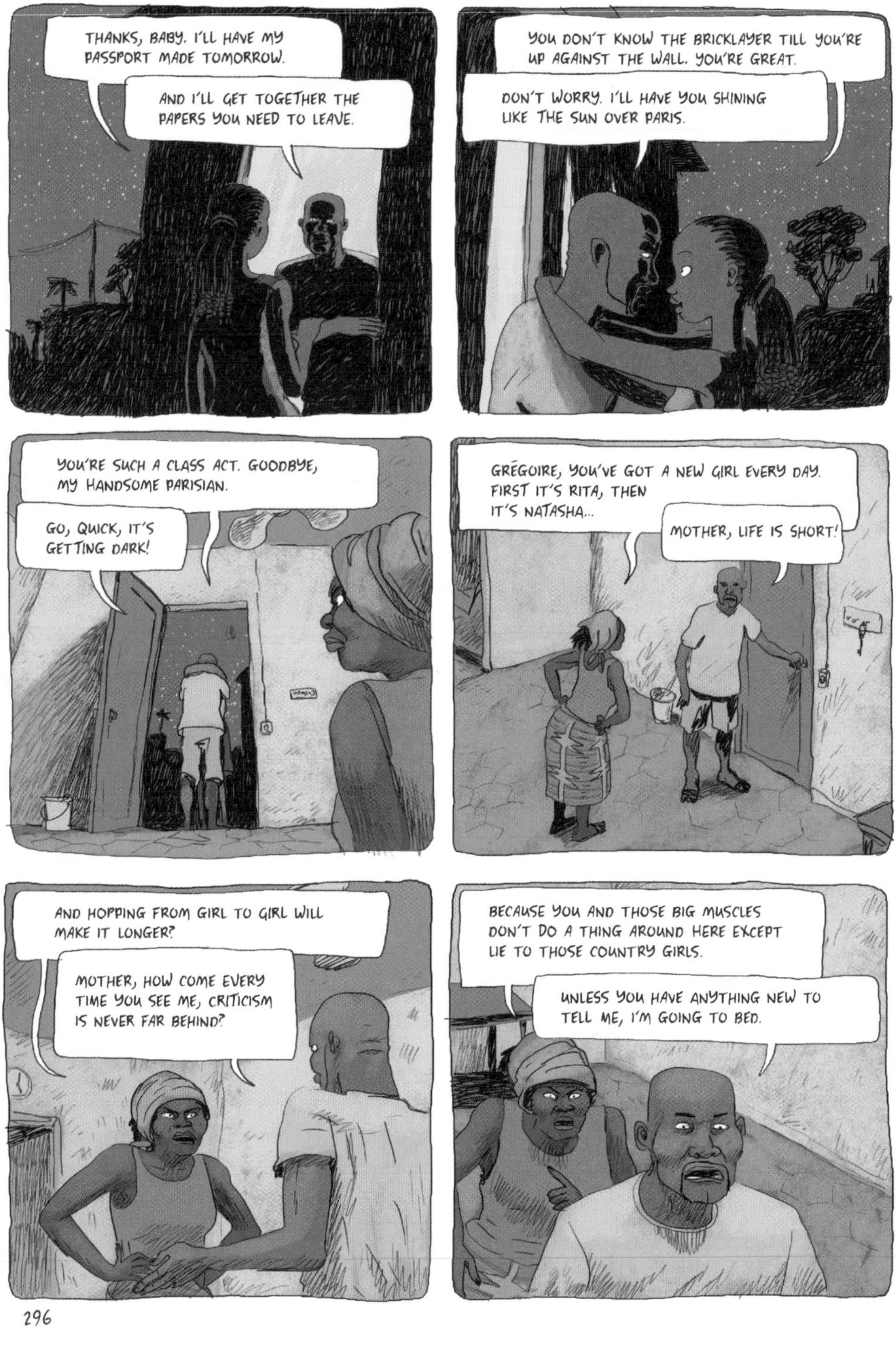
THANKS, BABY. I'LL HAVE MY PASSPORT MADE TOMORROW.
AND I'LL GET TOGETHER THE PAPERS YOU NEED TO LEAVE.
YOU DON'T KNOW THE BRICKLAYER TILL YOU'RE UP AGAINST THE WALL. YOU'RE GREAT.
DON'T WORRY. I'LL HAVE YOU SHINING LIKE THE SUN OVER PARIS.
YOU'RE SUCH A CLASS ACT. GOODBYE, MY HANDSOME PARISIAN.
GO, QUICK, IT'S GETTING DARK!
GRÉGOIRE, YOU'VE GOT A NEW GIRL EVERY DAY. FIRST IT'S RITA, THEN IT'S NATASHA...
MOTHER, LIFE IS SHORT!
AND HOPPING FROM GIRL TO GIRL WILL MAKE IT LONGER?
MOTHER, HOW COME EVERY TIME YOU SEE ME, CRITICISM IS NEVER FAR BEHIND?
BECAUSE YOU AND THOSE BIG MUSCLES DON'T DO A THING AROUND HERE EXCEPT LIE TO THOSE COUNTRY GIRLS.
UNLESS YOU HAVE ANYTHING NEW TO TELL ME, I'M GOING TO BED.

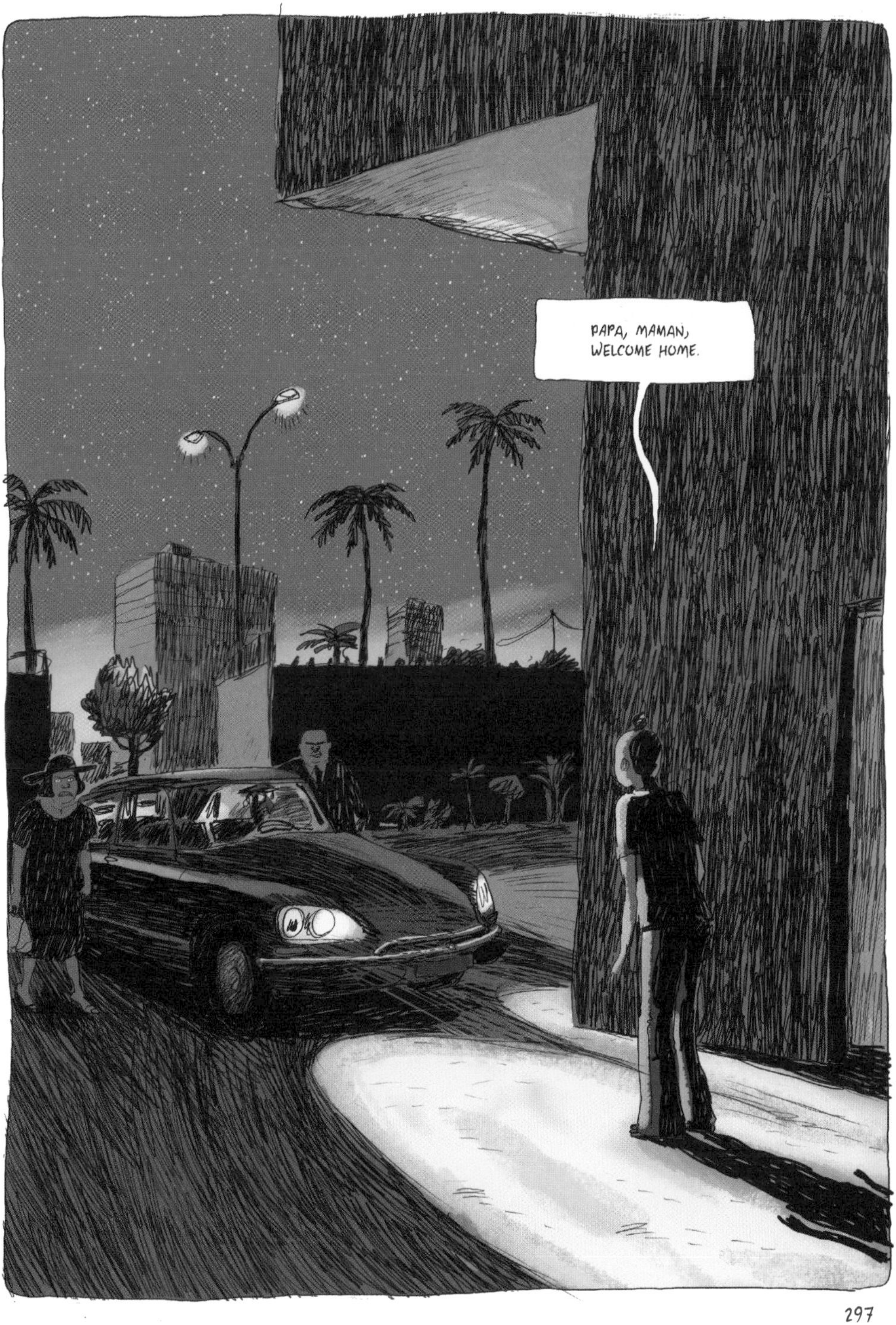
PAPA, MAMAN,
WELCOME HOME.

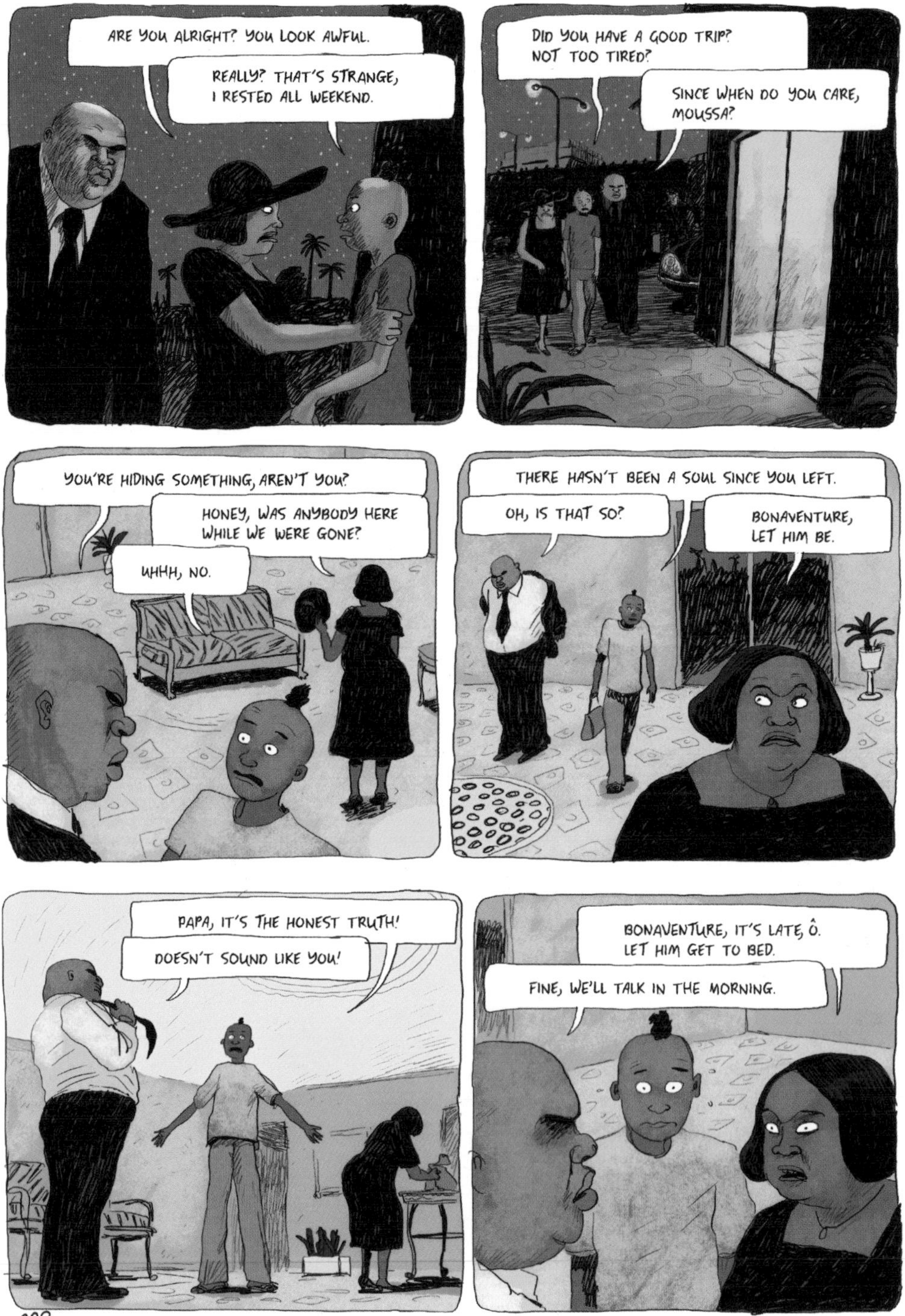
ARE YOU ALRIGHT? YOU LOOK AWFUL.
REALLY? THAT'S STRANGE, I RESTED ALL WEEKEND.
DID YOU HAVE A GOOD TRIP? NOT TOO TIRED?
SINCE WHEN DO YOU CARE, MOUSSA?
YOU'RE HIDING SOMETHING, AREN'T YOU?
HONEY, WAS ANYBODY HERE WHILE WE WERE GONE?
UHHH, NO.
THERE HASN'T BEEN A SOUL SINCE YOU LEFT.
OH, IS THAT SO?
BONAVENTURE, LET HIM BE.
PAPA, IT'S THE HONEST TRUTH!
DOESN'T SOUND LIKE YOU!
BONAVENTURE, IT'S LATE, Ô. LET HIM GET TO BED.
FINE, WE'LL TALK IN THE MORNING.

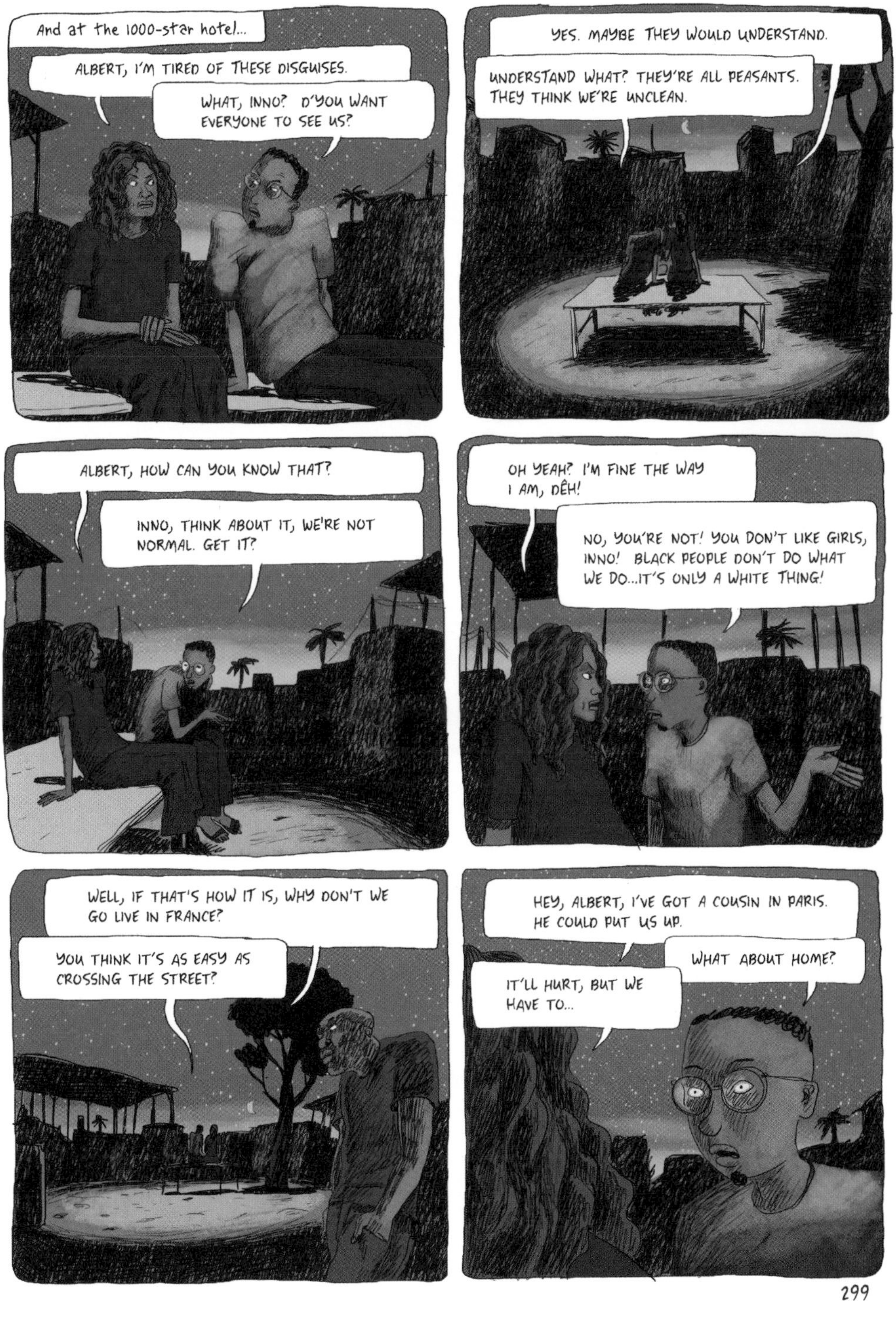
And at the 1000-star hotel...
ALBERT, I'M TIRED OF THESE DISGUISES.
WHAT, INNO? D'YOU WANT EVERYONE TO SEE US?
YES. MAYBE THEY WOULD UNDERSTAND.
UNDERSTAND WHAT? THEY'RE ALL PEASANTS. THEY THINK WE'RE UNCLEAN.
ALBERT, HOW CAN YOU KNOW THAT?
INNO, THINK ABOUT IT, WE'RE NOT NORMAL. GET IT?
OH YEAH? I'M FINE THE WAY I AM, DÊH!
NO, YOU'RE NOT! YOU DON'T LIKE GIRLS, INNO! BLACK PEOPLE DON'T DO WHAT WE DO...IT'S ONLY A WHITE THING!
WELL, IF THAT'S HOW IT IS, WHY DON'T WE GO LIVE IN FRANCE?
YOU THINK IT'S AS EASY AS CROSSING THE STREET?
HEY, ALBERT, I'VE GOT A COUSIN IN PARIS. HE COULD PUT US UP.
WHAT ABOUT HOME?
IT'LL HURT, BUT WE HAVE TO...

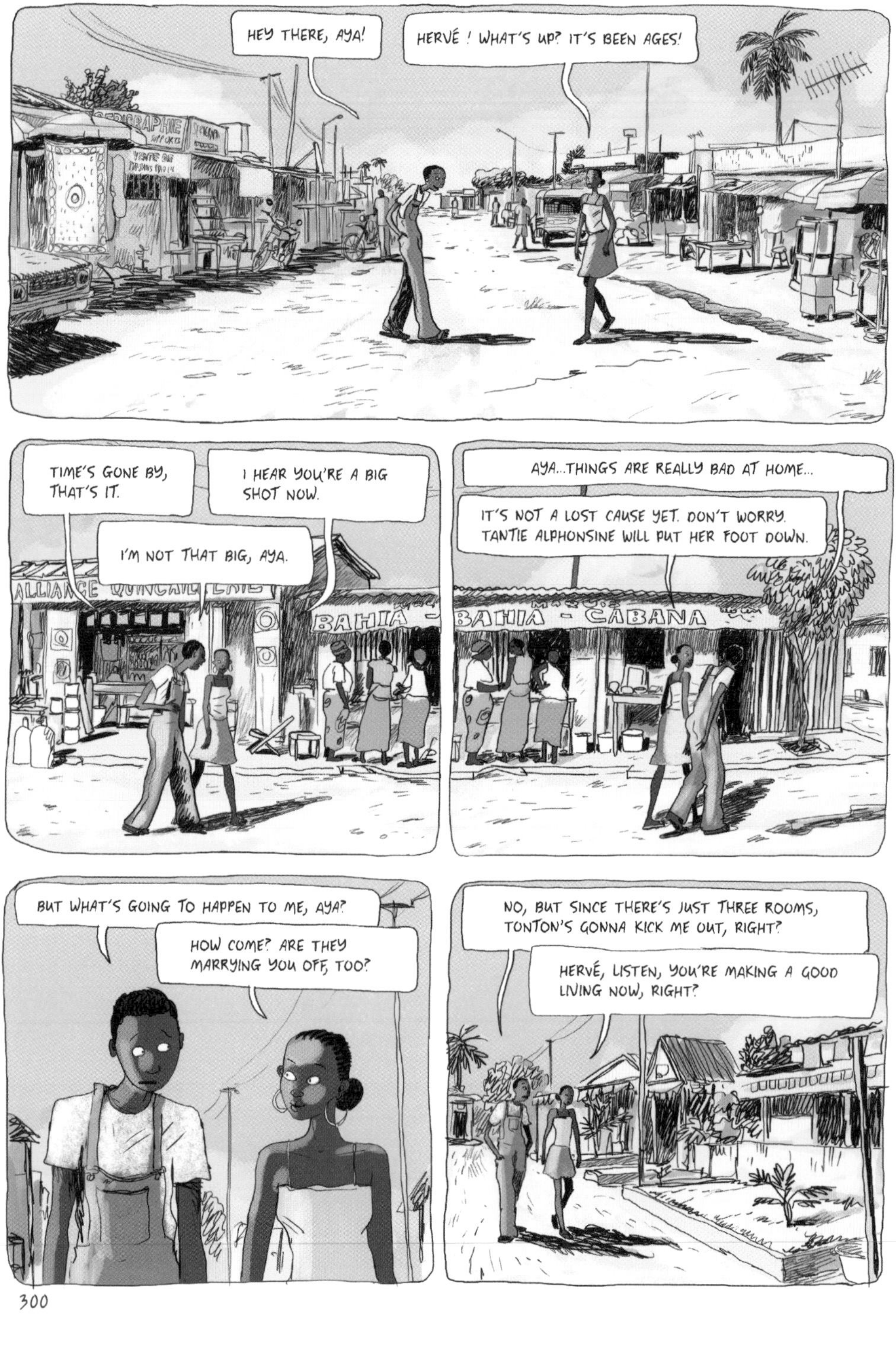
HEY THERE, AYA!
HERVÉ ! WHAT'S UP? IT'S BEEN AGES!
TIME'S GONE BY, THAT'S IT.
I HEAR YOU'RE A BIG SHOT NOW.
I'M NOT THAT BIG, AYA.
ALLIANCE QUINCAILLERIE
BAHIA - CABANA
AYA...THINGS ARE REALLY BAD AT HOME...
IT'S NOT A LOST CAUSE YET. DON'T WORRY. TANTIE ALPHONSINE WILL PUT HER FOOT DOWN.
BUT WHAT'S GOING TO HAPPEN TO ME, AYA?
HOW COME? ARE THEY MARRYING YOU OFF, TOO?
NO, BUT SINCE THERE'S JUST THREE ROOMS, TONTON'S GONNA KICK ME OUT, RIGHT?
HERVÉ, LISTEN, YOU'RE MAKING A GOOD LIVING NOW, RIGHT?

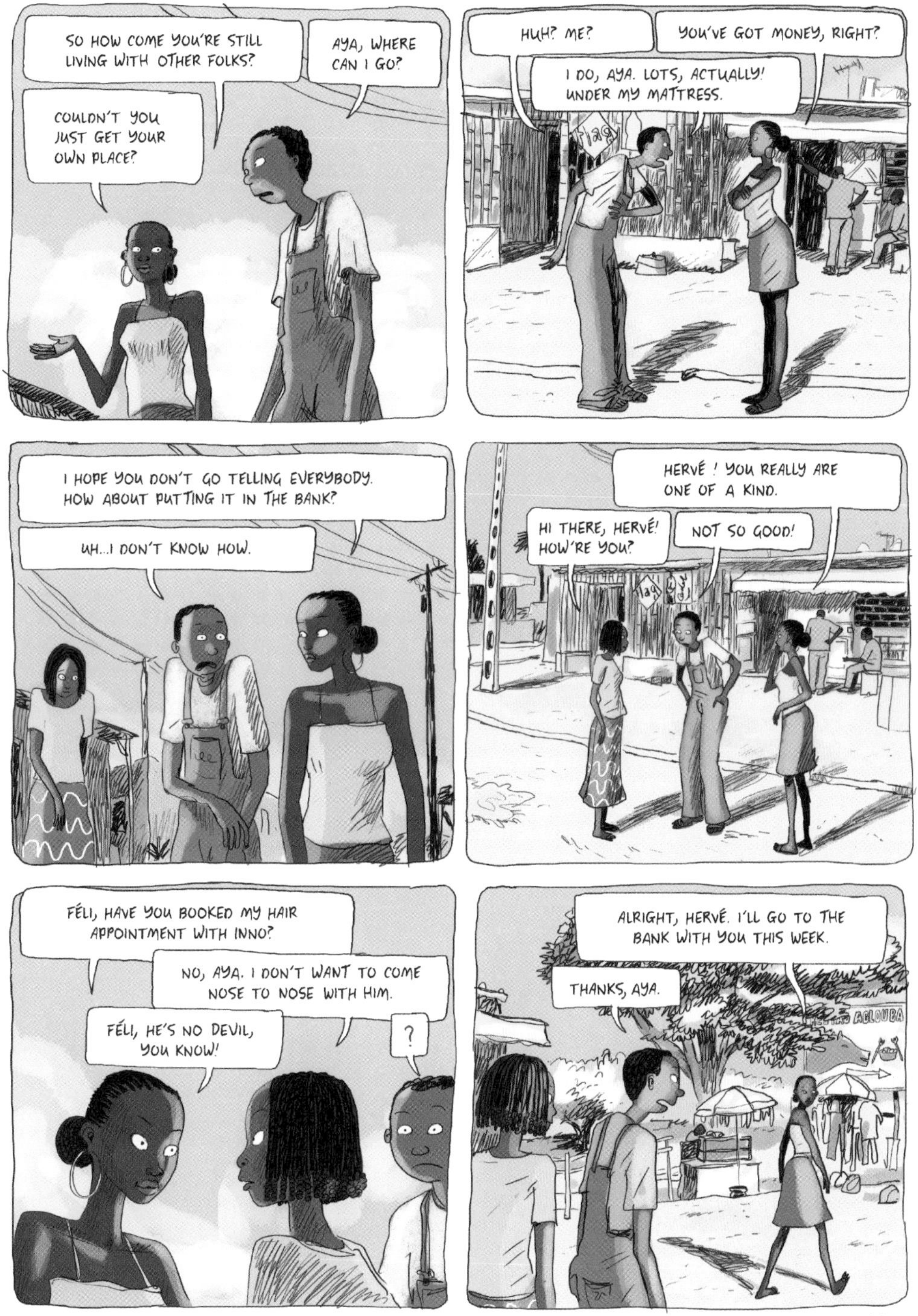
SO HOW COME YOU'RE STILL LIVING WITH OTHER FOLKS?
AYA, WHERE CAN I GO?
COULDN'T YOU JUST GET YOUR OWN PLACE?
HUH? ME?
YOU'VE GOT MONEY, RIGHT?
I DO, AYA. LOTS, ACTUALLY! UNDER MY MATTRESS.
I HOPE YOU DON'T GO TELLING EVERYBODY. HOW ABOUT PUTTING IT IN THE BANK?
UH...I DON'T KNOW HOW.
HERVÉ ! YOU REALLY ARE ONE OF A KIND.
HI THERE, HERVÉ! HOW'RE YOU?
NOT SO GOOD!
FÉLI, HAVE YOU BOOKED MY HAIR APPOINTMENT WITH INNO?
NO, AYA. I DON'T WANT TO COME NOSE TO NOSE WITH HIM.
FÉLI, HE'S NO DEVIL, YOU KNOW!
?
ALRIGHT, HERVÉ. I'LL GO TO THE BANK WITH YOU THIS WEEK.
THANKS, AYA.
AGLOUBA

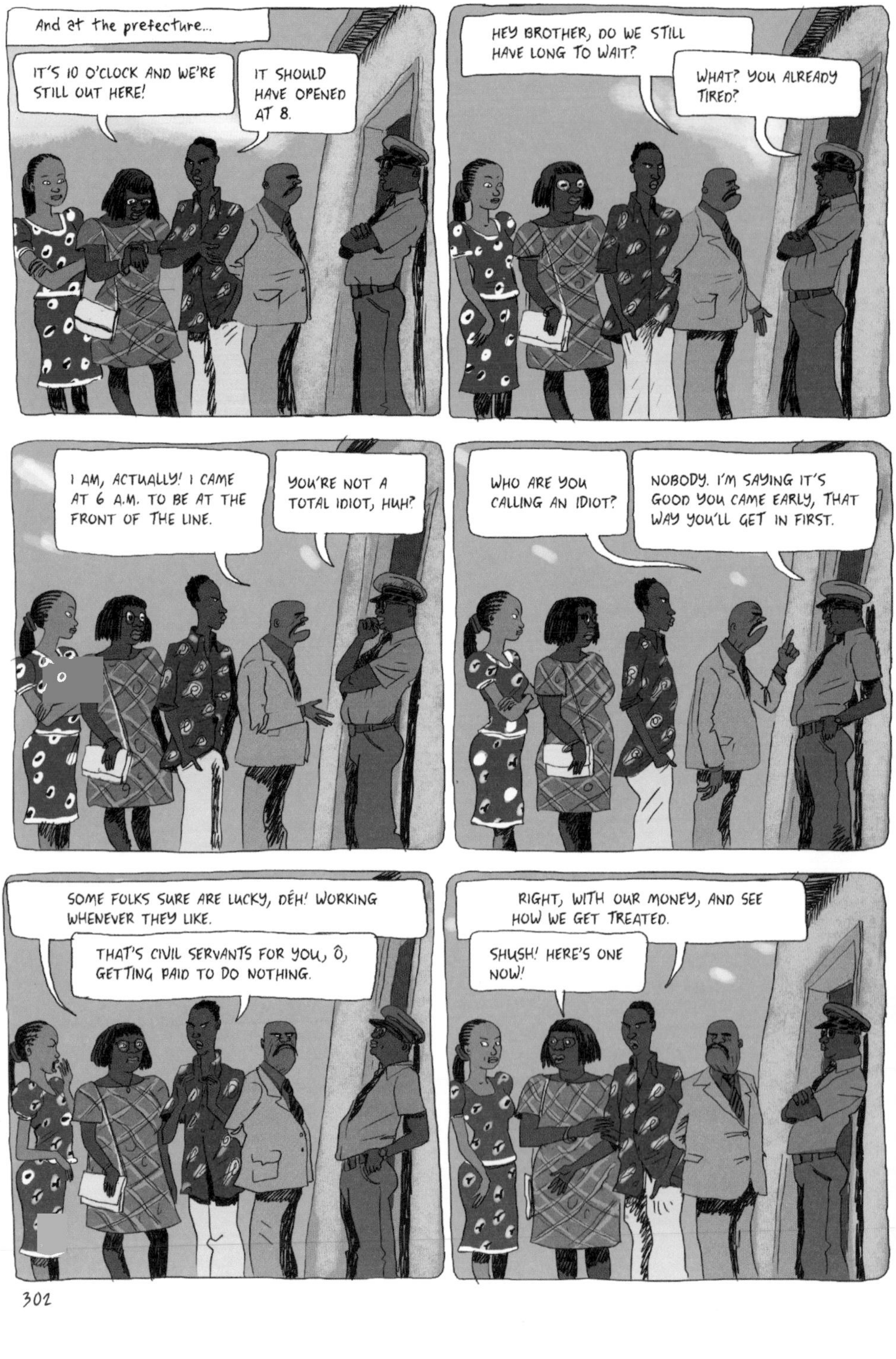
And at the prefecture...
IT'S 10 O'CLOCK AND WE'RE STILL OUT HERE!
IT SHOULD HAVE OPENED AT 8.
HEY BROTHER, DO WE STILL HAVE LONG TO WAIT?
WHAT? YOU ALREADY TIRED?
I AM, ACTUALLY! I CAME AT 6 A.M. TO BE AT THE FRONT OF THE LINE.
YOU'RE NOT A TOTAL IDIOT, HUH?
WHO ARE YOU CALLING AN IDIOT?
NOBODY. I'M SAYING IT'S GOOD YOU CAME EARLY, THAT WAY YOU'LL GET IN FIRST.
SOME FOLKS SURE ARE LUCKY, DÉH! WORKING WHENEVER THEY LIKE.
THAT'S CIVIL SERVANTS FOR YOU, Ô, GETTING PAID TO DO NOTHING.
RIGHT, WITH OUR MONEY, AND SEE HOW WE GET TREATED.
SHUSH! HERE'S ONE NOW!

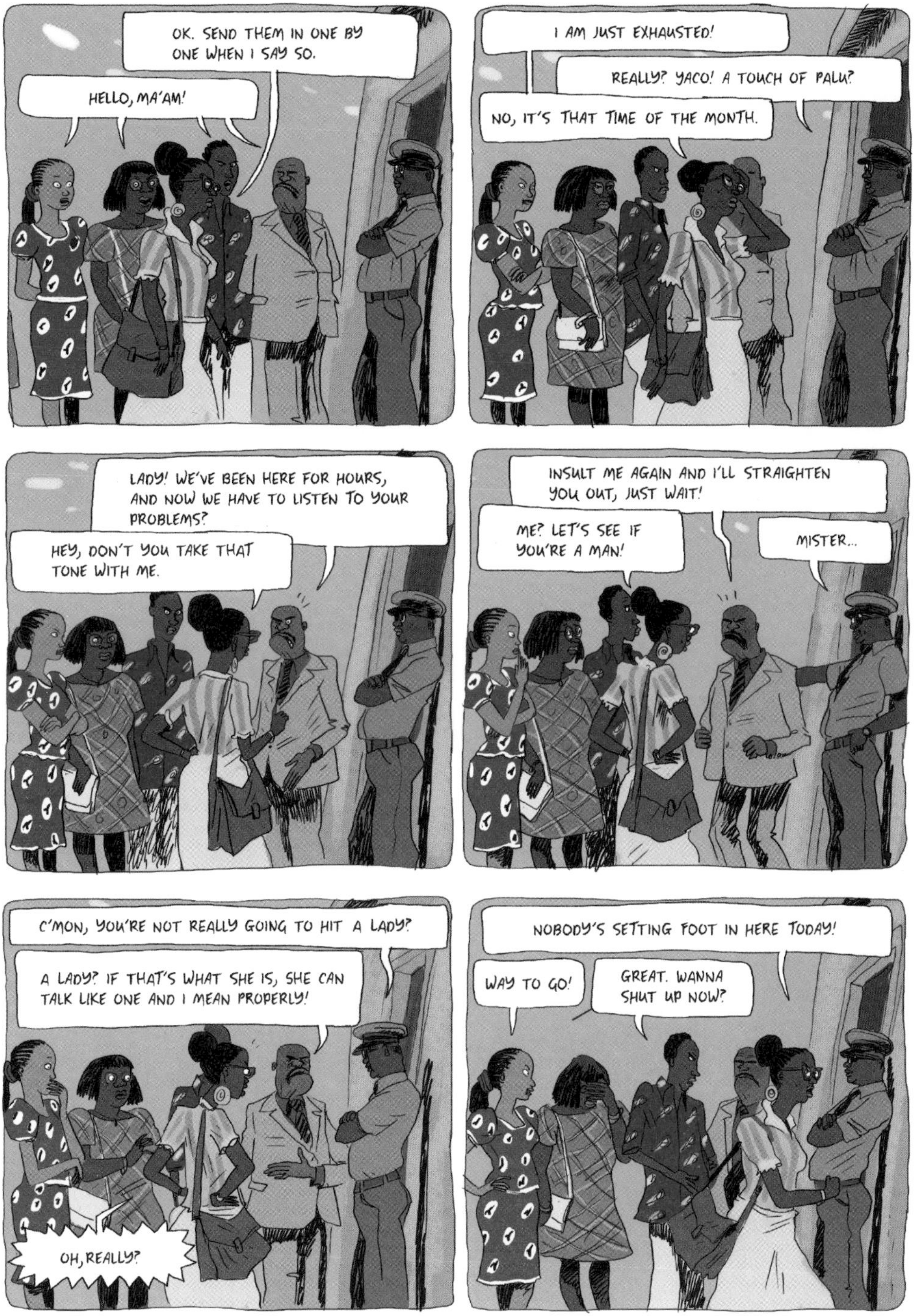
OK. SEND THEM IN ONE BY ONE WHEN I SAY SO.
HELLO, MA'AM!
I AM JUST EXHAUSTED!
REALLY? YACO! A TOUCH OF PALU?
NO, IT'S THAT TIME OF THE MONTH.
LADY! WE'VE BEEN HERE FOR HOURS, AND NOW WE HAVE TO LISTEN TO YOUR PROBLEMS?
HEY, DON'T YOU TAKE THAT TONE WITH ME.
INSULT ME AGAIN AND I'LL STRAIGHTEN YOU OUT, JUST WAIT!
ME? LET'S SEE IF YOU'RE A MAN!
MISTER...
C'MON, YOU'RE NOT REALLY GOING TO HIT A LADY?
A LADY? IF THAT'S WHAT SHE IS, SHE CAN TALK LIKE ONE AND I MEAN PROPERLY!
OH, REALLY?
NOBODY'S SETTING FOOT IN HERE TODAY!
WAY TO GO!
GREAT. WANNA SHUT UP NOW?

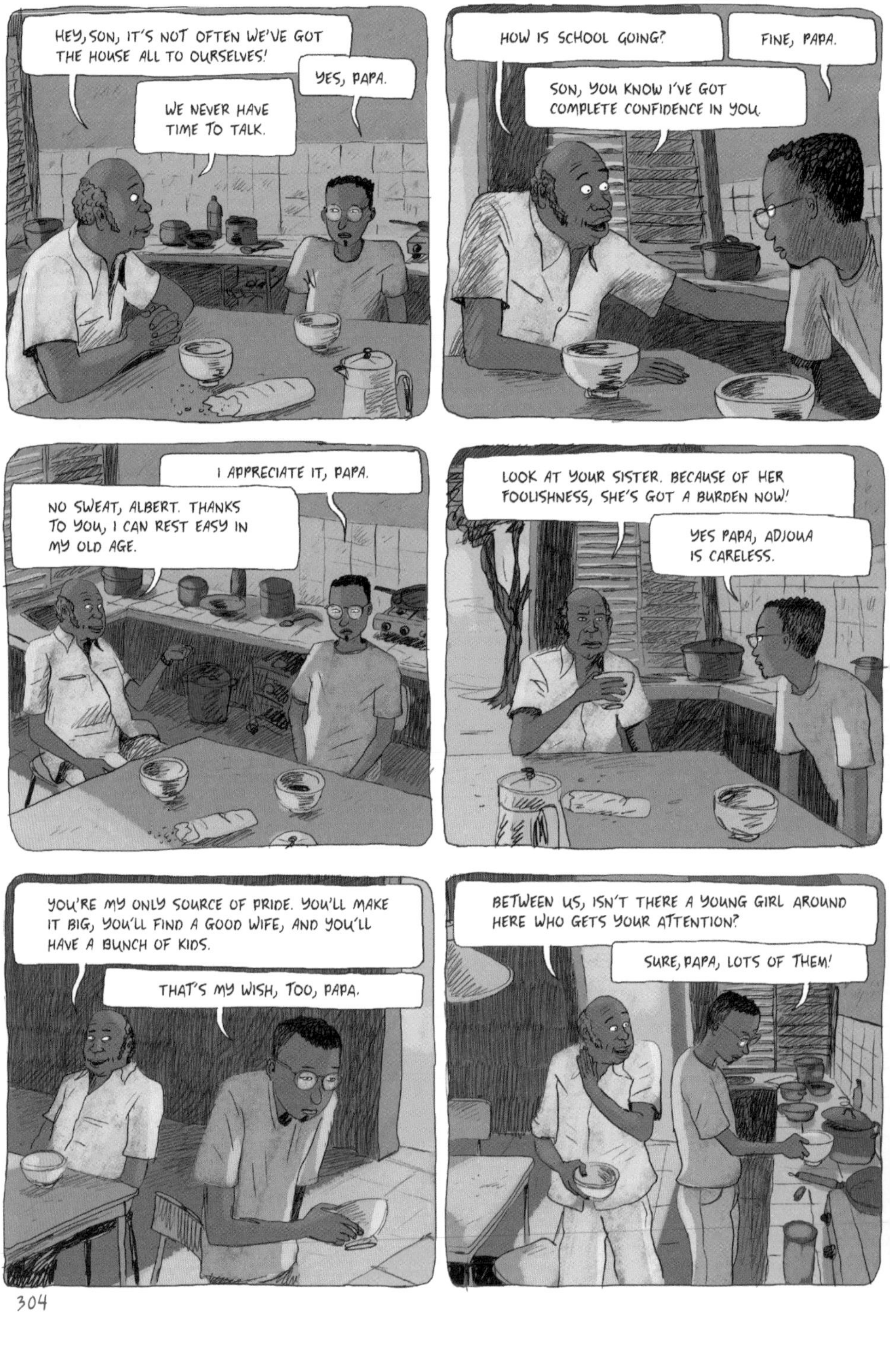
HEY, SON, IT'S NOT OFTEN WE'VE GOT THE HOUSE ALL TO OURSELVES!
WE NEVER HAVE TIME TO TALK.
YES, PAPA.
HOW IS SCHOOL GOING?
FINE, PAPA.
SON, YOU KNOW I'VE GOT COMPLETE CONFIDENCE IN YOU.
I APPRECIATE IT, PAPA.
NO SWEAT, ALBERT. THANKS TO YOU, I CAN REST EASY IN MY OLD AGE.
LOOK AT YOUR SISTER. BECAUSE OF HER FOOLISHNESS, SHE'S GOT A BURDEN NOW!
YES PAPA, ADJOUA IS CARELESS.
YOU'RE MY ONLY SOURCE OF PRIDE. YOU'LL MAKE IT BIG, YOU'LL FIND A GOOD WIFE, AND YOU'LL HAVE A BUNCH OF KIDS.
THAT'S MY WISH, TOO, PAPA.
BETWEEN US, ISN'T THERE A YOUNG GIRL AROUND HERE WHO GETS YOUR ATTENTION?
SURE, PAPA, LOTS OF THEM!

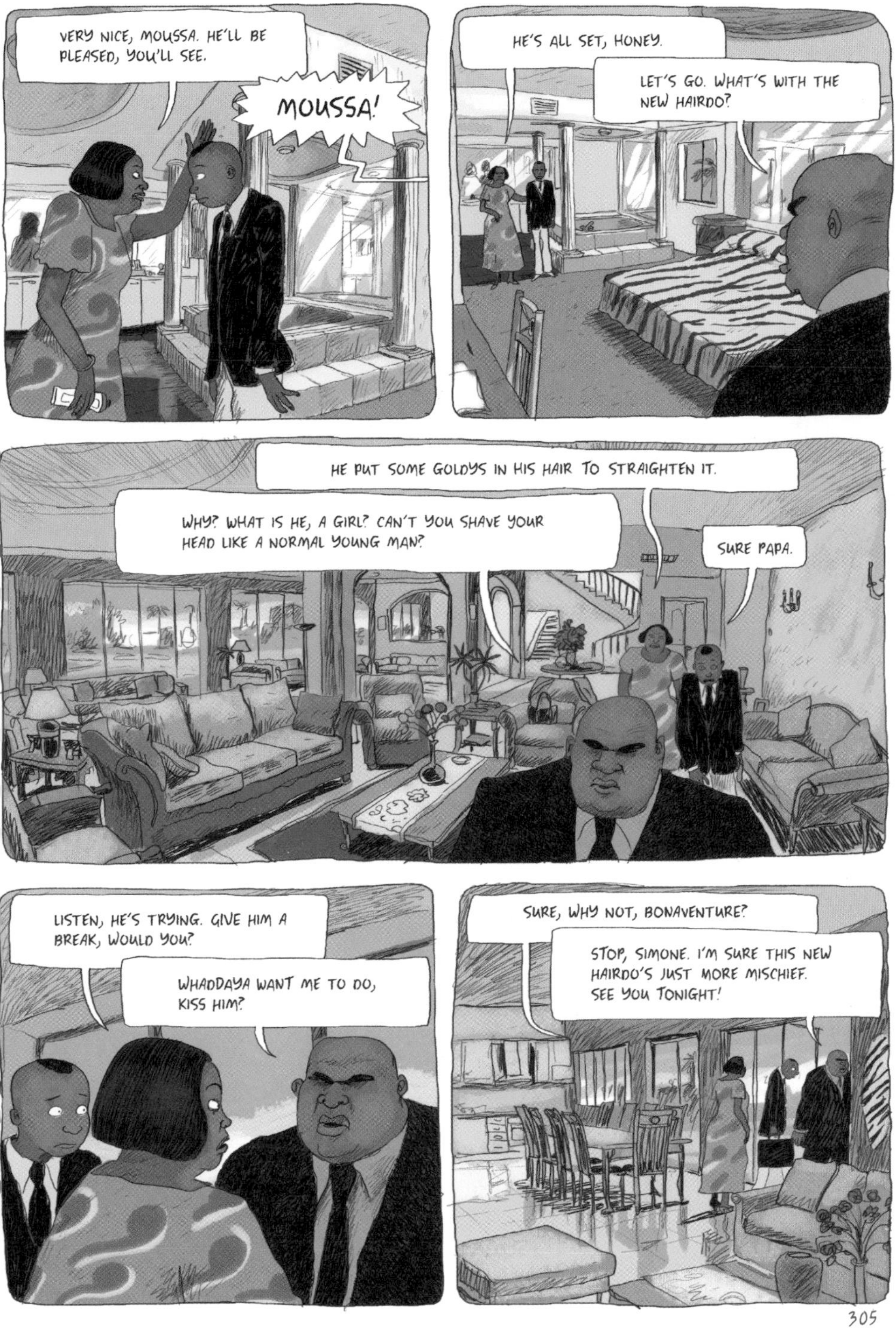

VERY NICE, MOUSSA. HE'LL BE PLEASED, YOU'LL SEE.
MOUSSA!
HE'S ALL SET, HONEY.
LET'S GO. WHAT'S WITH THE NEW HAIRDO?
HE PUT SOME GOLDYS IN HIS HAIR TO STRAIGHTEN IT.
WHY? WHAT IS HE, A GIRL? CAN'T YOU SHAVE YOUR HEAD LIKE A NORMAL YOUNG MAN?
SURE PAPA.
LISTEN, HE'S TRYING. GIVE HIM A BREAK, WOULD YOU?
WHADDAYA WANT ME TO DO, KISS HIM?
SURE, WHY NOT, BONAVENTURE?
STOP, SIMONE. I'M SURE THIS NEW HAIRDO'S JUST MORE MISCHIEF. SEE YOU TONIGHT!

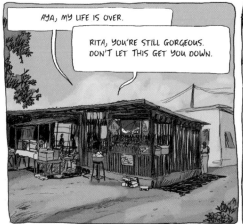

AYA, MY LIFE IS OVER.

RITA, YOU'RE STILL GORGEOUS. DON'T LET THIS GET YOU DOWN.

AYA, MY FATHER'S MAD THAT I CAME BACK FROM FRANCE SO FAST WITH NO MONEY.

BUT THINGS WERE TOO HARD FOR YOU THERE.

I KNOW, AYA, BUT HE DOESN'T BELIEVE ME. THAT'S WHY HE'S HAVING ME MARRY, SO HE'S GOT ONE MOUTH LESS TO FEED.

WE WON'T LET HIM, RITA.

HE MADE UP HIS MIND SO FAST, I DIDN'T EVEN HAVE TIME TO SORT THINGS OUT.

WHAT WERE YOU PLANNING, RITA?

CAFETERIA
LE CHARME
RESTAURATION & DIVERS
CABINE Téléphonique

YOU KNOW, MY GUY IS HERE AT THE MOMENT. I HOPE HE CAN HELP ME.

WELL, YOU CAN COUNT ON THE OLD LADIES TO NEGOTIATE.

THEY'RE GETTING ALL THE PARENTS TOGETHER TO TALK TO YOUR FATHER.

YOU MEAN EVERYBODY'S GOING TO KNOW?

SORRY TO SAY, BUT THEY ALREADY DO.

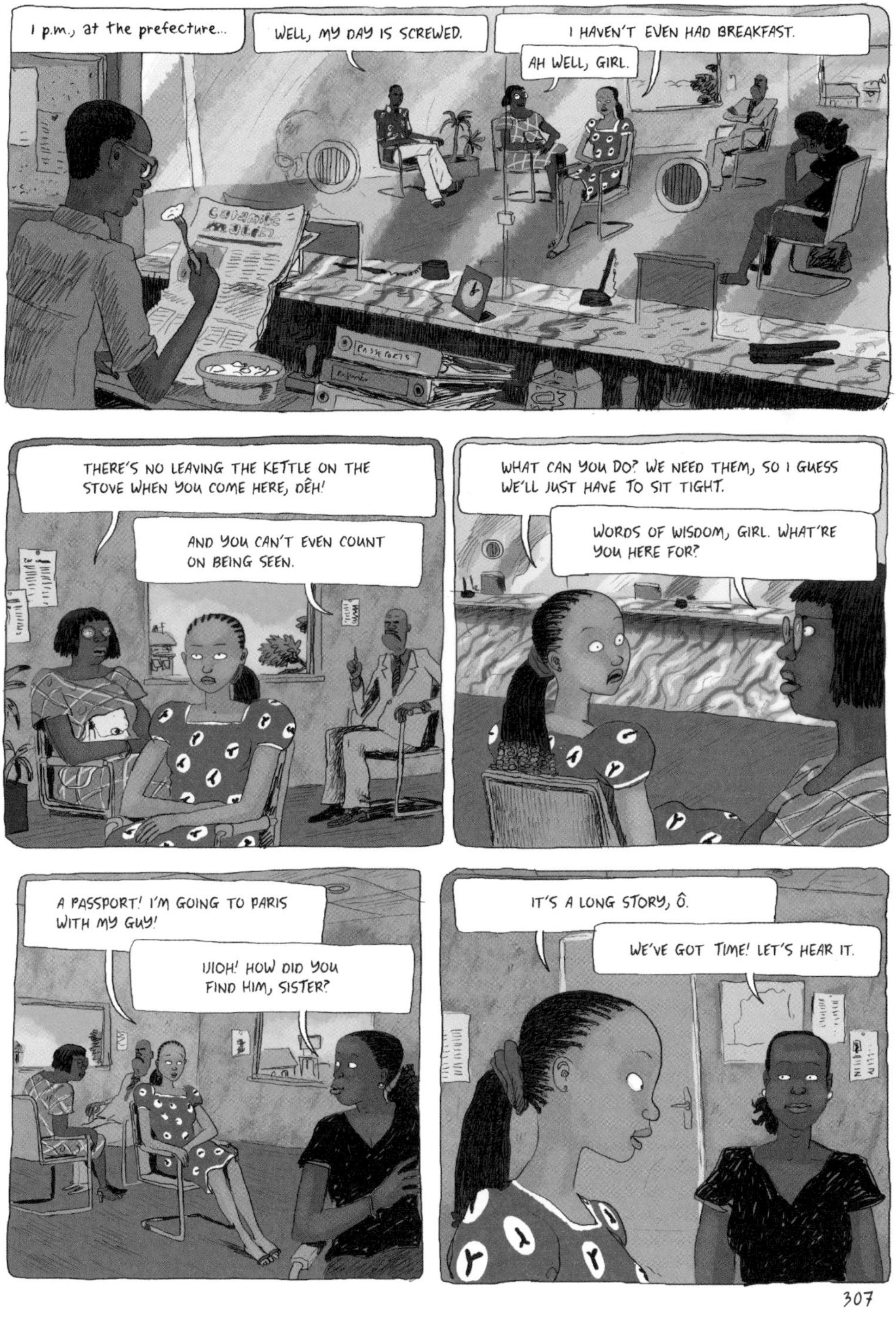
1 p.m., at the prefecture...
WELL, MY DAY IS SCREWED.
I HAVEN'T EVEN HAD BREAKFAST.
AH WELL, GIRL.
THERE'S NO LEAVING THE KETTLE ON THE STOVE WHEN YOU COME HERE, DÊH!
AND YOU CAN'T EVEN COUNT ON BEING SEEN.
WHAT CAN YOU DO? WE NEED THEM, SO I GUESS WE'LL JUST HAVE TO SIT TIGHT.
WORDS OF WISDOM, GIRL. WHAT'RE YOU HERE FOR?
A PASSPORT! I'M GOING TO PARIS WITH MY GUY!
IJIOH! HOW DID YOU FIND HIM, SISTER?
IT'S A LONG STORY, Ô.
WE'VE GOT TIME! LET'S HEAR IT.

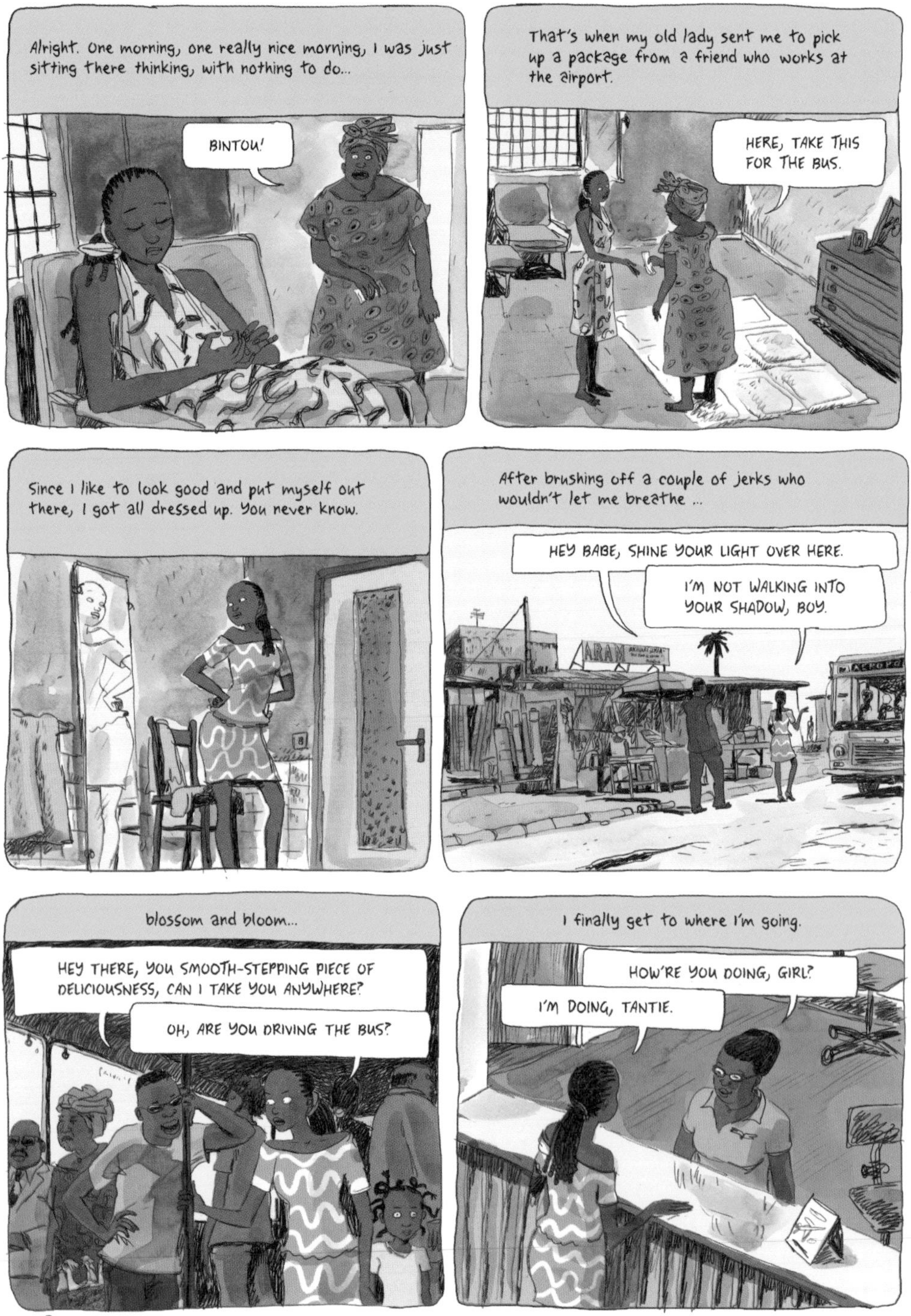
Alright. One morning, one really nice morning, I was just sitting there thinking, with nothing to do...
BINTOU!
That's when my old lady sent me to pick up a package from a friend who works at the airport.
HERE, TAKE THIS FOR THE BUS.
Since I like to look good and put myself out there, I got all dressed up. You never know.
After brushing off a couple of jerks who wouldn't let me breathe ...
HEY BABE, SHINE YOUR LIGHT OVER HERE.
I'M NOT WALKING INTO YOUR SHADOW, BOY.
blossom and bloom...
HEY THERE, YOU SMOOTH-STEPPING PIECE OF DELICIOUSNESS, CAN I TAKE YOU ANYWHERE?
OH, ARE YOU DRIVING THE BUS?
I finally get to where I'm going.
HOW'RE YOU DOING, GIRL?
I'M DOING, TANTIE.

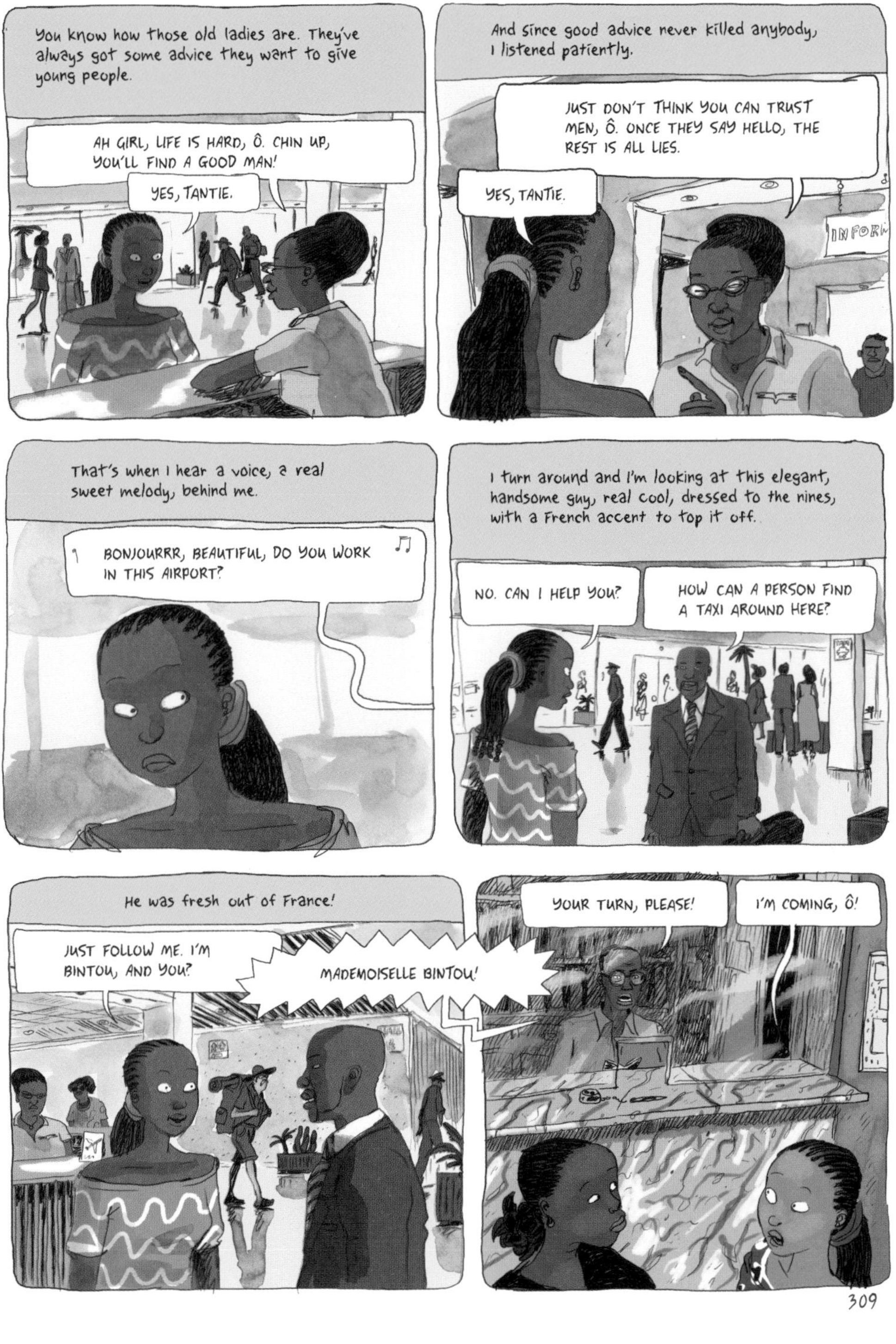

You know how those old ladies are. They've always got some advice they want to give young people.
AH GIRL, LIFE IS HARD, Ô. CHIN UP, YOU'LL FIND A GOOD MAN!
YES, TANTIE.
And since good advice never killed anybody, I listened patiently.
JUST DON'T THINK YOU CAN TRUST MEN, Ô. ONCE THEY SAY HELLO, THE REST IS ALL LIES.
YES, TANTIE.
INFORM
That's when I hear a voice, a real sweet melody, behind me.
BONJOURRR, BEAUTIFUL, DO YOU WORK IN THIS AIRPORT?
I turn around and I'm looking at this elegant, handsome guy, real cool, dressed to the nines, with a French accent to top it off.
NO. CAN I HELP YOU?
HOW CAN A PERSON FIND A TAXI AROUND HERE?
He was fresh out of France!
JUST FOLLOW ME. I'M BINTOU, AND YOU?
MADEMOISELLE BINTOU!
YOUR TURN, PLEASE!
I'M COMING, Ô!

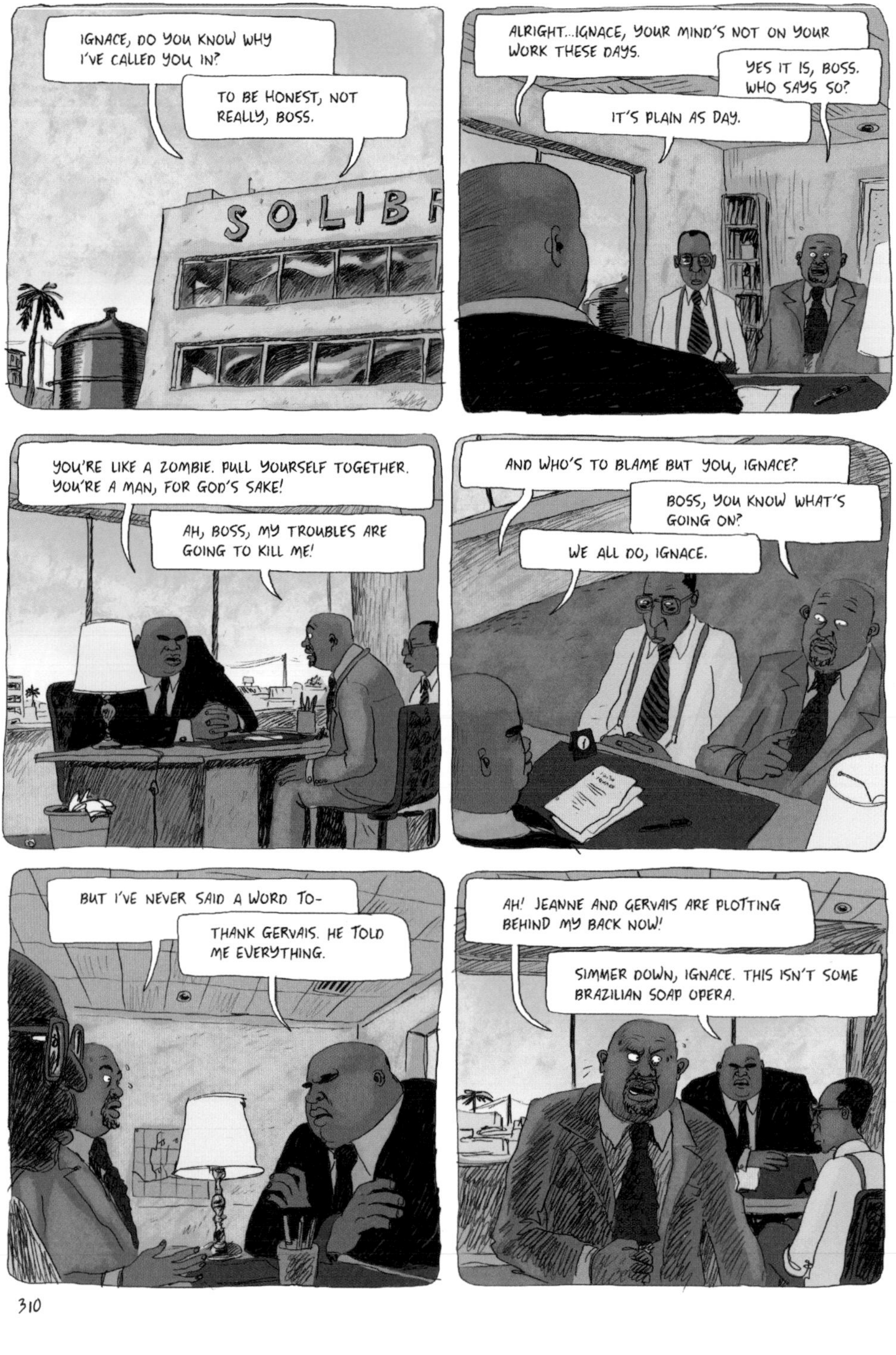
IGNACE, DO YOU KNOW WHY I'VE CALLED YOU IN?
TO BE HONEST, NOT REALLY, BOSS.
SOLIB
ALRIGHT...IGNACE, YOUR MIND'S NOT ON YOUR WORK THESE DAYS.
YES IT IS, BOSS. WHO SAYS SO?
IT'S PLAIN AS DAY.
YOU'RE LIKE A ZOMBIE. PULL YOURSELF TOGETHER. YOU'RE A MAN, FOR GOD'S SAKE!
AH, BOSS, MY TROUBLES ARE GOING TO KILL ME!
AND WHO'S TO BLAME BUT YOU, IGNACE?
BOSS, YOU KNOW WHAT'S GOING ON?
WE ALL DO, IGNACE.
BUT I'VE NEVER SAID A WORD TO-
THANK GERVAIS. HE TOLD ME EVERYTHING.
AH! JEANNE AND GERVAIS ARE PLOTTING BEHIND MY BACK NOW!
SIMMER DOWN, IGNACE. THIS ISN'T SOME BRAZILIAN SOAP OPERA.

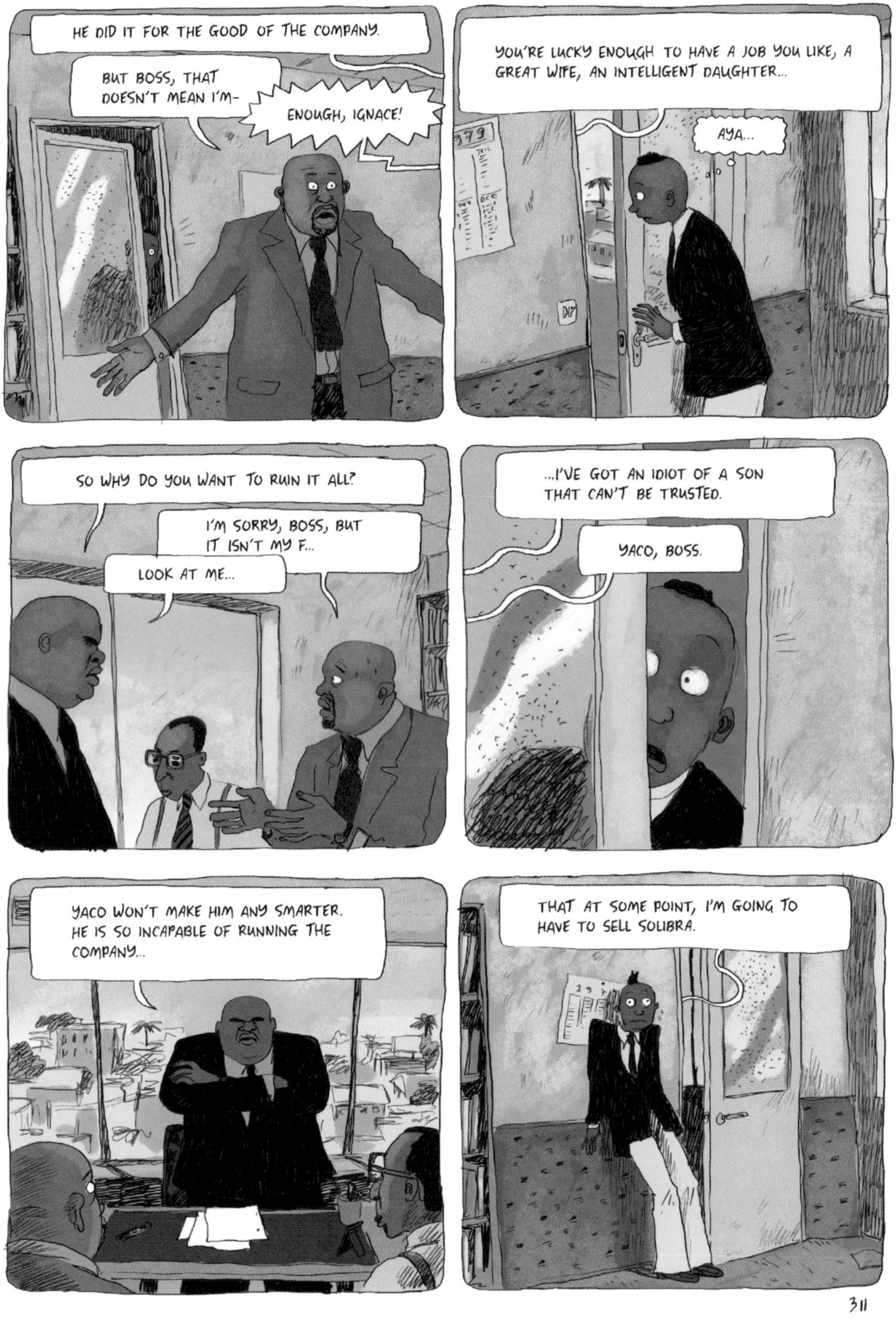
HE DID IT FOR THE GOOD OF THE COMPANY.
BUT BOSS, THAT DOESN'T MEAN I'M-
ENOUGH, IGNACE!
YOU'RE LUCKY ENOUGH TO HAVE A JOB YOU LIKE, A GREAT WIFE, AN INTELLIGENT DAUGHTER...
AYA...
SO WHY DO YOU WANT TO RUIN IT ALL?
I'M SORRY, BOSS, BUT IT ISN'T MY F...
LOOK AT ME...
...I'VE GOT AN IDIOT OF A SON THAT CAN'T BE TRUSTED.
YACO, BOSS.
YACO WON'T MAKE HIM ANY SMARTER. HE IS SO INCAPABLE OF RUNNING THE COMPANY...
THAT AT SOME POINT, I'M GOING TO HAVE TO SELL SOLIBRA.

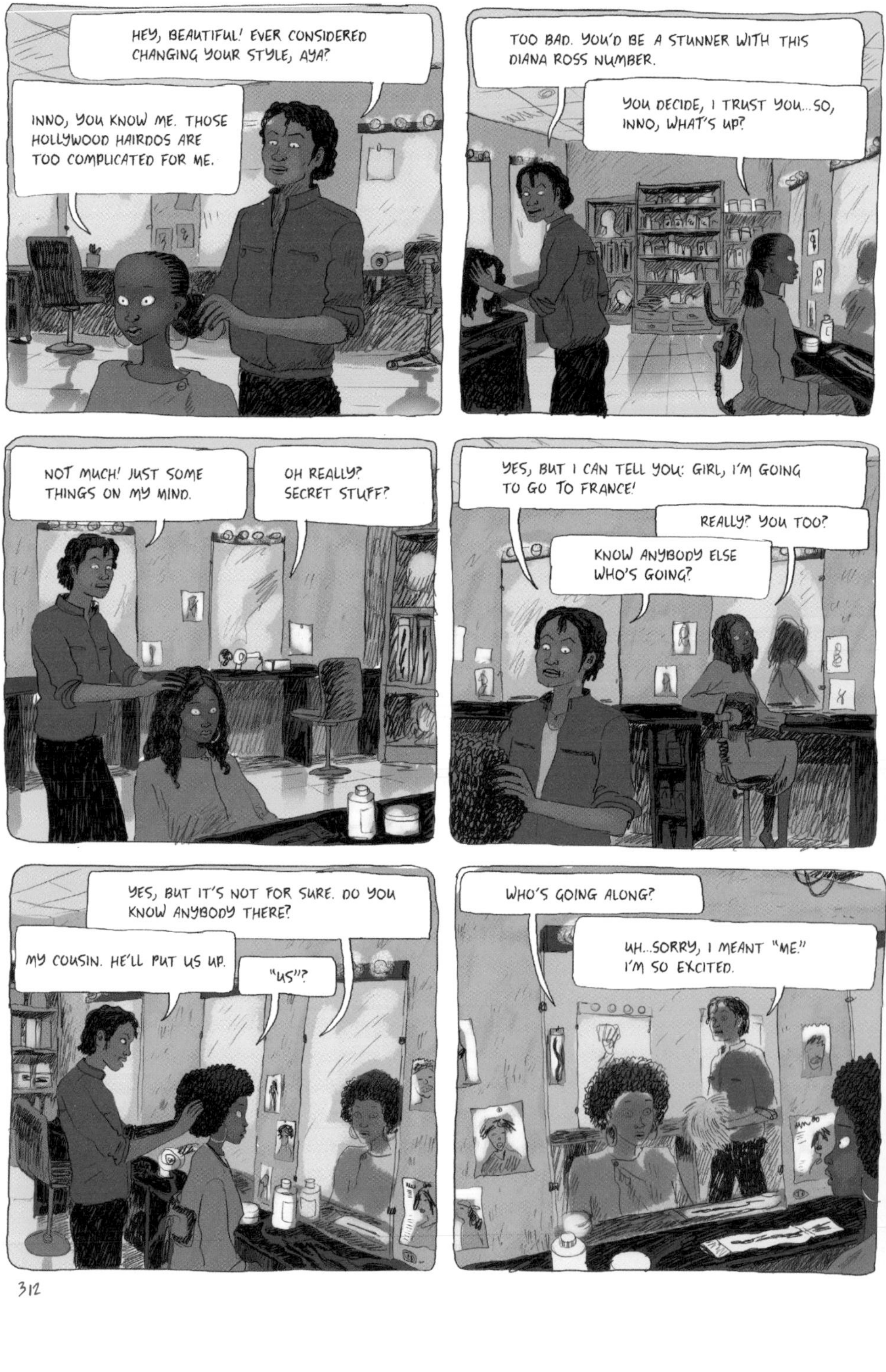
HEY, BEAUTIFUL! EVER CONSIDERED CHANGING YOUR STYLE, AYA?
INNO, YOU KNOW ME. THOSE HOLLYWOOD HAIRDOS ARE TOO COMPLICATED FOR ME.
TOO BAD. YOU'D BE A STUNNER WITH THIS DIANA ROSS NUMBER.
YOU DECIDE, I TRUST YOU...SO, INNO, WHAT'S UP?
NOT MUCH! JUST SOME THINGS ON MY MIND.
OH REALLY? SECRET STUFF?
YES, BUT I CAN TELL YOU: GIRL, I'M GOING TO GO TO FRANCE!
REALLY? YOU TOO?
KNOW ANYBODY ELSE WHO'S GOING?
YES, BUT IT'S NOT FOR SURE. DO YOU KNOW ANYBODY THERE?
MY COUSIN. HE'LL PUT US UP.
"US"?
WHO'S GOING ALONG?
UH...SORRY, I MEANT "ME." I'M SO EXCITED.

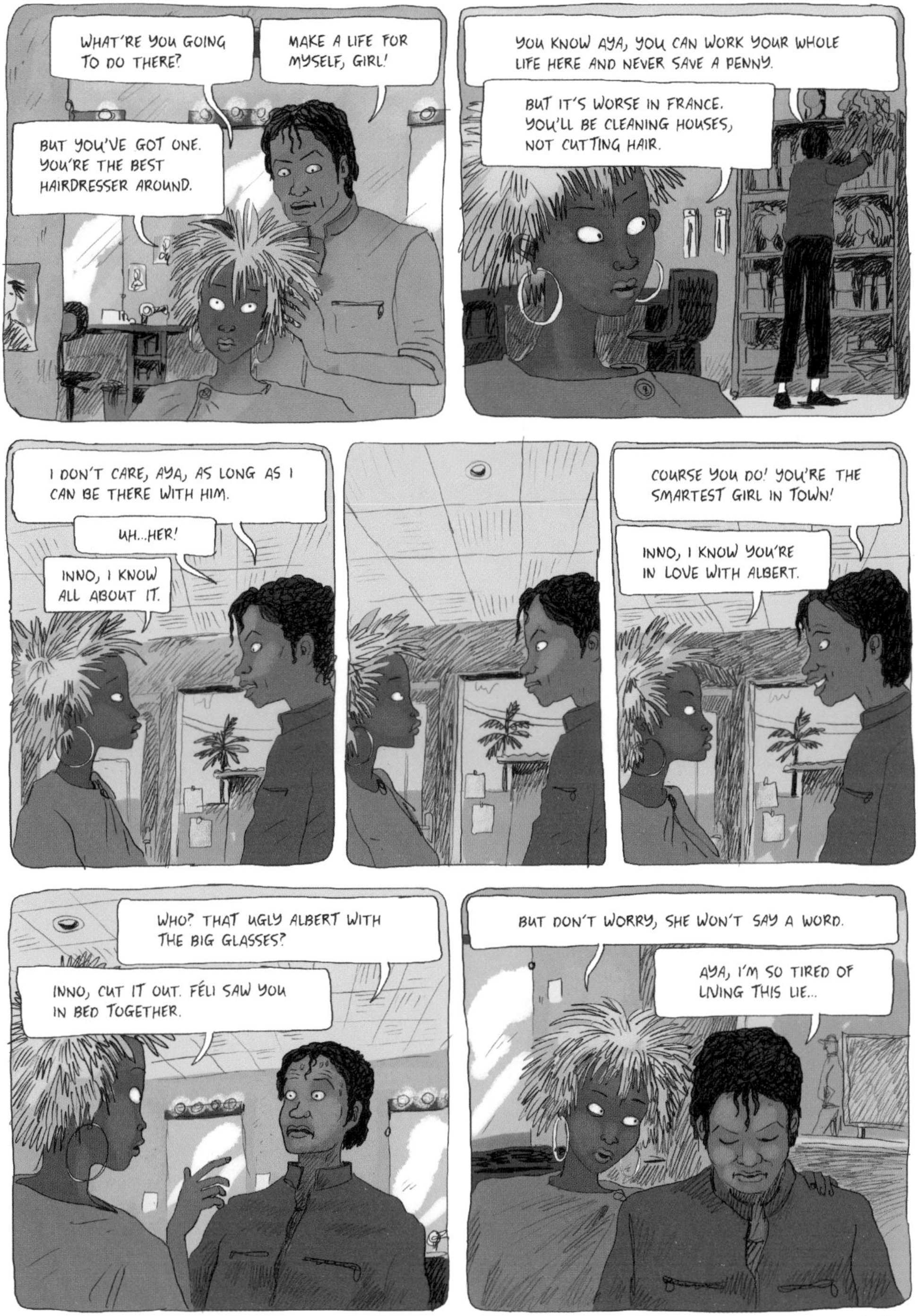

WHAT'RE YOU GOING TO DO THERE?
MAKE A LIFE FOR MYSELF, GIRL!
BUT YOU'VE GOT ONE. YOU'RE THE BEST HAIRDRESSER AROUND.
YOU KNOW AYA, YOU CAN WORK YOUR WHOLE LIFE HERE AND NEVER SAVE A PENNY.
BUT IT'S WORSE IN FRANCE. YOU'LL BE CLEANING HOUSES, NOT CUTTING HAIR.
I DON'T CARE, AYA, AS LONG AS I CAN BE THERE WITH HIM.
UH...HER!
INNO, I KNOW ALL ABOUT IT.
COURSE YOU DO! YOU'RE THE SMARTEST GIRL IN TOWN!
INNO, I KNOW YOU'RE IN LOVE WITH ALBERT.
WHO? THAT UGLY ALBERT WITH THE BIG GLASSES?
INNO, CUT IT OUT. FÉLI SAW YOU IN BED TOGETHER.
BUT DON'T WORRY, SHE WON'T SAY A WORD.
AYA, I'M SO TIRED OF LIVING THIS LIE...

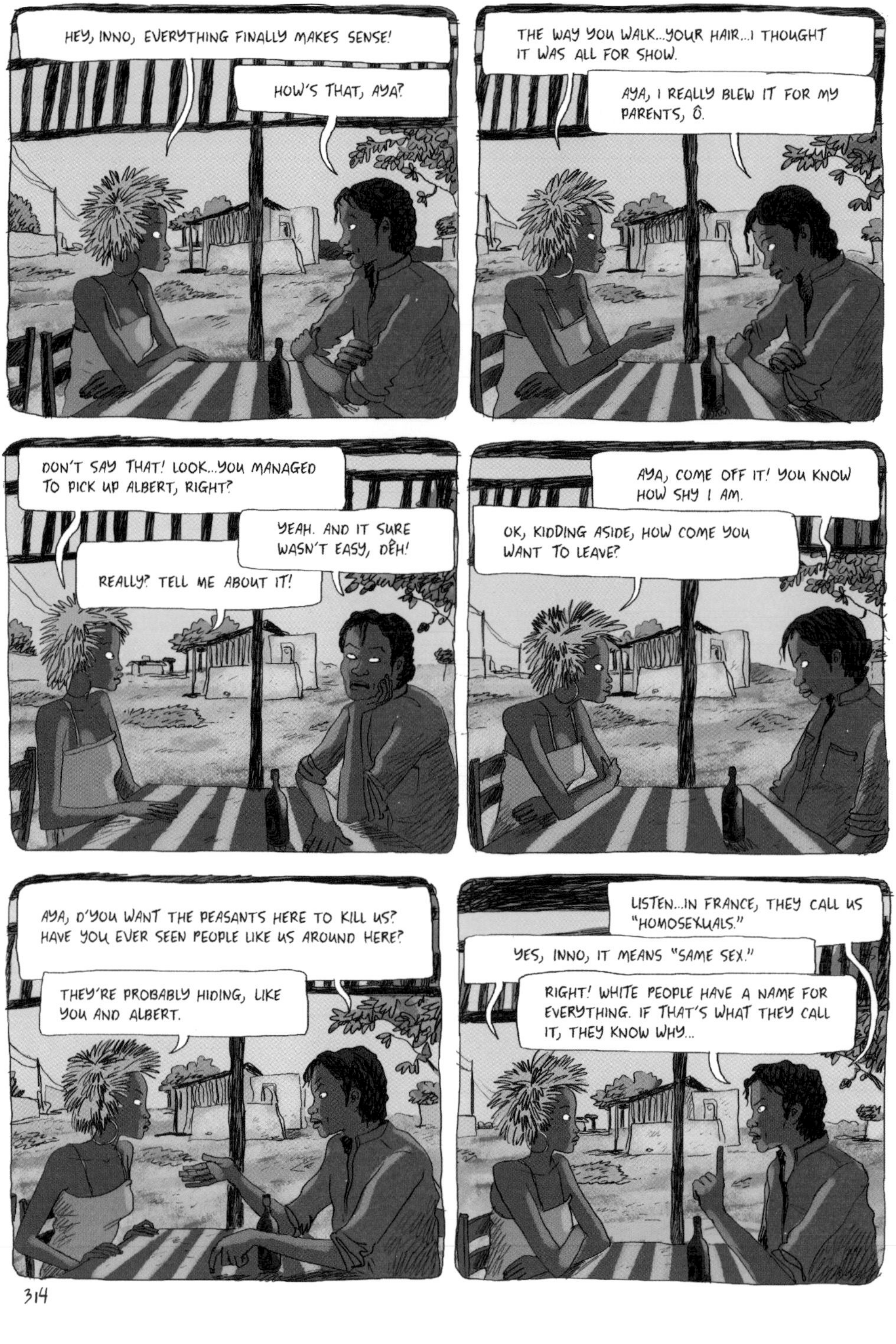
HEY, INNO, EVERYTHING FINALLY MAKES SENSE!
HOW'S THAT, AYA?
THE WAY YOU WALK...YOUR HAIR...I THOUGHT IT WAS ALL FOR SHOW.
AYA, I REALLY BLEW IT FOR MY PARENTS, Ô.
DON'T SAY THAT! LOOK...YOU MANAGED TO PICK UP ALBERT, RIGHT?
YEAH. AND IT SURE WASN'T EASY, DÊH!
REALLY? TELL ME ABOUT IT!
AYA, COME OFF IT! YOU KNOW HOW SHY I AM.
OK, KIDDING ASIDE, HOW COME YOU WANT TO LEAVE?
AYA, D'YOU WANT THE PEASANTS HERE TO KILL US? HAVE YOU EVER SEEN PEOPLE LIKE US AROUND HERE?
THEY'RE PROBABLY HIDING, LIKE YOU AND ALBERT.
LISTEN...IN FRANCE, THEY CALL US "HOMOSEXUALS."
YES, INNO, IT MEANS "SAME SEX."
RIGHT! WHITE PEOPLE HAVE A NAME FOR EVERYTHING. IF THAT'S WHAT THEY CALL IT, THEY KNOW WHY...

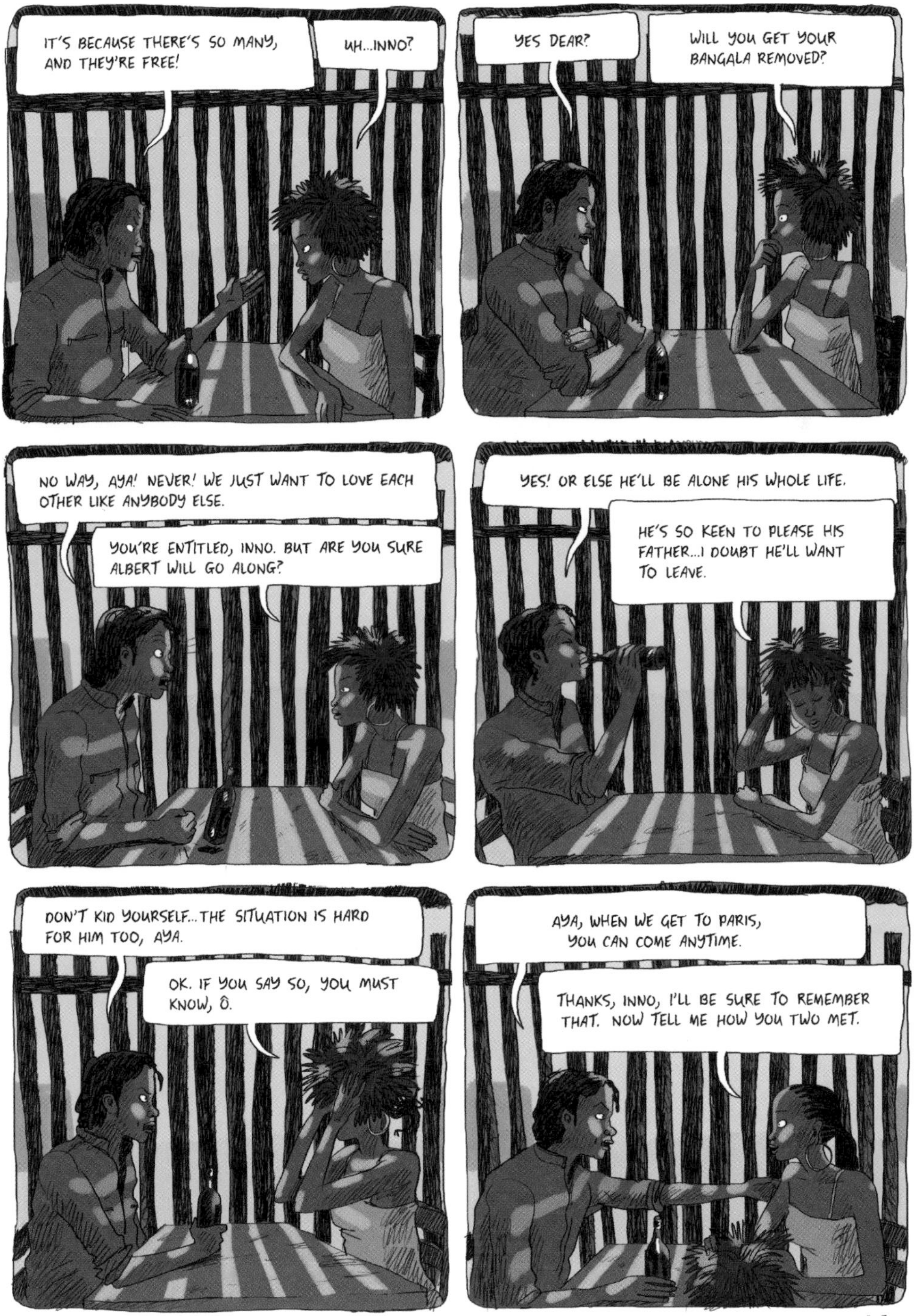
IT'S BECAUSE THERE'S SO MANY, AND THEY'RE FREE!
UH...INNO?
YES DEAR?
WILL YOU GET YOUR BANGALA REMOVED?
NO WAY, AYA! NEVER! WE JUST WANT TO LOVE EACH OTHER LIKE ANYBODY ELSE.
YOU'RE ENTITLED, INNO. BUT ARE YOU SURE ALBERT WILL GO ALONG?
YES! OR ELSE HE'LL BE ALONE HIS WHOLE LIFE.
HE'S SO KEEN TO PLEASE HIS FATHER...I DOUBT HE'LL WANT TO LEAVE.
DON'T KID YOURSELF...THE SITUATION IS HARD FOR HIM TOO, AYA.
OK. IF YOU SAY SO, YOU MUST KNOW, Ô.
AYA, WHEN WE GET TO PARIS, YOU CAN COME ANYTIME.
THANKS, INNO, I'LL BE SURE TO REMEMBER THAT. NOW TELL ME HOW YOU TWO MET.

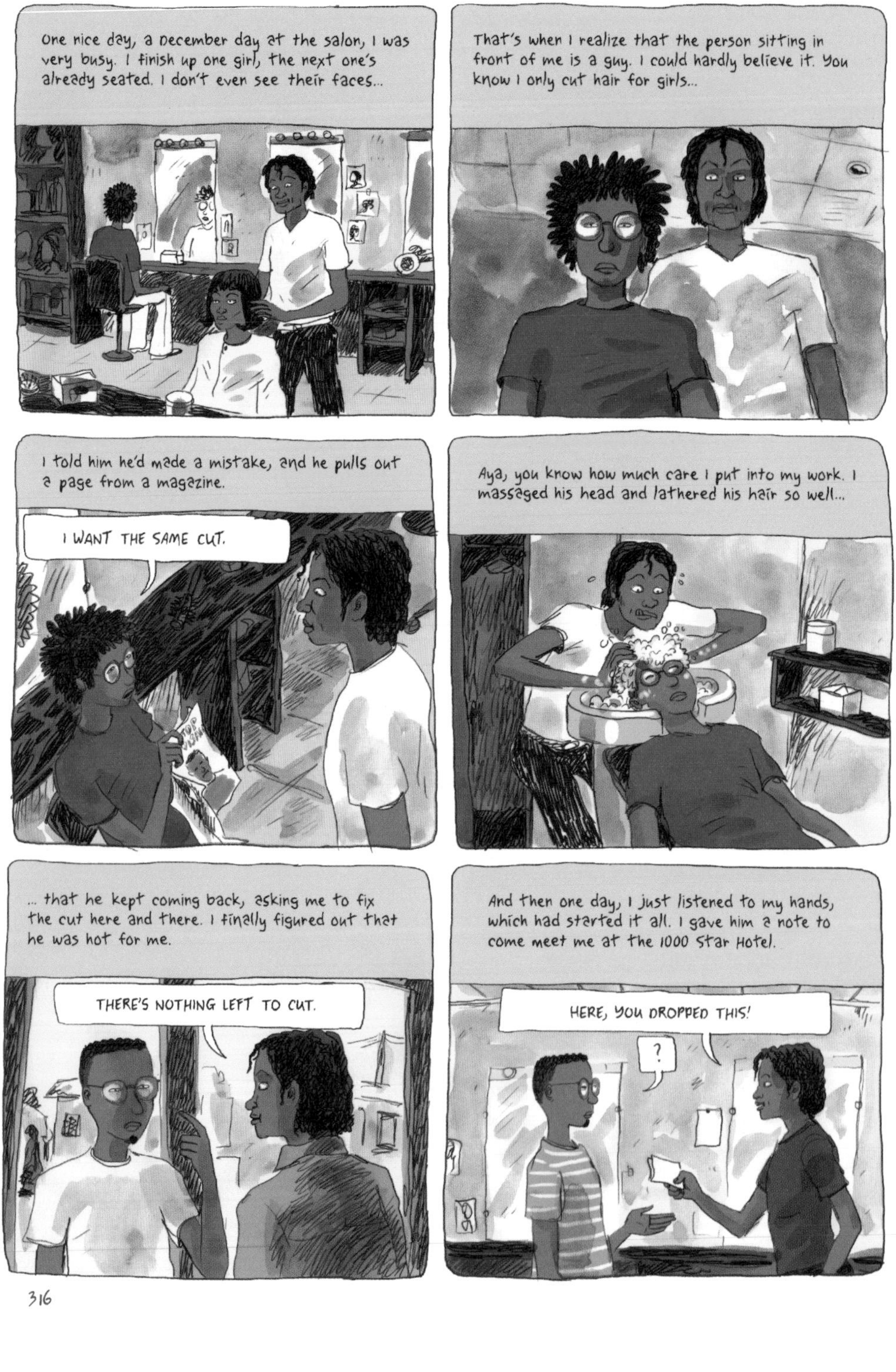
One nice day, a December day at the salon, I was very busy. I finish up one girl, the next one's already seated. I don't even see their faces...
That's when I realize that the person sitting in front of me is a guy. I could hardly believe it. You know I only cut hair for girls...
I told him he'd made a mistake, and he pulls out a page from a magazine.
I WANT THE SAME CUT.
Aya, you know how much care I put into my work. I massaged his head and lathered his hair so well...
... that he kept coming back, asking me to fix the cut here and there. I finally figured out that he was hot for me.
THERE'S NOTHING LEFT TO CUT.
And then one day, I just listened to my hands, which had started it all. I gave him a note to come meet me at the 1000 Star Hotel.
HERE, YOU DROPPED THIS!
?

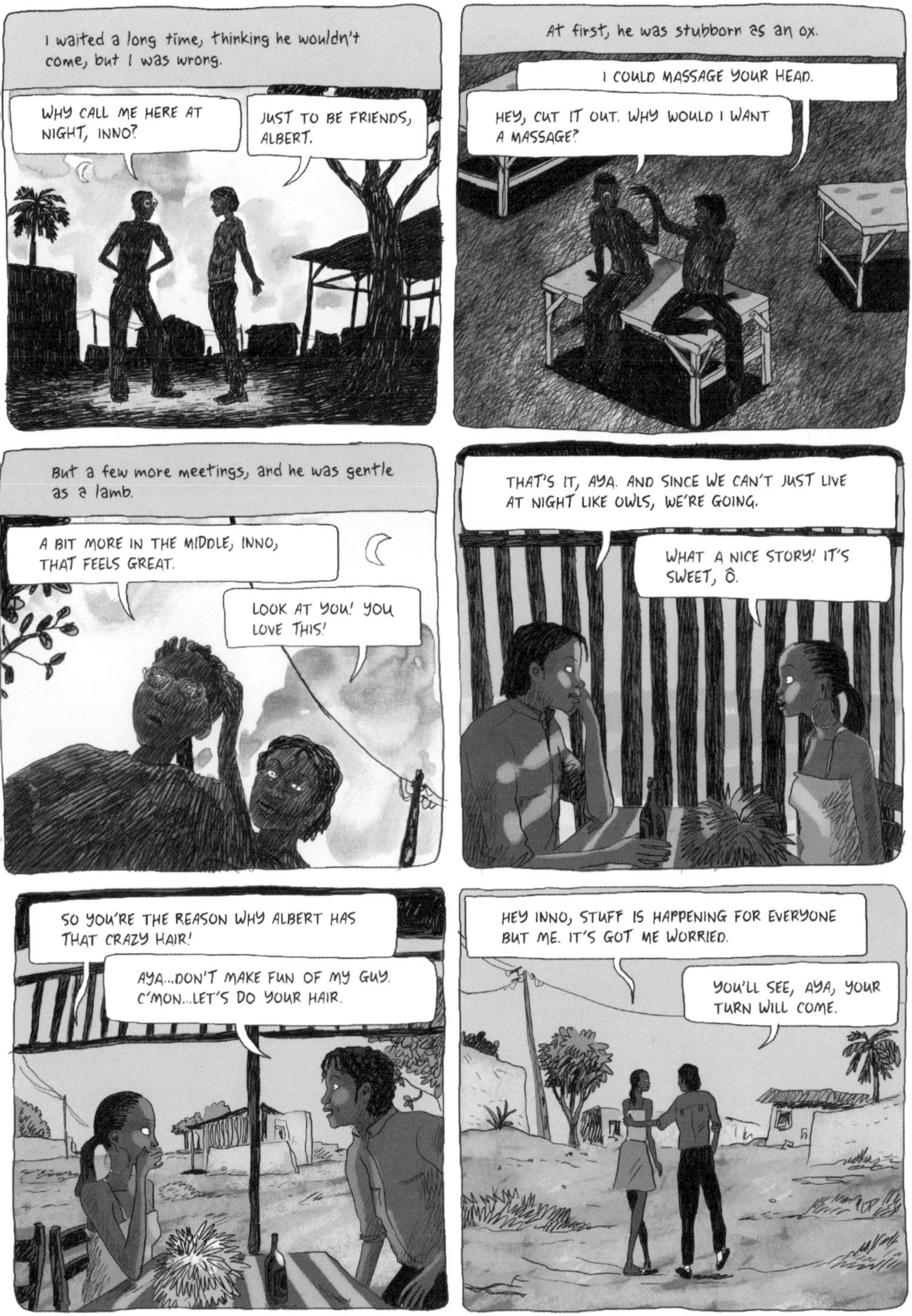
I waited a long time, thinking he wouldn't come, but I was wrong.
WHY CALL ME HERE AT NIGHT, INNO?
JUST TO BE FRIENDS, ALBERT.
At first, he was stubborn as an ox.
I COULD MASSAGE YOUR HEAD.
HEY, CUT IT OUT. WHY WOULD I WANT A MASSAGE?
But a few more meetings, and he was gentle as a lamb.
A BIT MORE IN THE MIDDLE, INNO, THAT FEELS GREAT.
LOOK AT YOU! YOU LOVE THIS!
THAT'S IT, AYA. AND SINCE WE CAN'T JUST LIVE AT NIGHT LIKE OWLS, WE'RE GOING.
WHAT A NICE STORY! IT'S SWEET, Ô.
SO YOU'RE THE REASON WHY ALBERT HAS THAT CRAZY HAIR!
AYA...DON'T MAKE FUN OF MY GUY. C'MON...LET'S DO YOUR HAIR.
HEY INNO, STUFF IS HAPPENING FOR EVERYONE BUT ME. IT'S GOT ME WORRIED.
YOU'LL SEE, AYA, YOUR TURN WILL COME.

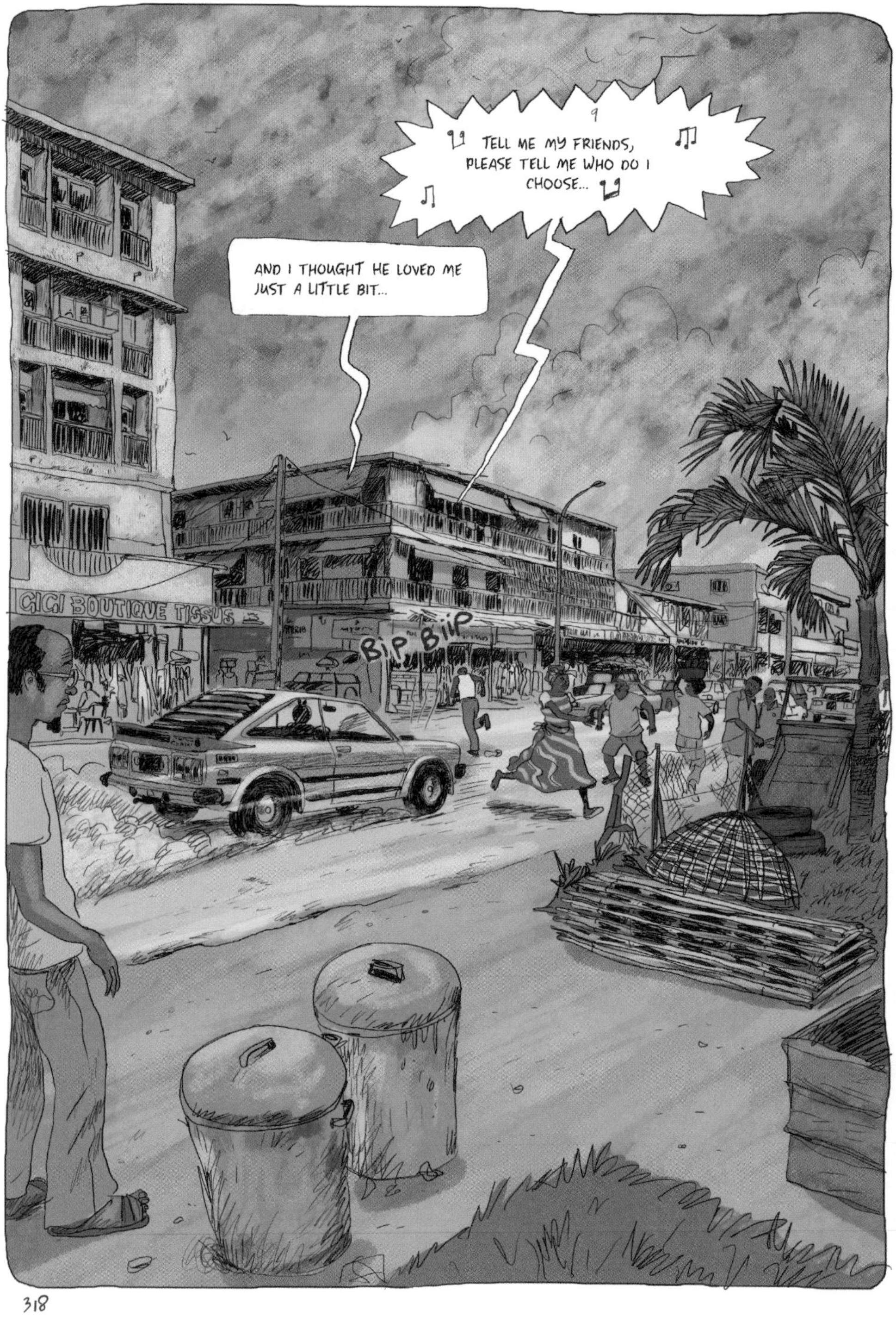
TELL ME MY FRIENDS, PLEASE TELL ME WHO DO I CHOOSE...
AND I THOUGHT HE LOVED ME JUST A LITTLE BIT...
CICI BOUTIQUE TISSUS
BIP BIIP

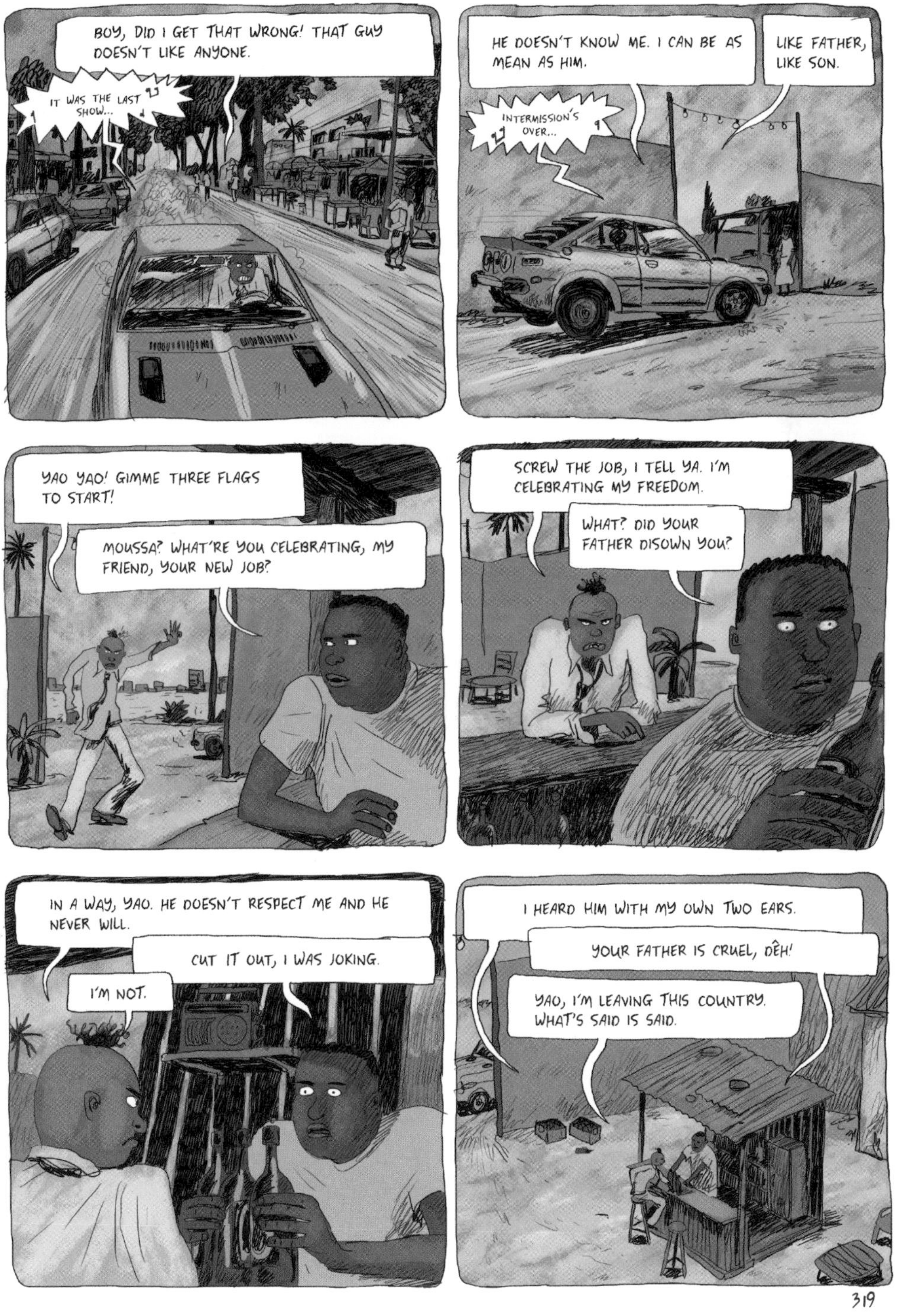
BOY, DID I GET THAT WRONG! THAT GUY DOESN'T LIKE ANYONE.
IT WAS THE LAST SHOW...
HE DOESN'T KNOW ME. I CAN BE AS MEAN AS HIM.
LIKE FATHER, LIKE SON.
INTERMISSION'S OVER...
YAO YAO! GIMME THREE FLAGS TO START!
MOUSSA? WHAT'RE YOU CELEBRATING, MY FRIEND, YOUR NEW JOB?
SCREW THE JOB, I TELL YA. I'M CELEBRATING MY FREEDOM.
WHAT? DID YOUR FATHER DISOWN YOU?
IN A WAY, YAO. HE DOESN'T RESPECT ME AND HE NEVER WILL.
CUT IT OUT, I WAS JOKING.
I'M NOT.
I HEARD HIM WITH MY OWN TWO EARS.
YOUR FATHER IS CRUEL, DÊH!
YAO, I'M LEAVING THIS COUNTRY. WHAT'S SAID IS SAID.

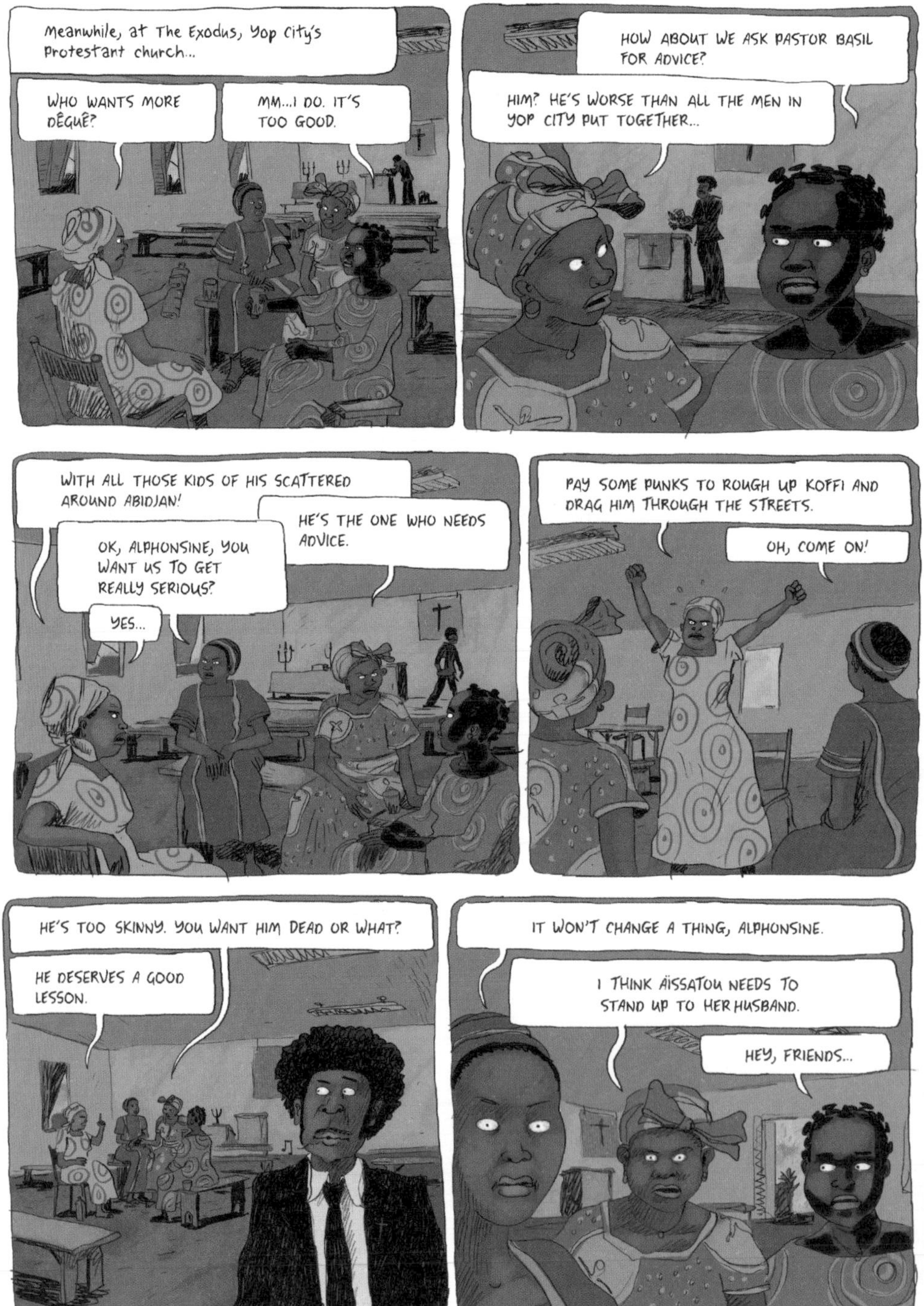
Meanwhile, at The Exodus, Yop City's Protestant church...
WHO WANTS MORE DÊGUÊ?
MM...I DO. IT'S TOO GOOD.
HOW ABOUT WE ASK PASTOR BASIL FOR ADVICE?
HIM? HE'S WORSE THAN ALL THE MEN IN YOP CITY PUT TOGETHER...
WITH ALL THOSE KIDS OF HIS SCATTERED AROUND ABIDJAN!
HE'S THE ONE WHO NEEDS ADVICE.
OK, ALPHONSINE, YOU WANT US TO GET REALLY SERIOUS?
YES...
PAY SOME PUNKS TO ROUGH UP KOFFI AND DRAG HIM THROUGH THE STREETS.
OH, COME ON!
HE'S TOO SKINNY. YOU WANT HIM DEAD OR WHAT?
HE DESERVES A GOOD LESSON.
IT WON'T CHANGE A THING, ALPHONSINE.
I THINK AÏSSATOU NEEDS TO STAND UP TO HER HUSBAND.
HEY, FRIENDS...

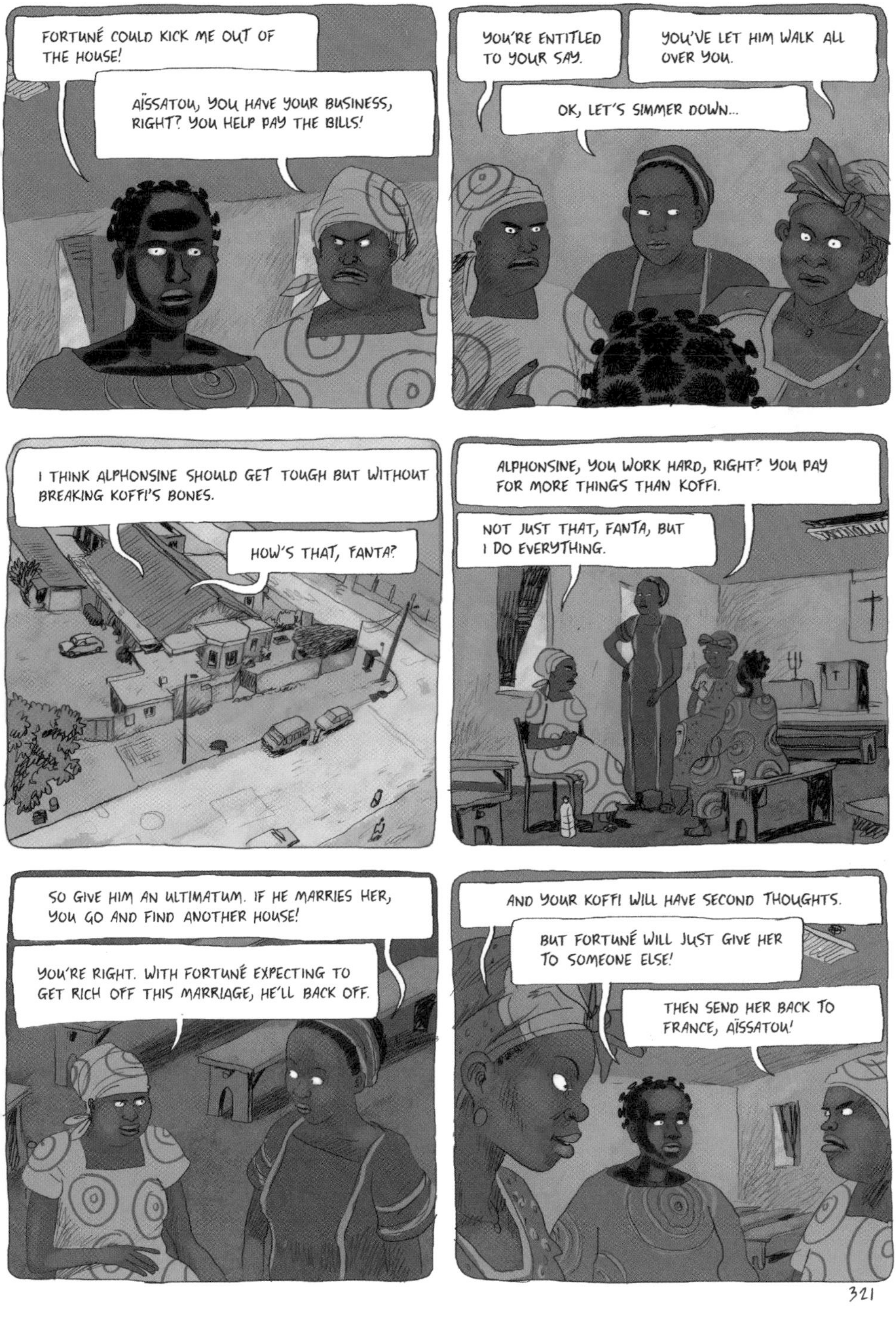
FORTUNÉ COULD KICK ME OUT OF THE HOUSE!
AÏSSATOU, YOU HAVE YOUR BUSINESS, RIGHT? YOU HELP PAY THE BILLS!
YOU'RE ENTITLED TO YOUR SAY.
YOU'VE LET HIM WALK ALL OVER YOU.
OK, LET'S SIMMER DOWN...
I THINK ALPHONSINE SHOULD GET TOUGH BUT WITHOUT BREAKING KOFFI'S BONES.
HOW'S THAT, FANTA?
ALPHONSINE, YOU WORK HARD, RIGHT? YOU PAY FOR MORE THINGS THAN KOFFI.
NOT JUST THAT, FANTA, BUT I DO EVERYTHING.
SO GIVE HIM AN ULTIMATUM. IF HE MARRIES HER, YOU GO AND FIND ANOTHER HOUSE!
YOU'RE RIGHT. WITH FORTUNÉ EXPECTING TO GET RICH OFF THIS MARRIAGE, HE'LL BACK OFF.
AND YOUR KOFFI WILL HAVE SECOND THOUGHTS.
BUT FORTUNÉ WILL JUST GIVE HER TO SOMEONE ELSE!
THEN SEND HER BACK TO FRANCE, AÏSSATOU!

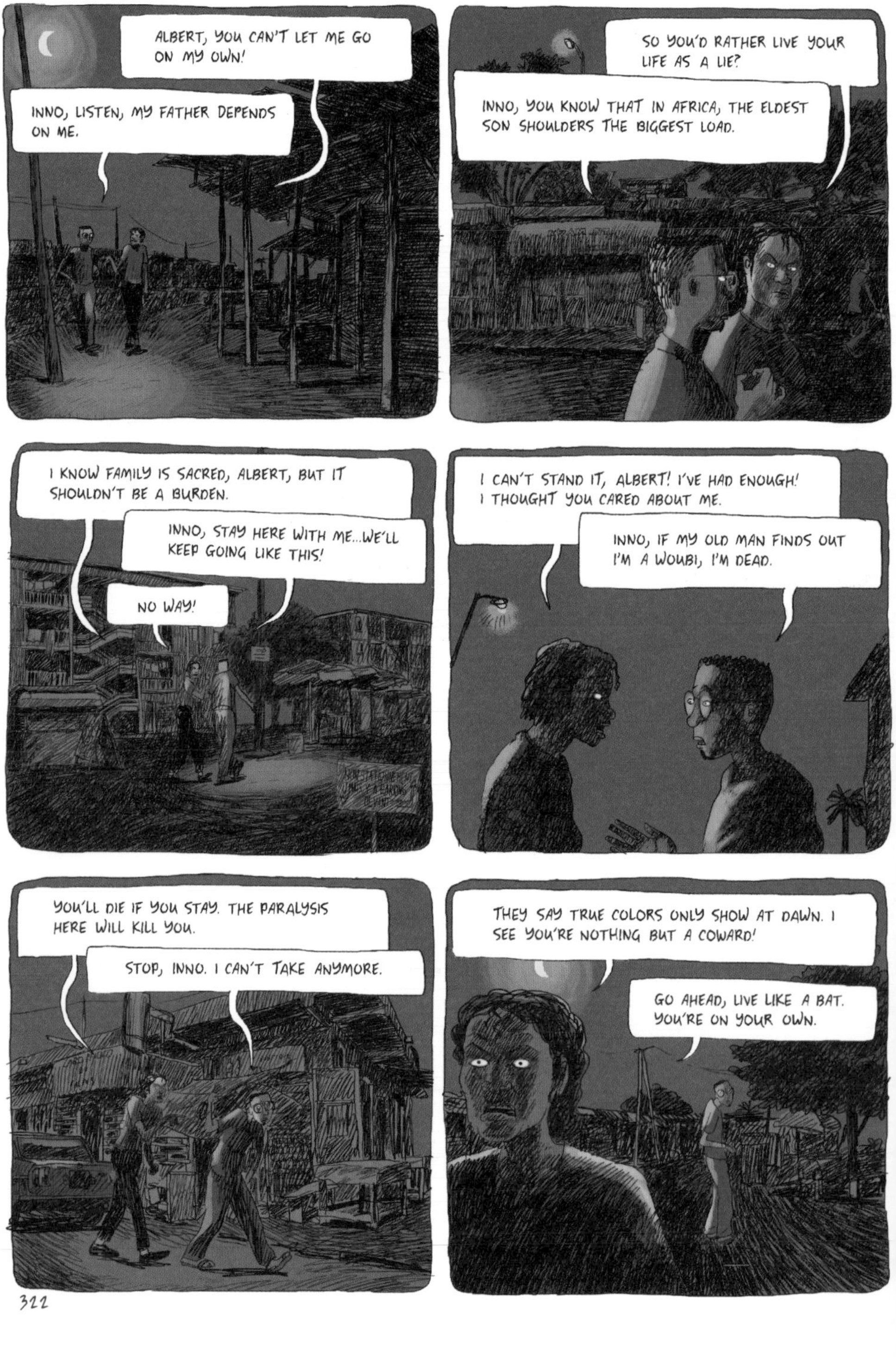
ALBERT, YOU CAN'T LET ME GO ON MY OWN!
INNO, LISTEN, MY FATHER DEPENDS ON ME.
SO YOU'D RATHER LIVE YOUR LIFE AS A LIE?
INNO, YOU KNOW THAT IN AFRICA, THE ELDEST SON SHOULDERS THE BIGGEST LOAD.
I KNOW FAMILY IS SACRED, ALBERT, BUT IT SHOULDN'T BE A BURDEN.
INNO, STAY HERE WITH ME...WE'LL KEEP GOING LIKE THIS!
NO WAY!
I CAN'T STAND IT, ALBERT! I'VE HAD ENOUGH! I THOUGHT YOU CARED ABOUT ME.
INNO, IF MY OLD MAN FINDS OUT I'M A WOUBI, I'M DEAD.
YOU'LL DIE IF YOU STAY. THE PARALYSIS HERE WILL KILL YOU.
STOP, INNO. I CAN'T TAKE ANYMORE.
THEY SAY TRUE COLORS ONLY SHOW AT DAWN. I SEE YOU'RE NOTHING BUT A COWARD!
GO AHEAD, LIVE LIKE A BAT. YOU'RE ON YOUR OWN.

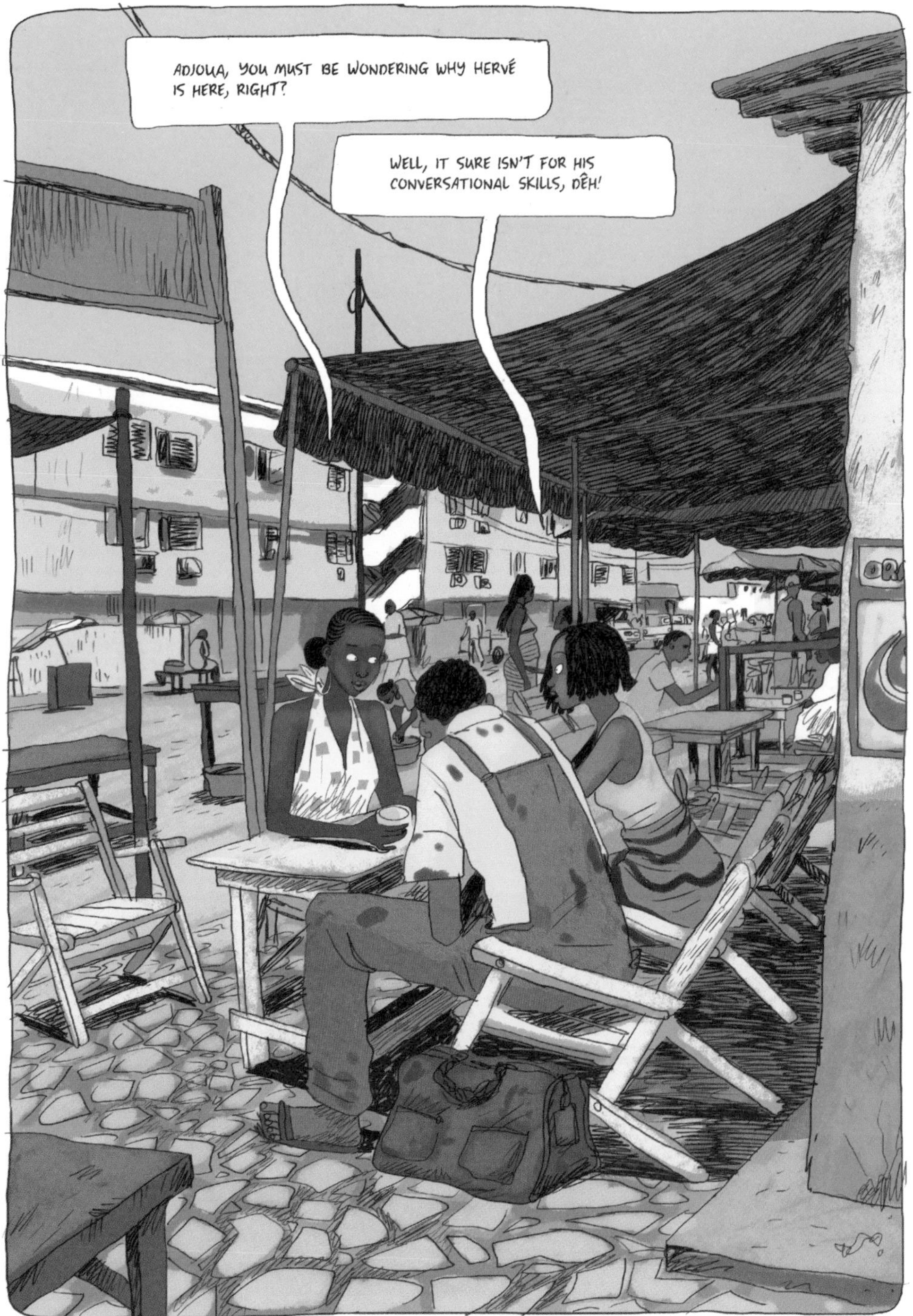
ADJOUA, YOU MUST BE WONDERING WHY HERVÉ IS HERE, RIGHT?
WELL, IT SURE ISN'T FOR HIS CONVERSATIONAL SKILLS, DÊH!

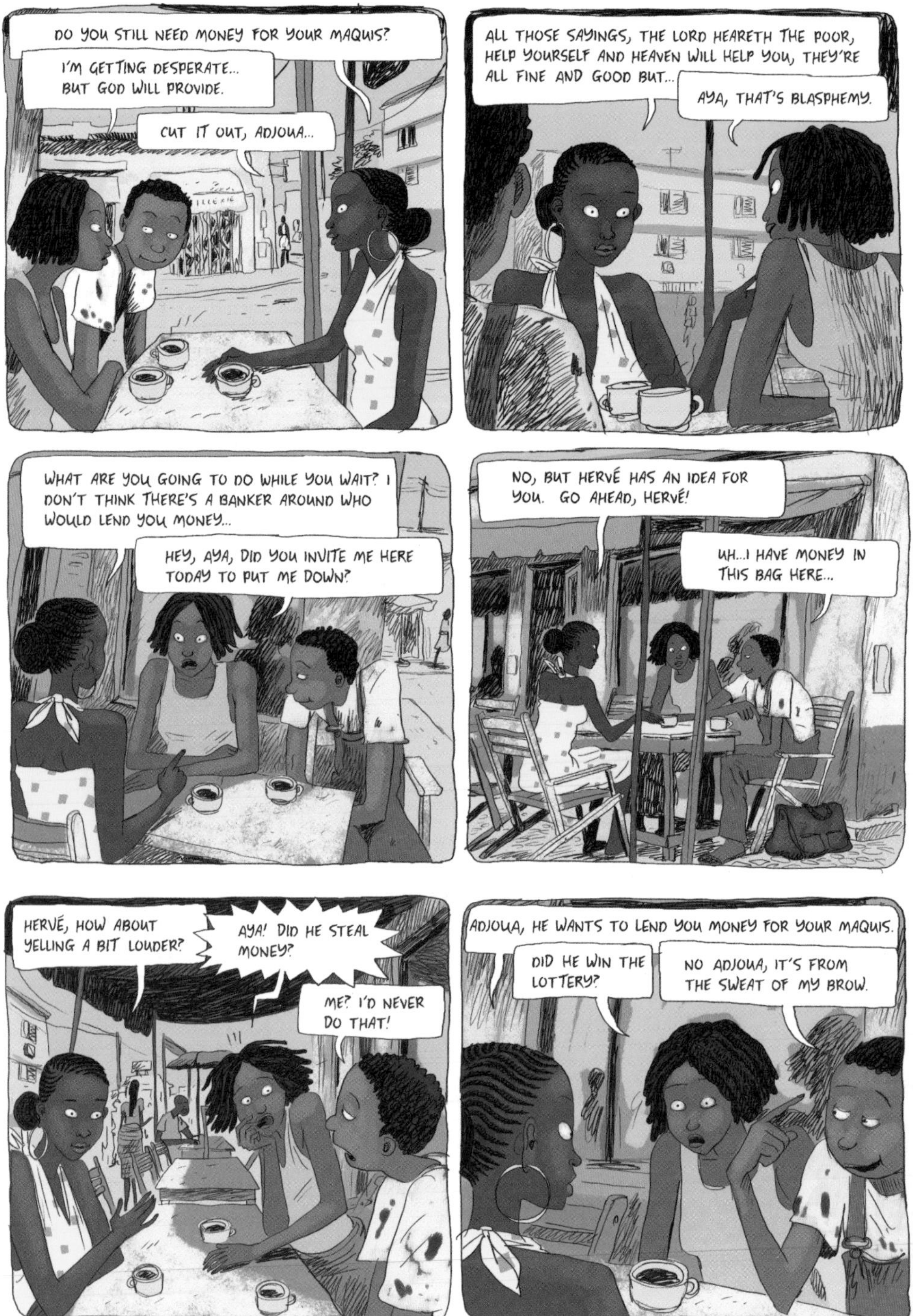
DO YOU STILL NEED MONEY FOR YOUR MAQUIS?
I'M GETTING DESPERATE... BUT GOD WILL PROVIDE.
CUT IT OUT, ADJOUA...
ALL THOSE SAYINGS, THE LORD HEARETH THE POOR, HELP YOURSELF AND HEAVEN WILL HELP YOU, THEY'RE ALL FINE AND GOOD BUT...
AYA, THAT'S BLASPHEMY.
WHAT ARE YOU GOING TO DO WHILE YOU WAIT? I DON'T THINK THERE'S A BANKER AROUND WHO WOULD LEND YOU MONEY...
HEY, AYA, DID YOU INVITE ME HERE TODAY TO PUT ME DOWN?
NO, BUT HERVÉ HAS AN IDEA FOR YOU. GO AHEAD, HERVÉ!
UH...I HAVE MONEY IN THIS BAG HERE...
HERVÉ, HOW ABOUT YELLING A BIT LOUDER?
AYA! DID HE STEAL MONEY?
ME? I'D NEVER DO THAT!
ADJOUA, HE WANTS TO LEND YOU MONEY FOR YOUR MAQUIS.
DID HE WIN THE LOTTERY?
NO ADJOUA, IT'S FROM THE SWEAT OF MY BROW.

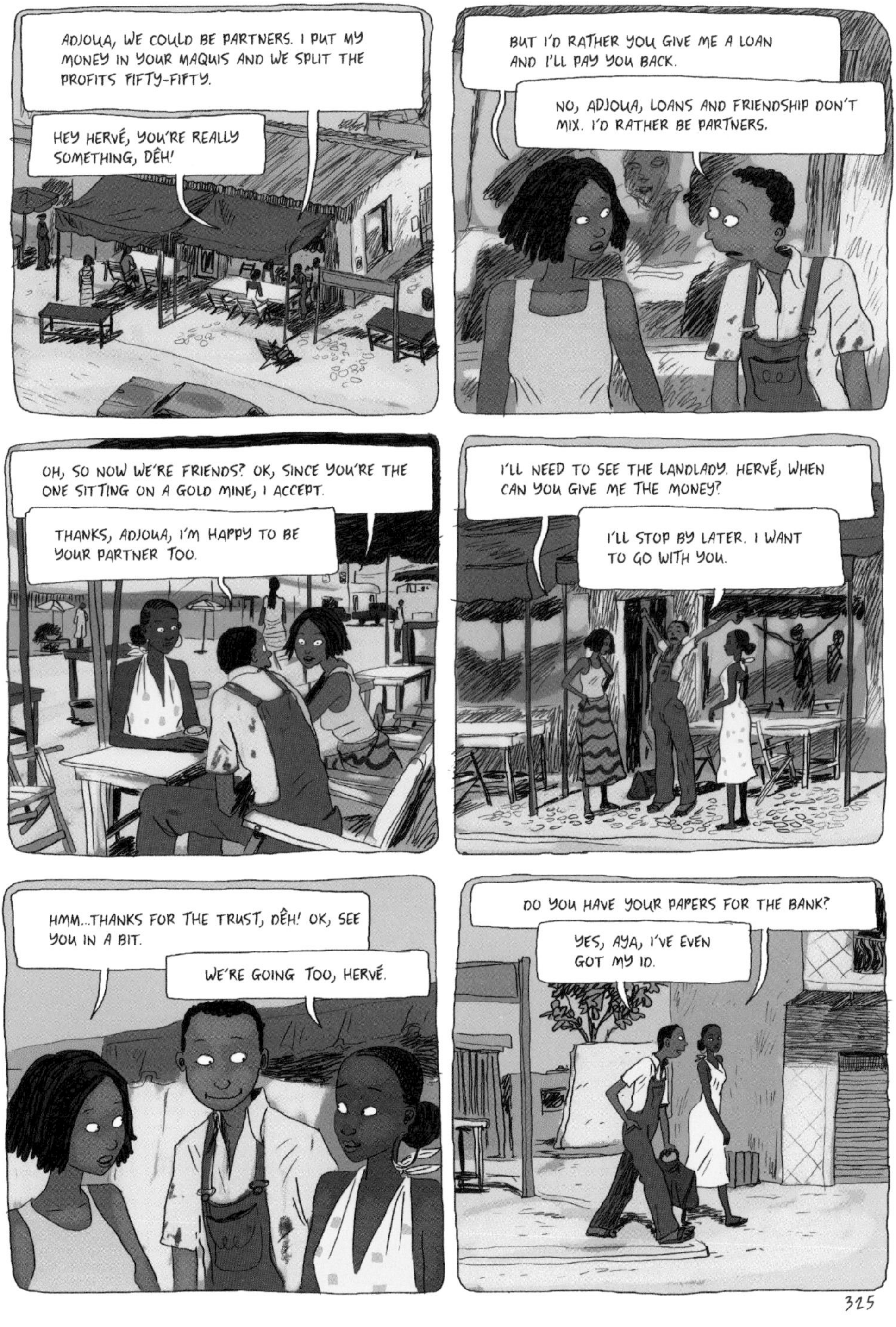
ADJOUA, WE COULD BE PARTNERS. I PUT MY MONEY IN YOUR MAQUIS AND WE SPLIT THE PROFITS FIFTY-FIFTY.
HEY HERVÉ, YOU'RE REALLY SOMETHING, DÊH!
BUT I'D RATHER YOU GIVE ME A LOAN AND I'LL PAY YOU BACK.
NO, ADJOUA, LOANS AND FRIENDSHIP DON'T MIX. I'D RATHER BE PARTNERS.
OH, SO NOW WE'RE FRIENDS? OK, SINCE YOU'RE THE ONE SITTING ON A GOLD MINE, I ACCEPT.
THANKS, ADJOUA, I'M HAPPY TO BE YOUR PARTNER TOO.
I'LL NEED TO SEE THE LANDLADY. HERVÉ, WHEN CAN YOU GIVE ME THE MONEY?
I'LL STOP BY LATER. I WANT TO GO WITH YOU.
HMM...THANKS FOR THE TRUST, DÊH! OK, SEE YOU IN A BIT.
WE'RE GOING TOO, HERVÉ.
DO YOU HAVE YOUR PAPERS FOR THE BANK?
YES, AYA, I'VE EVEN GOT MY ID.

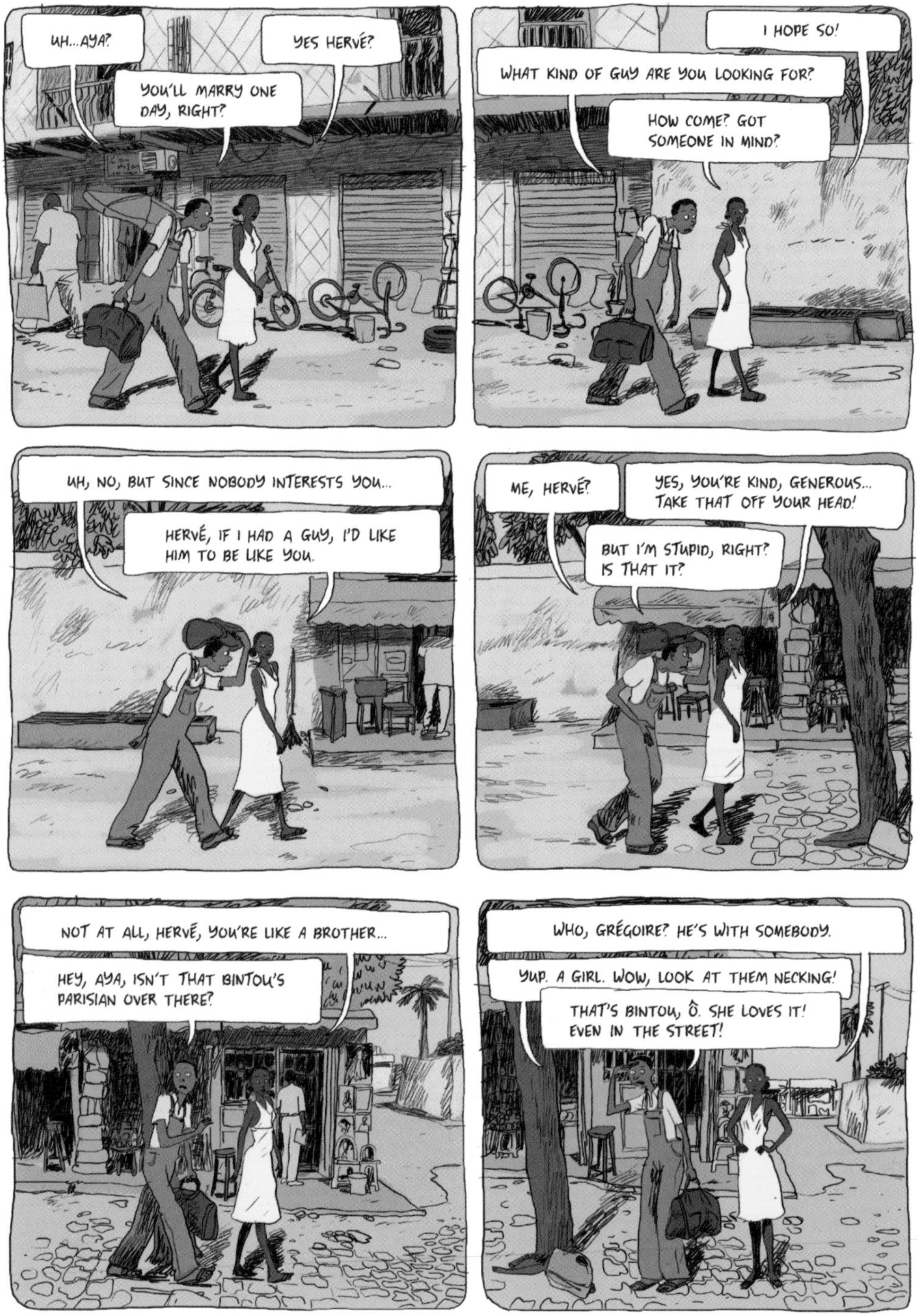
UH...AYA?
YES HERVÉ?
YOU'LL MARRY ONE DAY, RIGHT?
I HOPE SO!
WHAT KIND OF GUY ARE YOU LOOKING FOR?
HOW COME? GOT SOMEONE IN MIND?
UH, NO, BUT SINCE NOBODY INTERESTS YOU...
HERVÉ, IF I HAD A GUY, I'D LIKE HIM TO BE LIKE YOU.
ME, HERVÉ?
YES, YOU'RE KIND, GENEROUS... TAKE THAT OFF YOUR HEAD!
BUT I'M STUPID, RIGHT? IS THAT IT?
NOT AT ALL, HERVÉ, YOU'RE LIKE A BROTHER...
HEY, AYA, ISN'T THAT BINTOU'S PARISIAN OVER THERE?
WHO, GRÉGOIRE? HE'S WITH SOMEBODY.
YUP. A GIRL. WOW, LOOK AT THEM NECKING!
THAT'S BINTOU, Ô. SHE LOVES IT! EVEN IN THE STREET!

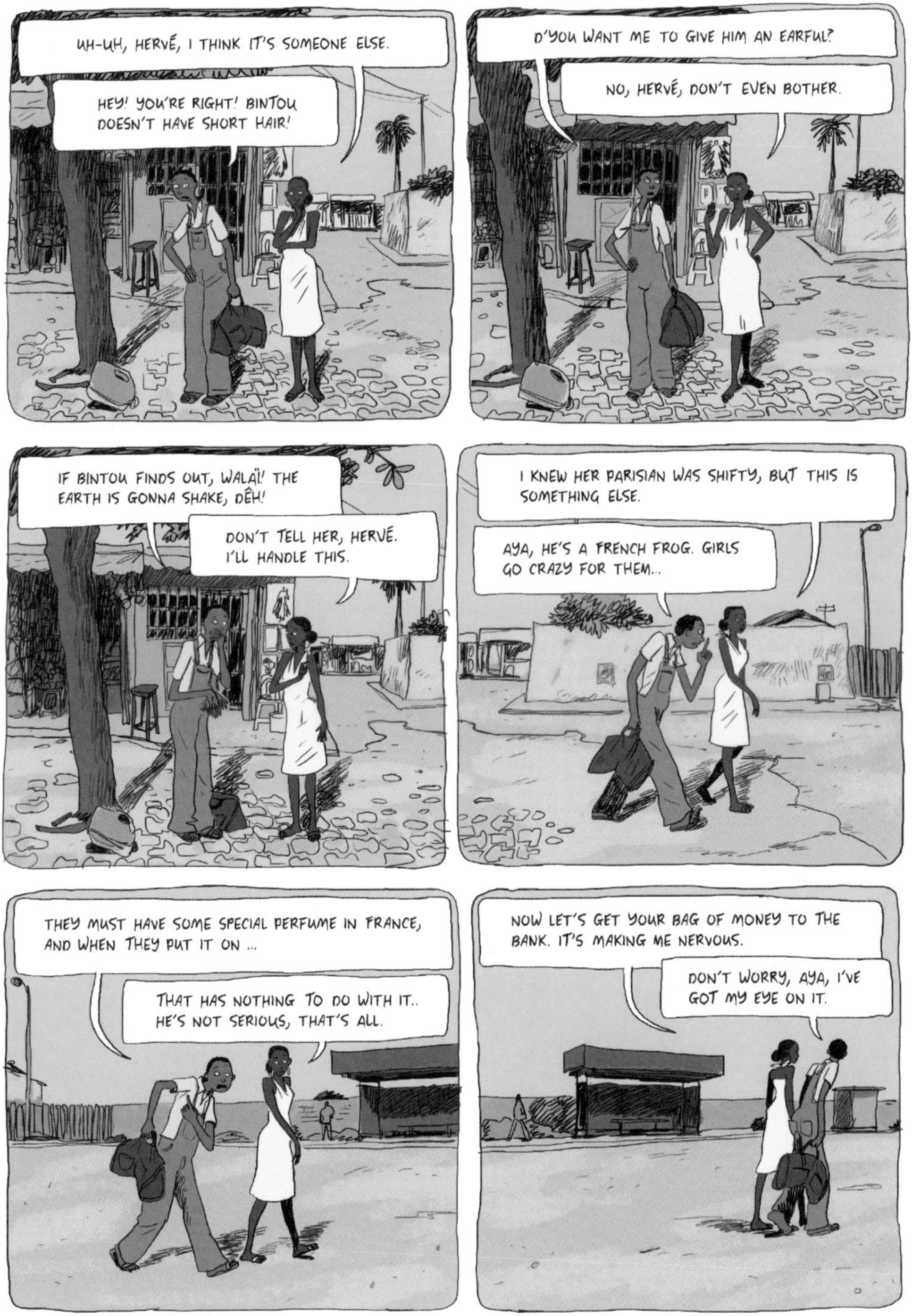
UH-UH, HERVÉ, I THINK IT'S SOMEONE ELSE.
HEY! YOU'RE RIGHT! BINTOU DOESN'T HAVE SHORT HAIR!
D'YOU WANT ME TO GIVE HIM AN EARFUL?
NO, HERVÉ, DON'T EVEN BOTHER.
IF BINTOU FINDS OUT, WALAÏ! THE EARTH IS GONNA SHAKE, DÊH!
DON'T TELL HER, HERVÉ. I'LL HANDLE THIS.
I KNEW HER PARISIAN WAS SHIFTY, BUT THIS IS SOMETHING ELSE.
AYA, HE'S A FRENCH FROG. GIRLS GO CRAZY FOR THEM...
THEY MUST HAVE SOME SPECIAL PERFUME IN FRANCE, AND WHEN THEY PUT IT ON ...
THAT HAS NOTHING TO DO WITH IT.. HE'S NOT SERIOUS, THAT'S ALL.
NOW LET'S GET YOUR BAG OF MONEY TO THE BANK. IT'S MAKING ME NERVOUS.
DON'T WORRY, AYA, I'VE GOT MY EYE ON IT.

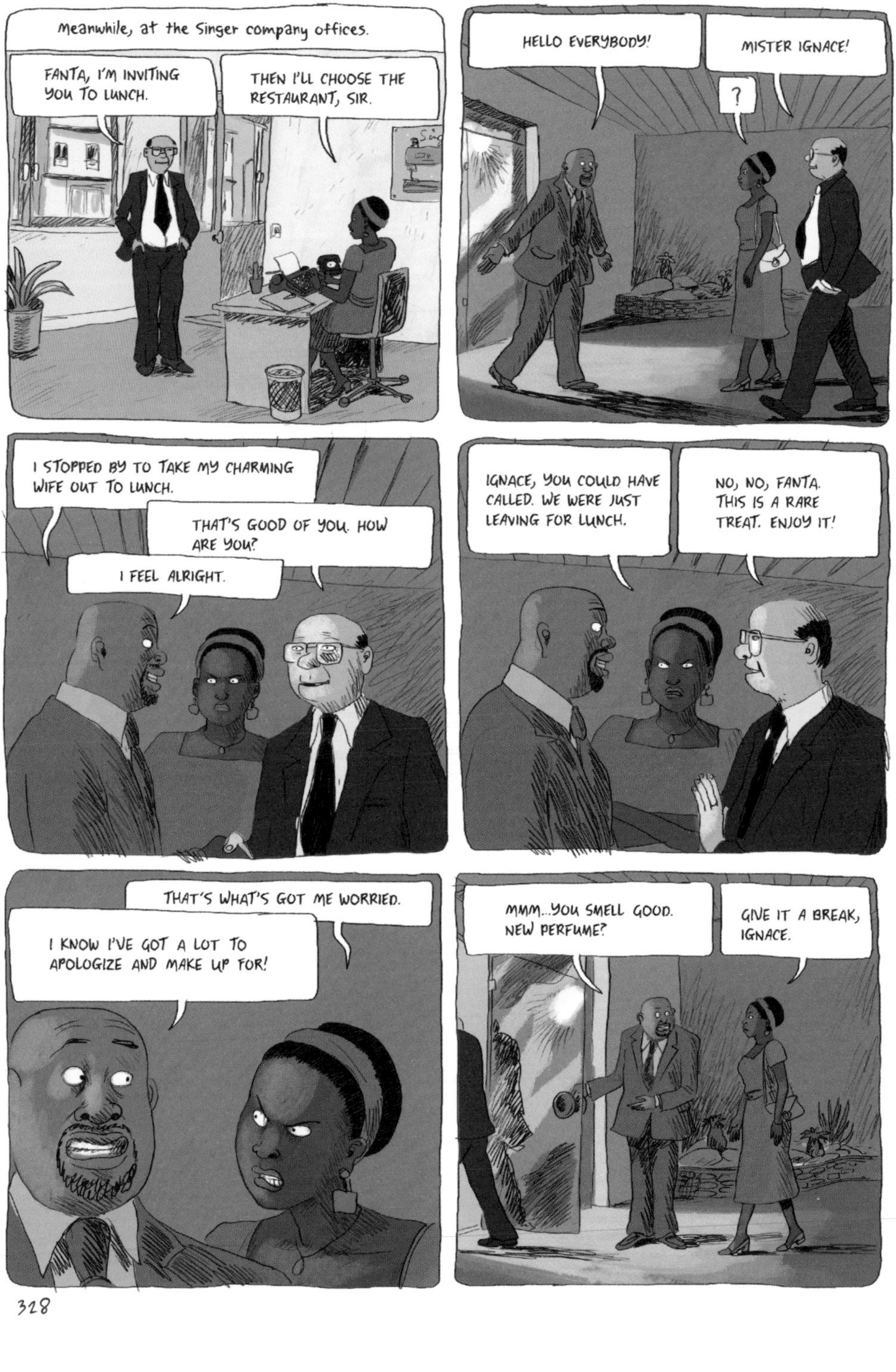
Meanwhile, at the Singer company offices.
FANTA, I'M INVITING YOU TO LUNCH.
THEN I'LL CHOOSE THE RESTAURANT, SIR.
HELLO EVERYBODY!
MISTER IGNACE!
?
I STOPPED BY TO TAKE MY CHARMING WIFE OUT TO LUNCH.
THAT'S GOOD OF YOU. HOW ARE YOU?
I FEEL ALRIGHT.
IGNACE, YOU COULD HAVE CALLED. WE WERE JUST LEAVING FOR LUNCH.
NO, NO, FANTA. THIS IS A RARE TREAT. ENJOY IT!
THAT'S WHAT'S GOT ME WORRIED.
I KNOW I'VE GOT A LOT TO APOLOGIZE AND MAKE UP FOR!
MMM...YOU SMELL GOOD. NEW PERFUME?
GIVE IT A BREAK, IGNACE.

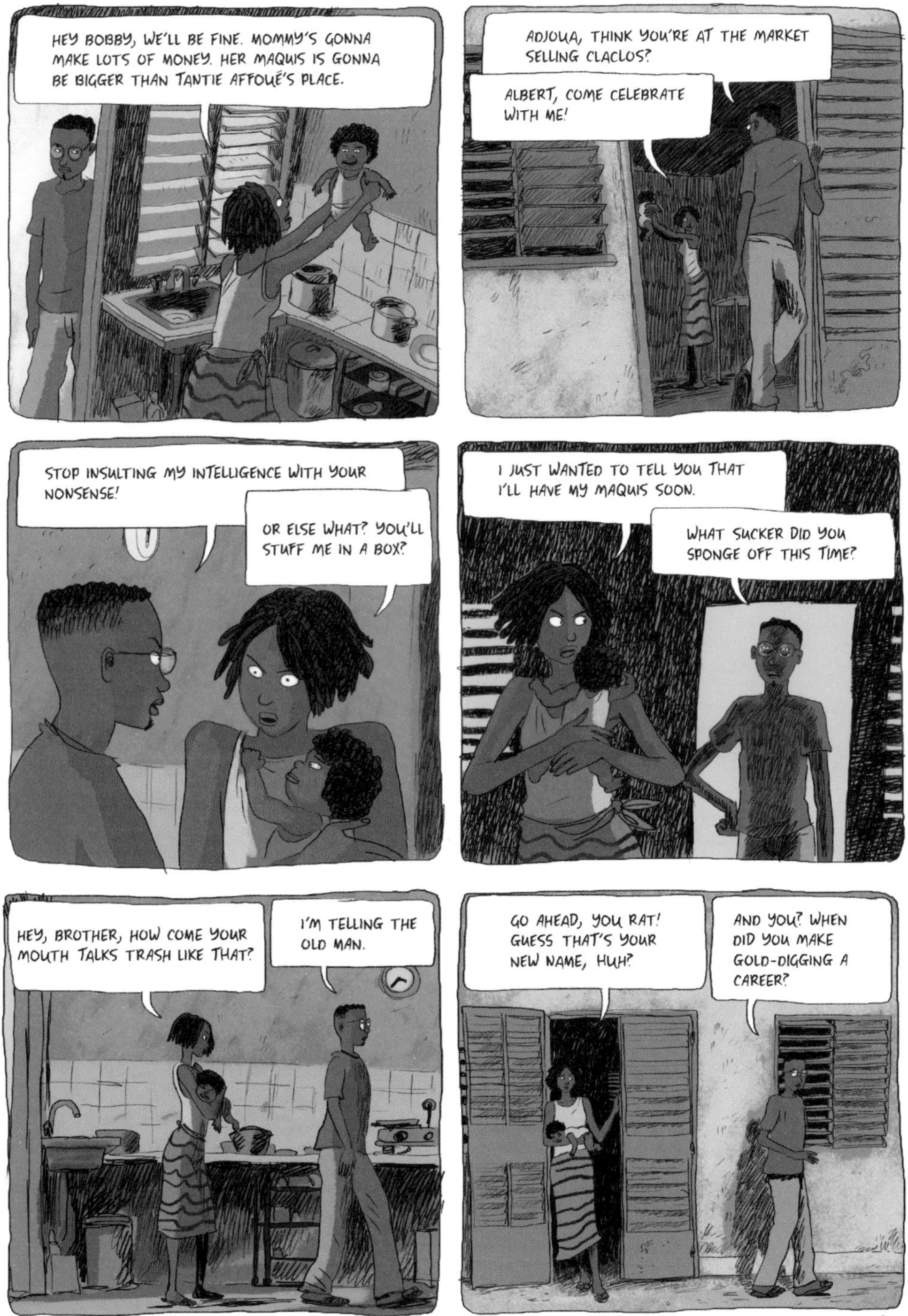
HEY BOBBY, WE'LL BE FINE. MOMMY'S GONNA MAKE LOTS OF MONEY. HER MAQUIS IS GONNA BE BIGGER THAN TANTIE AFFOUÉ'S PLACE.
ADJOUA, THINK YOU'RE AT THE MARKET SELLING CLACLOS?
ALBERT, COME CELEBRATE WITH ME!
STOP INSULTING MY INTELLIGENCE WITH YOUR NONSENSE!
OR ELSE WHAT? YOU'LL STUFF ME IN A BOX?
I JUST WANTED TO TELL YOU THAT I'LL HAVE MY MAQUIS SOON.
WHAT SUCKER DID YOU SPONGE OFF THIS TIME?
HEY, BROTHER, HOW COME YOUR MOUTH TALKS TRASH LIKE THAT?
I'M TELLING THE OLD MAN.
GO AHEAD, YOU RAT! GUESS THAT'S YOUR NEW NAME, HUH?
AND YOU? WHEN DID YOU MAKE GOLD-DIGGING A CAREER?

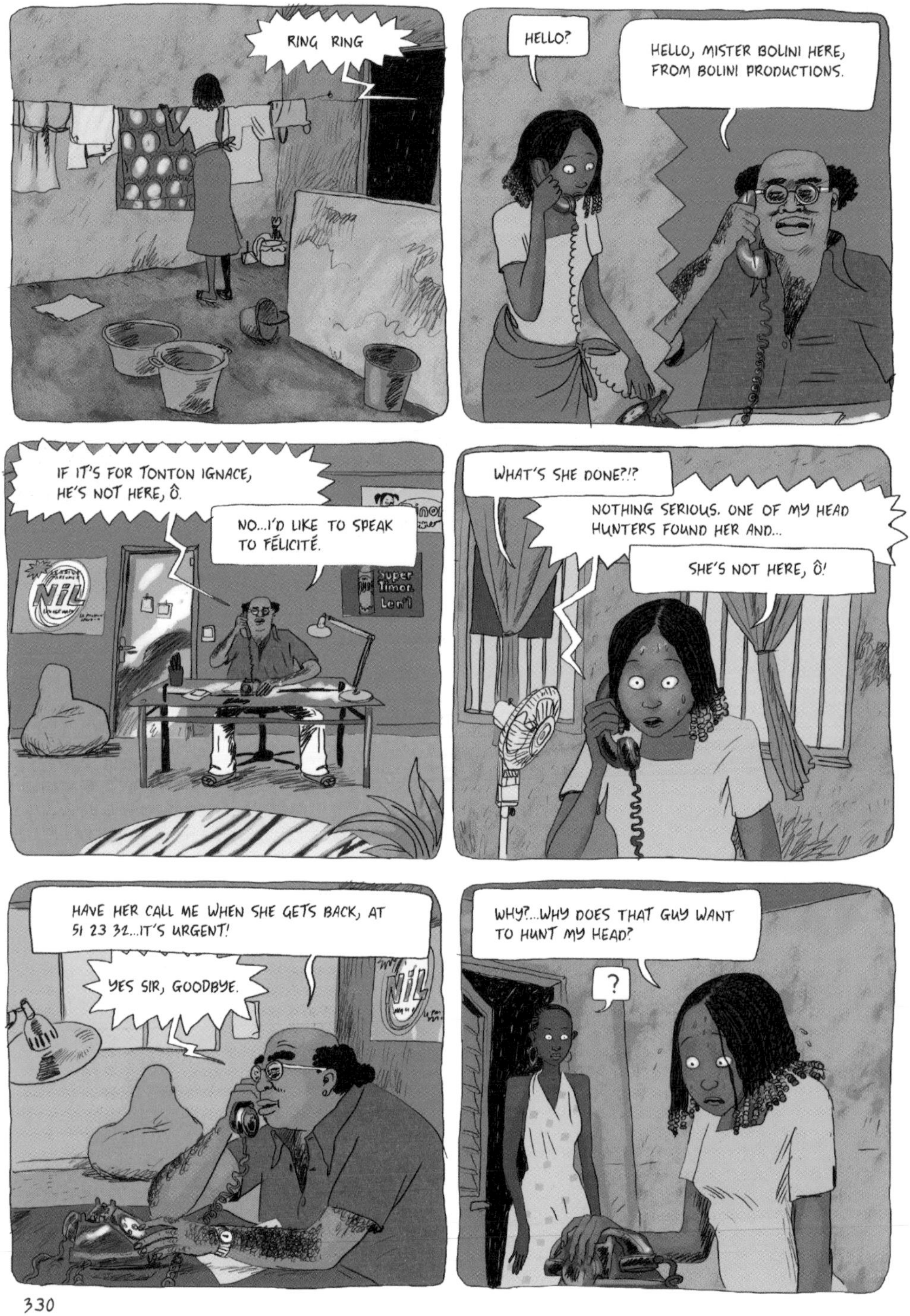
RING RING
HELLO?
HELLO, MISTER BOLINI HERE, FROM BOLINI PRODUCTIONS.
IF IT'S FOR TONTON IGNACE, HE'S NOT HERE, Ô.
NO...I'D LIKE TO SPEAK TO FÉLICITÉ.
WHAT'S SHE DONE?!?
NOTHING SERIOUS. ONE OF MY HEAD HUNTERS FOUND HER AND...
SHE'S NOT HERE, Ô!
HAVE HER CALL ME WHEN SHE GETS BACK, AT 51 23 32...IT'S URGENT!
YES SIR, GOODBYE.
WHY?...WHY DOES THAT GUY WANT TO HUNT MY HEAD?
?

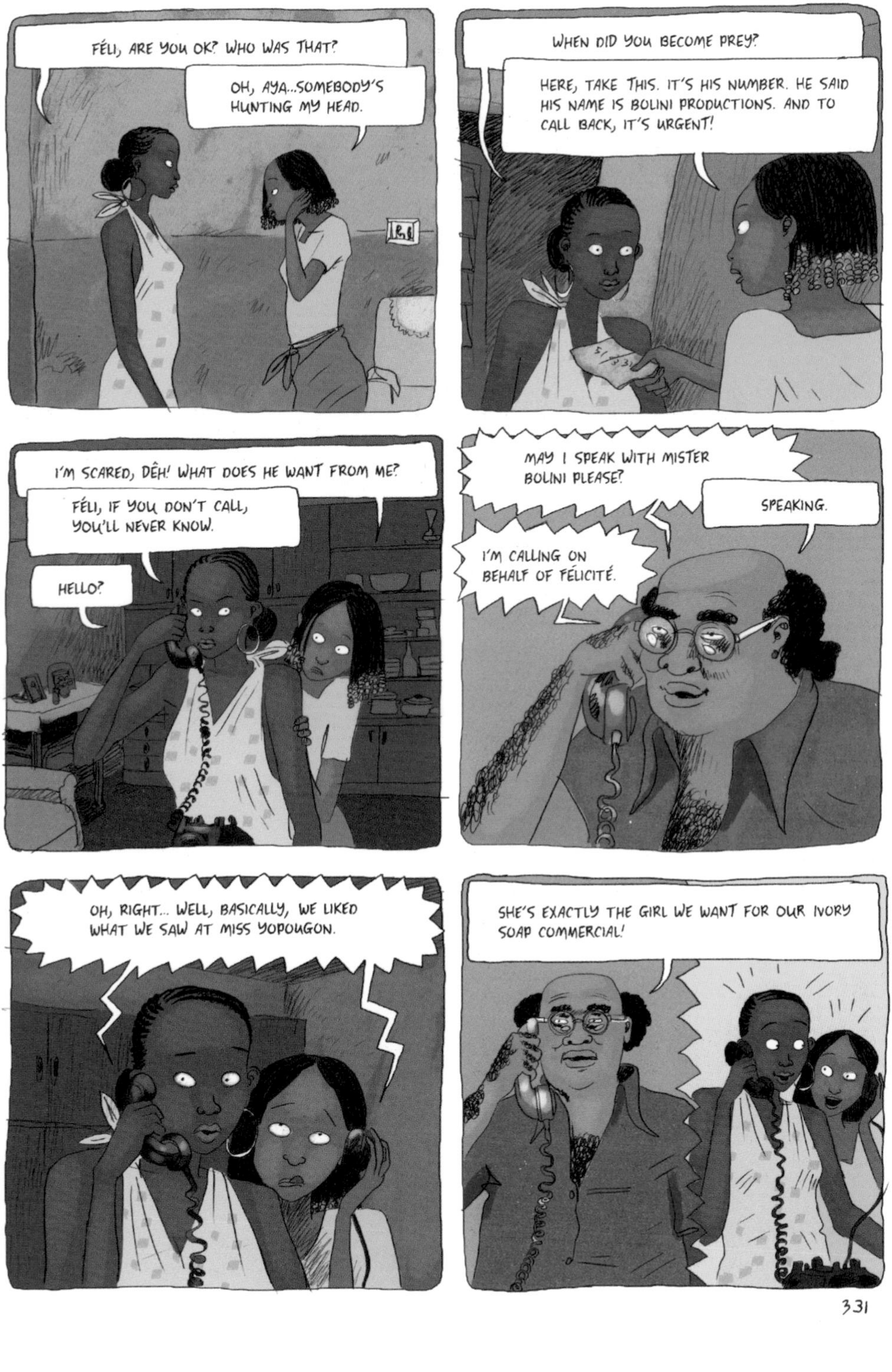
FÉLI, ARE YOU OK? WHO WAS THAT?
OH, AYA...SOMEBODY'S HUNTING MY HEAD.
WHEN DID YOU BECOME PREY?
HERE, TAKE THIS. IT'S HIS NUMBER. HE SAID HIS NAME IS BOLINI PRODUCTIONS. AND TO CALL BACK, IT'S URGENT!
I'M SCARED, DÊH! WHAT DOES HE WANT FROM ME?
FÉLI, IF YOU DON'T CALL, YOU'LL NEVER KNOW.
HELLO?
MAY I SPEAK WITH MISTER BOLINI PLEASE?
SPEAKING.
I'M CALLING ON BEHALF OF FÉLICITÉ.
OH, RIGHT... WELL, BASICALLY, WE LIKED WHAT WE SAW AT MISS YOPOUGON.
SHE'S EXACTLY THE GIRL WE WANT FOR OUR IVORY SOAP COMMERCIAL!

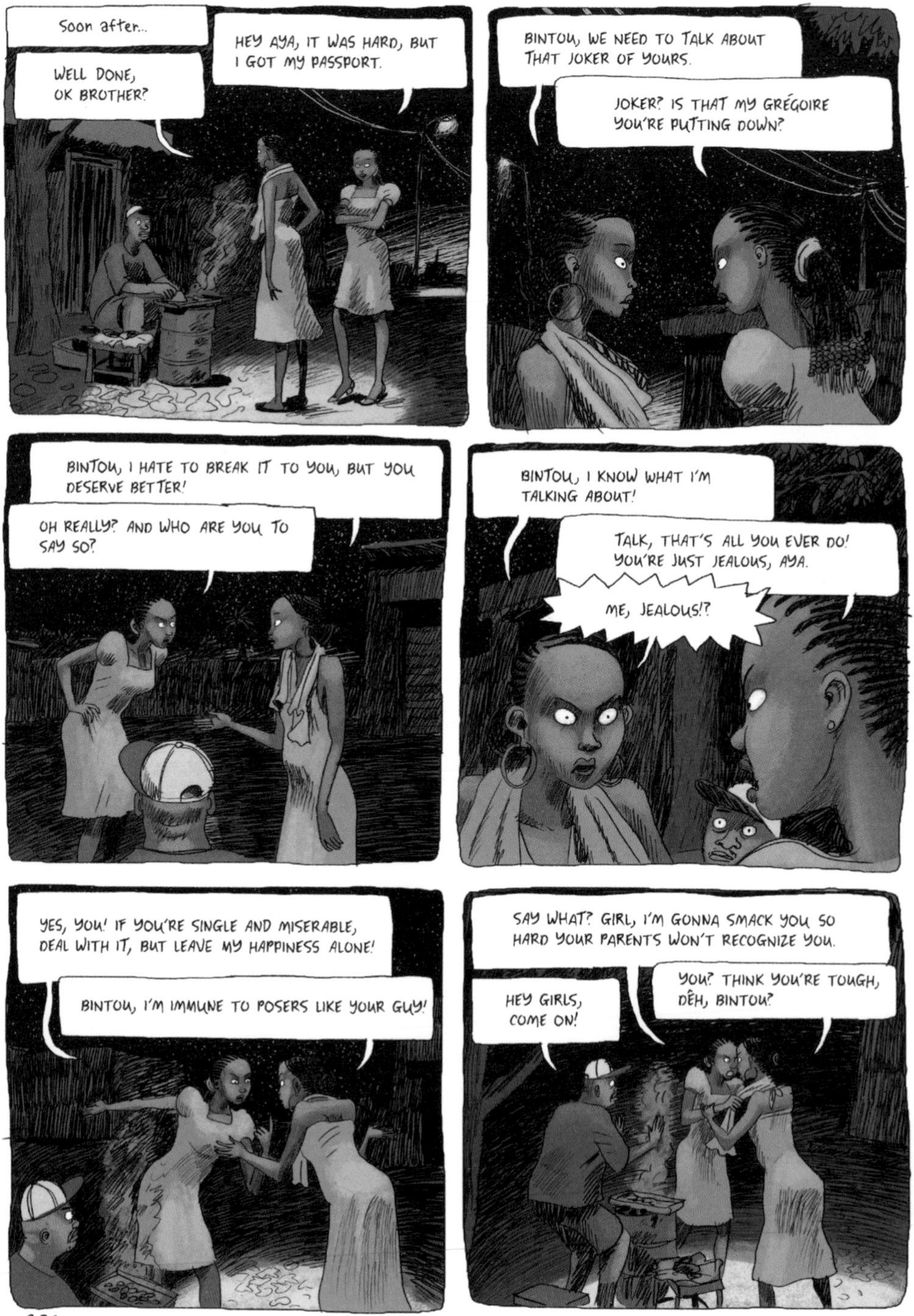
Soon after...
WELL DONE, OK BROTHER?
HEY AYA, IT WAS HARD, BUT I GOT MY PASSPORT.
BINTOU, WE NEED TO TALK ABOUT THAT JOKER OF YOURS.
JOKER? IS THAT MY GRÉGOIRE YOU'RE PUTTING DOWN?
BINTOU, I HATE TO BREAK IT TO YOU, BUT YOU DESERVE BETTER!
OH REALLY? AND WHO ARE YOU TO SAY SO?
BINTOU, I KNOW WHAT I'M TALKING ABOUT!
TALK, THAT'S ALL YOU EVER DO! YOU'RE JUST JEALOUS, AYA.
ME, JEALOUS!?
YES, YOU! IF YOU'RE SINGLE AND MISERABLE, DEAL WITH IT, BUT LEAVE MY HAPPINESS ALONE!
BINTOU, I'M IMMUNE TO POSERS LIKE YOUR GUY!
SAY WHAT? GIRL, I'M GONNA SMACK YOU SO HARD YOUR PARENTS WON'T RECOGNIZE YOU.
HEY GIRLS, COME ON!
YOU? THINK YOU'RE TOUGH, DÊH, BINTOU?

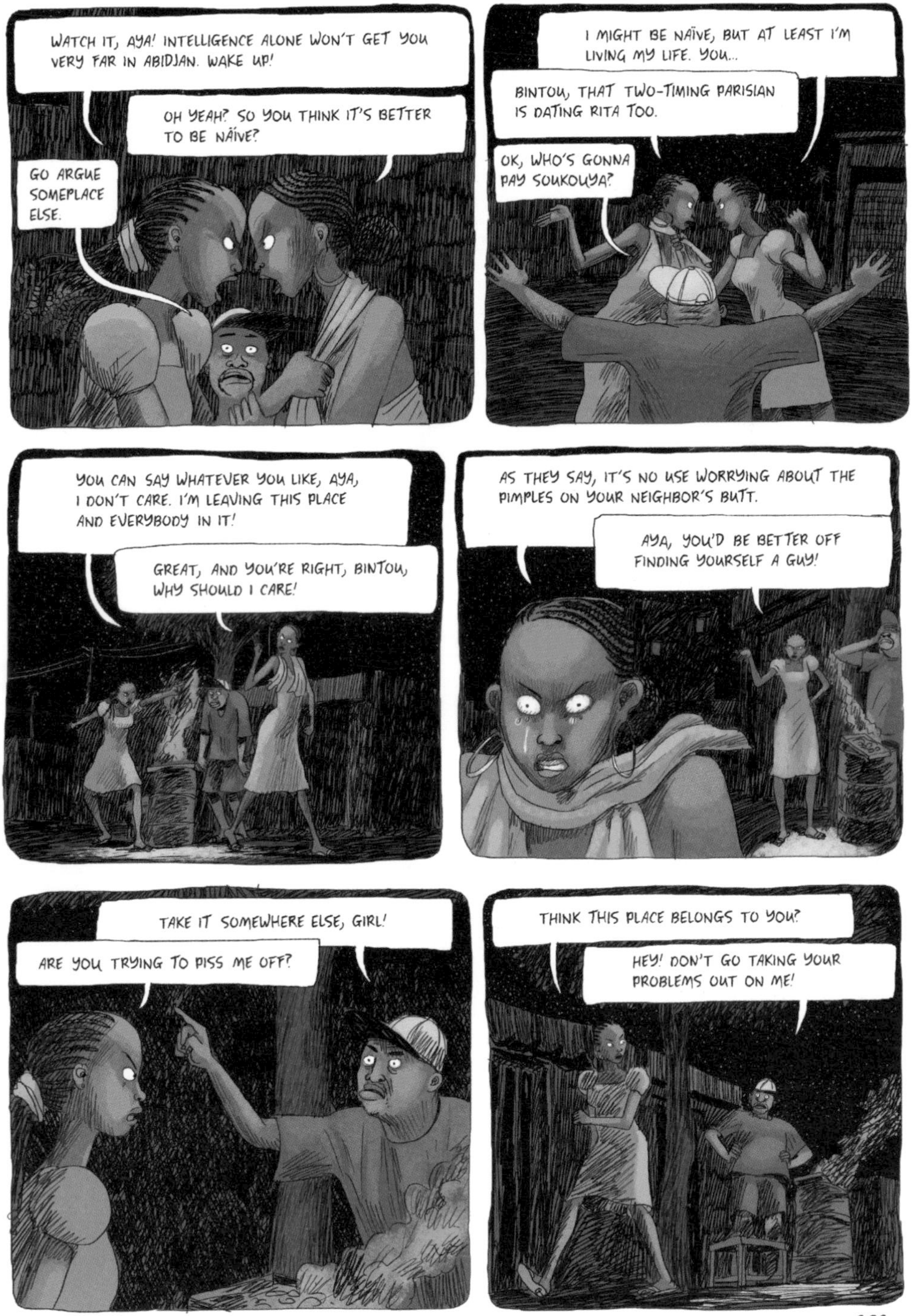
WATCH IT, AYA! INTELLIGENCE ALONE WON'T GET YOU VERY FAR IN ABIDJAN. WAKE UP!
OH YEAH? SO YOU THINK IT'S BETTER TO BE NAÏVE?
GO ARGUE SOMEPLACE ELSE.
I MIGHT BE NAÏVE, BUT AT LEAST I'M LIVING MY LIFE. YOU...
BINTOU, THAT TWO-TIMING PARISIAN IS DATING RITA TOO.
OK, WHO'S GONNA PAY SOUKOUYA?
YOU CAN SAY WHATEVER YOU LIKE, AYA, I DON'T CARE. I'M LEAVING THIS PLACE AND EVERYBODY IN IT!
GREAT, AND YOU'RE RIGHT, BINTOU, WHY SHOULD I CARE!
AS THEY SAY, IT'S NO USE WORRYING ABOUT THE PIMPLES ON YOUR NEIGHBOR'S BUTT.
AYA, YOU'D BE BETTER OFF FINDING YOURSELF A GUY!
TAKE IT SOMEWHERE ELSE, GIRL!
ARE YOU TRYING TO PISS ME OFF?
THINK THIS PLACE BELONGS TO YOU?
HEY! DON'T GO TAKING YOUR PROBLEMS OUT ON ME!

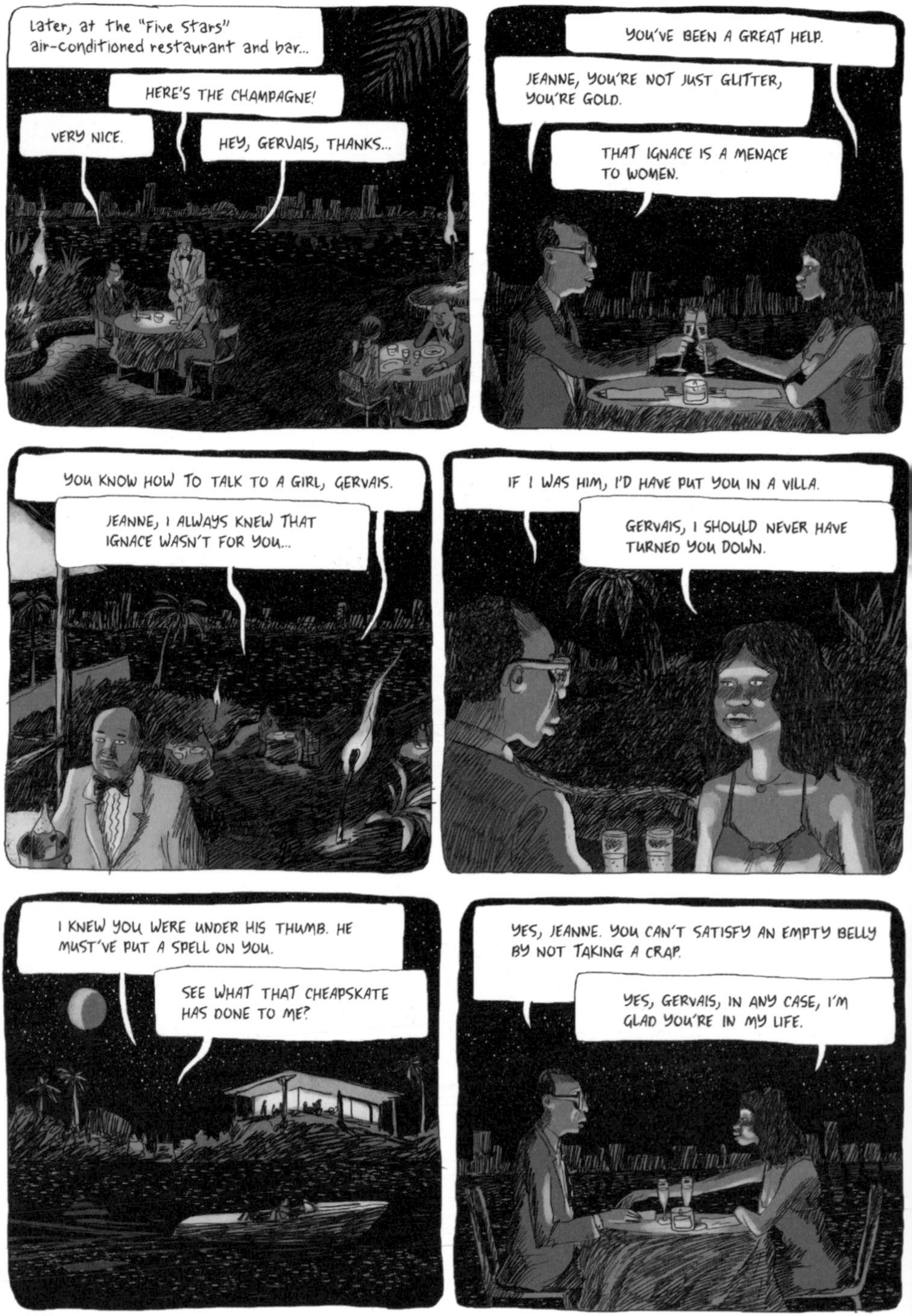
Later, at the "Five Stars" air-conditioned restaurant and bar...
HERE'S THE CHAMPAGNE!
VERY NICE.
HEY, GERVAIS, THANKS...
YOU'VE BEEN A GREAT HELP.
JEANNE, YOU'RE NOT JUST GLITTER, YOU'RE GOLD.
THAT IGNACE IS A MENACE TO WOMEN.
YOU KNOW HOW TO TALK TO A GIRL, GERVAIS.
JEANNE, I ALWAYS KNEW THAT IGNACE WASN'T FOR YOU...
IF I WAS HIM, I'D HAVE PUT YOU IN A VILLA.
GERVAIS, I SHOULD NEVER HAVE TURNED YOU DOWN.
I KNEW YOU WERE UNDER HIS THUMB. HE MUST'VE PUT A SPELL ON YOU.
SEE WHAT THAT CHEAPSKATE HAS DONE TO ME?
YES, JEANNE. YOU CAN'T SATISFY AN EMPTY BELLY BY NOT TAKING A CRAP.
YES, GERVAIS, IN ANY CASE, I'M GLAD YOU'RE IN MY LIFE.

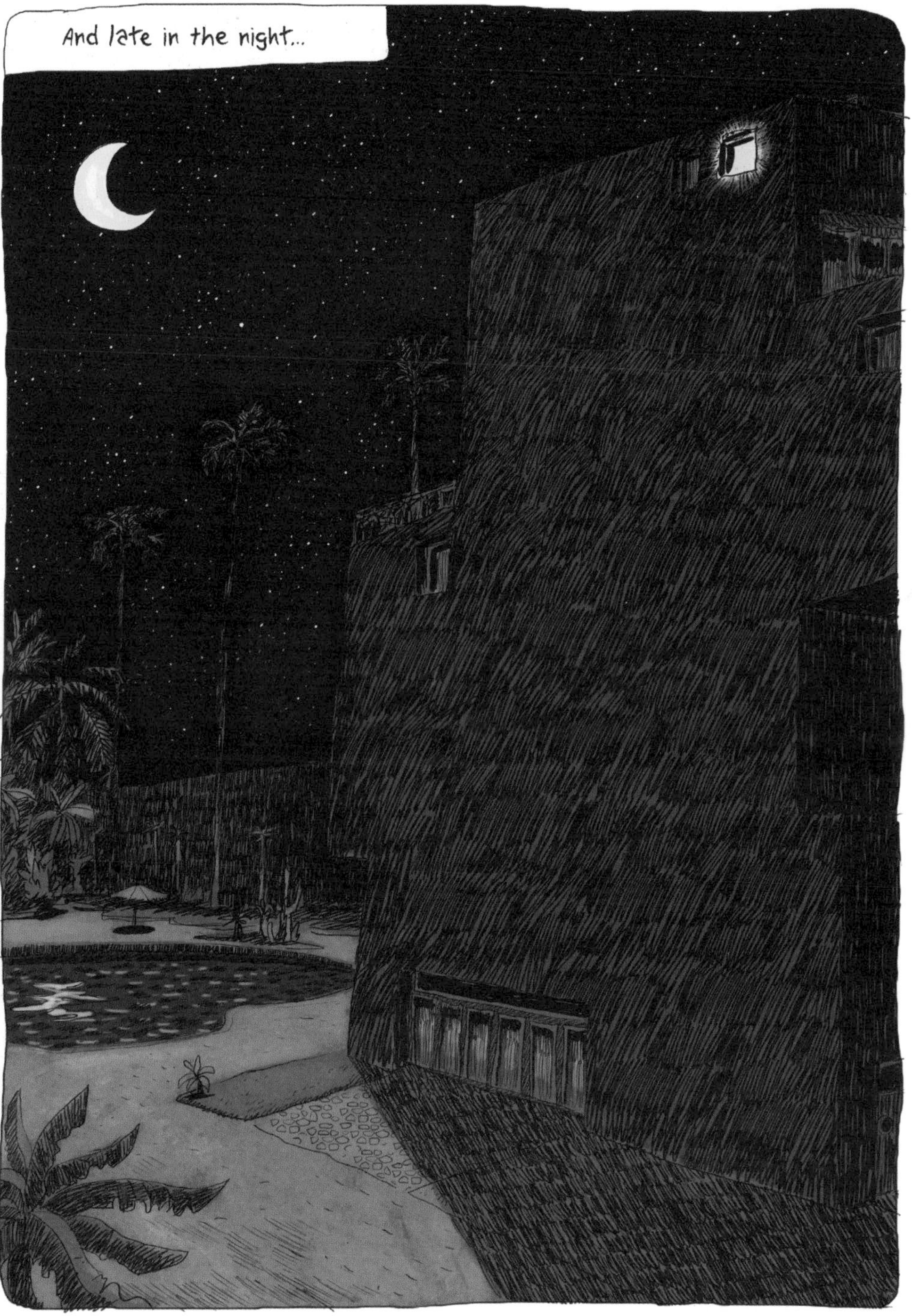
And late in the night...

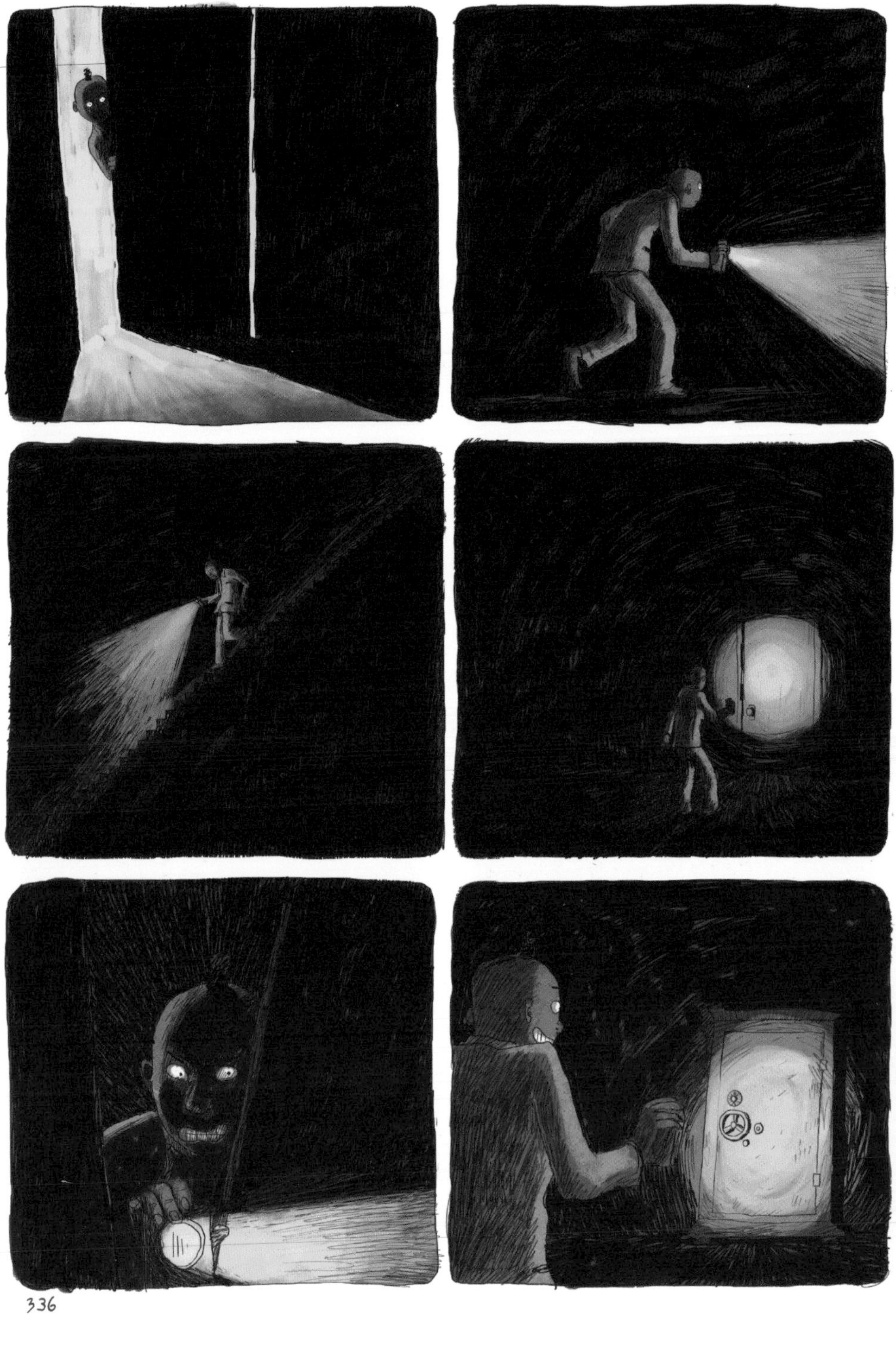

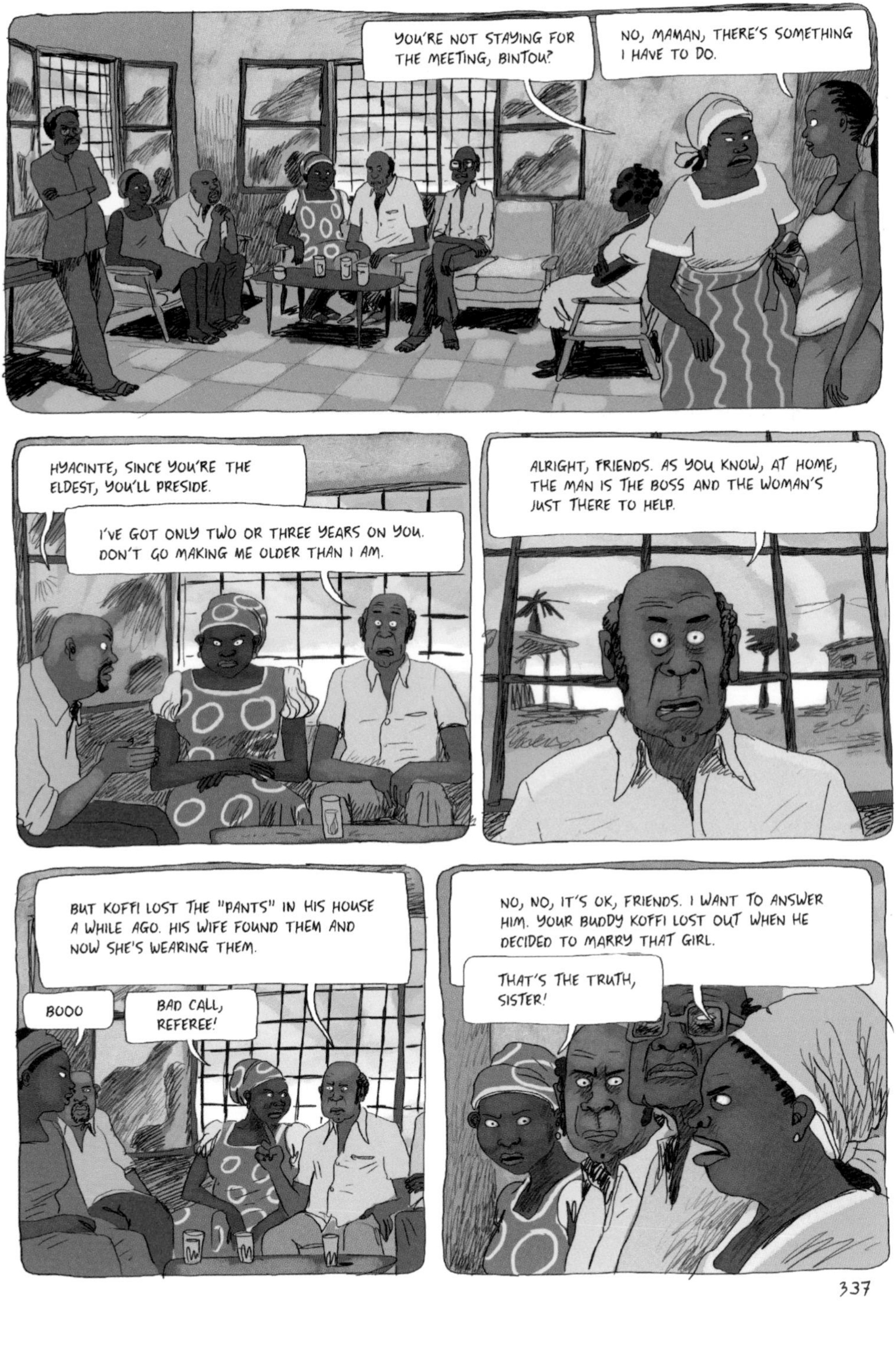
YOU'RE NOT STAYING FOR THE MEETING, BINTOU?
NO, MAMAN, THERE'S SOMETHING I HAVE TO DO.
HYACINTE, SINCE YOU'RE THE ELDEST, YOU'LL PRESIDE.
I'VE GOT ONLY TWO OR THREE YEARS ON YOU. DON'T GO MAKING ME OLDER THAN I AM.
ALRIGHT, FRIENDS. AS YOU KNOW, AT HOME, THE MAN IS THE BOSS AND THE WOMAN'S JUST THERE TO HELP.
BUT KOFFI LOST THE "PANTS" IN HIS HOUSE A WHILE AGO. HIS WIFE FOUND THEM AND NOW SHE'S WEARING THEM.
BOOO
BAD CALL, REFEREE!
NO, NO, IT'S OK, FRIENDS. I WANT TO ANSWER HIM. YOUR BUDDY KOFFI LOST OUT WHEN HE DECIDED TO MARRY THAT GIRL.
THAT'S THE TRUTH, SISTER!

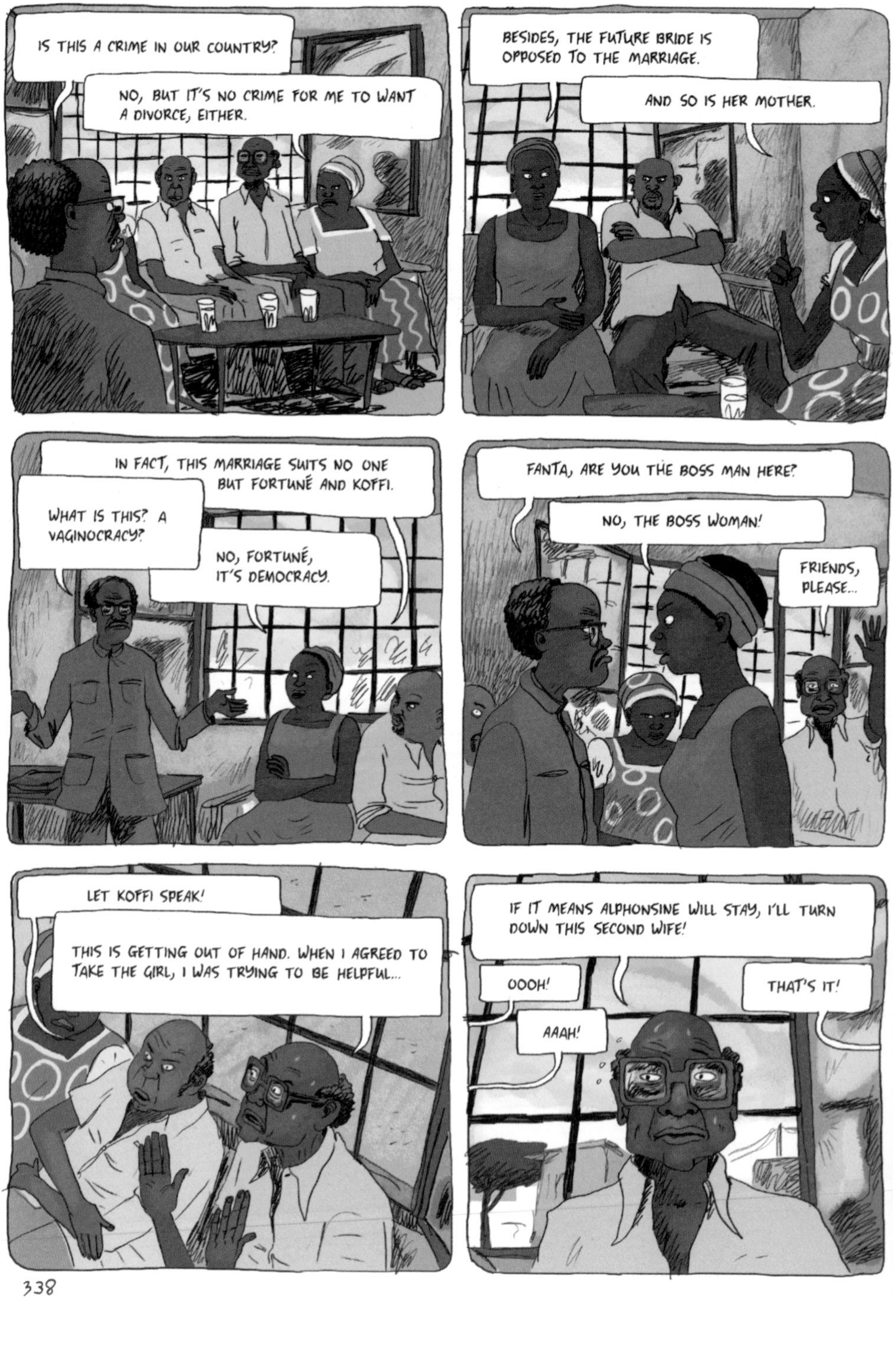
IS THIS A CRIME IN OUR COUNTRY?
NO, BUT IT'S NO CRIME FOR ME TO WANT A DIVORCE, EITHER.
BESIDES, THE FUTURE BRIDE IS OPPOSED TO THE MARRIAGE.
AND SO IS HER MOTHER.
IN FACT, THIS MARRIAGE SUITS NO ONE BUT FORTUNÉ AND KOFFI.
WHAT IS THIS? A VAGINOCRACY?
NO, FORTUNÉ, IT'S DEMOCRACY.
FANTA, ARE YOU THE BOSS MAN HERE?
NO, THE BOSS WOMAN!
FRIENDS, PLEASE...
LET KOFFI SPEAK!
THIS IS GETTING OUT OF HAND. WHEN I AGREED TO TAKE THE GIRL, I WAS TRYING TO BE HELPFUL...
IF IT MEANS ALPHONSINE WILL STAY, I'LL TURN DOWN THIS SECOND WIFE!
OOOH!
AAAH!
THAT'S IT!

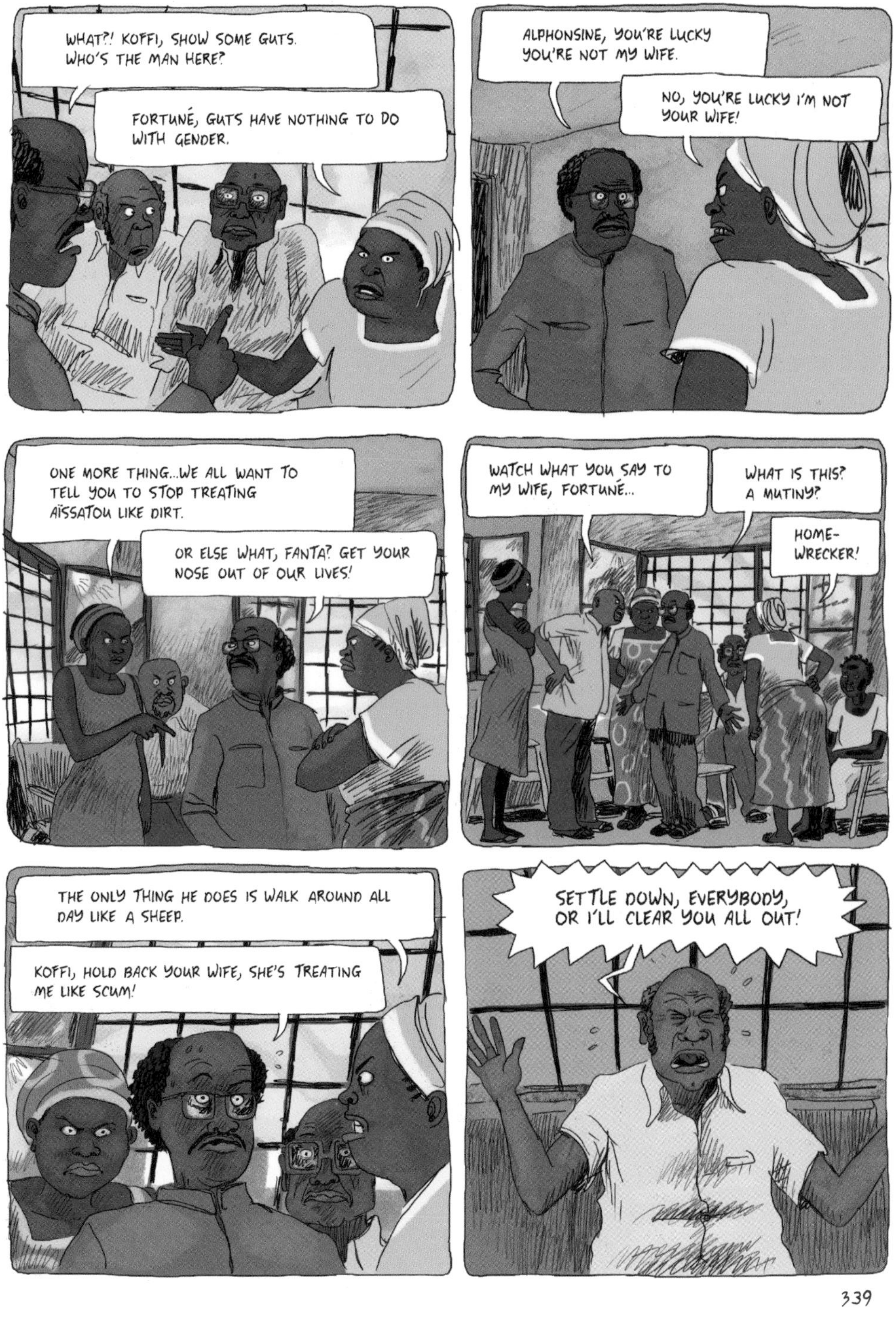
WHAT?! KOFFI, SHOW SOME GUTS. WHO'S THE MAN HERE?
FORTUNÉ, GUTS HAVE NOTHING TO DO WITH GENDER.
ALPHONSINE, YOU'RE LUCKY YOU'RE NOT MY WIFE.
NO, YOU'RE LUCKY I'M NOT YOUR WIFE!
ONE MORE THING...WE ALL WANT TO TELL YOU TO STOP TREATING AÏSSATOU LIKE DIRT.
OR ELSE WHAT, FANTA? GET YOUR NOSE OUT OF OUR LIVES!
WATCH WHAT YOU SAY TO MY WIFE, FORTUNÉ...
WHAT IS THIS? A MUTINY?
HOME-WRECKER!
THE ONLY THING HE DOES IS WALK AROUND ALL DAY LIKE A SHEEP.
KOFFI, HOLD BACK YOUR WIFE, SHE'S TREATING ME LIKE SCUM!
SETTLE DOWN, EVERYBODY, OR I'LL CLEAR YOU ALL OUT!

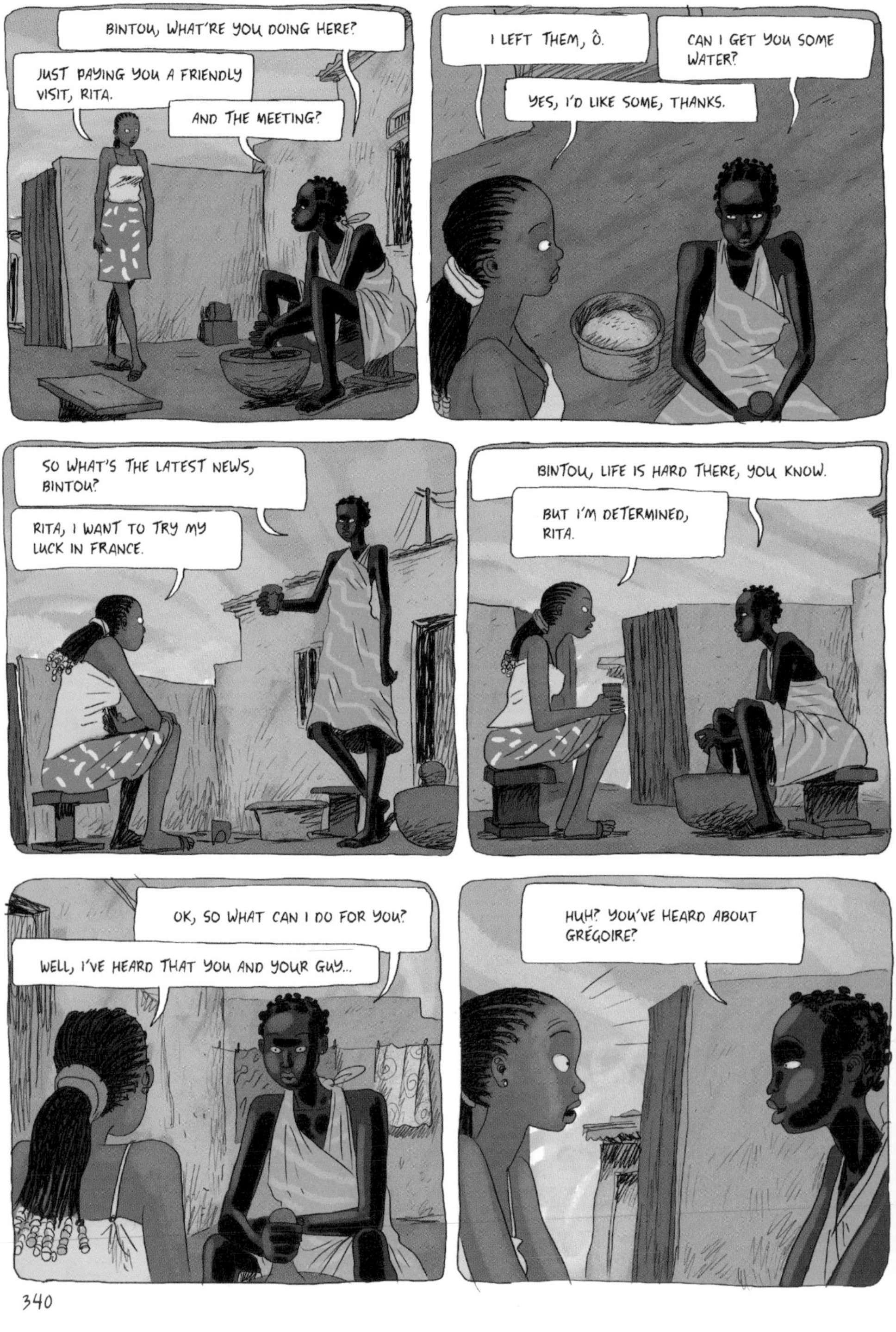
BINTOU, WHAT'RE YOU DOING HERE?
JUST PAYING YOU A FRIENDLY VISIT, RITA.
AND THE MEETING?
I LEFT THEM, Ô.
YES, I'D LIKE SOME, THANKS.
CAN I GET YOU SOME WATER?
SO WHAT'S THE LATEST NEWS, BINTOU?
RITA, I WANT TO TRY MY LUCK IN FRANCE.
BINTOU, LIFE IS HARD THERE, YOU KNOW.
BUT I'M DETERMINED, RITA.
OK, SO WHAT CAN I DO FOR YOU?
WELL, I'VE HEARD THAT YOU AND YOUR GUY...
HUH? YOU'VE HEARD ABOUT GRÉGOIRE?

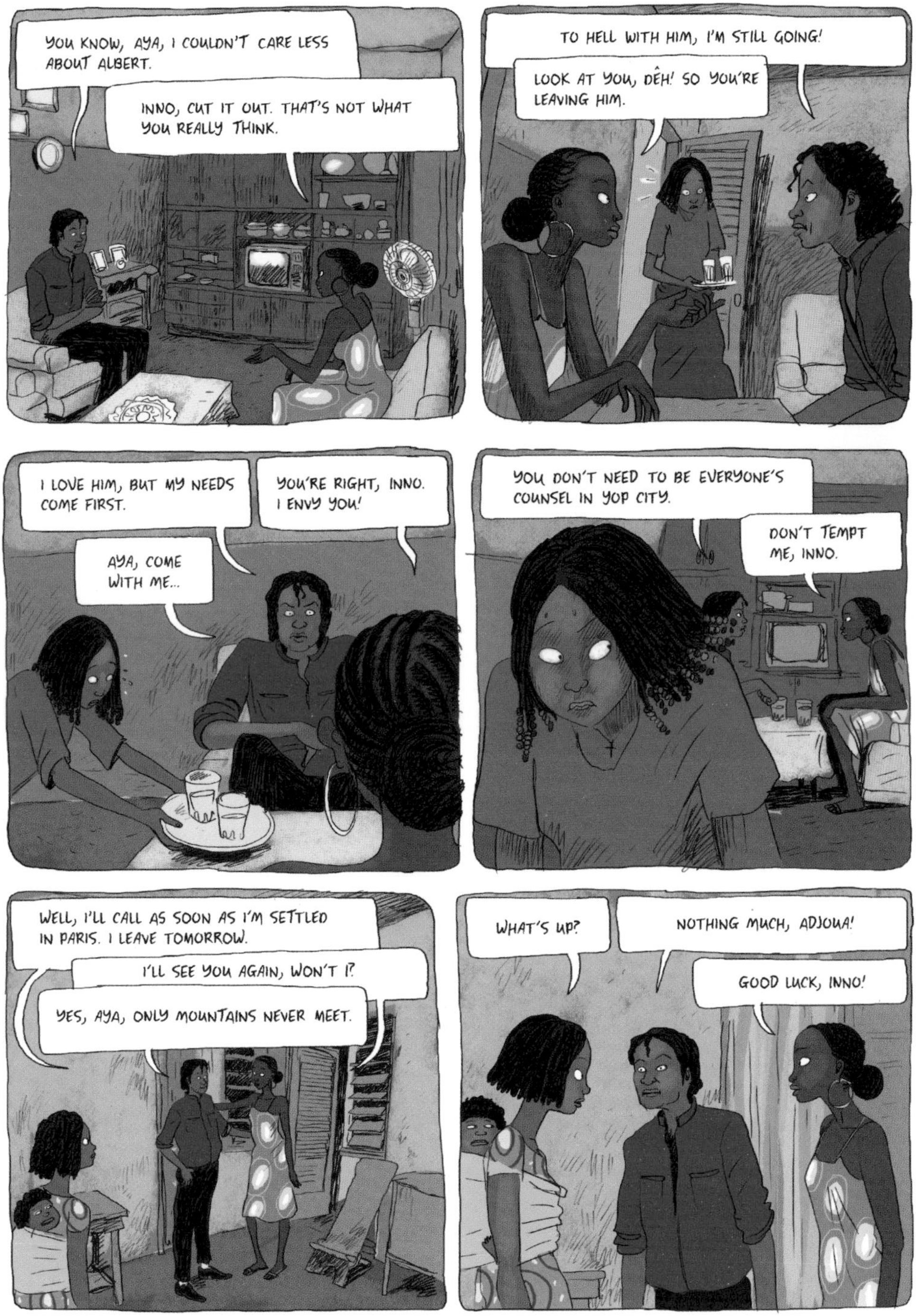
YOU KNOW, AYA, I COULDN'T CARE LESS ABOUT ALBERT.
INNO, CUT IT OUT. THAT'S NOT WHAT YOU REALLY THINK.
TO HELL WITH HIM, I'M STILL GOING!
LOOK AT YOU, DÊH! SO YOU'RE LEAVING HIM.
I LOVE HIM, BUT MY NEEDS COME FIRST.
YOU'RE RIGHT, INNO. I ENVY YOU!
AYA, COME WITH ME...
YOU DON'T NEED TO BE EVERYONE'S COUNSEL IN YOP CITY.
DON'T TEMPT ME, INNO.
WELL, I'LL CALL AS SOON AS I'M SETTLED IN PARIS. I LEAVE TOMORROW.
I'LL SEE YOU AGAIN, WON'T I?
YES, AYA, ONLY MOUNTAINS NEVER MEET.
WHAT'S UP?
NOTHING MUCH, ADJOUA!
GOOD LUCK, INNO!

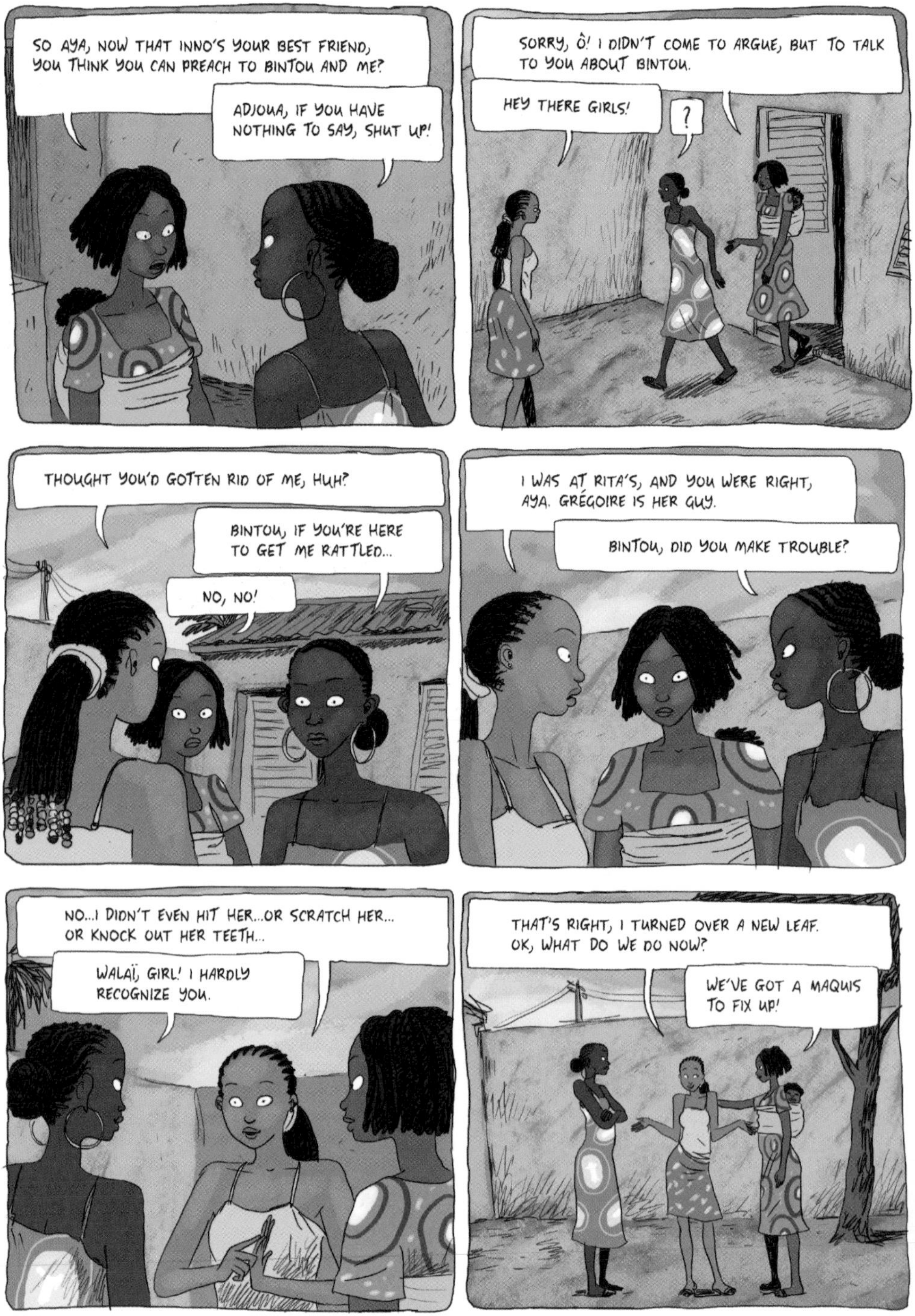
SO AYA, NOW THAT INNO'S YOUR BEST FRIEND, YOU THINK YOU CAN PREACH TO BINTOU AND ME?
ADJOUA, IF YOU HAVE NOTHING TO SAY, SHUT UP!
SORRY, Ô! I DIDN'T COME TO ARGUE, BUT TO TALK TO YOU ABOUT BINTOU.
HEY THERE GIRLS!
?
THOUGHT YOU'D GOTTEN RID OF ME, HUH?
BINTOU, IF YOU'RE HERE TO GET ME RATTLED...
NO, NO!
I WAS AT RITA'S, AND YOU WERE RIGHT, AYA. GRÉGOIRE IS HER GUY.
BINTOU, DID YOU MAKE TROUBLE?
NO...I DIDN'T EVEN HIT HER...OR SCRATCH HER... OR KNOCK OUT HER TEETH...
WALAÏ, GIRL! I HARDLY RECOGNIZE YOU.
THAT'S RIGHT, I TURNED OVER A NEW LEAF. OK, WHAT DO WE DO NOW?
WE'VE GOT A MAQUIS TO FIX UP!

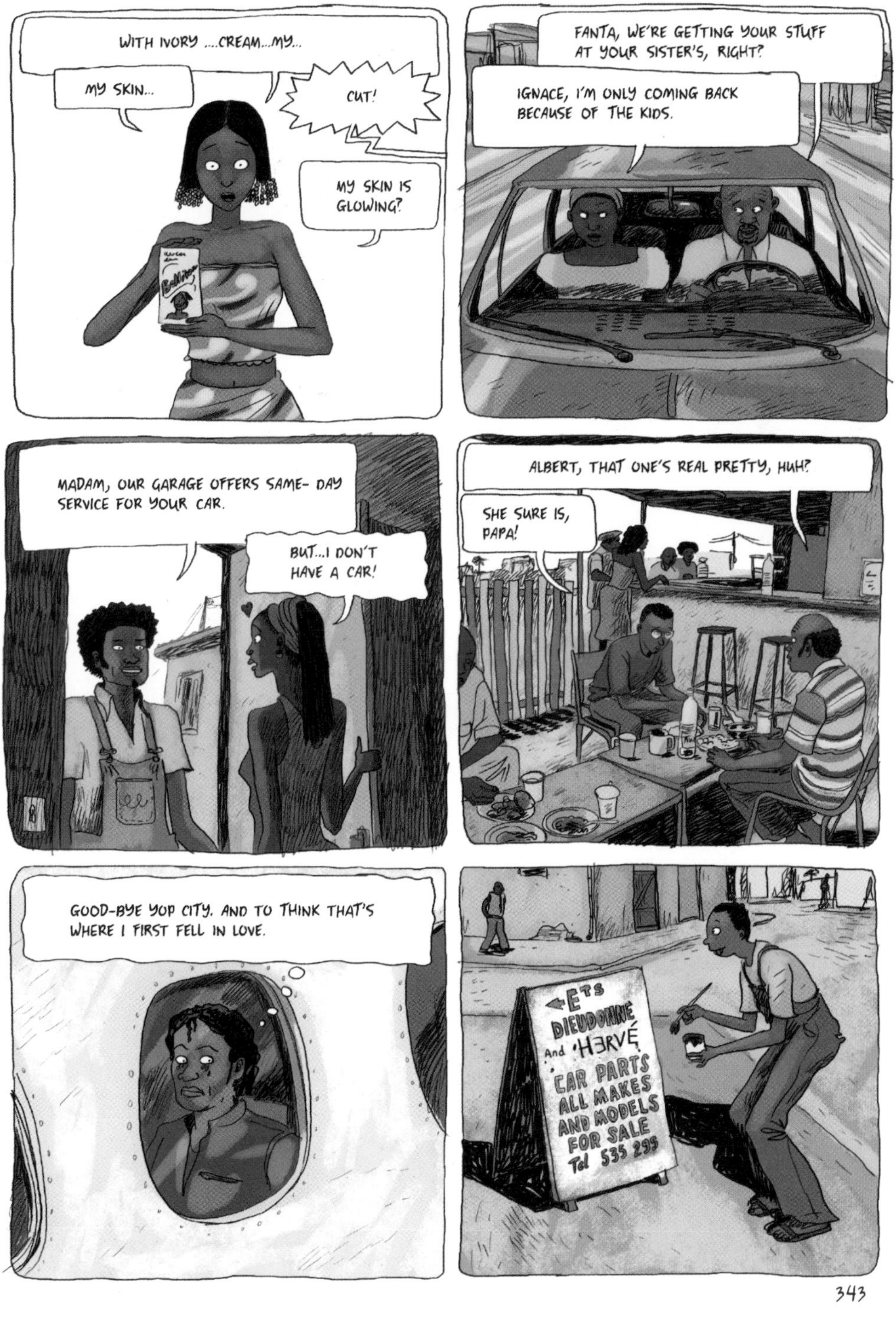

WITH IVORY ....CREAM...MY...
MY SKIN...
CUT!
MY SKIN IS GLOWING?
FANTA, WE'RE GETTING YOUR STUFF AT YOUR SISTER'S, RIGHT?
IGNACE, I'M ONLY COMING BACK BECAUSE OF THE KIDS.
MADAM, OUR GARAGE OFFERS SAME- DAY SERVICE FOR YOUR CAR.
BUT...I DON'T HAVE A CAR!
ALBERT, THAT ONE'S REAL PRETTY, HUH?
SHE SURE IS, PAPA!
GOOD-BYE YOP CITY. AND TO THINK THAT'S WHERE I FIRST FELL IN LOVE.
ETS DIEUDONNÉ And HERVÉ
CAR PARTS ALL MAKES AND MODELS FOR SALE
Tel 535 295

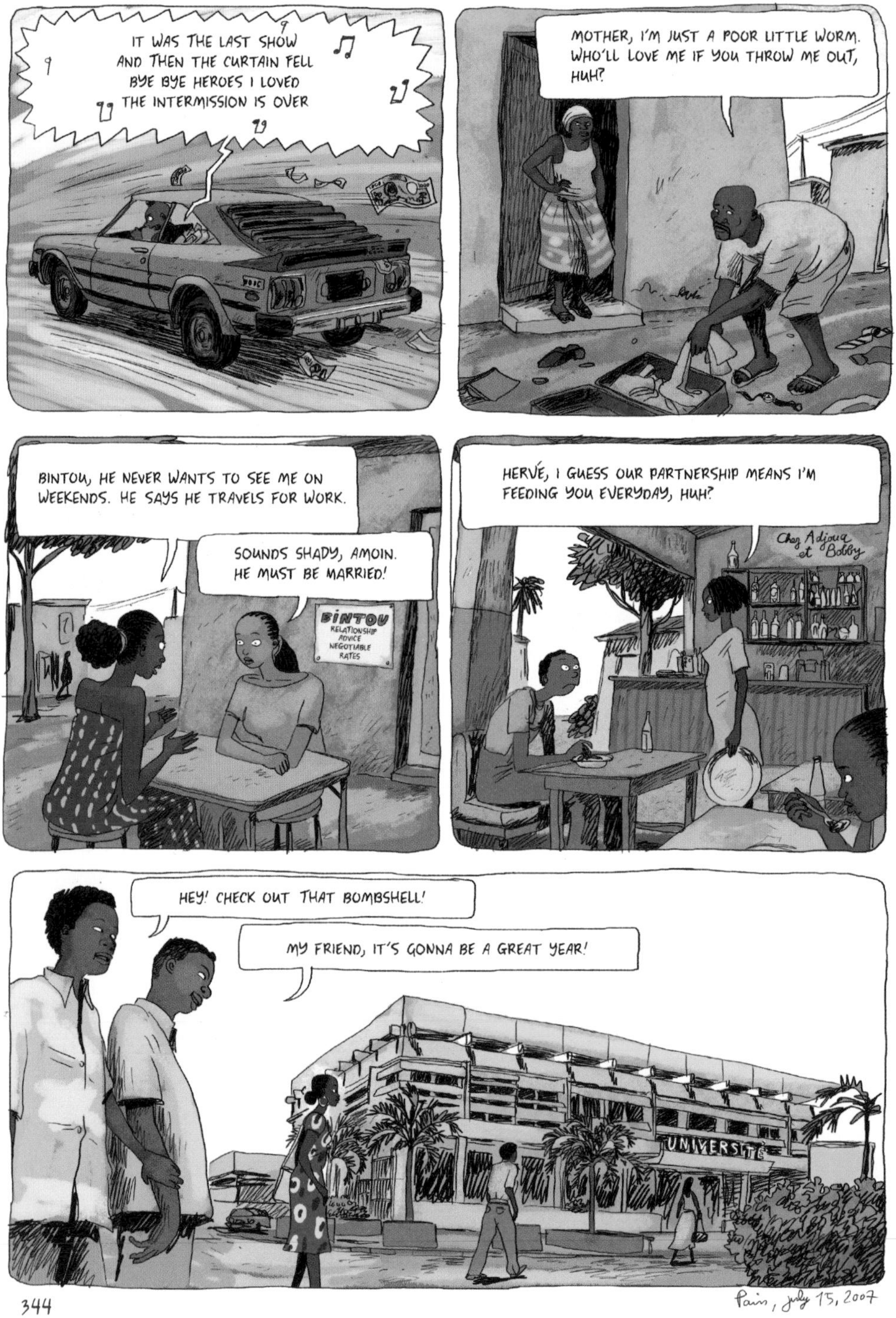
IT WAS THE LAST SHOW
AND THEN THE CURTAIN FELL
BYE BYE HEROES I LOVED
THE INTERMISSION IS OVER
MOTHER, I'M JUST A POOR LITTLE WORM. WHO'LL LOVE ME IF YOU THROW ME OUT, HUH?
BINTOU, HE NEVER WANTS TO SEE ME ON WEEKENDS. HE SAYS HE TRAVELS FOR WORK.
SOUNDS SHADY, AMOIN. HE MUST BE MARRIED!
BINTOU
RELATIONSHIP ADVICE
NEGOTIABLE RATES
HERVÉ, I GUESS OUR PARTNERSHIP MEANS I'M FEEDING YOU EVERYDAY, HUH?
Chez Adjoua et Bobby
HEY! CHECK OUT THAT BOMBSHELL!
MY FRIEND, IT'S GONNA BE A GREAT YEAR!
UNIVERSITÉ

Paris, July 15, 2007

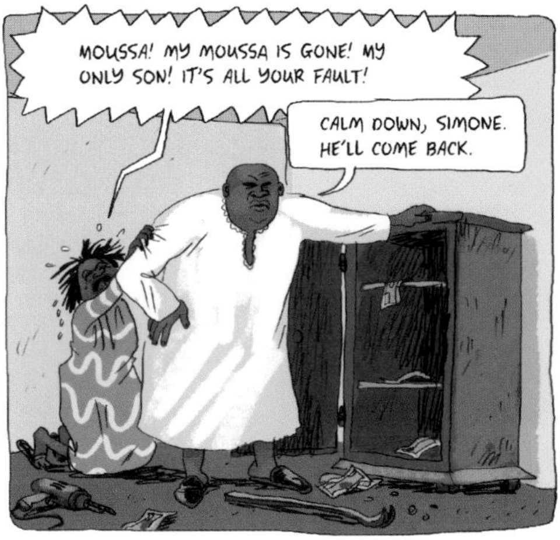
MOUSSA! MY MOUSSA IS GONE! MY ONLY SON! IT'S ALL YOUR FAULT!
CALM DOWN, SIMONE. HE'LL COME BACK.

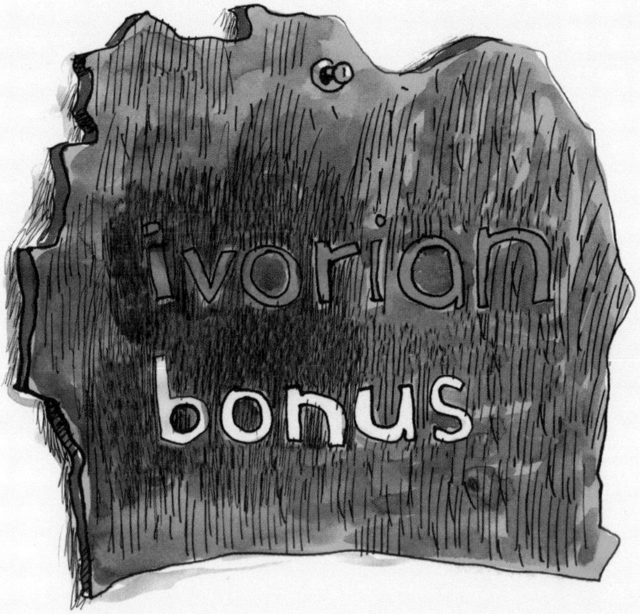
ivorian
bonus

HERE'S A LITTLE GLOSSARY TO HELP YOU BETTER UNDERSTAND THE STORY

ALLOCO: DEEP FRIED SLICES OF PLANTAIN, A FAVORITE STREET FOOD.

BANGALA: SLANG, MALE REPRODUCTIVE ORGAN—YOU KNOW.

CHOCODI: BRAND OF IVORIAN CHOCOLATE.

CLACLOS: SMALL FRIED DUMPLINGS MADE OF RIPE PLANTAINS MIXED WITH FLOUR, ONIONS AND SALT, WITH OR WITHOUT A LITTLE CHILI PEPPER.

CÔCÔTA: NOOGIE

DÈGUÉ: BEVERAGE MADE OF MILLET, CURDLED MILK AND SUGAR.

DÊH: AN EXCLAMATION THAT INTENSIFIES MEANING. "SHE'S BEAUTIFUL, DÊH!" (SHE IS SOOO BEAUTIFUL!)

DJO: A GUY, DUDE.

FAMILY BOOK: MARRIAGE CERTIFICATE AND OFFICIAL RECORD OF PARENTAGE AND RELATIONSHIPS AMONG FAMILY MEMBERS.

FOUTOU: DISH OF MASHED PLANTAIN AND CASSAVA.

FRESHNIE: A NICE LOOKING GIRL.

GAZELLE: A REAL BEAUTY.

GÔ: GIRL.

IJIHO!: OOH LA LA!

KAKABA: SOMETHING TINY; AN INSECT. ALSO USED AS AN INSULT TO MEAN INSIGNIFICANT OR RIDICULOUS.

KÊH: A CLIPPED EXCLAMATION ADDED TO THE END OF A WORD OR PHRASE FOR EMPHASIS, LEAVING NO ROOM FOR AMBIGUITY.

KOUTOUKOU: AN ALCOHOLIC BEVERAGE MADE FROM FERMENTED PALM JUICE.

MAGGI CUBE: A BRAND OF BOUILLON CUBES COMMONLY USED IN IVORIAN COOKING.

MAMAN: INFORMAL, MOTHER.

MAQUIS: AN INEXPENSIVE OPEN-AIR RESTAURANT WITH MUSIC AND ROOM TO DANCE.

PALU: SHORT FOR THE FRENCH "PALUDISME," MEANING MALARIA. "PALU" IS ALSO USED MORE GENERALLY TO REFER TO INFECTIONS INVOLVING FEVER, CHILLS, AND ACHES.

TANTIE: INFORMAL, AUNT. ALSO USED TO SHOW RESPECT OR AFFECTION WHEN TALKING TO AN OLDER WOMAN.

TASSABA: SLANG, BEHIND. "MOVE YOUR TASSABA!" (MOVE YOUR BUTT!)

TONTON: INFORMAL, UNCLE.

WALAÏ: GOOD LORD!

WOUBI: GAY.

YACO: I'M SORRY.

IN OUR COUNTRY, WE HAVE A FAMOUS PROVERB THAT GOES LIKE THIS:

"WHEN A BABY IS IN THE BELLY, IT BELONGS TO ITS MOTHER. WHEN IT'S BORN, IT BELONGS TO EVERYONE."

THE "IT BELONGS TO EVERYONE" PART IS REALLY GREAT, BELIEVE ME. AND HERE'S WHY.

FIRST, WHEN YOU GIVE BIRTH, YOU ONLY STAY IN THE MATERNITY WARD FOR A DAY, UNLESS YOU HAVE A CAESARIAN, IN WHICH CASE YOU GO HOME THE DAY AFTER (NOT ENOUGH ROOM AND IT'S EXPENSIVE).

BUT THAT DOESN'T MATTER BECAUSE AS SOON AS YOU GET HOME, YOU ARE WELCOMED LIKE A QUEEN BY EVERYONE.

YOUR FAMILY WILL TAKE CARE OF YOU AND YOUR BABY FOR A WHILE, AND THAT'S GREAT, BECAUSE YOU WON'T HAVE TIME TO GET THOSE FAMOUS POSTPARTUM BLUES.

THE BABY AND YOU ARE PROMPTLY LOOKED AFTER.

YOUR MOTHER HEATS SOME WATER AND MASSAGES YOUR WHOLE BODY, ESPECIALLY THE BELLY. NEXT SHE SLATHERS YOU IN SHEA BUTTER AGAIN AND WRAPS YOUR BELLY (IF YOU HAVEN'T HAD A CAESARIAN, OF COURSE). AFTERWARD, SHE DRESSES YOU AND DOES YOUR HAIR (YOU COULDN'T GET BETTER TREATMENT AT A SPA).

DURING THIS TIME, A TEAM MADE UP OF YOUR GRANDMOTHER (IF YOU STILL HAVE ONE) AND GREAT-AUNTS TAKES CARE OF YOUR BABY. THEY MASSAGE ITS HEAD WITH A WARM WASHCLOTH (SO THAT ITS HEAD BECOMES NICE AND ROUND) AND THEN ITS WHOLE BODY (TO MAKE IT NICE AND FIRM). WHEN THAT'S DONE, THE BABY IS WASHED, SLATHERED IN LOTION AND DUSTED WITH "BÉBÉ D'OR" TALCUM POWDER OR OTHER THINGS, THEN DRESSED IN PRETTY CLOTHES.

MEANWHILE, ANOTHER TEAM MADE UP OF FEMALE COUSINS, SISTERS-IN-LAW, AND TANTIES MAKES A DELICIOUS MEAL, AND THEN IT'S TIME TO SIT DOWN TO EAT! YOU COME OUT OF YOUR ROOM BEAUTIFUL AND GLOWING (THANKS TO THE SHEA BUTTER) AND YOU ENJOY THE SPECIAL MEAL THAT YOU REQUESTED UNDER THE HAPPY GAZE OF YOUR WHOLE FAMILY.

WHEN YOU HAVE FINISHED THE MEAL, YOUR BEAUTIFUL BABY IS RETURNED TO YOU SO YOU CAN NURSE IT (YUP, YOU'VE GOT TO WORK JUST A LITTLE BIT). AFTER IT BURPS, YOU PUT IT DOWN TO SLEEP, AND YOU CAN TAKE A WELL-DESERVED NAP AND REST EASY BECAUSE YOUR BABY IS BEING WATCHED OVER BY DOZENS OF PEOPLE.

AND WHAT DOES THE FATHER DO IN ALL OF THIS? DON'T THINK HE'S EXCLUDED. ON THE CONTRARY, HE'S GOT A TON OF THINGS TO DO. HE CAN CARRY HIS BABY (IF HE'S NOT TOO SCARED ABOUT CRUSHING IT), OR HUG HIS WIFE (IF HE'S NOT TOO EMBARRASSED IN FRONT OF EVERYONE). BUT MOST OF THE TIME, HE'S BUSY SERVING DRINKS TO ALL THE FRIENDS AND NEIGHBORS WHO'VE COME TO CONGRATULATE HIM. HE'S PROUD AND HAPPY TO TELL ANYONE WHO'LL LISTEN THAT HE'S A FATHER, AND SPENDS HIS EVENINGS AT THE MAQUIS CELEBRATING, AND WHEN HE COMES HOME LATE AND TIPSY, YOU LISTEN TO HIM SAYING HOW HAPPY HE IS TO BE A FATHER, AND YOU CURL UP WITH HIM BECAUSE YOU'RE RESTED ENOUGH TO DO SO, AND ESPECIALLY SO YOU DON'T GET RILED UP ABOUT HIS ANTICS.

YOU'RE HELPED IN THIS WAY FOR SOME TIME. A FEW DAYS BEFORE THE AUNTS, FEMALE COUSINS, AND SISTERS-IN-LAW LEAVE (YOUR MOTHER AND GRANDMOTHER CAN STAY MUCH LONGER), YOU INTRODUCE YOUR BABY TO ALL THE PEOPLE IN YOUR NEIGHBORHOOD (EVEN THOUGH THEY'VE ALL COME BY YOUR HOUSE ALREADY TO SEE YOU). THIS RITUAL IS VERY IMPORTANT BECAUSE YOU BRING THEM YOUR BABY AS A SIGN OF RESPECT AND CONSIDERATION. THAT'S HOW YOU GET EVERYONE TO ADOPT YOUR BABY.

THAT'S HOW CHILDREN GROW UP IN THIS COMMUNITY. WHEN YOUR
CHILDREN ARE OLD ENOUGH TO PLAY OUTSIDE, THEY'LL ALWAYS BE
WATCHED BY SOMEONE AND THEY'LL GET SCOLDED BY A TANTIE OR
TONTON THE MINUTE THEY'RE UP TO SOME MISCHIEF.

YOUR CHILDREN WILL INVITE OTHER NEIGHBOR KIDS TO COME EAT AT YOUR
HOUSE BECAUSE YOUR CHILDREN HAVE HAD MEALS AT THEIRS. THEY'LL
LEARN ABOUT SHARING AND LIFE AS PART OF A COMMUNITY. YOU'RE
PROBABLY WONDERING ABOUT THE "MOTHER-FATHER-CHILD" BOND.
DON'T WORRY, THE OTHERS WILL NEVER GET IN THE WAY OF THAT BOND.
JUST BECAUSE YOU GIVE YOUR CHILDREN TO OTHERS FOR A SHORT TIME,
DOESN'T MEAN THEY'LL LOVE YOU ANY LESS.

IN ANY EVENT, IN OUR COUNTRY, WE DON'T HAVE TO DEAL WITH THOSE
KINDS OF QUESTIONS, BECAUSE WE DON'T EVEN THINK ABOUT THEM, AND
EVERYTHING GOES REALLY WELL.

AFTER ALL, WE ALL WANT OUR CHILDREN TO BE HAPPY.

"SO WHERE ARE ALL THE PSYCHOLOGISTS IN AFRICA?"

- "HEY ADJARA, GIRLFRIEND, IT'S BEEN A WHILE, Ô. YOU JUST VANISHED. WHAT WAS THAT ALL ABOUT?"
- "AFFÓUE, YOU DIDN'T HEAR WHAT HAPPENED TO ME?"
- "WHAT? DID YOU HAVE A DEATH IN THE FAMILY?"
- "EVEN WORSE, GIRLFRIEND, YOU GOTTA HEAR THIS..."
- "GO AHEAD, I'M LISTENING."
- "MY HUSBAND CHEATED ON ME...WITH MY YOUNGER SISTER!!!"
- "WALAÏ, ARE YOU KIDDING ME?"
- "AFFOUÉ, I WAS TRAUMATIZED."
- "I CAN IMAGINE, POOR THING."
- "IT HURT SO MUCH, I EVEN HAD TO GO SEE A PSYCHOLOGIST."
- "A WHAT?"
- "A PSYCHOLOGIST. PEOPLE WHO DEAL WITH MENTAL PROBLEMS..."
- "NO WAY! I CAN SEE HOW IT WAS HARD ON YOU, BUT WHY GO TO A PSYCHOPSY...?"
- "A PSYCHOLOGIST? AFFOUÉ, I WAS IN SUCH PAIN, I THOUGHT OF ENDING IT ALL. SOMEBODY HAD TO HELP ME."
- "SURE, BUT THAT'S YOUR FAMILY'S JOB. AND YOU DIDN'T GO CRAZY. ONLY CRAZY PEOPLE GO TO THE PSYCHOLOCO... OR DID YOU GO NUTS?"
- "AFFOUÉ, HOW CAN YOU SAY THAT?"
- "BECAUSE IF THAT'S THE CASE, GIRLFRIEND, YOU'VE GOT TO TELL ME... THROWING AWAY MONEY WHEN SO MANY PEOPLE NEED IT. NOW THAT'S CRAZY!"

 POOR ADJARA! IF SHE'D KNOWN, SHE NEVER WOULD HAVE TOLD AFFOUÉ THAT SHE HAD GONE TO SEE A PSYCHOLOGIST. THANKS TO AFFOUÉ, THE WHOLE NEIGHBORHOOD'S GOING TO HEAR THAT SHE ALMOST ENDED UP IN THE LOONY BIN. HER NAME WILL BE DIRT IN ALL OF ABIDJAN!

AROUND HERE, IF YOU DECIDE TO STUDY PSYCHOLOGY, PSYCHIATRY, CHILD PSYCHIATRY OR ANYTHING ELSE THAT STARTS WITH "PSY-", IT'S BECAUSE YOU DON'T WANT TO WORK AFTER YOUR STUDIES OR YOU JUST WANT TO WASTE YOUR TIME ON SCHOOL BENCHES, WEARING A HOLE IN THE SEAT OF YOUR PANTS OR SKIRT. BECAUSE ONCE YOU GET YOUR DIPLOMA, YOU WON'T FIND ANY PATIENTS. THAT'S FOR THE GOOD AND SIMPLE REASON THAT AFRICANS THINK YOU MUST BE ON THE VERGE OF LOSING YOUR MIND IF YOU GO SEE THESE DOCTORS. AND FOR AFRICANS, LOSING YOUR MIND IS THE WORST ILLNESS IN THE WORLD, EXCEPT MAYBE NOT BEING ABLE TO EAT CHICKEN KÉDJÉNOU, OR PEANUT SAUCE, OR GRILLED FISH...

SO NOW YOU'RE WONDERING, HOW DO ALL THESE KIDS COPE WHEN THEY FIND OUT THEY HAVE NEW BROTHERS AND SISTERS? HOW DO THESE WOMEN WHO HAVE BEEN CHEATED ON CONTINUE WITH THEIR LIVES? AND HOW DO THE MEN KEEP GOING-MEN WHO LOSE THEIR JOBS OVERNIGHT OR END UP ON THE STREET BECAUSE THEY HAVE NO MONEY TO PAY THE RENT?

AS FAR AS THE KIDS GO, WELL, THEY SIMPLY DEAL WITH IT.

WITH SO MANY NEIGHBORS AND FAMILY MEMBERS GOING THROUGH SIMILAR SITUATIONS, THEY GET USED TO THESE SOAP OPERAS. IT'S ALL PART OF DAILY LIFE.

SO IF THE FATHER NEXT DOOR LIVES WITH THREE WIVES AND ALL THEIR MANY CHILDREN, OR IF THE KIDS' FRIENDS INTRODUCE THEM TO NEW BROTHERS AND SISTERS FROM THE SAME FATHER BUT NOT THE SAME MOTHER, THEY'RE NOT SHOCKED IN THE LEAST. AND IT'S NO BIG DEAL FOR CHILDREN TO COME LIVE WITH THEM WITHOUT THEIR PARENTS AND TO BE INTRODUCED AS COUSINS. THE KIDS ARE TOLD TO CONSIDER THEM AS BROTHERS AND SISTERS, BECAUSE ULTIMATELY, WHAT REALLY MATTERS IS FORMING A REAL FAMILY.

IN AFRICA, CHILDREN ARE THE ONES WHO ARE MOST RESILIENT IN THESE SITUATIONS. THAT'S BECAUSE THEY'RE LUCKY ENOUGH TO BE PART OF A LARGE FAMILY.

THERE'S THE LARGE FAMILY AT HOME, OF COURSE, BUT THE NEIGHBOR-HOOD MAKES UP A LARGE FAMILY AS WELL. SO CHILDREN DON'T HAVE TO BEAR THE BRUNT OF ADULT QUARRELS.

THEY HAVE MORE INTERESTING THINGS TO DO THAN TO FRET ABOUT FAMILY DRAMAS, LIKE PLAYING WITH FRIENDS OR - THIS IS A FAVORITE - SIZING EACH OTHER UP BY COUNTING HOW MANY BROTHERS AND SISTERS THEY HAVE. OUR PSYCHOLOGISTS ARE THE PEOPLE AROUND US.

IT'S A WHOLE OTHER STORY FOR THE ADULTS, THOUGH. THEY SUFFER SO MUCH THAT SOME GO SEE WITCH DOCTORS. NOT TO HEAL THEIR EMO-TIONAL PAIN; THERE'S NO SENSE IN IT AND THAT'S NOT THE MOST IMPOR-TANT THING. INSTEAD, WITCH DOCTORS ARE ASKED TO BRING BACK LOVED ONES WHO STRAY, HELP A WIFE MAKE HER HUSBAND MORE VIGOROUS IN BED, DISPENSE A MAGIC POTION THAT WILL LET YOU GET A RAISE OUT OF YOUR BOSS OR MAKE SOMEONE LOVE YOU MORE THAN ANOTHER.

BUT DO ANY OF THESE REALLY WORK...ESPECIALLY THE POTION TO IMPROVE SEXUAL PERFORMANCE? I COULDN'T TELL YOU BECAUSE I'VE NEVER TRIED THEM!

- AYA

THE FIRST TIME I WENT TO SEE A PSYCHOLOGIST WAS IN PARIS. I HAD JUST ARRIVED FROM MY HOME COUNTRY OF IVORY COAST. I WAS 12 YEARS OLD AND I WAS GOING INTO 6TH GRADE. THE PRINCIPAL, WHO KNEW THAT I'D LEFT MY PARENTS, TOOK PITY ON ME AND ASKED THAT I BE MONITORED BY A CHILD PSYCHIATRIST. TWICE A WEEK FOR AN HOUR, I FOUND MYSELF SITTING IN FRONT OF A STRANGE MAN WHO DIDN'T TALK MUCH AND ALWAYS START- ED THE CONVERSATION WITH "SO HOW ARE YOU DOING TODAY?"

YOU CAN IMAGINE HOW PROUD I WAS! I HAD SOMEONE ALL TO MYSELF WHO LISTENED WITHOUT SAYING A WORD AND SMILED AT EVERY SEN- TENCE I UTTERED. I HAD BECOME A VERY IMPORTANT PERSON IN FRANCE. BUT THE BEST THING ABOUT OUR MEETINGS WAS THE PASTRIES AND CANDIES ON HIS DESK THAT I WAS ALLOWED TO EAT. THOSE SWEETS HELPED ME A LOT IN TELLING HIM THE WHOLE STORY OF MY SHORT 12-YEAR OLD LIFE (WHICH WAS ALREADY PRETTY FULL OF EXPERIENCE, RIGHT?). I TOLD HIM ABOUT MY FAMILY (IN ALL THE DETAILS), THINGS THE NEIGHBORS HAD DONE (SPICY), AND MY MISFORTUNES (MEMORABLE) WITH MY GIRLFRIENDS (HOW WE'D MEET UP TO HAVE A FIGHT OR HOW WE MADE A LITTLE MONEY BY DANCING, AND SO ON). IN A NUTSHELL, I TOLD HIM ANYTHING AND EVERYTHING. IN FACT, HE GOT TO HEAR WHATEVER WAS PASSING THROUGH MY POOR HEAD, AND WHEN I HAD NOTHING LEFT TO TELL, I'D MAKE UP STORIES. I DIDN'T WANT HIM TO STOP OUR SESSIONS JUST BECAUSE I DIDN'T HAVE ANYTHING LEFT TO SAY. DID HE BELIEVE ME OR NOT? WHAT WAS HE DOING WITH ALL THOSE NOTES AND ALL MY STORIES? WOULD HE MENTION THEM TO THE SCHOOL PRINCIPAL OR THE PRESIDENT OF FRANCE? I NEVER FOUND OUT. BUT MY TEETH GOT TO KNOW WHAT CAVITIES FEEL LIKE. WHEN I TOLD MY MOTHER OVER THE PHONE THAT I WAS SEEING A PSYCHOLOGIST, AND HOW GREAT IT WAS, AND HOW I NEVER WANTED IT TO END, AND THAT HE WAS SO KIND TO ME BECAUSE HE LET ME GO ON FOR HOURS AND GAVE ME TASTY TREATS TO EAT, AND THAT I HAD FINALLY FOUND SOMEONE WHO WAS INTERESTED IN WHAT I HAD TO SAY IN THIS NEW COUNTRY, SHE BURST INTO TEARS. FRANCE HAD DRIVEN HER LITTLE GIRL CRAZY. BUT I THINK SHE WAS CAREFUL TO NOT MENTION ANY OF IT TO PEOPLE IN THE NEIGHBORHOOD.

- MARGUERITE ABOUET

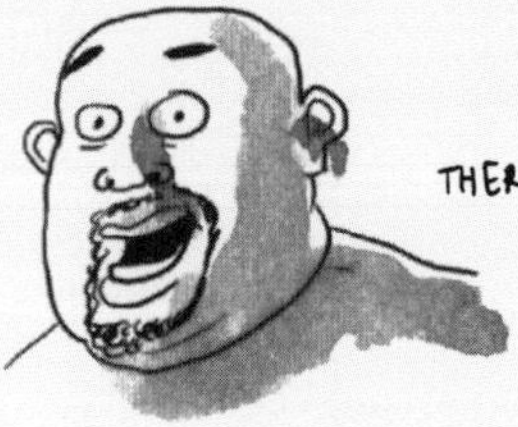

THERE'S SOMETHING I'VE GOT TO TELL YOU: I DON'T REALLY LIKE BEER.

MY FAVORITE DRINK IS "GNAMANKOUDJI," ALSO KNOWN AS GINGER JUICE. IT TASTES GREAT, OF COURSE, AND IT'S ALSO... A LOVE POTION.

HERE'S THE RECIPE:

PEEL 4 POUNDS OF FRESH GINGER.

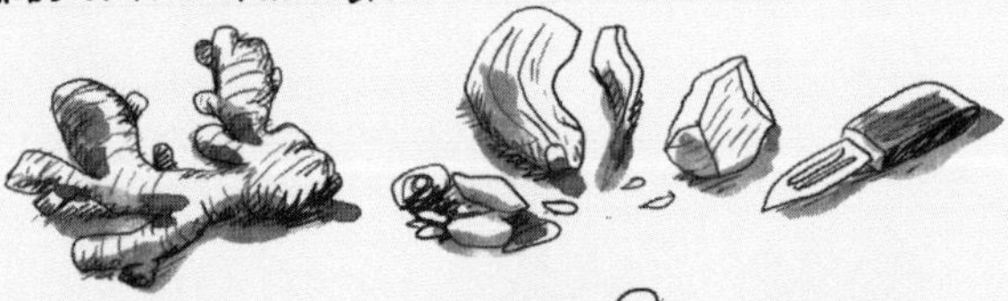

CRUSH OR POUND THE GINGER TO EXTRACT THE JUICE.

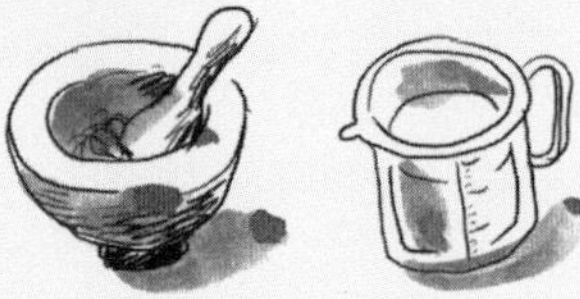

ADD WATER (A HALF OR WHOLE GALLON, DEPENDING ON HOW SPICY YOU WANT IT.)

LET THE MIXTURE REST FOR A WHILE, UNTIL THE STARCH SETTLES.

ADD SUGAR TO TASTE AND A FEW VANILLA BEANS.

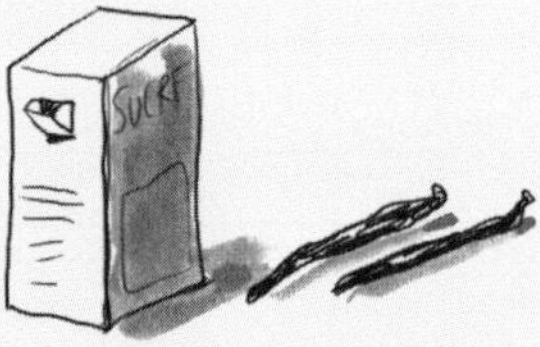

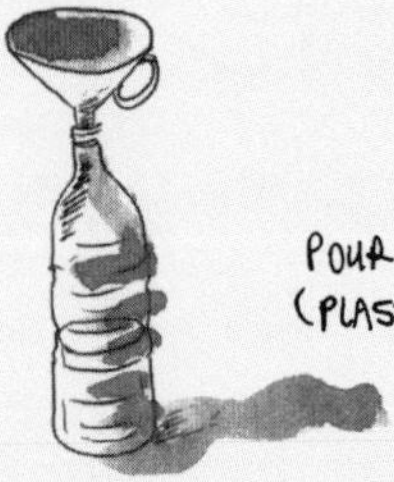

POUR THE JUICE INTO BOTTLES (PLASTIC IS FINE) AND REFRIGERATE.

YOU'RE DONE!

THE BEST ADVICE COMES LAST: YOU CAN MAKE FABULOUS COCKTAILS BY ADDING... YUM YUM... RUM, VODKA... WHATEVER YOU LIKE. BELIEVE ME, YOU ARE IN FOR A GREAT TIME. SEE YOU AROUND SOON!

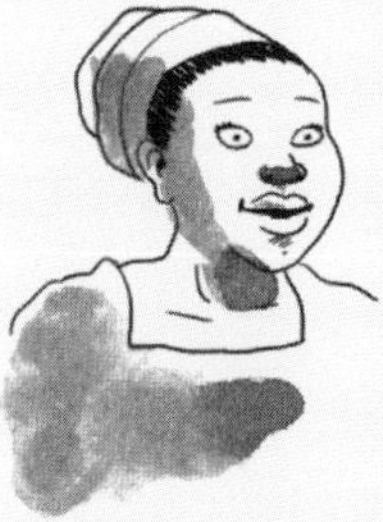

FRIENDS, ONE OF MY (MANY) SECRETS FOR GETTING MY HUSBAND TO HURRY HOME AND STAY HOME AFTER WORK IS MY FAMOUS **PEANUT SAUCE**, ALSO KNOWN AS "BACK AND FORTH"– TASTE IT AND YOU'LL BE BACK FOR MORE. HERE'S THE RECIPE.

TO SERVE 6 PEOPLE:

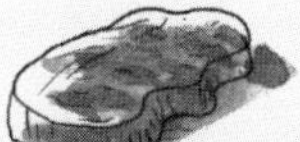

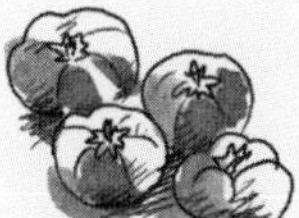

- 2 LBS BEEF (OR 1 FREE RANGE CHICKEN)
- 4 LARGE TOMATOES
- 1 CAN OF TOMATO PASTE

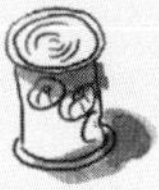

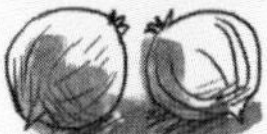

- 2 LARGE ONIONS
- 1/4 LB JAR OF UNSWEETENED PEANUT BUTTER (DAKATINE OR BONMAFÉ BRANDS IF YOU CAN FIND THEM)

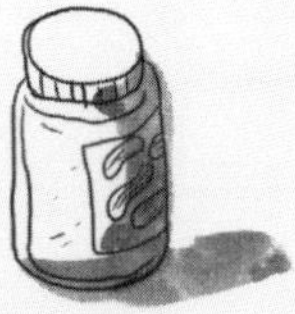

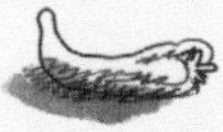

- 1 HOT PEPPER
- SALT

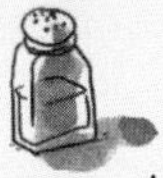

- 2 MAGGI CUBES (OR OTHER BOUILLON)

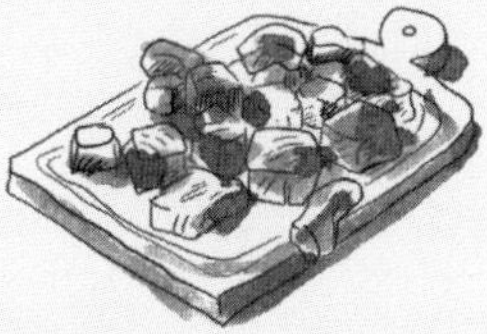

1) START BY TRIMMING AND CUBING THE MEAT.

DICE 1 ONION.

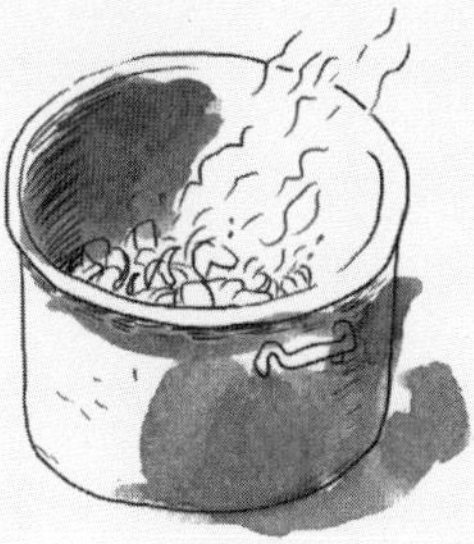

BROWN THE MEAT AND ONION IN A HEAVY POT (A CROCKPOT OR SKILLET), ADD A BIT OF SALT, COVER AND SIMMER FOR 15 MINUTES.

2) WHEN ALL THE LIQUID HAS EVAPORATED, ADD 4 TOMATOES, CUT INTO QUARTERS, THE SECOND ONION, CUT IN HALF, AND A CAN OF TOMATO PASTE.

3) AFTER 10 MINUTES, ADD WATER TO COVER THE MEAT. STIR IN THE PEANUT BUTTER, A PINCH OF SALT AND THE HOT PEPPER (DON'T SLICE OR CRUSH — THE PEPPER IS MEANT TO PERFUME THE SAUCE.) REMOVE THE PEPPER AFTER A WHILE (SERVE IT SEPARATELY FOR PEOPLE WHO LIKE THEIR FOOD SPICY), COVER, AND SIMMER FOR HALF AN HOUR.

4) AFTER THE 30 MINUTES, REMOVE THE TOMATOES AND ONIONS, BLEND THEM IN A FOOD PROCESSOR AND RETURN TO THE SAUCE. ADD A MAGGI CUBE. TOP OFF WITH ENOUGH WATER TO BARELY COVER THE MEAT. PLACE A LID ON THE POT AND SIMMER FOR ANOTHER 30 MINUTES.

5) WHEN A FILM OF OIL APPEARS ON THE SURFACE OF YOUR SAUCE, IT'S DONE.

SKIM OFF THE OIL IF YOU LIKE AND SEASON TO TASTE. ADD THE SECOND MAGGI CUBE. YOUR SAUCE SHOULD BE RICH AND FLAVORFUL. SERVE WITH RICE.

LET ME KNOW WHAT YOU THINK! ENJOY!

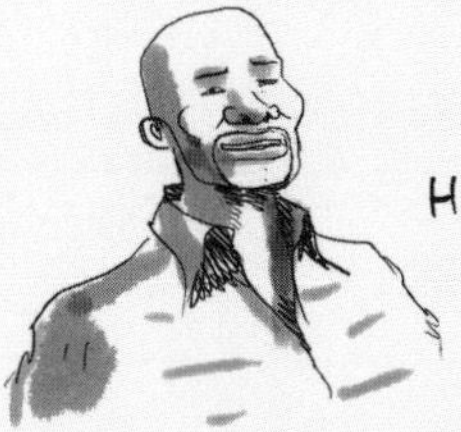

HI FRIENDS! ONE OF MY SECRETS (AMONG MANY OTHERS) THAT LETS ME SCORE WITH WOMEN IN PARIS AND ELSEWHERE IS MY DELICIOUS

CHICKEN KÉDJÉNOU.

IT'S VERY SIMPLE TO MAKE AND IT WILL POSITIVELY FLOOR THEM (PROBABLY THANKS TO THE CHICKEN). HERE'S THE RECIPE:

SERVES 2:

- 1 CHICKEN

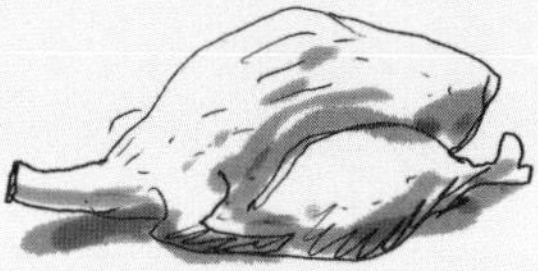

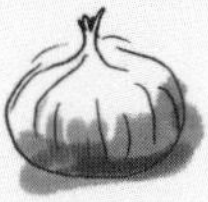

- 1 LARGE ONION
- 2 TOMATOES

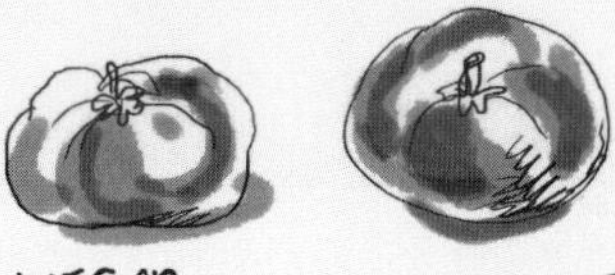

- 1 TABLESPOON OF VINEGAR

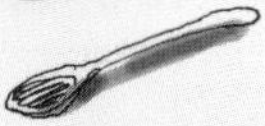

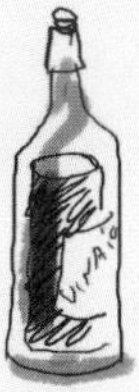

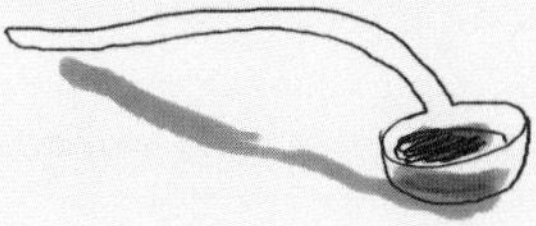

- 1 LADLE OF RED WINE
- SALT

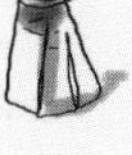

- 1 BOUILLON CUBE (MAGGI BRAND)

- 1 CHILI PEPPER (NOT REQUIRED, ONLY FOR THE BRAVE)

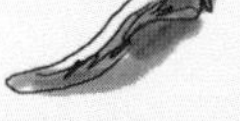

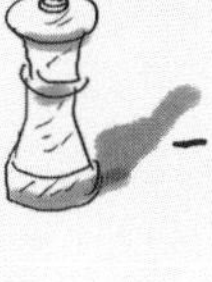

- PEPPER

1) WASH AND CUT UP THE CHICKEN, ONION, AND TOMATOES.

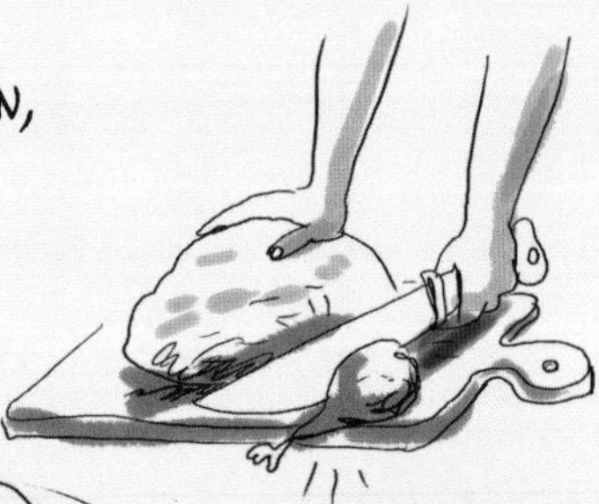

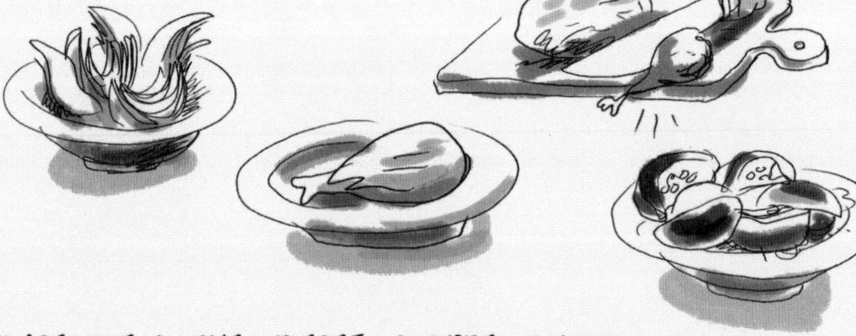

2) PLACE THE CHICKEN PIECES, CHOPPED ONION, QUARTERED TOMATOES, SALT, MAGGI CUBES, CHILI PEPPER, PEPPER, VINEGAR, AND RED WINE IN A LARGE POT, AND LET YOUR STEW COOK WITH THE LID ON FOR ONE HOUR.

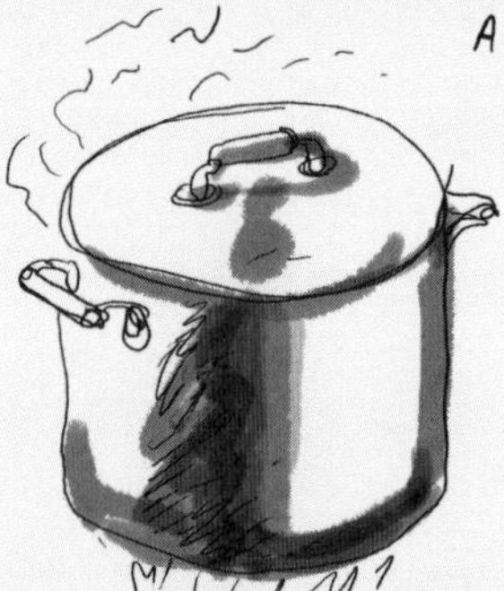

THAT'S IT, IT'S READY TO SERVE!

YOU CAN ACCOMPANY THIS DISH WITH RICE, ATTIÉKÉ (GROUND CASSAVA), CORN, COUSCOUS, YAMS OR POTATOES...

IT'S A WINNER EVERY TIME!

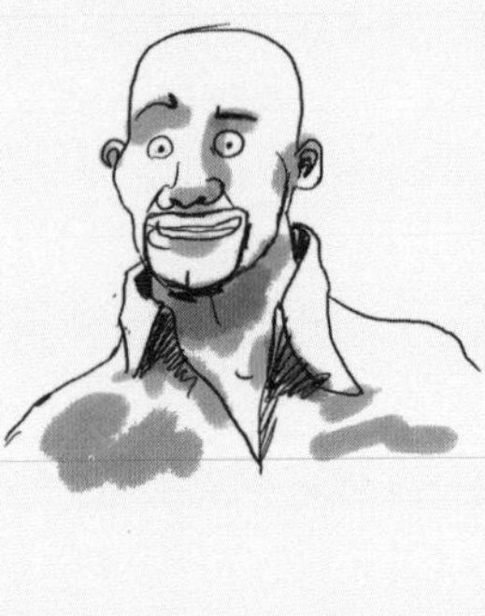

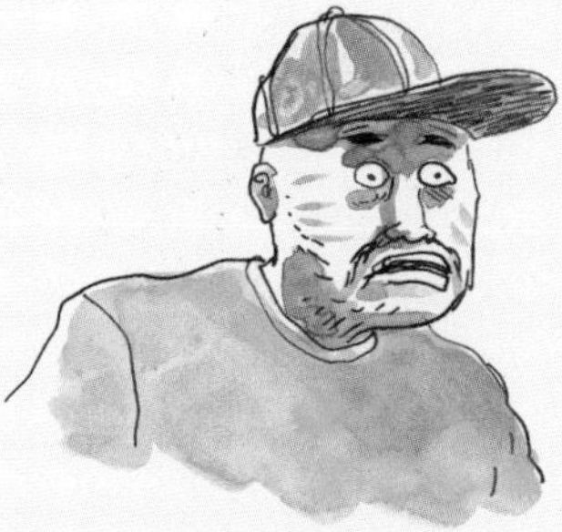

HEY, I'M IN THE BOOK TOO, Y'KNOW. ALRIGHT, I'M GOING TO SHOW YOU HOW TO MAKE "SOUKOUYA." WITH ME BEING A SMALL-TIME SOUKOUYA VENDOR, THIS RECIPE WILL MAKE ME FAMOUS, WHICH WOULD BE GREAT!

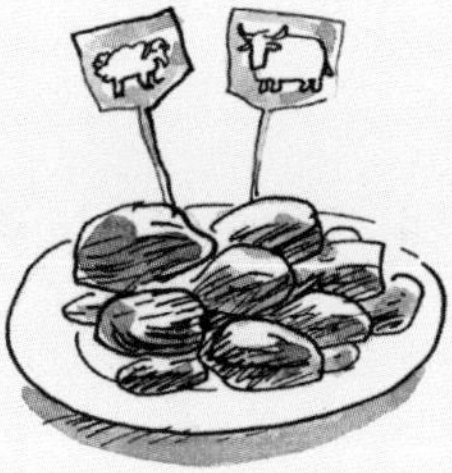

FOR 2 PEOPLE:

- 500 GRAMS OF MUTTON
(OR OTHER MEAT, BUT MUTTON IS THE MOST TENDER, DÊH!)

- 1 LARGE ONION

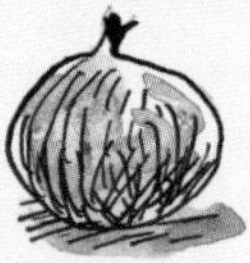

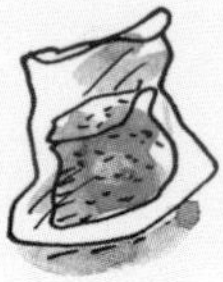

- CHILI PEPPER

(THIS IS FOR YOU TO SEE IF YOU'RE MAN ENOUGH TO HANDLE IT, DÊH!)

- 1 MAGGI CUBE

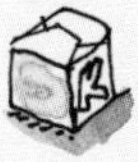

CUT THE MEAT INTO PIECES, PLACE THEM IN A BOWL, ADD THE MAGGI CUBE AND MIX WELL. THEN PLACE THE MEAT IN A GRILL PAN AND TURN IT OVER FROM TIME TO TIME. WHEN THE MEAT IS ALMOST COOKED THROUGH, ADD THE CHOPPED ONION AND THE CHILI PEPPER, STIR AND SERVE HOT, DÊH, AND EAT IT WITH ANYTHING YOU WANT. ENJOY YOUR SOUKOUYA!

GIRLFRIENDS MY BRAISED CHICKEN IS BETTER THAN
TANTIE AFFOUÉ'S.
I'LL GIVE YOU MY RECIPE SO YOU CAN SEE FOR
YOURSELF HOW DELICIOUS MY COOKING IS.

"ADJOUA'S BRAISED CHICKEN"

SERVES 4:

- 4 THIGHS FROM FREE-RANGE CHICKENS

- 1 BUNCH OF PARSLEY

- 2 LARGE ONIONS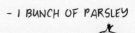

 - 1 SMALL PIECE OF GINGER

- OIL, SALT, AND PEPPER

 - A MAGGI CUBE

- 2 GARLIC CLOVES

PURÉE GINGER, PARSLEY, GARLIC, AND ONION IN A BLENDER AND PLACE THE
MIXTURE INTO A BOWL. ADD SALT, PEPPER, AND THE MAGGI CUBE. COAT THE
CHICKEN PIECES, PLACE THEM ON THE GRILL AND COOK, TURNING THEM FROM
TIME TO TIME.

MY SPECIAL TOUCH: IN A FRYING PAN, BRAISE THE GRILLED CHICKEN PIECES
AND THE REMAINING SPICE MIX IN A BIT OF OIL FOR 15 MINUTES. SERVE HOT.

YOU CAN ACCOMPANY THIS DISH WITH ATTIÉKÉ (CASSAVA SEMOLINA), RICE,
FRIED OR MASHED YAMS, FRIED OR BOILED POTATOES, OR COUSCOUS. ENJOY!

BACK HOME, WE HAVE A SAYING THAT GOES:

"YOU CAN ALWAYS TELL A WOMAN BY HER **PAGNE**."

A PAGNE (PA-NYE) IS A PIECE OF BRIGHTLY COLORED, WAX-PRINTED CLOTH. EVERY PATTERN HAS A MEANING, SO YOU NEED TO WATCH WHAT YOU WEAR. FOR EXAMPLE, NOW THAT I'M A RESPECTABLE, MARRIED WOMAN, I WOULD CHOOSE "CAPABLE HUSBAND" OR "SORRY, TAKEN."

- BINTOU, WHO IS SINGLE AND LOOKING FOR LOVE, MIGHT CHOOSE "FREE AS A BIRD" OR "YOU DON'T KNOW WHAT YOU'RE MISSING."

- AYA, WHO IS SINGLE AND PREFERS TO KEEP MEN AT A DISTANCE, WOULD CHOOSE "WATCH MY BITE!" OR "GO PLAY SOMEWHERE ELSE."

- A JEALOUS OR POSSESSIVE WOMAN WOULD WEAR A PAGNE THAT SAYS "MY ENEMY IS WATCHING" OR "YOUR FOOT, MY FOOT, IF YOU GO OUT, I'LL GO OUT TOO" - A CLEAR MESSAGE THAT SHE INTENDS TO KEEP A CLOSE EYE ON HER HUSBAND.

A PAGNE CAN BE SEWN INTO A SKIRT, A DRESS, OR A PAIR OF PANTS.

YOU CAN ALSO TAKE A SMALLER PAGNE AND WRAP IT AROUND YOUR HEAD. VERY CLASSY!

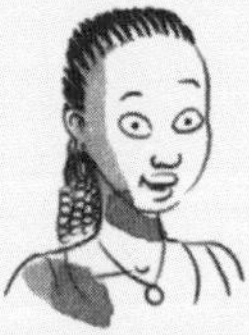

WHEN THEY SEE ME ROLL MY TASSABA, MEN FALL AT MY FEET. I'LL TELL YOU MY TRICK, BUT IT'S JUST ONE OF THE SPECIAL SECRETS I'VE GOT. AFTER ALL, I'M LOOKING FOR A GOOD CATCH, TOO. FIRST, YOU NEED TO LET YOUR HIP JUT OUT A BIT, AND YOU DON'T NEED A BIG BEHIND. NO, EVEN GIRLS WITH A SMALL OR FLAT BOTTOM CAN DO THIS.

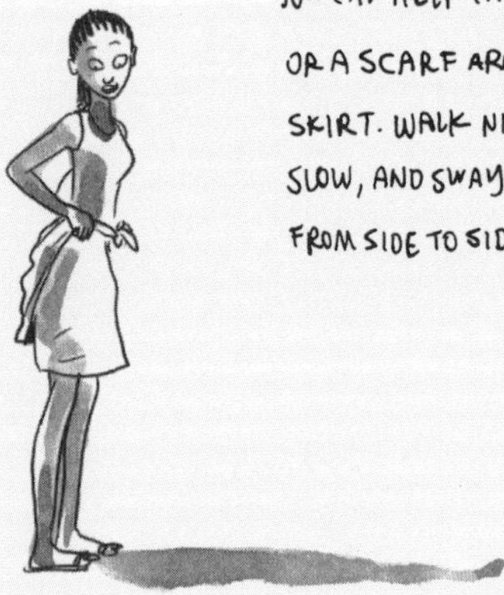

YOU CAN HELP THINGS ALONG BY WEARING A BELT ON YOUR PANTS, OR A SCARF AROUND YOUR DRESS OR SKIRT. WALK NICE AND SLOW, AND SWAY YOUR BUTT FROM SIDE TO SIDE.

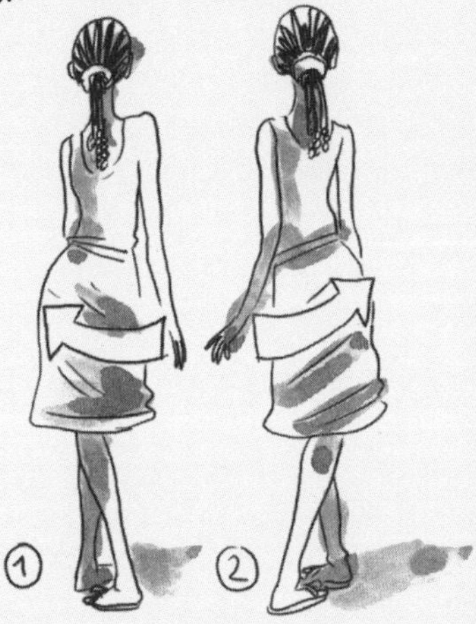
1
2

SAME THING ON THE DANCE FLOOR, BUT FASTER; YOU NEED TO REALLY SHAKE YOUR BEHIND. IT'S A MOVE WE CALL THE BUTT ROLL OR BUTT SHAKE.

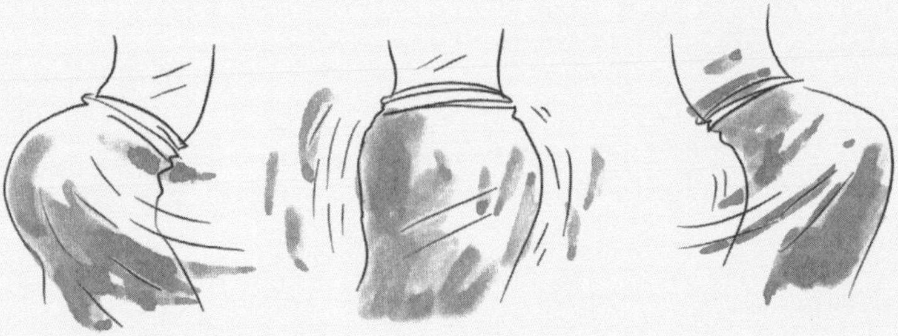

GOOD LUCK!

GIRLFRIENDS, IT'S NOT EASY LOOKING AFTER A BABY, ESPECIALLY WHEN THERE ARE NO TANTIES OR YOUNG GIRLS IN THE NEIGHBORHOOD TO HELP OUT.

SO HOW DOES ONE RUN ERRANDS, DO HOUSEWORK, AND COOK WITH A BABY THAT'S CRYING ALL THE TIME (ESPECIALLY IF IT'S COLICKY)?

I'M GOING TO HELP YOU BY TELLING YOU MY SECRET (WHICH IS KNOWN THROUGHOUT AFRICA BY THE WAY):

YOU CARRY YOUR BABY ON YOUR BACK.

NO MORE STROLLERS THAT GET IN THE WAY, NO MORE LATE DINNERS... YOUR LIFE WILL CHANGE! THE HARDEST THING IS FINDING A PAGNE (A PIECE OF BRIGHTLY COLORED, WAX-PRINTED CLOTH).

① WRAP THE PAGNE AROUND YOUR WAIST BEFORE PICKING UP THE BABY.

② PLACE THE BABY ON YOUR HIP.

③ MOVE IT TOWARDS YOUR BACK AS YOU BEND OVER (WITHOUT LETTING GO OF THE BABY).

④ THE BABY IS NOW ON YOUR BACK, YOU'RE STILL BENT OVER, AND YOU SQUEEZE THE BABY'S ARMS UNDER YOUR ARMPITS.

⑤ STILL BENT OVER, YOU NOW LIFT THE UNWRAPPED PAGNE OVER THE BABY UP TO ITS NECK TO HOLD ITS HEAD UP (IF THE BABY IS SMALL) OR UNDER ITS ARMPITS (FOR A BIGGER BABY).

⑥ YOU STAND UP STRAIGHT AND FASTEN THE PAGNE AROUND YOUR CHEST BY ROLLING IT OR MAKING A KNOT.

⑦ THEN, YOU RAISE THE BOTTOM OF THE PAGNE UP TO THE BABY, AND YOU MAKE A KNOT.

THERE YOU GO, NOW YOU CAN TEND TO WHATEVER NEEDS TO BE DONE.
OBVIOUSLY, IT LOOKS COMPLICATED, BUT WITH A LITTLE PRACTICE, YOU'LL MANAGE...
JUST TO PLAY IT SAFE, YOU MIGHT WANT TO PRACTICE FIRST ON A TEDDY BEAR OR A DOLL.

DRAWING ON THE UNIVERSAL IN AFRICA
An Interview with Marguerite Abouet
BY ANGELA AJAYI

Reprinted with permission from the *Wild River Review*.

Too often, it is easier than we realize to forget the intimate details of a childhood, especially one lived thousands of miles away in a different country. As the years pass by, distance and time make fading memories more difficult to recall. Slowly, a new—and hopefully better—life takes over our days, making it even harder to remember little details.

Like Marguerite Abouet, I left West Africa at an early age. And like her, I too, long to remember and write about what it was like then, for in the back of my mind West Africa is always present. It comes as no surprise to me that Abouet's only comic book in English, Aya, is her very powerful visual and literary expression of this longing, this deep need to hold onto childhood memories filled with "unbelievable" stories about neighbors, families, friends—all in an Ivory Coast that had recently gained independence from France and was enjoying a new middle class society.

HOLD STILL.

Set in a bustling city in Ivory Coast, Aya is a witty, urban story. One that, Abouet says, could have taken place anywhere in the world. She is right, in theory, for there is a universalizing force that seems to drive Marguerite Abouet, the writer.

So come along and let her show you why, and literally through pictures, how, just as they might do in Europe or America, young girls sneak out to meet guys at night—or go to a party and flirt with the most attractive guy there. Around the world, it's really all the same.

And yet, Aya is also an urban story that takes place, specifically, in Ivory Coast—a country which is now experiencing what many other African countries have faced after decades of colonial rule: political corruption, disease, civil strife, and staggering poverty.

Days after I finished this interview with Abouet,

I realized that in it I had brought attention to the current harsh realities for Africans in Ivory Coast, and for those who migrated to Europe. Perhaps, as someone who was raised in Africa, I felt I had to...and it was the responsible thing to do. Perhaps it may always remain so; I don't know. Thankfully, Abouet was generous and warm in her response to my questions, always unapologetically reaching for honesty in her own reflections.

At a panel discussion at the 2007 PEN World Voices Festival in New York City, Abouet spoke of how she often feels a certain responsibility as an African writer because she wrote the book Aya. It was unclear to me whether this feeling of responsibility, like mine, had everything to do with addressing the current crisis in many parts of Africa. But I secretly wished it didn't, and that part of it also meant continuously drawing attention to the universal and relatable aspects of Africa, which Abouet has indeed successfully done in her engaging work, Aya—and in her interview with me.

ANGELA AJAYI: *Tell me about moving from Ivory Coast to France at a very young age (seven?)—and how this experience, coupled with living in France from thereon, might have influenced the course of your life and your writing of Aya (if at all).*

MARGUERITE ABOUET: I came to France at the age of twelve. Because the Ivory Coast is an old French colony, I spoke French very well—obviously with an accent! Culturally speaking, I also did not have great difficulty integrating into the society.

Then, as the years went by, I had the desire to write Aya. I had always felt the need to recollect my youth down there, the mischief I got into, the unbelievable stories about the *quartier* (neighborhood), the families, the neighbors. I did not want to forget that part of my life. I wanted to hold on to those memories, and the desire to recount them got stronger with age. I felt a little guilty for being content in another country, far away from my family; in addition, I got so annoyed at the way in which the media systematically showed the bad side of the African continent, habitual litanies of wars, famine, of the 'sida,' (AIDS) and other disasters, that I wished to show the other side, to tell about daily modern life that also exists in Africa. *Aya* is therefore an urban story which could have taken place anywhere in the world.

AJAYI: *Ivory Coast enjoyed what some have called* la belle époque *in the 1970s when President Houphouët-Boigny's free land policies brought about an economic boom—and thus the emergence of a middle class was possible. This is indeed something that is sorely lacking in many African countries today. In* Aya *you capture the middle class society so well that I wondered if your family was part of it. If yes, what were some of its societal norms at that time? I ask this because in* Aya, *there is a focus on societal norms and a testing of them by some of the main characters like Bintou, Adjoua, and even Aya herself. For instance, in the book, Aya tells her father she wants to become a doctor and he discourages her because "university is for men, not girls."*

ABOUET: After gaining independence, a new middle class appeared on the Ivory Coast. Many peasants' children had the opportunity to study in the city. Thus it was necessary to provide housing for these young people, and new additions and areas began to crowd Abidjan. Helped along by the economy of the time, all these new graduates found jobs. For relaxation, they formed clubs where they met after work or on weekends. That is also where they socialized and married. Their parents no longer had much influence on their life choices; they had been surpassed by the changes in the country and by this new freedom brought about by the "Ivorian miracle."

Women above all were influenced by the Western media and were emancipated. They no longer yielded to their parents' authority in choosing a husband. Their level of education made them aware of their rights: the right to divorce, access to the pill, opportunities for professional careers.

It is true that Africans had a strong desire for a male as the eldest child. It is he who would carry on the family name and would contribute to the support of the family by caring for aging parents. As far as a girl was concerned, she was often a liability and was married very quickly, mostly to the advantage of the parents.

But here, as in the Ivory miracle, men justifiably chose women from these clubs; they knew that they were very modern and cultivated, and financially independent. My parents were a part of that middle class. They were well off before they met. When they decided to get married, their parents both approved the match because their children already had a place to live and a job. It is true that in *Aya* the father tells his daughter that great accomplishments are made by men. This comment must be taken in context: this is only fiction, and fortunately not all African fathers are like Ignace. His only goal is to marry his daughter to the son of his boss. He is so intent on this that he urges her not to go too far in her studies.

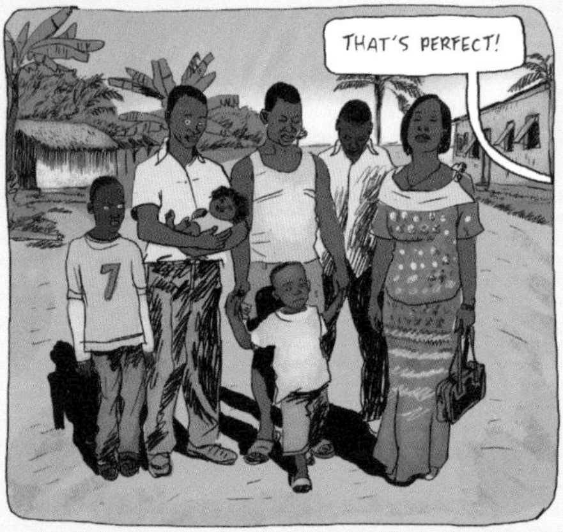
THAT'S PERFECT!

AJAYI: *In* Aya, *the modern (telephones, fancy dresses, and cars from Paris, etc.) and the traditional (wearing of traditional waxed cloth-like pagne, etc) seem to coexist well and without much friction (except perhaps when norms are obviously challenged). You seem to be saying something about the impact of modernity on women in African society in the book though, both good and bad. Please elaborate more on this if you can.*

ABOUET: It is true: Africa is torn between

tradition and modern times. That is the logical result of the meeting between Africa and the West in the media where many European and Brazilian programs are replayed. Actually, the women in *Aya* avail themselves of certain rights, even though they are subject to numerous patriarchal dictates: the right and choice of working (that is true for all Yopoupan mothers), control over household funds, also the choice to have fewer children (true for Bintou's mother), the right not to accept polygamy, access to a basic level of education (true for Aya's mother), also the right to divorce.

It is the good side of modern times that can coexist well with tradition. The tradition of Ivorian hospitality that is characteristic to young and old is one of respect for family environments and for the aged. That is why girls adhere to traditional values in *Aya*, in spite of the freedoms they have.

WHO'S GOT THE PERFUME ON?

PLEASE, NO SMILING.

AJAYI: *You've chosen the comic book to convey your story. Is there a specific reason for this or was it coincidental? I read that you are currently working on some novels. Do you find the creative process different from when you wrote a comic book like* Aya? *Harder? Easier? Not comparable at all?*

ABOUET: Novels written for young people are subject to a host of commercial constraints such as age, purpose, themes, and editors who do not shy away from endless correcting and reworking of the text. That is a problem that I did not face in *Aya*. By addressing adults as well as the young, I had great freedom to create.

AJAYI: *There is a lot of humor in* Aya, *even when the characters show questionable moral behavior like promiscuity and infidelity. It seems to me that humor could be the vehicle you've used to draw attention to these particular aspects of 1970s urban life in Ivory Coast. Please elaborate on your use of humor in the book.*

ABOUET: The people of the Ivory Coast are known for their sense of humor, particularly with regard to things that are not humorous. Their motto is: as long as no one has died, life continues. Whatever the conflicts or the problems, they will be resolved by following the advice of the sages at the foot of the talking tree (tree of advice), and then one can reconcile by celebrating with a feast.

The humor in *Aya* is not limited to the 70s; it is equally appropriate for today, because there are new sources of humor (all the *coup d'états* and their successive presidents, the unexpected fates of immigrants in Europe and the United States, escapades with hookers, brazen corruption, and so on.) Moreover, one need go no further than listening to the songs and reading the humor magazines like 'GBICH' to realize that Ivorian humor has grown. In *Aya* I only paid homage to the kind of humor that is part of me and with which I grew up.

AJAYI: *What is your life in France like at the moment? And as an African woman who immigrated to France, what do you think of the current socio-political situation in the country in regards to immigrants, especially North Africans?*

ABOUET: My life is quite normal. I live with my husband and our two-month-old son. I stopped working as a legal assistant and I am trying to write every day.

From the very beginning, I believed that the socio-political situation in North Africa and that in West Africa are totally different.

As an African from the West, I would like to point out that the French had the black Africans brought over to do the jobs that no one else wanted to do. As long as the Blacks stayed in their assigned place—as supermarket attendants, house maids, street sweepers, in child and geriatric care, or at most, as artists and athletes—all went very well. But now some of the offspring and young children of those first arrivals are doing more than that. At the price of a difficult struggle, they are becoming company owners, managers, intellectuals, and they are more visible. These Blacks sense more discrimination because they have abandoned their role. This kind of racism is more frequent when the economy is doing poorly.

Today's real danger is not idiotic racism and the increase in nationalists. We know how to deal with it—it is evident in ordinary attitudes which convey the worst paternalistic and condescending clichés that symbolically destroy Blacks even more surely than the overtly racist insults.

I believe that Blacks have just need for a Republic that is accessible to all and allows each one to find his place in society according to his talents.

AJAYI: *Today, many people in Africa are obviously experiencing serious economic hardship and struggle to survive on a daily basis—and the American media via films such as* Blood Diamonds *and* The Constant Gardener *continuously portray an Africa that is wrought with violent civil war, corruption, etc. The post-colonial Ivory Coast in* Aya *is a totally different one—almost unrecognizable, especially given the media's images. Life was refreshingly simple, peaceful, and people were obviously enjoying themselves. What do you think of how the West (more so America, I think) portrays Africa in general nowadays—and was* Aya *an attempt to respond to that at all? If not, inadvertently, you have portrayed an Africa that seems almost non-existent now, one that we really don't see or hear much of anymore. Wonderful, I think.*

ABOUET: We are often told that Africans live in famine, illness, tribal wars, poverty, with a hand extended, begging the West for aid.

It is interesting to confirm that the easygoing and careless impression of Africa that is found

STOP SHAKING, PÉPÉ!

WAAH!

in *Aya* fortunately still exists, even today. It would be nice if the African continent were evoked dropping the stereotypes of suffering because Africa is really quite a large and diverse continent, and as everywhere else—particularly in the United States, there are enormous differences in social classes...

Paradoxically, it is a form of well-disposed racism when I hear some people say that they will never go to Africa for fear of seeing this suffering.

One needs to know that Africans are about more than the side of misery that is persistently shown of their continent. Africans have only had their independence for forty years, compared to a century for France; it seems fair to give Africans time to free themselves of old crocodiles in power and to evolve.

I can assure you that the Ivory Coast remains a beautiful country with nice *quartiers* (neighborhoods), superb beaches, and a magnificent fauna and flora, despite its disasters. African women finally share the same dreams of other women on the planet, and all I want to do is show their daily lives along with their hopes and desires to find fulfillment as modern women in Africa.

Born in Nigeria, Angela Ajayi came to the United States to attend college and discovered an undeniable love for literature—and books. after completing a B.A. in English literature, she spent six weeks at the Radcliffe publishing course in Cambridge, Massachusetts, and then moved to New York City where she worked in scholarly publishing for a number of years and completed an M.A. in comparative literature at Columbia University. She currently works for a publishing house in New Jersey and edits mainly scholarly books on Africa.

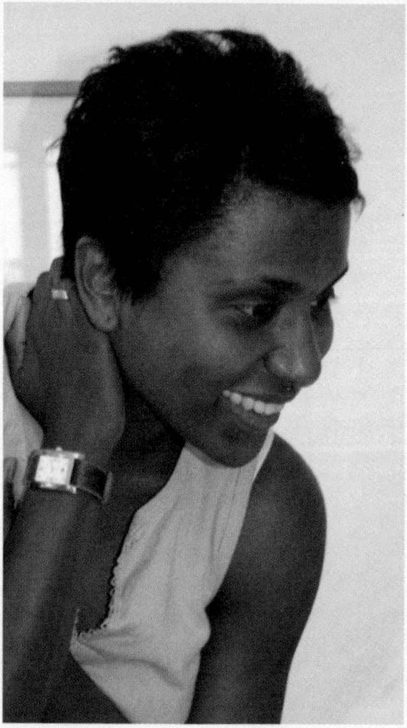

© Antoine Delesvaux

Marguerite Abouet was born in Abidjan in 1971. Her mother was a management secretary at Singer and her father was a salesman at Hitachi. She grew up with her family in the working-class neighborhood of Yopougon. When she was twelve, her parents sent her and her older brother to Paris to live with their great-uncle and pursue "extensive studies." Breaking off her studies earlier than expected, she began to write novels that she didn't show to anyone, and was by turns a punk, a super-nanny for triplets, a caregiver for the elderly, a waitress, a data entry clerk, and a legal assistant at a law firm. She now lives in Romainville, a suburb of Paris, and spends all of her time writing. *Aya* and *Aya of Yop City* were her first graphic novels, written in a fresh voice and with a keen sense of humor, and telling the story of an Africa far removed from clichés, war and famine. In 2006, Marguerite Abouet and Clément Oubrerie received the prize for best first comic book at the prestigious Angoulême International Comics Festival.

Clément Oubrerie was born in Paris in 1966. After completing high school, he enrolled at the Penninghen School of Graphic Arts, breaking off his studies after four years to visit the United States. He stayed there for two years, holding down various odd jobs and seeing his work published for the first time before landing in a New Mexico jail for working without papers. Back in France, he went on to a prolific career in illustration as the author of more than forty children's books and as a digital animator. He is the graphic talent behind several television series, including *Moot-Moot*, produced by Eric Judor and Ramzy Bedia. He is also the co-founder of the La Station animation studio and Autochenille Productions, which is working on the screen adaptation of Joann Sfar's *The Rabbi's Cat*. In the *Aya* books, his first graphic novels, his unique talent brings Marguerite Abouet's stories to life with vibrant spirit and authenticity.

His work can be found online at clementoubrerie.blogspot.com

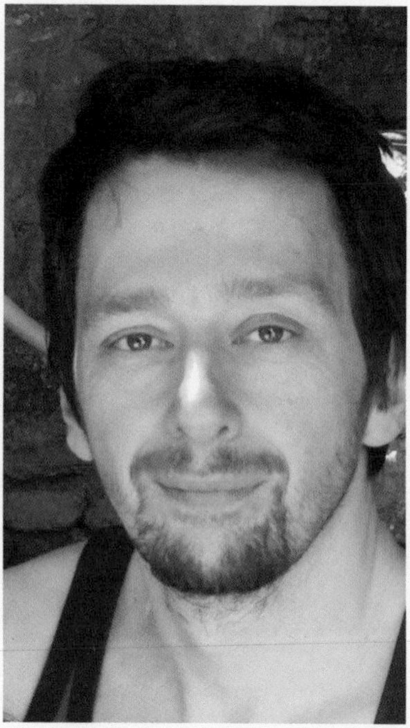

AYA

LOVE IN YOP CITY

THE DRAMATIC CONCLUSION TO THE AWARD-WINNING SERIES

Aya: Love in Yop City comprises the final three chapters of the Aya story, episodes never before seen in English. While its stories maintain their familiar tone, quick pace, and joyfulness of the first three chapters, we see Aya and her friends beginning to make serious decisions about their future. With a little help from the tight-knit community of Yopougon, Aya comes through various trials stronger than ever.

$24.95 USD/CDN • ISBN : 978-1-77046-092-8

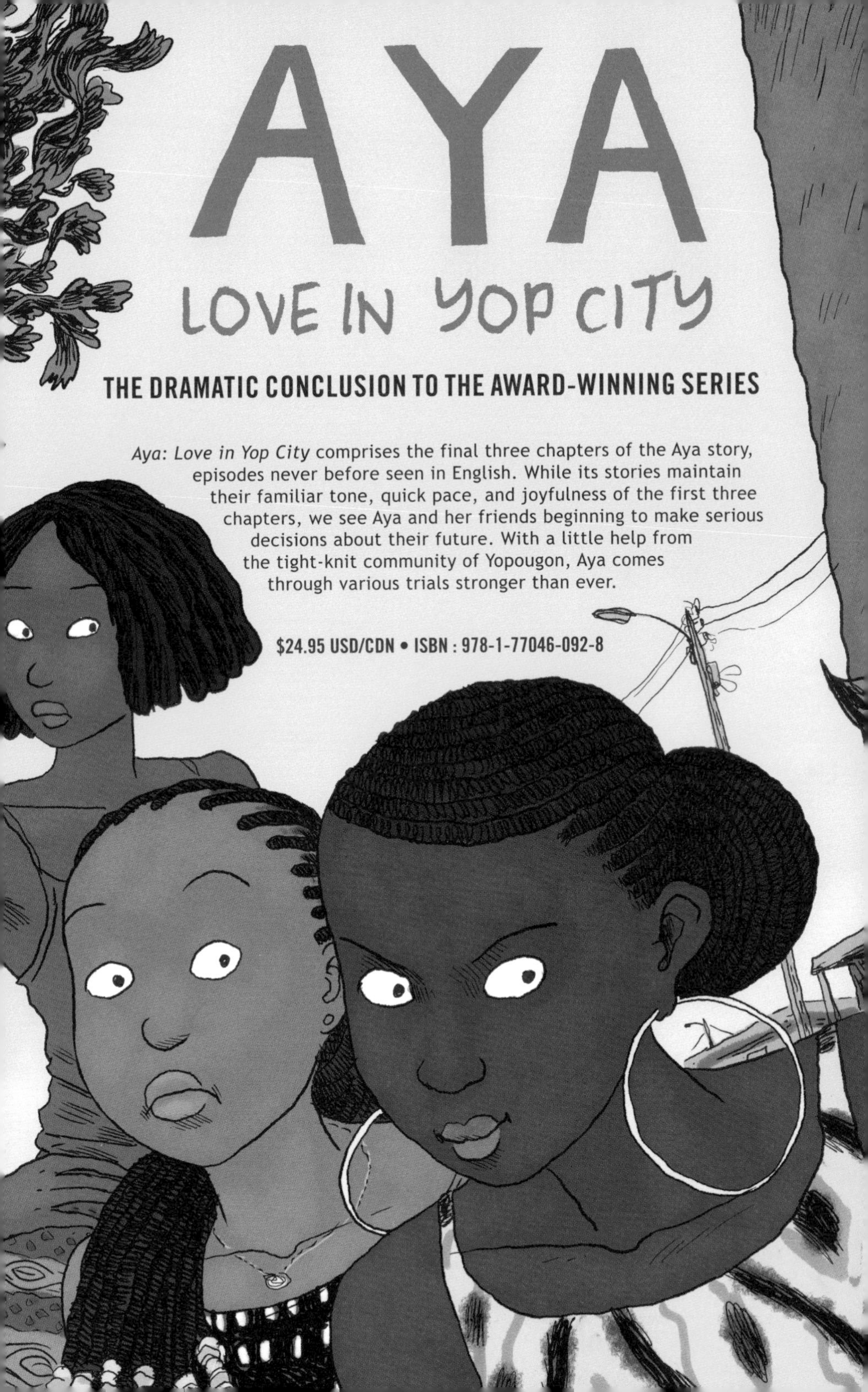

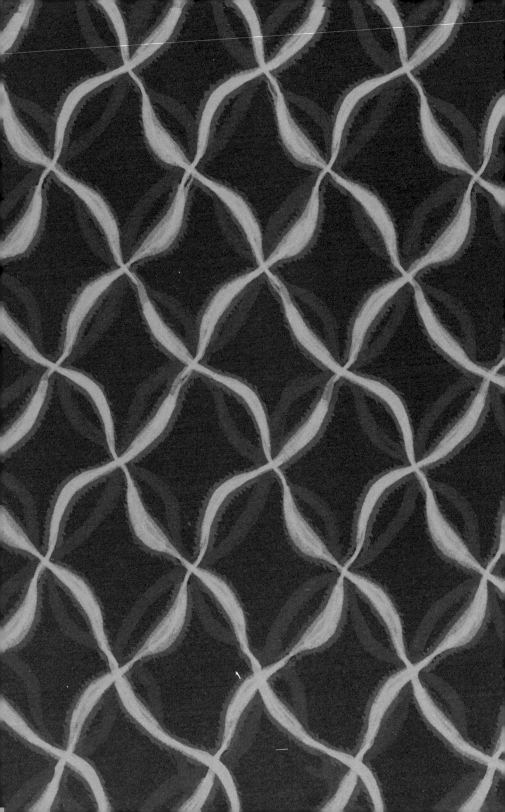